The Gateway

A Conference Sponsored Jointly by the
American Enterprise Institute for Public Policy Research
and the College of Business Administration,
University of Illinois at Chicago Circle

The Gateway

U.S. Immigration Issues and Policies

Edited by Barry R. Chiswick

American Enterprise Institute for Public Policy Research
Washington and London

Library of Congress Cataloging in Publication Data

Main entry under title:

The gateway.

    (AEI symposia ; 81I)
    Proceedings of a conference cosponsored by the American
Enterprise Institute for Public Policy Research and the College of
Business Administration, University of Illinois at Chicago Circle,
and held Apr. 10–11, 1980 at the UICC campus.
    Includes index.
    1. United States—Emigration and immigration—Congresses.
2. Emigration and immigration law—United States—
I. Chiswick, Barry R. II. American Enterprise Institute for Public
Policy Research. III. University of Illinois at Chicago Circle.
College of Business Administration. IV. Series.
JV6493.G37   325.73   81-8009

ISBN 0-8447-2221-9   AACR2
ISBN 0-8447-2220-0 (pbk.)

AEI Symposia 81I

Printed in the United States of America

Participants

José Alberro
Department of Economics
University of Illinois at Chicago Circle

James Bass
Inter-American Development Bank

Jagdish N. Bhagwati
Department of Economics
Columbia University

Barry R. Chiswick
Department of Economics and Survey Research Laboratory
University of Illinois at Chicago Circle

Carmel U. Chiswick
Department of Economics
University of Illinois at Chicago Circle

Walter Fogel
Graduate School of Business Administration
University of California at Los Angeles

Bruce L. Gardner
Department of Agricultural Economics
Texas A & M University

Harry J. Gilman
Bureau of International Labor Affairs
U.S. Department of Labor

Robert S. Goldfarb
Department of Economics
George Washington University

Andrew M. Greeley
National Opinion Research Center
University of Chicago

Michael J. Greenwood
Department of Economics
University of Colorado

Thomas F. Johnson
American Enterprise Institute for Public Policy Research

Allan G. King
Department of Economics
University of Texas at Austin

Linda S. Liner
Planning and Evaluation
Immigration & Naturalization Service

Philip L. Martin
Department of Agricultural Economics
University of California, Davis

John F. McDonald
Department of Economics
University of Illinois at Chicago Circle

John M. McDowell
Department of Economics
Arizona State University

Jacob Mincer
Department of Economics
Columbia University

Larry C. Morgan
Department of Agricultural Economics
Texas A & M University

Joan Nelson
School of Advanced International Studies
Johns Hopkins University

David S. North
Center for Labor and Migration Studies
New TransCentury Foundation

Siobhan Oppenheimer-Nicolau
Ford Foundation

David M. Reimers
Department of History
New York University

Walter G. Rest
Immigrants Service League
Travelers Aid Society

Edwin P. Reubens
Department of Economics
City College, City University of New York

George Rosen
Department of Economics
University of Illinois at Chicago Circle

Warren C. Sanderson
Department of Economics
State University of New York at Stony Brook

Julian L. Simon
Department of Economics
University of Illinois at Urbana/Champaign

Nigel Tomes
Department of Economics
University of Western Ontario

Andrea Tyree
Department of Sociology
State University of New York at Stony Brook

Dan Usher
Department of Economics
Queen's University

Ralph Westfall
College of Business Administration
University of Illinois at Chicago Circle

Jeffrey G. Williamson
Department of Economics
University of Wisconsin

Lorene Yap
Urban Institute

Contents

PART THREE
THE ECONOMIC IMPACT OF IMMIGRANTS

PART FOUR
ALTERNATIVE IMMIGRATION POLICIES

The Gateway

U.S. Immigration Issues and Policies

Introduction

Barry R. Chiswick

This volume contains the proceedings of a conference, "U.S. Immigration Issues and Policies," cosponsored by the American Enterprise Institute for Public Policy Research and the College of Business Administration, University of Illinois at Chicago Circle (UICC). The conference was held April 10–11, 1980, at the UICC campus.

The conference was organized in part because of the importance of immigration and immigration policy to a wide range of U.S. domestic economic and social issues, as well as relations with other countries. Immigrants have an impact on nearly all aspects of domestic life, including wages and employment, population growth, housing prices, and intergroup relations. Immigration policy is also linked to foreign policy, not only with Mexico but also more recently with countries in the Caribbean, Asia, and Eastern Europe and in coming decades with sub-Saharan Africa.

Equally important for organizing the conference, however, was the scarcity of substantive research on which to base public policy. Since the Dillingham Commission report in 1911, there has been little systematic substantive research on immigration issues and policies, although in this seventy-year interval important research studies have periodically appeared. In the past five years, at least four federal policy committees (under various titles—interagency task forces, congressional committees, select commissions) have studied the issue. The research efforts by these committees have been minimal because of the short duration of their mandates and the requirement that a group representing diverse political interests offer specific policy recommendations. A research effort freed from the constraints necessarily imposed on policy-oriented committees could be a fruitful means of stimulating substantive research that would help fill the research void and increase our understanding of the issues and policy trade-offs in immigration.

Those invited to prepare papers, serve as formal discussants, and participate in the conference discussion included researchers well-versed in the intricacies of immigration law, policy, and analysis, as well as experienced researchers in closely related fields who could provide a fresh perspective and alternative research methodologies. To avoid the parochialism of a group of technicians in a single discipline talking their own jargon to each other and losing sight of the broader aspect of

1

the issues, a wide range of researchers were invited. By academic discipline, the majority of participants were economists, but historians, political scientists, sociologists, and social workers were also active participants.

Within the mutually approved research topic, the authors were given complete freedom in developing their contributions. It was understood that this would be a research conference and that all participants would be expressing their own views, rather than those of the organizations or agencies with which they are affiliated. By not requiring the conference to develop a policy consensus, we were able to achieve a wider exchange of ideas and a more uninhibited discussion.

The authors were given the opportunity to revise their papers after the conference. To reduce the number of iterations, however, the formal discussant comments, the general discussion, and author responses are based on the original conference papers. Any inconsistencies that might arise from this procedure are likely to be minor and detectable by the alert reader. The general discussion encompassed a wide range of issues related to the papers under discussion. The transcription was edited to bring the text closer to written than to spoken English, while at the same time preserving the substance, tone, and flavor of the original.

The conference consisted of four sessions: the supply and demand for immigrants, the progress of immigrants, the economic impact of immigrants, and alternative immigration policies. There were two or three papers and three or four discussants per session. This volume follows the order of the conference presentations. It is hoped that the papers and discussions in this volume will stimulate additional research on the various dimensions of immigration and help provide a research base for the thoughtful development of public policy.

The Supply of and Demand for Immigrants

The session on the supply of and demand for immigrants began with a paper by David M. Reimers, "Recent Immigration Policy: An Analysis." Using historical analysis, Professor Reimers reviews the post–World War II liberalization of the restrictive immigration legislation of the 1920s. He shows how struggles over the Displaced Persons Law of 1948, the Immigration and Nationality (McCarran-Walter) Act of 1952, and the various special laws of the 1950s and early 1960s led to the 1965 amendments that abolished the national origins quota system and the severe restrictions on Asians and substituted a preference system. The new law, while still selective, emphasized family unification, with a smaller role for occupational requirements and refugee status.

2

Congress amended the law several times, most recently in 1980, to provide for a uniform worldwide system of 320,000 immigrants subject annually to numerical limitation, in addition to visas for immediate relatives of U.S. citizens, who are not subject to numerical limitation (now about 125,000 per year), and "conditional" admission of refugees over and above this limit.[1] The changes in the law in 1965 were accompanied by a gradual increase in immigration and shifting patterns of immigration. After World War II, southern and eastern Europeans began to replace northern and western Europeans, and both in turn gave way, after 1965, to immigration from the third world.

Immigration policy responded to economic forces and fears, foreign policy (especially the cold war), and ethnic politics. Arguments about race and ethnicity gave way to cold war arguments and family concerns. The old-line restrictionist groups, like the veterans and patriotic organizations, took a back seat to the growing influence of ethnic and religious agencies and the executive branch in shaping immigration policy. Economic interest groups were more vociferous in discussions about the bracero program (1942–1964) and the illegal alien issue.

The discussion of the Reimers paper focused on why economic issues appeared to play so small a role in the immigration reform debate; the effects of changing attitudes toward religious, ethnic, and racial discrimination on U.S. immigration policy; and the role of religious agencies in reforming basic immigration law.

Michael J. Greenwood and John M. McDowell studied "The Supply of Immigrants to the United States." They take a short-run perspective by analyzing a cross section of international migration flows to the United States from as many origin countries as the available data allow. They first develop and estimate a model to explain the international distribution of emigration from each of several countries of origin around the world to the receiving countries. A major conclusion emerging from this analysis is that observed emigration from many countries to the United States is substantially less than is predicted by the model, suggesting that U.S. immigration law is a binding constraint. If entry barriers were removed, Western Hemisphere nations appear most likely to supply the United States with large increases in immigrants.

Professors Greenwood and McDowell then examine immigration to the United States from the perspective of the United States; that is, using U.S. data on immigration, they analyze migration to the United States from various countries of origin. The model includes variables designed

[1] The Refugee Act of 1980, which increased the number of visas for refugees and introduced other changes to facilitate refugee resettlement, was immediately shown to be inadequate by the "unscheduled" influx of 120,000 Cuban refugees.

to capture the influences of differential economic advantage and variables intended to reflect the costs of transferring skills to the United States from abroad (as measured by the similarity of occupational structure). Distance and the earnings differentials appear to be important factors affecting the rate of migration from various countries to the United States. Another factor increasing the rate of immigration is a higher level of economic development in the sending country. Similarly, the availability of social security for the aged in the countries of origin discourages migration by the aged. Finally, the ability of prospective immigrants to transfer their occupational knowledge from their native country to the U.S. labor market is also an important influence on U.S. immigration rates.

The discussion of the Greenwood-McDowell paper was primarily concerned with the econometric problems of estimating a supply equation for immigrants when legislation is a binding constraint and when there are little data. Alternative specifications of the dependent variable, the number of immigrants, and the explanatory variables were considered.

Jagdish N. Bhagwati's paper, "Taxation and International Migration: Recent Policy Issues," is concerned with two issues. The first is the question of the appropriate exercise of income tax jurisdiction, whether it ought to be on the basis of citizenship, as in the United States and the Philippines, or on the basis of residence, as in the European countries and most less-developed countries. This question arises from the theoretical and policy discussions of the proposal to tax the "brain drain," or emigration of skilled labor. The sending countries could impose the tax on their emigrants. Such a tax would require a change in U.S. policy only insofar as the sending countries seek bilateral treaties for a sharing of tax information to facilitate their enforcement. The second issue is one of sharing revenue in proportion to the taxes paid by the immigrants. Under such a scheme, the receiving countries, for example, the United States, would share the tax revenues raised in the normal course of events from immigrants with the countries of origin.

From the discussion, it became clear that the sending countries could institute emigrant taxes unilaterally, although enforcement problems would be severe if the tax rates were too high. The difficulty of implementing the revenue-sharing scheme, including the determination of how the funds would be distributed (for example, through bilateral treaties or an international organization), was discussed. Also considered were the objections to indirectly contributing to their countries of origin by persons whose emigration was induced by political, religious, or social repression.

The Progress of Immigrants

Barry R. Chiswick's analysis, "The Economic Progress of Immigrants: Some Apparently Universal Patterns," was not formally presented at the conference.[2] It is included in this volume, however, because of its relevance to the topic of the second session, the progress of immigrants. Also it served as a point of departure for some analysis in the other two papers in the session and much of the ensuing discussion. On the basis of assumptions regarding the international transferability of skills and the favorable self-selection of migrants, hypotheses are generated regarding the progress of economic migrants and refugees in comparison with the native born. These hypotheses are found to be consistent with data from the United States (by racial and ethnic groups) and other countries.

Data on males from the 1970 Census of Population indicate that, although economic migrants initially have an earnings disadvantage in comparison with the native born, their earnings rise sharply with post-immigration labor market experience and they reach earnings equality with native-born men of the same ethnic group and the same demographic characteristics for those in the United States about eleven to fifteen years. Economic migrants in the United States for more than fifteen years tend to have higher earnings than the native born. Refugees have lower earnings than economic migrants or the native born with the same characteristics, but the large differential shortly after immigration narrows with the duration of residence. The earnings of refugees approach but do not overtake those of the native born. The sons of immigrants are found to earn 5 to 10 percent more than the sons of native-born parents with the same demographic characteristics.

Andrew M. Greeley's study, "Immigration and Religio-Ethnic Groups: A Sociological Reappraisal," considers the sociological concept of "social disorganization" elaborated by W. I. Thomas, especially in his *Polish Peasant* volumes. Thomas argued that the trauma of immigration destroyed the old agricultural values of the Polish peasant and provided him with no new set of values with which to cope with the demands of urban industrial life in the United States. The result was a collapse of the intimate social structures that make life possible and success achievable. Dr. Greeley believes that the social disorganization theory, sometimes drastically oversimplified, has had enormous impact on both policy makers and educated Americans.

A consideration of the history of the Polish-Americans whom Thomas described suggests that he may well have confused the pathology

---

[2] It originally appeared in William Fellner, ed., *Contemporary Economic Problems 1979* (Washington, D.C.: American Enterprise Institute, 1979).

of a minority with the culture of the majority of the group. Using data from the General Social Surveys and other sources, Professor Greeley shows that Polish-Americans rapidly acculturated into American life, achieving educational, occupational, and income parity in a relatively brief period of time without necessarily shedding many of their Polish cultural characteristics. Dr. Greeley believes that the success of Polish-Americans and other European Catholics raises serious questions about the claims that other "disorganized" groups cannot be successful in American life. Some preliminary data on several ethnic groups presented by Dr. Greeley from another analysis indicate that there may be many different roads to economic success. Some immigrants first acquire high income and then high levels of schooling, while others seem to use large investments in schooling as a path to high incomes.

The discussion was primarily concerned with ethnic group differences in economic success. Some groups subject to discrimination (Jews, Japanese, and Chinese) have demonstrated substantial achievements, while some others (Mexicans, American-Indians, and Puerto Ricans) have been far less successful than average. Several hypotheses, not all mutually exclusive, that might explain these patterns were considered.

Session 2 closed with Walter Fogel's paper, "Twentieth-Century Mexican Migration to the United States." He believes that contemporary migration from Mexico is quite different from migration in the 1920s and 1950s, two decades with high rates of immigration from Mexico. Mexico's population is 70 million, compared with 25 million in 1950 and 16 million in 1920. Thus, the number of potential migrants is much larger. Similarly, the Mexican-American population of the United States is 8 to 10 million compared with under 3 million in 1950. The larger Mexican population of the United States provides a cultural and knowledge environment that facilitates additional migration.

Professor Fogel argues that the current migration is not very sensitive to shifts in the demand for labor in the United States but, more than in the past, is driven by population and labor-force growth in Mexico. He believes the analysis of the data on Mexican migration is consistent with this conclusion, although the available data do not permit definitive results. These findings have important implications for the United States because Mexican immigrants have much lower earnings than other immigrants and their offspring fail to catch up with other native-born white Americans. The current large migration from Mexico amounts to a rapid enlargement of a disadvantaged group.

The discussion of the Fogel paper centered on whether there had been a shift in favor of supply-push as compared with demand-pull factors in determining Mexican migration or whether both factors were operative in the past and in the present. The discussion also explored the number and demographic characteristics of illegal Mexican aliens.

The Economic Impact of Immigrants

The third session began with Jeffrey G. Williamson's "Immigrant-Inequality Trade-Offs in the Promised Land: Income Distribution and Absorptive Capacity Prior to the Quotas." There is abundant time-series evidence confirming a high, positive, simple correlation between immigration rates and income inequality in America since the early nineteenth century. From such correlations it can be inferred that America was trading off equality to absorb Europe's mass emigrations. Professor Williamson's paper suggests that the data do not warrant such inferences.

Professor Williamson applies a multisectoral general-equilibrium two-factor (labor and land-capital) model to the period 1839–1966. This confirms that immigration did indeed tend to increase income inequality among the native population as well as among the labor force augmented by the immigrants. Demand forces, however, appear to have been far more important than immigrants in driving America over the increasing inequality part of the Kuznets curve after the 1830s. Professor Williamson believes that the timing of the immigration quotas correlates well with American experience with immigrant-absorptive capacity; political pressure in support of quotas and their subsequent enactment were a consequence of decreases in the elasticity of the demand for labor and in the supply of native labor that implied that immigration had a substantial depressing effect on wages.

The discussion of the Williamson paper primarily concerned the technical aspects of the multisector econometric model (including the appropriate specifications of the factors of production) and the reasons why labor demand and supply elasticities may have fallen after the 1890s. There was also discussion of whether the political forces could have perceived the decline in absorptive capacity quickly. Alternative explanations for the enactment of restrictive legislation were considered.

Barry R. Chiswick's study, "The Impact of Immigration on the Level and Distribution of Economic Well-Being," is based on two-factor and three-factor (high-level manpower, low-level manpower, and capital) aggregate production functions. It shows that immigration tends to raise the income of the native population but to change the distribution of this income. The different impacts of high-skilled and low-skilled immigrants are considered. A dynamic element is introduced when the model allows for changing impacts as the relative skills of immigrants increase with their duration of residence.

INTRODUCTION

When an income transfer system (welfare, social services, and social overhead capital financed prior to the immigration) is introduced, income redistribution programs can make all native-born groups at least as affluent as before the migration. This cannot occur, however, if the immigrants themselves are substantial net recipients of these transfers. It could not occur, for example, if the immigrants were low-skilled workers and had equal access to the income transfer system as native-born low-skilled workers. An immigrant tax (large visa fee or immigrant income tax surcharge) that captures some of the economic rent that visa recipients receive would raise the aggregate income of the native population and increase the annual number of visas that the United States would be willing to issue. Such a scheme would still provide opportunities for refugee and family reunification migration.

The discussion focused on whether income redistribution programs would be developed to compensate the groups that lose from immigration. The issue of externalities was raised; it was generally agreed that pecuniary externalities (for example, falling wages for low-skilled natives due to immigration of low-skilled workers) do not warrant correction on the grounds of economic efficiency, while physical externalities (for example, increased traffic congestion) warrant correction because they involve a waste of resources.

Julian L. Simon's paper is "The Overall Effects of Immigrants on Natives' Incomes." It presents estimates of the composite impact in each year following the immigrants' entry and then a present-value estimate of the entire stream of positive and negative effects in various years. The paper discusses what Professor Simon believes are the three most important elements. The first is the capital-dilution effect, where a new approach is sketched to estimate the proportion of the returns to capital captured by immigrants who arrive without capital. The second is the social security transfer effect, that is, the current benefits to the native population of the immigrants' social security tax contributions. Third, it considers the impact on productivity of economies of scale, the sum of learning by doing, creation of new knowledge, and other aspects of economies of scale.

Professor Simon's estimates suggest that the life-cycle saving-and-transfer process has a positive effect on the income of natives and is of the same order of magnitude as his estimates of the capital-dilution effect. Assessing the effect of immigrants on productivity, together with the other effects, requires a dynamic macromodel; a simple one is simulated in the paper. The results indicate that within a few years the productivity effect comes to dominate and thereafter dwarfs the capital-dilution and saving-and-transfer effects. Seen as an investment, Professor

Simon estimates that immigrants yield a high return to the native population.

In the discussion, reservations were raised regarding the validity of Professor Simon's procedures for estimating the savings-transfer effect of the social security system. There was also a discussion of Simon's implicit assumptions regarding the financing of social overhead and of other capital and the receipt of benefits from this capital. Whether economies of scale with respect to population size do (or still) exist in the United States was discussed at considerable length without resolution.

Alternative Immigration Policies

The closing session consisted of two papers, one by Larry C. Morgan and Bruce L. Gardner on the U.S.-Mexico bracero (temporary farm worker) program (1942–1964) and the other by Robert S. Goldfarb on the role of occupation (skills) in issuing immigration visas under current law. Professors Morgan and Gardner indicate in their paper, "Potential for a U.S. Guest-Worker Program in Agriculture: Lessons from the Braceros," that, in dealing with the problem of illegal immigration from Mexico, neither a policy of strictly policing the border nor a policy of opening the border seems acceptable. An alternative is to permit temporary migration by Mexican guest workers. The authors assess the possible consequences of this policy by analyzing the earlier experience with the bracero program under Public Law 78 in the 1950s and 1960s.

Using an econometric model of the supply of and demand for farm labor in the seven states that received almost all the braceros, Professors Morgan and Gardner estimate that the bracero program on average reduced farm wages by about 8 percent and imposed losses of about $140 million per year on U.S. farm workers. The estimated gains to U.S. employers and consumers of farm products sum to about $185 million per year, for a net gain to the U.S. population of about $45 million per year. The effects of the braceros on other aspects of social welfare and on illegal immigration are also discussed. They conclude that the more pessimistic warnings about the ill effects of a guest-worker program are unsupported by the U.S. experience with the bracero program.

The discussion focused on several themes. One was the appropriate level of aggregation for the analysis of the impact: individual crops or agriculture in general. Another was the extent to which guest workers or temporary migrants gradually become permanent immigrants. There were also discussions of the feasibility of a large agricultural guest-worker program in the coming decade, given the decline in labor intensity of U.S. agriculture, and the feasibility of an urban guest-worker program.

The final paper was by Robert S. Goldfarb, "Occupational Preferences in the U.S. Immigration Law: An Economic Analysis." After a description of current immigration law, Professor Goldfarb argues that the provisions limit skilled immigration but fail (because of illegal immigrants) to limit unskilled immigration effectively. A number of conceivable economic rationales for such provisions are identified, and the relevance of each rationale is explored. "Aggregate output" rationales viewing immigration as a way of maximizing an objective such as national output or per capita income are found to be relevant, while rationales focusing on special conditions in specific occupations (labor shortages, monopoly elements, etc.) are not considered a useful basis for a general immigration policy. As part of the discussion, the U.S. use of immigration to ameliorate the so-called doctor shortage is described and evaluated.

Broad policy implications of the aggregate output rationale are explored, with simple models. Optimal immigration levels do exist and vary with the precise policy objective. The current system's ability to apply an aggregate output rationale effectively is then investigated. Sources of difficulty include the inability to set numerical limits on immigration by occupation group and the lack of incentives for selecting "high-quality" potential immigrants. Finally, there is the issue of who gets the "economic rents" generated by the nonprice rationing system. The author argues that there is at present no mechanism for the native population to capture some of these economic rents and that probably a substantial proportion of these rents not retained by the immigrants are received by immigration lawyers or are otherwise dissipated in misallocations of resources designed to increase the probability of receiving a visa.

The discussion of Professor Goldfarb's paper focused on the technical and political feasibility of implementing meaningful visa rationing criteria based on occupation or skills. One issue was whether the occupational classifications should be broad or narrow. Several definitions of "absorptive capacity" of immigrants were considered as this term, or a variant of it, was used in several conference papers.

Part One

The Supply of and Demand for Immigrants

Recent Immigration Policy:
An Analysis

David M. Reimers

The immigration acts of the 1920s ended virtual unrestricted migration from Europe. Previously, Asians had been barred, beginning with the Chinese in 1881, the Japanese in 1908 (the Gentlemen's Agreement), and most others in 1917. Congress excluded certain classifications of Europeans prior to the 1920s, but the national origins quota laws of that decade reduced the flow from Europe drastically. When the quota provisions of the Johnson-Reed Act of 1924 were fully operative, approximately 150,000, mostly Northern and Western Europeans, were permitted to enter annually, in addition to a nonquota flow from the Western Hemisphere.[1]

Because of feelings of Pan-Americanism and regional economic concerns, Congress hesitated to halt immigration from the Western Hemisphere by the use of quotas. Yet the health and "likely to become a public charge" provisions could be used to limit potential immigration from the Western Hemisphere. At first, these restrictions were not effectively employed. During the 1920s, about 1½ million persons emigrated to the United States from the Western Hemisphere. Most scholars believe, however, that a large number of illegals, over 500,000, also entered from Mexico. Until 1925, the United States had no significant force to halt illegal immigrants along the Mexico border; Congress then created the border patrol. A small group hampered by a lack of funds, the patrol earned a reputation for efficiency in its early years.[2]

The author wishes to thank Barry Chiswick and Carmel Chiswick for their comments, as well as Len Dinnerstein, who read an earlier draft. My research assistant, Nancy Perlman, was also helpful.

[1] The basic history of immigration restriction and nativism is in John Higham, *Strangers in the Land* (New York: Atheneum, 1963). Higham can be supplemented with Thomas J. Curran, *Xenophobia and Immigration, 1820-1930* (Boston: Twayne Publishers, 1975); Barbara Miller Solomon, *Ancestors and Immigrants: A Changing New England Tradition* (Cambridge, Mass.: Harvard University Press, 1956); and Marion T. Bennett, *American Immigration Policies: A History* (Washington, D.C.: Public Affairs Press, 1963).

[2] Abraham Hoffman, *Unwanted Mexican Americans in the Great Depression: Repatriation Pressures, 1929-1939* (Tucson: University of Arizona Press, 1974), pp. 31-32.

After World War II, Americans modified their harsh laws. Despite changing post–World War II immigration policy, much of the old structure remains. When Congress enacted the restrictions, quotas permitted approximately 150,000 annually; an equal number came from the Americas, totaling about 300,000 per year. The worldwide ceiling—290,000, established in 1978 by combining the Eastern (170,000) and Western (120,000) Hemisphere ceilings and amended by the Refugee Act of 1980 to be 320,000—is similar to the total envisioned at the end of the 1920s. Exemptions in the law for certain classifications of relatives and refugees make the current annual immigration larger than 320,000.

Immigration slumped drastically during the Great Depression and World War II and then gradually increased. In the 1950s, it averaged 250,000 annually; in the 1960s, about 320,000; and in the 1970s, more than 400,000. In 1978, partly because of the adjustment of the status of the refugees from Indochina, it topped 600,000, and in 1980 over 750,000 newcomers arrived. The American population has grown since the 1920s. One could argue that the policy of the late 1920s was more generous in terms of the total immigration to the United States in relation to population size, compared with that of the 1970s. In the late 1920s, when immigration averaged about 300,000, there were about 400 persons here for each newly arrived immigrant. In 1970, there were 544 persons here for each of the 373,000 entering immigrants.

The overall limit to immigration is important. Despite the changes in immigration policy after the 1940s and the gradual increase in immigrants, few advocated a radical increase in numbers. Nor did many suggest that America could absorb many more than are currently coming.

What follows is an analysis of the post-1940 liberalization of immigration policy, including the major changes in law and an explanation of why the laws changed. The issues during this period have been about the kinds of immigrants the nation should receive rather than the numbers. Hence, discussion has focused on the national origins quotas, refugees, family unification, and, to a lesser extent, economics. The fact that economic issues were not stressed as much as others does not mean that they are unimportant. About some issues, such as the bracero program and illegal aliens, economic interest groups were especially vociferous. The bracero program, however, dealt with temporary workers rather than permanent immigrants. Economic matters also count in the determination of permanent and legal immigration. In the debates about immigration, most congressmen, without many scholarly studies to support them, took for granted that large increases in immigration would have an undesirable economic effect on the United States.

Once Congress agreed on a vague top figure—not too different from that envisioned in the late 1920s—that the nation could absorb without serious economic repercussions, the debates centered on who would receive the coveted visas. Ethnic issues, the cold war, and foreign policy played the key roles. The executive branch was important in determining policy as were a host of patriotic and veterans groups as well as ethnic, religious, and humanitarian organizations. The political give-and-take among these groups and forces gradually led to a more liberal immigration policy, symbolized by the 1965 act. The change in the law has also led to the present pattern of immigration—away from a European orientation to a third world one, with most immigrants coming from Asia and Latin America. This was not necessarily the design of Congress, but it was typical of the way in which immigration policy was formulated—the product of compromises in the political arena, often on an ad hoc basis with little scientific study. American society was prepared to accept the third world immigrants because the society had become more tolerant.

The Great Depression and World War II

The establishment of a new immigration policy in the 1920s was followed by the Great Depression, when few wanted to emigrate to the United States. Indeed, among some groups, more voluntarily returned than came during the first years of the depression. Even if they wanted to emigrate, the government used the "likely to become a public charge" provision to keep them out. For Mexicans in the United States, like others, the depression brought lean years. As jobs dried up, they returned to Mexico. American officials, local as well as federal, took an active role in Mexican repatriation. Rather than give relief, local officials in Los Angeles and elsewhere provided transportation for the return trip. One scholar estimated that over 400,000 Mexican aliens (and their American-born children) were repatriated during the decade.[3]

Although economic issues were paramount in the early years of the depression, the triumph of Nazism in Germany and its expansion created new pressures for emigration to America. By the mid-1930s, many Jews and others persecuted by the Nazis were eager to escape, and they looked to America as a haven. Only a minority of Americans were willing to help; they urged either a humanitarian enforcement of the immigration laws or new legislation to aid refugees in getting to

[3] Ibid., p. ix.

15

America. Some victims of Nazism got in, but efforts for large-scale assistance remained unsuccessful. Quotas went unused; thousands who wanted to emigrate to the United States were unable to do so. Those from nations with small quotas were handicapped because so few slots were available. But even the fairly large German quota went unused. The Department of State frequently refused to grant visas because it was not satisfied that prospective immigrants could guarantee they would not become public charges once in the United States, or because the consuls believed these immigrants might turn out to be subversives or German agents.[4]

Nor did many refugees find America a haven during the early 1940s. By then, of course, circumstances were different, as the nation was at war with Nazi Germany. The basic fact remains, however, that the United States did little to aid the refugees from Europe either during the 1930s or during the war years.

In two other respects, however, immigration policy changed during World War II. The acute manpower shortage created by the war opened the door for the utilization of temporary workers from Mexico. Southwestern growers and others agitated for the recruitment of temporary laborers. As mobilization proceeded rapidly, it was clear that an agricultural labor shortage was developing. The administration responded sympathetically to these demands and in 1942 negotiated the bracero agreement with the Mexican government. Braceros were also recruited from the Bahamas, Barbados, Canada, Jamaica, and Newfoundland, but the bulk were Mexican.[5]

A second change in immigration during the war was minor, almost symbolic, but it foreshadowed shifts in postwar immigration policy and politics. This was the repeal of the Chinese exclusion acts in 1943. The first ethnic group to be banned, the Chinese virtually ceased coming to the United States after the 1880s; some here returned to China. Moreover, Chinese immigrants and their children experienced widespread hostility in the late nineteenth and early twentieth centuries. The opposition included violence, legal restrictions, and social, educational and economic discrimination. By the 1930s, Chinese immigrants

[4] For refugee policy in the 1930s, see David S. Wyman, *Paper Walls: America and the Refugee Crisis, 1938-1941* (Amherst: University of Massachusetts Press, 1968); Henry Feingold, *The Politics of Rescue: The Roosevelt Administration and the Holocaust, 1938-1945* (New Brunswick: Rutgers University Press, 1970); and Arthur D. Morse, *While Six Million Died: A Chronicle of American Apathy* (New York: Random House, 1968).

[5] For a general discussion of the bracero program, see Richard B. Craig, *The Bracero Program: Interest Groups and Foreign Policy* (Austin: University of Texas Press, 1971); and Ernesto Galarza, *Merchants of Labor: The Mexican Bracero Story* (Santa Barbara, Calif.: McNally & Loftin, 1964).

and American-born Chinese were locked into the nation's Chinatowns, facing limited possibilities for social mobility.

By the 1940s, certain developments enabled repeal of the exclusion acts. The number of Chinese in America was so small that arguments about cheap labor threatening the American standard of living seemed absurd. The Chinese-American community had also changed. No longer exclusively a bachelor society, the Chinese had formed families, learned English, and adapted many American ways. To other Americans, they appeared less different and mysterious. Finally, there was the issue of foreign policy, a key matter in the repeal. The pro-China foreign policy of the Roosevelt administration made Americans look differently at China. When Japan attacked the United States in 1941, China became an ally.

Representative Walter Judd, a Republican congressman from Minnesota and former missionary to China, and a number of scholars and authors like Pearl S. Buck began a campaign to repeal the exclusion acts. These individuals organized the Citizens Committee to Repeal Chinese Exclusion, with Richard Walsh, editor of *Asia and the Americas*, as chairman. Although it lacked a large budget and ran a modest campaign, the committee nonetheless successfully helped steer the repeal bill through Congress. A few wanted the ban on all Asians repealed, but the more conservative members, mindful of the current attitude toward Japan and Japanese-Americans, believed that this was too controversial and urged instead a limited approach. Playing upon the wartime sympathy for China reaped results; Congress repealed the ban without much debate. Traditional West Coast opposition to the Chinese largely disappeared. Although organized labor and patriotic groups remained unenthusiastic or hostile to shifts in immigration policy, the measure granting China a quota of 105 annually was not a drastic change in American immigration; hence, the bill was not a major issue.[6] Legislation after the war admitted other Asians.[7]

Early Postwar Policy: Displaced Persons, McCarran-Walter, and the First Cold War Refugees

The debate over repeal of the Chinese exclusion acts indicated that it was primarily a matter of wartime policy and not a significant innova-

[6] For a detailed discussion of the repeal of the Chinese exclusion, see Fred W. Riggs, *Pressures on Congress: A Study of the Repeal of Chinese Exclusion* (New York: King's Crown Press, 1950). See also U.S. Congress, House, Committee on Immigration and Naturalization, *Repeal of the Chinese Exclusion Acts: Hearings,* 78th Congress, 1st session, 1943.

[7] In 1946, Congress repealed the ban on Indians and permitted the president to grant the Philippine Islands a quota of 100 after independence.

tion in immigration law. The same can be said for the passage of the so-called War Brides Act at the end of the war. This act, under which 117,000 aliens were eventually admitted, waived the visa requirements and provisions of the law excluding physical and mental defectives for those married to American service personnel. Since the law covered soldiers who had married Asians as well as Europeans, it did open the door for the admission of aliens from Japan and Korea.[8]

The War Brides Act was not especially controversial, but this was not the case with the Displaced Persons (DP) Act of 1948, its amended version in 1950, and the McCarran-Walter Act of 1952. The long debates about these laws revealed congressional reluctance to change American immigration policy; indeed, Congress reaffirmed the restrictions and national origins quotas of the 1920s when it passed the McCarran-Walter Act. Yet, the DP act was a crack in the door; it set in motion a long battle over American immigration policy that eventually led to the amendments of 1965 liberalizing immigration laws.

The devastation of World War II was staggering. Thirty million died. Much of Germany and Russia and parts of Eastern Europe lay in ruins. Americans, or at least high officials, had become aware of the Holocaust well before the end of the war. Millions of others had not perished. Several hundred thousand concentration camp inmates and millions of forced laborers or ex-prisoners of war were left without homes. The American government expected that these persons would be repatriated; most were. About 1 million displaced persons refused repatriation. The vast bulk were Poles, Balts, and Yugoslavs who did not want to return to their homelands. A small minority were Jews who had escaped Hitler's destruction. Their numbers swelled after the war when many Jews confronted anti-Semitism in Poland. Some were Jews who had spent the war years in Russia. They were not welcome in Poland; during 1945–1946, ugly anti-Semitic incidents sent thousands fleeing into the western zones of Germany. Thus, the U.S. area of occupation had a large number of displaced persons, many living in DP camps under appalling conditions. One government investigator in 1945 reported totally inadequate camp conditions. He found some former concentration camp victims still wearing their camp uniforms and living behind barbed wire.[9]

[8] Elizabeth J. Harper, *Immigration Laws of the United States* (Indianapolis: Bobbs-Merrill Co., 1975), p. 16.

[9] *New York Times*, September 30, 1945, p. 38. For a general discussion of the displaced persons issue, see Robert A. Divine, *American Immigration Policy, 1924-1952* (New Haven: Yale University Press, 1957), chaps. 6-7; and U.S. Displaced Persons Commission, *The DP Story*, 1952. I am especially indebted to Professor Leonard Dinnerstein of the University of Arizona for permitting me to see his forthcoming book, "America and the Survivors of the Holocaust," a detailed analysis of the entire DP issue.

Considerable favorable—but cautious—opinion existed toward the DPs. By the summer of 1946, leading newspapers and journals began to support efforts to allow these people to come to America. The *Saturday Evening Post*, for example, declared in February 1947 that

> if our efforts to protect these people in their right of asylum in Europe are anything more than wind, we are bound to consider whether or not some of them could come to our shores without evasion of immigration-quota restriction. Careful screening would, of course, be necessary but surely a nation whose population is mainly composed of immigrants and their descendants cannot logically maintain that the only "good" immigrants are those who are already here.[10]

Pro-displaced persons sentiments recognized that the United States was the richest nation in the world and that America, as a nation of immigrants, had a special humanitarian contribution to make in resolving this particular problem. The growing cold war buttressed this mood. As hostility replaced cordial relations between the Union of Soviet Socialist Republics and the United States, the American government became unwilling to resettle refugees forcibly behind the iron curtain.

Right after the war, President Truman dispatched Earl G. Harrison, who had experience with refugees, to examine the situation in Europe. Mr. Harrison found appalling conditions. He urged that 100,000 Jews be allowed to go to Palestine, an idea that the president found acceptable. This proposal involved Great Britain, which opposed more than token Jewish emigration to Palestine, and the future of the Near East. Moreover, Jewish emigration to Palestine would not solve the problem of the other DPs. As a short-term measure, on December 22, 1945, President Truman directed new consulate offices in Europe to give preference to DPs within the existing quota system.[11]

This action ultimately admitted about 41,000 by June 1948, but it did not come to the heart of the problem, for many DPs remained in the camps and more kept arriving. Despite much public sympathy toward the DPs, many Americans did not want to alter immigration laws, especially the national origins quota system. It took a bitter political fight in Congress and powerful lobbying efforts to enact, and then amend, the displaced persons legislation and eventually admit over 400,000 by the end of 1952.

American Jews were especially concerned about the survivors of the Holocaust. Under the leadership of the American Jewish Committee, a Citizens Committee on Displaced Persons (CCDP) was formed to

[10] Displaced Persons Commission, *DP Story*, pp. 9-11.
[11] Divine, *Immigration Policy*, pp. 112-113.

pressure Congress for legislation. Chaired by Earl Harrison and supported by a large number of Christian as well as Jewish groups, the CCDP campaigned vigorously for the enactment of DP legislation.

The CCDP had cautious support from the administration, but President Truman did indicate in October 1946 that he would ask for legislation to admit DPs outside the regular quota system. The citizens committee had hoped for leadership from key congressional leaders but had to settle for Congressman William Stratton of Illinois to introduce its proposal. Because the Stratton bill provided for the admission of immigrants outside the quota system, it stirred immediate opposition. A few thousand coming under the quotas was one issue; the specter of 400,000 outside the quotas, as called for by the Stratton bill, was another.

The Earlier Emotional Issues Emerge. The battle over the legislation revealed that many of the emotional issues of the 1920s and 1930s surrounding immigration were by no means dead. Economic issues bothered both proponents and opponents of the measure. Many feared that the nation would plunge into a depression after the end of the war, a possibility made menacing by the millions of ex-servicemen attending school or seeking employment. Even without the fear of depression, there was the postwar housing shortage. As one congressman put it,

> If you are going to continue to bring people into the country while GIs are walking the streets without homes to live in and when our economy is geared in such a way that if you have a sudden depression, you will have more unemployed than any other country in the world, then we are not doing our duty toward our country. What we need today is someone to stand on the floor of Congress and stand up for America. What we need is some more real, genuine Americanism.[12]

Proponents of the bill worked hard to meet these arguments and to convince organized labor to reverse its traditional stand on immigration restriction. They were relieved when William Green, president of the American Federation of Labor, endorsed the Stratton bill.[13] Moreover, the legislation itself sought to meet the economic arguments by special provisions. Forty percent of those coming were to be agricultural workers, a provision in part inspired by the belief that immigrants could be more easily employed in farming than elsewhere. The act also

[12] *Congressional Record,* June 10, 1948, p. 7774.
[13] U.S. Congress, House, Subcommittee on Immigration and Naturalization of the Committee on the Judiciary, *Permitting Admission of 400,000 Displaced Persons into the United States: Hearings,* 80th Congress, 1st session, 1947, p. 161.

required that officials give evidence that jobs and housing were available for the immigrants. Congressman Frank Fellows of Maine, who later sponsored the compromise law of 1948, told the House,

> To those who say our first duty as to jobs and housing is to our own veterans, I would say I wholeheartedly agree. Provisions of the bill require evidence by a State official that necessary housing and jobs are available before admission of these immigrants.[14]

While some opponents of the Stratton proposal battled along economic lines, others suggested that opening the door for the admission of immigrants outside the quotas would mean that thousands of undesirable and unassimilable refugees would be given asylum in America. Especially vociferous in opposing the admission of DPs were the veterans and Proponents of the bill worked hard to meet these arguments and to Legion, and those who liked to trace their ancestors to colonial America. When it was suggested that America might have a special moral obligation to take a fair share of the DPs, the American Legion spokesman said that our responsibility was to protect Americans first. "Displaced veterans, displaced Americans have first claim upon America's conscience," he declared.[15] Although the American Legion eventually changed its stand on the displaced persons issue, the traditional restrictionist groups and a hard core in Congress formed the center of its opposition.[16]

The arguments used by the patriotic groups and those of many congressmen against DP legislation frequently insisted that the DPs were undesirable. Of key importance was anti-Semitism. Although the vast bulk of the DPs were not Jews, in the public's mind the DP issue was often seen as a Jewish issue, an idea that the CCDP worked hard to overcome.[17]

Given the opposition to displaced persons, DP supporters realized that the Stratton bill would not pass without changes. Opposition was especially strong in the Senate where Senator Chapman Revercomb of West Virginia chaired the Immigration Subcommittee of the Senate Judiciary Committee. DP opponents managed to stall action and urged instead that congressional committees be sent to Europe to investigate the DP camps. The investigation provided support for the DPs, for both

14 *Congressional Record,* June 10, 1948, p. 7740.

15 House, Subcommittee on Immigration and Naturalization of the Committee on the Judiciary, *Permitting Admission of Displaced Persons,* p. 330.

16 Divine, *Immigration Policy,* chap. 6.

17 Leonard Dinnerstein, "Anti-Semitism in the Eightieth Congress: The Displaced Persons Act of 1948," *Capitol Studies,* vol. 6 (Fall 1978), pp. 15-17.

21

the House and the Senate committees suggested that something should be done to bring DPs to America.[18] In the second session of the Eightieth Congress, Congressman Frank Fellows, who chaired the Subcommittee on Immigration of the House Judiciary Committee, proposed that 200,000 be admitted from those who were registered in the camps by April 21, 1947. A compromise proposal, Fellows's bill called for those admitted to be charged against future immigration quotas for their country of origin. This was a key provision, for a majority in Congress was unwilling to disregard the national origins quotas. Mortgaging future quotas was an acceptable way to get the DPs in and keep the national origins quotas intact.

The Senate bill was less liberal. The Revercomb committee suggested that 100,000 DPs be admitted over a two-year period and that the cutoff date be December 22, 1945, the date of President Truman's directive. Both dates were after the war, but the House used the date when the camps were closed. The difference was significant; many Jews who had fled from Eastern Europe had done so in 1946, after the president's directive. Hence, the date became an important issue. Moreover, the Senate proposal reserved 50 percent of the visas for agricultural workers and suggested that half of those admitted come from those areas (Estonia, Latvia, and Lithuania) annexed by Russia after the war. This was more a cold war issue than a DP one, but both of these provisions would have further limited the chances of Jewish DPs coming to America.[19]

Attempts to alter the Senate bill were only partially successful. The senators increased the total to 200,000 but the cutoff date and other restrictions were left largely intact. The vote against changing the cutoff date was decisive.[20] The Senate also amended the bill to give preference to the Volksdeutsche, those Germans expelled from Eastern European states after the war. The House refused to accept the Senate bill, however, and the two chambers conferred to break the deadlock.

The Enactment of the Displaced Persons Act. Although accepting some minor changes, the Senate conferees wanted to include the Volksdeutsche, strongly opposed changing the cutoff date, and in essence told the House to take the bill or nothing. One particular provision that revealed the discrimination against Jews was that, although the cutoff for DPs generally was December 22, 1945, the Volksdeutsche would be eligible if they resettled by July 1, 1948. The inclusion of ethnic Germans also

[18] Ibid.
[19] Ibid.
[20] Divine, *Immigration Policy,* pp. 121-124.

22

revealed the impact of the cold war and a shifting attitude toward Germany and Germans. At the end of the war, considerable hostile public opinion existed toward Germans and the Volksdeutsche, who were thought to have been pro-Nazi during the war. Several congressmen proposed using the German immigration quota for the victims of Nazism.[21] By 1948, however, the Volksdeutsche were seen in a different light.

Not a few House members were angry. Four refused to sign the conference report. Congressman Fellows told the House,

> The real bone of contention is this date December 22, 1945. The House bill had the cut-off date of April 21, 1947. We felt that that was a fairer date, taking into consideration all of the circumstances. But we could not and have not changed the date of December 22, 1945.[22]

Congressman Emanuel Celler of New York bluntly said that the cutoff date of December 22, 1945, "would make the act utterly unworkable and that it would deliberately discriminate against the Jews who crowded into the DP camps after that date." He went on to attack the Volksdeutsche.[23]

Disappointed though the liberals were, the bill was all they could get. President Truman reluctantly signed it but noted that it was "flagrantly discriminatory," especially against Jews, because of the 1945 cutoff date. He also insisted that the bill discriminated against Catholics, which was not true and was denied by Roman Catholic spokesmen.[24]

The enactment of the Displaced Persons Act did not end the controversy; Democratic liberals wanted to amend the law immediately. The Republicans defended the bill, though the Republican presidential nominee, Governor Thomas Dewey, spoke cautiously in the 1948 campaign. Hopes for amendment were high in early 1949. The obstructionist tactics of Senator Pat McCarran, who was the new chairman of the Senate Judiciary Committee, blocked changes for that year. He could not hold back amendments indefinitely, however. In 1950, Congress changed the law to increase the numbers and eliminate the discriminatory provisions. The cutoff date was extended to January 1, 1949, although by the time Congress amended the law most Jewish DPs had gone to Israel. The agricultural and Baltic preferences were also eliminated and a number of groups were added, such as World War II Polish veterans

---

[21] See U.S. Congress, House, Subcommittee No. 1 of the Committee on Immigration and Naturalization, *Study of Problems Relating to Immigration and Deportation and Other Matters: Hearings,* 79th Congress, 1st session, 1945.

[22] *Congressional Record,* June 18, 1948, p. 8858.

[23] Ibid., p. 8861.

[24] Divine, *Immigration Policy,* pp. 128, 131.

23

in exile in Great Britain.[25] The inclusion of such refugees other than the original DPs indicates a further shift in the political climate from 1945, when the DP issue was first raised. These new groups clearly reflected the growing influence of the cold war on American immigration policy.

The Displaced Persons Act of 1948 and its amendments in 1950 did not fundamentally alter American immigration policy. The fight over the act was a preview of forces shaping American immigration for the next two decades. This bill marked a major congressional effort to admit refugees, whether the victims of World War II or the cold war. As the Displaced Persons Commission put it,

> The DP Act of 1948 marked a turning point in American immigration policy, and in American foreign policy. For the first time in this century, restrictive and exclusionary legislation was relaxed in order to facilitate the admission of refugees into this country.[26]

That the act was a cautious turning point can easily be seen in the battle over the McCarran-Walter Act of 1952, only two years after the 1950 amendments. Proponents of immigration liberalization had been heartened by the DP act and by the repeal earlier of some of the exclusions against Asians. At the same time, fears of a major depression after the end of the war lessened. Some also noted that the nation had just defeated Nazi Germany and its ugly racism and that American immigration laws with their odious national origins quotas seemed in contradiction with the goals of the war.

In the face of these forces and with a general consensus emerging about the need for a comprehensive review of American immigration policy, Congress moved to investigate and ponder the whole issue of immigration. In 1947, Senator Chapman Revercomb proposed an investigation of immigration laws. At first under Senator Revercomb and then under Senator McCarran, the committee gathered mounds of information and produced a lengthy report in 1950. It was the most comprehensive study of immigration since the 1911 Dillingham commission.[27]

Following the issuance of the report, both the Senate and House began two years of debate on the McCarran bill that accompanied the

[25] Ibid., chap. 7.

[26] Displaced Persons Commission, *DP Story,* p. 345.

[27] Two general accounts of immigration policy covering the 1950s are Bennett, *American Immigration Policies;* and U.S. Congress, Senate, *U.S. Immigration Law and Policy: 1952-1979,* a report prepared at the request of the Committee on the Judiciary upon formation of the Select Commission on Immigration and Refugee Policy, 96th Congress, 1st session, 1979.

report. The debate over the proposed legislation, which was finally passed in revised form, continued the restrictionist-liberalization argument; it revealed that hopes for liberalization faced an uphill battle. Although the McCarran-Walter Act did modify immigration policy, it was basically a restatement of the legislation of the 1920s.

At the heart of the 1952 act were the national origins quotas and overall ceiling for Eastern Hemispheric immigration of approximately 150,000. The 1950 Senate report avoided the racist arguments of the past but nonetheless accepted the national origins plan:

> Without giving credence to any theory of Nordic superiority, the subcommittee believes that the adoption of the national origins formula was a rational and logical method of numerically restricting immigration in such a manner as to best preserve the sociological and cultural balance in the population of the United States. There is no doubt that it favored the peoples of western Europe over those of southern and eastern Europe, but the subcommittee holds that the peoples who had made the greatest contribution to the development of this country were fully justified in determining that the country was no longer a field for further colonization, and henceforth further immigration would not only be restricted but directed to admit immigrants considered to be more readily assimilable because of the similarity of their cultural background to those of the principal components of our population.[28]

Most congressional proponents of national origins similarly avoided direct racist arguments. Senator McCarran came closest to such a defense when he told the Senate that

> the cold hard truth is that in the United States today there are hard-core indigestible blocs who have not become integrated into the American way of life, but who, on the contrary, are its deadly enemy. The cold, hard fact is, too, Mr. President, that this Nation is the last hope of western civilization; and if this oasis of the world shall be overrun, perverted, contaminated, or destroyed, then the last flickering light of humanity will be extinguished. A solution of the problems of Europe and Asia, Mr. President, will not come as we transplant these problems en masse to the United States of America.[29]

[28] U.S. Congress, Senate, Committee on the Judiciary, *The Immigration and Naturalization Systems of the United States,* 81st Congress, 2nd session, 1950, S. Rept. 1515, p. 455.

[29] *Congressional Record,* May 16, 1952, p. 5330.

Criticisms of the McCarran-Walter Act. Liberals, led by Herbert Lehman and Hubert Humphrey in the Senate and Emanuel Celler in the House, attacked the national origins formula as

> a racist philosophy. It is a philosophy of fear, suspicion, and distrust of the foreigners outside our country, and of the aliens within our country. . . . This philosophy is founded on the assumption that America is under the constant threat of losing her Anglo-Saxon character because of immigration, and that the so-called bloodstock of America, described as Anglo-Saxon and Nordic, is the basis of America and must be preserved from contamination by foreign immigrants.[30]

Senator Lehman insisted that the philosophy of national origins was "strikingly similar to the basic racial philosophy officially espoused so unfortunately and with such tragic consequences in Nazi Germany a few short years ago."[31]

Major ethnic organizations, except for the Japanese American Citizens League (JACL), usually denounced the bill while patriotic groups defended it. Proponents warned against the economic consequences of large immigration, pointed to the dangers facing America in the cold war, and especially defended the tight security provisions of the act. Some defended the national origins provisions as well. Witnesses and congressional speakers who opposed the bill were equally vociferous and outspoken, but they clearly lacked the votes to block its passage or uphold President Truman's veto. Recognizing their relatively weak position, the Lehman-Humphrey forces proposed a substitute bill calling for pooling unused quotas (which were mainly from Northern and Western Europe), making them available to countries with small quotas, and increasing slightly the total volume of immigration by using the 1950 rather than the 1920 census as a basis for quotas.

Even these modest changes had little chance of enactment; Congress rejected them along with attempts to block the McCarran-Walter Act. Only a handful of senators were present when the Senate passed the act by a voice vote on May 22, 1952.[32]

The low ceiling on immigration and national origins quotas prompted most debate and were the most important parts of the law. Yet Congress debated other provisions and made some changes in

[30] *Congressional Record,* May 11, 1952, p. 5102.

[31] Ibid.

[32] The most complete discussion of the McCarran-Walter Act can be found in Marius A. Dimmitt, "The Enactment of the McCarran-Walter Act of 1952" (Ph.D. diss., University of Kansas, 1970). See also, Bennett, *American Immigration Policies,* chaps. 10-13; and Divine, *Immigration Policy,* chap. 9.

policy. The act repealed the racial ban on citizenship, and proponents of the law insisted that this proved the act was not racist. This provision prompted JACL to defend the act. Mike Masaoka of the league said that his organization believed the bill had limitations but supported it because thousands of Japanese immigrants, most of them elderly, would be eligible for citizenship.[33] Repeal of a racial ban on citizenship was not especially controversial. Several Asian groups had already been made eligible for citizenship. Led by Congressman Judd, the House had repealed the racial ban in 1949, and repeal had wide support in the Senate.[34]

The bill also incorporated Congressman Judd's suggestion for the creation of an Asia Pacific triangle, a region composed of Asian nations. Each Asian country in the triangle was granted a minimum quota of 100 annually; the total for the triangle was 2,000. The act's supporters hailed these quotas as further proof that the bill was not discriminatory. Opponents agreed that both the removal of the race ban and the introduction of Asian quotas were desirable, but they noted that sections pertaining to the Asia Pacific triangle perpetuated racial discrimination. Whereas alien quotas were usually charged to the country of birth, persons of half or more Asian ancestry were charged to that Asian quota. A person born in Colombia of Japanese parents, for instance, would not enter as a Colombian but rather as part of the small Japanese allotment. Colombia was a Western Hemisphere nation without a quota. The intent of the law was no secret; its drafters and supporters worried about hundreds of thousands of persons of Asian ancestry living in South America or Canada who, without this special provision, would be eligible to come in as nonquota immigrants from the Western Hemisphere.[35]

The law also limited colonies and dependent areas to 100 annually, a section that sharply reduced immigration from the West Indies. Formerly, West Indians came under the large British quota, but now, West Indians, as colonists of Great Britain, were limited to 100 per year. Defenders of the bill claimed that all colonies were subject to the same restrictions. The fact that black West Indians were those most affected by the change was not lost on the bill's critics.[36]

---

[33] U.S. Congress, Subcommittees of the Committees on the Judiciary, *Revisions of Immigration, Naturalization and Nationality Laws: Joint Hearings,* 82nd Congress, 1st session, 1951, pp. 45-65.

[34] Divine, *Immigration Policy,* pp. 173-174; and Dimmitt, "McCarran-Walter Act," pp. 133-134.

[35] Congress, *Revisions of Immigration Laws,* p. 574; *Congressional Record,* May 15, 1952, p. 5234; and Divine, *Immigration Policy,* pp. 181-182.

[36] *Congressional Record,* May 13, 1952, p. 5111; May 15, 1952, p. 5291; April 23, 1952, p. 4440; and Dimmitt, "McCarran-Walter Act," pp. 136, 240.

If quotas, national origins, and racism received most attention, the 1952 bill contained other important parts. Building upon prior legislation, the act included stringent security procedures for admission because its supporters wanted to preclude the possibility of communist subversion through immigration. Critics claimed the law was too harsh. President Truman did single out some of these provisions in his veto message, but the cold war climate was conducive to such legislation. Indeed, one of the main arguments in favor of the bill was that it protected America from subversive immigrants. Moreover, Senator McCarran and others frequently insisted that radicals and Reds were the chief groups opposing the bill, by implication suggesting that nonradical opponents were duped. This was, of course, a familiar tactic of the politics of the 1950s.[37]

Finally, the act included a preference system for immigrants within the quotas themselves, based on relatives and economics. Although not an important issue in 1952, it became important in the 1965 amendments liberalizing immigration policy.

The McCarran-Walter Act did not impose a quota system for the Western Hemisphere but rather relied upon the general categories of exclusions, such as "likely to become a public charge," to regulate Western Hemisphere immigration. Nor did the McCarran subcommittee of 1950 pay much attention to braceros or illegal immigration. Unions were concerned about these issues, and they became key immigration matters in the years to follow. The McCarran subcommittee did favor the use of temporary workers and tighter enforcement of the border, but in general these were not pressing issues surrounding the 1952 act and were seldom discussed.[38]

Following President Truman's veto, the antirestrictionists concentrated their efforts on upholding the president. In the House, they had little chance; the representatives passed the measure by a vote of 278 to 113. In the Senate, however, the margin was only 57 to 26. A switch of two senators would have sustained the president.[39]

President Truman's Commission on Immigration. In rejecting the bill, President Truman called for a special commission to reexamine the whole issue of immigration.[40] Congress did not want another commission, but President Truman appointed one anyway, in September 1952. The commission held hearings in several major American cities and

[37] Dimmitt, "McCarran-Walter Act," p. 234.

[38] Senate, Committee on the Judiciary, *Immigration and Naturalization Systems,* pp. 573-585.

[39] Dimmitt, "McCarran-Walter Act," pp. 234-235.

[40] U.S. President's Commission on Immigration and Naturalization, *Whom Shall We Welcome?* 1953, pp. 275-284.

finally issued a report—*Whom Shall We Welcome?*—which, not surprisingly, criticized the McCarran-Walter Act's approach.[41]

While the commission was getting under way, President Truman and some Democrats tried to inject the McCarran-Walter Act into the 1952 presidential election. While supporting Adlai Stevenson and the Democratic party, President Truman attacked the Republicans for their support of the act and called for revision. (The vote in the Senate had been twenty-five Democrats to override the veto, mainly from the South, and eighteen against. The Republicans had voted thirty-two to eight to override.) The president charged that Dwight Eisenhower was morally blind on this issue and that the act contained racist ideas.[42] General Eisenhower appeared typically vague but flexible on immigration.[43]

The 1952 election was hardly fought over immigration and party divisions were not clear. The victory of Dwight Eisenhower and the Republicans indicated that there would be no popular demand in the 1950s for another major effort to overhaul immigration policy. By the time the President's Commission on Immigration and Naturalization made its report in January 1953, the issue was dead. Yet *Whom Shall We Welcome?* clearly stated the liberal position on immigration, one which would find increased support by the 1960s.

Citing the contributions that immigrants had made to American society and dismissing economic fears, the commission argued that the nation needed more immigrants, not fewer, and suggested that 250,000 quota immigrants be admitted yearly. It was especially critical of the national origins provision as applied to Europe, the limit on immigration from colonies, and sections of the McCarran-Walter Act charging those of Asian ancestry, regardless of country of birth, to Asian quotas.[44] Pointing to the cold war, the commission also suggested that immigration be geared to a humanitarian refugee policy. Perhaps a forerunner of the 1965 act, the report called for categories of preferences, with the reunification of families, American needs, and those seeking asylum included in the nation's immigration policy.[45]

Congress was in no mood to reform immigration policy. Proposals like *Whom Shall We Welcome?* fell on deaf ears. Yet immigration did

---

[41] Ibid., passim.

[42] *New York Times,* October 18, 1952, p. 14.

[43] *New York Times,* September 9, 1952, p. 16; October 17, 1952, p. 19; October 18, 1952, p. 8; and October 22, 1952, p. 16.

[44] President's Commission on Immigration and Naturalization, *Whom Shall We Welcome?* pp. 42-43, 88-90.

[45] Ibid., pp. 117-120. Many of these arguments had already been suggested in William S. Bernard, ed., *American Immigration Policy—A Reappraisal* (New York: Harper Brothers, 1950).

receive attention in the 1950s and resulted in several acts that weakened the McCarran-Walter Act. The various exemptions—sometimes called tinkerings—to the law became so significant that most newcomers were coming as nonquota immigrants by the 1960s.

President Eisenhower had rejected the harsh criticism of the McCarran-Walter Act, but he nonetheless favored acceptance of refugees from communism and a more flexible immigration policy. One of his first proposals to Congress was revision of the immigration laws, with special provisions to admit escapees from behind the iron curtain, numbering 120,000 per year for two years. In calling for additional legislation for increased immigration, President Eisenhower emphasized that this plea was based on humanitarian grounds to help refugees from communism and was part of American foreign policy. The proposed law, he claimed, would help ease overpopulation and economic problems of our allies in Western Europe; at the same time, care would be taken to protect the United States against undesirable immigrants.[46] The president's supporters in Congress assured their colleagues that

> the entire concept of the program and its administration is placed within the framework of the Immigration and Nationality Act, commonly referred to as the McCarran-Walter Act. The security provisions of the Immigration Act are to be fully complied with and the screening process proposed in the bill is, in fact, even more rigorous than that which applies under normal immigration procedures. . . . Additional requirements regarding the submission of assurances of employment and housing are further designed to protect the domestic economy and social welfare of the United States.[47]

The president's suggestion was similar to the DP act, for it called for the admission of refugees outside the annual quotas.

Even this cautious approach from a Republican president found enemies in Congress. The House minority report warned that the bill "involves incalculable danger to this Nation."

Specifically, the minority insisted

> to superimpose this special scheme of assisted immigration upon regular quota and nonquota immigration systems means actually to destroy the principle of national origins upon which our immigration system is based. This destruction of the basis of our immigration system is to be achieved under this bill, without regard to the vital security interests of this

[46] *Congressional Record,* July 28, 1953, p. 10150.
[47] U.S. Congress, House, Committee on the Judiciary, *Emergency Immigration Program,* House Report 974, 83rd Congress, 1st session, 1953, p. 9.

Nation and at a considerable expense to the American tax-payer.[48]

With Congressman Francis Walter leading the opposition, the House was unwilling to accept the original bill to admit 240,000 nonquota migrants. Senator McCarran was also eager to amend the Eisenhower plan; after considerable debate and some changes, the House and Senate agreed to accept 214,000 special immigrants by the end of 1956. The largest group was German ethnic expellees, but Poles, Italians, Greeks, and some Arabs and Asians were included. As in the case of the DP act, prospective immigrants required assurances from U.S. citizens of jobs and housing (unless they were close relatives) and elaborate screening to make certain that no subversives would sneak through.[49]

The debate over the Refugee Relief Act of 1953 was typical of the immigration discussions in Congress until the early 1960s. General proposals to alter the national origins system or overhaul the McCarran-Walter Act went nowhere; measures pushed on grounds of national security, the cold war, or humanitarianism had better prospects. Even the 1953 act became controversial after its enactment. Special Advisor of Refugees Edward J. Corsi, formerly head of the Immigration and Naturalization Service, charged that the State Department, especially Scott McLeod, was hindering the admission of refugees because of excessive concern about security.[50] Mr. Corsi lost his job, but the process was speeded. He perhaps exaggerated in his public charges and statements before a Senate committee, but there is no doubt that the fear of communism was strong both in Congress and in the State Department of the 1950s. They were deeply concerned lest any Reds get through the golden door.

The minority who worried about the impact of special refugee legislation upon the basic national origins quota system was correct about one thing: The special laws were undercutting the McCarran-Walter Act in fact, if not in principle. Italy, for example, had a quota of 5,645 under the 1952 act, but two to three times that number were admitted annually in the early 1960s. Congress rejected major revisions of the law again in 1956, but the Hungarian Revolution produced a mass exodus of freedom fighters, some of whom President Eisenhower wanted to admit to the United States. The President sent Vice-President Richard Nixon to Vienna to make a study and recommendations. Mr. Nixon stressed that the freedom fighters were strongly anti-communist and

48 Ibid., p. 19.
49 Bennett, *American Immigration Policies,* pp. 194-196.
50 *New York Times,* April 21, 1954, p. 1.

would make good citizens.[51] In early 1957, President Eisenhower asked for special legislation and some broader changes in the basic immigration laws. Sympathy for the freedom fighters was limited. Congress did not agree to major changes but did grant the president latitude in admitting refugees, including about 38,000 freedom fighters. Another change, though perhaps minor, indicated the further disintegration of the quota system, for Congress in that year cancelled the mortgaged quotas required under the Displaced Persons Act.[52]

The remainder of President Eisenhower's term and the first days of the Kennedy administration did not witness major shifts in immigration policy. Still, Congress amended the laws to admit more refugees. Events overseas put further pressure on the president and Congress to open the immigrant door more. The collapse of the Batista regime and the triumph of Fidel Castro in Cuba propelled thousands of Cubans to seek asylum in the United States. Their numbers were eventually to exceed 800,000. The president used the parolee status to enable many to enter and also to help Chinese arriving via Hong Kong. The admission of Cuban refugees was another sign of the growing importance of the executive branch in the formulation of immigration policy. In 1962, Congress enacted the Migration and Refugee Assistance Act to aid the president in these matters.[53]

Immigration Reform: The 1965 Act and Its Aftermath

The additions to the 1952 law enacted in the ten years following the fight over the McCarran-Walter Act had eroded the basic law sufficiently so that President Kennedy, like Harry Truman and to a lesser extent Dwight Eisenhower, made a frontal attack on the national origins system itself. With most immigrants coming outside the quotas and with Congress being besieged by private member bills to circumvent rigid immigration restrictions, the time was ripe for change.

Two other facts are important in explaining the significant changes enacted in 1965. First, the healthy economy in the 1960s dampened opposition to immigration. Labor groups, for example, favored a more liberal policy. One should not overemphasize economics, however. The reforms of 1965 did lead to increases in immigration, but the main effort of reformers was to rid the laws of ethnic discrimination. A great number of ethnic, religious, and humanitarian groups objected to the

[51] Richard M. Nixon, "Providing for the Needs of the Hungarian Refugees," *Bulletin of the Department of State,* vol. 36 (January 21, 1957), pp. 94-96.

[52] Bennett, *American Immigration Policies,* pp. 200-203.

[53] Senate, *U.S. Immigration Law,* pp. 44-48.

McCarran-Walter Act and they lobbied to change it. Polls indicated that Americans did not want more immigrants but favored changes in the selection process.[54] Still, a growing economy generally lessened antagonism toward immigrants.

The second fact was a growing toleration of ethnic minorities—and their growing political power. It is no accident that the 1965 changes occurred during the decade when the nation elected its first Roman Catholic president and experienced a major civil rights movement, including important legislation to eradicate white racism. Bigotry and even vague defenses of national origins quotas for immigration, so easily enacted by lopsided majorities in 1952, were simply not publicly acceptable in the mid-1960s. Nor were the traditional supporters of national origins well organized. Senator Edward Kennedy, the Senate leader for changing the law, wrote,

> During the course of the hearings I personally met with representatives from several of these organizations, including the American Coalition of Patriotic Societies, the American Legion, the Daughters of the American Revolution, and the National Association of Evangelicals. There was a candid exchange of views between myself and those who joined the discussion. While most of those with whom I met were skeptical regarding the various reform channels, and for reasons which varied among the organizations represented at the meetings, I believe it is fair to say that all recognized the unworkability of the national-origins quota system and at the close of the meeting expressed a willingness to cooperate in finding a new formula for the selection of immigrants. No significant opposition to eliminating the national-origins quota system was organized by any of their organizations.[55]

In July 1963, President John Kennedy sent to Congress his proposals for immigration reform. They included several key parts but the most important was the phase-out of the national origins system. In addition, the president wanted the Asia Pacific triangle eliminated. He asked for a continuation of the nonquota status for the Western Hemisphere and requested a nonquota status for newly independent nations of Jamaica and Trinidad and Tobago.[56]

[54] *Immigration,* American Institute of Public Opinion: Gallup Political Index, report no. 3 (Princeton, N.J.: August 1965).
[55] Edward Kennedy, "The Immigration Act of 1965," *Annals of the American Academy of Political and Social Science: The New Immigration,* vol. 367 (September 1966), p. 142.
[56] *New York Times,* July 24, 1963, p. 1.

33

These provisions were in keeping with the tone of *A Nation of Immigrants,* a short book John Kennedy had authored in 1958, and reformers like the administrator of the Bureau of Security and Consular Affairs, Abba Schwartz.[57] Senator Philip Hart of Michigan and Representative Celler introduced companion bills. The death of President Kennedy and some opposition in Congress held up the reforms briefly and eventually produced modifications in the original proposals, but President Lyndon Johnson also supported immigration reform. He told Congress in January 1965,

> We must lift by legislation the bar of discrimination against those who seek entry into our country, particularly those with much needed skills and those joining their families. In establishing preferences, a nation that was built by immigrants of all lands can ask those who now seek admission: "What can you do for your country?" But we should not be asking: "In what country were you born?"[58]

Although Congress took several years to enact the original Kennedy reforms, the eventual outcome was not in serious doubt about the end of the national origins quotas and the establishment of a preference system to replace it. Indeed, the number of congressmen climbing on the anti-national origins bandwagon in 1964 and 1965 was staggering, as dozens of bills and their sponsors proposed the abolition of national origins. Still, some discussion took place over the eventual bill, and the Johnson administration was forced to accept provisions it did not want. Congress was busy with other measures in 1963 and 1964; hence, immigration reform suffered a further delay.

The most acceptable changes in policy were the substitution of a preference system for the national origins system and the elimination of the Asia Pacific triangle. The administration marshaled foreign policy arguments against national origins and so did the growing number of groups favorable to reform. A few patriotic groups warned against change; in the Senate, Sam Ervin fought a rear guard action for the old way. The senator said, for example, that the proposed bill eliminating national origins

> is discriminatory against those [English-speaking] people because it puts them on exactly the same plane as the people of Ethiopia are put, where the people of Ethiopia have the

---

[57] Abba P. Schwartz, *The Open Society* (New York: William Morrow & Co., 1968), chap. 6. See also Charles Keely, "The Immigration Act of 1965: A Study of the Relationship of Social Science Theory to Group Interest and Legislation" (Ph.D. diss., Fordham University, 1970); and Jethro K. Lieberman, *Are Americans Extinct?* (New York: Walter & Co., 1968).

[58] *New York Times,* January 14, 1965, p. 38.

same right to come to the United States under this bill as the people from England, the people of France, the people of Germany, the people of Holland, and I don't think—with all due respect to Ethiopia—I don't know of any contributions that Ethiopia has made to the making of America.[59]

New Emphasis on Family Unification. Even Senator Ervin, after winning some changes, knew that the national origins system was doomed. Most of the debate on discrimination centered on Europe, but the repeal of the Asia Pacific triangle was also a key part of reform. The bill as eventually enacted permitted a ceiling of 170,000 for the Eastern Hemisphere, with a maximum of 20,000 per country, which put Asian countries on the same footing as those from Western Europe. The preference system emphasized family unification. Seventy-four percent of the places were reserved for family preferences. The largest was the fifth preference (24 percent) for brothers and sisters of U.S. citizens, a provision that prompted some to label the bill "the brothers and sisters law."

The family preferences aided those countries that had already sent people to America, but the law did open the door for the large influx of immigration from the Far East in recent years. It is doubtful whether Congress or the administration saw the triangle's repeal as significantly changing patterns of immigration. Not too much was said about it. Attorney General Robert Kennedy told the House subcommittee investigating immigration in 1964 that the most important impact would be on nations like Greece, Italy, and Portugal. In answering a question about potential immigration from Asia, Mr. Kennedy said,

> I would say for the Asia-Pacific triangle it would be approximately 5,000, Mr. Chairman, after which immigration from that source would virtually disappear; 5,000 immigrants could come in the first year, but we do not expect that there would be any great influx after that.[60]

Nor was the preference system especially controversial. The administration had originally stressed occupational preferences but was willing to compromise. Because the final bill gave priority to the unification of families, it appeared humanitarian and satisfied domestic pressures. Ethnic groups from nations with low quotas and large backlogs had a way to increase their immigration.

[59] U.S. Congress, Senate, Subcommittee on Immigration and Naturalization of the Committee on the Judiciary, *Immigration: Hearings,* 89th Congress, 1st session, 1965, p. 63.
[60] U.S. Congress, House, Subcommittee No. 1 of the Committee on the Judiciary, *Immigration: Hearings,* 88th Congress, 2nd session, 1964, p. 418.

The number (10,200) reserved for refugees recognized the continuing world refugee problem, but the future would prove this figure unrealistic. The bill also allowed preference for professionals and other skilled workers needed in the United States. The limited number for occupational skills—a maximum of 20 percent—and the tight procedures for labor certification appeased traditional fears about the impact of immigration on the labor market. Actually, considerably fewer than 20 percent came with labor certification because members of the worker's family were charged to the occupational preferences.[61] On the other hand, many immigrants coming as refugees or under family preferences eventually entered the labor force without labor certification.[62]

Some parts of the bill did draw fire from Congress, particularly from Michael Feighan, chairman of the House Subcommittee on Immigration. Although he knew his own committee and Congress generally favored abolition of national origins, Congressman Feighan was partly responsible for placing family unification at the top of the preference list and for tighter labor certification. Prior to the Democratic landslide in 1964, his delaying tactics were effective, but he was fighting a lost cause if he hoped to halt reform. One architect of the bill, Abba Schwartz, said,

> It was no longer possible for Congressman Feighan to fail to bring to a vote the Administration's proposal or variations which would accomplish the major object—abolition of the national origins quota system. The overwhelming Democratic majorities in the Congress following the 1964 landslide elections made possible enlargement of the committees, and Attorney General-designate Katzenbach was the first to assure me that there was no need for concern about Feighan's sabotaging our efforts.[63]

Katzenbach was right. Although Congressman Feighan secured changes in the administration's bill, the fight moved to the Senate, where the opposition to one key issue was stronger. Congressman Feighan had been persuaded to accept the continuation of a nonceiling and nonquota status for the Western Hemisphere, but the strong opposition of Senators Everett Dirksen of Illinois and Ervin forced a change. The Johnson

[61] For a discussion of the occupational preference system, see Robert S. Goldfarb, "Occupational Preferences in the U.S. Immigration Law: An Economic Analysis," in this volume.

[62] David North and Allen LeBel found that, within two years, about one-half of the immigrants had entered the labor market. David North and Allen LeBel, *Manpower and Immigration Policies in the United States,* National Committee for Manpower Policy, Special Report no. 20, 1978, p. 56.

[63] Schwartz, *The Open Society,* p. 121.

administration accepted the overall ceiling of 120,000 for the Western Hemisphere as the price for a consensus bill.[64] Some face-saving was involved. The final bill established a Select Commission on Western Hemisphere Immigration to make a recommendation about that issue. Neither Senator Dirksen nor Senator Ervin expected the commission to reject the 120,000 limit. The commission noted the disagreements surrounding the issue and did not make a definitive recommendation. Rather, it suggested that the implementation of the ceiling be postponed for a year. Congress took no action, and the 120,000 maximum became part of immigration policy.[65]

The proponents of a Western Hemisphere ceiling were not always precise in their arguments, but they were anxious about growing immigration from the Western Hemisphere and the rapid population growth there.[66] The administration claimed that no absolute limit was necessary, as traditional methods of control would regulate immigration from this region, and that the imposition of a ceiling would injure the Good Neighbor Policy. The figure of 120,000 was a compromise representing the approximate annual flow of immigration from the Western Hemisphere in the years just prior to 1965.[67]

Once the House changes were accepted and the Western Hemisphere issue resolved, the bill passed easily. The senators accepted their version 76 to 18, with the opposition being mainly southerners. In post–World War II America, southerners have been less enthusiastic about immigration reform than the rest of the nation. Southern representatives have constituencies generally composed of old-stock Americans; they are less susceptible to pressure for liberalization. Moreover, racial attitudes, which do bear on immigration policy, have been less tolerant in the South. Finally, the fact that immigrants traditionally have settled outside the South has also meant a loss of political power for southern states in terms of congressional representation.

The Senate passed the conference bill by a voice vote, while the House agreed to it by a vote of 320 to 69.[68] To emphasize the dramatic

[64] Schwartz, *The Open Society*, p. 124; *New York Times*, August 28, 1965; and *Congressional Record*, September 30, 1965, p. 25657. For an interesting discussion of the Western Hemisphere ceiling, see Gerald M. Rosberg, "Legal Regulation of the Migration Process: The 'Crisis' of Illegal Immigration," in William H. McNeill and Ruth S. Adams, eds., *Human Migration: Patterns and Policies* (Bloomington: Indiana University Press, 1978), pp. 343-347.

[65] U.S. Congress, Select Commission on Western Hemisphere Immigration, *Report January 1968*, 1968, p. 9.

[66] *Congressional Record*, September 22, 1965, pp. 24739, 24776.

[67] Rosberg, "Migration Process," pp. 343-347.

[68] *Congressional Record*, September 22, 1965, p. 24783; September 30, pp. 25616, 25663-25664.

nature of the repeal of national origins quotas and immigration reform, only thirteen years after the one-sided 1952 reaffirmation of the national origins quota system, President Johnson signed the bill on October 3, 1965, at the base of the Statute of Liberty. Somewhat accurately he said,

> This bill is not a revolutionary bill. It does not affect the lives of millions. It will not reshape the structure of our daily lives, or add importantly to our wealth and power. Yet it is still one of the most important acts of this Congress and this Administration. For it repairs a deep and painful flaw in the fabric of American justice. . . . The days of unlimited immigration are past. But those who come will come because of what they are—not because of the land from which they sprung.[69]

Backlogs in southern and eastern Europe were the most immediate beneficiaries of the changes. As a result of the amendments, after 1968 the bulk of European immigrants came from southern and eastern rather than northern and western Europe, which prompted one Irish-American organization to complain about the new law.[70] Abolition of national origins quotas and the introduction of the preference system accounted for this shift. By ending small quotas on new nations in the Caribbean (such as Jamaica, Trinidad and Tobago, and the smaller West Indian islands) and repealing the Asia Pacific triangle, Congress made immigration from those areas easier. Table 1 indicates the shift in immigration since 1965.

Barriers to Africa and Asia. The family preference system, the 20,000 nation, and the 170,000 Eastern Hemisphere limits were barriers. Since 74 percent of the slots were reserved for family unification preferences, nations such as those in Africa and Asia, with low rates of prior emigration to America, were handicapped. There were ways for some Asian nations to get around these barriers. Exemptions for immediate family members, such as parents, children, and spouses of adult U.S. citizens, permitted nations to exceed the 20,000 limit.

Pre-1965 communities of Koreans, Filipinos, and Chinese provided the contacts in America for the development of immigrant networks. The Chinese were the most notable because they had been here since the mid-nineteenth century and were, along with the Japanese, the largest of the Asian-American groups. The Chinatown populations of

---

[69] *New York Times,* October 4, 1965.

[70] See the statement of John P. Collins, national chairman of the American Irish National Immigration Committee, in U.S. Congress, House, Subcommittee No. 1 of the Committee on the Judiciary, *Immigration: Hearings,* 90th Congress, 2nd session, 1968, pp. 2-8.

TABLE 1

IMMIGRANTS ADMITTED BY COUNTRY OR REGION OF BIRTH,
FISCAL YEARS ENDED SEPTEMBER 30, 1977, AND JUNE 30, 1965

	Number		
Country of Birth	1977	1965	Percent change
All countries	462,315	296,697	+55.8
Europe	70,010	113,424	−38.3
Austria	400	1,680	−76.2
Belgium	377	1,005	−62.5
Czechoslovakia	575	1,894	−69.6
Denmark	433	1,384	−68.7
France	1,618	4,039	−59.9
Germany	6,372	24,045	−73.5
Greece	7,838	3,002	+161.9
Hungary	853	1,574	−45.8
Ireland	1,238	5,463	−77.3
Italy	7,510	10,821	−30.6
Netherlands	1,014	3,085	−67.1
Norway	334	2,256	−85.2
Poland	4,010	8,465	−52.6
Portugal	9,657	2,005	+381.6
Romania	2,015	1,644	+22.6
Soviet Union	5,742	1,853	+209.9
Spain	2,487	2,200	+13.0
Sweden	571	2,411	−76.3
Switzerland	610	1,984	−69.3
United Kingdom	12,477	27,358	−119.3
Yugoslavia	2,791	2,818	−.96
Other Europe	1,088	2,438	−55.4
Asia	157,759	20,683	+662.7
China and Taiwan	19,764	4,057	+387.2
Hong Kong	5,632	712	+691.0
India	18,613	582	+3,098.1
Iran	4,261	804	+430.0
Japan	4,178	3,180	+31.4
Korea	30,917	2,165	+1,328.0
Pakistan	3,183	187	+1,602.1
Philippines	39,111	3,130	+1,149.6

(Table continues)

TABLE 1 (continued)

Country of Birth	Number 1977	Number 1965	Percent change
Thailand	3,945	214	+1,743.5
Vietnam	4,629	226	1,948.2
Other Asia	23,526	5,426	+333.6
North America	187,345	126,729	+47.8
Canada	12,688	38,327	−66.9
Mexico	44,079	37,969	+16.1
West Indies	114,011	37,583	+203.4
Cuba	69,708	19,760	+252.8
Dominican Republic	11,655	9,504	+22.6
Haiti	5,441	3,609	+50.8
Jamaica	11,501	1,837	+526.1
Trinidad and Tobago	6,106	485	+1,159.0
Other West Indies	9,600	2,388	+302.0
Other North America	16,567	12,350	+28.9
South America	32,954	30,962	+6.4
Argentina	2,787	6,124	−54.5
Brazil	1,513	2,869	−47.3
Colombia	8,272	10,885	−24.0
Other South America	20,382	11,084	+83.9
Africa	10,155	3,383	+200.2
Oceania	4,092	1,512	+170.6
Other countries	—	4	—

SOURCE: United States Department of Justice, Immigration and Naturalization Service.

New York and San Francisco grew rapidly in the 1970s as immigrants from Hong Kong and Formosa flocked to the United States. Koreans, who, after the Filipinos, were the second largest Asian group to come by the end of the 1970s, managed to build an immigrant network. In 1950, the Korean population of the United States was small. Then came students, a few businessmen, and brides of U.S. servicemen after the Korean War. The 1965 act opened the door for the health professionals. Once these early groups settled, they began to use family preferences to bring in other Koreans.[71]

[71] For an excellent discussion of Koreans, see Illsoo Kim, "Immigrants to Urban America: The Korean Community in the New York Metropolitan Area" (Ph.D. diss., City University of New York, 1979).

The Koreans were not unique; the preference for skilled workers or professionals aided other potential emigrants of the third world. The so-called brain drain to America had largely been from Europe immediately after World War II. After 1965, a number of scientists and other professionals, especially doctors and nurses, from the third world began to emigrate. By the late 1970s, over 70,000 doctors had arrived; there were more Filipino physicians here than native-born black ones.[72]

Cold war refugee policy continued to lead to immigration even though the annual preference for refugees under the 1965 changes was only 10,200. Cubans were the largest group to arrive in the 1960s, but others followed in the next decade. The law defined refugees as those fleeing communism or from the Middle East; this hurt the chances of those, like Haitians, claiming refugee status from right-wing dictatorships. Troubles in the Middle East drove people from there. The collapse of the American-backed regime in South Vietnam in the spring of 1975 created a new pool of refugees fleeing communism. Over 200,000 Vietnamese came to America from 1975 to 1979. The "boat people" began to arrive in 1979; the administration committed itself to take in another 168,000 in 1980.[73] Cubans began a new exodus, rather dramatically, by boat to Florida in the spring of 1980.

In a number of years, the number of refugees exceeded the 6 percent preference because the president and the attorney general used the executive parolee power to permit Cubans, Vietnamese, and others to enter outside the refugee quota. Congress responded with funds to support the parolees and passed legislation to adjust their emergency status. Congress, the president, and relief agencies all realized that the refugee quota was too low and the law too rigid. Congress responded by enacting the Refugee Act of 1980. This bill broadened the definition of refugees to include those from any part of the world, not just from communist countries and the Middle East. It increased the annual normal refugee figure to 50,000 and total immigration from 290,000 to 320,000. It also attempted to streamline refugee procedures and granted the president power to deal with emergencies.[74]

---

[72] See Rosemary Stevens, *The Alien Doctors: Foreign Medical Graduates in American Hospitals* (New York: John Wiley & Sons, 1978); and Patricio R. Mamot, *Foreign Medical Graduates in America* (Springfield, Ill.: Charles Thomas, 1974).

[73] For the Vietnamese, see Gail Kelly, *From Vietnam to America: A Chronicle of the Vietnamese Immigration to the United States* (Boulder, Colo.: Westview Press, 1977); and Darrell Montero, *Vietnamese Americans: Patterns of Socioeconomic Adaptation in the United States* (Boulder, Colo.: Westview Press, 1979).

[74] *Congressional Quarterly,* vol. 38 (March 8, 1980), p. 690.

The administration announced that a total of 231,000 refugees would be permitted to enter in 1980, mostly from Indochina. The exodus of Cubans in the spring of that year upset these plans and seemed to make the 1980 law inadequate. It had been enacted only a few weeks before President Carter's commissioner for refugee affairs, Victor H. Palmieri, told a congressional committee that the latest Cuban arrivals "in this country without having undergone the proper screening and documentation present serious legal as well as humanitarian problems for which we were not frankly prepared." [75]

The influx of the Vietnamese was the most dramatic single episode involving immigration after 1965, but it was indicative of the overall shift of American immigration toward a third world orientation. As the cold war moved to the Western Hemisphere and Asia, concern over displaced persons and refugees from behind the iron curtain shifted to helping Cubans and Vietnamese. Some eastern Europeans still looked to America as a haven. Russian Jews attracted most attention and congressional action; they became the center of foreign policy as well as immigration debate.[76] But, the big numbers of refugees from communism after 1960 were no longer Europeans.

Congress pondered issues other than refugee policy. In one area, the question of illegals, no agreement could be reached. Congress did return periodically to immigration policy and make changes during the 1970s. Although a ceiling had been placed for the first time on the Western Hemisphere by the 1965 changes, that region lacked a country limit and a preference system. Reformers focused on developing a uniform policy for both hemispheres and finally were successful, with some minor exceptions, when Congress amended the Immigration and Nationality Act again in 1976. Effective in 1977, the Western Hemisphere acquired a modified preference system along with a 20,000 annual limit for each nation.[77]

The introduction of the preference system was not controversial. Administration officials and others argued that the lack of a Western Hemisphere preference system created hardships and inconsistencies. As the House committee supporting the changes noted, the 1965 act had created two immigration systems that were inconsistent.[78]

---

[75] *New York Times,* May 4, 1980.

[76] See William W. Orback, *The American Movement to Aid Soviet Jews* (Amherst: University of Massachusetts Press, 1979).

[77] Senate, *U.S. Immigration Law,* pp. 62-64.

[78] U.S. Congress, House, Committee on the Judiciary, *Immigration and Nationality Act Amendments,* 94th Congress, 2nd session, 1976, House Report 94-1553, pp. 3-4.

The Controversy on the Mexican Limit

The issue causing controversy, and opposition by the State Department, was the 20,000 limit, which affected Mexico, the nation sending the largest number of immigrants to the United States from 1965 to 1976. In several years, the number of Mexican immigrants was more than twice the proposed limit. Legal Mexican immigration to the United States would have been drastically cut, even allowing for the exemptions of immediate family members. The cutting of Mexican immigration, however, would have aided immigrants from other Latin American countries. The pressure for change appeared irresistible and even the departments of State and Justice recognized the realities. In a joint statement issued in 1975, they said,

> Based on a review of existing data, a uniform ceiling for each country . . . would be preferable. This would permit an equitable distribution of immigration from throughout the hemisphere and from throughout the world. Problems with illegal immigration will exist whether immigration from Mexico is limited to 20,000 or 35,000 or not at all.[79]

When Congress finally enacted the bill, President Gerald Ford rejected the idea of a 20,000 maximum for Mexico even though he signed the 1976 amendments. The president told Congress,

> The United States has a very special and historic relationship with our neighbor to the south. In view of this special status we have with the Mexican Government and the Mexican people, I will submit legislation to the Congress in January to increase the immigration quotas for Mexicans desiring to come to the United States.[80]

Congress was content, however, to give Mexico only 20,000 even though President Ford and later President Jimmy Carter endorsed a higher total for both Mexico and Canada. Congress legislated one more change in 1978 that virtually completed the reforms begun in 1965. This was to combine the two hemisphere ceilings of 120,000 and 170,000 into a world total of 290,000, and establish a uniform preference system.[81]

Apart from the Western Hemisphere, uniformity issues, and the admission of refugees, perhaps the major shift in immigration policy of the 1970s was the cutoff of the influx of foreign doctors. The growing

---

[79] Ibid., p. 9.
[80] U.S. Weekly Compilation of Presidential Documents, vol. 12, no. 43 (October 21, 1976), p. 1548.
[81] Senate, U.S. Immigration Law, pp. 66-67.

number of foreign medical graduates practicing in the United States had caused apprehension about the quality of medical care. American hospitals were increasingly relying upon these graduates; their reliance was increased by the passage of Medicare and Medicaid and the lack of an adequate number of graduates from American medical schools who could staff hospitals. If "quality" were the only issue, means could have been found to regulate the immigrant doctors. The American Medical Association (AMA) has traditionally exercised a tight control over the practice of medicine and controlled the entry of new physicians. The AMA was interested in the quality of medical care and the distribution of doctors, but clearly it was also trying to control the supply and income of its members. American medical schools expanded in the 1960s and 1970s; this helped ease the problem. In any event, organized medicine convinced Congress that "there is no longer an insufficient number of physicians and surgeons in the United States such that there is no further need for affording preference to alien physicians and surgeons into the United States under the Immigration and Nationality Act." [82] Accordingly, the Health Professions Educational Assistance Act of 1976 provided for cuts in the number of immigrant doctors.

As the 1970s came to a close, Congress took a step in examining immigration. Sensing a need for a thorough overhaul of immigration policy and procedures and recognizing that the last major study was carried out prior to the enactment of the McCarran-Walter Act, which was still the basic immigration law, in the fall of 1978 Congress established a Select Commission on Immigration and Refugee Policy. Senator Edward Kennedy, in introducing the bill to create the commission, said, "The time is past due for us to approach the revision of our antiquated immigration law like we have approached the revision of the criminal code—to dump the old, and start anew." [83] Armed with an original budget of $700,000 (later increased), the select commission set out to examine American immigration policy so that Congress would be able to reform immigration laws—again (the Commission's report was issued in 1981, after this volume went to press). Congress did not appear to be in a mood to increase immigration or change seriously the broad outlines of policy but rather to examine procedures and administration and seek a simpler and more lasting system. The establishment

[82] U.S. Code: Congressional and Administrative News, Public Law 94-484, *Health Professions Educational Assistance Act of 1976*, 94th Congress, 2nd session, October 12, 1976, p. 2243. See also Goldfarb, "Occupational Preferences," in this volume; and Lauren LeRoy and Philip R. Lee, eds., *Deliberations and Compromise: The Health Professions Act of 1976* (Cambridge, Mass.: Ballinger Publishing Co., 1977), especially pp. 46-76.

[83] *Congressional Record,* September 20, 1978, pp. 15599-15600.

of the commission did not preclude all reforms while awaiting the final report; Congress did pass the Refugee Act of 1980.

The Refugee Act of 1980 broadened the definition of refugee, provided for procedures for admission and funding, and increased the "normal flow" of refugees to 50,000 annually. It also permitted the president to admit additional refugees after consulting with Congress, and President Carter did so in planning to admit 217,000 in 1981. Yet Carter decided not to use the act when facing the Cuban-Haitian influx in the spring of 1980. Instead of consulting with Congress and invoking the act, the president created a new category, "Cuban-Haitian Entrant (status pending)" to care for the approximately 130,000 Cubans and Haitians in Florida. This emergency status was good for six months, but it was later extended into 1981. Although Congress did not make these people regular refugees, in October 1980 it did provide funding for them. Hence their status was left pending but they were entitled to the same financial assistance as were other refugees.

The Illegal or Undocumented Issue

Refinement of laws on legal immigration and refugee policy characterized congressional policy after 1965, but Congress could not agree on the most controversial form of immigration—illegal or undocumented immigration.[84] Illegals had crossed the loosely controlled Mexican-American border in the 1920s, and they began to appear again in the late 1940s and early 1950s. Most observers believe that the bracero agreement begun during World War II encouraged the flow because many braceros got a taste of American wages; if they could not work again as braceros, they came illegally.[85] Others simply heard of better economic conditions to the north and went there in search of work. American growers in the Southwest, moreover, were not fussy about

[84] Recently some observers have insisted the term "illegals" is pejorative and have suggested "undocumented aliens" be used instead. Many of the so-called undocumented aliens have unauthorized documents, which makes that term unsatisfactory as well. I have used both terms without intending to imply a negative meaning to either. The literature on illegals or the undocumented is vast and growing. For a summary of some of the issues, consult U.S. Department of Justice, Office of Policy and Planning, *U.S. Domestic Council Committee on Illegal Aliens, Preliminary Report,* 1976. See also U.S. Congress, House, *Illegal Aliens and Alien Labor: A Bibliography and Compilation of Background Materials (1970-June 1977),* committee print no. 9, prepared at the request of the Committee on the Judiciary, 95th Congress, 1st session, 1977.

[85] Julian Samora, *Los Mojados: The Wetback Story* (Notre Dame: University of Notre Dame Press, 1971), pp. 43-46. For a general assessment of the bracero program, see Larry C. Morgan and Bruce L. Gardner, "Potential for a U.S. Guest-Worker Program in Agriculture: Lessons from the Braceros," in this volume.

whether their employees were legal. During the war, the Mexican government refused to cooperate with Texas on the bracero program; Texas growers hired whom they could. If illegals worked for lower wages, so much the better. An agreement between the United States and Mexico in 1949 led to many illegals gaining legal status, as braceros. The 1951 President's Commission on Migratory Labor noted that more braceros were being obtained this way than by actual recruitment.[86]

Labor unions, especially those dealing with agriculture, and their liberal allies were unhappy about both the wetbacks and braceros and agitated to terminate the program and halt the influx of illegals. Until the 1960s, growers and other business interests who wanted a steady supply of reliable and low-cost labor successfully fought attempts to end the agreement.[87]

Action against the wetbacks was more successful, however, in the 1950s. In part, this was due to the fact that the bracero program functioned well and provided needed labor. In June 1954, Attorney General Herbert Brownell announced that the Eisenhower administration was moving to rid parts of the Southwest of wetbacks. Under the vigorous direction of Immigration and Naturalization Commissioner Joseph May Swing, the government rapidly and precisely conducted a successful Operation Wetback campaign that deported over 1 million people in that year.[88] The INS functioned like a small army; its agents ventured into large cities as well as the agricultural areas. Many illegals left voluntarily as the INS used the fear-of-God tactic it had employed in the 1930s.[89]

Operation Wetback was largely an administration program, for Congress paid more attention to refugees and the politics of the McCarran-Walter Act than to illegals. Congress did make it a felony to import or harbor illegal aliens; this was not particularly effective in stemming the flow. Proposals to make it a crime to hire illegals did not pass in the 1950s, nor later for that matter. Congress provided funds for INS and approved the bracero agreement, which supplied workers. Generally, the issue of illegals was not a major one in Congress in the 1950s.

The success of the INS in 1954 in removing illegals was so dramatic that the question of illegal immigration remained unimportant throughout the 1960s. Those wanting to help domestic farm workers

---

[86] Samora, *Mojados,* pp. 47-48; and President's Commission on Migratory Labor, *Migratory Labor in American Agriculture,* 1951, p. 53. See also Galarza, *Merchants of Labor.*

[87] Craig, *Bracero Program,* passim.

[88] Samora, *Mojados,* pp. 51-55.

[89] Ibid., pp. 52-53.

concentrated instead on ending the bracero agreement. The antibracero forces gained organizational and congressional allies during the 1950s, and in 1960 were nearly successful in killing the program. The election of John F. Kennedy that year was a bad sign for both the growers and the braceros.[90]

The new Secretary of Agriculture Orville Freeman, replacing Ezra Taft Benson, did not sympathize with the growers; the Kennedy administration generally listened to organized labor. The attack on the program began early in the Kennedy years. After renewal with limiting amendments and extended hearings in Congress, the program was finally allowed to die in 1964. The probracero forces used foreign policy and consumer price arguments to urge its extension, but the concern over American domestic farm labor won out.[91]

National attention about illegals, and to a lesser extent a possible renewal of a bracero-type agreement, reemerged in the 1970s. By the mid-1970s, most congressional concern about immigration centered on illegal immigration. Growers were increasingly faced with the prospect of farm workers' unions and higher costs; they turned to mechanization and the employment of illegals to keep their costs down. Still, some growers as well as other businessmen suggested that a new bracero program would be helpful.

A bracero, or guest-worker program, as in the 1950s, was tied to the question of illegal or undocumented workers. Some argued that, since the flow of illegals could not be halted, it was better to recognize the problem and provide for a stable work force with minimum protection for these workers.

There were differences, however, in the undocumented workers of the 1950s and those of the 1970s. The 1950s issue was an agricultural one. In the 1970s, the bulk of these people were not in agriculture; an Operation Wetback sweep of the 1950s would not have been possible. Moreover, in the 1970s, the courts had limited some of the procedures of the INS. Still, the growing number of undocumented workers (as they were coming to be called) being caught, largely along the Mexican border, signaled a growing problem of immigration regulation and prompted considerable public debate.

Several issues explain this concern. First, the obvious growth in apprehensions, numbering over 1 million in 1978, indicated that many illegals were again coming to the United States, largely, but not exclusively, from Mexico. There was little the nation could do about social and economic conditions in Mexico or the Caribbean, where so many

[90] Craig, *Bracero Program,* chap. 5.
[91] Ibid.

faced acute poverty, unemployment, and a growing population and hence looked to the United States as a place to work either temporarily or permanently.

The Impact of the American Economy. A second important issue was the American economy in the 1970s. Both inflation and unemployment troubled Americans. Immigrants are convenient scapegoats during difficult economic times. Most legal immigrants came under the relative preferences or as refugees. Although a large proportion eventually worked, they were usually not attacked for causing economic burdens or for taking jobs from American citizens. Americans generally saw their immigration policy as humanitarian. Many experts were aware of larger issues, but the humanitarian impulse and the awareness of domestic pressures made unification of families and the admission of refugees acceptable. Of course, Americans knew that there were economic implications to immigration. Public opinion polls revealed, for example, opposition to the admission of Vietnamese refugees, especially because people believed they might cause unemployment.[92]

The unsettled economic situation and growing numbers of illegals made the situation ripe for immigration politics. Many played the numbers game with the undocumented aliens; claims varied in the 1970s, with some estimating that up to 12 million illegals resided in the United States. The *New York Times* in early 1980 said that the State Department estimated there were 10 million illegals in the United States.[93] A study prepared by the Bureau of the Census for the Select Commission on Immigration and Refugee Policy cautioned that "there were no reliable estimates" of illegals, but suggested that the number might be 6 million or less.[94] The select commission decided against making a full study of illegals because of the cost and difficulty in obtaining reliable data.[95]

Increasingly, politicians and others were forced to admit that they did not know how many undocumented aliens lived here and that they

[92] Harris Survey, news release, June 26, 1975; and the *New York Times*-CBS Poll, reported in the *New York Times*, July 15, 1979. For evidence of hostility to the 1980 Cuban refugees, see *New York Times*, May 10, 1980.

[93] *New York Times*, January 16, 1980.

[94] For a discussion of the counting issue, see Charles Keely, "Counting the Uncountable: Estimates of Undocumented Aliens in the United States," *Population and Development Review*, vol. 7, no. 4 (December 1977), pp. 473-481. The Bureau of the Census's statement can be found in U.S. Department of Commerce, Bureau of the Census, *Preliminary Review of Existing Studies of the Number of Illegal Residents in the United States,* report prepared for the Select Commission on Immigration and Refugee Policy, January 1980, introduction.

[95] Select Commission on Immigration and Refugee Policy, *Semi-Annual Report,* March 1, 1980, p. 13.

lacked data about their social and economic impact on the nation. Still, political officials carelessly threw figures around. Evelyn Mann, of the Population Office of the City Planning Department of New York City, told a House committee in 1978 that an estimated 750,000 undocumented aliens resided in New York City. When asked about data, she answered, "Frankly, we have no data on which to build a precise estimate." She further admitted that the city acknowledged political pressures: "Each year we have to respond to the revenue sharing entitlement figures." [96]

In addition to the numbers game, a variety of charges, some mutually exclusive, were made about these people. When he was INS commissioner, Leonard Chapman claimed that the removal of illegals would create at least 1 million jobs for native Americans. This line of thinking that illegals took jobs from American citizens was especially popular.[97] Others took a different tack and said that the undocumented were loafers and drained the public treasury. State and city officials at times did not choose sides but wanted to make sure that illegals were counted so that their communities were not shortchanged when federal funds were being distributed. Counting illegals became a constitutional issue when the newly formed Federation for American Immigration Reform (FAIR) and several congressmen challenged inclusion of illegals in the 1980 census as a basis for congressional representation.[98] A few groups, like Zero Population Growth, wanted the flow halted because of its impact on future population growth. This concern was part of a general one emerging in the 1970s: the impact of

[96] U.S. Congress, House, Select Committee on Population, *Immigration to the United States: Hearings,* 95th Congress, 2nd session, 1978, p. 176.

[97] General Leonard Chapman, head of the INS in 1975, estimated the number as being between 4 million and 12 million and said a study by Lesko Associates put the figure at slightly over 8 million. Since little hard data were given, these estimates, although widely reported in the media, have been viewed with skepticism. For an example of General Chapman's reporting, see Leonard Chapman, Jr., "Illegal Aliens: Time to Call a Halt," *Reader's Digest,* October 1976, pp. 188-192. The INS under Lionel Castillo stopped making estimates and admitted that hard data were lacking. He told a House committee in 1978 that the parameters were between 3 million and 6 million illegal aliens. Select Committee on Population, *Immigration to the United States,* p. 138. For a recent statement about illegals taking jobs from American citizens, see the statement by Secretary of Labor Ray Marshall, who told the *Los Angeles Times* that unemployment could be brought from 6 percent to below 4 percent if half the jobs held by illegals were taken by Americans. *Los Angeles Times,* December 1, 1979, I, p. 1.

[98] The *Bergen County* (N.J.) *Record,* January 11, 1980, p. 1; and *New York Times,* February 7, 1980, p. 21. See the statement of FAIR's executive director, Roger Connor, in *FAIR: Immigration Report,* vol. 3 (Washington, D.C.: December 1979), p. 1.

immigration, legal and illegal, on American population and the environment. First raised to national prominence in 1972 by the Commission on Population Growth and the American Future, it was picked up by other groups and some government spokesmen dealing with immigration.[99]

Not all discussion about undocumented aliens was hostile. Hispanic and other groups treated the illegals with sympathy, as did some media presentation. Popular books, such as Grace Halsell's *The Illegals,* published in 1978, viewed the undocumented favorably. Trade unions, traditionally opposed to illegals, also shifted and began organization drives among them.[100] The official stand of the AFL-CIO still supported halting the flow, however. Nor was all discussion about illegal or undocumented aliens mere guesswork. Scholars such as David North and Wayne A. Cornelius attempted to collect data and analyze the impact of illegals. Their work, though limited, was often cited by others discussing the issue.[101]

In addition to the sensational media coverage, political rhetoric, and scholarly studies, Congress pondered the matter but could not devise a solution, except more funds for the INS. A variety of committees investigated, held hearings, and made suggestions. The most popular proposal, sponsored by Peter Rodino, congressman from New Jersey, made it a crime for employers to hire illegals knowingly. In the early 1970s, the House passed the Rodino bill twice, but the Senate did not even hold hearings until 1976. There the bill fell under the jurisdiction of Senator James Eastland of Mississippi, who traditionally was no

[99] U.S. Commission on Population Growth and the American Future, *Final Report,* 1952, pp. 203-206; Paul Ehrlich et al., *The Golden Door: International Migration, Mexico and the United States* (New York: Ballantine Books, 1979), pp. 352-355; and *Questions and Answers on U.S. Immigration and Population* (Washington, D.C.: Zero Population Growth, 1978). The 1978 Select Commission on Immigration and Refugee Policy was charged to examine the impact of immigration on demographic trends.

[100] *New York Times,* June 3, 1979, p. 1; *Los Angeles Times,* March 11, 1979, II, p. 6; and Grace Haskell, *The Illegals* (New York: Stein and Day, 1978). See also John Davidson, *The Long Road North* (Garden City: Doubleday & Co., 1979); and the articles by Robert Scheer in the *Los Angeles Times,* November 11, 1979, I, p. 1, and November 12, 1979, I, p. 1.

[101] David S. North and Marion F. Houstoun, *The Characteristics and Role of Illegal Aliens in the U.S. Labor Market: An Exploratory Study* (Washington, D.C.: Linton, 1976); and Wayne A. Cornelius, *Illegal Migration to the United States: Recent Research Findings, Policy Implications, and Research Priorities* (Cambridge: Center for International Studies, Migration and Development Study Group, MIT, 1977). For examples of broader works that use these studies, see Ehrlich et al., *Golden Door;* and Michael J. Piore, *Birds of Passage: Migrant Labor and Industrial Societies* (Cambridge, England: Cambridge University Press, 1979).

friend of immigration. Illegals were another matter, however. He did not favor the Rodino bill. Political observers said this was because Senator Eastland spoke for those employers who wanted to have a supply of cheap labor.[102] Some businessmen insisted that American citizens would not work for the wages that illegals received. As one restaurant owner said about hiring dishwashers, "I'd like to hire Americans, but when you are in a bind you hire who you can."[103] Others also opposed the bill. Even after the retirement of James Eastland, the Senate did not pass it.

By the late 1970s, opposition to the Rodino bill grew. Employers stressed that it put the burden of enforcement on them and was impossible to fulfill. Hispanic groups suggested that employers would discriminate against them rather than run afoul of the law. Civil libertarians also wondered about discrimination against Hispanics and worried that the law might require a national identification card, which was not popular in the post-Watergate era.[104] In 1977, President Carter renewed the pleas for the Rodino plan and coupled it with a call for amnesty for illegals here before 1970 and for a temporary status for those arriving between 1970 and 1977. Congress held hearings on President Carter's proposals, but they went nowhere.[105]

As Congress could not agree, the problem of controlling illegal entry was left to the INS, which was unable to police the Mexican border effectively. Various INS commissioners complained of understaffing and of the impossible situation; Congress did increase the INS's budget. Even Lionel Castillo, INS commissioner until October 1979 and supposedly sympathetic to illegal Mexicans, realized the difficulty

---

[102] *Congressional Digest,* vol. 54 (June 1975); and *New York Times,* September 29, 1975. For a sampling of the debate on the Rodino bill, see *Congressional Record,* September 12, 1972, pp. 30160, 30168, and May 3, 1973, pp. 14187, 14190-14191, 14204; *Los Angeles Times,* March 27, 1973; and Department of Justice, Domestic Council, Committee on Illegal Aliens, *Preliminary Report,* pp. 111-115.

[103] *New Orleans Times-Picayune,* October 2, 1974.

[104] For the late 1970s, see the testimony in U.S. Congress, House, Subcommittee on the Departments of State, Justice, Commerce, the Judiciary and Related Agencies of the Committee on Appropriations, *Undocumented Aliens: Hearings,* 95th Congress, 2nd session, 1978; U.S. Congress, House, Subcommittee on Inter-American Affairs of the Committee on International Relations, *Undocumented Workers; Implications for U.S. Policy in the Western Hemisphere: Hearings,* 95th Congress, 2nd session, 1978; and U.S. Congress, Senate, Committee on the Judiciary to Amend the Immigration and Nationality Act and for Other Purposes, *Alien Adjustment and Employment Act of 1977: Hearings,* 95th Congress, 2nd session, 1978.

[105] *U.S. Weekly Compilation of Presidential Documents,* vol. 13, no. 32 (August 4, 1977), pp. 1169-1175. The Gallup poll also found a majority against an amnesty for illegal aliens. See *New York Times,* October 30, 1977.

of the task. Under his supervision, the INS proposed to build a huge fence at El Paso, one of the key crossing spots, even though this caused diplomatic complications and probably offered limited effectiveness.[106]

The difficulties of determining how many undocumented aliens resided in the nation and what economic and social impact they had were so great that accurate information was not available for Congress to make a sensible decision. In 1978, the Select Committee on Population of the House concluded that, before action could be taken, a major project be created to determine the facts. Recalling past estimates, the committee said, "All these estimates were the product of intuition and so-called professional judgment. None were based on hard data, which were lacking, nor were any developed on the basis of scientific procedures." [107] Even if Congress and the experts developed hard data, given the complexity of enforcement and its foreign and domestic implications, it is doubtful whether congressional action would be forthcoming.

Complications of Existing Policy

The headlines created by the 130,000 Cuban refugees arriving in Florida in the spring of 1980 dramatized the illegal issue. If the government gave these newcomers immigrant status, why not Mexicans, Haitians, and others who came without visas? Over 10,000 undocumented Haitians resided in the same state; their case for asylum was being pleaded by voluntary agencies and fought in the courts. Yet the issue was not simply one of proper legal status. The Cuban exodus symbolized many of the issues of American immigration policy after 1945.

Here were third world, Hispanic refugees from communism seeking asylum in America. Like some of those from Indochina they were boat people. Their families and friends in America and voluntary agencies such as the Catholic Church were assisting them. As in the past, the executive branch was playing an important role. President Carter avoided using the new refugee act and admitted them with a special status. Congress provided funds for their adjustment. Ultimately, a solution would have to be found to resolve their status and a way to deal with still other Haitians landing in Florida.

The complications of the Cuban refugees had been played before, as the cold war, foreign policy, the attractiveness of American society

106 Construction on the 9- to 10-foot-high fence began in June 1979. It was also proposed to build a new fence separating Tijuana, Mexico, and San Ysidro, California. *New York Times,* June 22, 1979. See the coverage of this controversy in the *Los Angeles Times,* March 17, 1979, and April 29, 1979.

107 U.S. Congress, House, Select Committee on Population, *Legal and Illegal Immigration to the United States: Report,* 95th Congress, 2nd session, 1979, p. 16.

to others, and domestic ethnic and voluntary agency pressures influenced the development and shape of American immigration after World War II. The results were political compromises leading to revisions of the laws. These revisions were a general liberalization that, somewhat inadvertently, made for a shifting pattern of immigration from the third world to the United States. Some congressmen might have hoped that the 1978 Select Commission on Immigration and Refugee Policy's forth-coming recommendations would suggest a more permanent policy, but that was not likely. It was possible that solid studies about the impact of immigration upon American society would guide Congress in making immigration laws, but upheavals in Cuba or Vietnam or the devaluation of the peso in Mexico seem to have more influence on the policy than studies.

Liberalization did not mean a return to the nineteenth-century pattern of free immigration; few advocated that. Rather, the changes after the war leading to the 1965 act and its modifications ended the national origins quota system, lifted the restrictions on Asians, and re-placed them with a preference system emphasizing family unifications and, to a lesser extent, occupations and refugees. To deal with the small refugee preference, Congress and the president took special action when emergencies arose. For some peoples, such as those in Africa, it was still difficult to get into America; for many "refugees," like black Haitians, the road was not easy. Hence the policy, altered from the rigidity of the 1920s, was still selective.

What will happen in the 1980s? The nation seems to face too many economic problems for many to advocate sizable increases in immigration. The most likely pattern in the 1980s is a continuation of the 1965 selectivity with modifications to admit more refugees and tinkering with the laws to make the process efficient. If Congress ap-pears reluctant to make major changes in legal immigration, it is also unwilling to do much about illegal immigration, unless its magnitude grows substantially. Sealing the entry for illegals is difficult because of the inability of Congress to resolve conflicting groups and interests. Hence, the nation will probably handle this phenomenon in the 1980s the way it dealt with it in the 1970s: to discuss and debate it, control the borders as best it can with limited resources, but not take any drastic action.

The Supply of Immigrants to the United States

Michael J. Greenwood and John M. McDowell

An examination of the potential supply of immigrants to the United States might take any number of different perspectives. Several prior studies dealing with this issue have taken a long-run perspective and have analyzed the determinants of international migration over long sweeps of history. Harry Jerome, for instance, examined both the timing and composition of U.S. immigration from Europe over roughly a 100-year period prior to the imposition of U.S. immigration quotas in 1924; Brinley Thomas has included the international flow of manpower as a critical element in his detailed examination of long swings in the Atlantic economy.[1] It has been suggested that both push factors in origin countries and pull factors in the United States have been responsible for the volume and composition of U.S. immigration flows over time.[2]

While a complete analysis of U.S. and indeed of worldwide migration must incorporate temporal factors, in the present study we have followed a much more modest approach by taking a short-run perspective and by analyzing in a cross-sectional framework international migration flows to the United States from as many origin countries as the available data allow. In this sense, our study follows Robert E. B. Lucas.[3]

We are grateful to Barry R. Chiswick for making a number of helpful comments on an earlier draft of this paper.

[1] Harry Jerome, *Migration and Business Cycles* (New York: National Bureau of Economic Research, 1926); and Brinley Thomas, *Migration and Economic Growth: A Study of Great Britain and the Atlantic Economy,* 2nd ed. (Cambridge: Cambridge University Press, 1973).

[2] Jerome, *Migration and Business Cycles;* Thomas, *Migration and Economic Growth;* Dorothy Swain Thomas, *Social and Economic Aspects of Swedish Population Movements* (New York: Macmillan, 1941); Simon Kuznets and E. Rubins, *Immigration and the Foreign Born,* National Bureau of Economic Research, occasional paper, no. 46 (New York, 1954); and R. A. Easterlin, "Influences in European Overseas Emigration before World War I," reprinted in R. W. Fogel and Stanley Engerman, eds., *The Reinterpretation of American Economic History* (New York: Harper and Row, 1971).

[3] Robert E. B. Lucas, "The Supply-of-Immigrants Function and Taxation of Immigrants' Income," in J. N. Bhagwati, ed., *The Brain Drain and Taxation: Theory and Empirical Analysis* (Amsterdam: North-Holland Publishing Co., 1976).

FIGURE 1

THE EFFECTS OF IMMIGRATION QUOTAS ON WAGE RATES IN THE UNITED STATES

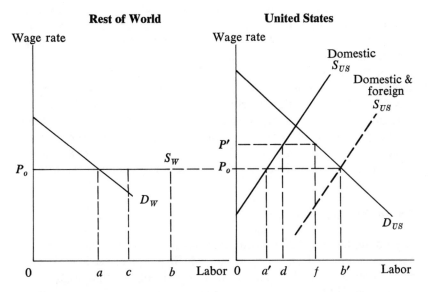

Let us begin by considering a simple model of international migration, where the United States is able to maintain a wage rate above the world equilibrium wage rate by imposing an immigration quota. Figure 1 depicts a situation in which labor supply in the rest of the world is perfectly elastic and in which the United States imposes an immigration quota of df workers per period. In the presence of this quota, the United States is able to maintain its wage rate at p', whereas the world equilibrium wage rate is lower at p_o. If labor were homogeneous, if transportation costs were negligible, and if other impediments to the free flow of immigrants were nonexistent, then $ac = df$ workers would immigrate to the United States under the quota system. If the quota were removed, $ab = a'b'$ workers would move to the United States, and U.S. wages would fall to p_o, the world equilibrium level.

This discussion suggests two alternative and, in a sense, equivalent approaches to estimating the number of U.S. immigrants in the absence of barriers to entry. One approach is demand oriented and would aim at estimating the U.S. excess demand for labor ($a'b'$) at the world equilibrium wage rate. The second approach is supply oriented and would aim at estimating the change in labor supply that would occur in the absence of entry barriers. The approach that we have followed is more supply oriented. However, rather than assuming that the

55

United States is the only viable destination for potential international migrants, we have taken the position that the United States is only one of many potential destinations, especially when the money and non-money costs of moving are taken into consideration. Furthermore, we have taken the position that labor is not homogeneous and that differential costs and differential returns to migration to the United States exist for individuals with different occupational skills.

In the following section, we examine the institutional framework in the United States during 1970, the period on which the study focuses. Specifically, in this section we consider the Immigration and Nationality Act Amendments of 1965. Section 3 presents a simple model of immigration from each of twenty-three foreign countries that supplied the United States with immigrants. It also develops a model that explains the pattern of origin countries from which U.S. immigrants with an occupation are drawn.

The Institutional Framework

The Immigration and Nationality Act Amendments of 1965 provide the basic institutional framework within which our analytical work must be considered. The 1965 act repealed the existing national origin quota system that had formed the basis for the numerical restrictions on immigration since the 1920s. Furthermore, when the 1965 act became effective on July 1, 1968, immigration from the Western Hemisphere was numerically restricted for the first time. Thus, the annual numerical limitations on the issuance of immigrant visas are generally applicable to both the Western and Eastern Hemispheres.

Prospective immigrants, other than immediate relatives of U.S. citizens, must compete in the geographic hemisphere to which they belong by birth for a restricted number of visas. This distinction by hemisphere is important because the 1965 act maintained the policy of a different formula for allocating visas in each hemisphere. For natives from the Western Hemisphere, the annual limit for the issuance of immigrant visas was set at 120,000. Within this annual ceiling, immigrant visas for those other than immediate relatives are allocated on a first-come, first-served basis in the order in which applicants are found qualified for immigration.

The criteria used for selecting qualified recipients of immigrant visas are not evident in all circumstances, since no preference system was initially established for natives from the Western Hemisphere. In order to qualify for admission to the United States, however, a prospective immigrant who intends to work (except a parent, spouse, or child of a citizen or lawful permanent resident of the United States)

56

must obtain labor certification from the Department of Labor. The secretary of labor must certify that there is a need for the prospective immigrant's type of occupational skills in the United States and that allocating the visa will not displace United States workers nor adversely affect the economy of the United States.

The available evidence suggests that the 1965 act has restricted the total number of immigrants from the Western Hemisphere. By July 1969, one year after the numerical limitation became effective, Western aliens had applied for more immigration visas than were available. As a consequence, the waiting period, which was nine months in 1969, lengthened to fourteen months by 1970. Later, in 1976, a House report indicated that nearly 300,000 individuals were on the waiting list of those intending to immigrate to the United States from the Western Hemisphere and that their waiting time was more than two years.[4]

Though the aggregate number of immigrants from the Western Hemisphere appears to have been reduced, the effect of the 1965 act on the flow of immigrants from specific countries in the Western Hemisphere is not clear. The numerical restrictions in the 1965 act did not apply a quota per country on the Western Hemisphere until a later amendment in 1976. Therefore, due to the allocation of special visas on a first-come, first-served basis, the flow of immigrants from any single country is not affected in any obvious way.

In addition to limiting the number of immigrant visas from the Western Hemisphere, the Immigration and Nationality Act Amendments of 1965 set an annual limit of 170,000 on the number of immigrant visas available throughout the rest of the world. As mentioned, the 1965 act also repealed the existing national origins quota system.[5] The U.S. law specified that no more than 20,000 visas are to be available to individuals from any specific country in the Eastern Hemisphere and no more than 200 visas to any dependent country (in either hemisphere).

Within the limit of 20,000 per country and the ceiling of 170,000 total immigrants, visas to natives of the Eastern Hemisphere are allocated under a seven-category preference system with a first-come, first-served basis within each preference. This preference system includes four categories providing for reuniting families (74 percent of the

[4] U.S. Congress, House Report no. 94-1553, 94th Congress, 2nd session, September 15, 1976, pp. 3-4.

[5] The national origins quota system, which was codified in the Immigration and Nationality Act of 1952, restricted the number of immigrants from any specific Eastern Hemisphere country to one-sixth of 1 percent of the inhabitants in the continental United States whose ancestry or national origin was attributable to the country. Under the 1952 act, a minimum quota of 100 and a ceiling of 2,000 immigrants was placed on most natives of countries in the Asia Pacific triangle.

visas); two preferences for professional, skilled, and unskilled workers needed by the United States (20 percent of the visas); and one category for refugees (6 percent of the visas). Any visas not used by these seven preferences are made available to other immigrants ineligible for a preference but otherwise qualified for visas. In 1976, an amendment to the law slightly modified this preference system and applied it to natives of the Western Hemisphere as well as the Eastern Hemisphere.

A visa petition for an occupational preference (third or sixth preference) cannot be approved unless a labor certification is issued by the secretary of labor, who must certify that sufficient qualified workers are not available in the area (occupational or geographic) of the United States to which the alien is destined and that wages and working conditions will not be adversely affected for persons employed in similar occupations. An additional restraint is placed on immigrants who seek to enter under an occupational preference. Any family members who accompany workers entering the United States under an occupational preference are also charged to the occupational preference category. In 1970, the spouses and children of workers admitted accounted for 44.4 percent of the visas allocated to an occupational preference.[6] In many years since 1970, the spouses and children of aliens admitted under an occupational preference have actually outnumbered the workers admitted in these preference categories.

The Analytical Framework

Data on international migration are limited; consequently, many types of migration models commonly estimated in studies of internal migration cannot meaningfully be estimated in studies of international migration. Because the limitations of existing data had much to do with shaping our approach, we first consider the migration data utilized in this study. We then discuss a simple model of the geographic distribution of emigrants from various, specific origin countries. A major conclusion emerging from this analysis is that emigration from many countries to the United States is substantially less than predicted by a simple economic model of international migration.

In our final substantive section, we take the perspective of the United States and examine the determinants of immigration to the United States from various nations. Distance and earnings appear to be important factors affecting the rate of immigration from various countries to the United States. Another factor affecting the rate of

[6] U.S. Department of Justice, *1970 Annual Report of the Commissioner of Immigration and Naturalization*, 1972, p. 6.

immigration is the sending country's level of economic development. Finally, the ability of prospective immigrants to transfer their occupational knowledge from their native countries to the U.S. labor market importantly influences U.S. immigration rates.

The Data on International Migration. The use of published data relating to international migration involves a number of serious problems that make intercountry comparisons of superficially comparable information quite hazardous. Not only do national sources of information on the international flow of migrants differ greatly, but also emigrants and immigrants are in practice defined quite differently, even when the sources of such information are similar. The most common source of data on international migration is administrative records, which include border control, population registers, employment registers, alien registration, exit or entry visas, and others. Certain countries use censuses or sample surveys to collect the relevant information.

Many countries base their definitions of emigrants on intended duration in the country of destination, but this duration varies widely, from permanent residence to residence of six months. Other countries base their definitions on the expressed intention to give up residence in the country of emigration, and still others on the expressed intention to establish residence in the country of immigration. Certain countries require that the emigrant intend to take employment in the country of destination. This list is not exhaustive. While some countries count all departing persons who fall within their definition of an emigrant, others count only residents or only nationals or only aliens or only persons with an exit visa. Still other classifications are common. For some countries, the mode of transportation used by those parting is relevant, presumably because of the specific type of administrative record that is utilized. Furthermore, many countries, such as the United States and Canada, do not even attempt to compile data on emigration.

The situation regarding the definition and measurement of immigration is equally complex. Because of the multitude of differing conditions that enter into the definition and measurement of emigrants and immigrants, it is not surprising that the number of emigrants recorded by country i as moving from country i to country j virtually never equals the number of immigrants recorded by country j as moving from i to j. The differences between the two numbers are frequently extreme. In 1960, for example, Mexico reported that 647,557 persons emigrated to the United States, while the United States reported that 35,223 persons immigrated from Mexico. In 1970, these two countries reported respective figures on emigration and immigration of 36,635 and

59

47,500.[7] Mexico's published international migration data show a net movement of 78,379 persons from the United States to Mexico in 1970, but one strongly suspects that unenumerated movements from Mexico to the United States are such that Mexico is a heavy net supplier of U.S. immigrants.

To demonstrate the lack of comparability of national data on international migration, the Economic Commission for Europe prepared two matrices of 1972 international migration between member countries, one for 342 flows as reported by the country of immigration and one for the same potential 342 flows as reported (and in some cases not reported) by the country of emigration.[8] The total number of immigrants reported was 57 percent higher than the total number of emigrants reported.

This discussion suggests that the pooling of data on international migration for the purpose of developing a matrix of international migration flows is a questionable procedure. Because of the severity of the data problems, we have followed two fairly distinct approaches in our examination of international migration. The rationale that underlies each approach is that the most comparable and consistent data that can be utilized for analytical purposes are those reported by a given country. Thus, we first develop and estimate a model to explain the international distribution of emigrants from *each* of several countries around the world. Second, we examine immigration to the United States from the perspective of the United States; that is, using U.S. data on immigration, we analyze migration to the United States from various origin countries. No country with a centrally planned economy has been selected as either an origin or a destination.

In each approach, we have focused on the year 1970 because for many countries the most recent population census data relate to this year. In our study of emigration, data availability has forced us to examine 1971 flows in certain instances, 1972 flows in one important case (the Philippines), and 1975 flows in another important case (the United Kingdom). The two basic sources of migration data utilized here are United Nations, Department of International Economic and Social Affairs, *Demographic Yearbook: 1977*, and U.S. Department of Justice, *1970 Annual Report: Immigration and Naturalization Service.*

---

[7] One reason for the large difference between the 1960 and 1970 reported figures on Mexican emigration to the United States is that Public Law 78 was in effect in 1960. Under this law, the United States admitted 315,846 Mexican nationals in 1960 as braceros (temporary workers). The reason for the remaining tenfold difference in reported Mexican emigration is unclear.

[8] United Nations, Department of International Economic and Social Affairs, *Demographic Yearbook: 1977*, 1978, p. 16.

The Distribution of Foreign Emigrants. The models developed in this study are essentially based on the notion that, given their constraints, migrants are free to seek their maximum economic advantage. The major problem is that the models are estimated with real world data that reflect all sorts of international barriers to the free flow of migrants. We offer two justifications for following the procedures we developed in the presence of this problem.

First, when international migration is considered from the perspective of the country of emigration (i), the number of emigrants from i to country j is frequently greater than the number of official immigrants that j reports as having been accepted from i. To demonstrate this point, we have compared 1970 data on U.S. immigration provided in the annual report of the Immigration and Naturalization Service with 1970 emigration data provided by fourteen countries that enter our analytical work. The total number of immigrants reported by the United States as coming from these countries was 70.9 percent of the total number of emigrants reported by these countries as moving to the United States.[9] When Mexico is removed from the group of fourteen countries, this percentage falls to 48.7. Numbers provided by countries of emigration differ from those provided by countries of immigration for many reasons, including nonparallel concepts of emigrants and immigrants, different measurement procedures, lags in reporting, differences between the country of departure and the country of chargeability, and differences between the country that the emigrants report as their destination and the country to which they actually go. Nevertheless, while recognizing that problems still exist, we feel that emigration data better reflect what would occur in a free market.

Second, in this section we show reasonably strong evidence that higher wages are attractive to international migrants. In the presence of international barriers to the free flow of migrants, such results could be obtained if countries with higher wage levels established higher immigration quotas. If higher wage levels reflect situations in which labor is in relatively short supply, then internal political processes in high-wage countries may establish higher quotas as a means of satisfying labor demand (presumably at lower wage rates than would otherwise prevail in such countries). If countries with relatively abundant labor supplies imposed relatively low quotas to "protect" their workers, then the real world pattern of international migration flows could be at least roughly the same as the pattern that would be produced by a free market.

[9] The countries included in this list are Greece, Spain, Austria, Luxembourg, Netherlands, West Germany, Finland, Norway, Sweden, Iceland, Mexico, Bolivia, Australia, and Japan. These are the same countries for which we have analyzed 1970 emigration flows.

TABLE 1

TOTAL EMIGRANTS REPORTED BY VARIOUS COUNTRIES AND
THE U.S. SHARE OF EACH COUNTRY'S EMIGRANTS

Country/Year	Total Emigrants	U.S. Share (percent)
Greece (1970)	92,681	12.4
Italy (1971)	167,721	8.8
Spain (1970)	114,430	1.0
Austria (1970)	22,652	20.2
Luxembourg (1970)	6,270	4.1
Netherlands (1970)	45,746	6.8
United Kingdom (1975)	238,300	9.3
West Germany (1970)	498,397	4.7
Denmark (1971)	31,626	7.4
Finland (1970)	44,495	1.4
Norway (1970)	18,352	15.5
Sweden (1970)	28,653	5.3
Iceland (1970)	2,192	14.8
Mexico (1970)	62,713	58.4
Costa Rica (1971)	169,605	24.4
Bolivia (1970)	14,557	19.7
Venezuela (1971)	239,728	34.5
Australia (1970)	120,236	6.5
New Zealand (1971)	38,165	3.8
Philippines (1972)	21,036	43.8
Japan (1970)	45,234	51.3
Korea (1971)	167,605	34.2
Malaysia (1970)	538,059	0.0

SOURCE: United Nations, Department of International Economic and Social Affairs, *Demographic Yearbook 1977,* table 29.

Table 1 indicates both the total number of emigrants from each of twenty-three foreign countries and the share of each country's emigrants who were reported to be departing for the United States. The twenty-three countries included in table 1, as well as in the empirical work to be discussed, are as follows:

1. Europe: Greece, Italy, Spain, Austria, Luxembourg, Netherlands, United Kingdom, West Germany, Denmark, Finland, Norway, Sweden, and Iceland

2. North America: Mexico and Costa Rica
3. South America: Bolivia and Venezuela
4. Oceania: Australia and New Zealand
5. Asia: Philippines, Japan, Korea, and Malaysia

The data refer to the years 1970 (fifteen countries), 1971 (six countries), 1972 (one country), and 1975 (one country), depending on availability.

The United States gained a somewhat higher share of emigrants from Mexico (58.4 percent) than from any other country. Japan (51.3 percent), Philippines (43.8 percent), Venezuela (34.5 percent), and Korea (34.2 percent) also had over one-third of their emigrants declare the United States as their destination. In fact, the U.S. share of Mexican emigrants is probably considerably higher than 58.4 percent because of the failure of Mexican authorities to account for illegal flows across Mexico's border with the United States. In 1960, Mexico reported 803,277 emigrants (compared to 62,713 in 1970), 80.6 percent of whom declared the United States as their destination. This latter percentage is likely to be a somewhat more accurate indication of the share of Mexican emigrants that is gained by the United States.

In an attempt to explain the spatial distribution of each country's emigrants, we have estimated the following relationship for each of twenty-three countries:

$$EMIG_{ij} = F(DIST_{ij}, WAGE_j, POP_j, e_{ij}),\qquad(1)$$

where $EMIG_{ij} =$ the number of emigrants from country i who declared country j as their destination[10]; $DIST_{ij} =$ the airline mileage between the nearest major cities in i and j[11]; $WAGE_j =$ average weekly earnings in the manufacturing sector of country j, expressed in dollars[12]; $POP_j =$ population of country j; and $e_{ij} =$ random errors.

This relationship contains three explanatory variables that frequently provide reasonable explanations of place-to-place migration flows within various countries. Distance serves as a proxy for both economic and noneconomic factors. The greater the distance between i and j, the greater the expected money and nonmoney costs of moving between i and j. Money costs include out-of-pocket costs for transportation and foregone earnings. Nonmoney costs include psychic factors, such as separation from family and friends, that should also increase with

[10] UN, *Demographic Yearbook: 1977,* table 29.

[11] *Air Tariff,* Computaprint Ltd., Worldwide Book, no. 1 (London, 1978).

[12] United Nations, Department of International Economic and Social Affairs, *Statistical Yearbook: 1977,* ST/ESA/STAT/SER.S/5 1978, tables 182 and 195.

increased distance from a person's home. Finally, information is likely to decrease with increased distance, which should make longer moves more risky, ceteris paribus. Thus, the greater the distance between i and j, the less the expected migration from i to j.

Higher expected wage or earnings levels should be attractive to migrants. While international comparisons of wage and earnings levels present a number of problems, we have employed such a variable as a crude indicator of economic advantage. Wage data are reported for the manufacturing sector of many countries; we have utilized these data in our analysis. We calculated both annual manufacturing earnings and average weekly manufacturing earnings from separate data sources and examined relationship (1) with each measure. Little difference exists between the relationships estimated with the two measures; consequently, we have reported only those relationships that utilize weekly earnings.[13]

For a number of reasons, the more populous a country is, the more likely it is to experience a greater volume of immigration from any given origin country. Population serves as a reasonable proxy for size of the destination labor market and hence, other things being equal, for the expected number and variety of job opportunities. Through trade, financial arrangements, and past migration, larger nations are also likely to have established more ties with the rest of the world. Furthermore, to the extent that countries with larger populations set higher absolute limitations on immigration, presumably because of their ability to absorb more migrants without seriously jeopardizing existing economic and social relationships, larger countries should experience greater immigration.

For each country of emigration, we have utilized as many observations on countries of destination as the reported data allow. Largely because of differences in the number of destination countries reported for each origin country, the number of observations underlying each regression differs widely, from a minimum of fourteen for Finland to a maximum of forty-six for Japan. For each country of emigration, the United States was reported to be a recipient of out-migrants.

Relationship (1) has been estimated in double-log form by ordinary least squares. Table 2 presents the estimates of this relationship for each of the twenty-three countries indicated previously. The signs on the

[13] Because of the noncomparability of national cost-of-living indexes, no attempt has been made to adjust the wage data for inernational cost-of-living differences. To the extent that such differences are reflected in international exchange rates, however, some adjustment is implicit in our wage measure, especially in the analysis of migration to the United States, because all wage data are expressed in U.S. dollars.

explanatory variables are almost always as expected, with twenty-one of twenty-three distance elasticities, twenty-two of twenty-three wage elasticities, and twenty-two of twenty-three population elasticities having the anticipated signs. Moreover, the coefficients are generally quite significant, with forty-six of the sixty-nine estimated coefficients being significant at better than the 2.5 percent level and five more being significant at better than the 5 percent level.

With the exception of Spain, the model does reasonably well at explaining the distribution of emigrants.[14] The average adjusted coefficient of multiple determination is 0.515. We have also used each regression to predict the value of emigration to the United States from each origin country. The sum of the predicted flows to the United States (409,018), reported in table 2, is approximately 16 percent greater than the sum of the actual flows to the United States (351,272). The model predicts somewhat greater flows than those observed for Italy (27,119 predicted versus 14,747 observed), Netherlands (7,124 versus 3,128), Venezuela (127,772 versus 82,796), Australia (14,766 versus 7,776), and Costa Rica (135,266 versus 41,440). It is noteworthy that the predicted flow to the United States is considerably greater than the actual flow for the few Western Hemisphere countries incorporated in the analysis.

Because the United States is a major recipient country for emigrants from many nations included in our analysis and because the United States has both a relatively high wage rate and a binding immigration quota, the wage coefficients reported in table 2 may be biased in a downward direction. If this bias exists, then unbiased predicted emigration flows to the United States would be higher than the biased predicted flows reported here. This point may be particularly relevant for Western Hemisphere countries, since the United States is clearly the major high-wage destination for emigrants from these countries. Note that if predicted and actual flows to the United States are separately summed for Mexico, Venezuela, Costa Rica, and Bolivia and compared, the predicted (285,091) exceeds the actual (163,741) by 74.1 percent. If this argument concerning bias is correct, the 74.1 percent figure is a conservative estimate of potential migration to the United States from Western Hemisphere countries.

14 Note that, because the model estimated here focuses separately on each country of origin, the results can be interpreted either as indicating absolute emigration to each destination country or the share of total emigration that goes to each destination country. If the latter interpretation were followed, each observation on emigration would be divided by total emigration from the given country to the set of destination countries used here, which is a constant for any given year. The empirical results reported below would differ only in the constant term, which would be greater by the value in $\ln\Sigma_j EMIG_{ij}$.

TABLE 2

GROSS COUNTRY-SPECIFIC EMIGRATION: LOGARITHMIC REGRESSION COEFFICIENTS AND t-RATIOS

Country/Year	No. of Observations	Const.		Explanatory Variables			Adj. R^2	U.S. Observation	
		β: t:	D_{ij}	W_j	P_j			Actual	Predict
Greece (1970)	39	−2.919 (1.043)	−0.392 (1.205)	2.199 (6.190)	0.654 (3.494)	0.515	11,484	2,955
Italy (1971)	16	1.029 (0.439)	−0.520 (2.114)	2.219 (5.135)	0.473 (2.056)	0.646	14,747	27,119
Spain (1970)	25	5.213 (0.779)	−0.286 (0.516)	−0.015 (0.014)	0.838 (1.926)	0.039	1,120	1,420
Austria (1970)	15	−18.963 (4.810)	0.972 (3.055)	3.694 (5.622)	0.224 (0.705)	0.715	4,565	4,572
Luxembourg (1970)	22	6.714 (2.589)	−1.397 (6.127)	0.500 (1.031)	1.432 (5.600)	0.733	255	210
Netherlands (1970)	28	1.572 (0.810)	−0.304 (1.788)	1.327 (3.910)	0.619 (3.553)	0.469	3,128	7,124
United Kingdom (1975)	19	4.447 (1.857)	−0.076 (0.327)	0.947 (2.057)	0.192 (0.983)	0.159	22,100	13,223
West Germany (1970)	45	8.481 (5.415)	−0.886 (6.220)	0.911 (3.913)	0.822 (5.610)	0.655	23,444	22,494
Denmark (1971)	43	7.806 (4.287)	−0.890 (5.233)	0.615 (2.598)	0.645 (5.008)	0.601	2,332	1,047
Finland (1970)	14	−3.311 (0.737)	−0.523 (1.045)	2.989 (3.034)	0.038 (0.088)	0.334	621	1,305

Country (year)								
Norway (1970)	29	5.850 (3.878)	−0.882 (5.504)	1.167 (5.575)	0.542 (3.763)	0.701	2,837	3,517
Sweden (1970)	45	7.580 (3.770)	−1.257 (6.562)	1.300 (4.838)	0.784 (5.467)	0.694	1,529	1,974
Iceland (1970)	24	−0.591 (0.135)	−0.382 (0.803)	1.707 (3.690)	−0.146 (0.526)	0.417	325	262
Mexico (1970)	28	3.429 (0.578)	−0.648 (1.271)	1.410 (3.453)	0.733 (3.099)	0.558	36,635	21,651
Costa Rica (1971)	36	12.185 (3.822)	−1.760 (5.620)	1.724 (5.719)	0.646 (3.399)	0.720	41,440	135,266
Bolivia (1970)	24	14.777 (5.378)	−1.566 (4.030)	0.110 (0.180)	0.742 (2.728)	0.505	2,870	402
Venezuela (1971)	35	14.511 (4.232)	−1.683 (4.381)	1.099 (2.950)	0.739 (4.571)	0.507	82,796	127,772
Australia (1970)	28	13.587 (2.269)	−1.377 (1.973)	1.293 (3.375)	0.371 (1.487)	0.255	7,776	14,766
New Zealand (1971)	42	22.790 (4.750)	−2.699 (5.110)	1.395 (4.551)	0.327 (1.927)	0.500	1,445	1,006
Philippines (1972)	27	−1.481 (0.287)	0.034 (0.054)	0.736 (1.745)	0.644 (2.951)	0.221	9,222	393
Korea (1971)	39	12.984 (3.984)	−1.804 (5.177)	1.698 (6.962)	0.725 (5.014)	0.731	57,346	10,636
Japan (1970)	46	10.027 (4.810)	−1.244 (5.133)	1.140 (6.205)	0.806 (7.963)	0.726	23,225	9,780
Malaysia (1970)	18	37.267 (3.926)	−4.381 (3.199)	1.206 (1.318)	0.270 (0.605)	0.434	30	124

The Distribution of U.S. Immigrants. Differential earnings is only one factor that may influence the decision to emigrate. As discussed previously, the institutional framework is also important. U.S. laws have apparently limited the total number of immigrants and may also have altered the mix of those who ultimately gain immigrant status in the United States.[15] Moreover, the ease with which a worker can transfer his occupational skills to the U.S. labor market is likely to be of some importance.

The models that we develop in this section focus not only on variables designed to capture the influences of differential economic advantage but also on variables intended to reflect the costs of transferring skills to the United States from abroad. Let us begin by considering the following two models:

$$\ln\left(\frac{I_i}{MP_i}\right) = \ln C_0 + \sum_{j=1}^{10} \beta_j X_{ji} + e_{2i} \quad \text{and} \quad (2)$$

$$\ln\left(\frac{M_i}{MP_i}\right) = \ln C'_0 + \sum_{j=1}^{10} \beta_j' X_{ji} + e_{3i}, \quad (3)$$

where I_i = the gross number of U.S. immigrants from country i who declared an occupation when entering the United States during fiscal year 1970; MP_i = the 1969 male population of country i, aged twenty through forty-nine; M_i = the gross number of male immigrants, aged twenty through forty-nine, who entered the United States from country i during fiscal year 1970; X_{1i} = the estimated minimum airline mileage from country i to the United States, expressed as a logarithm; X_{2i} = 1970 average weekly manufacturing earnings in country i measured in U.S. dollars, expressed as a logarithm; X_{3i} = country i's percentage growth in real per capita Gross National Product (GNP) from 1965 to 1970, expressed as a logarithm; X_{4i} = the percentage of country i's 1970 labor force engaged in manufacturing, expressed as a logarithm; X_{5i} = the number of natives of country i who attended a U.S. university in 1970 as a proportion of the number of males aged twenty to twenty-four in country i (1969), expressed as a logarithm; X_{6i} = the number of under- and postgraduate university degrees granted in country i (1970) as a proportion of the total population of country i, expressed as a logarithm; X_{7i} = the percentage of total male population of country i aged twenty to twenty-four in 1969, expressed as a logarithm; X_{8i} = the percentage of males aged twenty to twenty-four in country i (1969) divided by the percentage of males twenty to twenty-four in

[15] See Charles B. Keely, "Effects of U.S. Immigration Law on the Manpower Characteristics of Immigrants," *Demography*, vol. 12, no. 2 (May 1975), pp. 179-191.

country i (1960), expressed as a logarithm; $X_{9i} =$ a dummy variable that equals one if country i's official United Nations language is English, and otherwise equals zero; $X_{10i} =$ a dummy variable that equals one if country i is in the Eastern Hemisphere, and otherwise equals zero; $C_0, C'_0 =$ constants; and $e_{2i}, e_{3i} =$ random errors.

The model has been estimated on a sample of thirty-four nations.[16] These countries were selected because the data on the independent variables were available. The appendix to this chapter contains a complete description of the data on the independent variables, as well as an indication of all data sources.

As pointed out in the previous section, increased costs of migration, for which distance can serve as a proxy, are expected to reduce the rate of migration from country i to the United States. Moreover, since a higher wage in country i reflects a smaller wage differential between country i and the United States, the rate of migration from higher wage countries to the United States should be lower. Hence, we expect that $\beta_1 < 0$ and $\beta_2 < 0$. More rapid expansion of country i's economy, as indicated by the percentage growth in real GNP, should serve to enhance job opportunities in the sending country and thus retard migration from country i to the United States $(\beta_3 < 0)$. The strength of this relationship may be moderated somewhat, if an expanding economy is conducive to personal asset accumulation that can be used to support migration.

The percentage of males aged twenty to twenty-four is a proxy for the relative magnitude of new labor force entrants in country i (X_7). The higher this percentage, the more depressed are likely to be labor market conditions faced by new entrants, partly because relative initial wages are likely to be lower and partly because unemployment rates are likely to be higher. Consequently, the propensity to migrate is increased. This effect may differ across occupations, since the market conditions faced by new entrants will be less attractive the greater the relative number of new entrants in any given skill category. Moreover, the propensity to migrate should be higher the less substitutable the skills of new entrants for the occupational skills of older workers who are employed in the entrant's particular occupation. Finally, younger persons are known to be considerably more mobile than older persons for a variety of reasons. We therefore expect that $\beta_7 > 0$.

[16] The European countries include Austria, Denmark, France, Germany, Greece, Ireland, Italy, Portugal, Spain, Sweden, Switzerland, and the United Kingdom. The Asian countries include Hong Kong, India, Israel, Japan, Korea, the Philippines, Syria, Thailand, and Turkey. The North and Central American countries include Canada, El Salvador, Guatemala, Mexico, and Nicaragua. The South American countries include Brazil, Chile, Colombia, Ecuador, and Venezuela. The Oceanian countries include Australia and New Zealand. The only African country included is South Africa.

The growth over time in the relative number of new entrants is also expected to affect the incentive to migrate. Suppose the relative number of new entrants is high in a given year. Emigration should be stimulated since labor market conditions will tend to be depressed. If the new entrants follow preceding cohorts of new entrants whose numbers were also relatively high (a low value of X_{8i}), then market conditions should be even more depressed. Therefore, given the number of new entrants in 1969, the rate of emigration should be inversely related to the growth over time of new entrants. Otherwise stated, the conditions in the sending country that enhance the likelihood of emigration are a large relative number of new entrants to the labor force, especially if the entrants have been relatively large in number for some period of time. Therefore, we expect, other things being equal, that $\beta_8 < 0$.

Impact of knowledge and occupation. The ease with which a prospective migrant can transfer his occupational skills to the U.S. labor market should influence his propensity to migrate. Knowledge and occupational skills are not perfectly transferable between countries; the lower the cost of this adjustment, the greater the incentive to migrate to the United States. Barry R. Chiswick, for instance, observed that net downward occupational mobility was least for immigrants from developed English-speaking countries.[17] The cost of adjusting to the U.S. labor market appears to be lower for such individuals; consequently, other things being equal, their incentive to migrate should be enhanced $(\beta_9 > 0)$.

Similarly, a higher proportion of individuals attending U.S. universities will increase the probability that accumulated occupational knowledge will be easily transferable to the U.S. labor market. It should be noted that merely increasing the number of individuals attending a U.S. university does not directly increase the number of immigrants who enter the United States with an occupation, since foreign students would not typically be included in the totals for these workers. However, acquiring knowledge specific to the U.S. labor market would increase the probability of acquiring a future occupation in the United States. Therefore, to the extent the relative flow of foreign students to the United States is reasonably stable, the number of current immigrants entering the United States with an occupation is expected to be positively related with the flow of foreign students $(\beta_5 > 0)$.

[17] Barry R. Chiswick, "Immigrants and Immigration Policy," in William Fellner, ed., *Contemporary Economic Problems 1978* (Washington, D.C.: American Enterprise Institute, 1978).

The percentage of the labor force engaged in manufacturing may reflect the state of economic development in a country. To the extent that greater economic development serves to enhance job opportunities in the sending country, migration should be retarded and, hence, β_4 should be less than zero. Other considerations, however, make the interpretation of the expected relationship between the labor force in manufacturing and immigration flows less clear. The incentive to migrate to the United States, for instance, should be enhanced for individuals whose occupational skills are similar to those used in U.S. labor markets. If the percentage of the labor force engaged in manufacturing serves as a crude index for the mix of occupational skills in a sending country, then a larger fraction of labor force in manufacturing may suggest a mix of occupational skills that is closer to that found in the United States. As a consequence, the incentive to migrate to the United States should be increased. The strength of this latter effect will therefore moderate or, conceivably, reverse the expected sign on β_4.

A common finding in studies of migration is that better educated individuals have a higher propensity to migrate. This finding may be due partly to more educated individuals being more likely to have better information concerning alternative areas. Moreover, persons with higher educational attainment may be better able to adapt to the requirements faced when entering a new occupational environment. Thus, if more educated individuals are better equipped to adjust to changing environments, then their transaction costs associated with international moves will be moderated. Furthermore, persons with higher educational attainment may also find substantial demand for their skills in the United States. For each of the above reasons, we expect $\beta_6 > 0$.

This expectation should, however, be qualified. The incremental value that the U.S. labor market assigns to a prospective immigrant's education, which is acquired in his respective home country, may be less than the incremental value of the education if used in the native country. If this argument is valid, the effect of education is less clear. Another important consideration is that the effect of educational attainment may differ considerably across occupational categories.

Let us now turn to our empirical findings. As mentioned, our primary focus is on the immigrants who entered the United States with an occupation during fiscal year 1970.[18] On entering the United States,

[18] Some individuals may have had an adjustment of status to that of immigrant after living in the United States for some period of time. Of the 376,326 immigrants to the United States in 1970, 55,761 were already in the United States and were adjusted to permanent resident alien status. Some of those changing their

42.1 percent of the 1970 immigrants reported an occupation. Of those not reporting an occupation, housewives and children under fourteen made up most of the group, with students and retired persons also contributing in lesser numbers.[19] Excluding housewives and children from our dependent variable should not seriously affect the estimation. Later, we will provide some evidence on factors affecting the flow of older and retired workers to the United States.

The breakdown by continent for immigrants who enter the United States with an occupation shows some difference. While 45.5 percent of the European immigrants and 42.7 percent of the Asian immigrants entered in 1970 with an occupation, only 38.4 percent of those entering from the Western Hemisphere declared an occupation. These figures suggest that relatively more of the European immigrants, as compared with natives from the Western Hemisphere, are in the ages primarily associated with working. Further evidence of this contention is available. While 58.4 percent of the European immigrants were aged twenty through forty-nine, only 46.0 percent of the immigrants from the Western Hemisphere were.

Table 3 presents estimates of factors that influence the rate of immigration from various countries to the United States. In regression (1), the dependent variable is calculated as a rate $\ln(I_i/MP_i)$, where the numerator is the number of U.S. immigrants from country i who declared an occupation when entering the United States during fiscal year 1970. The denominator in this expression is the 1969 male population in the sending country aged twenty through forty-nine. Again, the relationships have been estimated in double-log form by ordinary least squares.

No estimated coefficient has an unexpected sign. However, certain factors seem particularly noteworthy. Distance to the United States (X_1) appears to discourage migration to the United States.[20] Other important factors affecting the rate of immigration are the earnings level and the percentage of the labor force in manufacturing in the sending country. Lower earnings in the sending country increase the

status entered the United States with student, diplomatic, or tourist visas, while others were illegal aliens. Those individuals who adjusted status are not subject to the transactions costs and economic differentials incorporated in our model and, since these individuals are not excluded from our immigration flows, our results are biased on the conservative side.

[19] U.S. Department of Justice, *1970 Annual Report of the Commissioner of Immigration and Naturalization*, 1972, p. 5.

[20] Lucas, "Supply-of-Immigrants Function," also found that the various costs associated with longer distances deter immigration. Furthermore, the findings by Lucas support our evidence on English-speaking nations as well as the effect of income in the country of origin on the incentive to migrate.

TABLE 3

RATES OF MIGRATION TO THE U.S. OF PERSONS WITH AN OCCUPATION:
LOGARITHMIC REGRESSION COEFFICIENTS (β) AND t-RATIOS (t)

	Regression	
	1	2
	Migrants who declare	Male migrants aged
Independent Variables	an occupation at entry	20 to 49 at entry
X_1: distance to U.S.	β: $-$ 1.280	$-$ 1.358
	t: (2.996)	(3.329)
X_2: average weekly earnings	$-$ 1.264	$-$ 1.465
	(2.613)	(3.174)
X_3: change real per capita GNP	$-$ 0.224	$-$ 0.182
	(0.627)	(0.534)
X_4: labor force in	1.259	1.461
manufacturing (%)	(2.069)	(2.515)
X_5: foreign students at	0.482	0.486
U.S. colleges	(2.556)	(2.701)
X_6: college graduates	0.070	0.061
	(0.205)	(0.190)
X_7: entrants to labor force (1969)	2.612	3.725
	(0.759)	(1.134)
X_8: entrants (1969) $\div$	$-$ 2.210	$-$ 2.454
entrants (1960)	(0.982)	(1.143)
X_9: English language	1.063	1.089
	(1.482)	(1.592)
X_{10}: Eastern Hemisphere	0.717	0.645
	(0.977)	(0.921)
C: constant	$-$ 2.462	$-$ 4.633
	(0.317)	(0.626)
R^2	.51	.56
Adjusted R^2 (obs. = 34)	.30	.37
Dependent variable	$\ln\left(\dfrac{I_i}{MP_i}\right)$	$\ln\left(\dfrac{M_i}{MP_i}\right)$

relative economic gain resulting from migration; consequently, the incentive to migrate is enhanced. The evidence is consistent with this expectation. Furthermore, if a country's occupational mix is similar to that of the United States, as evidenced by a high proportion of labor force in manufacturing, the rate of immigration from country i to the United States is increased.

Occupational knowledge is not perfectly transferable from another country to the United States. It is therefore noteworthy that the rate of immigration to the United States is higher for persons from English-speaking countries. This evidence is compatible with the hypothesis that, if a prospective immigrant is from an English-speaking country, the costs of adjustment to the U.S. labor market are reduced. Hence, the incentive to migrate is greater. Moreover, receiving an education at a U.S. university would certainly increase the probability that the accumulated knowledge will be transferable, without substantial losses, to the U.S. labor market. As a consequence, increasing the proportion of natives from a country who receive a college education in the United States (X_4) appears to increase the flow of immigrants who enter the United States to perform work. In this relationship, however, the causality may be subject to question. If a prospective immigrant wants to migrate to the United States, the move may be facilitated by first coming to the United States as a student. We have not isolated this causal effect in our cross-sectional model of immigration flows.

Employment after arrival. An alternative approach, which also studies the flow of individuals migrating for occupation-related reasons, is to examine the flow of immigrants who are likely to be employed workers after arrival in the United States. Such a group is male immigrants who are aged twenty through forty-nine. In regression (2) of table 3, these immigrants are expressed as a proportion of the 1969 male population aged twenty through forty-nine in the sending country.

The adjustment in regression (2) seems to improve the explanatory power of the model; the approach in regression (1) of looking only at those who declare occupations adds random error to the dependent variable. Furthermore, the males who migrate for economic gain may not necessarily declare an occupation on entering the United States. Natives from the Eastern Hemisphere, for instance, are not required to obtain labor certification unless they are in one of the occupational preference categories (third or sixth preference). These individuals may therefore enter the United States under a "relative preference"; apparently, there is no requirement for them to declare an occupation. On the other hand, the improved explanatory power in regression (2) may merely reflect that some immigrants who declare an occupation, such as older workers and women, may have minor differences in the elasticity of their response to economic incentives. As a consequence, the model performs better after isolating a more homogeneous worker category.

Given the available data, it was not possible to separate by sex or age those individuals who declared an occupation. Therefore, we could estimate either the response of those declaring an occupation or a sex-age group that we expect to be moving for occupational gain. Though the estimated parameters are similar in regressions (1) and (2), the latter specification appears to be better in performance.

It is of interest to examine how the flows of immigrants by specific occupations are affected by the explanatory variables of the model. The complete study of this question is not contained in the current paper. We have examined, however, the flow for a specific group of highly skilled occupations: professionals, technical workers, managers (except farm), officials, proprietors, and kindred workers $(occ(1)_i)$. Professional and technical workers make up 88.8 percent of this selected group. The immigrants in these occupations were expressed as a proportion of total immigrants from country i with an occupation (I_i). Once again, the same variables are used to explain the proportion of immigrants from country i who are in the highly skilled occupations.

The results of this test are provided in the following regression

$$\ln\left(\frac{occ(1)_i}{I_i}\right) = \begin{array}{l} -6.0355 + 0.4947\,X_1 + 0.3341\,X_2 - 0.2423\,X_3 \\ \quad(1.4110)\quad(2.1002)\quad\;\;(1.2532)\quad\;\;(1.2324) \\ -5.5956\,X_4 + 0.1662\,X_5 + 0.3051\,X_6 + 0.5117\,X_7 \\ \;\;(1.7758)\quad\;\;(1.6009)\quad\;\;(1.6331)\quad\;\;(0.2697) \\ +0.7787\,X_8 + 0.0080\,X_9 + 0.3543\,X_{10} \\ \;\;(0.6279)\quad\;\;(0.0203)\quad\;\;(0.8765) \\ \qquad\qquad R^2 = .58 \end{array} \qquad (4)$$

where the independent variables are the same as in table 3.

Two of the explanatory variables seem particularly interesting, namely, distance to the United States (X_1) and college graduates in the sending country (X_6). In the results presented in table 3, the variable for college graduates failed to show any significant effect on the flow of immigrants. An increase in the proportion of college graduates in the sending country, however, does appear to influence the occupational distribution of those who migrate to the United States with a declared occupation. Increasing the percentage of college graduates increases the relative number of immigrants in the professional and technical fields. This finding may suggest that the incremental value that the U.S. labor market assigns to a prospective immigrant's educational attainment is greater than the incremental value of the education if used in the native country.

As distance to the United States is increased, the number of immigrants in highly skilled occupations rises relative to the number of immigrants in other occupations. It is likely that the workers in the highly skilled occupations are also more educated; more educated individuals tend to invest more in acquiring knowledge concerning employment prospects in distant locations. In addition, more educated individuals may be better able to adjust to the conditions that they face upon moving long distances from their native environments. Therefore, as distance is increased, the relative attractiveness of migrating apparently increases for individuals in highly skilled professions.

Two other explanatory variables are of interest. A higher proportion of natives attending U.S. universities (X_5) appears to increase the proportion of immigrants in highly skilled occupations. Also, as the percentage of the labor force in manufacturing (X_4) increases, the number of highly skilled migrants decreases relative to the number of other workers. This latter evidence seems to support the hypothesis that greater economic development serves to enhance job opportunities and reduce the incentive to migrate, especially for individuals in highly skilled professions. In considering the variable X_5, the issue of causality may be particularly important. A move to the United States as a professional or technical worker would likely be facilitated by first coming to the United States as a student. Furthermore, having acquired higher education in the United States, a foreign student may face substantial transactions costs in attempting to transfer his accumulated knowledge back to a native country. These considerations suggest that a positive bias may be introduced in our coefficient.

Older Immigrants. The final group of immigrants examined in our paper are those individuals aged fifty or older at the time of their arrival in the United States. In 1970, 14,093 of these individuals were reported to have gained immigrant status. Some of the explanatory variables, such as distance, may be expected to have the same qualitative effect on the older individuals as for total immigrants with an occupation. However, since these individuals are either retired or close to retirement, the model used to examine the flow of these individuals is different.

Our model for the flow of older immigrants is

$$\ln\left(\frac{OI_i}{OP_i}\right) = \ln K_0 + \sum_j \alpha_j X_{ji} + e_{5i}$$
$$\text{where } j = 1, 3, 9, 10, 11, 12 \tag{5}$$

and where $OI_i =$ the gross number of immigrants, aged fifty or older, who entered the United States from country i during fiscal year 1970; $OP_i = 1969$ population of country i, aged fifty or older; $X_{11i} =$ the amount of social assistance in country i (expressed in U.S. dollars) divided by the population aged sixty-five or older in country i, expressed as a logarithm[21]; X_{12i} = the total number of immigrants from country i to the United States between the years 1960 and 1970, expressed as a logarithm; K_0 = a constant; and e_{5i} = random errors.

The model has been estimated on a sample of twenty-six nations.[22] Once again, this sample of countries was selected because the data are available. A complete description of the data and sources may be found in the appendix to this chapter.

Regression (1) of table 4 presents estimates of this model. The per-capita social assistance variable (X_{11}) is of particular interest. In our data, we are not able to distinguish the international portability of this social assistance, which is primarily in the form of social security benefits.[23] If these social security benefits are portable across international borders, then the income effect may actually serve to stimulate international migration. On the other hand, if these benefits are not portable, as the amount of social assistance per individual is increased, the flow of immigrants to the United States should be reduced. The estimates in table 4 seem consistent with this latter hypothesis.

Two other factors appear to influence the flow of older immigrants to the United States. Higher costs associated with longer travel distance to the United States appear to reduce the flow of immigrants to the United States. Moreover, a larger total flow of immigrants to the United States from country i (1960 through 1970) increases the rate at which older individuals migrate. This finding may be due to older migrants following their children or other younger relatives who have preceded them to the United States. This hypothesis, however, is not directly tested here.

Regression (2) of table 4 presents estimates of the factors that influence the flow of older immigrants (OI_i) as a proportion of the total immigrants (TI_i) who arrived from country i during fiscal year 1970. Again, the social assistance variable has an expected negative sign.

[21] Social assistance includes social security benefits (general government), social assistance grants, and government transfers to private nonprofit institutions serving households.

[22] The European countries include Austria, Belgium, Denmark, France, Germany, Ireland, the Netherlands, Norway, Portugal, Spain, Sweden, Switzerland, and the United Kingdom. The Asian countries include Israel, the Philippines, and Turkey. The North and Central American countries include Canada, Honduras, Jamaica, and Panama. The South American countries include Argentina, Chile, Colombia, Ecuador, and Peru. The Oceanian countries include Australia.

[23] For those countries that reported a separate category for social security benefits ($n = 17$), the social security benefits were 84.6 percent of the total social assistance benefits.

TABLE 4

RATES OF MIGRATION OF OLDER PERSONS TO THE U.S.:
LOGARITHMIC REGRESSION COEFFICIENTS (α) AND t-RATIOS (t)

	Regression	
	1	2
	Immigrants who	Older persons as
	are aged fifty	percent of total
Independent Variables	or older	U.S. immigrants
X_1: distance to U.S.	α: $-$ 0.809	$-$ 0.533
	t: (1.922)	(2.501)
X_3: change real per capita GNP	0.508	0.557
	(0.979)	(2.120)
X_9: English language	0.064	$-$ 0.271
	(0.108)	(0.898)
X_{10}: Eastern Hemisphere	0.081	1.183
	(0.129)	(3.720)
X_{11}: social assistance $\div$ population aged 65 or older	$-$0.448 (3.460)	$-$0.247 (3.768)
X_{12}: total immigrants from country i to the U.S. (1960 through 1970)	0.366 (1.584)	0.060 (0.515)
K_0: constant	1.777	0.253
	(0.334)	(0.094)
R^2	.62	.59
Adjusted R^2 obs. $= 26$	.50	.47
Dependent variable	$\ln \left(\dfrac{OI_i}{OP_i} \right)$	$\ln \left(\dfrac{OI_i}{TI_i} \right)$

The evidence also suggests that an increase in distance to the United States serves to reduce the flow of older immigrants relative to total immigrants. Distance therefore appears to deter the migration of older individuals relatively more than younger prospective migrants. This finding may be due to the higher costs associated with moving the greater amount of physical assets that tend to accumulate with age. Moreover, social and cultural ties develop with age; as a consequence, older individuals may become reluctant to move long distances from their native environments. Also, with shorter remaining life, as well as greater country-specific investment, the incentive for older individuals to move is less.

Two additional factors appear to influence the proportion of total immigrants who are aged fifty or more, namely, the expansion of the sending country's economy and the fact that the sending country is in the Eastern Hemisphere. The reason for the highly significant effect of the Eastern Hemisphere variable is not clear. Perhaps this finding reflects, in part, a spillover effect resulting from the 1965 change in the U.S. immigration laws. Prior to the 1965 amendments, natives from countries in the Eastern Hemisphere were restricted by country quotas with 30 percent of each quota reserved for parents of U.S. citizens. After the 1965 amendments became effective in 1968, parents of U.S. citizens, regardless of origin, were free to migrate to the United States without the necessity of waiting for a restricted visa number. The change in the law may therefore have allowed some older individuals to migrate, where previously they may have been restrained from doing so.

A more rapid expansion of a sending country's economy, as represented by a high percentage change in real per-capita GNP, serves to enhance job opportunities in the sending country and should thus reduce the flow of migrants to the United States. The influence of this factor, however, should be relatively stronger for an individual who considers migration primarily in terms of its effects on immediate economic gain in his current occupation. Expansion of a sending country's economy should therefore deter the migration of retired individuals, or those who are close to retirement, relatively less. The positive and significant coefficient on X_3 may therefore suggest that, if relatively more young persons are deterred from migrating due to expanding labor demand in their native countries, the age distribution of migrants tends to shift toward older persons.

Estimates of Possible Immigration

Our initial objective in this paper was to estimate the magnitude of immigration to the United States if U.S. entry barriers were removed. If other nations were to maintain their barriers, one is hard pressed to imagine why any given country should send fewer persons to the United States, although the rate of flow might well tend to decline over time as initial U.S. economic advantages are eroded.[24] Our tentative conclusion, based on an examination of data provided by various countries of emi-

[24] This statement presumes decreasing returns to scale as new migrants enter the United States. Fairly general agreement appears to exist that decreasing returns to (population) scale have prevailed in the U.S. economy since perhaps 1900 or, at the latest, 1920. See Allan C. Kelley, "Demographic Changes and American Economic Development: Past, Present and Future," in E. R. Morss and R. H. Reed, eds., *Economic Aspects of Population Change,* Commission on Population Growth and the American Future, Research Reports, vol. 2 (Washington, D.C.: Government Printing Office, 1972), pp. 10-44.

gration, is that a simple economic model of international migration predicts roughly 16 percent more migration to the United States than actually occurred in a given year. Western Hemisphere nations appear most likely to supply the United States with large increases in immigrants. The models we have used conservatively predict that emigration from such nations to the United States should be over 74 percent higher than the emigration that was actually observed.

For several reasons, these estimates are subject to sizable error. The magnitude of the error that results from estimating a model that assumes free choice with data reflecting all sorts of real-world barriers to free choice is unknown. Many potential origin countries are not included in our analysis; for the origin countries that are included, many important potential destination countries had to be eliminated because of a lack of data. Immigration flows to the United States are known to have varied over time, when they were freer to do so, as economic conditions in the United States and in source countries changed; we have in no way accounted for such influences in our analysis. Finally, our simple model accounts for an average of about one-half of the variance in international emigration.

Certain factors seem particularly noteworthy in our model designed to explain the pattern of origin countries from which U.S. immigrants with an occupation are drawn. Distance to the United States appears to discourage migration to the United States. Our evidence is also consistent with the expectation that lower earnings in the sending country increase the relative economic gain resulting from migration and therefore induce more immigration. Furthermore, if a country's occupational mix is similar to that of the United States, as evidenced by a high proportion of the labor force in manufacturing, the rate of immigration from country i to the United States is increased. As noted, this variable is open to alternative interpretations. As the percent of the labor force in manufacturing in a sending country increases, for instance, the number of highly skilled migrants decreases relative to the number of other workers. This evidence seems to support the hypothesis that greater economic development serves to enhance job opportunities and reduce the incentive to migrate, especially for individuals in highly skilled occupations.

Our evidence is also compatible with the hypothesis that, if a prospective migrant is from an English-speaking country, the cost of adjustment to the U.S. labor market is reduced and, hence, the incentive to migrate is greater. Moreover, the proportion of natives from a country who receive a college education in the United States is positively related to the flow of immigrants who enter the United States to perform work. Finally, the level of social assistance in a sending country is inversely related to the rate at which older individuals migrate to the United States.

Appendix: Sources and Notes

I. Independent variables:

$X_1 =$ the estimated minimum airline mileage from country i to the United States.

SOURCE: *Air Tariff,* Worldwide Book 1 (July 1978).

$X_2 =$ 1970 average weekly manufacturing earnings in country i.

SOURCE: United Nations, *Statistical Yearbook: 1977,* table 182, pp. 673–676.

NOTES: Series generally related to the average (male-female) earnings of wage earners in manufacturing industries. Earnings normally include bonuses, cost-of-living allowances, taxes, social insurance contributions payable by employed persons, and, in some cases, payments in kind. Earnings normally exclude social insurance contributions payable by employers, family allowances, and other social security benefits. Special problems were encountered in the following cases:

A. Three countries (Australia, El Salvador, and Switzerland) recorded data for only the separate categories male and female. The percentages of males and females in the labor force (International Labor Organization [ILO], *Yearbook of Labour Statistics: 1973,* table 2) were used as weights in order to calculate the combined male-female average earnings.

B. Ten countries reported monthly earnings. In order to convert these data to weekly earnings, the data were multiplied by a factor equal to $12 \div 52$. These countries are Austria, Brazil, Chile, India, Japan, Korea, Mexico, the Philippines, South Africa (white population), and Venezuela.

C. Eighteen countries reported only hourly earnings. For these countries, hourly wages in each country are multiplied by the number of hours worked in manufacturing industries in the respective country (ILO, *Yearbook of Labour Statistics: 1973,* table 13). These countries are Canada, Colombia, Denmark, Ecuador, El Salvador, France, Germany, Greece, Guatemala, Ireland, Italy, Nicaragua,

Portugal, Spain, Sweden, Switzerland, Thailand, and United Kingdom. One exception is Nicaragua, for which the hours worked per week are calculated as the average hours worked in manufacturing in data recorded for Central and South American countries.

D. Three countries (Hong Kong, Israel, and Turkey) reported daily earnings. For these countries, daily earnings are multiplied by a factor of five.

E. Portugal and New Zealand presented special problems: For Portugal, 1971 weekly earnings are used; for New Zealand, weekly earnings refer to male earnings.

F. National currencies have been converted to U.S. dollars. The source used for the 1970 exchange rates is United Nations, *Statistical Yearbook: 1977,* table 192.

$X_3 =$ country i's percentage growth in real per-capita GNP from 1965 to 1970.

SOURCE: United Nations, *Statistical Yearbook: 1977,* table 185, pp. 692–696.

NOTES: Numbers refer to the change in the index of per-capita domestic output at constant prices in terms of the system of national accounts. It should be noted that the numbers are subject to some imprecision. The methods used to measure the estimates in constant prices differ widely, for instance. Nevertheless, the numbers seem appropriate for indicating general trends.

$X_4 =$ percentage of country i's labor force in manufacturing.

SOURCES: United Nations, *Demographic Yearbook: 1972,* table 10, pp. 296–327; United Nations, *Demographic Yearbook: 1973,* table 40, pp. 666–685; and U.S. Bureau of Labor Statistics, *Handbook of Labor Statistics,* table 162, pp. 576–579.

NOTES: Data for years other than 1970 are used for the following countries: Ecuador (1962), El Salvador (1971), Guatemala (1964), Hong Kong (1971), Korea (1966), and Nicaragua (1963). Special problems were also encountered in the following cases:

A. For Switzerland, the definition of manufacturing includes mining and quarrying, electricity, gas and water, construction, and manufacturing.

B. Data are for South African white population.

$X_5 =$ the number of natives of country i who attended a U.S.

university in 1970, expressed as a proportion of country i's male population aged twenty through twenty-four.

SOURCES: Unesco, *Statistical Yearbook: 1972,* table 4.8, pp. 463–489; and United Nations, *Demographic Yearbook: 1970,* table 6, pp. 166–407 (and other volumes).

NOTES: The population data are for years other than 1969 for the following countries: Brazil (1970), El Salvador (1971), France (1968), India (1970), Italy (1968), Germany (1968), Nicaragua (1971), the Philippines (1968), Syria (1970), Thailand (1970), Turkey (1970), and Venezuela (1968). Moreover, for Guatemala and Colombia, the 1969 estimated population is interpolated from 1964 and 1973 data.

$X_6 =$ the number of first- and postgraduate university degrees granted in country i (1970), expressed as a proportion of the total population of country i (1969).

SOURCES: Unesco, *Statistical Yearbook: 1972,* table 4.5, pp. 446–456; and United Nations, *Demographic Yearbook: 1970,* table 6, pp. 166–407 (and other volumes).

NOTES: The number of graduates is recorded for years other than 1970 in the following countries: Brazil (1969), Colombia (1969), El Salvador (1975), France (1971), Germany (1969), India (1967), Ireland (average of 1965 and 1975), Mexico (1969), New Zealand (average of 1969 and 1971), Nicaragua (1969), the Philippines (1971), Portugal (1975), South Africa (1963), and Venezuela (1969). For notes on population estimates, see variable X_7.

$X_7 =$ the percentage of male population aged twenty to twenty-four in country i (1969).

SOURCE: United Nations, *Demographic Yearbook: 1970,* table 6, pp. 166–407 (and other volumes).

NOTES: The data are for years other than 1969 for the following countries: Brazil (1970), El Salvador (1971), France (1968), India (1970), Italy (1968), Germany (1968), Nicaragua (1971), the Philippines (1968), Syria (1970), Thailand (1970), Turkey (1970), and Venezuela (1968). Also, for Guatemala and Colombia, the 1969 estimated population is interpolated from 1964 and 1973 data.

$X_8 =$ the percentage of males aged twenty to twenty-four in

83

country i (1969) divided by the percentage of males aged twenty to twenty-four in country i (1960).

SOURCES: United Nations, *Demographic Yearbook: 1970,* table 6, pp. 166–407; and United Nations, *Demographic Yearbook: 1961,* table 5, pp. 138–161 (and other volumes).

NOTES: See notes for variable X_7. Also the 1960 estimates are for years other than 1960 in the following countries: Colombia (1965), Ecuador (1962), Guatemala (1965), and South Africa (1965).

$X_9 =$ a dummy variable that equals one if country i's official United Nations language is English.

SOURCE: United Nations, *Who's Who in the United Nations: 1975,* pp. 701–704.

$X_{10} =$ a dummy variable that equals one if country i is in the Eastern Hemisphere.

$X_{11} =$ the amount of social assistance in country i (expressed in U.S. dollars) divided by the population aged sixty-five or older in country i.

SOURCES: United Nations, *Yearbook of National Account Statistics: 1977,* system of national accounts (SNA) standard tables 14; and United Nations, *Demographic Yearbook: 1970,* table 6, pp. 166–407 (and other volumes).

NOTES: Social assistance includes social security benefits (SNA standard tables 14) and social assistance grants (SNA standard tables 14). Social security benefits are defined as payments to individuals under the social security arrangements that are imposed, controlled, or financed by the government for the purposes of providing social security benefits for the community or large sections of the community. Social assistance grants are cash grants to individuals or households by public authorities, private non-profit institutions, and corporate and quasi-corporate enterprises, except social security benefits and unfunded employee benefits. Also, it should be noted that the population estimates used in calculating this variable are for 1968 instead of 1969 in the following countries: Belgium, Denmark, France, Germany, Greece, Italy, and the Philippines. 1973 population estimates are used for Costa Rica.

$X_{12} =$ the gross number of immigrants from country i to the United States between the years 1960 through 1970.

SOURCE: U.S. Department of Justice, *1970 Annual Report: Immigration and Naturalization Service.*

II. Dependent Variables:

I_i = gross number of immigrants born in country i and admitted to the United States, with an occupation, for permanent residence during fiscal year 1970.

SOURCE: U.S. Department of Justice, *1970 Annual Report: Immigration and Naturalization Service,* table 8, p. 49.

M_i = gross number of male immigrants born in country i, aged twenty through forty-nine, admitted to the United States during fiscal year 1970.

SOURCE: U.S. Department of Justice, *1970 Annual Report: Immigration and Naturalization Service,* table 9, p. 52.

OI_i = gross number of total immigrants born in country i, aged fifty or older, admitted to the United States during fiscal year 1970.

SOURCE: U.S. Department of Justice, *1970 Annual Report: Immigration and Naturalization Service,* table 9, pp. 52 and 53.

P_i, MP_i,
and OP_i = country i's 1969 total population, 1969 male population aged twenty through forty-nine, and 1969 population aged fifty or older, respectively.

SOURCE: United Nations, *Demographic Yearbook: 1970,* table 6, pp. 166–407.

NOTES: All population totals are estimates and, where necessary, volumes other than the 1970 *Demographic Yearbook* are used to calculate these estimates.

85

Taxation and International Migration: Recent Policy Issues

Jagdish N. Bhagwati

Among the recent developments in the theory of international migration and its implications for public policy have been questions relating to the exercise of tax jurisdiction by nation-states over migrants, that is, people who move across national borders. These questions raise not merely narrowly economic but also moral-philosophical and sociological issues since they involve in an essential way the relationship between individuals and nation-states.

More precisely, the questions that have been addressed are the following. First, should nation-states exercise income tax jurisdiction over citizens abroad, quite regardless of status concerning residence and "migration," as indeed the United States and the Philippines do, or should they follow the "schedular" system, under which taxation is levied by residence qualification alone? Second, should nations that receive foreign nationals as migrants of one kind or another share the tax revenues raised from such nationals with the countries of origin? Both these questions have immediate policy relevance in the United States; they have been aired recently in international forums dealing with north-south relations, on which they bear.

The first section of this paper is addressed to developing the historical background of these questions. The second section then considers the first issue, tax jurisdiction of nation-states vis-à-vis migrants. The third section addresses the second issue, revenue sharing by receiving countries with the sending countries.

A Backward Glance

The *economic* issues in taxation and migration have their counterparts in the political issues that have surfaced about the voting rights of

This paper was prepared for the "Conference on U.S. Immigration Issues and Policies," sponsored by the American Enterprise Institute and University of Illinois, Chicago Circle, April 10-11, 1980. Thanks are due to the National Science Foundation for partial financial support of the research underlying this paper (grant no. SOC77-07541). Barry R. Chiswick's comments have been valuable.

migrants in receiving countries. As economic analysts have raised the issue whether migrant citizens ought to be allowed total exemption (as with the schedular tax system) from the tax jurisdiction of their countries of nationality—whether there should be "representation without taxation"—political analysts have raised the reverse question in regard to voting: Should not immigrant aliens who have retained their foreign nationality get the right to vote in their countries of residence—should there be "taxation without representation?"

Interestingly, there are important and telling contrasts between these two sets of questions that are worth spelling out. The political analysts have come to their question by observing the plight of the unskilled *Gastarbeiters,* guest workers, in western Europe, captured beautifully by Brusati in his poignant portrayal of the Italian immigrant workers in Switzerland in *Bread and Chocolate.* Can one protect the civil rights and liberties of these immigrants if they do not have the vote in a pluralistic democracy?[1] While the United States has seen no public or even academic debate on this issue of granting voting rights to (legal) aliens, the European scene has witnessed rapid progress on the issue, with Sweden granting the vote in local elections to foreign workers in the general election of September 1976.[2]

The neglect of this issue in the United States is an interesting phenomenon that may be explained by the following factors. First, the exploitation of gastarbeiters, who are legal, unskilled aliens, has not been a major factor on the U.S. scene, where the economic-need criterion for setting immigration quotas has played a much more limited role. The adoption of the familial and refugee-oriented immigration system in regard to importation of unskilled labor, in face of internal need for labor, has spawned a large illegal immigration, where the question of voting rights runs into the immediate and insuperable objection that the presence of the illegal immigrants is not formally sanctioned by the society. The emphasis therefore shifts much more to questions such as the illegals' rights to social security, health, and safety and the implications for census counting and apportionment of seats and federal funds. Second, the legal immigration has largely been familial and refugee oriented, and the economic-need criterion has been applied for the rest mainly to let in the PTK (professional, technical, and kindred)

---

[1] The grant of the vote is only a necessary, not a sufficient, condition for the guarantee of such rights, of course.

[2] See the account of it in Tomas Hammar, "The First Immigrant Election," *International Migration,* vol. 15 (February/March 1977). Professor Hammar, of the department of political science in Stockholm University, is engaged in a detailed study of this election. The question of following Sweden's example is being actively considered in Norway as well.

type of brain-drain immigrant, these being categories that (except possibly in the case of large-scale refugee inflows from one source, as with the boat people) plainly do *not* undergo the kind of exploitative experience that the gastarbeiters have experienced. Third, the naturalization process in the United States is probably much easier than in western Europe, so that the anomaly of having resident aliens and foreign workers in one's midst without giving them the right to vote in elections at any level does not appear to be particularly grotesque, if it enters U.S. consciousness at all.

By contrast, the tax and international migration questions have come up historically, almost entirely in the context of highly *skilled* migration. They are couched in completely general economic and moral-philosophical terms. Specifically, the present policy formulations derive from my early proposal to tax the brain drain. The specific, and all-too-critical, dimensions of the proposal in regard to who would levy and collect the tax were not spelled out in the original proposal, as briefly stated in a *Daedalus* paper.[3] The basic notion that the migrants themselves would pay the tax levied on their incomes in the country of immigration, was, however, spelled out in a later paper in *World Development*.[4] The proposal distinguished sharply from the notion of an "exit tax," which would presumably be levied prior to the migration and, at least in the versions that became current when the Soviet Union was flirting with the notion of its implementation, related to expended educational costs embodied in the migrant. Moreover, the proposal was addressed to highly skilled migrants from the LDCs (less developed countries) to the DCs (developed countries). The underlying moral rationale at the time was twofold. The highly skilled migrants from LDCs ought to make a contribution to LDC development through such an institutionalized tax system. These migrants improved their incomes greatly from the migration across the immigration barriers of the DCs, and it was arguable that, in several cases, their being allowed to migrate resulted in some difficulties—with losses for the countries of emigration. Both these reasons applied with much less force for the DC-to-DC migration; hence the proposal was confined only to the PTK-style immigrants from LDCs to DCs.

A subsequent conference on the proposal, organized at Bellagio, Italy, February 15–19, 1975, with the Rockefeller Foundation's support, led to further variations on the theme, largely as a result of the inter-

[3] Jagdish N. Bhagwati, "United States in the Nixon Era: The End of Innocence," *Daedalus*, vol. 101, no. 4 (Fall 1972), pp. 25-48.

[4] Jagdish N. Bhagwati and William Dellalfar, "The Brain Drain and Income Taxation," *World Development*, vol. 1, no. 1 (1973).

national-tax-legal, human-rights, and constitutional-legal input provided by distinguished lawyers present at the conference. In particular, such a tax on immigrants, which would be levied differentially on them and not on natives of the countries of immigration, could not be levied without considerable difficulty, if at all, by the United States, as it was most likely to be challenged successfully in the U.S. courts. No such constitutional barrier would present itself in the United Kingdom, where the Parliament is effectively sovereign in a world of an unwritten constitution. Since the *tax* would apply to immigrants predominantly from the non-white part of the commonwealth, the possibility of tax legislation being enacted to support the levy of such a tax on PTK-type immigrants was remote, however, in a context of increasing racial tension.

LDCs' Taxes on Own Migrants. The feasible format for such a proposal, therefore, seemed to be one whereby the LDCs would themselves levy the tax on their migrants. This, in turn, raised the question, Could such a tax be *collected* by the countries of emigration? If it could not, the responsibility for collection would be entirely that of the levying country; this raises questions, in turn, as to the feasibility of such a tax system. At the time, therefore, I summarized the situation concerning how the tax might be collected by the DCs:

> Thus, if the brain drain tax is to be levied by LDCs, there would be insuperable practical difficulties unless the DC governments were to agree to utilize their revenue agencies to collect it. To do this, clearly a treaty between the DC and the LDC in question would have to be executed making it legally feasible to have the tax enforced in the DC. A major problem that would then be raised by such bilateral treatymaking, which in turn would have to be consistent with domestic constitutional law and with public opinion, is that in this bilateral version the proceeds of the tax would be routed *individually* back to LDCs of origin: for it is easy to imagine several LDCs to which the public opinion in the United States, for example, would condemn the making of such a bilateral "contribution" and which would therefore be likely to be reflected in the judicial view of the matter if the enforceability of such an LDC-tax were challenged in the courts.
>
> It was thus clear that if for no other reason than purely on the ground of making the tax as judicially acceptable as possible, a *multilateral* version of it would be the best, and this meant that the preferred version of the original *World Development* paper, i.e., the version under which the United Nations would get involved in the brain drain tax in an essential way, became the optimal version of the Bellagio discussions as well.

Given the fact that the LDCs could in principle exercise tax jurisdiction over their nationals abroad, it could then be proposed that the LDCs would delegate their jurisdiction to the United Nations. At the same time, the DCs would make their contribution to the implementation of the tax by offering the UN their collection facilities. The tax revenues would then be routed to the UN, to be disbursed in the LDCs en bloc, according to the usual criteria for developmental spending as followed by UNDP [United Nations Development Programme] for example. The rationale behind the tax implementation would consist of two arguments, in order of their importance:

(1) Firstly, one would assert the moral principle that, in a world of imperfect mobility, those few who manage to get from LDCs into DCs to practice their professions at substantially-improved incomes ought to be asked to contribute a fraction of their gains for the improved welfare of those left behind in the LDCs; this would effectively be extending the usual principle of progressive taxation across national borders.

(2) Moreover, since there is a widely-held presumption, based on several sound arguments and embodied in numerous international resolutions, that the brain drain creates difficulties for the LDCs, it would also constitute a simple and rough-and-ready way for the emigrating professionals to compensate the LDCs for these losses. In fact, the moral obligation to share one's gains with those who are unable to share in these gains would be reinforced if these others were also hurt by one's emigration.

The tax proposal, in routing the proceeds via UN to LDCs en bloc, would also affirm the growing trend on the part of the LDCs, since the 1964 UNCTAD [United Nations Conference on Trade and Development] Conference, to emphasise their Third World "bloc," thus enabling them to go beyond their nationalist confines in this act of international policymaking. Furthermore, by bringing together the LDCs and DCs into joint action under UN auspices, it would also affirm the interdependent nature of the present world economy and the need to have coordinated and cooperative action among LDCs and DCs.

It is also clear that, once the tax is made into such a "global," cooperative policy measure, it could be embodied into a treaty or charter at the United Nations, with the DCs and LDCs signatories to it. This would then increase significantly, and almost certainly guarantee, the possibility of its being politically acceptable, and simultaneously being able to withstand challenges to its constitutionality in the United States.[5]

Fundamentally, therefore, the version of the tax proposal that I emerged with from Bellagio—though not by any means with many converts to the proposal at the conference—was a rather complex one, and one that was hardly calculated to secure a great following. Nonetheless, the basic idea of taxing the highly skilled migrants in some manner found a niche in the concerns at UNCTAD in its work on the brain drain or what it rather describes as the reverse transfer of technology. Thus, at the expert group meeting, February 27 to March 7, 1978, the Group of 77 in the draft recommendations urged the DCs to

> render assistance, either on a bilateral or multilateral basis, to developing countries which exercise or wish to exercise their internationally recognised jurisdiction to tax their citizens abroad under a "global" tax system; such assistance could take the form either of "tax collection assistance" and/or of access to information.[6]

Moreover, at the last UNCTAD conference in Manila, the DCs and LDCs adopted, in a rare unanimous affirmative vote, resolution 102(V), which for the first time introduced a reference to tax policies in the context of international migration, providing UNCTAD with a mandate to investigate further the range of questions that have been opened by the proposal to tax the brain drain.[7]

---

[5] Jagdish N. Bhagwati, ed., *The Brain Drain and Taxation: Theory and Empirical Analysis,* vol. 2 (Amsterdam: North-Holland Publishing Co., 1976), pp. 21-22. Note that as argued in the second section, my views on this question have changed a great deal, and I now favor a different format that does not involve the DCs in any essential way at all.

[6] Ibid.

[7] Paragraph 9b. of this resolution, adopted on May 30, 1979, states:

> Developed countries which admit skilled migrants should:
>
> (i) consider assisting, within national constraints, in the building up of better data on skilled migration and explore ways of systematizing the collection and dissemination of statistical information;
>
> (ii) consider, in the light of the in-depth study by the Secretary-General of the United Nations and his decisions referred to in paragraphs 5 and 6 above, measures related to social security, pension rights, currency control, tax policies and remittances with a view to encouraging contributions to the economic development of developing countries, recognizing that the issues mentioned above involve more than the problems of development and the reverse transfer of technology and recognizing existing national competences in these matters.

TAXATION AND INTERNATIONAL MIGRATION

On Taxing Citizens Working Abroad

The problem of whether migrant citizens abroad ought to be taxed by the government of their nationality is not confined to PTK-type citizens with high skills, just as the political problem of voting rights for aliens is not a question confined in the end to the unskilled gastarbeiters. This frees one from worrying about whether the brain drain causes losses to the sending countries that require "compensation." The rationale for the adoption of the global system of tax jurisdiction that encompasses all citizens regardless of their residences is independent, in principle, from whether the foreign residence of the citizen inflicts a loss on the country of emigration. In the unskilled gastarbeiter case, there was initial complacency about the good effects on the sending countries that soon gave way to extreme alarm about its deleterious effects. The inevitable seesaw of opinion has gone the other way for the skilled brain drain. The initial alarm about the disruption and losses in the sending countries has yielded to naively optimistic assessments of its beneficial effects on the sending countries.

The Grubel-Scott type of corrective was necessary;[8] the concepts and models used to buttress the Panglossian viewpoint were themselves simplistic. The view, for example, that the brain drain often represents a "spillover of unemployment" phenomenon has used a naive model of unemployment in LDCs that makes the unemployment exogenous to the possibility of external migration. One's answers can change dramatically if the possibility of migration across national borders to earn the high wages enjoyed by those who surmount the immigration quotas is seen as generating an expectations-induced augmentation of unemployment.[9] Nor, for instance, were considerations such as equality accorded the weight that specific LDC societies might wish to place on them in their objective functions.[10] On balance, the effects on the sending countries will vary with the kinds of skills being discussed,[11] with the objectives that the society has (for example, in regard to the relative weights

[8] Herbert G. Grubel and A. D. Scott, "The International Flow of Human Capital," *American Economic Review, Papers and Proceedings,* vol. 56 (May 1966), pp. 268-274.

[9] See, for example, Jagdish N. Bhagwati and Koichi Hamada, "The Brain Drain, International Integration of Markets for Professionals and Unemployment," *Journal of Development Economics,* vol. 1, no. 1 (1974).

[10] For a more sustained discussion of these themes, see Jagdish N. Bhagwati, "International Migration of the Highly Skilled: Economics, Ethics and Taxes," *Third World Quarterly,* July 1979.

[11] See Koichi Hamada and Jagdish N. Bhagwati, "Domestic Distortions, Imperfect Information and the Brain Drain," in Bhagwati, *Brain Drain and Taxation.*

assigned to equality of success as against equality of access), with the time horizon over which they seek to pursue those objectives (for example, a government may be distressed by the short-run inefficiency caused by the immediate outflow of a large fraction of its skilled force in one field even though it may be built up to its old level some time later), and so on.

Second, it is not possible to tax migrants for a grand social purpose such as developmental spending in the LDCs simply because the immigration quotas of the receiving DCs confer on them substantial rents that, according to the oldest argument for taxation in economic science, constitute an inviting tax base. The migration of both skilled and unskilled people, whether temporary or permanent in intention, is regulated by restrictions on entry that have developed from legislation enacted in various developed countries in the early part of the twentieth century. Indeed, the free flow of human beings has practically ceased to be regarded as part of the "liberal" international economic order.[12] Interestingly, a fundamental asymmetry of concerns has been accepted, even among proponents of human rights, regarding restrictions on emigration and restrictions on immigration; this reflects an implicit philosophical position founded perhaps on territoriality. An *economic* result of the spread of immigration quotas is that the forces tending to narrow the wage differentials directly across nations are held in abeyance, with the result that the lucky migrants, by and large, enjoy windfall gains in the nature of economic rent. I originally felt that these rents, like all economic rents (for instance, the monoply profits enjoyed by those who manage to get the scarce import licenses in exchange control regimes that confer scarcity premiums on imports of goods rather than people), could be taxed to social advantage without distorting resource-allocational incentives. Thus, migrants (especially, the generally successful PTK-type) from LDCs may be taxed to raise resources for developmental spending in the LDC en bloc, much as profits from the sale of International Monetary Fund gold stocks at the high market prices have been used to assist the needier member countries. While this argument is economically and morally sound, it fails to persuade. There is, in the end, no LDC-wide solidarity to justify

---

[12] This was not always so. Some may recall the universalist single-planetary philosophical position on international mobility formulated during the sixteenth century and expressed by Franciscus a Victoria in his *Reflections Theologicae*. Asserting what he graphically termed the "Right of Natural Society and Communication," he sought to provide the ethical rationale for the Spaniards proceeding to the Indies to settle there by arguing that "it has been the custom from the beginning of the world for anyone to go into whatever country he chooses and prohibition of entrance is a violent measure not removed from war."

taxing LDC migrants, who typically come from a *limited* set of LDCs, to promote developmental spending in *all* LDCs.

The essence of my proposal for taxing migrants makes sense, however, on a different rationale that requires *neither* that the countries of emigration be damaged by the outmigration *nor* that the incomes received abroad by the migrants represent economic rents. There is no reason why citizens who reside or work abroad, no matter what their legal status as migrants or their intentions about the length of stay, should be exempt from the national tax obligation of the country whose nationality they hold. That the PTK-type migrants from LDCs are, after migration (and often before as well, given the inequality of access to higher education and hence of success in many LDCs), among the more prosperous of the LDC citizens largely because the immigration quotas lead to high wages makes any exemption of these particular citizens from the LDC tax net that much more incongruous. The rationale extends beyond the PTK to *all* categories of citizens; my original proposal gets into a more general format with the transition to this particular rationale. This is the particular format in terms of which the issues are being debated.

As it happens, the income tax system of the United States exactly reflects the equitable way to tax citizens, that is, to make no exception for citizens because they reside abroad. This global system of income taxation that assesses taxability on the basis of citizenship is also practiced by the Philippines and (in theory, though without attempt at enforcement) by Mexico, a point of some interest to those who seek to understand how historical or geographical affinity can diffuse ideas. By contrast, the European countries, and their excolonies such as India, have adopted the schedular income tax system that exempts citizens from taxation by several rules of residence, making residence the essential criterion for taxability.[13]

The Political Issue. The question of taxability of citizens abroad raises a basic political issue that must be addressed. If one asserts that the citizens abroad are part of the society that the nation-state represents, it follows that the national tax system ought to embrace them as well. Questions of equity of tax burden, for example, would have to be defined by reference to a population set that cannot properly exclude the citizens abroad. The retention of nationality is often regarded as an index of such membership in the society represented by the nation-state,

---

[13] For a detailed description, see Oliver Oldman and Richard Pomp, "The Brain Drain: A Tax Analysis of the Bhagwati Proposal," in Bhagwati, *Brain Drain and Taxation*.

hence the justification for the adoption of the global tax system based on citizenship.[14] The nature of modern migration is such that the retention of ties to one's nation of origin or emigration is far more common than before. Among the gastarbeiters, this is fostered by the ghettos and the threatening prospect of forced return to one's country. Among the PTKs, the to-and-fro travels promoted by cheap fares and the fact that countries such as the United States do not discriminate seriously between natives and resident aliens seem to be among the factors that encourage people to retain their ethnic identities and ties to their own nations. The modern migrants seem to be a part, not merely in a legal-citizenship but also in an emotional and cultural sense, of the societies of their countries of emigration.[15]

Today the economist must construe national welfare as being defined over a population set including the citizens abroad. This precept both runs counter to the concentration in many theoretical studies on the welfare of those left behind and also implies that, in some cases where the imigrants have close affinity to the countries of both immigration and emigration, it would be necessary to (double) count them in the population sets of both countries for analyzing the welfare impact of international migration.

Certainly, it is a perfectly appropriate procedure to adopt the global tax system, since the equity issues defined in the context of income taxation should be discussed without excluding the migrants from the population. As Senator Proxmire has reportedly emphasized, there is no reason why the Americans living in Parisian luxury ought not to pay their share of the U.S. tax burden and leave it to be borne only by the proletariat in Detroit. This particular viewpoint has led some public finance theorists such as John Wilson, Koichi Hamada and myself, and James Mirrlees recently to explore the impact of migration on the trade-

---

[14] In fact, Barry R. Chiswick has reminded me that military conscription is a form of "tax" that *is* widely levied on nationals living abroad by those countries that do have a draft.

[15] For some empirical evidence on the fact that many gastarbeiters respond to sociological inquiries by saying that they would not accept naturalization in the receiving countries even if they were to settle permanently in these countries, see the studies cited in Rosemarie Rogers, "On the Process of International Migrants' Integration into Host Societies: A Hypothesis and Comments," Migration and Development Study Group, Discussion paper no. C/78-16 (Cambridge, Mass.: Massachusetts Institute of Technology, December 1978). For the migrants in the highly skilled categories, see William Glaser, *The Brain Drain: Emigration and Return* (Oxford, England: Pergamon Press, 1978). Glaser's United Nations Institute for Training and Research project underlines similar conclusions. Of course, refugees may be an exception to the point being made. However, it is not unknown for refugees to return to their home countries en masse as the causes that led to their exodus are reversed, as in, for example, Bangladesh and Uganda.

off between equity and efficiency in the Atkinson model (where the trade-off arises because the income tax is collected to redistribute income for equity but affects efficiency by distorting the choice to educate oneself as more education means more social-and-private income) and in the Mirrlees model (where the efficiency distortion comes from distortion of choice between income and leisure instead).[16] Hamada and I also explored in the Atkinson model the precise implications of the schedular system on distorting the efficiency choices concerning education and migration since it virtually absolves those who work abroad from the domestic tax net.

Taxing Firms, Not Individuals. One interesting complication from the viewpoint of U.S. policy—also confronting the countries wishing to use the global system of income taxation—is that the incidence of the tax on citizens abroad may fall on U.S. firms rather than on the nationals. This may happen when, say, a U.S. construction firm tenders for a contract in Saudi Arabia. That firm must pay its U.S. citizen-employees salaries that are going to be the net of whatever tax liability follows from the global system, if those employees are to be induced to go abroad. Its rival French firm does not have to pay the French income tax on its French employees; this puts the French firm at a competitive advantage. This is, strictly speaking, a harmonization issue. Since harmonization is not possible as there are two different tax systems involved, the answer is plain. The General Agreement on Tariffs and Trade should allow countries on the global tax system to subsidize their firms' tenders for external contracts, to restore "true" comparative advantage. In short, given two different objectives, one needs two instruments. The equity issue requires the use of the global tax system; the efficiency-in-comparative-advantage issue requires an appropriate export subsidy (related to U.S. labor use).

The two models, however (the equity model that favors the global tax system and the external-comparative-advantage model that favors the schedular system given its existence in rival countries), have played a tug of war in the United States in an endless struggle through most of this century; the construction lobby (occasionally joined by citizens abroad, of course) asks for the adoption of something close to the schedular system, and the equity-minded legislators such as Senator Proxmire ask for the opposite. The exact debate has centered around

[16] John Wilson, "The Effect of Potential Emigration on the Optimal Linear Income Tax," *Journal of Public Economics,* December 1980; James Mirrlees, "A Theory of Taxation and Migration" (Paper presented to the Ford Foundation Conference on Taxation of Citizens Working Abroad, held in New Delhi, January 1981).

section 911 of the tax law that states the allowable exclusions from gross taxable incomes of U.S. citizens abroad (not in employ of the U.S. government). Christine Heckman of the Harvard Business School has provided the following capsuled version of the seesaw between restricting and liberalizing this exclusion, that is, between getting closer to or away from the scope of the global system. The period up to the Tax Reform Act of 1976 provides the flavor of the two sets of forces and how, in fact, from a full-fledged global system at the inception, the United States moved to the schedular system in 1926 and then, prompted by equity considerations, gradually wound its way back to the global system, with exemptions whose scope has been changed and debated ever since.

A. *History of 911*

(1) *1900–1942*: Up to 1925, extreme pressure was placed upon Congress by American industry to develop incentives for industrial expansion overseas. There was concern that many foreign companies doing business in the U.S. had unfair advantages, since foreign nationals generally were exempt from domestic taxes in their home countries. In 1926, as a result of these concerns, the first foreign earned income exclusion law, Section 213(b)(14), was enacted by Congress. The law permitted U.S. overseas workers to exclude or subtract from their gross taxable income "amounts derived and received from sources (business conducted) without the United States"; that is, if a person had lived 6 months or more abroad, income earned while residing abroad was exempt from taxation. Up to that time, overseas workers had only been allowed to credit against their U.S. tax bill their income taxes paid to foreign governments.

In 1928, Section 213(b)(14) was designated Section 116(a). Senator Reed of the Senate Finance Committee moved to repeal this section in 1932. He contended that while the intent of the law was to promote American business activity abroad, a foreign income exclusion was not necessary to help foreign trade, and was unfair to citizens resident in the U.S., who received no similar privilege. Senator Reed further argued that the intent of Section 116(a) had been distorted. He cited cases where American ambassadors, ministers, and officials of the foreign service had used the law to sidestep income taxes. After some debate and compromise, Section 116(a) was amended so that income paid by the U.S. government or its agencies could no longer be excluded or deducted.

(2) *1942–1951*: Continued concern with abuses of the law led Congress to amend Section 116(a) again in 1942. As amended, Section 116(a) applied only to "an individual citizen of the U.S., who established to the satisfaction of the Commissioner, that he was a bonafide resident of a foreign country during the entire taxable year," not just 6 months.

(3) *1951–1962*: Residency requirements were again changed in 1951. The amended law established that any income earned overseas by a U.S. citizen could be excluded if (s)he resided abroad for 17 out of 18 months. This part of the law was designated Section 116(a)(2). The purpose of the change was to encourage citizens "to go abroad on a short term basis to increase technical knowledge in backward areas."

At the same time another subtle addition to the law, Section 116(a)(1), clarified when certain foreign residents could actually start to claim income exclusion.

In 1953, the amount of excludable income under Section 116(a)(2) was limited to a $20,000 ceiling. In 1954, Section 116(a)(1) became Section 911(a)(1). Section 116(a)(2) was renumbered and subdivided: the residency portion of Section 116(a)(2) became Section 911(a)(2). The provision for a $20,000 ceiling became Section 911(c).

(4) *1962–1975*: In 1963, Congress changed the ceiling to an income exclusion of $20,000 for the first 3 years of residence and $35,000 for each year thereafter. The $35,000 limit was lowered in 1965 to $25,000. By 1975, Section 911 provided for the following:

(i) A $20,000 income exclusion for those who had resided in a foreign country for 17 out of 18 months. A $25,000 exclusion for those with 3 or more years of bonafide residency.

(ii) Permission to subtract the exclusion off the top of earned income; the remainder was the income base for tax calculations. In effect this left the taxpayer in a lower rate bracket than would otherwise have been the case.

(iii) A tax credit on all foreign income taxes paid. However, those claiming the U.S. standard deduction could not claim the foreign tax credit. For example, a worker earning $50,000 paid $230 under the 1975 law (Exhibit 1). While the 1975 law was more stringent than earlier laws, many felt it still gave unfair tax advantages to a special class of Americans.

(5) *The 1976 Tax Reform Act*: The sweeping Tax Re-

form Act of 1976, which changed several areas of U.S. tax laws, also altered Section 911 significantly. Among other things, the amended Section 911 provided that:

(i) A maximum of $15,000 could be excluded from earned income by a U.S. citizen who was present in a foreign country for at least 17 out of 18 months. An employee of a charity was allowed a $20,000 exclusion.

(ii) Taxable income remaining after the application of the earned income exclusion was subject to tax at higher-bracket rates. Specifically, the remaining income was to be taxed at the rate applicable before the exclusion.

(iii) Any foreign taxes paid on the $15,000 of excluded income could not be included as part of the foreign tax credit.

(iv) Individuals applying the standard deduction could also apply foreign tax credits.

Thus, as a result of this legislation the exclusion was dropped to $15,000 and income was taxed at higher rates. Under the 1976 law, the family earning $50,000 would now pay $4,214 (Exhibit 1).

As originally enacted, the 1976 Act made the changes effective for the 1976 tax year. However, the sweeping changes in Section 911 brought about by the Tax Reform Act elicited such strong negative reaction that Congress delayed the effect of the 1976 law for one year until January 1, 1977. Further delays were later effected to allow a thorough examination of opposing views of the law. These delays were supported and publicly encouraged by the Treasury. In February 1978, the law was still dormant and scheduled for further debate.[17]

The controversies over what the exemptions ought to be, for schooling, cost-of-living differences, etc., have preoccupied the U.S. legislators and the U.S. Treasury. The adoption of the global tax system is fully consistent with the adoption of treaties to prevent double taxation, so that the net burden of the migrant increases under this formula *only* insofar as the tax liability under the tax system of the country of nationality exceeds the liability in the country of residence/work. For many LDCs, however, this will be the case, even with generous exemptions à la the present U.S. provisions.[18]

[17] Christine Heckman, "Taxation of Americans Working Overseas," in Robert S. Carlson, H. Lee Remmers, Christine Heckman, David K. Eiteman, and Arthur I. Stonehill, *International Finance: Cases and Simulation* (Reading, Mass.: Addison-Wesley Publishing Co., 1980), chap. 25, pp. 327-344. The material cited in the text is based on the section entitled *Historical Perspectives*.

[18] Compare Koichi Hamada, "Taxing the Brain Drain: A Global Point of

U.S. Role in Adoption of Global Tax System by LDCs. Since this conference is focused on U.S. policies concerning immigration, presumably into the United States rather than from it, the question of the appropriateness of the global system, as it applies to U.S. citizens abroad, is not a relevant issue. The issue, however, of whether the United States ought to shift to the schedular system has certainly come to the forefront again, with the controversies over the 1976 act. What should concern us at this conference rather is the *reverse* possibility, namely, the possibility that some LDCs might wish to move to the *global* system. The United States is involved in this issue only insofar as the question of tax collection and enforceability may come up in this connection.

At Bellagio, where the lawyers argued that the tax be levied by the LDCs, the question of enforceability and collection was viewed with particular alarm. We were thinking of how to use the DC tax agencies to collect the tax for the LDCs. It may be possible to employ techniques that do not make such demands on the DCs. In particular, the Philippines operates a simple version of the global tax system, by utilizing three graduated rates of 1 percent, 2 percent, and 3 percent, which are applied to the earned income of the Filipinos in the United States, for example. The tax is estimated and collected annually by making annual passport renewal conditional on submission of the W-2 form and the tax payment. This system, generally described as the one-two-three system in the Philippines, seems to have worked well. At the rates levied, it does not seem to have led to any significant change in nationality to escape the implied tax burden.[19] It is not beyond the scope of normal bilateral treaties between nations, for the United States to extend assistance by way of information (and systematizing thereof if necessary) on legal, foreign nationals from a particular country in its midst and perhaps even investigating the possibility of sharing tax information between countries to make such collection efforts by LDCs easier and more efficient. That, in fact, is the burden of the recommendation of the UNCTAD expert group meeting.

View," in J. Bhagwati, ed., *The New International Economic Order: The North-South Debate* (Cambridge, Mass.: MIT Press, 1977), table 1. Note also that the Filipino system, described later in this paper, adds a small tax of 1 percent, 2 percent, or 3 percent on the taxable earned incomes of Filipinos abroad, *on top of* whatever they pay to foreign governments, thus avoiding raising the double taxation complication by keeping the Filipino tax assessment moderate.

[19] Professor Richard Pomp is engaged on an extended study of the Filipino one-two-three tax system as a consultant to the World Bank and is scheduled to present his report on it to a Ford Foundation Conference on Taxation of Citizens Working Abroad, in New Delhi, January 4-9, 1981.

Sharing "Normal" Tax Revenues

The proposal to tax the incomes of the migrants themselves, as with the adoption of the global system, must be distinguished from the idea of getting the developed countries of immigration to share income tax revenues (raised from the migrants simply by the routine taxation apparatus) with the less developed countries of origin. The rationale for such migration-related taxation on developed countries can be provided in two alternative ways. Either the developed countries ought to compensate the less developed countries for the losses that the brain drain imposes on them or, since the developed countries gain from such migration, they ought to share these gains (based on the inflow of less developed country nationals) with the less developed countries that need development resources, regardless of whether there is any loss to the less developed countries.

The latter moral argument reflects a Nozick type of ethical criterion: The human resources "belong" to the less developed countries and the division of the gains from their working in the developed countries ought rightfully to be shared with the former. This form of argument, evidently not utilitarian in nature, holds if it is contended that these human resources would have been utilized less profitably or not at all in the less developed countries.

Of these two notions, the former (suggesting compensation for the less developed countries) would appear to be the main motivating force behind recent pronouncements from spokesmen of the less developed countries calling for a brain-drain–related transfer of resources/revenues by the less developed countries. One LDC leader said,

> I would also like to propose the establishment of an International Labour Compensatory Facility (ILCF). It could be elaborated along the lines of the Trust Fund for Compensatory Facilities of the IMF. The proposed Facility would draw its resources principally from labour importing countries, but in a spirit of solidarity and goodwill, other ILO members may contribute to it. The accumulated resources will be diverted to developing labour exporting countries in proportions relative to the estimated cost incurred due to the loss of labour.[20]

Further, a 1977 report stated that

> the Commission on Development recommends that, in order to compensate for the reverse transfer of technology, resulting

[20] Address by Crown Prince Hassan bin Talal of Jordan to the sixty-third meeting of the International Labor Organization, Geneva, June 10, 1977. Note the emphasis on "compensation" and the notion of losses suffered by loss of manpower.

from such exodus, amounting to several billions of dollars for the last decade, special arrangements including the possibility of establishing special funds, should be made to provide the necessary resources for strengthening the technological capabilities of the developing countries.[21]

Given, however, the controversy that surrounds the question as to the magnitude, if not the existence, of losses to less developed countries in a meaningful and measurable sense, it would appear pertinent to rest the case for a migration-related transfer of funds from developed countries to less developed countries on the latter moral rationale, namely, the gains by developed countries from the influx of highly skilled migrants.

Skilled immigrants in particular are generally admitted on an economic-needs criterion. To some extent, even within the United States, which is otherwise on a familial-criterion system, there is a prima facie presumption that there is indeed some net gain, however defined, to the United States from the influx of PTKs.[22]

Thus, by bilateral or multilateral tax treaties, the United States could agree, for example, to share tax revenues that it earns from the PTK nationals of less developed countries on the basis of some formula.[23] There is legal precedent for such tax sharing, of course. The revenues from taxing the French workers in the canton of Geneva, for example, are shared with the French principalities from which the workers come. Again, the proposal to have the developed countries share their tax revenues with the less developed countries of nationality/origin fits in well with the notion that the less developed countries are self-reliant. These revenues are, after all, paid by their own talented and skilled manpower, which constitutes their "natural resources." Their taxes may

---

[21] Report of the Contact Group on Industrialisation and Transfer of Technology, Conference on International Economic Cooperation, Paris, May 14, 1977 (Paris: Conference on International Economic Cooperation, 1979).

[22] The presumption that the developed countries gain from PTK immigration has recently been challenged by Dan Usher, "Public Property and the Effects of Migration upon Other Residents of the Migrants' Countries of Origin and Destination," *Journal of Political Economy*, vol. 85, no. 5 (October 1977), on the ground that the immigrants receive more from their share in public expenditures than they give up by way of taxes. His calculations, however, are not persuasive. The general presumption in this regard is that PTK immigrants, belonging generally to the developed country groups that are subject to progressive taxation in developed countries, are likely to be making a net contribution to, rather than a net claim on, the developed countries through the tax system. The presumption of gain by the developed countries from PTK immigration can only be reinforced on this account.

[23] The ways in which this can be done have been discussed in Richard D. Pomp and Oliver Oldman, "Tax Measures in Response to the Brain Drain," *Harvard International Law Review*, vol. 60 (Winter 1979), pp. 1-60.

well be utilized partially to redistribute to the poor in their own countries of nationality rather than fully to redistribute to the poor in the countries of their residence.

I have focused only on two major types of *international* tax issues that have been raised recently in the literature on international migration and are still relatively unfamiliar in American literature. The first issue, concerning the exercise of income tax jurisdiction by nations over their nationals abroad, does not directly concern the United States as far as immigrants to the United States are concerned. As already discussed, the LDCs can do this entirely by themselves in principle. The role of the United States, however, in terms of policy accommodation would be to undertake bilateral tax treaties facilitating the flow of information in order to ease the task of tax collection by these countries on their nationals in the United States. The second issue, on the other hand, involves *sharing* tax revenues, pro rata in some agreed fashion to the number of highly skilled migrants. This would involve United States tax policy much more directly, of course.

From the viewpoint of the United States, its *internal* tax policy has ramifications also for issues that have recently come to the forefront and are more familiar on the academic scene, the rights of illegal aliens to federal and local tax-funded benefits being one of them. These are specific to the United States, and of considerable relevance indeed.

Commentaries

Carmel U. Chiswick

David Reimers's paper is both informative and stimulating. My purpose here is to consider from the perspective of an economist the debates over immigration legislation described so vividly in the paper. Although my intention is to consider separately the economic incentives faced by the supporters of liberalization and by its opponents, economic self-interest along the traditional lines of employers versus workers as we usually articulate it appears weak as an explanatory model. It is a tribute to Professor Reimers's lucid presentation and analysis of the facts that this is apparent and that an alternative model suggests itself.

Let me list briefly the most puzzling findings, and then I shall go to my economic hypotheses. First, and most strikingly, arguments of economic self-interest, when used at all, are used pejoratively. One might expect that each side of the debate over immigration policy would argue its own economic self-interest, at least implicitly. Instead, it seems that each side accuses the other of being concerned with "crass" economic motives. The supporters of liberalization accuse the unions of wanting to induce labor shortages, while the supporters of restriction accuse employers of trying to import cheap labor and thus undermine earnings gains made by American labor. The clear implication is that proof of economic self-interest is sufficient to undermine the credibility of other arguments.

A second striking anomaly is that those provisions of the law that are "economic" in their intent are inept in their design. The occupational preference system is an obvious case in point. Occupational preferences are supposed to protect us as consumers from shortages of "scarce" skills, while at the same time they are supposed to protect us as workers from "unfair" competition by immigrants. The law is poorly written and implemented. Moreover, the flaws in economic logic are the kind of elementary ones that can be discussed in a course on the principles of economics. It is hard to believe that any economic expertise was brought to bear on this so-called economic provision.

104

A third feature, and one consistent with the first two, is that the economic aspects of the law are clearly peripheral. An overall limit to immigration is justified on economic (absorptive-capacity) grounds, but the exceptions to the overall limit are so numerous as to raise the question of its relevance. Occupational preferences are presumably there for economic reasons, but they account for less than 10 percent of the entire immigration flow, when one takes into account the fact that even within the "occupational preference" allotment most people come in as family members. Even the bracero program, which was surely economic in its intent and design, appears to have been peripheral to the concerns of the people involved in immigration law and is in many ways peripheral to the whole question of immigration flows.

Finally, and perhaps not entirely accidentally, economists have not paid much attention to questions relating to immigration, either to the progress of immigrants or to their impact on the American economy. In the debates discussed by Professor Reimers, it is generally assumed that there is an absorptive-capacity limit that would be costly to exceed. This has not, however, been seriously discussed in the economic literature, although many would take strong issue with either the notion itself or with the arbitrariness of the numerical limit.

The Support for Liberalization

Each of these puzzles constitutes an important datum that has to be taken into account in a model of the motives and incentives structuring the debate. Both employers' and workers' groups have varied over time in the intensity of their interest in immigration and have typically concentrated on some subset of the liberalization debates. In contrast, the humanitarian not-for-profit organizations, which typically concentrate on charities and relief works, have consistently played a central, long-term role lobbying for liberalization. The refugee-relief organizations have their own economic self-interest, of course, that provides them with an incentive for making their central focus humanitarian. Many of them also have religious affiliations, formal or informal. Whether religious or secular, their spokespersons tend to be people who are not comfortable making arguments of economic self-interest to support their position. Thus, even though the immigrants themselves may be quite concerned and articulate about seeking economic advantage, the people who are lobbying on their behalf have tended to avoid calling attention to their aspirations in that regard.

To the extent that the most active of these organizations are structured along religious lines, there is also an understandable tendency for the problems concerning them to be those most important for members of the same faith. This suggests a number of hypotheses with which the evidence presented by Professor Reimers would be consistent. Relaxation of the severe restrictions against the immigration of Asians, for example, was clearly the accomplishment of missionary groups that cared enough to mount an intensive lobbying effort in the 1940s and early 1950s. Christian organizations were also concerned in the 1940s and 1950s with problems of religious oppression in communist countries. They successfully used cold-war foreign policy self-interest, rather than economic self-interest, as their handle for opening the door to immigrants, working through the State Department to have refugees from communism classified as exemptions to the immigration quotas.

This State Department avenue was not available to the Jewish organizations trying to admit immigrants from the displaced persons camps in Europe in the late 1940s; they had to face a much more difficult debate in the Senate. There is something intriguing about this debate as Professor Reimers describes it. Given the emotional force of the arguments, one wonders why the favorable economic impact of immigrants in the United States did not figure more prominently. One hypothesis is that the Jewish organizations were sensitive to anti-Semitic accusations of greed and rapacity. An alternative hypothesis is that, despite their genuine and passionate commitment to helping the refugees, their strong commitment to union ideology may have effectively blinded them to a potentially persuasive line of attack. Effectively viewing the United States as one great big closed shop whose workers needed solidarity to protect their own interests, they did not seriously question the absorptive-capacity notion that raising the number of immigrants would be opening the flood gates to cheap labor. Instead, they tried to argue that our country was sufficiently rich that it could "afford" to let in more refugees.

The Restrictionist Forces

The serious, consistent, and overwhelming opposition to liberalization of immigration policy has come from people concerned with preserving the "social and cultural balance of the population of the United States."[1] The arguments are blatantly racist in their essence and were immediately labeled as such by the opposition; there does not seem to be much denial of that on either side. Discrimination as a consumption good seems to be the appropriate economic model to apply to the behavior of the opponents of liberalization. (Although they also may have been concerned about diluting their voting power, that is, losing their property

[1] U.S. Congress, Senate, Committee on the Judiciary, *The Immigration and Naturalization Systems of the United States,* 81st Congress, 2nd session, 1950, S. Rept. 1515, p. 455.

rights, this concern seems to have been focused along racial and religious lines.) Moreover, this model gives a hypothesis as to why arguments regarding the favorable economic impact of immigrants in the United States would have carried so little weight: The discriminating consumer was simply willing to pay the price.

In the interest of analytical clarity, we should distinguish racism per se, whether antiblack or anti-Asian, from religious prejudice. The distinction has not often been made because many politically powerful people appeared to have both prejudices. It seems, however, that changes in the support for a restrictionist immigration law in the United States can be explained by growing religious tolerance as distinct from racial amity. This distinction is essential for understanding the simultaneous liberalization and restriction observed during the 1960s and 1970s.

The de facto implications for black immigration of recent changes in quotas are not at all obvious, perhaps reflecting the ambiguous nature of growing racial tolerance in the United States. We are much more liberal in our policy toward immigration from Africa, but the serious black immigration in terms of numbers is from the Caribbean, where our policy is more restrictive. In contrast, increased religious tolerance is an important dimension of the "growing ethnic tolerance" referred to by Professor Reimers, which is clearly evident in the observed change in public sympathy towards immigrants from non-Protestant countries. There is no question that in 1924, when the national origins quotas were established, a great deal of the sentiment behind that system was anti-Catholic. Religious prejudice is also a more accurate description than racism of the anti-Semitism expressed so clearly in the debates over refugees in the 1930s and 1940s. The fact that John F. Kennedy was president when the major liberalizations were begun is in itself evidence of the decline in religious prejudice as a political force.

Implications for the Future

To what extent is this model only of historical interest, and to what extent are these forces still relevant for today's debates over immigration policy? Religious prejudice is not nearly as relevant as it was. Racial prejudice has also become less important, though the case for this assertion is not as strong as for the change in religious attitudes. Reapportionment in the 1960s, however, has effectively broken up the power blocs in the Senate that once had a stranglehold on much social legislation. Demographic change and changes in voting patterns mean that people from erstwhile nonpreferred groups are no longer politically dominated in the same way as before.

Economists are more articulate in the media and more powerful in the halls of government than in the past, although neither case should be overstated. It is both reassuring and indicative of the change, however, that economists are beginning to show an interest in immigration policy. Thus, a second difference between the historical experience and today's situation is that economic self-interest as an argument is much more respectable and plays an explicit role. Our social transfer programs imply different economic costs; they also imply that the economic costs and benefits of immigration affect more of us than used to be the case. Professor Reimers mentioned in his remarks that a bracero program and the undocumented workers from Mexico have become central issues in the immigration debate and will become even more so. The braceros are not immigrants in the traditional sense but rather guest workers; this in itself is something of a new dimension.

Now that support for liberalization is no longer the exclusive domain of the humanitarian organizations, the distinction between refugees and other immigrants is becoming blurred. Humanitarian organizations that want to bring in refugees will have to make more of an argument as to how these refugees will be contributing to the economic well-being of those already here. Family reunification as a criterion for admission to the United States is going to be less easy to present as self-evident; the case will have to be made that we can (and wish to) support these brothers, sisters, uncles, and aunts. We will have to justify on economic grounds why we should expand the occupational categories at the expense of the kinship categories. These are important elements that do change the nature of the debate.

Lorene Yap

I will focus my comments on the paper by Professors Greenwood and McDowell but will also comment briefly on Professor Bhagwati's efforts to tax immigrants.

I like the Greenwood-McDowell paper because it attempts to extend what we know about immigration beyond the usual, aggregate model that explains flows from one place to another in terms of general wage differentials, distance, and population. Economic motivation is important for virtually all kinds of migration flows. Therefore, I am primarily interested in other aspects of these migration flows. Professors Greenwood and McDowell have two methods for providing more information:

- Examining determinants of immigration to the United States that go beyond the usual wage, distance, and population variables (their U.S.-determinants model)

- Estimating the magnitude of migration to the United States if U.S. barriers were removed (their world-emigration model).

They are more successful with their first task than with their second. Their contribution in their U.S. determinants model is to show the importance of skill transfer in the migration flow. The regressions would be more informative, however, if the flow of skilled migrants were separated from the flow of unskilled migrants. While both flows are economically motivated, they can be explained with different kinds of factors; trying to explain the combined flow masks interesting differences. The signs of the coefficients in regression (5) for migrants with professional and technical skills, for instance, are quite different from those in regressions (1) through (3) for all migrants. As the authors themselves note, a college education matters more to skilled migrants and distance is less of a deterrent to skilled migrants, because of a more international market for their skills, than to unskilled migrants. Coming from an English-speaking country, on the other hand, would not be as much of an advantage to a professional migrant, who probably has learned English regardless of his native language, as to an unskilled migrant.

As their second task, they try to estimate how much migration would come into the United States if U.S. barriers to migration were removed (their world emigration model). They were not successful in convincing me, because of the problems with conceptualization and with the data. With their world emigration model, they are not just *explaining* the factors that affect immigration; they are trying to *predict* the level of immigration that would occur if immigration barriers were removed. A predictive model is much harder to do than an explanatory one. If one is trying to identify the major explanatory factors, then even if he has poor data and problems in interpreting the magnitude of the coefficients or their statistical significance, he can usually show that the sign of the coefficient is accurate.

In contrast, with a predictive model, one must show that the magnitude of the coefficients is accurate. The size of their coefficients is not believable. First, the quality of the immigration data is poor. The migration flows being analyzed are only legal flows. Therefore, the wage coefficient (plus other coefficients) show only the responsiveness of legal migration to wage differentials. Second, the authors are using essentially a free flow model to depict a situation that contains many restrictions to free movement. There are restrictions in a number of receiving countries, not just the United States. In addition, there are restrictions on outflow in some of the originating countries. Consequently, one cannot really get a sense of what the free flow would be if U.S. quotas were reduced from this kind of model, given the fact that no attempt is made to model any of these specific barriers directly.

There are two possible ways to incorporate the barriers. If the existing model is used, it would be desirable to know not only the going wage in a particular country but also the probability that a prospective migrant will actually be able to enter the country to receive that wage. The probability would depend on such factors as existence of waiting lists or time needed to obtain a visa. Then, the model could be used to predict the immigration level that would occur if the probability of entry were raised. In fact, it would be difficult to collect this information for all countries. Therefore, a different approach might be more fruitful. Consider looking at the problem exclusively in terms of the U.S. labor market. As the authors point out, a reduction in U.S. immigration barriers, by stimulating migration, would lower the U.S. wage rate toward the world price (with adjustments for transportation costs, labor unions, and other kinds of wage restraints). With a labor supply and demand model for the United States, one can estimate how much more labor would be needed to reduce the wage from the actual wage to a lower wage.

This method of estimating the flow of free immigration to the United States is attractive for several reasons. In the first place, there is an enormous literature on U.S. labor market models on which to draw. One might even be satisfied using the estimates of wage elasticities in other studies; if not, the results of an analysis can be checked easily against the others. Second, the quality of the data would be better. One would need U.S. labor data only, which the Bureau of Labor Statistics has been collecting for years, rather than the less reliable immigration data. Of course, there is still the problem of the extent to which our labor data reflect illegal immigration. Illegal workers, however, are a smaller percentage of the labor force relative to the illegal immigrants in the immigration flow. Third, there is more potential for policy analysis because one can distinguish among different kinds of migrants. The current skill mix of migrants, for instance, has particular welfare implications for the country. If the labor market model were differentiated by skills, one could then examine some of the interactions between the skill categories as well as the skill mix that might result if migration barriers were eliminated.

Professor Bhagwati's paper is particularly interesting for two reasons: as an introduction to the subject of taxing migrants, since I am not familiar with the literature, and as an example of advocacy economics, where Professor Bhagwati is trying to persuade us to tax migrants. He probably is suffering from the frustrations that come with advocacy economics; despite the merits of his argument, people still are

110

probably not convinced. There are several possible reasons why countries are slow to adopt such a tax. Pragmatically, the issue is probably of low priority to a less developed country and certainly to a developed country, especially since it is so difficult to collect. The objectives are good; efficient schemes to collect the tax can be devised. But the payoff probably is quite low relative to other things in which less developed countries could put their resources. As mentioned, it is hard enough to tax individuals and corporations within a country, much less try to collect them outside. One might say, therefore, that it is more cost-effective for a less developed country to concentrate on the biggest elements of the tax system, rather than on an extension like this one.

In addition, it is not clear that the additional revenue from this tax is that large for the less developed countries. Even without a migrant tax, countries are probably receiving a number of benefits from emigrants. Remittances for some countries are reasonably large. The developed countries also have little motivation to collect the tax. Not only is it difficult to collect; the argument that the more developed country is benefiting from the skills of immigrants from less developed countries also is not persuasive. It is no different from other charges of exploitation of less developed countries by the developed countries, such as the colonial exploitation argument of earlier years and the terms of trade arguments of the 1950s. The developed countries have never been terribly excited about paying compensation. They would say, in fact, that they are paying—with foreign aid.

Discussion

GEORGE ROSEN, University of Illinois at Chicago Circle: I have several questions and comments on the Greenwood-McDowell paper. First, are there data on the immigrant's level of education and the extent of education in the United States? Second, one variable was the proportion of the population educated in the country. For large countries such as India, the proportions are quite low, whereas the absolute figures are large. Aren't the absolute figures more important for determining the number of potential immigrants? Finally, regarding the distance variable, one might want to separate Eastern and Western hemispheres. There has been sufficient difference in U.S. immigration policy regarding the two hemispheres for the period under study that one might want to estimate separate equations by hemisphere.

MR. McDOWELL: With the summary data in the Immigration and Naturalization Service (INS) annual reports, it is not possible to identify the immigrant's level of education. It might be possible to do this in other data sources. Why did we look at the proportion rather than absolute number of persons with higher education? The number of college graduates would be highly correlated with the population of the country; we were trying to isolate the effect of the relative level of education in the country. Regarding the separate effects of the distance variable for the two hemispheres, you may have a good point. It would be simple to interact the hemisphere dummy variable with the distance variable to see if anything significant occurs.

MR. ROSEN: Why can't India tax its emigrants directly?

MR. BHAGWATI: This is precisely what I am discussing. I have this particular version of a brain drain tax that is based on the countries exercising their tax jurisdiction. It is practiced by the United States and the Philippines. The LDCs are beginning to think about taxing emigrants. They can collect the taxes without developed country

112

collaboration. The United States could get involved in sharing tax information, which is done bilaterally under international tax treaties.

DAVID S. NORTH, New TransCentury Foundation: Regarding the taxing of emigrants' earnings, Jamaica and Barbados have an interesting technique regarding the foreign fruit pickers who enter under one small guest worker program usually referred to by the name of the visa, H2. There is a contract that the Department of Labor more or less accepts; it requires something like 20 percent of the worker's earnings be sent back to Jamaica and Barbados. This is an automatic withholding from the worker's wages; it goes to national banks in Jamaica and Barbados. The workers get their earnings when they return, but they do not receive interest on the funds on deposit.

The Greenwood-McDowell paper is dealing with the elite within an elite. It is dealing with the legal immigrants who are an elite among all migrants to the United States. Then it deals with the people who have stated occupations. William Weissert and I did some work a couple years ago with the 1970 cohort of immigrants.[1] We found that, on the basis of data on the annual alien registration cards a couple of years after immigration, the number of people who were working was substantially larger than the ones who stated occupations on their visa application forms. The people who were additions to the immigrant labor force were somewhat different from the ones who stated their occupations on those forms. There are many more women, for instance. This is a somewhat less skilled labor force than the one perceived because of that anomaly in the reporting technique. Many arriving immigrants who are workers do not record their occupation on their visa application forms.

Noticing the relationship between the presence of a social security (old age pension) system in the nations of emigration and the movement to the United States was particularly interesting. The number of people over the age of sixty-five arriving in the United States, particularly from the Eastern Hemisphere, is much larger than it had been in 1970. This is largely because of the number of people from the Philippines who have learned about Supplemental Security Income (SSI). They are entitled to it on arrival, and they are making use of it.

BRUCE L. GARDNER, Texas A & M University: On the supply of immigrants, the Greenwood-McDowell paper found that the percent of the population in manufacturing is a powerful variable. The rationale was

[1] U.S., Department of Labor, *Immigrants and the American Labor Market,* by David North and William Weissert, Manpower Research Monograph, no. 31, 1974.

that it means the sending country is a lot like the United States. With that rationale, why not use something like the difference between their manufacturing proportion and ours rather than the level? Also, what is the rationale for thinking that a country more like the United States would send more immigrants? In trading commodities, one would have to say he would expect more trade from countries that produce a list of commodities a lot like the United States. It seems to be the opposite.

MR. McDOWELL: The interpretation of the manufacturing variable is open to some more explanation. It is strong throughout the regressions and it is strongly positive. I put it into the category of transferring of skills—the more similar the occupational mix, the greater the transferability of skills to the U.S. market. In fact, we did measure the difference between the country of origin and the U.S. manufacturing proportion because we took the percentage of manufacturing for each country relative to the United States, which was the country we were using as a base.

MR. CHISWICK: I am concerned about the econometric problem of "adding up." We know that the total number of immigrants into the United States in a particular year has a ceiling. The number coming from each individual country is then related to the number coming from other countries. Doesn't this create econometric problems?

The effect of social insurance on international emigration for the aged is related to the portability of the social insurance. Social security in the United States is portable, Supplemental Security Income (SSI) is not portable. We find aged Americans returning to their home countries or going to Mexico; the social security check follows. The SSI check, if they were eligible for SSI, would not follow. This should affect incentives for emigration among older Americans. The portability of benefits is an important factor to consider in constructing a social insurance variable for other countries.

MR. McDOWELL: For the Western Hemisphere in 1970, there were no country quotas nor was there a preference system. The visas were distributed on a first-come, first-served basis, and therefore there was open competition from any particular country. We took a perspective that within the Western Hemisphere quota an individual was able to compete for a visa with persons from other countries. Our model did not include an upper bound on immigrants from an individual country, but there was an upper limit.

In terms of the Eastern Hemisphere, there was a specific country quota as well as the aggregate quota; in fact, there were two countries that one could argue were bound by that constraint, the Philippines and Italy. We felt unsure about putting in a control variable for those two countries—whether we would indeed be saying something about the binding constraint of the quota or about the specific countries since we only had two observations.

We considered doing a Tobit analysis in which we could look at an upper-bound constraint. That would have required a time-series model and would have taken the quota laws into account.

The comment on the portability of social security benefits is relevant. We did not obtain information on the specific institutional arrangements for the twenty-four countries.

MR. REIMERS: Not being an economist, I am struck that so much of the argument and discussion at this conference is in terms of economics. So much immigration policy, however, is determined by noneconomic considerations.

Let me cite one historical example. The Dillingham commission (1909) turned out forty-two volumes of enormously useful materials for historians and others. Yet Congress did not pass a major immigration law until twelve years later. Then Congress was not concerned about what the data said because it had decided that people from southern and eastern Europe were inferior and it was best to keep them out.

Some of the same is true today. One can get into elaborate discussions about the economic impact of immigration, whether one should tax this person or that and so forth. Immigration policy is made in other ways. It has so much more to do with family unification. Who can oppose unification of families? Who can oppose refugees? The "economic" categories get a low priority. There seems to be almost a level of political reality that in many cases has to do with emotional concerns, has to do with myth. There is the level where social scientists analyze the effect, but in many ways that is not relevant when policy is made.

The Select Commission on Immigration and Refugee Policy is going to turn up a great deal of useful information. It may not have much impact when it comes to rewriting the law. It might be useful for all of us, but Congress may not pay much attention to it.

MR. GREENWOOD: I agree with Dr. Yap that the demand approach to estimating the number of immigrants that the United States might expect in the absence of any legal constraints on immigration is probably quite fruitful. One of the major reasons we did not follow that approach is that we did not feel we had the expertise in the area of macro-econometric modeling to do the job in the available length of time. The macroeconomic approach, however, is not without pitfalls. The world equilibrium wage is likely to be much lower than the U.S. wage, but macroeconomic models are estimated under a regime of U.S. wages. The structure of the macroeconomic models would be drastically different under a world equilibrium wage. We are therefore reluctant to use these models to simulate immigration to the United States.

The results associated with our supply approach are, of course, tentative. The data limitations are so severe that we felt satisfied in finding that the predicted immigration was greater than the observed values for the United States. In other words, it appeared that our models were telling us that the laws are constraining. Perhaps we did not need a model to tell us that.

MR. BHAGWATI: In the version I am considering, the taxation of migrants is not something that involves the countries of immigration except in terms of sharing tax information. Bilateral tax treaties have been and can be negotiated, but whether in fact any specific country will do this is a political issue. Because these are prosperous migrants, whether they are short-run migrants, long-run migrants, or to-and-fro migrants, it is worth doing. One may raise only $200 million. This is small compared with the size of an average country's national income or the size of its budget, but this is not a reason for not instituting the tax. I do not expect the migrants themselves to support it. The elites are closely integrated with the migrants that come from essentially the same upper-class background, so they too may oppose it. I do not know why the Philippines has such a system, unless it is U.S. influence. We should not assert that historically we have this system and it is politically the only ideal one because it happens to be here.

Part Two

The Progress of Immigrants

The Economic Progress of Immigrants: Some Apparently Universal Patterns

Barry R. Chiswick

U.S. immigration policy has historically been based primarily on the premise that immigrants have a favorable impact on the country's economic development.[1] This was the basis of the Open Door policy practiced from colonial times until the late nineteenth century. The earliest restrictions were intended to bar the entry of persons who would lower the nation's productivity—the sick, disabled, indigent, and criminal. Even the ethnocentric national origins quota system was influenced by concerns with productivity, although apparently based on a prejudiced reading of the data.[2]

The 1965 amendments to the Immigration and Nationality Act sharply changed U.S. immigration policy. The end of the national origins quota system that had been applicable to the Eastern Hemisphere (and Western Hemisphere dependencies) since the 1920s resulted in a relative decline in immigration from Europe and a substantial increase in immigration from South and East Asia and from the current and former dependencies in the Caribbean. For other reasons immigration from Mexico, Cuba, and other parts of Latin America has also increased. From 1955 to 1965, half the nearly 3 million immigrants were born in Europe, but in the next decade the proportion declined to 28 percent of nearly 4 million immigrants (see table 1). Whereas at the turn of the century the term "new immigration" referred to those from southern and eastern Europe, it now refers to immigration from third world countries. In the decade 1955–1965, 7.5 percent of the immigrants were from Asia,

NOTE: This paper was not part of the formal conference program. It originally appeared in William Fellner, ed., *Contemporary Economic Problems 1979* (Washington, D.C.: American Enterprise Institute, 1979), pp. 359-399.

[1] For a summary of U.S. immigration policy since colonial times, see Barry R. Chiswick, "Immigrants and Immigration Policy," in William Fellner, ed., *Contemporary Economic Problems 1978* (Washington, D.C.: American Enterprise Institute, 1978), pp. 285-325.

[2] For a sense of the debate at the time, see the article by Paul H. Douglas (then a professor and later senator from Illinois), "Is the New Immigration More Unskilled than the Old?" *Journal of the American Statistical Association,* vol. 16 (June 1919), pp. 393-403. Douglas's answer was no.

TABLE 1
Immigration to the United States by Country of Origin, Fiscal Years 1956–1975

Place of Origin	1956–1965 Number (thousands)	1956–1965 Percent	1966–1975 Number (thousands)	1966–1975 Percent
Europe	1,409	49.0	1,067	28.0
Germany	310	10.8	102	2.7
Greece	58	2.0	129	3.4
Italy	197	6.8	217	5.7
Poland	87	3.0	50	1.3
Portugal	29	1.0	121	3.2
United Kingdom	249	8.8	157	4.1
Other	479	16.6	291	7.6
Asia	215	7.5	944	24.8
China [a]	49	1.7	205	5.4
India	5	0.2	101	2.7
Japan	49	1.7	43	1.1
Korea	16	0.6	138	3.6
Philippines	28	1.0	239	6.3
Other	68	2.3	218	5.7
Africa	23	0.8	59	1.6
Egypt	7	0.2	25	0.7
Other	16	0.6	34	0.9
North America [b]	1,051	36.5	1,492	39.2
Canada	322	11.2	160	4.2
Mexico	420	14.5	538	14.1
Cuba	132	4.6	290	7.6
Dominican Republic	40	1.4	126	3.3
Haiti	13	0.5	55	1.4
Jamaica	15	0.5	124	3.3
Other	109	3.8	199	5.3
South America	168	5.8	216	5.7
Colombia	47	1.6	64	1.7
Ecuador	23	0.8	43	1.1
Other	98	3.4	109	2.9
Oceania	12	0.4	28	0.7
Total	2,878	100.0	3,808	100.0

NOTE: Detail may not add to totals because of rounding.
[a] China includes Taiwan and Hong Kong.
[b] For North America other than Canada, there were 729,000 immigrants (25.3 percent) for 1956-1965 and 1,332,000 immigrants (35.0 percent) for 1966-1975.
SOURCE: Immigration and Naturalization Service, U.S. Department of Justice, 1978.

but in the next decade 25 percent were from Asia. The share of immigration from Mexico and the Caribbean increased from 25 percent to 35 percent. Hispanic, black, and Asian immigrants are likely to continue to play an increasing role in U.S. immigration.

These amendments, together with subsequent legislation, also changed the mechanism for rationing immigration visas among the applicants from a country. The system is now more heavily weighted toward accepting those who are related to a U.S. citizen or resident alien, with less emphasis given to the immigrant's skills.

The 1965 amendments were passed at an unusual time in American history. In an era of expanding civil liberties, the racial and ethnic discrimination implicit in the national origins quota system was becoming increasingly inconsistent with both the domestic antidiscrimination legislation and the desired friendly relations with the emerging third world countries. It was also an era of optimism in public policy. The amendments may have had a favorable impact on productivity in the United States by providing opportunities for immigration to skilled and highly motivated workers from countries which previously had very small quotas. The greater emphasis that it placed on kinship ties than on productivity may have had the opposite effect.

More than a decade has passed since the 1965 amendments, and there is a different perspective on the limitations of America's resources. In addition, the issue of illegal aliens has heightened public interest in immigration policy. Interagency and congressional task forces and commissions have been formed, or are soon to be formed, to study immigration policy. Even if legislation is not changed because these studies conclude that current law is optimal, the periodic reevaluation of policy is fruitful.

An analysis of the impact of immigrants on the average level and distribution of income among the native population shows that immigrants with higher levels of skill are more likely to raise the average level of income and decrease the inequality of income among the native population. A preliminary analysis of the earnings of foreign-born white men in the United States also showed that the skills of immigrants are not static. Foreign-born men were compared with native-born men with the same demographic characteristics. Although the immigrants had lower earnings when they first arrived, as time passed they acquired skills relevant to the U.S. labor market, and the earnings gap between the foreign and native born narrowed. After about thirteen years in the country the earnings of the foreign born actually exceeded those of the native born.[3]

3 See Barry R. Chiswick, "The Impact of Immigration on the Level and Distribu-

Can the findings regarding the economic progress of white men be generalized to other immigrant groups? If these findings, which suggest an overall favorable impact of immigrants, are relevant only for white male immigrants they are of little value for policy makers, regardless of their value to historians of contemporary America. On the other hand, if it appears that these findings are not unique to a single demographic group at a single point in time, but rather reflect broad patterns that are likely to be reproduced in new immigrant groups, then they are of considerable value.

In addition, it is useful to know whether the criteria for admitting immigrants into the United States are relevant for understanding their economic progress and impact. Immigration visas may be rationed on the basis of the person's likely productivity in the country, whether the person has relatives in the country, or for humanitarian reasons, such as refugee relief. It is important to understand more fully the progress of immigrants admitted under different criteria in order to aid their adjustment more effectively, to recognize more accurately the costs and benefits of alternative policies, and to help form an overall immigration policy. While a humane immigration policy must surely include a recognition of the importance of kinship ties and refugee relief, the implications of these policies as distinct from one giving a greater weight to productivity need to be recognized.

We cannot currently analyze the economic progress in the United States of future immigrants. To gain some insights into the future, however, it is possible to analyze the progress in the contemporary United States of Hispanic, black, and Asian immigrants, and to examine the progress of immigrants in other times and in other places. In this analysis it will be possible to differentiate economic migrants from refugees. If similar patterns of progress are found in a variety of settings, there is greater confidence that these patterns will persist in the future.

The purpose of this chapter is to extend the analysis of the economic progress of immigrants. The analysis is in terms of the earnings of male immigrants of various racial-ethnic groups in various settings, in comparison with native-born men with similar demographic characteristics. The earnings of the native-born sons of immigrants are also compared with the earnings of the sons of native-born parents. The first section discusses the international transferability of skills and self-selection on the part of immigrants. This leads to the development of hypotheses regarding the pattern of earnings between the native and the foreign born,

tion of Economic Well-Being," this volume; idem, "The Effect of Americanization on the Earnings of Foreign-Born Men," *Journal of Political Economy,* October 1978, pp. 879-921.

and how this varies by country of origin, time in the place of destination, and type of immigration. The section closes with a discussion of the statistical framework.

The next section tests these hypotheses through a detailed examination of the economic progress of seven immigrant groups in the contemporary United States—foreign-born whites (singling out Cubans and Mexicans for special attention), blacks, Chinese, Japanese, and Filipinos. The analysis generally uses a one-in-a-hundred sample from the *1970 Census of Population* to compare the earnings in 1969 of these foreign-born men with their native-born counterparts.

This is followed by an analysis of the economic progress of immigrants in other times and other places: the United States at the turn of the century, and contemporary Canada, Great Britain, and Israel.

The final section sets out some implications for immigration policy that emerge from this study.

Hypotheses and Statistical Framework

For the comparative analysis of the earnings of foreign-born and native-born men with the same demographic characteristics, it is hypothesized that the earnings differential would depend, in part, on the transferability to the United States of the skills acquired by the foreign-born in school and on the job in the country of origin. It would also depend on the extent to which there is self-selection in favor of those with greater innate ability or work motivation. The transferability of skills and the self-selection of immigrants are key factors in the analysis. Their implications for the earnings of the foreign born are first developed; then the statistical framework used to test these hypotheses is presented. Although the discussion in this section is in terms of immigrants to the United States, the points are applicable to immigrants to any country.

Transferability of Skills. In general, those with more schooling appear to have more allocative efficiency, that is, they are more efficient in making decisions regarding the optimal allocation of resources.[4] They also appear to have more worker efficiency, that is, they are better able to perform tasks, perhaps because they learn skills in a shorter time and perform them with less error. The extent to which schooling enhances productivity would, in part, be related to the quality of the schooling itself: up to some point more hours of schooling per year, a lower student-teacher ratio, and more knowledgeable teachers increase the productivity of schooling. The productivity also depends, however, on where and how the worker applies the knowledge acquired in school.

[4] See, for example, Theodore W. Schultz, "The Value of the Ability to Deal with Disequilibria," *Journal of Economic Literature,* September 1975, pp. 827-846.

123

For the present purposes, the international transferability of the skills acquired in school is of considerable interest. For a given cohort of immigrants this transferability may be thought of as having two components: the extent to which skills acquired in school are transferable from one country to another within occupational or training categories and the occupational composition of that cohort. Presumably, all schooling has some elements that are country specific and some that are transferable internationally, but their relative importance would vary among the levels and types of education. A Russian criminal lawyer, for example, may have received a high-quality education in Moscow, but the training will have little market value in the United States. On the other hand, a mathematician from Russia with the same number of years of schooling may find his skills well rewarded in the United States. An immigrant cohort of persons with readily transferable skills will achieve greater and more rapid success in the United States than an otherwise identical cohort consisting of workers with skills that are of value primarily in their country of origin.

Immigrants can acquire schooling in either the country of origin or in the country of destination. Schooling acquired in the United States is more likely to be relevant for U.S. labor markets. But since the quality and transferability of previous schooling in part determines the productivity of U.S. schooling, those with previous schooling that is less transferable to the United States may gain less from schooling here.

This discussion suggests that it is useful to classify immigrants by the extent to which immigrant cohorts are weighted toward transferable skills or occupations. For the classification according to transferability of skills two country-of-origin groups are used, English-speaking countries and all other countries. The presumption is that for any given occupation the skills (including language) acquired in London, England, and Kingston, Jamaica, are more likely to be readily transferred to the U.S. labor market than the skills acquired during the same number of years of schooling in Berlin, Germany, or Port-au-Prince, Haiti.

For the classification according to the distribution of skills, it is useful to think in terms of "economic" and "noneconomic" migrants. All immigrants may be said to base their decision on the optimization of their economic well-being, if this is defined broadly to include personal safety and freedom. But here the distinction between economic and noneconomic motivations is the extent to which real money income (narrowly defined economic well-being) rather than political or social factors influences the migration decision.[5]

---

[5] For analyses of the motivations and skills of the Cuban and Vietnamese refugees, see Richard Brody and others, *Cubans in Exile: Disaffection and the Revolution*

Since the earning power of one's skills plays a primary role in economic migration and a secondary role in refugee migration, a cohort of the latter is likely to include a larger proportion of workers with skills that have little international transferability. Refugee migration generally arises from a sudden or unexpected change in political conditions, which appear to change more suddenly and more sharply than economic conditions. As a result, refugees are less likely than economic migrants to have acquired readily transferable skills and are more likely to have made investments specific to their country of origin. Economic migrants are younger on average than refugees, since migration tends to be more profitable the sooner it is done. Delay involves forgoing the higher earnings in the place of destination and shortening the remaining working life. In addition, delay results in increasing investments specific to the country of origin, thereby reducing the gain from migration.

It is not always easy to identify individuals as either economic migrants or refugees, because the classification depends in part on the person's motive for migrating. It is possible, however, judgmentally to classify immigrants from some countries at some points in time as predominantly refugees and others as predominantly economic migrants. In the 1970 U.S. census data the primary refugee group among whites is the Cubans (since 1959), while among Asian-Americans the largest proportions of refugees are Chinese. There were no major refugee movements to the United States from English-speaking countries in the past several decades. Because one cell in our two-by-two classification is empty, there are three categories of immigrants; economic migrants from English-speaking countries, economic migrants from other countries, and refugees.[6]

The effect of the transferability of schooling on earnings implies the hypothesis outlined in the first row of table 2. That is, the effect of schooling on earnings is expected to be greatest for those whose schooling is most transferable to the U.S. labor market (the native born) and would decline with the degree of transferability—next highest for English-speaking economic migrants, then other economic migrants, and least for refugees.

(Stanford, Calif.: Stanford University Press, 1968); and William T. Liu, *Transition to Nowhere: Vietnamese Refugees in America* (Nashville, Tenn.: Carter House Publishers, 1978). For a review of refugee migrations in the post-World War II period, see Gaynor I. Jacobson, "The Refugee Movement: An Overview," *International Migration Review*, vol. 2, no. 4 (Winter 1977), pp. 514-523.

[6] For the purpose of this analysis, among whites the English-speaking countries are Britain, Ireland, Canada, Australia, and New Zealand. Among blacks the English-speaking countries are in the Caribbean area.

TABLE 2

HYPOTHESES REGARDING THE ECONOMIC PROGRESS OF IMMIGRANTS
TO THE UNITED STATES

Partial Effect on Earnings, or Parameter	Native Born	Economic Migrants		Refugees
		English-speaking countries	Other countries	
Partial effect on earnings of:				
schooling	1	2	3	4
labor market experience in country of origin (T)	1	2	3	4
years since migration (YSM) (T constant)	—	3	2	1
Parameter				
YSM at which earnings of migrants and native born are equal	—		1	2

NOTE: 1 = highest or earliest; 4 = lowest or latest.

The discussion of the effect of the transferability of the skills acquired in school applies with equal force to the skills acquired through formal or informal on-the-job training in the country of origin. In this analysis there is no direct measure of the magnitude of job-related training, but the indirect measure, years of labor market experience in the country of origin, is used in its place. The native born will of course have their labor market experience in the United States; among the foreign born, those from countries with technologies and economic systems that most closely resemble the United States will tend to have skills that are readily transferable. Refugee populations will include a larger proportion of workers with skills acquired on the job in the country of origin that have little applicability in the United States. These hypotheses are summarized in the second row of table 2.

The weaker the transferability of skills, the lower the earnings and the greater the probability of unemployment for the immigrant when he first arrives. With the passage of time in the United States the immigrant acquires knowledge, habits, and skills that increase his productivity on the job and reduce the incidence and duration of unemployment. This may occur through an informal learning-by-living adjustment process, by a more formal job training (or retraining) program, or by formal schooling. The Cuban emigré lawyers and doctors who found dish-

126

washing their best job opportunity when they first arrived have, over time, either acquired new skills or gradually acquired American licenses.

The effect on earnings of years since migration is expected to be inversely related to the extent to which country-of-origin skills are transferable to the U.S. labor market. In the extreme case, if skills are perfectly transferable across countries, time in the place of destination would have no effect on earnings over and above the effect of total labor market experience.[7] Thus, for the same schooling and age, the number of years an immigrant has been in the United States is likely to be least important as a determinant of earnings for economic migrants from English-speaking countries and most important for non-English-speaking refugees. This hypothesis is summarized in the third row of table 2 and is shown schematically by the slopes of the earnings profiles in figure 1.

Self-Selection of Immigrants. There is substantial support for the hypothesis that immigrants tend to have a higher level of innate ability and work motivation than their fellow countrymen with similar characteristics who remain at home. In his study of immigration to the United States in the century before World War I, Marcus Lee Hansen wrote: "Countries of origin were dismayed by their loss when they saw their ports thronged with the sturdiest of their peasantry. Efforts to stem the movement were attempted."[8] More recently, theoretical and empirical studies suggest a higher propensity to migrate among those who are more able, are more achievement motivated, or have a higher level of schooling.[9]

[7] Time in the United States could even have a negative effect on earnings. Bartel and Borjas found that among adult men who engage in voluntary job change in the United States, earnings are initially higher than would be predicted on the basis of their demographic and skill characteristics, but that with the passage of time their earnings regress toward the predicted value. See Ann P. Bartel and George Borjas, "Middle-Age Job Mobility: Its Determinants and Consequences," in Seymour Wolfbein, ed., *Men in Pre-Retirement Years* (Philadelphia: Temple University Press, 1977).

[8] Marcus Lee Hansen, *The Immigrant in American History,* Arthur M. Schlesinger, ed. (Cambridge, Mass.: Harvard University Press, 1940), p. 212.

[9] For a theoretical exposition of why migration rates would be higher for those with greater earnings potential, see Barry R. Chiswick, "The Effect of Americanization on the Earnings of Foreign-Born Men," *Journal of Political Economy,* October 1978, p. 900. For some empirical studies, see June A. O'Neill, "The Effect of Income and Education on Inter-Regional Migration," Ph.D. dissertation, Columbia University, 1970; Abba Schwartz, "Migration, Age, and Education," *Journal of Political Economy,* August 1976, pp. 701-719; Kathryn Tidwick, "Need for Achievement, Social Class, and Intention to Emigrate in Jamaican Students," *Social and Economic Studies,* March 1976, pp. 52-60; Anthony M. J. Yezer and Lawrence Thurston, "Migration Patterns and Income Change: Implications for the Human Capital Approach to Migration," *Southern Economic Journal,* vol. 42 (April 1976), pp. 693-702. See also, Schultz, "Value of Ability."

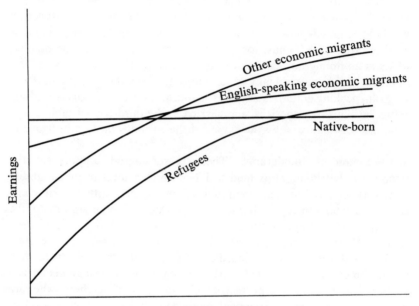

Years since migration

The extent of the self-selection of migrants in favor of the more able will vary across countries. The self-selection would be more pronounced the larger the costs of migration, including the costs of the subsequent adjustment in the new environment. The smaller costs of migration for economic migrants from English-speaking countries implies that the favorable self-selection will be less intense, which at least partially offsets the greater transferability of their skills. In comparison with economic migrants, refugees are less likely to be self-selected on the basis of high labor market ability and work motivation, because factors other than labor market success are important determinants of their migration. This is shown schematically in figure 1 by the lower earnings profile for refugees than for economic migrants.

If the distribution of innate ability and motivation is similar across countries, the average level of ability and motivation would be higher for the immigrants (particularly economic migrants) than for the native born in a population. Then the question arises: Are the advantages of greater ability sufficient to offset the disadvantages of the less than perfect

128

international transferability of knowledge and skills so that the earnings of immigrants eventually equal that of the native born? The years since migration at which this earnings crossover occurs, if it does occur, is a parameter of considerable interest that will be estimated. Because of the less favorable self-selection of refugees, the earnings crossover will occur later for them than for economic migrants, if it occurs at all. This hypothesis is summarized in the fourth row of table 2. The schematic earnings profiles in figure 1 are drawn under the assumption that the earnings crossover occurs sooner for economic migrants than for refugees.

There is likely to be a regression toward the mean in the distribution of ability from one generation to the next. That is, the children of high (low) ability parents have an average level of ability less (greater) than that of their parents, but greater (less) than the average level of ability in the population. This would arise if some aspects of ability are transmitted from one generation to the next through genetic or environmental factors.[10] In this case, the earnings of the children of immigrants would exceed those of the children of native-born parents to the extent that their greater level of innate ability and motivation outweighs disadvantages from having parents with a foreign origin. If the favorable self-selection of immigrants is less intense for refugees than for economic migrants, the earnings advantage of the children of refugees would be smaller than that of the children of economic migrants. This issue will be examined through a comparison of the earnings of the native born on the basis of their parents' place of birth.

Statistical Framework. The statistical framework for analyzing the earnings of immigrants and testing the hypotheses has been developed elswhere and will be described only briefly here.[11] By the use of the human capital earnings function, annual earnings (in natural logarithms) are expressed as a function of a set of explanatory variables, which

[10] If the children of high (low) ability parents had higher (lower) ability than their parents, the variance of ability would increase from one generation to the next. Intuitively, this seems unlikely. For some recent evidence on the well-established principle of regression to the mean in standard measures of ability from one generation to the next, see Lloyd G. Humphrey, "To Understand Regression from Parent to Offspring, Think Statistically," *Psychological Bulletin,* vol. 85 (1978), pp. 1317-1322.

[11] See Chiswick, "Americanization," pp. 897-921; and Barry R. Chiswick, "Sons of Immigrants: Are They at an Earnings Disadvantage?" *American Economic Review,* February 1977, pp. 376-380. For an analysis of occupational change, see Barry R. Chiswick, "A Longitudinal Analysis of the Occupational Mobility of Immigrants," in Barbara Dennis, ed., *Proceedings of the 30th Annual Winter Meeting, Industrial Relations Research Association* (Madison: University of Wisconsin Press, 1978).

include years of formal schooling, years of labor market experience (measured by the number of years since age five that the person was not in school), weeks worked, marital status, area of residence, whether the person is foreign born, and, if foreign born, the number of years since migrating to the United States. Earnings include wage, salary, and self-employment income.

The training variables of interest are years of schooling, years of labor market experience, and years since migrating to the United States. Preliminary analyses indicated that the effect of schooling on earnings for the foreign born is the same whether the schooling is acquired in the United States or in the country of origin. For this reason, the analysis below will not distinguish where the schooling was acquired.[12]

In a cohort of immigrants, among those with the same number of years of schooling, those who are older have had more work experience in their country of origin. On the other hand, for those with the same amount of schooling and total labor market experience, having been in the United States longer means less training in the country of origin and more of it here. The effect on earnings of years since migration, when total labor market experience is held constant, measures the differential effect of U.S. over country-of-origin experience.

Two demographic variables, marital status and area of residence, are included to control statistically for characteristics that affect earnings and may vary systematically with nativity, but that may not be related to differences in productivity.[13] Ignoring these variables can provide misleading interpretations. For example, a very high proportion (68 percent) of the black male immigrants live in metropolitan areas in New York State, compared with 10 percent of native-born blacks. On the other hand, 8 percent of the foreign-born and 44 percent of the native-born black men live in the urban South. Wages tend to be high in metropolitan areas in New York State and low in the southern states for all workers. If region of residence is ignored, black immigrants would appear to be much more productive than native-born blacks, not because of greater skills or work motivation, but because they are more likely to live in a high-wage area.

---

[12] Although the effect of schooling on earnings is smaller for immigrants than for the native born (with the exception of black immigrants), the effect of schooling is similar for the sons of immigrants and the sons of native-born parents. This suggests that the smaller effect on earnings of U.S. schooling for immigrants may arise from their previous schooling having been acquired in another country, rather than from having parents with foreign schooling.

[13] The area control variables used in the analysis are generally urban/rural and South/non-South residence, but this varies somewhat by racial-ethnic group.

The Contemporary United States

Having developed the hypotheses to be tested and having set out the statistical framework, we can now proceed to the analysis of the economic progress of male immigrants and sons of immigrants in the contemporary United States.[14] The data are from the *1970 Census of Population*. The analyses are performed separately for seven racial-ethnic groups: whites, two Hispanic subsets of whites (Cubans and Mexicans), blacks, and three groups of East Asian origin (Chinese, Japanese, and Filipinos).

The intragroup procedure adopted here permits an analysis of earnings among immigrant generations without confounding the findings with differences in the racial-ethnic mix of first-, second-, and higher-generation Americans. The procedure tests the proposition that the substantial differences in the immigration histories of the seven groups do not call for separate stories or hypotheses to explain the relative progress of the foreign born in each group. Rather, the findings indicate that a single, relatively simple model can explain the economic progress of immigrants regardless of their racial-ethnic group. This proposition is further tested in the next section when the progress of immigrants in four other settings is examined.

White Immigrants.[15] Among adult men in the United States in 1970, 5 percent were foreign born, and of these, 91 percent were white. The white immigrants earned slightly less than the native born in 1969, about 1 percent less when measured by mean earnings and 3 percent less when measured by the mean natural logarithm of earnings (the logarithm of the geometric mean). The white immigrants had about a year less schooling than the native born, were three years older, and were more likely to live in an urban area outside the South. They have been in the United States on average for about twenty-two years (see table 3).

If other variables are held constant, the white immigrants earned 3 percent more than the native born. However, white immigrants who have been in the United States for ten years earned about 3 percent less than the native born, while those in the United States twenty years earned about 6 percent more than the native born. The earnings crossover occurred at thirteen years of residence in the United States.

---

14 For the purpose of this analysis, persons born abroad of American parents are excluded from the data. Few people are in this category. If one parent is a U.S. citizen, the children are entitled to U.S. citizenship.

15 This discussion is based on Chiswick, "Americanization."

TABLE 3

COMPARISON OF EARNINGS FOR NATIVE- AND FOREIGN-BORN ADULT MEN IN THE UNITED STATES, BY RACIAL-ETHNIC GROUP, 1970

Racial-Ethnic Group and Nativity[a]	Means				Relative Difference in Earnings[b]			
	Annual earnings (dollars)	Schooling (years)	Age (years)	Years since migration (YSM)	Overall	Other variables held constant[c] YSM = 10	YSM = 20	Years since Migration at Earnings Crossover[d]
White								
native	9,738	11.9	42.8	—	−0.03	−0.03	+0.06	13
foreign	9,662	10.8	45.6	21.7				
Cuban								
native	10,341	12.3	43.6	—	−0.44	−0.16	+0.03	18
foreign	6,857	10.8	42.2	7.2				
Mexican								
native	6,523	8.9	39.6	—	−0.21	−0.05	+0.04	15
foreign	5,474	6.1	41.9	18.0				
Black								
native	6,138	9.9	41.8	—	+0.05	−0.02	+0.10	11
foreign	6,585	11.0	40.4	11.3				

Asian							
Japanese							
native	10,389	12.6	43.6	—	−0.14	−0.12	+0.03	18
foreign	9,191	14.3	38.4	10.9				
Chinese							
native	10,745	12.7	41.8	—	−0.35	−0.26	−0.08	—[e]
foreign	8,019	11.9	42.8	16.8				
Filipino							
native	7,010	11.1	36.8	—	−0.08	−0.06	+0.11	13
foreign	7,086	11.0	44.6	18.9				

NOTE: The table refers to men aged twenty-five to sixty-four years in 1970 who worked and had nonzero earnings in 1969 and, for the analyses for black and Asian immigrants, were not enrolled in school in 1970.

[a] Racial-ethnic identity is defined by the questions on race and Spanish origin. White men are used as the native-born comparison group in the Cuban analysis. The Mexican analysis is for the five southwestern states. The Cuban and black analyses are for urban areas.

[b] The difference in the means of the natural logarithm of earnings. A negative coefficient indicates lower earnings for the foreign born. For small differences, when multiplied by 100, the parameter is the percentage difference in earnings.

[c] Other variables are years of schooling, labor market experience and its square, the logarithm of weeks worked, marital status, and geographic distribution. The variable for years since migration and its square are evaluated at $YSM = 10$ and $YSM = 20$.

[d] The number of years in the United States at which the earnings of the foreign born equal the earnings of the native born, when other variables (note c) are held constant.

[e] The earnings of Chinese immigrants approach but do not equal the earnings of native-born Chinese-Americans.

SOURCE: 1970 Census of Population, Public Use Sample, 5 percent questionnaire, 1/100 sample except for a 1/1,000 sample for the white analysis.

TABLE 4

PARTIAL EFFECTS ON EARNINGS OF SCHOOLING, LABOR MARKET
EXPERIENCE IN COUNTRY OF ORIGIN, AND YEARS SINCE MIGRATION FOR
ADULT MEN IN THE UNITED STATES, 1970
(percent)

Racial-Ethnic Group	Schooling		Labor Market Experience in the Country of Origin [a]		Years since Migration to the United States [b]
	Native born	Foreign born	Native born	Foreign born	
White	7.2	5.7	2.13	1.14	1.12
Cuban (urban)	7.3	3.1	2.22	0.33	2.37
Mexican (southwest)	5.2	3.9	1.80	1.67	1.34
Black (urban)	4.6	3.3	0.78	1.18	1.60
Asian					
Japanese	6.3	5.9	1.73	1.52	2.38
Chinese	6.7	4.8	2.73	−0.60 [c]	2.70
Filipino	5.8	6.4	1.30	1.46	1.94

NOTE: The foreign born are compared with native-born men of the same racial-ethnic group, except for the Cubans where the comparison is with native-born urban white men. Unless noted otherwise, the data are for men aged twenty-five to sixty-four years in 1970 who worked at least one week and had nonzero earnings (wage, salary, and self-employment income) in 1969. The analyses for black and Asian men exclude persons enrolled in school in 1970. The parameters are estimated from a linear regression of the natural logarithm of earnings on schooling, labor market experience and its square, the logarithms of weeks worked, marital status, and geographic area, and, for the foreign born, years since migration and its square.

[a] The quadratic experience variable (T, T^2) is evaluated at $T = 10$.

[b] The quadratic years since migration variable (YSM, YSM^2) is evaluated at $YSM = 10$.

[c] Set of country-of-origin experience variables (T, T^2) has no significant effect on earnings.

SOURCE: *1970 Census of Population*, Public Use Sample, 5 percent questionnaire, 1/100 sample, except for a 1/1,000 sample for the white analysis.

Schooling has a smaller effect on earnings in the United States for the foreign born than for the native born (see table 4). Earnings rise by 5.7 percent per year of schooling for the foreign born and by 7.2 percent for the native born. Among the foreign born, however, the effect

134

of schooling on earnings is larger for men from the English-speaking developed countries than for other white immigrants, 6.6 percent compared with 5.2 percent.

The effect on earnings in the United States of labor market experience acquired in the country of birth is also smaller for the foreign born than the native born. Living in the United States an extra year, however, raises earnings by more for the foreign than the native born. The differential effect on earnings of job training in the United States as compared with training in the country of origin is small for immigrants from the English-speaking developed countries, but larger for those from other countries. After ten years in the United States, the partial effects are 0.35 percent for the former and 1.40 percent for the latter.

Among the native-born adult white men, one-fifth have a foreign-born parent. Parentage makes virtually no difference in the level of schooling, but those with a foreign-born parent are more likely to live in urban areas outside the South. The 12 percent difference in earnings in favor of those with foreign-born parents is reduced to 5 percent when training and demographic variables are held constant (table 5).

These findings for white men are consistent with the hypotheses developed above. A country-of-origin analysis for white men indicates that those born in Cuba and Mexico have earnings that are substantially lower than those of other white immigrants. Among the second-generation white men, earnings are substantially lower for those of Mexican parentage and are substantially higher for Jews.[16] The earnings of white men born in Cuba and Mexico are studied before proceeding to the analysis for black and Asian immigrants.

Cuban immigrants. Unlike the other major immigrant groups in the United States Cuban immigrants came recently and migrated at an older age. Nearly half the Cuban immigrants live in urban Florida and another one-fifth live in urban areas in New York State. The

[16] The country-of-origin analysis is based on a one-in-a-hundred sample of the population. Approximately 98 percent of men of Cuban and Mexican origin in the 1970 census are classified as white in the question on race. Parents' country of birth is the father's if he was foreign born, otherwise it is the mother's. There are too few adult second-generation Cuban-Americans for a separate country variable.

Religion is not asked in the census. The Jewish variable is for a subset of Jews, those raised in a home in which Yiddish, Hebrew, or Ladino (Judeo-Spanish) was spoken either in addition to or instead of English. Although in general having a non-English mother tongue is associated with 2 percent lower earnings for second-generation Americans, if other variables are held constant, a Jewish mother tongue is associated with 15 percent higher earnings. Because the information on mother tongue does not exist in the data set with year of immigration for the foreign born, no separate analysis of the earnings of immigrants can be made for Jews.

TABLE 5

DIFFERENCE IN EARNINGS BETWEEN FOREIGN PARENTAGE AND
NATIVE PARENTAGE ADULT MEN BORN IN THE UNITED STATES, 1970
(percent)

Racial-Ethnic Group	Relative Difference[a]
White	4.9
Mexican[b]	5.1
Mexican[b,c]	8.6
Black (urban)	
All states	8.4[c]
New York State	10.7[c]
Asian	
Japanese	5.2[c,d]
Chinese	4.3[c,d]
Filipino	9.0[c,d]

NOTE: Earnings in 1969 for native-born men aged twenty-five to sixty-four years in 1970 who worked and had nonzero earnings in 1969.

[a] The parameter is 100 times the coefficient of a foreign parentage dichotomous variable when the natural logarithm of earnings is regressed on schooling, experience, marital status, the log of weeks worked, geographic area, nativity of parents, and, in some equations, mother tongue. For small values the parameter is the percentage difference in earnings. A positive value indicates higher earnings for those with foreign-born parents.

[b] Men with Spanish surnames living in the five southwestern states.

[c] Mother tongue is held constant. Evaluated for a Spanish mother tongue in the Mexican analysis and an English mother tongue in the black analysis.

[d] Coefficient is not significantly different from zero. The sample size is small for native-born men with native-born parents.

SOURCE: 1970 Census of Population, Public Use Sample, 15 percent questionnaire, 1/1,000 sample for white men, and 1/100 sample for other groups.

analysis for Cubans provides a means of studying the experience in the United States of a refugee population. Their migration was stimulated by Castro's accession to power in 1959 and the subsequent social, political, and economic changes that were a consequence of converting Cuba into a Marxist-Leninist state.[17] Seventy-eight percent of adult Cuban-born men in the United States in 1970 were in the country for ten or fewer years. Among adult foreign-born men in 1970, the average number of years since migrating was seven for the Cubans, as compared

[17] See Brody, Cubans in Exile.

with eighteen for the Mexicans and twenty-two for all white immigrants. Since there are very few native-born men with Cuban-born parents, the benchmark for comparison with the native born is all white men living in urban areas.

Cuban-born men had very low earnings in 1969, $6,857 compared with $10,341 for native-born white men (table 3). Some of this earnings differential is attributable to their lower level of schooling (one-and-a-half fewer years of schooling) and the greater proportion living in a low-wage state, Florida. Adjusting for differences in schooling, age, place of residence, and other demographic factors substantially reduces the earnings disadvantage of the Cuban born (the difference in the mean logarithm of earnings is reduced from 0.44 to 0.24).

The key factors for understanding the lower earnings of the Cuban refugees are the small effect on earnings of training received in Cuba and the short time they have lived in the United States. The effect of an additional year of schooling on earnings in the United States is 3.1 percent for the Cubans (table 4). This can be compared with 7.3 percent for native-born urban white men, 5.2 percent for white immigrants from all non–English-speaking countries, and 3.9 percent for Mexican immigrants. Years of labor market experience in Cuba have virtually no effect on earnings in the United States. Labor market experience in the United States, on the other hand, has a substantial effect on earnings.

The earnings of Cuban immigrants do eventually reach parity with native-born white men. For those in the United States ten years, earnings are lower by about 16 percent, while earnings are higher by 3 percent for those in the United States for twenty years. Earnings equality is reached at about eighteen years in the United States (immigrated in 1951), that is, for the small cohort of immigrants who came to the United States before Castro came to power. It remains to be seen in the *1980 Census of Population* whether the Cuban refugees who arrived in the United States between 1960 and 1964 will attain earnings parity with the native born.

The earnings pattern for the Cuban immigrants is consistent with our expectations for a refugee population. Schooling and labor market experience acquired in Cuba have a small effect on earnings in the United States, whereas U.S. labor market experience has a large effect on earnings. Other things the same, the Cuban immigrants who came here after Castro came to power have lower earnings than other white immigrants and the native born. The earnings gap is narrower, however, the longer the refugees have been in the United States. The Cubans who came here in the early 1950s did have the same earnings in 1969 as the native born.

Mexican immigrants. The Mexican-American population includes some of the "oldest" and some of the most recent immigrants to the United States. About one-quarter of Mexican-origin adult men were born in Mexico, and of the three-quarters born in the United States half have a foreign-born parent. Among those with native-born parents, many can trace their ancestry to migrations from Mexico in the seventeenth century to what is now the southwestern region of the United States.

Mexican-Americans earn less than other white men of the same immigrant generation. Other things the same, first-, second-, and later-generation Mexican-Americans earn about 15 to 25 percent less than Anglos, and the difference does not appear to diminish between successive generations. Although the earnings of Mexican immigrants do not catch up to the earnings of native-born whites, the patterns found among successive generations for whites as a group also appear among successive generations for Mexican-Americans.

Compared with native-born Mexican-Americans, Mexican immigrants have low earnings ($5,474 as compared with $6,523 in 1969) and nearly two years less schooling (table 3).[18] When other variables are held constant, however, the earnings disadvantage of Mexican immigrants narrows sharply to 5 percent. Compared with native-born Mexican-origin men, the immigrants who have been in the United States ten years have 5 percent lower earnings while those in the United States twenty years have 3.4 percent higher earnings. After about fifteen years in the United States the earnings of Mexican immigrants equal that of native-born Mexican-origin men.

Mexican immigrants are disadvantaged not only by a low level of schooling, but also by a small effect of schooling on earnings (3.9 percent compared with 5.2 percent for native-born Mexican-origin men) and a smaller effect on earnings of labor market experience in the country of origin (table 4). Labor market experience acquired in the United States, however, has a substantial favorable effect on the earnings of Mexican immigrants.

Many of the earnings-related characteristics of native-born men with parents born in Mexico are very similar to those of Mexican-origin men with both parents born in the United States. They have about the same level of schooling and are about the same age. The latter are, however, more likely to live in rural areas. Among native-born men of Mexican origin, nearly all (98 percent) of those with native-born

18 This section reports findings for the 86 percent of Mexican-origin men living in the five southwestern states. Similar conclusions emerge if the analysis is performed for all states.

138

parents were : ¡ed in a home in which Spanish was spoken, either exclusively or together with English.

Overall, second-generation Mexican-Americans earned 9 percent more than those with parents born in the United States. Even when the training and demographic variables are held constant their earnings advantage ranges from 5 to 9 percent (table 5). The sons of Mexican immigrants have a clear earnings advantage over the sons of native-born parents of Mexican origin.

Penalosa arrives at a similar conclusion in his analysis of the family income of native-born Mexican-Americans using data from the *1960 Census of Population.*[19] He attributed this finding to self-selection in migration when he wrote:

> Until fairly recently both Hispanos and Californios [descendents of 17th century settlers from Mexico] were largely located in their ancestral rural areas, and attended isolated and largely *de facto* segregated schools. . . . Immigration in itself ordinarily implies some desire for change, a desire not necessarily shared by a conquered people. It would appear that foreign immigrants and their families have been acculturating more rapidly to dominant Anglo society than the native-born members of ethnic enclaves of centuries standing.

Black Immigrants. From the end of the period of the legal importation of slaves in 1808 until recently there was little immigration by blacks into the United States. In the post–World War II period, and particularly since the mid-1960s, the immigration of blacks has increased sharply, although blacks are still a small proportion of the nation's annual stream of immigrants. In 1976, for example, only 40,000 persons, or 10 percent of the immigrants, were from the predominantly black countries of the Caribbean and sub-Saharan Africa.[20] As a result, in 1970 only 1.1 percent of the blacks in the country were foreign born and another 1.1 percent (disproportionately children) were native born with a foreign-born parent.[21] It is likely, however, that black immigrants and their children will become an increasing proportion of the population in the coming decades.

[19] See Fernando Penalosa, "Education Income Discrepancies between Second and Later Generation Mexican-Americans in the Southwest," *Sociology and Social Research,* July 1969, pp. 448-454.

[20] U.S. Department of Justice, Immigration and Naturalization Service, *1976 Annual Report* (Washington, D.C., 1978), table 14.

[21] U.S. Bureau of the Census, *1970 Census of Population,* Subject Report no. PC(2)-1A, "National Origin and Language" (Washington, D.C., 1973), table 1.

Black immigrants are primarily from the Caribbean area. Forty percent were born in the English-speaking West Indies (present and former dependencies of Britain) while 50 percent were born in non-English-speaking countries in the Caribbean basin, including Cuba. Less than one-tenth were born in Africa or the Atlantic islands. Among native-born blacks with a foreign-born parent there is a less intense concentration of parent's country of birth in the Caribbean area (about 60 percent), with a larger proportion from Africa and other parts of the Eastern Hemisphere.

On average, foreign-born black men had substantially higher earnings than native-born black men in 1969, $6,585 compared with $6,138 (table 3). This arises from several advantages in earnings-related characteristics. Foreign-born black men have more schooling (by one year) and are more likely to live in urban areas in the Northeast. Nearly all foreign-born blacks, as compared with four-fifths of the native-born blacks, live in urban areas. Two-thirds of the foreign born live in New York State (8 percent of the blacks in the state) compared with one-tenth for native-born blacks. Because earnings are higher in urban New York than in urban areas of other non-southern states, the analysis is computed for all states and for New York State to test the sensitivity of our findings to the different geographic distribution of native- and foreign-born blacks.

Compared with native-born black men with similar earnings-related characteristics, foreign-born urban black men earned 2 percent less if they were in the United States for ten years, but 10 percent more if they had lived here for twenty years. Among those blacks living in metropolitan areas in New York State, the earnings of the foreign born were 5 percent lower at ten years since migration and 6 percent higher at twenty years. The earnings crossover occurs at eleven years since migration in an all-state analysis and at thirteen years among persons living in metropolitan areas of New York State.

The effect of schooling on earnings is larger for black immigrants from the English-speaking West Indies than it is for other black immigrants, as predicted by the hypothesis that there is a greater transferability to the United States of the skills acquired in English-speaking, British-oriented school systems.[22] Among black immigrants an extra year of labor market experience in the country of origin has a larger effect on U.S. earnings for those from the English-speaking

[22] The partial effects for schooling are 5.4 percent for English-speaking immigrants and 3.0 percent for other immigrants. Moreover, the effect of schooling on earnings is greater among blacks from the English-speaking West Indies than for native-born blacks. This may reflect the poor quality of schooling received by native-born blacks when the 1970 cohort of adults were youths.

West Indies. The differential effect on earnings of living in this country an extra year is smaller for the English-speaking immigrants. That is, U.S. labor market experience is more productive relative to a similar exposure in the country of origin the less similar are the two countries.[23]

Second-generation black Americans earn 26 percent more than urban blacks whose parents were born in the United States, $7,719 compared with $6,110. This arises in part because of the former's higher level of schooling (by two years) and greater tendency to live in a high-wage region of the country. Other things the same, for those raised in a home in which English was the only language spoken, second-generation black Americans earned 8 percent more than those with native-born parents, and the differential is 11 percent if the data are limited to metropolitan areas in New York State (table 5).

The earnings pattern among blacks of different immigrant generations is very similar to the pattern that was hypothesized on the basis of the international transferability of skills and the favorable self-selection of immigrants.

East Asian Immigrants. Nearly 1.4 million persons in the United States in 1970 were racially of East Asian origin, primarily Chinese, Japanese, Filipino, or Korean.[24] The timing of immigration to the United States has been influenced not only by economic circumstances here but also by war and the economic and political circumstances in the countries of origin.

The migration of East Asians to the United States began with the movement of Chinese laborers to California as part of the Gold Rush of 1849. Chinese immigration reached a peak in the 1870s (123,000 immigrants) and then declined as restrictive legislation was enacted. Contracts to supply unskilled ("coolie") labor were prohibited by legislation in 1875. The Chinese Exclusion Act of 1882 and its subsequent amendments barred the immigration of Chinese laborers, and as a result immigration from China declined sharply. The annexation of

---

[23] Evaluated at ten years after migration, the partial effects are 1.0 percent for blacks from the English-speaking West Indies and 1.8 percent for other black immigrants. The very weak effect on earnings of labor market experience for U.S. blacks when measured by cross-sectional data has been attributed to the sharply improved economic prospects of younger cohorts of blacks.

[24] The question on race in the *1970 Census of Population* elicited that there were about 590,000 Japanese, 435,000 Chinese, 340,000 Filipinos, and 70,000 Koreans in the United States. (U.S. Bureau of the Census, *1970 Census of Population,* Subject Report, "Japanese, Chinese, and Filipinos in the United States," 1973, table 1, p. x.) Since then, in addition to substantial immigration from China, the Philippines, and Korea, about 500,000 Indochinese refugees have been admitted to this country.

Hawaii in 1898 ended large-scale Chinese immigration to these islands. It was not until World War II (December 1943) that the Chinese Exclusion Act and its amendments were repealed, China was given a small quota (105 per year), and foreign-born Chinese were made eligible for citizenship. Immigration from China (including Taiwan and Hong Kong) increased as a result of the end of the national origins quota system with the 1965 amendments and special refugee relief programs since 1949 (table 1).

There was little immigration from Japan to the United States until the 1890s (1891–1900, 26,000 immigrants), and this immigration reached a peak at the turn of the century (1901–1910, 130,000 immigrants). Starting with the "Gentlemen's Agreement" of 1907 between the government of Japan and the executive branch of the U.S. government, with few exceptions Japanese laborers were barred from migrating to the United States.[25] The exclusion was set into law with the 1917 immigration amendments and remained in effect until Japan was given the minimum quota of 100 in 1952. The end of the national origins quota system with the 1965 amendments had relatively little effect on immigration from Japan, presumably because the country had already attained a high level, and a high rate of increase, of income.

Following the annexation of the Philippines as a result of the Spanish-American War (1898) and until 1935, Filipinos were nationals of the United States and were not subject to immigration restrictions. Filipino migration to Hawaiian sugar and pineapple plantations increased as they were substituted for the restricted Chinese and Japanese laborers. The migration of Filipinos to the mainland increased in the 1920s from Hawaii and the Philippines. With independence, the Philippines was given a small quota, although immigration was facilitated by special provisions for joining the armed forces. The 1965 immigration amendments, however, have resulted in substantially increased Filipino immigration (see table 1).

The historical pattern of immigration from East Asia has determined the distribution of Asian-Americans by immigrant generation. Among adult men, the Japanese are predominantly second-generation Americans, while the Chinese and Filipinos are predominantly foreign born (see table 6).

Adult Chinese and Japanese men born in the United States earned more than native-born white men in 1969, in part because of the

---

[25] The annexation of Hawaii in 1898 had less of an effect on Japanese migration to these islands because it was two decades before formal legal restrictions were imposed and the Gentlemen's Agreements were less stringently enforced with regard to the Hawaiian Islands.

TABLE 6

DISTRIBUTION OF JAPANESE, CHINESE, AND FILIPINO MEN AGED
TWENTY-FIVE TO SIXTY-FOUR YEARS, BY IMMIGRANT GENERATION, 1970
(percent)

	Foreign Born	Native Born with a Foreign-Born Parent	Native Born, Both Parents Native Born	Total
Japanese	12.8	68.8	18.3	100.0
Chinese	64.8	23.9	11.3	100.0
Filipino	73.0	21.4	5.6	100.0

SOURCE: *1970 Census of Population,* 5 percent and 15 percent questionnaires, 1/100 sample.

former's higher level of schooling and tendency to live in high-wage states, California and Hawaii (table 3). Other things the same, there is little difference in earnings among native-born whites, Chinese, and Japanese. Foreign-born Chinese and Japanese men, however, earned less than foreign-born white men, despite advantages of schooling and geographic location.[26] They are, however, at an earnings disadvantage in having been in the United States for fewer years. Other things the same, including time in this country, Japanese immigrants earn about the same as white immigrants, but the Chinese immigrants earn less. Filipino men, whether native or foreign born, have much lower earnings than white men or other men of Asian origin, both overall and when other variables are held constant. The reasons for the very low earnings of Filipino men are as yet unclear.

Years of schooling and years of labor market experience in the country of origin have a smaller effect on U.S. earnings for the foreign born than the native born among the Japanese and Chinese, although not among the Filipinos (table 4). Among foreign-born Asian men, schooling and labor market experience in the country of origin has the smallest effect on earnings for the Chinese. Indeed, among Chinese immigrants work experience in the country of origin (primarily China) has no effect on earnings, while that acquired in the United States has the largest differential impact. These patterns are consistent with the Chinese having the largest proportion of refugees.

[26] Foreign-born Chinese and Filipino men have an exceptionally large inequality of years of schooling, with unusually high proportions of men having high and very low levels of education.

143

Do the earnings of the foreign-born Asian men ever reach or exceed the earnings of native-born men with similar demographic and geographic characteristics? For Japanese immigrants the earnings crossover occurs at eighteen years in the United States, after which the foreign born have higher earnings (table 3). Among the Filipinos the earnings crossover occurs at thirteen years. Only among the Chinese do the earnings of the foreign born never equal that of the native born, although the difference becomes quite small.

When the data are limited to native-born men it is possible to analyze whether it matters where one's parents were born. Other things the same, Asian-Americans with a foreign-born parent earn 4 to 9 percent more than those of the same race with native-born parents (table 5). This is essentially the same finding as for the other racial-ethnic groups.

Because of this earnings advantage of second-generation Americans and the very high proportion of native-born Asian-Americans who are second generation in comparison with the white population, the earnings crossover between the foreign and native born comes later for the Asian-Americans. That is, if the relative weight of second-generation Americans among the native born were the same as for the white population, the earnings crossover for the Asian foreign born would come sooner. The rankings among the three Asian groups would not change. The Filipinos would be at the lower end and the Japanese at the upper end of the eleven- to fifteen-year interval found for other racial-ethnic groups. For the Chinese, the earnings crossover would not occur until somewhat more than twenty years after migration. That is, it occurs for those who came to the United States before the Communist takeover of China in 1949.

The most recent group of East Asian immigrants are the refugees from Indochina. Since the fall of Saigon in April 1975 about 500,000 Indochinese refugees have entered the United States. Many of these refugees acquired skills in their home country that are not readily transferable to the United States. At present there is little systematic data on the economic progress of these refugees. A panel survey of over 400 Vietnamese refugee families conducted in August/September 1975 and in July/August 1976 suggests that they are making substantial progress.[27] The proportion of men aged sixteen years and over who were employed increased from 67 to 86 percent. Of the employed household heads, the proportion in white-collar and craft jobs increased from 35 to 71 percent. The proportion of employed household heads with monthly earn-

[27] Opportunity Systems, Inc., *Third Wave Report: Vietnam Resettlement Operational Feedback,* prepared for HEW Refugee Task Force (Washington, D.C., September 1976), tables 33, 35, and 36.

ings exceeding $600 increased from 19 to 41 percent. It is still too early, however, to determine their ultimate economic success in the United States.

The findings of the comparative analysis of earnings for the three largest groups of East Asian origin are consistent with the hypotheses developed above. Skills acquired prior to immigration are less productive in the United States than the skills of the native born. This is shown among the Chinese and Japanese by the smaller effect on earnings of schooling and experience acquired in the country of origin for the foreign than the native born. These training variables have a particularly small effect for Chinese immigrants, among whom are a disproportionate number of refugees.[28] For all three East Asian immigrant groups, and particularly for the Chinese, labor market experience in the United States has a larger effect on earnings than experience prior to migration.

The implications for earnings of the favorable self-selection of immigrants, particularly economic migrants, emerge from the data. The earnings of the foreign born eventually equal and then exceed those of the native born for the Japanese and Filipinos in roughly the same length of time as for the non-Asian immigrants that were studied. Among the cohort of Chinese immigrants, which is expected to have a less intensely favorable self-selection because of the high proportion of refugees, the crossover either does not occur or occurs much later (that is, for those who came to the United States before 1949). The favorable self-selection of immigrants apparently affects the second generation. Within each of the three East Asian groups the sons of immigrants earn more than the sons of native-born parents.

Other Times, Other Places

The previous section examined in detail the economic progress of foreign-born men in the contemporary United States. Stable patterns consistent with the previously developed hypotheses were observed across racial-ethnic groups regarding the effect on earnings of time in the United States, language and skills acquired in the country of origin, and type of immigration. This section extends the analysis to see if these hypotheses are supported by data from other times and from other places. To do this, the earnings of immigrants in four different settings are studied. These are the United States at the turn of the century, and contemporary Canada, Great Britain, and Israel.

---

[28] The patterns for the Filipinos differ and are similar to those found in the comparison of native-born blacks and blacks from the English-speaking West Indies.

United States at the Turn of the Century. Starting in the 1870s and accelerating in the next two decades, the number of immigrants to the United States increased sharply, with an increasing proportion coming from southern and eastern Europe. These developments heightened concern as to the effect of immigration on the country and led to the establishment of the U.S. Immigration Commission to study the progress and impact of immigrants and issue policy recommendations. The commission conducted a survey in 1909 of over a half million wage and salary workers in mining and manufacturing, primarily in the northeast and north central states. Sixty percent of the sample were foreign born.

The commission's report, issued in 1911, was one of the bases for the literacy requirements in the 1917 amendments and the quota systems introduced in the 1920s. Although it has been alleged that the commission's interpretations of the data, and hence their policy recommendations, were based on prejudice against the "new immigrants" from southern and eastern Europe, it has also been alleged that the data themselves are untainted by this prejudice.[29] In recent years, modern statistical techniques have been applied to the detailed cross-tabulations published by the commission, even though the randomness of the sample has not been established. Francine Blau's study, the most recent, uses a methodology closest to the one used above for the analysis of the contemporary United States.[30]

Blau was concerned, in part, with earnings differences among four groups of men, the native born with a native-born father, the native born with a foreign-born father, immigrants from "advantaged countries" (Group 1 immigrants, from English-speaking Canada and northern and western Europe, excluding Ireland), and immigrants likely to be subject to discrimination (Group 2 immigrants, from southern and eastern Europe, Ireland, and French-speaking Canada). Several variables that determine earnings were held constant. These include the proportions that were literate, English-speaking, married, and living in the central states, as well as the average age and industry characteristics.

Blau found that, other things the same, the wages of the foreign born in 1909 were higher by 1.1 percent for each extra year of residence in the United States. A similar value is obtained for white foreign-born men in the contemporary United States ten years after migration (table 3).

[29] For a sense of some of the emotions surrounding the debate in the professional literature, see Douglas, "New Immigration."

[30] See Francine D. Blau, "Immigration and Labor Earnings in Early Twentieth Century America," in Julian L. Simon and Julie da Vanzo, eds., *Research in Population Economics,* vol. 2 (Greenwich, Conn.: JAI Press, 1980), pp. 21–41, and the references therein.

Blau estimated the number of years in the United States that it takes for the wages of the foreign born to equal (and then surpass) the wages of the native born. It was eleven years for Group 1 immigrants (northern and western Europe) and sixteen years for Group 2 immigrants. These are the end points of the interval found in the analysis for the contemporary foreign-born population of the United States.

In the comparison between the native born with a native-born father and those with a foreign-born father Blau found that, other things the same, the earnings of the latter were higher by 2.4 percent, although the difference is not statistically significant. For the contemporary population, native-born adult white men with a foreign-born parent have a statistically significant 5 percent earnings advantage, which is not significantly different from Blau's 2.4 percent.

The earnings patterns for the foreign born relative to the native born in the United States at the turn of the century appear to be consistent with our expectations and are very similar to the patterns found for the contemporary United States.

Canada. For an examination of the economic progress of immigrants in other places, it is useful to study a country with a socioeconomic structure and recent immigration experience similar to those of the United States. Over the past few decades, Canadian and U.S. immigration policies have been similar in several respects.[31] In the decades prior to the 1960s Canadian policy was based on country of origin and was not very different from the U.S. national origins quota system. During the 1960s both countries abandoned their ethnocentric policies. Although the United States maintained hemisphere and country quotas for the Eastern Hemisphere and extended them to the Western Hemisphere, Canada did not adopt formal limits on the number of persons who may enter. As a result, in the past twenty-five years annual immigration has ranged from a peak of 282,000 in 1957 to a low of about 70,000 in the early 1960s, with immigration being higher during periods of economic expansion.

In the postwar period, until 1962, the primary criteria for immigration into Canada were the person's nationality, country of birth, and kinship ties with a Canadian citizen or permanent resident. Citizens of the English-speaking white countries and France experienced little dif-

---

[31] The discussion of Canadian policy is based on John Hucker, "A Synopsis of Canadian Immigration Law," *Syracuse Journal of International Law and Commerce*, vol. 3, no. 1 (Spring 1975), pp. 47-76; Canadian Department of Employment and Immigration, *Twenty Questions about Canada's New Immigration Act*, 1979, and *New Directions: A Look at Canada's Immigration Act and Regulations*, 1978.

ficulty entering Canada. Immigration from other European countries by persons without a Canadian sponsor was generally tied to the business cycle, with more visas issued in periods of economic expansion and fewer in recessions. By special agreements with the newly independent South Asian and later also the West Indian governments (former British colonies) a small number of immigrants could enter without sponsors if they met certain occupational requirements. There were racial differences in the extent to which Canadian citizens and permanent residents could sponsor the immigration of close relatives.

As a result of these policies, the foreign born who arrived in Canada prior to the 1960s were predominantly white and of U.S., British, Irish, or other European origin. This situation was not unlike that in this country, except that the United States had a large proportion of Mexican immigrants in the Southwest because of the common border.

Canadian immigration policy changed sharply in the 1960s. Legislation in 1962 and 1967 ended the emphasis on country of origin and the racial discrimination in the requirements for sponsored immigrants (close relatives). For persons other than sponsored immigrants, selection criteria were based primarily on the applicant's personal characteristics and were weighted toward the person's productivity and likely success in adjusting to Canada. Persons scoring above a certain number of points are granted immigration visas. In recent years between one-fifth and two-fifths of the immigrants have been without a Canadian relative and were thus admitted under the point system, as were another quarter with only distant relatives.[32]

The change in immigration policies in the 1960s, together with factors external to Canada, altered the distribution of immigrants by country of origin and skill level.[33] The proportion of immigrants from Asia, Africa, and the West Indies increased from 4 percent in 1951–1960 to 11 percent in 1961–1966, to 26 percent in 1967–1973. An increased proportion of immigrant workers are professional or technical workers, from less than 10 percent during the 1950s to 20 to 30 percent in the 1960s and 1970s. It is too early to determine, however, whether immigrants entering under the new program will be more successful in Canada than earlier cohorts of immigrants.

Fortunately, there is a recent study by B. B. Tandon of the earnings of foreign-born males in Toronto, Canada, using data from the 1971 census of Canada and methodology similar to the one applied to the United States. Toronto is an important immigrant-receiving metro-

[32] Canadian Department of Employment and Immigration, *Annual Report to Parliament on Immigration Levels,* 1978, pp. 20 and 22.
[33] Louis Parai, "Canada's Immigration Policy: 1962-1974," *International Migration Review,* Winter 1975, pp. 470-471.

148

politan area. Of the immigrants arriving in Canada in 1971, 30 percent settled in Toronto, and half the adult population of the metropolitan area is foreign born.[34]

Tandon analyzed the average hourly earnings in 1970 of Canadian and foreign-born males who were full-time members of the civilian labor force (that is, aged sixteen to sixty-four years and not enrolled in school or in the military). Using separate equations for the native and foreign born he regressed the logarithm of hourly earnings on years of schooling, years of total labor market experience, and, for the foreign born, years living in Canada. He found that a year of schooling had a larger effect on earnings in Canada for the native than the foreign born, 7.1 percent compared with 3.4 percent. The effect on earnings in Canada of an extra year of labor market experience in the country of origin is also larger for the native born, 3.5 percent compared with 1.1 percent when evaluated at ten years of experience. Among the foreign born with the same amount of schooling and labor market experience, earnings are higher the longer the period of residence in Canada, although additional years have a decreasing marginal effect on earnings (2.1 percent when evaluated at ten years since migration).

The earnings difference between native- and foreign-born Canadians can be related to the latter's duration of residence in Canada. With ten years of schooling (the mean schooling level for the foreign born) and twenty years of postschool labor market experience, the foreign born in Canada for ten years earned 10 percent less than the native born, while those in Canada twenty years had 4 percent higher earnings. The earnings crossover, the number of years in Canada at which the earnings of the native and foreign born are equal, occurs at sixteen years. This is not very different from the earnings crossover at thirteen years estimated for white immigrants in the United States. A somewhat later earnings crossover may not be unexpected, however, if the subsequent migration of the foreign born in Toronto (an important first stop for immigrants) to other parts of Canada and to the United States is self-selected in favor of those who have made the best adjustments to North American labor markets.

The earnings of the foreign born in Canada in comparison with the native born are as predicted by the hypotheses developed above. The parallels between the immigration policies and the economic progress of the foreign born in Canada and the United States are striking. It cannot be determined at this time how the recent divergence in

---

[34] B. B. Tandon, "Earnings Differentials among Native-Born and Foreign-Born Residents of Toronto," *International Migration Review,* vol. 12, no. 3 (Fall 1978), pp. 406-10.

immigration criteria—whereby the Canadian emphasis is more on productivity and that of the United States more on kinship ties—will affect the economic progress and impact of immigrants.

Great Britain. Although often thought of as a country of emigration, Great Britain is currently and historically also a recipient of immigrants from outside the British Isles.[35] Toward the end of the nineteenth century and in the early twentieth century many immigrants came from southern and eastern Europe, some to stay permanently, and others for a brief spell as they continued on to North America or to British colonies. In subsequent decades, although migration from the European continent continued, immigration increased from what is now referred to as the New Commonwealth countries of Asia, Africa, and the Caribbean. In the 1950s and 1960s the New Commonwealth countries became the major source of immigration.

According to the *1971 Census of Britain*, 4.5 percent of all males were born outside the British Isles, a proportion not very different from the 5 percent foreign born in the United States. About half the foreign-born men in Britain were born in the New Commonwealth countries, three-tenths were born in Europe (non-Commonwealth), and one-tenth were born in the Old Commonwealth countries (Canada, Australia, and New Zealand) or the United States. Although race is not asked in the British census, survey data indicate that about a third of the foreign-born men were classified by the interviewer as colored, that is, black or of South or East Asian origin. Hence, many of the immigrants born in the New Commonwealth are white, presumably descendants of Europeans returning to Britain.

To what extent are the earnings of immigrants in Britain relative to the native born consistent with our hypotheses as to the economic progress of immigrants? According to the *1972 General Household Survey,* adult (aged twenty-five to sixty-four) foreign-born white men earned 6 percent more than adult native-born white men, but this difference disappears when other things, such as schooling (the white foreign born have a half year more schooling) and demographic variables, are held constant. The colored foreign born earn about 19 percent less than the white native born, and this increases to about 24 percent when other factors (including the higher level of schooling of the colored immigrants) are held constant. The earnings disadvantage of the colored is smaller (about 4 percent) when the small

[35] This section is based on Barry R. Chiswick, "The Earnings of White and Coloured Immigrants in Britain," *Economica,* February 1980, pp. 81-87, using data from the *1972 General Household Survey.* For the purpose of this discussion, immigrants from Ireland are included in the native-born population of Great Britain.

sample of native-born colored men, who are primarily the sons of immigrants, is compared with the white native-born men, whose ancestors have lived in Britain for generations.

The effect of schooling on earnings is larger in Britain for the native born than for the foreign born—7.5 percent for the native born, 6.9 percent for the white foreign born, and about 4 percent for the colored foreign born. The racial difference may reflect a lower quality of schooling or a weaker transferability to Great Britain of the skills acquired in school. An extra year of British labor market experience also has a larger effect on earnings for the native than the foreign born.[36]

There appears to be little differential effect on earnings, for either the white or colored foreign born, of labor market experience acquired in Great Britain rather than in the country of birth. This implies that most immigrants, particularly in the last two decades, were well Anglicized before they came. Indeed, according to the *1971 Census of Britain* two-thirds of the foreign-born males were born in the New or Old Commonwealth, the Republic of South Africa, or the United States, and nearly four-fifths of those living in Great Britain for twenty or fewer years were born in these countries.[37] Most of the immigrants from non-English-speaking countries (primarily the non-Commonwealth countries of Europe) have lived in Britain for more than twenty years. Beyond two decades, an extra year of labor market experience in the country of destination has little additional effect on earnings compared with an extra year of experience in the country of origin.

The earnings patterns for male immigrants in Great Britain are consistent with the hypotheses and with the patterns observed for foreign-born white and black men in the United States from English-speaking countries.

Israel.[38] The Jewish population of Israel is primarily foreign born or native born with a foreign-born parent. It has been estimated that in

[36] After ten years of work experience in the country of origin, an extra year of labor market experience raises earnings by 2.2 percent for the native born and by 1.5 percent for the foreign born.

[37] *Census, 1971, Great Britain, Country of Birth Tables* (London: Her Majesty's Stationery Office, 1974), table 4.

[38] The analysis for Israel is limited to the Jewish population. Jewish immigrants in Israel are often classified by their continent of origin, that is, Europe and America (primarily Europe) or from Asia and Africa (primarily North Africa and the Middle East). The demographic data on immigration are from Roberto Bachi, *The Population of Israel* (Jerusalem: Hebrew University, 1977), particularly chapters 8, 9, and 14. The data used in the regression analysis of earnings are from the *1976 Income Survey* and were provided by the Central Bureau of Statistics, Jerusalem, Israel. The regression analysis is based on a collaborative effort with Itzhak Goldberg, whose comments were extremely helpful.

1975, 49 percent of the Jewish population were foreign born, 41 percent were native born with a foreign-born father, and 10 percent (disproportionately youths) were third- or higher-generation residents of the area. Just over half the Jewish population is of Asian-African origin: 47 percent of the foreign born, 58 percent of the second generation, and 30 percent of the third-generation Israelis.[39]

A model of conventional economic migration, of persons moving from one country to another in response to an earnings differential, would be of limited value for explaining migration to Israel. The large-scale emigration of Jews from eastern Europe from the 1880s to World War I resulted primarily in migration to North America. The few who went to Palestine, at that time a poverty-stricken corner of the Ottoman Empire, were almost certainly not motivated by economic considerations. After World War I the territory became a British Mandate. Immigration increased in response to the promise of a Jewish homeland, tighter U.S. immigration restrictions, and the spread of active anti-Semitism in Europe, although from 1930 until independence in May 1948 the British attempted to limit sharply Jewish immigration. During the period of the British Mandate the proportion of refugees among the immigrants increased.

Israeli government policy, as expressed in the Declaration of Independence (1948) and the Law of Return (1950), has been to provide all Jews the right to immigrate and become citizens, with minor reservations to protect the health and safety of the population. This objective was promoted by subsidizing migration and through intergovernmental negotiations. As a result, the proportion of refugees among the immigrants was quite high. Many of the European immigrants in the immediate postindependence period were displaced persons and former concentration-camp inmates. During the three-year period from May 1948 to 1951, 18 percent of the Jews in Asia (including nearly the entire Jewish communities in Yemen and Iraq), 20 percent of the Jews in the Balkans, and 12 percent of the Jews in eastern Europe (excluding the U.S.S.R.) migrated to Israel. Primarily as a result of the migration of Jews from Moslem countries to Israel, the Jewish population of Asia and Africa (outside of Israel) declined from 1.3 million persons in 1945 to 0.3 million by 1975.[40]

Reemigration, that is, migration out of Palestine and Israel has also been characteristic of the Jewish population since Ottoman times. The proportion of the foreign born among emigrants is large and exceeds their proportion in the Jewish population. During the 1948–1969

[39] Bachi, *Population,* pp. 264-266.
[40] Ibid., pp. 75 and 84.

period, the foreign born were 75 percent of the emigrants but only 63 percent of the population. The rate of reemigration is highest among American and western European immigrants and very low among immigrants from the Arab countries of the Middle East. The rate of emigration among the foreign born declines with the length of time spent in the country. Among the immigrants who arrived in 1962–1969, for example, the emigration rate (that is, the number emigrating as a proportion of those still in the country) within one year of arrival was 2.7 percent; between one and two years, 3.7 percent; between two and three years, 2.1 percent; between three and four years, 1.6 percent; between four and five years, 1.4 percent.

Although the subsequent emigration of immigrants is in part a consequence of the inability of some to adjust to a new environment, Bachi writes that "emigration movements have a prevalently economic motivation."[41] Within country-of-origin categories the reemigration rates are higher among the young adults, the single, the more educated, and the less religious, and among those for whom "Jewish motivation" was a weaker factor in the original migration. The destinations of emigrants have been primarily high-income areas. Among the emigrants (native and foreign born) in the 1948–1972 period, 43 percent went to North America, 37 percent went to western Europe, and 10 percent to Australia, New Zealand, and other parts of the Americas.

These data suggest that migration to Israel is less likely to have been self-selected in favor of persons with high labor market ability and economic motivation in comparison with migration to the United States and Canada. Even if the emigration from the country of origin were favorably self-selected, the possibility of more favorable self-selection among those going to high-income countries rather than to Israel cannot be dismissed. Emigration out of Israel appears to have a more economic basis and is more likely to be self-selected in favor of those with ability and motivation to generate high earnings.

The foregoing has implications for our comparative analysis of the earnings of immigrants and natives in the place of destination. A migration stream composed primarily of refugees (whether Cuban refugees in the United States or Jewish refugees in Israel) in which the favorable self-selection is less intense implies a relatively lower earnings profile for the immigrants and an earnings crossover with the native born at a later time, if it occurs at all. The subsequent emigration of the more able among the immigrants also suggests a smaller effect on earnings of time in the country and a later earnings crossover when cross-sectional data are used. Finally, any earnings advantage of the native born with

41 Ibid., p. 126; see also pp. 120-126.

foreign-born parents would be weaker if the favorable self-selection among immigrants is less intense, or is even reversed.

The analysis of earnings is for data from a 1976 household survey for Israel and replicates the methodology applied to the United States. The data are for Jewish men aged twenty-five to sixty-four years in 1976 who were not enrolled in school and who worked and had positive earnings in 1975. The data permit the identification of the person's ethnic origin (European-American or Asian-African) on the basis of his country of birth or his father's country of birth if he is native born.[42] The ethnic origin distinction is useful because the skills acquired in Europe or the United States may be more readily transferable to Israel than the skills acquired in North Africa and the Middle East.

Overall, the foreign born earned 18 percent less than the native born (table 7). Although the foreign born have two and a half fewer years of schooling, they have more labor market experience. Other things the same (schooling, age, marital status, weeks worked, and ethnic origin), the foreign born earned 17 percent less than the native born if they were in Israel for ten years and 9 percent less if they had lived in Israel for twenty years. The earnings crossover occurs very late, between thirty-five and forty years in the country. Immigrants of Asian-African origin earned 12 percent less than those of European-American origin, other things the same.

Schooling has a smaller effect on earnings for the foreign born. Earnings rise by 3.6 percent for an extra year of schooling for the foreign born and by 5.2 percent for the native born (table 7). Experience (years) in the country of origin also has a smaller effect on earnings in Israel for the foreign born. The relative difference between the foreign born and natives in the effects on earnings of schooling and labor market experience in the country of origin is larger in Israel than it is for the racial-ethnic groups in the United States or Canada, with the exception of the Cubans and Chinese in the United States (compare tables 4 and 7). That is, the parameters for Israel are comparable to the relationships found for refugee groups in the United States.

Duration of residence in the country has a somewhat smaller differential effect on earnings for the foreign born in Israel (0.9 percent per year when evaluated at $YSM = 10$) than in the United States (table 4), other things the same. This finding in cross-sectional data may arise from the reemigration of the more able, more economically motivated immigrants. And the reemigration of the more able immi-

---

[42] Among the small sample of third- and higher-generation Israeli Jews it is not possible to identify ethnic origin. Because of intermarriage among Jews, by the third generation continent of origin has less meaning.

TABLE 7

ANALYSIS OF EARNINGS FOR NATIVE- AND FOREIGN-BORN JEWISH MEN IN ISRAEL, 1976

Nativity	Means of Variables					Partial Effects of Variables[a] (percent)			Relative Difference in Earnings[b]	
	Sample size	Earnings (Israeli pounds)	Schooling (years)	Age (years)	Years since migration (YSM)	Schooling	Experience in country of origin	Years since migration	YSM = 10	YSM = 20
Total	3,228	33,072	9.6	42.3	—	—	—	—	—	—
Native born	681	38,446	11.5	35.3	—	5.2	2.9	—	—	—
Foreign born	2,546	31,641	9.0	44.2	22.7	3.6	1.2	0.9	-0.17	-0.09

NOTE: The table refers to the earnings in 1975 of Jewish men aged twenty-five to sixty-four years in 1976 who worked, had positive earnings in 1975, and were not enrolled in school.

[a] The partial effects were computed from separate regressions for the native and foreign born. The natural logarithm of earnings was regressed on schooling, experience (years since age five not in school), experience squared, log of weeks worked, marital status, Asian-African origin, and, for the foreign born, years since migration (YSM) and its square. The effects of experience and years since migration are evaluated at ten years.

[b] The parameter is the difference in the natural logarithm of earnings from a pooled regression including the same variables as in note a, evaluated at ten and twenty years since immigration. For small values, when multiplied by 100 the parameter is the percentage difference in earnings. A negative coefficient indicates lower earnings for the foreign born.

SOURCE: Israel Central Bureau of Statistics, *1976 Income Survey*.

155

grants appears to be a relatively more important characteristic of Israel than of the United States.

Among the native born, the earnings of second-generation Israelis (father foreign born) can be compared with those with a native-born father. The earnings advantages of the second generation found in the U.S. data and attributed to the favorable self-selection of immigrants is apparently not found in the Israeli data. For the same schooling and demographic characteristics, men with an Asian or African father have lower earnings (by 16 percent) than men with a native-born father, while men with a European or American father have the same earnings (lower by 1 percent, but the t-ratio is only 0.3) as those with a native-born father.

The earnings pattern for the foreign born as compared with the native born in Israel is consistent with our expectations for an immigration that is primarily not based on conventional economic factors. Israeli immigration has, in fact, been primarily of ideologically motivated individuals or the consequence of large-scale migrations of nearly entire communities as a result of political factors. The favorable self-selection of Jewish migrants to high-income third countries and the reemigration of immigrants has also been an important factor. As with refugees in the United States, it takes much longer for the earnings of the foreign born to catch up to the earnings of the native born.

Policy Implications

This study has been concerned with the economic progress of immigrant groups in the United States and elsewhere. Although the background and historical experiences of these groups vary, certain persistent patterns emerge, apparently from differences in the international transferability of the skills acquired in the country of origin and from the self-selection of immigrants in favor of those with more innate ability and economic motivation.

The analysis indicates substantial, perhaps impressive, economic progress of immigrants. The earnings disadvantage of male economic migrants when they first arrive is relatively short-lived. They catch up to the native born with similar demographic characteristics by the time they have been in the country eleven to sixteen years, and thereafter the immigrants have higher earnings. Their native-born sons earn 5 to 10 percent more than the sons of native-born parents, other things being equal. Among refugees, however, because of the weaker transferability of their skills and the less intensely favorable self-selection, earnings are lower. It takes several decades for their earnings to catch up with those of the native born, if it occurs at all.

There are clear patterns of racial-ethnic group differences in economic success, even though there is substantial variation in the earnings of individuals within each group. Among the U.S. immigrant groups (first- and second-generation Americans) studied here, non-Hispanic whites, Japanese, and second-generation Chinese have been the most successful, then blacks, and among the least successful are the Mexicans and Filipinos. An understanding of these differences may be important for domestic social policy as well as for immigration policy and are an important subject for future research.

In the empirical analysis it was not possible to distinguish immigrants who would be admitted under a kinship criterion, currently the primary basis for rationing immigration visas to the United States, from those who would be admitted under a productivity criterion.[43] There is a presumption, however, that a properly functioning productivity criterion would be more successful than a kinship criterion in identifying those who would have greater skills, with greater transferability to the United States, and more innate ability and work motivation relevant for this country.

Economic migrants selected under a productivity criterion are likely to have the highest earnings and easiest adjustment to U.S. labor markets—the immigrants would have highly transferable skills and would be very favorably self-selected. Their impact on the overall economic well-being of the native population is likely to be more favorable than an equal number of refugees or immigrants admitted under a kinship criterion. Immigrants admitted under a kinship criterion may have a more successful economic adjustment than refugees with the same demographic characteristics, because economic factors are likely to be more important in their migration decision and their U.S. relatives may ease the adjustment. Admitting refugees and those with relatives in the United States does satisfy other important social objectives, in

---

[43] Of the nearly 400,000 immigrants to the United States each year in the past decade, excluding those admitted under the special Cuban and Vietnamese refugee programs, nearly three-quarters have come under kinship criteria. The two "occupational preferences," in principle designed to facilitate the immigration of skilled workers and professionals, provide a maximum of 54,000 visas each year for qualifying workers and their immediate family members. Under regulations in effect in 1980, however, except for those in preferred occupations (dieticians and physical therapists with college degrees), a cumbersome and costly administrative procedure must be followed, which requires considerable effort by a prospective employer. Since workers cannot be compelled to remain with their employer-sponsor, personal ties or whether the person is currently working for the employer (legally or not) may be important in encouraging an employer to help a worker obtain a labor certificate. For the regulations on occupational preferences in effect in 1980, see "Employment of Aliens in the United States: Labor Certification Program," *Federal Register,* January 19, 1977, pt. IV, pp. 3440-3450.

particular, humanitarian considerations and, for refugees, U.S. foreign policy concerns. The current emphasis on kinship, however, makes those citizens and resident aliens with relatives in other countries, whether immediate or more remote, the greatest beneficiaries of U.S. immigration policy.

U.S. immigration policy can be expected to be based on a balancing of productivity and humanitarian considerations. The number of immigrants and the relative emphasis of these broad criteria will be determined through the political process. This should be done, however, with a more complete knowledge of the costs and benefits of the alternatives. This study has been one step in this direction.

Immigration and Religio-Ethnic Groups: A Sociological Reappraisal

Andrew M. Greeley

In a number of papers, Barry Chiswick has demonstrated the success of immigrants in contemporary America. After a relatively limited number of years, immigrants do about as well as comparable native born. The sons of immigrants seem to earn more money than do the sons of native born even after the appropriate standardizations have been applied to the data. Recently, Professor Chiswick has argued that this phenomenon seems to be worldwide for economic immigrants.[1] He suggests that the economic immigrants have been preselected both by themselves and by the receiving country, so that they have skills matching the economic needs of the receiving country.

The Chiswick analysis of the data on the United States, however, based as it is on the U.S. census, does not enable us to address directly the question of religio-ethnic groups in American society. First of all, the census does not ask a religious question (Polish Catholics and Polish Jews are combined, as are Irish Catholics and Irish Protestants). Second, the census provides information only about the foreign born and the native born of foreign parents and, hence, offers no data on the third- and fourth-generation ethnic.

There are a number of reasons for raising the question of the American religio-ethnic groups. First, they immigrated at a different time in American history, when educational qualifications did not exist for immigrants. Hence, one cannot be sure that Professor Chiswick's preselection theory could have applied to them, particularly since so many of the turn-of-the-century immigrants were landless, rural, proletarian products of the late nineteenth-century demographic revolution in eastern and southern Europe. Second, both the research of the National Immigration Commission in the first decade of the century and later the findings of the University of Chicago School of Sociology contend that the assimilation of these immigrant groups would be a difficult process

---

[1] Barry R. Chiswick, "The Economic Progress of Immigrants: Some Apparently Universal Patterns," in William Fellner, ed., *Contemporary Economic Problems 1979* (Washington, D.C.: American Enterprise Institute, 1979), reprinted in this volume.

between 1915 and 1930 and, perhaps, an impossible one. The Dillingham commission based its argument on a theory of racial inferiority.
The eastern Europeans were "inherently unstable" and the southern
Europeans were "inherently criminal." The Chicago School of Sociology
argued that the problem of the immigrant was not one of racial but of
cultural inferiority. They lacked the cultural and personality skills to
be able to cope with urban, industrial society.

American social science has not followed up seriously either of
these contentions. While no one today (presumably) would argue the
racial inferiority of Italians or Polish Catholics, the assumption of
cultural inferiority is still widespread, if implicitly, for instance, in the
blue-collar ethnic so often discussed in the national media. The Polish
and Italian jokes; the assumption, even in academic circles, that the
ethnics lag behind other groups in social and economic achievement;
and even a recent article in *Science* contending that Catholicism is a
barrier to educational achievement[2]—all would indicate that American
society is not yet fully persuaded that the "wretched refuse of the earth"
are as successful in America as some other groups.

To put the matter at a more general level, the sociological approach
to immigration still emphasizes the "social disorganization" phenomenon.
The controversy during the 1960s over the so-called war on poverty in
books, for example, by Cloward and Plivin, on the one hand, and Daniel
Patrick Moynihan, on the other, on the subject of the social disorganization of urban communities indicates that the term first introduced to
American social sciences by W. I. Thomas is still an important category
for explaining the origin of urban problems. It seems appropriate to ask
whether the categories were useful in describing the assimilation problem
of those groups for which it was first invented. Chiswick's model assumes
a relatively easy path to economic success for immigrants. The social
disorganization model presumes, explicitly in the case of W. I. Thomas
and implicitly in the case of those who still use it, that the assimilation
of immigrants is a long, difficult, and perhaps, impossible task, a task
often requiring that outside agents help to organize them in order to
compensate for their own social disorganization.

Francine Blau (reviewing work by Robert Higgs, Peter J. Hill and
Paul F. McGoulderick, and Michael B. Tanner) reanalyzed the data
collected by the immigration commission and found that one-fourth of
the difference between wages paid to Irish, French Canadian, and
eastern and south European immigrants and to natives could be

[2] Kenneth R. Hardy, "Social Origins of American Scientists and Scholars," *Science*,
vol. 185 (August 9, 1974), pp. 497-506.

attributed to labor market discrimination.[3] Neither the commission itself nor later sociological analysis considered the possibility of discrimination.

Finally, if the turn-of-the-century immigrant groups have been more or less easily assimilable, then questions must be raised about other impoverished and despised immigrants currently coming legally or illegally into the United States. Obviously, one would not want to draw a strict parallel between turn-of-the-century "disadvantaged" immigrants and contemporary ones. Yet, those who doubt that the capacity of American society to absorb today's "wretched refuse" can have no more powerful misgivings than did those turn-of-the-century observers who thought that the eastern and southern European Catholics were either racially or culturally inferior.

There are four sections to this paper. The first section presents the traditional sociological perspective on immigration; this relies to a great part on the actual words of William Isaac Thomas. While sociologists talk about social disorganization and occasionally refer to W. I. Thomas, they rarely read him and, hence, are unaware of the enormous impact he has had on their thinking and, indeed, on the thinking of many Americans who are not sociologists. Thomas's images, pictures, and theories have become part of the collective imagination of Americans and are rarely examined, either inside or outside the sociological profession.

Second, I present some cohort analysis, attempting to place in perspective the change in the educational and occupational status of the Catholic immigrant groups relative to the host population since the early years of the century. Third, I describe their contemporary educational, occupational, and income status. Finally, I investigate the possibility that, while all the various immigrant groups may eventually achieve success in America, they walk different paths to that success.

W. I. Thomas and the Theory of Social Disorganization

The Polish Peasant is a five-volume work published between 1918 and 1920.[4] The two authors described it as follows:

> The work consists of five volumes, largely documentary in their character. Volumes I and II comprise a study of the

[3] Francine D. Blau, "Immigration and Labor Earnings in Early Twentieth Century America," *Research in Population Economics,* vol. 2 (Greenwich, Conn.: JAI Press, 1980).

[4] W. I. Thomas and Florian Znaniecki, *The Polish Peasant in Europe and America: Monograph of an Immigrant Group,* 5 vols. (Boston: The Gorham Press, 1920).

161

organization of the peasant primary groups (family and community), and of the partial evolution of this system of organization under the influence of the new industrial system and of immigration to America and Germany. Volume III is the autobiography (with critical treatment) of an immigrant of peasant origin but belonging by occupation to the lower city class, and illustrates the tendency to disorganization of the individual under the conditions involved in a rapid transition from one type of social organization to another. Volume IV treats the dissolution of the primary group and the social and political reorganization and unification of peasant communities in Poland on the new ground of rational cooperation. Volume V is based on studies of the Polish immigrant in America and shows the degrees and forms of disorganization associated with a too-rapid and inadequately mediated individualization, with a sketch of the beginnings of reorganization.[5]

Volume 1 has a long and rather opaque methodological note on social disorganization, a description of peasant society in Poland, and a large collection of Polish letters intended to support (not exactly prove and not merely illustrate) the analysis. Volume 2 continues the letters (for 600 more pages) under the heading of primary group disorganization. Volume 3 is a long life history of a peasant named Waldek. Volume 4 is devoted to social disorganization and reorganization in Poland. Volume 5—our main concern—is an analysis of the "disorganization" of the Polish peasant in America, supported again by extensive case studies.[6]

Thomas was intensely interested in social problems as well as social analysis. Indeed, he rarely bothered to separate the two interests, as Morris Janowitz notes. He chose the Poles for study in part because they seemed to be the most intractable of the problem groups in Thomas's Chicago (in *Old World Traits,* Thomas describes sympathetically and with considerable wisdom why they seemed intractable to American social service agencies).

It must be understood that much of Thomas's dialogue was with the racists who dominated American intellectual life in the early years of this century and who exercised determining influence on the National Commission on Immigration (which reported that southern Italians were innate criminals and Poles innately "unstable"). Intellectual racism is so abhorrent to Americans today that we have a difficult time

[5] Herbert Blumer, *Critiques of Research in the Social Sciences,* vol. 1 (New York: Social Science Research Council, 1946), p. 3.

[6] Blumer provides an excellent critique of the methodological weaknesses and obscurities of the analysis, issues beyond our immediate focus in this paper. Ibid.

comprehending what an academic environment might be like when racism was the conventional wisdom. In his 1912 *American Journal of Sociology* article, Thomas concedes to that wisdom the possibility of racial influence and then proposes his own psychological and cultural approach:

> Without ignoring economic determinism or denying the importance of specific race characters, I have assumed that individual variation is of more importance than racial difference, and that the main factors in social change are attention, interest, stimulation, imitation, occupational differentiation, mental attitude, and accessibility to opportunity and copies. In other words, I have emphasized the social rather than the biological and economic aspects of the problem.

The basic theme of this article, which is the preprogram for the Polish peasant just as *Old World Traits* is the postscript and the summary, is that racial or national groups may appear inferior physically when in fact they are inferior culturally, either because they come from a culture that is inferior in itself, because their culture is deteriorating around them, or because their culture does not prepare them to cope with the problems that they encounter in a new set of circumstances. In *The Polish Peasant*, the latter two explanations for the problems of the Polish-American community are advanced as a response to the biological inferiority argument of the racists.

While he collected materials from other Polish communities in America and from other Polish neighborhoods in Chicago, Thomas's principal area of interest was the Polish community on the northwest side of Chicago, which originated around St. Stanislaus Kotska Church on Noble Avenue—the heart of American Polonia. Indeed, because of its size, its early beginnings, and its influence on the rest of Polish America, the community could be considered Polonia par excellence.

The situation in that neighborhood, when Thomas began his investigations, was not promising. First, the immigrants were already partially disorganized, that is, their primary group relationships and social controls were eroding. (Thomas did not note that they were the land-hungry rural proletarians who resulted from the late nineteenth-century population explosion in eastern Europe, an effect, in part of the relative peace that followed the Congress of Vienna earlier in the century.)

> The great majority of emigrants is thus recruited from those peasant and small town communities in which the contacts with the outside world are relatively numerous and the process of disorganization of the old social structure has been already

163

going on for some time, whereas the work of social reconstruction by which the peasants are made active members of the nationwide system has either only begun or has embraced only the most advanced members, who then normally abstain from emigrating. This means that, generally speaking, the Polish immigrants whom America receives belong mostly to that type of individuals who are no longer adequately controlled by tradition and have not yet been taught how to organize their lives independently of tradition. This kind of material may easily go to pieces if rational social control and encouragement are lacking, but it may also easily be shaped by proper methods into useful elements of some new social construction. It is less reliable but more adaptable than the more advanced or more conservative part of the lower classes of Polish society.[7]

Second, the Polish-American community was not able to deal with its own problem members and, indeed, ignored their existence:

No one bothers about the innumerable cases of family decay, juvenile delinquency, alcoholism, vagabondage, crime. Few know the full extent of the demoralization going on among American Poles. We expect that the study of demoralization which constitutes the second part of this volume and is based on American sources will be a painful surprise to most of the constructive elements of Polish-American society.[8]

Social Problems in Polonia. What was this demoralization that he found in Polonia? Basically, it was the inability of an individual to control his own actions:

All those attitudes which enable the individual to lead a normal social life are directly or indirectly the result of a long series of social influences which have acted upon the original stock of his temperament and fashioned it into a character, that in other words these attitudes are institutional rather than spontaneous.[9]

An individual, who, like the peasant, has been brought up as a member of a permanent and coherent primary-group and accustomed to rely for all regulation of conduct upon habit and the immediate suggestions and reactions of his social milieu is much more helpless when his milieu fails to give him stimuli sufficiently continuous, varied and coercive for socially

[7] Thomas and Znaniecki, *Polish Peasant*, pp. 6-7.
[8] Ibid., p. 54.
[9] Ibid., pp. 166-167.

normal action than an individual who, like a city intellectual, has been accustomed to be satisfied with such superficial social stimulations as can be obtained from mere acquaintances or business contacts, has been trained to foresee and to be influenced by distant and indirect social consequences of his behavior, knows how to regulate his conduct consciously in accordance with general and abstract schemes and supplements any insufficiency of present social influences by personal ideals which society has helped him to develop in the past.[10]

Nor could one expect much of the second generation, those who were born in America:

The second generation, unless brought in direct and continuous contact with better aspects of American life than those with which the immigrant community is usually acquainted, degenerates further still, both because the parents have less to give than they had received themselves in the line of social principles and emotions and because the children brought up in American cities have more freedom and less respect for their parents. The second generation is better adapted intellectually to the practical conditions of American life, but their moral horizon grows still narrower on the average and their social interests still shallower. One might expect to find fewer cases of active demoralization, of anti-social behavior, than in the first generation which has to pass through the crisis of adaptation to new conditions. And yet it is a well-known fact that even the number of crimes is proportionately much larger among the children of immigrants than among the immigrants themselves.[11]

The authors then considered five major problems of the Polish-American community. Incidentally, they never gave anything approaching an estimate of either the incidence or prevalence of the problems but hinted sometimes that they are universal (as in references to *the* Polish family) and at other times seemed to assert that they were dealing with deviant cases. (The method of the book compels them to rely on the case method so that they could understand the psychology of the people involved without ever seeing a need to establish the "representativeness of the case.")

1. *Economic independence.* The most fundamental problem facing the peasant immigrant was that the economic systems in the new country and the old were so different:

[10] Ibid., p. 167.
[11] Ibid., pp. 168-169.

The most important feature of the conditions of economic life of the Polish peasant at home as compared with those of the immigrant in this country is the high stability of the former, naturally leading to the formation of steady habits.[12]

The immigrant, unless he settles on land, finds himself suddenly without any definite and permanent social scheme for economic activities. His "job" is seldom in his old line and he can change it any time and start on something quite different. Often the work is harder and always more monotonous than what he has been used to doing, so that he is seldom if ever kept within a certain line by the attraction of the work itself. There is no security attached to any job; he may lose it from week to week and can only seldom base on its continuation any plans for the distant future. On the other hand, he is not very much afraid of losing it because he feels sure of finding something else sooner or later. He sees also that he can make debts much more easily than in the old country, both because of his increased earning power and because of the wider use of credit in American society. And these debts mean less because it is easier for him to escape the responsibility.[13]

The problem can finally be remedied when the peasant is purged of his old economic ideals and permanently incorporated into a "new, coherent and normal primary-group, Polish, or, *better* still, American."

In short, the only really efficient remedy against the economic disorganization of the immigrant when the latter is no longer susceptible to economic ideals is his complete, exclusive and permanent incorporation into a new, coherent and normal primary-group, Polish or, better still, American.[14]

2. *Break of the conjugal relation.* The values that held the Polish peasant family together in the Old World were not sustained in the New. On the contrary, the dramatic change undermined the values that might have held the *average* Polish family together.

The moral status of the average Polish-American individual or marriage-group in matters of conjugal life can be thus briefly characterized as that of a very unstable balance of temperamental attitudes and personal habits, which determines whether the traditional social schematization—now almost reduced to a mere form—will be preserved or not. As long

[12] Ibid., p. 173.
[13] Ibid., p. 174.
[14] Ibid., p. 220.

as the natural tendencies and habits of the man and of the woman work more or less in accordance with this schematization, their relation is still defined as of old, since it is easier to accept the ready and usual definition than to work out a new one. But there is no social prestige behind this definition and no higher motive which would induce the individual to accept and maintain it when it disagrees with his temperament and habits. Therefore, any cause producing disharmony between the old social schemes and the individual's natural or habitual tendencies may lead him to reject the traditional definition and either prevent him from establishing a conjugal relation where according to all the social rules it should be established or make him break a conjugal relation already existing.[15]

Again, there was no hope for the average (and here Thomas seemed to be saying that his case materials were representative) Polish family other than by replacing its values with American values, giving "the Polish-American society new ideals of family life, or helping it develop such ideals. This can only be done by its actual incorporation into American society, not merely into the American state and economic systems. . . ." [16]

3. *Murder.* Crime rates were higher in the Polish neighborhoods but not, according to Thomas, for racial reasons. Poles were not inherently unstable; rather, their instability was the result of the disorganization in which they were trapped:

The immigrant gets into contact with outsiders, with people not belonging to his family, community or even race incomparably more than he ever did, and even the members of his old community living in changed conditions and no longer constituting one coherent group often become estranged from him. His usual attitude toward this social environment is not that of mere indifference. It is essentially defensive, full of mistrust, of a vague feeling of danger, of a continual expectation of wrong or offense. Mistrust toward strangers was the habitual attitude of the peasant, developed by centuries of cultural isolation and by a subordinate social status which made the peasant community often suffer from unexpected social evils whose source it could not control. The immigrant's experiences in this country, sometimes involving exploitation, often humiliation, always full of things and happenings and human acts whose meaning he only vaguely grasps, contribute,

[15] Ibid., p. 224.
[16] Ibid., p. 270.

of course, to maintain and develop this attitude of general mistrust and his first movement is usually one of apprehension or implicit hostility. Furthermore, the nervousness brought by the unsettled conditions of life makes him easily exaggerate the slightest wrong.[17]

In such cases, an individual whose fundamental attitudes were still in accordance with an old tradition was "in a close personal relationship with another whose behavior is a product of the partly disorganized conditions of American society." Murder resulted because "for the unadapted [there] is a personal injury and a moral wrong to be tragically avenged."

4. *Vagabondage and delinquency among boys.* The young men who grew up in such a situation of little social control were ill suited for both societies:

The wild boy is in a rather hopeless position. His salvation would be in his being accepted—and forced to stay—in a social milieu above the normal which would give him better training and higher standards than those which are sufficient for the more passive or better prepared types, whereas he is either left to his former non-constructive milieu or put in a milieu below the normal.[18]

5. *Sexual immorality of girls.* The same problems appeared in a different guise for young women:

The significance of sexual immorality in girls of the second generation is perfectly obvious. Illicit sexual tendencies are simply a component—sometimes predominant, oftener subordinate— of a powerful desire for new experience and for general excitement which under the given conditions cannot be satisfied in socially permitted ways. It depends in some measure on individual temperament whether in a given case this desire for new experience will be successfully counteracted by a desire for security which tends to make the girl stay in the beaten path and follow the rules laid down by society.

The girl's problem was that she was not completely cut off from the "high life" (Thomas's words) as she would have been in Europe but did not have full access to it either:

She feels that some small part at last of this gorgeousness actually is within her reach, and her imagination pictures to

17 Ibid., pp. 276-277.
18 Ibid., pp. 316-317.

her indefinite possibilities of further advance in the future. Sooner or later, of course, she will be forced back into her destined channel by society, by the state, by economic conditions, will be forcibly "reformed" and settled, not into a satisfied, positively moral course of life but to a more or less dissatisfied acceptance of the necessary practical limitations of her desires and of the more or less superficial rules of decorum.[19]

Thus, the Polish peasant was demoralized in the New World because he was disorganized. He had no sense of responsibility and security because he had nothing to which to belong.

First, the peasant was adapted to the life of a permanent agricultural community, settled for many hundreds of years in the same locality and changing so slowly that each generation adapted itself to the changes with very little effort or abstract reflection. Secondly, the peasant was not accustomed to expect unfamiliar happenings in the course of his life within his community, and if they came relied upon his group, which not only gave him assistance, when necessary, in accordance with the principle of solidarity, but helped him regain his mental balance and recover the feeling that life in general was normal in spite of the unexpected disturbance. Further, the peasant drew all his social stimulations, checks and suggestions from direct social contact with his milieu, and the steadiness and efficiency of his life-organization depended on the continuity of his social intercourse with his own group. Finally, he was until quite recently a member of a politically and culturally passive class, did not participate consciously, even in the slightest measure, in any of the impersonal institutions that ever existed in his country.[20]

Only one solution could check demoralization, make the immigrants valuable and culturally productive members of the American society, and imperceptibly, without violence, lead to their real Americanization; that solution was to integrate them totally into American society.[21]

The power of Thomas's analysis is awesome, especially when one considers that he was articulating the first effective sociological response to the racists. Consider, for example, a quotation from Emily Balch, which is relatively benign in its racism:

[19] Ibid., p. 339.
[20] Ibid., p. 342.
[21] Ibid., p. 343.

Yet amid all these complicated variations there gradually forms in the mind of the observer what is felt to be a type, such as a composite photograph is made up by the merging of many impressions on the sensitive plate. This type, as it is shaped in my mind, is short, thick-set and stocky, rather than the reverse; not graceful nor light in motion. The face is broad, with wide-set eyes and marked cheekbones; the nose broad and chiseled or aquiline, the forehead rather lowering, the expression ranging from sullen to serene but seldom animated or genial. The eyes are of a distinctive shade, grey inclining to blue. . . . The hair, in my typical Slav, is light in childhood, though never the pure flaxen of the Scandinavian; with added years it turns to deep brown, darkening gradually through successive ashen-brown shades. The whole suggestion is of strength, trustworthiness, and a certain solidarity, until excitement or emotion lights up the naturally rather unexpressive features.

The Social Science Research Council in 1939 concluded that *The Polish Peasant* was one of the six most important social science works of the century (the others were Adolph A. Berle and Gardner Means's *The Modern Corporation,* Franz Boas's *Primitive Art,* Dickinson's *Administrative Justice,* Mill's *Behavior of Price,* and Webb's *The Great Plains*). Thomas was no more a naive "anglo-conformist" or a supporter of "assimilation" than he was a racist; he was extremely skeptical of some of the "social work" programs and movements in support of which his own volumes would later be cited.[22] If it is possible to correct Thomas's view of the immigrant poor, the reason is that we have been able to build on the intellectual foundations that he has given us. It is both anachronistic and ungrateful to blame him for not knowing what we know, since much of that would not be known unless he had prepared the way for us. If I return to W. I. Thomas, it is not to bury him, nor necessarily to praise him, but to continue the work he began.

The basic mistake in Thomas's argument, it would appear, is not that he saw pathology that was not there but that the pathology he saw was not typical. The symptoms of social disorganization can surely be found in most immigrant communities, but most of the members are not socially disorganized. Thomas saw the pathology and assumed that it would interfere with the upward mobility of the Polish immigrants. So fascinated was he by the tragedy that he did not see the nonpathology. In particular, he did not see the large numbers of people who were working industriously and urging their children to education and achievement. If asked whether the pathology was typical, Thomas would probably have responded that it was not but that it revealed much about

[22] Thomas and Znaniecki, *Polish Peasant,* vol. 5, pp. 216-217.

the community. A random sample of Polish families—and the concept of random sample was not available to Thomas—would have doubtless revealed much. Thomas's "error" was to miss the ordinary.

Cohort Analysis

This section uses the National Opinion Research Center (NORC) General Social Survey (GSS) to trace the outline of the social history of three of the Catholic ethnic immigrant groups in this century. By way of preliminary, I must say something about the NORC General Social Survey, the capacity of respondents to identify themselves ethnically, and the survival of ethnic groups in American society despite the assimilation dynamics at work in society.

Between 1972 and 1978, NORC collected data in seven different General Social Surveys. (Each General Social Survey was based on national probability samples.) Funded by the National Science Foundation, the GSS was designed to provide data on questions previously asked in survey research in order that time-series analysis might take place. The data are available to all social scientists in America. The survey cycles certain key questions every one to three years. In addition to providing material for time-series analysis, it also enables us to ask questions about minority groups that do not normally appear in sufficient numbers in the typical 1,500-respondent national survey, so that statistically safe generalizations might be made about them. Irish Catholics, for example, are little less than 5 percent of the American population. In the typical national survey, one could expect somewhere between 60 and 85 Irish Catholics. In the accumulated GSS, with more than 10,000 respondents, however, there are 500 Irish Catholics; statistically significant comparisons may be made between the Irish and other ethnic groups. Unlike the census, the GSS asks the religious question. Religioethnic analysis becomes possible with it.

Only the last two of the seven currently available General Social Surveys, however, asked the generational question. Therefore, it is impossible to replicate precisely Chiswick's technique. There are only forty-four Irish Catholics, sixty-six Slavic Catholics, and seventy-six Italian Catholics on whom we have generational information. The cohort analysis presented in the present section, however, is in some sense a substitute. Incidentally, in the General Social Survey population, 22 percent of Americans are first and second generation, and 78 percent third and fourth generation. Twenty-seven percent of Irish Catholics are first and second generation, 70 percent of Slavic Catholics, and approximately the same proportion of Italian Catholics.[23]

[23] See the appendix to this chapter for the exact wording of the questions.

171

Half of the American population are able to give a primary ethnic group background in immediate response to a survey question, more than 80 percent of first- and second-generation respondents and a little under half of third- and fourth-generation respondents. Another quarter of the population are able to choose among the various ethnic groups the primary respondent's background. The three-quarters of the American population can give, with little trouble, an explicit ethnic identification; more than 90 percent of the first and second generation, more than 80 percent of the third generation, and 66.7 percent of the members of the fourth and subsequent generations have a readily available ethnic identification.

It is often argued that ethnic identification is diminishing in America. The ethnic groups are vanishing if only because of ethnic intermarriage. Nathan Kantrowitz and Fred Wacker have argued in recent articles that this assertion merely reveals the assimilationist bias built into much of American social science. Bias turns a researchable proposition into either a preconceived assumption or a foregone conclusion in advance of the empirical data. Nor do the recent articles on ethnic intermarriage prove what the authors of such articles assert.[24] They do no more than beg the question; the question is not whether there is ethnic intermarriage but whether the offspring of the ethnic intermarriage identify simply as Americans or choose one or the other of their ancestral groups as their primary ethnic identification. The available evidence indicates that most do the latter.

Furthermore, the available evidence indicates that ethnically linked cultural traits (such as drinking behavior) are not eliminated or even notably reduced by generation in America, by education, by moving from a heavily ethnic neighborhood, or even by ethnic intermarriage. Having one Irish parent is as good (or as bad) as having two Irish parents as far as inheriting the Irish drinking culture is concerned. Similarly, having one Jewish parent is as good as having two Jewish parents in inheriting the Jewish nondrinking culture.

Finally, as Kantrowitz has vigorously pointed out in his recent paper, the indices of ethnic segregation have not notably changed in American cities during the last thirty years. People still tend to live in communities with relatively heavy concentration of their own kinds of people. Kantrowitz estimates that if blacks were white their index of similarity would descend from eighty to sixty; in large American cities, the segregation index between such relatively unempathetic ethnic groups

---

[24] See, for example, Steven Steinberg, "Ethnicity in the United States: A Sociological Perspective," *International Journal of Group Tensions*, vol. 8, nos. 3-4 (1977); and Fred R. Wacker, "Assimilation and Cultural Pluralism in American Social Thought," *Five on Forty*, 1979, pp. 25-33.

as Danes and Italians is around sixty. It is possible, of course, that ethnic groups will begin to disappear in America. The assertion that this is happening and is an inevitable process is a matter of faith and ideology, unsupported by empirical evidence.

Decisions on College Attendance. With the General Social Survey data, it is possible to reconstruct the changing social situation of the ethnic immigrant by looking at the decision about college attendance made by young people (and presumably, in many cases, by young people and parents together). This method assumes that certain decisions are made in the late teens and the early twenties of one's life. Doubtless, there are men and women who decide to attend college in the later years of life. For the overwhelming majority of Americans, the decision to go to college is made in the late teens and the early twenties. If one knows the college decision of people who are in their seventies during the 1970s, one can begin to recreate the atmosphere, the environment, the typical decisions being made by ethnic immigrant families fifty years ago.

Obviously, such reconstruction is not nearly as satisfactory as survey data collected from the Polish immigrants of the northwest side of Chicago in 1920, when Thomas and Znaniecki were studying them. Those ethnics who were born during the 1890s came to their college decision period around 1910 and shortly thereafter. In figures 1, 2, and 3, they are described as the World War I cohort. Successive cohorts born in the 1900s, the 1910s, the 1920s, the 1930s, the 1940s, and the 1950s are known respectively as the Roaring Twenties, the depression, World War II, the cold war, and the Vietnam generations. For statistical reasons, college attendance is represented in figures 1, 2, and 3 as an odds rate. This is a statistic, linear n's logarithm, whose numerator is the proportion of a given group and whose denominator is the proportion outside that category. Thus, if half of the group goes to college, the fraction is $0.5/0.5 = 1$, indicating the odds are even that a member of such group will be in college. If 25 percent of a given group chooses college, then the odds ratio is 0.33; the odds are 1 to 3 that a member of the group will have attended college. If, however, 75 percent of the members of the group chooses college, then the odds ratio is 3.0, and the odds are 3 to 1 that a member of the group will have attended college. Figures 1, 2, and 3 are drawn on logarithmic paper in order that the slope of college might be linear. In the World War I era, the odds of a typical American young person attending college were a little less than 2 to 10. Since then, the odds have risen to slightly better than 6 to 10 (about 40 percent of young Americans of college age, in fact, attended college during the 1960s).

174

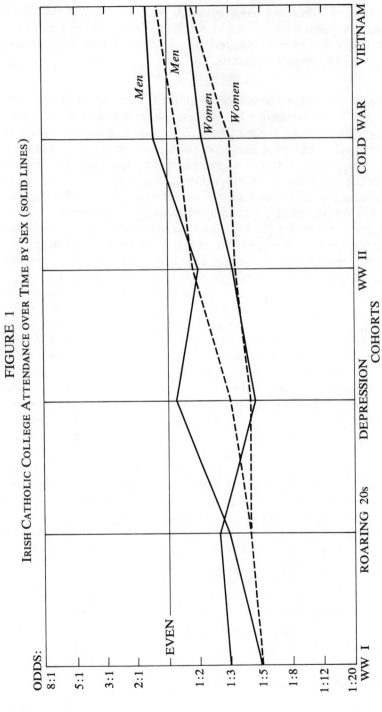

FIGURE 1
IRISH CATHOLIC COLLEGE ATTENDANCE OVER TIME BY SEX (SOLID LINES)

NOTE: The dashed trend represents the total non-Hispanic white population.

FIGURE 2

POLISH CATHOLIC COLLEGE ATTENDANCE OVER TIME BY SEX (SOLID LINES)

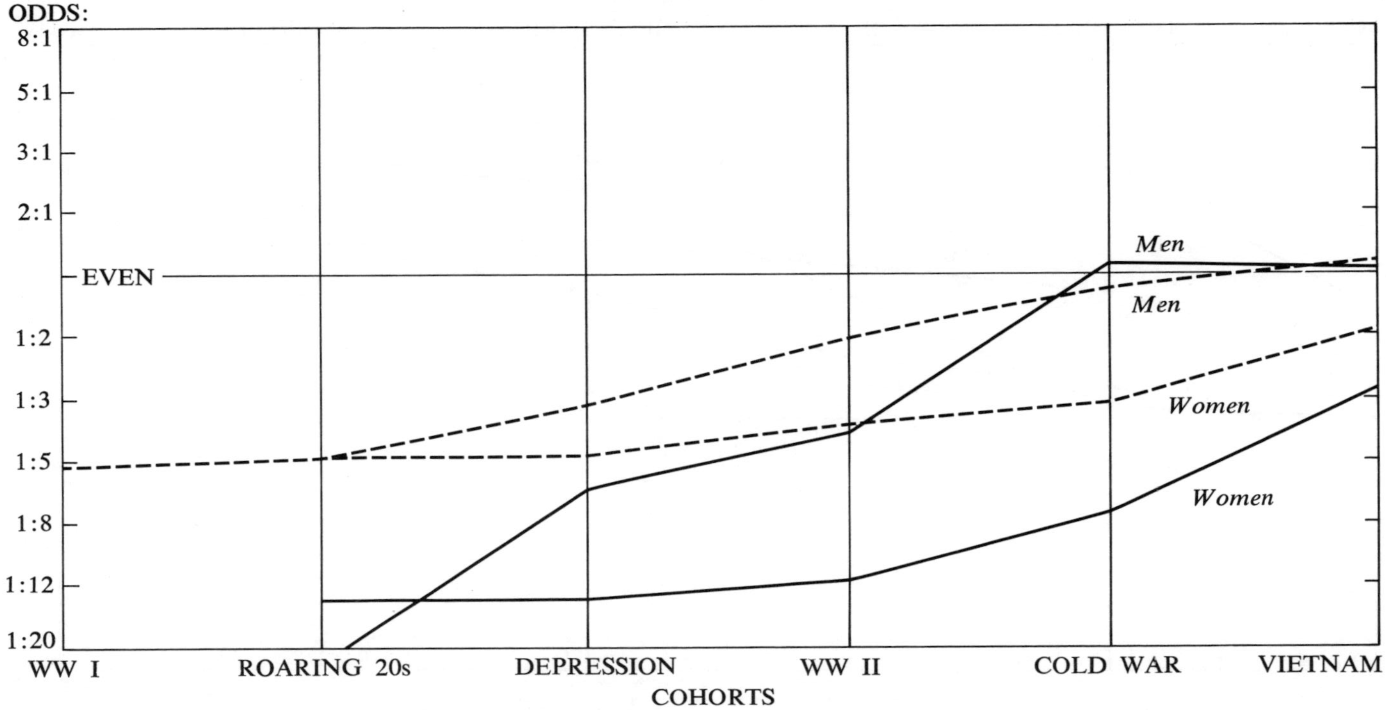

NOTE: The dashed trend represents the total non-Hispanic white population.

175

176

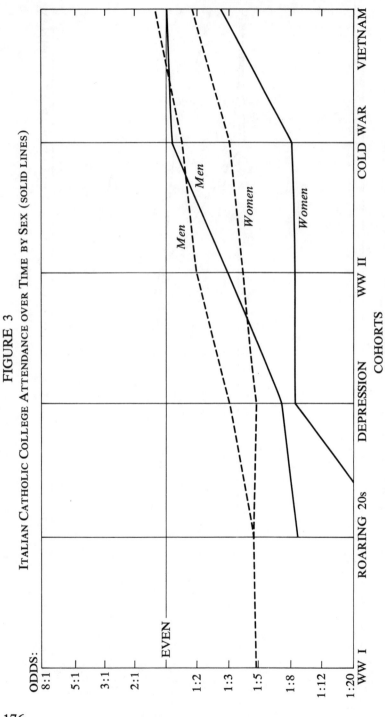

FIGURE 3

ITALIAN CATHOLIC COLLEGE ATTENDANCE OVER TIME BY SEX (SOLID LINES)

NOTE: The dashed trend represents the total non-Hispanic white population.

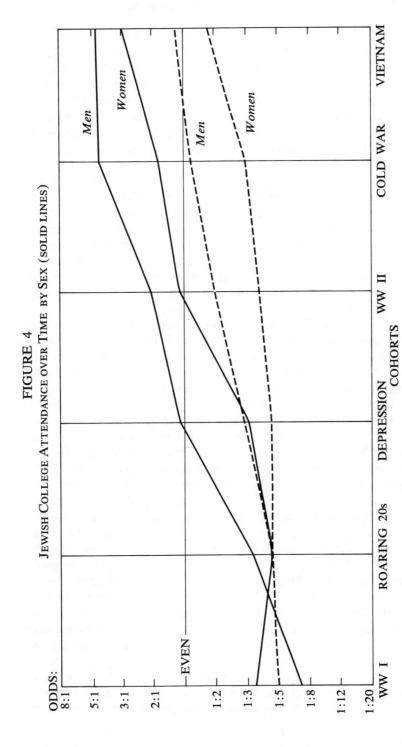

FIGURE 4

JEWISH COLLEGE ATTENDANCE OVER TIME BY SEX (SOLID LINES)

NOTE: The dashed trend represents the total non-Hispanic white population.

177

Figure 1 shows the college attendance slope for Irish Catholic men and women since the 1910s. For most of this century, Irish Catholic men and women have been either at or above the national slope in college attendance. One has to go back to the nineteenth century to find a time when Irish Catholics were less likely to attend college than comparable white Americans. If reaching the national average in college attendance is a sign of acculturation, the Irish were acculturated to American life by the beginning of the twentieth century (as were Jewish Americans).

For the Poles, however, the picture is quite different. In the 1920s, Polish college attendance increased for men but still remained substantially below the national slope. During the depression years, the Polish slope moved parallel with the ascending national slope. In the decades after World War II, however, college attendance of Polish males moved up sharply; by the 1950s, Polish men were as likely to attend college as other white American males. The college attendance ratio of Polish women moved up more slowly and converged with the national average only during the 1960s.

The Italian Catholic slope follows the same basic pattern as does the Polish Catholic slope. It is substantially below the national rate in the 1920s and 1930s, and then rapidly converges in the 1940s and 1950s. Italian Catholic women began to approach the national rate for college attendance of women only during the 1960s.

Two issues may arise in regard to this analysis: reverse migration and differential death rates. The unsuccessful ethnics of the first generation may have returned to Europe or have died early in life. There was considerable reverse migration, especially among the Italians. Furthermore, it would appear that the immigrant death rate in the Polish neighborhoods in Chicago was three times the city average. Both reverse migration and early death, however, would depress the odds of college education only among the first four cohorts. The cold war and Vietnam cohorts have so few foreign-born members that little impact could be expected on their achievements from either of these factors. Hence, the left-hand part of the slopes in figures 1, 2, and 3 might be lowered, but the right-hand end would remain virtually the same. Thus, even if one takes into account both reverse migration and higher death rates, the slopes remain significantly different from the national average.

During the nativist decade of the 1920s and the depression decade of the 1930s, then, the eastern and southern European ethnic group did not notably improve its relative position with regard to college attendance vis-à-vis the rest of America. Its slope of college attendance went up as did the slope for the rest of the country. The gap between southern and eastern European immigrant groups and the rest of the country did not notably close. In the years after World War II, however, the slope for the males from these ethnic groups turned sharply up; the difference in college attendance between the ethnic males and the other males was eliminated. The slope for women turned up somewhat less sharply, though at the present time they, too, seem to have caught up in college attendance decisions.

The striking feature of figures 1, 2, and 3 is the relatively brief period of time—fifteen years for men—required to eliminate the difference in college attendance decisions between the Poles, Italians, and other white Americans. Once the country escaped from the disastrous slump of the Great Depression, the young people born at the time *The Polish Peasant in Europe and America* was published set about disproving W. I. Thomas's brilliant theory.

We do not know how this happened. Was Thomas wrong in assuming that European immigrant traits would persist? Did he overestimate the importance of social disorganization? Did the Poles and Italians acculturate much more quickly than Thomas expected? Did they drop their "foreign" and "backward" cultural predisposition and become "Americans," even more quickly than the "Americanization" campaign of the 1920s demanded? Did the Polish peasants become achievement-oriented Protestants in the space of a generation? Is it possible that they clung to many of their Old World traits and were successful despite them? Is it possible, as Victor Green has suggested, that some of their Old World peasant traits (frugality, thrift, and industry, for example) actually facilitated their social success? It is difficult to answer any of these questions, though we do know that ethnic cultural residue has extraordinary durability; the Polish and Italian subcultures are still quite distinctive.

Further research on the social achievement of ethnic immigrants and their descendants will be required if we expect to understand the complex issues of assimilation and acculturation in American society. Minimally, however, it must be said that the southern and eastern European Catholics did move towards educational parity much more quickly than either the immigration commission or the authors of *The Polish Peasant* expected. If these groups could be successful, one surely must be skeptical about predictions that would deny the possibilities of parallel success for other groups. If there were cultural traits brought from Europe that actually facilitated their success, then American society would have to ask itself whether the national policy of Americanizing the immigrants, pursued so vigorously in the 1920s and 1930s, not only did not work but also might have been counterproductive, if it had worked. The implications of this question for our response to contemporary immigrants need hardly be detailed here.

179

Ethnic Groups and Economic Achievement

This section uses the General Social Survey data to investigate the annual income of various ethnic groups. I use dummy multiple variable regression analysis because this technique makes available tests of statistical significance. I compare the Catholic ethnic group with Protestant denominations because much of the discussion about religio-ethnicity in American society argues with some plausibility that denominational groupings for Protestants constitute subcultures comparable to the Catholic ethnic group (a parallel analysis using Protestant ethnic groups does not change appreciably the findings reported in this section). I shall also use American Methodists as the comparison group because they are both culturally a mainstream group and their annual income is virtually the same as the national average for white Americans (blacks and Hispanics are excluded from the analysis in order that the racial factor might be held constant).

Episcopalians, Presbyterians, Jews, and Irish Catholics all earn significantly more in annual income than do Methodists. Lutherans, non-denominational Protestants, other Protestants, and Baptists earn significantly less. However, both the other Protestants and the Baptists tend to be disproportionately located in rural areas or in the South, where economic advantages are less than in the North. Thus, the second column of table 1 introduces a control for region (South versus other) and size of city. The relatively disadvantaged Protestant groups continue to be significantly beneath the Methodists, but so too do the Italian and Slavic Catholics. Thus, if the eastern and southern European immigrants are compared with Methodists in terms of raw income, they both earn approximately $700 a year less than do the Methodists, but the difference is not statistically significant. However, when one takes into account the more favorable geographic distribution of these eastern and southern European Catholics, then their income does become significantly less than the comparison group.

If, however, the Protestant denominational groups are disadvantaged by reason of region, it might also be said that the Catholic groups are disadvantaged by reason of their more recent immigration to America and consequently lower level of educational background in the family of origin. In the third column of table 1, the father's education is taken into account. The Italian and Slavic Catholic once again are not significantly different from the white Methodist comparison group: the Italians are $106 a year above the Methodists; the eastern Europeans, $164 below the Methodists. Even though more than half of these two communities are first or second generation, their average

180

TABLE 1

MEAN INCOME OF CATHOLIC ETHNIC GROUPS, JEWS, AND PROTESTANT DENOMINATIONS
(Difference from mean for white Methodists, all respondents)

Group	Gross Difference (dollars)	(Significance)	Net of Region and Size of Place (dollars)	(Significance)	Father's Education (dollars)	(Significance)
Jews	4,358	(.000)	4,392	(.000)	4,491	(.000)
Episcopalians	3,724	(.000)	3,798	(.000)	2,893	(.000)
Presbyterians	3,231	(.000)	3,190	(.000)	2,846	(.000)
Irish Catholics	1,681	(.01)	1,462	(.03)	1,306	(.06)
French Catholics	454	*	247	*	517	*
Other Catholics	265	*	83	*	218	*
German Catholics	87	*	−201	*	81	*
Italian Catholics	−685	*	−935	(.011)	106	*
Slavic Catholics	−695	*	−864	(.01)	−164	*
Lutherans	−830	*	−1,117	(.02)	−672	*
Protestants without denomination	−1,131	*	−1,206	(.10)	−1,087	*
Other Protestants	−1,847	(.000)	−1,902	(.000)	−1,477	(.001)
Baptists	−2,953	(.000)	−2,416	(.000)	−1,791	(.000)

NOTE: Hispanics and blacks excluded.
* Not significant.

income is virtually the same as that of white Methodists; parental educational attainment is taken into account as well as region and city size.

The younger portion of the ethnic populations, however, might well be expected to do even better economically because they have benefited from the dramatic educational progress that the ethnic groups have made since 1945. If one, therefore, looks at respondents under forty (table 2), one sees that the three Catholic groups under consideration—the twentieth-century Italian and Slavic immigrants and the nineteenth-century Irish immigrants—all make significantly more money than do Methodists; this difference now measurable in thousands of dollars continues to be significant even after the standardization process has been applied. Standardization eliminates most of the diversity at the bottom end of the scale. Baptists and other Protestants catch up with Methodists. The advantage of the Irish, Italian, and Polish Catholics continues. Indeed, in the upper tenth of the population in income (more than $25,000 a year through the 1970s), there are slightly more Irish Catholics (6 percent) than there are Episcopalians and as many Polish and Italian Catholics (5 percent) as Presbyterians.

Chiswick's finding seems, thus, to be applicable even to the disadvantaged economic immigrants of the late nineteenth and early twentieth centuries. Members of these groups under forty do substantially better than typical white Americans in their economic achievement. One can, in other words, or, at least, one could at that time, be a severely disadvantaged economic immigrant and still look forward to a situation in which his children or his grandchildren would have as good an opportunity as anyone else to arrive at the economic elite and would on the average earn more than typical sons and daughters of the host population.

The National Immigration Commission, then, was simply wrong about the capacity of the eastern and southern European immigrants to succeed in America. While W. I. Thomas may have been right about the pathology among Polish peasant immigrants, that pathology did not prevent Polish (or Italian) achievement. One cannot, of course, make strict comparisons between 1915 and 1980. Yet one wonders if any contemporary immigrant group were as severely disadvantaged relative to the rest of the society as were the Poles that Thomas studied (with a death rate, he noted, three times that of the rest of Chicago).

The achievement of the Irish also is worth noting. A number of Irish-American writers, most notably William Shannon and Moynihan, have lamented the failure of the Irish to achieve notable success in the New World. This failure has been variously explained as the result of the alcohol problem, of the talented young men joining the priesthood, of the lack of ambition, and of the otherworldliness of the Irish Catholic

TABLE 2

MEAN INCOME OF CATHOLIC ETHNIC GROUPS, JEWS, AND PROTESTANT DENOMINATIONS
(Difference from mean for white Methodists, all respondents)

Group	Unadjusted Difference (dollars)	(Significance)	Adjusted for Size and Region (dollars)	(Significance)	Adjusted for Father's Education (dollars)	(Significance)	Adjusted for Own Education (dollars)	(Significance)
Jews	5,138	(.000)	5,071	(.000)	4,718	(.000)	3,735	(.000)
Presbyterians	4,475	(.000)	4,520	(.000)	4,275	(.000)	4,287	(.000)
Episcopalians	3,414	(.000)	3,416	(.000)	2,951	(.000)	2,511	(.000)
Irish Catholics	3,469	(.000)	3,179	(.000)	3,077	(.000)	3,022	(.000)
French Catholics	1,851	(.09)	1,997	*	1,890	*	2,334	(.05)
Italian Catholics	1,648	(.03)	1,398	(.08)	1,716	(.05)	1,892	(.03)
Slavic Catholics	1,643	(.06)	1,064	(.08)	1,159	(.07)	1,451	(.04)
German Catholics	1,515	*	965	*	945	*	946	*
Other Catholics	17	*	−123	*	67	*	646	*
Protestants without denomination	−144	*	−325	*	−250	*	114	*
Lutherans	−382	*	−747	*	−534	*	−233	*
Other Protestants	−1,200	(.02)	−1,201	(.02)	−786	*	−274	*
Baptists	−1,220	(.01)	−614	*	−100	*	−48	*

* Not significant.

183

religion. As long ago as the beginning of this century, the Irish had already exceeded the national rate of college attendance for young people of college age; present Irish Catholics under forty earn higher incomes than do Episcopalians. While the Irish were never quite as much victimized by stereotypes of prejudice as were the Poles or the Italians, their success in America was not anticipated, not even apparently by their own kind, and is still not fully believed (some authors—McCafferty and Fallows, for example—are prepared to admit the success of the Irish but argue that it has been achieved at the price of ceasing to be Irish, an assertion not supported by the evidence).

Predictions that the Irish or the Poles or the Italians would not be able to acculturate into American society were at least as systematic and as much a part of conventional wisdom as are parallel assertions about contemporary immigrant groups. It does not automatically follow, of course, that the assertions about contemporary immigrant groups are false; the economic situation in America may have changed since 1916 or even since 1945 to such an extent that it would be more difficult for despised, rejected, and stereotyped ethnic groups to succeed in our republic. If the conventional wisdom is not refuted by the evidence presented in tables 1 and 2 and in figures 1, 2, and 3, then it is at least rendered suspect. The burden of proof is on those who say that more recent immigrants cannot do what the Irish, the Italians, and the Poles did. It is not sufficient evidence merely to repeat stereotyped and bigoted assertions that were made at the end of the last century and in the first half of this century about the Catholic immigrants.

Barry Chiswick has, indeed, found evidence that Mexican immigrants have not had the same success as other immigrant groups (in his analysis of the 1970 census data). No satisfactory explanation for this difference has, however, been discovered. Some (Fernando, for example) attribute the lower achievement of Hispanic immigrants to inferior education and, in particular, the refusal of public schools to provide bilingual education (bilingual education was provided for Italian and eastern European Catholic immigrants in the parochial schools). Others (Pastora Cafferty, for example) think that the geographic proximity of Mexico makes possible a cyclic migration that impedes economic achievement. It may also be true in cyclic migration that handicapped, rural, white immigrants move back and forth from, let us say, the hills of Kentucky to cities such as Cincinnati, Detroit, and Chicago. Finally, the Mexican immigrant may be in a special way the victim of racial prejudice. At least one can say on the basis of the evidence presented in this paper, however, that one can fall back on the explanation that the Hispanic culture is somehow inferior or in some way inhibits economic achievement only when all the other explanations have failed.

The inferiority of Hispanic culture or Hispanic social "disorganization" ought not to be accepted on a priori grounds as an explanation to the condition of the "Hispanic peasant" any more than it seems relevant applied to the "Polish peasant."

Different Paths to Success

Professor Chiswick quite correctly points out in his recent paper that a rather parsimonious model is able to account for ethnic groups' success. The parsimony of the model, however, may conceivably obscure the different paths or walks by different groups as they seek success. Obviously, education facilitates more prestigious occupations; these occupations, in turn, produce greater income. Some family variables, however, may facilitate success for one group more than for others. Different occupational choices may represent alternative strategies for different groups. Thus, Christian Jacobsen and I discovered that Irish (whether Protestant or Catholic) men were more likely to choose governmental occupations than other groups, that Jews were more likely to choose professional occupations than other groups, and that Italians and Poles were more likely to choose corporate and industrial occupations.[25]

In a recent NORC study to be published shortly in a volume by William C. McCready,[26] a sample of six Chicago ethnic groups was investigated as an exploratory effort to determine whether there might be different strategies for success. White Protestant, Irish Catholic, Jewish, black, Korean, and Japanese subcultures were analyzed (table 3). Respondents' occupations and respondents' educations had a statistically significant impact on income for all educational groups, though father's education seemed to have an effect only for the three white groups; father's occupation had no independent impact for the Korean group. The fact that the respondent was married seems to have been of some importance for the Irish, Jewish, and blacks, but not for Protestants, Koreans, or Japanese. Whether a mother worked contributed to the income success of the Irish, blacks, and Japanese; the existence of a familial helping network contributed to Irish and Japanese success, but not to any of the other groups.

To look at the matter differently, white Protestants' achievement followed the standard model and was influenced by the occupation and education of the respondent, respondent's father, and spouse. Irish Catholics were influenced by three familial variables that did not affect

25 Andrew M. Greeley and Christian W. Jacobsen, "Editorial Research Note," *Ethnicity,* vol. 5, no. 1 (March 1978), pp. 1-13.
26 William C. McCready, *Ethnicity and Achievement* (Chicago: National Opinion Research Center, forthcoming).

TABLE 3

RELATIONSHIP BETWEEN INCOME AND INDEPENDENT
VARIABLES FOR SIX ETHNIC GROUPS
(beta coefficients)

	Protestant	Irish Catholic	Jewish	Black	Korean	Japanese
Respondent's occupation	.61	.45	.55	.32	.54	.49
Respondent's education	.43	.31	.35	(.16)*	.43	.35
Father's education	.38	.24	.26	(.12)	—**	—
Father's occupation	.38	—	.31	.24	—	.23
Married	—	.24	.31	.50	—	—
Spouse's education	.42	—	.38	.68	—	—
Siblings' education	—	.20	.21	(.18)	—	—
Mother worked	—	.27	—	.41	—	.20
Helping network	—	.27	—	—	—	.28
R^2	.63	.58	.61	.45	.50	.60

* These coefficients are slightly below the level at which they would be significant.
** These are not significant.

SOURCE: Data are from NORC Study 5090, *Family Life and Achievement in Six Ethnic Groups,* supported by a grant from the National Endowment for the Humanities.

the Protestants at all: siblings' education, a working mother, and the existence of a helping network. A helping network was important for the Japanese and Irish; a working mother for the blacks, Japanese, and Irish; and siblings' education for Jews. Protestants and Koreans (most of them immigrant professionals) are totally unaffected by anything other than income and education. Background variables, in other words, mean virtually nothing to the Korean and a great deal to the Irish. The fact that one is married and that one's spouse is well educated has more impact for blacks than for any other group.

TABLE 4

STANDARDIZED CORRELATIONS BETWEEN FAMILY BACKGROUND
AND GRADE POINT AVERAGE FOR ETHNIC GROUPS
(beta coefficients)

	Protestant	Jewish	Irish Catholic	Korean	Japanese	Black
Family income	.28	—	—	—	—	—
Affection	.14	.15	.18	.10	.19	.18
Democratic decision making	—	.11	.16	−.18	—	—
Number of rules for teen-agers	—	—	.21	.26	.30	.27

By way of summary, the Irish and blacks are the most influenced by family variables; the Koreans, least. The Japanese, Protestants, and Jews are somewhere in between. McCready's report is, as noted, preliminary; unfortunately, it did not include either Polish or Italian respondents. It does, however, lend some plausibility to the conclusion that there are different strategies and different paths to success for various ethnic groups.

Teen-age Academic Achievement

Similarly, there seem to be different dynamics at work in effective academic achievement of teen-age ethnics (table 4). The amount of affection in the family correlates moderately with achievement for all six groups. Family income correlates with grade point average (GPA) only for the Protestants, democratic decision making only for the Irish and Jews (and negatively for Koreans). The number of rules in the family has no impact on the GPA of Protestant or Jewish respondents and substantial impact for the other groups. The Irish, Koreans, Japanese, and blacks are able to use rules as a way of producing higher grade point averages, while the Jews and Irish are able to produce higher GPAs with democratic decision making. A Jewish family, in other words, seems to facilitate achievement among its teen-agers by being democratic, the Korean family by being authoritarian, the Irish family by blending the two principles, mixing democratic decision making with rules.

On the basis of McCready's research, some preliminary evidence suggests that, while the parsimony of Chiswick's model can account for

187

TABLE 5

INCOME FOR ETHNIC GROUP MEMBERS UNDER AGE 40
(Deviation from British and American Protestant Mean)

Group	Raw Difference (dollars)	(Significance)	Net of Region and City (dollars)	(Significance)	Net of Father's Education (dollars)	(Significance)
Jews	5550	(.000)	5240	(.000)	4546	(.000)
Irish Catholics	3527	(.000)	3527	(.000)	2715	(.004)
French Catholics	2210	(.07)	1715	—	1689	—
Italian Catholics	1893	(.02)	1494	(.04)	1520	—
German Catholics	1720	(.03)	1153	—	1064	—
Polish Catholics	1643	(.06)	1064	—	1159	—
German Protestants	406	—	62	—	62	—
Scandinavian Protestants	23	—	−621	—	−701	—
Irish Protestants	−1117	—	−980	—	−829	—

NOTE: British and American Protestant mean is $13,926.

ethnic achievement, it may mask the fact that different groups march towards achievement by different routes, though at the same pace. Social organization (opposed to social disorganization) seems to be more important for the Irish, blacks, and, to some extent, Japanese, than it is for Protestants, Jews, and Koreans. One might be tempted to hypothesize that, when the Poles and Italians can be studied in greater detail, communal support has an importance for them parallel to the Irish, Japanese, and blacks. In terms of public policy, one is inclined to suggest that attempts to undo social disorganization may be more necessary for some groups than for others, even if the social disorganization discussed by Thomas and Znaniecki did not prove a serious long-term obstacle to groups that may well have needed a helping network for adults and rules for teen-agers in order to facilitate success.

By way of summary, one can make the following observations:

1. While it is a brilliant intellectual enterprise and far superior to its racist predecessor, the Thomas and Znaniecki theory of social disorganization is not adequate as a description of the condition of the

European immigrants in the late nineteenth and early twentieth centuries. Doubtless, some social disorganization of the Thomas variety did exist among these communities as evidenced by Irish alcoholism, Polish patricide, and Italian criminality. Either the disorganization was not sufficiently widespread to impede the success of the ethnic group or the effects of the disorganization were quickly overcome.

2. To the extent that the picture of social disorganization exists in the collective preconscious of America, and particularly of American sociologists, it is an inadequate description of the story of the ethnic immigrants in the United States and an inadequate prescription for policy in response to the plight of more recent immigrants.

3. The widespread assumption of economic inferiority of Catholic ethnic groups does not stand the test of empirical evidence. That, of course, does not mean that the assumption will be abandoned.

4. Barry Chiswick's model of achievement seems to apply to disadvantaged ethnic immigrants who came to America at the end of the last century and the beginning of this one. It takes about a generation for immigrants to "catch up," whether they were migrating in 1970 or in 1870. The Irish had apparently caught up as early as 1910.

5. While the general explanation of immigrants' success, however, seems to hold for most groups (though not, unfortunately, for Mexicans), there is some possibility that different success strategies are perceived by different groups, with communal support and communal structure being less important for Jews and recent professional-class Koreans than for black or Catholic ethnics.

It is fair to say that American sociology has been remiss in acknowledging limitations on its analysis. No article on Polish-Americans has appeared in the three major sociological journals since the publication of *The Polish Peasant in Europe and America*, an astonishing phenomenon. As far as American sociology is concerned, the Poles are still poor, disorganized, and culturally inferior (and the Irish are still prone to alcoholism, although respectable members of the lower middle class). This paper is not the place for a sociological analysis of the neglect of the eastern and southern European and Irish Catholic immigrants. Nevertheless, the widespread assumption among sociologists and other Americans that Catholic ethnics have not quite measured up to American achievement standards persists. If sociology is to take seriously the study of newer immigrant groups and their adjustment to American life, it may have to correct its misconceptions about older immigrant groups.

189

Appendix

The questions used in the General Social Survey that are most pertinent to our analysis are the following:

---

30. From what countries or part of the world did your ancestors come?

IF SINGLE COUNTRY IS NAMED,
REFER TO NATIONAL CODES
BELOW, AND ENTER CODE
NUMBER IN BOXES:

IF MORE THAN ONE COUNTRY
IS NAMED, ENTER CODE
88 AND ASK A.

A. IF MORE THAN ONE COUNTRY NAMED:
Which one of these countries do you feel closer to?

IF ONE COUNTRY NAMED,
REFER TO CODES BELOW,
AND ENTER CODE NUMBER
IN BOXES:

IF CAN'T DECIDE ON ONE
COUNTRY, ENTER CODE 88.

APPENDIX TABLE 1

COUNTRY OF ORIGIN OF ANCESTORS OF RESPONDENTS, 1972–1978

Country	1972	1973	1974	1975	1976	1977	1978	All Years
Africa	137	64	92	71	57	99	68	588
Austria	14	11	7	9	11	15	6	73
Canada (French)	22	11	12	8	15	13	17	98
Canada (Other)	16	5	9	7	13	15	5	70
China	1	1	0	0	2	4	3	11
Czechoslovakia	6	22	20	24	16	18	24	130
Denmark	15	15	10	12	10	12	8	82
England and Wales	181	166	191	179	189	166	170	1242
Finland	10	13	13	11	6	12	10	75
France	29	25	36	31	27	26	31	205
Germany	223	225	249	244	225	253	249	1668
Greece	2	3	3	3	6	3	1	21
Hungary	10	12	10	10	14	12	10	78
Ireland	160	140	129	169	138	116	162	1014
Italy	77	84	64	59	93	69	64	510
Japan	0	2	3	3	2	4	1	15
Mexico	29	29	40	24	24	23	16	185
Netherlands (Dutch/Holland)	27	26	19	27	16	27	20	162
Norway	42	24	21	24	25	22	17	175
Philippines	1	1	3	1	6	4	6	22
Poland	54	39	45	32	44	34	46	294
Puerto Rico	6	7	12	13	10	9	8	65
Russia (USSR)	30	26	29	22	25	23	10	165
Scotland	33	40	37	40	43	44	37	274
Spain	6	9	6	9	6	9	6	51
Sweden	18	21	18	31	24	20	25	157
Switzerland	8	9	7	5	4	7	7	47
West Indies (Not Specified)	6	8	3	3	4	5	1	30
Other (Specify) (Remarks above)	10	8	6	2	6	10	12	54
American Indian	8	20	41	44	46	44	38	241
India	1	0	2	3	3	2	2	13
Portugal	2	7	1	3	3	6	5	27
Lithuania	4	4	2	6	10	5	4	35
Yugoslavia	4	3	3	1	4	7	5	27
Romania	3	4	1	4	4	2	0	18

(Table continues)

APPENDIX TABLE 1 (continued)

Country	1972	1973	1974	1975	1976	1977	1978	All Years
Belgium	3	2	1	4	2	2	2	16
Arabic	1	0	3	0	3	1	0	8
Other Spanish	3	8	1	4	3	4	5	28
West Indies (Non-Spanish)	1	3	4	0	3	3	3	17
America	29	91	30	44	38	26	48	306
No Answer	27	5	3	1	4	9	11	60
Not possible to code	354	311	298	303	315	345	369	2295

SOURCE: General Social Survey.

APPENDIX TABLE 2

DISTRIBUTION OF FAMILY INCOME, 1973–1978

Income Class	1972	1973	1974	1975	1976	1977	1978	All Years
Under $1,000	0	36	35	34	19	16	18	158
$ 1,000 to 2,999	0	107	109	97	101	53	72	539
$ 3,000 to 3,999	0	85	72	85	85	79	83	489
$ 4,000 to 4,999	0	83	66	72	60	53	54	388
$ 5,000 to 5,999	0	69	59	72	90	60	63	413
$ 6,000 to 6,999	0	54	67	73	66	67	68	395
$ 7,000 to 7,999	0	90	82	58	67	70	62	429
$ 8,000 to 9,999	0	153	112	133	115	114	103	730
$10,000 to 14,999	0	348	326	345	310	288	279	1896
$15,000 to 19,999	0	176	211	199	205	217	222	1230
$20,000 to 24,999	0	103	103	111	128	173	194	812
$25,000 or over	0	92	115	128	148	208	214	905
Refused	0	35	61	41	46	43	41	267
Don't Know	0	66	61	41	54	81	56	359
No Answer	0	7	5	1	5	8	3	29

NOTE: Incomes were estimated in dollars at the midpoint of each category. Incomes over $25,000 were estimated at $35,000. Since the wording of the General Social Survey question did not change as inflation depreciated the dollar, the figures cited in the text represent the average dollar income of the 1970s. The absence of an inflation deflator is a problem for our analysis only if one assumes that Poles would be less likely to be affected by inflation than other American groups.
SOURCE: General Social Survey.

Twentieth-Century Mexican Migration to the United States

Walter Fogel

This examination of Mexican migration is divided into several sections. The first presents the migration record of this century, by dividing Mexican migration into three distinct periods. The next part examines the forces that were, and are, behind the migration and offers a politico-economic interpretation of it. The third section develops the uniqueness of the contemporary period of migration from Mexico, and the fourth identifies some quantitative influences on current migration. The final section looks at the economic experience of Mexican immigrants and the generational progress of Mexican-Americans in the context of immigration impacts on the United States.

This paper suggests that contemporary migration from Mexico, especially unsanctioned migration, is having important, and unfortunate, effects on U.S. population size and on low-skilled labor markets. Various motives are sometimes imputed to those who write about immigration; my concern about Mexican migration has to do simply with its economic and population impacts and has nothing to do with a desire for racial or ethnic restriction of immigrants. Elsewhere, I have argued for a large increase in authorized immigration from Mexico, along with an end to unsanctioned migration.[1] These views are entirely consistent with a critical assessment of contemporary Mexican migration.

The Record in Brief

The Mexican-American (this term is used interchangeably with Chicano) population of the United States, like all population groups other than American Indians, is a product of migration—migration sanctioned by this country's immigration laws and regulations and also that outside those laws and regulations. While the territories that were transferred from Mexico to the United States by the treaty of Guadalupe Hidalgo in 1848 included Mexican citizens, their numbers were small—on the

---

[1] Walter Fogel, "United States Immigration Policy in an Era of Unsanctioned Migration," *Industrial and Labor Relations Review*, vol. 33, no. 3 (April 1980).

order of 75,000–100,000.[2] Thus, it has been migration between the two countries, rather than the natural increases of an indigenous population, that has produced the 8 to 10 million Mexican-heritage persons who live in the United States today.

The First Migration: 1900–1930. Some numbers would help to provide precision to the story of both early and later Mexican migration. Numbers are available, but they refer to only part of the actual migration. The numbers available refer to recorded immigration, that sanctioned under U.S. immigration law. Unrecorded and unsanctioned entry has been a large component of Mexican migration, frequently the largest component, since the existing border between the two nations was established, near the middle of the nineteenth century. Port-of-entry stations were not set up on the Mexican border until 1894, and no attempt was made to record Mexican entrants until 1908.[3] Complete recording of the Mexicans who immigrated through ports-of-entry probably did not occur until the visa control system was applied in 1925. Unsanctioned migration, with fraudulent documents or outside authorized entry stations, continued after that date to the present.

It is evident, then, that government immigration statistics greatly understate migration from Mexico and that their usefulness is largely confined to indicating the relative strength of migration forces at different periods of time. Counts of illegal alien apprehensions and contract laborers, as well as verbal assessments, help to flesh out the total picture but certainly not in a precise manner.

Migration from Mexico began rather slowly, at least in comparison with immigration from Europe. By the turn of the century, there were approximately 100,000 Mexican-born persons living in the United States, nearly three-quarters of them in south Texas near the Mexico-U.S. border.[4] The volume of Mexican migration began to increase prior to the end of the century, with the economic development of the southwestern states. The farming, mining, and construction industries in the border states employed Mexican workers for backbreaking, but unskilled, kinds of work. The completion of railroads that linked the interior of Mexico, where most of its people lived, with the United States, was fundamentally important to the expanded use of Mexican labor after 1890.[5] These

[2] Arthur F. Corwin, *Immigrants—and Immigrants* (Westport, Conn.: Greenwood Press, 1978), pp. 31-34.

[3] Ibid., p. 30.

[4] Ibid., p. 35.

[5] Leo Grebler, *Mexican Immigration to the United States: The Record and Its Implications* (Los Angeles: Mexican American Study Project, University of California, 1966), p. 19; and Victor S. Clark, "Mexican Labor in the United States," *Bulletin of the Department of Labor,* vol. 78 (September 1980), pp. 470-474.

railroads were used by Mexican laborers to reach American recruiters for farms and mines located near the border and were used by U.S. railroad employers to bring Mexican laborers to railroad construction and maintenance sites throughout the western United States. Tens of thousands of workers were sent to these sites during the early 1900s; the railroad employer practice of "lending" surplus workers to growers introduced the use of Mexican labor for agricultural work in many of the nonborder states.[6]

Coupling the available immigration statistics with historical accounts makes it evident that the pace of Mexican migration increased during the second decade of the twentieth century. Some of the increases, during the early part of that decade, were associated with the Mexican revolution, but the more important factor was a strong demand for labor in the United States, especially after World War I began and immigration from Europe was curtailed. Waiver of the $8.00 head tax and literacy requirements of the 1917 immigration control legislation facilitated the immigration of Mexican workers. Seventy-two thousand Mexican contract laborers were also brought in for emergency agricultural and railroad employment after 1917.[7]

The 1920s, however, saw a sharp rise in Mexican migration and provided a period of predecessor experience for contemporary migration. Sanctioned immigration during the decade was nearly half a million (table 1) and the unsanctioned variety was probably even larger.[8] Employment of Mexicans in northern manufacturing industries, which began in World War I, was enlarged; these industries included automobiles, steel, meatpacking, and fertilizers, as well as a number of agriculturally related food-processing activities.

Although Mexican workers were occasionally used as strikebreakers and for other labor divisive purposes, their principal function in the 1920s was to provide unskilled labor for economic growth. European immigration in the decade fell to 2.5 million from 4.3 million in the prior ten years and 8.1 million in the first decade of the century.[9] Mexicans, along with blacks from the South and Canadian immigrants,[10] helped to replace the European labor supplies. The Mexican contribution to their replacement was somewhat less direct than that of the other two groups,

---

[6] Clark, "Mexican Labor," p. 476; N. Roy and Gladys Gilmore, "Bracero in California," *Pacific Historical Review,* vol. 32 (August 1963), p. 268.

[7] Corwin, *Immigrants,* p. 180.

[8] Robert N. McLean, "Tightening the Mexican Border," *Survey,* vol. 54, no. 1 (April 1, 1930), p. 28. See also Manuel Gamio, *Mexican Immigration to the United States* (Chicago: University of Chicago Press, 1930).

[9] U.S. Immigration and Naturalization Service, *Annual Report 1976,* p. 87.

[10] Immigration from Canada rose from 180,000 in 1901-1910, to 742,000 in 1911-1920, and 925,000 in 1921-1930. Ibid.

TABLE 1
MEXICAN IMMIGRANTS TO THE UNITED STATES, 1900–1977

Fiscal Year	Mexican Immigrants
1900–1909	49,600
1910–1914	82,600
1915–1919	91,100
1920–1924	249,200
1925–1929	238,500
1930–1934	19,200
1935–1939	8,700
1940–1944	16,500
1945–1949	37,700
1950–1954	78,700
1955–1959	214,700
1960–1964	217,800
1965–1969	213,800
1970–1977	301,300
1970	44,500
1971	50,300
1972	64,200
1973	70,400
1974	71,900
1975	62,200
1976	58,400
1977	44,600

SOURCE: U.S. Immigration and Naturalization Service, *Annual Reports.*

since it was less frequently directed to the northern industrial centers that had been the destinations of many European immigrants.

The dominance on both sides of the border of economic motives for Mexican migration was vividly demonstrated by the Great Depression, which not only shut down the migration but also reversed it to the extent that perhaps half a million Mexicans were repatriated during the 1930s. Much of the movement back to Mexico was a voluntary response to economic malaise in the United States, but some of it was certainly coerced, either by local authorities or by a more general, depression-induced increase in racist sentiment toward Mexican workers.[11] The Great Depression reversed the direction of Mexican migration flows and, by doing so, also prevented the testing of U.S. control over immigration

[11] Abraham Hoffman, *Unwanted Mexican Americans in the Great Depression: Repatriation Pressures 1929-1939* (Tucson: University of Arizona Press, 1974).

from Mexico. In the late 1920s, the U.S. Department of State tightened its administrative controls over the issuance of immigrant visas to Mexicans, an alternative that the department greatly preferred to a congressionally threatened quota for Mexican immigration. Whether these controls could also have been applied to unsanctioned immigration seems doubtful in view of more recent experience. If experience on this matter could have been obtained, in the 1930s the United States might have been able to develop a policy for control of Mexican migration that would have avoided our current dilemma. The experience was not obtained, however, since the depression that began in 1929 and World War II made migration controls moot for the next fifteen years.

U.S. experience with Mexican migration in the first third of this century suggested that Mexicans constituted a highly flexible reserve of unskilled labor, one that would expand rapidly as the U.S. demand for labor increased, with or without the sanction of U.S. immigration law, and could be shrunk by return migration to Mexico when business conditions became slack. The latter attribution was only partially accurate; to the extent that it was accepted, it made Mexicans ideal labor reserves because it meant that they made relatively small demands upon community housing and public services. In brief, Mexican workers came to be regárded largely, if not completely, as a commodity, responsive to the labor demand of U.S. employers and without significant noneconomic needs of their own. These views dominated the de facto policy of the United States toward Mexican migration for the next forty years; their shortsightedness has only recently become apparent.

The Second and Third Migrations. The second period of migration from Mexico began with a wartime emergency contract labor program in 1942. That program was formalized and was extended by Congress, as the Bracero Program, through 1964, when it no longer had majority political support in the United States. At its peak, the Bracero Program brought over 400,000 Mexican laborers a year to U.S. growers (table 2). Following the previously established pattern, unsanctioned migration rose nearly hand in hand with authorized migration; in the early 1950s, the number of unsanctioned migrants began to exceed the number of laborers brought in under contract protection. This threatened the continuation of the contract program, produced public alarm, and, in 1954, brought about the apprehension and return to Mexico of over a million illegal entrants. With the help of Mexican authorities, the border was then secured against unlawful entry for the next ten years.[12] An expansion of the bracero program was permitted following the crackdown on un-

12 Corwin, *Immigrants,* p. 196.

TABLE 2
CONTRACT FARM LABORERS FROM MEXICO, 1943–1965

Year	Contract Laborers
1943	52,100
1944	62,200
1945	49,500
1946	32,000
1947	19,600
1948	35,300
1949	107,000
1950	67,500
1951	192,000
1952	197,100
1953	201,400
1954	309,000
1955	398,700
1956	445,200
1957	436,000
1958	432,900
1959	437,600
1960	315,800
1961	291,400
1962	195,000
1963	186,900
1964	177,700
1965	20,300

SOURCE: Leo Grebler, *Mexican Immigration to the United States,* Mexican American Study Project, p. 60.

sanctioned migrants; many workers who had been expelled from the country were able to reenter as contract laborers. Others were able to qualify for permanent immigration status under the sponsorship of American growers.[13]

Between 1954 and 1965, nearly all migration of workers and other persons from Mexico was sanctioned, either as permanent, lawful immigrants (at a rate of about 40,000 a year) or as contract laborers (at an annual average for the period of 300,000). The apparent control that existed over unlawful entry in this period is somewhat of an enigma because of both the prior history of this kind of entry and, especially, the subsequent great waves of illegal entry that have continued to the present.

[13] Ibid., p. 54.

TABLE 3
MEXICAN ILLEGAL ALIENS APPREHENDED, 1965–1978

Fiscal Year	Apprehensions
1965	55,300
1966	89,800
1967	108,300
1968	151,700
1969	201,600
1970	265,500
1971	348,200
1972	430,200
1973	576,800
1974	710,000
1975	680,000
1976	781,000
1977	954,800
1978	976,700

SOURCE: U.S. Immigration and Naturalization Service, *Annual Reports.*

This period of sanctioned migration ended in 1965 with the expiration of the Bracero Program. Apprehension of unsanctioned Mexican aliens rose rapidly from 55,000 in 1965 to 265,000 in 1970 and to over 1 million by the end of the 1970s (table 3).[14] The loss of Mexican contract workers to U.S. growers set off illegal migration in the 1960s; a strong U.S. demand for labor in the latter half of that decade (the national unemployment rate for the years 1966–1969 averaged 3.7 percent of the labor force) greatly increased its size. These events are not sufficient to provide a full understanding of contemporary migration from Mexico—that began in 1965 and should be considered as the third period of great Mexican migration in this century. A more complete analysis will be developed in the next section.

Although the unsanctioned variety dominates contemporary Mexican migration, there has also been a substantial amount of lawful immigration. Mexican immigration was 214,000 during the last five years of the 1960s and was 475,000, or nearly 60,000 a year, during the first eight years of the 1970s.[15] When the data become available, they will show that more Mexicans legally immigrated to the United States during the 1970s than in any prior decade, notwithstanding the 20,000 limita-

[14] U.S. Immigration and Naturalization Service, *Annual Report,* various years.
[15] Ibid.

tion for preference immigration placed on Mexico and all other Western Hemisphere countries in 1977.[16] Since the passage of the immigration amendments in 1965, more people have immigrated from Mexico than from any other country. Fifteen percent of all immigrants to the United States during the 1970s came from that nation.

Migration of Labor

The migration of Mexicans to the United States during the twentieth century is not difficult to explain. It has been an economic phenomenon, operating through labor demand within more or less competitive labor markets in the United States. Mexican workers have quickly responded as economic men and women to any indications that jobs were available to them; the pay that they could earn in the United States was many times greater than the sums that they received for subsistence farming, hired farm work, or other kinds of low-skilled employment in Mexico. With wages on the order of seven to ten times higher in the United States than in Mexico throughout the century, an extremely strong motive force for migration has existed and has produced actual migration whenever U.S. employers have beckoned.

Labor market incentives do not distinguish between sanctioned and unsanctioned migration. Therefore, unless statutory limitations on immigration are implemented and enforced in some fashion, we should expect to see both kinds operate. This has, indeed, been the case with respect to migration from Mexico. Throughout the twentieth century, with the single exception of the period 1954–1965, unsanctioned migration from Mexico has been at least as important as that authorized by immigration law and regulations. Weak, often half-hearted, attempts at immigration enforcement have not been able to deflect the powerful market incentives: cheap labor as seen by U.S. employers and high wages as seen by Mexican workers. These parties have managed to get together, with or without the imprimatur of legality.

The historical record makes evident that the availability of high-wage jobs in the United States has been the key element in Mexican migration. Whenever Mexican workers have received notice that they were wanted, they have responded in large numbers: from the first years of the twentieth century through the 1920s, again during and

16 The 20,000 limit does not apply to the admission of immediate relatives of U.S. citizens. Admission of immediate relatives from Mexico is now running at about 20,000-25,000 a year.

after World War II, and, most recently, from the mid-1960s to the present.

This does not mean that so-called push forces from Mexico have been unimportant. Poverty and underemployment in Mexico are conditions from which many workers have obviously wanted to escape, but escape is not possible until there is someplace to escape to. The United States at various times has put out a call for Mexican workers. Poverty in Mexico has meant that an ever-ready pool of labor has been available south of the border, waiting to be tapped; it is clear that U.S. economic agents, largely employers, have decided when that pool would be tapped. In other words, Mexican migration, at least until recently, has not been a case of workers and their families unilaterally overriding U.S. border and immigration control in order to escape impoverishment in Mexico. There has been a great deal of encouragement from the American side.

Recruitment by private U.S. employers has been the chief mechanism for initiating the migration flows. Employers have gone to the border themselves or have solicited labor contractors; they have always been successful in attracting supplies of Mexican labor.[17] Employers have occasionally been aided by the federal government, most notably, through the contract labor programs of World Wars I and II; government assistance has been at the request of private employers, usually growers, rather than independent of them. Consequently, it is not an exaggeration to say that in this century U.S. employers have been in control of de facto policy for immigration from Mexico.

The Political Economy of the Migration. While employer recruitment has initiated all three of the great waves of Mexican migration, it has not been able to regulate the flow satisfactorily once the migration has begun. Understandably, little direct recruitment is necessary to propel large-scale migration from low- to high-income areas. On the contrary, once descriptions of high-paying jobs are sent back by early migrants, the migration develops its own momentum and can exceed the employment and housing capacities of markets in the areas of destination.[18] When Mexican migration has produced excess supplies of labor, either by itself or in combination with U.S. recessionary shifts in labor demand, government, both federal and local, has stepped in to halt or reverse

---

[17] Corwin, *Immigrants*, pp. 50, 51, 54, 179.

[18] See Walter Fogel, *The Negro in the Meat Industry* (Philadelphia: Wharton School of Finance and Commerce, University of Pennsylvania, 1970), chap. 3; and Michael J. Piore, *Birds of Passage: Migrant Labor and Industrial Societies* (New York: Cambridge University Press, 1979), p. 19.

the flow. Qualitative controls over immigration and repatriation efforts did the job in the Great Depression; the border patrol and an expanded bracero program did it in the mid-1950s. The U.S. government has not been able to halt contemporary migration. International as well as domestic political considerations have made unacceptable the methods that worked earlier; effective alternatives have not been developed. There is, however, strong public sentiment for the government to reduce and control the existing flows; steps to accomplish these ends will eventually be taken, perhaps in a period of sharp recession.

Mexican migration is accurately characterized as a part of the U.S. market-oriented economy. Mexican labor has always been waiting to be called. Once called, the large wage differential between the two countries has done the rest; the market system has worked by moving labor from a low- to a high-valued use. The market has worked—producing beneficent results—only in the limited sense of moving labor. While this has been important for increases in economic output, it has not been the entire story by any means. From a politicoeconomic perspective, market-directed Mexican migration has not worked nearly as well.

In the first place, as noted, the volume of Mexican migration has placed great strain on labor market absorptive capacity, evidenced by local unemployment and downward pressure on wage rates. Although hard evidence on this point is difficult to produce, theory, observation, and the protests of labor groups all suggest that, at times, Mexican migration has lowered unskilled wage rates and has exacerbated local unemployment.[19]

Theoretically, competitive labor markets are supposed to employ migrants by means of the market mechanism of a falling wage, with an equilibrium of wages and mobility established when wages in the receiving area have fallen sufficiently to become more or less equal to wages in the sending area. It is apparent that U.S. labor markets have not always absorbed Mexican migrants in this classical manner and that, if they had been able to do so, the resultant wage for unskilled workers would have been seen as unacceptably low by a considerable segment of U.S. citizens. Wage differentials between Mexico and the United States have been so large that large numbers of people would have had to migrate to the United States to remove them.

Actual U.S. labor markets have always had some short-run rigidities. When dealing with large-scale Mexican migration, they have pro-

[19] See Walter Fogel, *Mexican Illegal Alien Workers in the United States* (Los Angeles: Institute of Industrial Relations, University of California, 1978), chaps. 6 and 7. It is certainly incorrect, however, to blame cyclical U.S. unemployment on Mexican migration.

duced a combination of rising unemployment and downward pressure on low-skilled wages. These effects, while quite mild compared to those that would accompany the equalization of unskilled wages between the two nations, have always become unacceptable to many U.S. citizens and officials well before any significant narrowing of wage differentials between the two countries has taken place. It is true that these unacceptable market impacts have been confined largely to periods of slow or nonexistent economic growth in the United States, but such periods are a part of the political-economic realities of this country, even if they tend to be of shorter duration than periods of strong growth.

Thus, the market system has been able to initiate the migration of needed Mexican labor, but it has not been able to keep the flow at a level acceptable to important segments of the U.S. community. Indeed, it could not possibly have done so, given the size of the wage disparities between the two countries. Periodic political sentiment for reversal of the migration flows has resulted. That fact belies one major argument for letting the market freely attract Mexican workers—the argument, always put forward by employers and their advocates, that these workers are like homing pigeons and, when there is no longer any work for them (as a result of either seasonal or cyclical shifts in the demand for labor), they return to Mexico.[20] This assertion has been inaccurate in the sense that many Mexican migrants, quite understandably, have become permanent residents of the United States, immovable by economic recession. Even those who have returned to Mexico after labor demand shifts frequently have been induced to do so by government authority or other nonmarket influences (including racism), rather than by a voluntary response to changed market conditions. Free markets have many virtues; in order to preserve them, it is best not to assert too much about their ability to affect human behavior in the best interests of the societies which they serve.

The market has also been inadequate as a regulator of Mexican migration because it has not taken into account impacts that occur outside the labor market, the so-called externalities. Mexican migrants have not been simply workers. They also invest in and consume housing and other durables, consume private and public outputs, add to population concentrations, provide cultural variety, and affect sociopolitical behavior. Their collective external impacts have been both positive and negative for the general welfare in the United States; I do not know how the net effects can possibly be assessed. Despite the assessment complexities, it is becoming increasingly apparent that, in an era of concern about popu-

[20] Corwin, *Immigrants,* pp. 137, 138, 143, 146.

lation and environmental limits, the U.S. populace is no longer willing to trust the market mechanism to bring about a salutary balance of Mexican migration impacts that are external to the market itself.[21] Market forces may still dominate Mexican migration by default because the externalities of that migration, including U.S.-Mexico governmental relations, are so complex. That result is not assured by any means, however.

Contemporary Migration

Twentieth-century Mexican migration is essentially a response to labor-market demand in the United States. This demand easily pulled in underemployed, largely surplus workers from Mexico. When the migration became politically unacceptable in the United States, it was halted and reversed, chiefly by government apprehension and removal of aliens who were unlawfully in the country but also by voluntary migrant returns to Mexico, especially in the Great Depression.

There are indications, however, that the contemporary wave of migration from Mexico, which began in 1965, does not fit this characterization quite so well as the two earlier migration periods. The obvious difference is that contemporary migration apparently cannot be stopped, at least without major new enforcement legislation. Contemporary migration from Mexico also appears to be larger in size than in the earlier periods, at least the unsanctioned component. These two differences suggest a third possibility—that the current migration may not be as much of a U.S. labor-market phenomenon and, thus, may not be as sensitive to shifts in the U.S. demand for labor as previously.

Differences between contemporary and earlier migrations from Mexico are likely because of changes within both Mexico and the United States. It is important to discuss these changes in some detail, not because they have fundamentally altered the nature of Mexican migration, but because they have greatly increased the importance and potential impact of Mexican migration on the United States.

Mexican Population Size and Location. The population of Mexico grew relatively slowly in this century, from 15 million in 1910 to 17 million in 1930 and 25 million in 1950.[22] Thus, the migrations of the 1920s and 1950s were from rather small population bases, at least in comparison

---

[21] For a description of some of the externalities associated with guest workers in Western Europe, see Stephen Castles and Godula Kosack, *Immigrant Workers and Class Structure in Western Europe* (Oxford: Oxford University Press, 1973).

[22] México, Dirección general de estadística, *Anuario estadístico de los Estados Unidos Mexicanos,* 1972-1974 (Mexico City, 1978).

with the United States. The U.S. population was seven times that of Mexico in 1920 and six times larger in 1950. Today, the population of Mexico is approximately 70 million, nearly three times as large as it was in 1950, and growing rapidly. Its population is projected to be at least 126 million by the year 2000, an estimate that takes into account some degree of success for its recent measures aimed at population control.[23] Mexico's population is nearly one-third that of the United States; by the end of this century, it may be almost one-half.

As an oversimplification for illustration purposes, if potential migration from Mexico is a constant function of the U.S.-Mexico wage differential and of the size of the underemployed labor force of the latter country, it is evident that this migration potential is much greater than during the 1950s; it will become substantially greater by the century's end. Implicit in this analysis is an assumption that the size of the underemployed labor force in Mexico will grow at least as rapidly as the total population. Barring rapid, job-creating economic growth, this is a safe assumption. The greatest population growth will be among the fifteen-to-thirty age group; increased female participation will further swell labor force size.[24] It is not impossible, of course, that Mexican economic development in the years ahead can absorb some of the surplus work force and thereby reduce the migration potential. No one familiar with the Mexican scene expects that to occur in this century, however, despite the rapid development of energy resources in that nation.[25]

The population of Mexico's six states that border the United States has also grown rapidly, from about 2 million in 1930 to nearly 8 million in 1970.[26] Most of this increase has been in cities immediately adjacent to the border. Between 1940 and 1974, Ciudad Juárez (opposite El Paso) grew from 55,000 to 650,000 people, Mexicali (opposite Imperial County, California) from 45,000 to 400,000, and Tijuana (opposite San Diego) from 25,000 to 750,000.[27] These extremely rapid population changes are indicative of the increasing economic integration of the U.S. and Mexico border economies. The integration includes joint manufacturing processes, with labor-intensive production carried

23 México, Dirección general de estadística, *Evaluación y Análisis*, no. 8, April 1978, pp. 54-63; and U.S. Department of Justice, Interagency Task Force on Immigration Policy, *Staff Report*, 1979, p. 222.

24 U.S. Department of Justice, Interagency Task Force on Immigration Policy, *Staff Report*, pp. 224-229.

25 See Dilmus D. James and John S. Evans, "Increasing Productive Employment in Mexico: Policy Options and Their Compatibility with Past Policies" (Paper presented to the North American Economics Association, Dallas, April 1977).

26 Corwin, *Immigrants*, pp. 118, 126.

27 Ibid., p. 68.

out in Mexico; daily commuting of 60,000–80,000 Mexican workers to employment in the United States; sizable retail sales to aliens on both sides of the border; and use of the Mexican cities to launch attempts at illegal entry to the United States. These activities and the sheer size of these border cities suggest that there has been an enhancement of potential migration from Mexico that goes beyond that produced by sheer population increase alone.

Potential migration has probably increased, as well, from greater knowledge within Mexico of life in the United States and from the higher material and other expectations of many Mexican workers, derived from their increased schooling and other aspects of modernity.[28] On the first point, the number of television receivers in Mexico grew from 1.2 to 4.9 million between 1965 and 1974;[29] many of the television programs viewed in Mexico are produced in the United States.

In sum, contemporary migration from Mexico occurs from a much larger population base and from a greater average propensity to migrate than existed in earlier migrations. Consequently, potential migration from Mexico is much larger than it was and is growing rapidly.

The U.S. Mexican-American Population. The Mexican-American population of the United States in 1920, at the time of the first substantial migration from Mexico, was about 1 million. It was under 3 million in 1950, near the period of the second migration. Five to 6 million Mexican Americans lived in the United States in 1970 and it is likely that 8 to 10 million are here today.[30]

If earlier migrations from Mexico were constrained by the alien culture of the United States, that is, by what have been called the psychic costs of adjustment, this kind of constraint is certainly less powerful now. The size and distribution of the Mexican-American (and other Hispanic) populations in the United States make it likely that the Mexican migrant will be able to find, and settle among, people who speak the same language and share the same culture. How important this is cannot be determined, but it must provide some facilitation for migration, not only because it eases psychic adjustment, but also because it reduces search costs for jobs, housing, and the other necessities of life.

Furthermore, it seems likely that the large size of the Mexican-American population has led to an increase in the proportion of Mexican

[28] Ibid., p. 59.
[29] U.S. Department of Justice, Interagency Task Force on Immigration Policy, *Staff Report,* p. 233.
[30] The 1920-1970 figures are based on data from the U.S. Bureau of the Census, *Census of Population,* various years, and include rough adjustments for census undercounts. The current figure is my own estimate.

migration that is permanent rather than temporary. Michael Piore has written that migration, at least in its early stages, tends to be temporary because migrants have difficulty developing social relationships in their new locations when they come from a culture differing from that of the host society.[31] As the size of the migrant group increases, its members have greater opportunities for intragroup social activities; they no longer find it necessary to return home to meet their social needs. The existence of sizable enclaves of Mexican-Americans in all medium- and large-sized cities of the Southwest, and in many cities in the rest of the country as well, eases the social and economic adjustment of migrants and reduces the likelihood that they will return to Mexico. Many still do return to Mexico seasonally or after short stays in the United States, but the proportion that does so is probably less than in earlier migrations.

Another factor operating to increase both Mexican migration and the proportion of permanent settlers is the fact that most Mexican migrants, whether sanctioned or unsanctioned, are obtaining employment in nonagricultural jobs—something not true in earlier migration periods. Reliable data on this point are not available, but it is estimated that less than 20 percent of the illegal Mexican aliens in the United States are employed in agriculture.[32] The availability of nonfarm jobs increases employment opportunities for migrants and, consequently, the rate of migration; it also increases the likelihood that the migration will be permanent since nonfarm jobs are less subject to seasonal fluctuations in employment than jobs in the farm sector.

The larger size of the Mexican-American population and the wider availability of jobs have made the migration decision for a resident of Mexico substantially similar to that of a U.S. resident who is contemplating a move from one part of the country to another. The Mexican resident probably has as much job information and can anticipate as much support from a social community as the U.S. resident. I do not want to draw this parallel too far because the psychic costs of adjustment must still be greater for the Mexican resident since he presumably has less familiarity with U.S. institutions, such as schools. Where sanctioned immigration is not possible, a major difference in the decision process may exist. The point remains, however, that, for the Mexican migrant, the United States has become much less of an alien place.

Supply-Driven Migration. Mexican migration is larger and involves more permanent settlers than formerly because of population and knowledge changes in both Mexico and the United States. It seems

[31] Piore, *Birds of Passage,* p. 233.
[32] Fogel, *Mexican Illegal Alien Workers,* pp. 85-86.

likely, also, that the current migration flows are less controlled by the U.S. demand for labor than in earlier periods of migration. The historical sketch presented in this paper shows that Mexican migration has been a response to U.S. labor market demand. The contemporary migration, beginning in the mid-1960s, was also set off by job vacancies in the United States. Undoubtedly, it will continue to be influenced by discrete shifts in the U.S. demand for labor, such as those in major recessions or business booms. Yet contemporary migration has built its own momentum, independent of demand forces in the United States, to a greater extent than the earlier migrations. This has occurred because of population growth, both in Mexico and in the Mexican-American population in the United States and because of reduced economic and psychic costs of migration. Also, unsanctioned migration has been allowed to continue at a high rate for a long time. The last factor has permitted millions of Mexicans to enter the United States, accumulate knowledge about entry and job search, and pass this information along to other potential migrants. The result of all these changes has been the development of a large migration stream from Mexico that remains large, regardless of small shifts in the demand for labor in the United States. Put another way, it appears that high unemployment in the United States, at the level of 7 or 8 percent of the labor force, would produce quite small effects on the size of the Mexican migration flows. Only a deep recession would reduce the flows substantially, and then the restraints would probably operate through immigration law enforcement as well as market forces.

Supply-driven migration can be theoretically explained. High wages in a labor-receiving area provide incentives for workers to move there from a low-wage area even without shifts (increases) in labor demand in the receiving area. Migrants are absorbed into employment in the receiving area, as wages fall, at a pace that depends only upon the elasticity of demand for labor. The migration stops when the wage differential between the two areas falls to a point where it just covers the costs of movement and job search.

If one believes that downward wage flexibility in U.S. markets is insufficient to validate this theory, an alternative explanation of supply-oriented migration can be given. With wages rigid, migrants can still be absorbed if they are considered to be more productive than indigenous workers. They will then displace the latter, who will become unemployed, leave the labor force, or delay entry to the labor force.

The restraints on migration that displace indigenous workers are as much political as economic. When unemployment and other indicators of an excess supply of labor reach certain levels, receiving areas will attempt to cut off the migrant flows and will usually be successful when the flows are of foreign, rather than domestic, workers. The amount of displacement needed to bring about political control of Mexican migration is not easily analyzed, but the sensitivity levels in the United States are probably higher than in earlier migration periods because much displacement now falls on youth, women, and minorities; these groups, however, have less political power than white males.

Supply-oriented Mexican migration during the 1970s has been absorbed in U.S. labor markets by both falling wages (in real terms) and displacement of resident workers. Inflation has facilitated the necessary wage adjustments. Where increases in the supply of migrant labor are sufficient to keep nominal wages from increasing but are unable to reduce them because of existing statutory minimums, income transfers, and worker expectations, obviously real wage reductions will depend upon the size of price increases. Those increases will be greater during inflation than otherwise. Migrant labor supplies during the 1970s have not eliminated nominal wage increases in labor markets that employ them, but they have no doubt reduced their size over what otherwise would have occurred. Thus, recent inflation apparently has helped bring about falling real and relative wages in markets that employ migrants and, consequently, has helped absorb migration from Mexico.[33] Some displacement absorption of this migration has undoubtedly occurred as well. Employers do prefer unsanctioned Mexican migrants for certain jobs and have employed them instead of the less productive resident workers who have been available.[34] This, in effect, shifts the latter to an unemployed or out-of-the-labor-force status.

Finally, the employment of Mexican migrants must produce aggregate income increases that, themselves, increase the demand for migrant workers (demand shifts). The income gains go to capital owners, skilled workers who are complemented by the migrant labor, and the migrants themselves, although some part of the migrant income is simply a substitution for income losses that fall on unskilled resident workers.[35] These increases in income enlarge aggregate demand for

[33] The incidence of illegal alien employment in the United States is probably greatest in the apparel industry. Average hourly earnings in that industry increased by 65 percent from 1970 to 1978, compared with an 84 percent increase for all U.S. manufacturing. See U.S. Bureau of Labor Statistics, *Employment and Earnings, United States, 1909-78,* bulletin 1312-11. On the recent widening of the U.S. wage structure, see Marvin Kosters, "Wages, Inflation, and the Labor Market," *Contemporary Economic Problems 1976* (Washington, D.C.: American Enterprise Institute, 1976), pp. 109-162.

[34] Fogel, *Mexican Illegal Alien Workers,* p. 85.

[35] For illustrative estimates of these effects in the U.S. economy, see George E. Johnson, "The Labor Market Effects of Immigration," *Industrial and Labor Relations Review,* vol. 33, no. 3 (April 1980), pp. 331-341.

goods and services, consequently increasing employment, including the employment of more migrants. Thus, the aggregate impacts of Mexican migration add to its self-sustaining nature.

Determinants of Migration

Contemporary migration from Mexico differs from that of earlier periods because it is influenced by larger population bases, in both the sending and receiving areas, and the greater knowledge relevant for migration of the current participants. It has become more self-sustaining and less subject to changes in labor demand in the United States. General evidence for the latter conclusion might be deduced from the fact that the contemporary large-scale migration has continued for so long—since 1965—through periods of recession and relatively high unemployment in the United States. This is not convincing evidence, however, since earlier migrations also continued through years of mild recession—1921 in the first migration period and 1949 during the second. The current migration has not been confronted with either a major depression, like that of the 1930s, or a major, uninhibited effort to enforce immigration laws, like that of the 1950s. In the absence of such tests, certainty about the different nature of the current migration is not possible. Some insights may be obtained, however, by subjecting the current period (data are for 1965–1977) to detailed empirical analysis.

Statistics on sanctioned immigration are of little help for this purpose because this kind of migration has long operated against a Mexican and total Western Hemisphere demand for immigration places that has greatly exceeded the number available. Consequently, the annual number of sanctioned immigrants from Mexico since 1965 does not provide insight into the demand or supply sensitivities of the immigration. Thus, the increases in Mexican-sanctioned immigration from 45,000 in fiscal 1970 to 72,000 in 1974 and then a decline to 58,000 in 1976, do not tell us that this immigration was sensitive to strong U.S. labor demand in the early 1970s and then to the recession of 1974–1975. Even if this judgment were wrong, it would have little importance since the sanctioned immigration component of total Mexican migration appears to be so small. Since 1976, of course, Mexican-sanctioned immigration has been further dampened by the extension of the limitation of 20,000 immigrants a year to each country of the Western Hemisphere.

Most current migration from Mexico appears to be of the unsanctioned variety, judging by the number of apprehensions made by the Immigration and Naturalization Service—approximately 1 million in

1978. Apprehension numbers, of course, do not measure the actual flow of migrants who are able to enter the United States and pursue employment or other activities for at least short periods of time; estimates by the U.S. border patrol indicate that the number of successful migrants is at least equal to the number of apprehensions.[36] The apprehension data can be used to analyze the annual flow of Mexican migration since 1965, although possible variations in border enforcement efforts make them less than ideal for this purpose.

First, the annual apprehension figures can be juxtaposed with U.S. annual unemployment rates (figure 1). Since apprehensions of Mexican aliens have grown rather steadily since 1965, while U.S. unemployment rates have fluctuated, a close relationship between movements in these two variables is not observed in this kind of simple analysis. The simple association between the two variables is, in fact, perversely positive—apprehensions and U.S. unemployment both rose secularly in the 1960s and 1970s. Apprehensions continued to rise through the 1970–1971 recession and they have remained high during the last few years of relatively great unemployment. The statistics for 1975 (table 1) suggest that the U.S. recession of 1974–1975 did temporarily reduce the migration flow. That conclusion is weakened by the fact that the INS budget was temporarily reduced during the first three months of 1975; that reduction rather than the recession may have caused the decline in apprehensions.[37]

It would be nonsensical to conclude from these facts that the high U.S. unemployment of the middle and the late 1970s brought about increased Mexican migration. Rather, there must have been other forces behind it, sufficiently powerful to overcome the dampening effect that rising U.S. unemployment would otherwise have had.

Statistical Results. Greater insight into the nature of recent unsanctioned migration from Mexico can be obtained through regression of apprehensions on various theoretical determinants of it. The period 1965–1977 was used for this purpose; it coincides with the upsurge in unsanctioned migration that followed the end of the Bracero Program and with the continued growth in that migration into the last half of the 1970s.

Illegal Mexican migration can be described by the following equation:

[36] Fogel, *Mexican Illegal Alien Workers,* p. 61. Estimates by border patrol officials of the ratio of successful entrants to apprehensions range from 2 to 1, to 5 to 1.
[37] Ibid., p. 65.

FIGURE 1
APPREHENSIONS OF MEXICAN ILLEGAL ALIENS AND THE
U.S. UNEMPLOYMENT RATE, 1965–1978

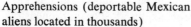

Apprehensions (deportable Mexican
aliens located in thousands)

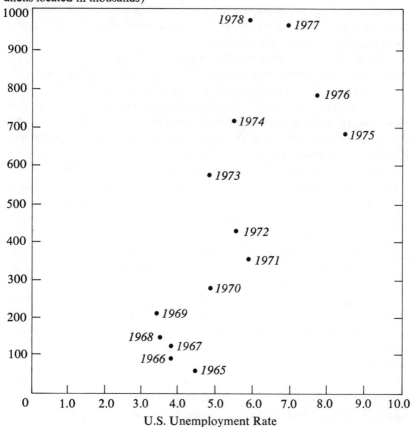

SOURCES:
   Apprehensions—U.S. Department of Justice, Immigration and Naturalization Service, *Annual Report of the Immigration and Naturalization Service* (years 1965-1978).
   U.S. Unemployment Rate—U.S. Department of Labor, Bureau of Labor Statistics, *Handbook of Labor Statistics, 1978* (Bulletin 2000), table 70, p. 213; *Employment and Earnings,* vol. 27, no. 1 (January 1980), table 12, p. 167.

$$M_t = \alpha_0 + \alpha_1 LF_t^{Mex} + \alpha_2 U_t^{U.S.}$$
$$+ \alpha_3 (W^{U.S.}/W^{Mex})_t + \varepsilon_t,$$

where M = annual apprehension of Mexican illegal aliens; LF^{Mex} = Mexican labor force; $U^{U.S.}$ = annual average unemployment rate in the

212

United States; $W^{U.S.}$ = annual manufacturing wage in the United States; W^{Mex} = annual manufacturing wage in Mexico; t = time (subscript); and ε_t = stochastic error term. The U.S. annual wage was obtained by multiplying average weekly earnings in manufacturing by fifty-two. The annual wage in Mexico was computed as average monthly earnings in manufacturing multiplied by twelve. Both wage rates were expressed in pesos and converted to real terms with the consumer price index for Mexico. This assumes that Mexican migrants evaluate the U.S. wage based on its purchasing power in Mexico.

Aside from the fact that apprehension of illegal aliens is not the same as actual migration, the major drawback of the dependent variable, M, is that it can be affected by variability in the enforcement of immigration law—the apprehension effort. A measurement of enforcement, the annual INS budget in constant dollars, was used to try to capture this possible effect but was not successful because of high correlations between the enforcement measure and the explanatory variables.

The estimated equation was (t statistics are in parentheses):

$$M = -3138.13 + 0.204LF^{Mex} - 4.603U^{U.S.} + 159.532(W^{U.S.}/W^{Mex})$$
$$(-16.2) \quad (29.9) \quad\quad (-0.71) \quad\quad (5.99)$$
$$R^2 = 0.997, F(3,9) = 1,082, \text{ and } DW = 2.89$$

All variables in the equation have the correct theoretical sign, but U.S. unemployment is not statistically significant. Since the apprehension of Mexican illegals has grown rather steadily since 1965, the equation was respecified with a time variable (T) to capture the upward time trend of migration that may have operated independently of economic factors. In this second estimation, the relative wage variable ($W^{U.S.}/W^{Mex}$) was split into its two components for the purpose of observing separately the influence of each country's wage rate; this procedure distinguishes between the two countries with respect to the source of a change in the relative wage. The results were:

$$M = -2705.80 + 0.202LF - 3.796U^{U.S.} + 0.0074W^{U.S.}$$
$$(-8.14) \quad (7.99) \quad\quad (-0.45) \quad\quad (5.04)$$
$$- 0.0170W^{Mex} - 5.221T,$$
$$(-1.48) \quad\quad (-0.55)$$
$$R^2 = 0.997, F(5,7) = 505, \text{ and } DW = 2.99$$

In this equation, there does not appear to be a time trend of migration independent of economic influences. Because of data limitations, however, this conclusion cannot be drawn. The only Mexican labor force data available were linear projections of 1960 and 1970 census figures. Consequently, the labor force variable itself is heavily time related, changing at a rate given largely by changes in the working age population in Mexico.[38] The migration effects of fluctuations in the Mexican labor force that are independent of population changes cannot be estimated.

Assessments can be made of the other economic variables. The U.S. wage has a small but statistically significant influence, much of it associated with the 1976 devaluation of the peso. The Mexican wage coefficient is negative and larger (in absolute value) than that of the U.S. wage, but it is statistically significant at only the 90 percent confidence level. The coefficient of the U.S. unemployment rate is not statistically significant in this equation.

The Durbin-Watson statistic for this regression suggested the possible presence of serial correlation; therefore, the equation was reestimated to include $U^{U.S.}$, $W^{U.S.}$, and W^{Mex} as two-year moving averages of observations that both followed and preceded M by six months. This procedure reduced the amount of serial correlation and changed the results slightly, as follows:

$$M = -1957.12 + 0.215LF^{Mex} - 16.484U^{U.S.} + 0.0046W^{U.S.}$$
$$\quad (-6.50) \quad\quad (6.95) \quad\quad\quad (-1.26) \quad\quad\quad (2.69)$$
$$\quad - 0.0510W^{Mex} + 7.849T$$
$$\quad (-2.90) \quad\quad\quad (0.82)$$
$$R^2 = 0.996, F(5,7) = 335, \text{ and } DW = 2.44$$

The net result of these regressions, leaving aside the Mexican labor force for the moment, is that the U.S. economic variables appear to have had little influence on recent Mexican migration. U.S. unemployment is not significant and the U.S. wage has a smaller effect than the Mexican wage (elasticities at the means are 0.9 and −2.6, respectively). These results support the view that the current migration from Mexico is not greatly influenced by changes in the conditions of U.S. labor markets, although great faith cannot be placed in regressions that include only thirteen observations. Of course, a conclusion that Mexican migration would not be influenced by a sustained high rate of U.S. unemployment, at the 10 percent level, for example, is not warranted; that kind of unemployment experience did not occur in the period 1965–1977.

Significance of Mexican Labor Growth. These statistical results are consistent with the view that growth in the Mexican labor force has been the principal force behind recent migration from that country (the labor force variable by itself is associated with 98 percent of the varia-

---

[38] The source of these data is *La Economía En Cifras, Nacional Financiera* (Mexico, D.F., 1978), pp. 13, 14.

tion in annual migration). The alternative view that migration would have increased greatly even without growth in the Mexican labor force seems unlikely but cannot be ruled out statistically. My regressions indicate that an increase of 1 million in the Mexican labor force is associated with a 200,000 increase in migration. With the Mexican labor force growing by about 700,000 persons a year, this source provides considerable impetus to the migration flow.

These results are similar to those of M. I. Blejer, H. G. Johnson, and A. C. Porzecanski. They found that the Mexican annual unemployment rate explained 82 percent of the variation in Mexican migration (apprehensions and sanctioned immigration) over the period 1960–1974 and that various relative wage measures were not significant.[39] Since their estimates of Mexican unemployment appear to have been derived from data on population growth, they must be highly correlated with this paper's labor-force variable. Both of these measures are dominated by Mexican population growth and lead to the conclusion that that growth has driven the migration increases of the 1970s. Changes in U.S. labor market tightness, as measured by unemployment and the U.S. manufacturing wage, have had relatively little influence on the migration increases.

Another variable thought by some to influence Mexican migration is the statutory minimum wage in the United States.[40] The proponents of this view suggest that either better enforcement or a higher minimum wage will reduce the employment of migrants by making affected employment more desirable to resident workers. When the statutory minimum was entered in the regression shown, it did have a negative sign but was not quite statistically significant at the 95 percent confidence level. Thus, alternative theories of its impact can be entertained. One of these, consistent with the negative sign, is simply that an increase in the minimum wage reduces the employment of all workers, resident and migrant alike. My own view is quite different, however. An increase in the U.S. minimum wage may well increase migration because of its incentive effects for migrants and because it may induce some U.S. employers to shift from resident to migrant workers. A minimum wage increase will raise labor costs above the marginal productivity of some resident workers and cause some employers who had not previously hired unsanctioned aliens to shift to that labor supply in the belief that

[39] M. I. Blejer, H. G. Johnson, and A. C. Porzecanski, "Un análisis de los determinantes económicos de la migración mexicano legal e ilegal hacia los Estados Unidos," *Demographia y Economía*, vol. 11, no. 3, pp. 326-340.

[40] See Piore, *Birds of Passage,* p. 185; and U.S. Department of Labor, *Minimum Wage and Maximum Hours Standards under the Fair Labor Standards Act,* 1979, p. 33.

unsanctioned migrants have higher productivities. A higher minimum wage cannot be considered an aid to immigration control while assessment of these alternative impacts remains unsettled.

This analysis, stressing Mexican population growth as the major force behind the contemporary migration increases, does suggest that contemporary migration differs from migration earlier in this century, because both the existing population of Mexico and increases in that population are now much larger. The self-sustaining quality of current migration may not be unique; earlier migrations, also, once set in motion, continued until halted by depression or vigorous enforcement of immigration laws. Yet, it is likely that the changes previously described—a larger and more rapidly growing Mexican population, a larger Mexican-American population, its greater political power, and the greater familiarity of potential migrants with the United States—have made Mexican migration less dependent on U.S. business cycles and immigration enforcement efforts. Even a deep recession might have only a small and brief impact. The enforcement measures that worked previously are not now acceptable on either political or humanitarian grounds. Indeed, there may no longer exist any enforcement measures that are both effective and widely acceptable to the U.S. citizenry, so difficult has immigration enforcement become. In short, barring new enforcement measures, Mexican migration will continue on a large scale and will be only mildly influenced by the kind of business cycles which the United States has experienced since World War II.

Temporary Migration? A popular view of Mexican migration is that most of the unsanctioned flow is temporary, geared to seasonal agricultural employment in the United States, and that, consequently, it does not have the kind of impacts on population and resources that result from permanent migration.[41] Although this paper suggests that more of the contemporary migration is permanent than was true earlier in this century, it does remain true that some of the Mexican migration is temporary in nature. It is important, however, to make several points about this fact and the assessments that are often placed upon it.

First, while temporary migration does not add to population or certain kinds of resource use, many of its economic impacts, good and bad, are the same as those resulting from permanent migration. The impacts on output, employment, wages, and resident worker displacement are largely the same whether the migration is permanent or temporary. A reputed advantage of temporary migration is that the

[41] See Wayne A. Cornelius, "Mexican Migration to the United States: The View from Rural Sending Communities" (Cambridge, Mass.: Center for International Studies, MIT, 1976), pp. 8-9.

TABLE 4

ILLUSTRATION OF U.S. POPULATION ADDITIONS FROM
UNSANCTIONED MIGRATION, 1965–1978, UNDER VARIOUS ASSUMPTIONS

| Apprehension Ratio | Percentage of Migration That Is Permanent | |
	25%	50%
1:1	1,600,000	3,200,000
2:1	3,200,000	6,400,000

NOTE: See text for derivation.

migrants will return home in a recession, consequently reducing the recessionary impact on resident workers. The experience of Western Europe with guest workers does not support this view.[42]

Second, the view that Mexican migration is temporary ought to be received with at least a little skepticism simply because it has always been promulgated by U.S. employers in support of their desire to employ Mexican labor, and has not been completely accurate.[43] A sizable contribution to the 8 to 10 million persons of Mexican origin who live in the United States has come from immigration, both sanctioned and unsanctioned, although available data do not permit estimates of the precise size of that contribution.

Third, even if the permanent component of unsanctioned migration is quite small, it does add a significant number of people to the U.S. population because the flow of unsanctioned migrants is so large. This is illustrated in table 4, where the first row and column number were constructed by assuming that only 25 percent of each year's unsanctioned entrants settle permanently in the United States and that the number of successful unsanctioned entrants in each year is equal to the number of INS apprehensions. Application of these assumptions to the fourteen years, 1965–1978, produces a total of nearly 1,600,000 additions to the U.S. population. This figure is more than twice total sanctioned immigration from Mexico in the same period and is about one-third of sanctioned immigration from all countries over that time span. If less conservative assumptions are made about either the permanent component of the migration or the ratio of successful illegal entrants to apprehensions, larger additions to population are obtained. The unavoid-

---

42 Philip L. Martin and Mark J. Miller, "Guestworkers: Lessons from Western Europe," *Industrial and Labor Relations Review,* vol. 33, no. 3 (April 1980).
43 Fogel, *Negro in the Meat Industry,* chap. 3; and Piore, *Birds of Passage,* p. 19.

able conclusion from this exercise is that permanent migration from Mexico is sizable even if only a small fraction of each year's unsanctioned migrants stay permanently in the United States.

Effects of Immigration and Mexican-American Progress

Several scholars have shown that a similar earnings pattern exists for all U.S. immigrant groups.[44] There are three elements in this pattern. First, within all national origin groups, immigrants match the earnings of native-born persons with like earnings characteristics after some ten to eighteen years of residence in the United States. Some refugees, as contrasted with economic immigrants, take longer. Second, within all national origin groups, persons born in the United States who have one or more parents born abroad (the second generation) earn 5 to 10 percent more than immigrants with the same earnings characteristics. Third, within all national origin groups, persons born in the United States who have native-born parents (the third and successive generations) earn 5 to 10 percent less than second-generation persons.

Assuming that these findings have not been greatly influenced by return migration and, thus, by the exclusion of unsuccessful immigrants from the analyses, they indicate, first, that immigrants generally can achieve earnings consistent with their earnings characteristics and, second, that the third generation earns less than the second. The latter finding seems anomalous in view of popular belief that generational succession itself opens up economic opportunities in the United States. Motivation differences, operating through "regression toward the mean," have been invoked to explain this finding, that is, the outstanding motivational characteristics possessed by immigrants are considerably reduced in their third-generation children.[45] This explanation may be correct. It is not clear, however, why the regression has no apparent effect on the second generation in comparison with its immigrant parentage, and, yet, enables that second generation to offset the putative advantages of

[44] Geoffrey Carliner, "Wages, Earnings and Hours of First, Second, and Third Generation American Males," *Economic Inquiry*, vol. 18, no. 1 (January 1980), pp. 87-101; Barry R. Chiswick, "The Economic Progression of Immigrants: Some Apparently Universal Patterns," in William Fellner, ed., *Contemporary Economic Problems 1979* (Washington, D.C.: American Enterprise Institute, 1979), pp. 357-399 and reprinted in this volume; and David L. Featherman and Robert M. Hauser, *Opportunity and Change* (New York: Academic Press, 1978), chap. 8.

[45] Barry R. Chiswick, "Sons of Immigrants: Are They at an Earnings Disadvantage?" *American Economic Review*, vol. 67, no. 1 (February 1977), p. 380; Barry R. Chiswick, "The Effect of Americanization on the Earnings of Foreign-Born Men," *Journal of Political Economy*, vol. 86, no. 5 (October 1978), p. 920; and Carliner, "Wages, Earnings and Hours," p. 90.

the third generation, such as reduced discrimination, greater market information, and the greater availability of parental wealth for human capital investment. Further investigation is needed.

The first finding in the pattern of immigrant earnings—the ultimate success of immigrants in comparison with U.S.-born persons of the same national origin—together with the fact that white male immigrants eventually match the earnings of *all* native-born white males with like skills, could produce a conclusion that white immigration, at least, has a favorable effect on average income and the inequality of income in the United States. Such a conclusion would be unwarranted, however, because it fails to take into account the average level and distribution of earnings characteristics possessed by immigrants compared with those of natives. When differences in earnings characteristics are accounted for, immigrants eventually do as well or better than anyone else. If the schooling and skills of immigrants are less than those of native-born persons, they are most unlikely to raise the average level and equality of income in the United States. Furthermore, a conclusion that the effect was favorable would be unwarranted because it does not take into account unsanctioned immigration.

The experience of the different Mexican-origin generations in this country illustrates this argument. Mexican-heritage persons fit neatly into the universal generation pattern in that second-generation males earn more than both Mexican immigrants and third-generation males. Also, Mexican immigrants match Mexican-Americans with like characteristics after fifteen years in this country.[46] Beyond these similarities, however, the Mexican experience departs sharply from that of immigrant groups of non Hispanic origins.

First, the annual earnings of sanctioned Mexican immigrants are well below those of all white male immigrants; they were only 57 percent of the latter in 1969.[47] Earnings of unsanctioned immigrants are even lower. The principal reason for the earnings difference is a difference in school levels—an average of 6.1 years for Mexicans compared with 10.8 years for all white male immigrants (one study found the average schooling of unsanctioned Mexican males to be 4.9 years).[48] Even when schooling and other earnings-related differences are taken into account, Mexican immigrants and their offspring earn substantially less than do other white persons. That is the second way in which the Mexican immigrant experience departs from the norm. Professor Chis-

[46] Chiswick, "The Economic Progression of Immigrants," p. 373.
[47] Ibid.
[48] David North and Marion T. Houstoun, *The Characteristics and Role of Illegal Aliens in the U.S. Labor Market* (Washington, D.C.: Linton and Co., 1976), chap. 3, p. 9.

wick states, "Other things the same, first, second, and later-generation Mexican Americans earn about 15 to 25 percent less than Anglos, and the difference does not appear to diminish between successive generations."[49] Mexicans earn less than most other immigrants because they have low amounts of human capital and because they suffer from language difficulties, discrimination, or other earnings handicaps. The same results and causes persist for their children and grandchildren.

These findings have tremendous implications for immigration and social policy. They mean that Mexican immigration brings a group of people to the United States who are disadvantaged at entry, who continue to be disadvantaged throughout their lives, and who will pass their disadvantages on to their children and grandchildren. Whether these disadvantages of schooling, language, and discrimination can be removed by special public programs is uncertain, as is public willingness to support such programs.

These findings and conclusions become more ominous when they are put in the context of unsanctioned migration from Mexico because that migration is so large, probably at least as large as all authorized immigration to the United States. What is occurring in U.S. history is the rapid expansion of a subpopulation—Mexican (and some other Hispanic groups)—that has low relative earnings and will continue to have low relative earnings for decades to come. Indeed, continued low relative earnings are assured simply by the migration itself because most Mexican migrants are low-skilled workers who compete with either earlier Mexican migrants or their children. The migration flow ensures that relative wages of the low-skilled in the United States, many of whom are Mexican Americans, will stay low.

It is not appropriate to speculate here on the consequences of developing another large low-income group within the U.S. population, while the already existing large low-income group, namely blacks, limps along with modest gains in its relative economic position. Clearly, this is something to consider.

The fact that Mexican generational economic progress is unsatisfactory to both Mexican Americans and the larger American society, together with the substantial amount of Mexican migration that is occurring, makes it quite evident that the effect of current immigration to the United States cannot be assessed by simply comparing immigrants and natives who have like earnings characteristics. Differences in earnings characteristics between immigrants and natives and rates of removal of these differences are also important. On neither score is it possible to be optimistic about the effects of Mexican migration.

[49] Chiswick, "The Economic Progression of Immigrants," p. 379.

Future Immigration Policy

There have been three distinct periods of heavy Mexican migration to the United States, including the contemporary one. All of these migrations have contributed importantly to the economic growth of this country, but they have also increased inequality of income since most Mexican migrants have been low skilled. The contemporary migration, in contrast to the earlier ones, is occurring from larger population and knowledge bases in Mexico and receives support from a larger Mexican-American population. Consequently, its income distribution and population impacts are greater than in earlier migrations, and it may be less sensitive to cyclical shifts in the U.S. demand for labor. Mexican migration also adds substantial numbers to the disadvantaged population of the United States. In view of these considerations and the projected growth of Mexico's population, the United States should develop policy and enforcement measures that greatly reduce unsanctioned migration from Mexico (and elsewhere). Subsequent to obtaining control of unsanctioned immigration, authorized immigration from Mexico should be increased, perhaps doubled or tripled from its current level of 20,000 a year (this assumes that the preferred alternative, a flexible ceiling for Mexican immigration that varies with U.S. labor market demand, cannot be enacted). The net effect of these actions would be greatly reduced migration from Mexico but uniquely large (within existing U.S. immigration law) authorized immigration from that country. The latter can be easily justified on historical, equitable, and pragmatic grounds.[50]

[50] Fogel, "Immigration Policy," pp. 306-308; and Fogel, "Illegal Aliens: Economic Aspects and Public Policy Alternatives," *San Diego Law Review,* vol. 15, no. 1 (1977), pp. 74-76.

Commentaries

Nigel Tomes

Professor Greeley has presented empirical results regarding the economic progress of earlier immigrant groups in terms of educational attainment and income; they are both interesting and intriguing. He has shown that the educational attainment of Jews and Irish Catholics was as good as or better than that of other Americans throughout the present century. Polish and Italian Catholics remained disadvantaged vis-à-vis natives until the post–World War II birth cohort. These results are consistent with previous studies of ethnic minorities[1] and of the economic progress of immigrants.[2] Indeed, an economic historian concluded his study of the progress of Jewish immigrants to the United States from eastern Europe around the turn of the century with the following statement: "Despite their initial disabilities of language and skills, each cohort of Jewish immigrants caught up in earnings with native American workers of the same age and in similar occupations within 10–15 years."[3] This accords well with the "stylized facts" concerning the progress of immigrants.[4] The children and grandchildren of Jewish immigrants appear to have succeeded beyond what would be predicted on the basis of the progress of the descendants of all immigrants.[5]

There are two possible explanations for the apparently slower progress of the Polish and Italian immigrant groups. First, the latter

---

[1] B. Duncan and O. D. Duncan, "Minorities and the Process of Stratification," *American Sociologicial Review,* vol. 33 (June 1968), pp. 356-364.

[2] Barry R. Chiswick, "The Effect of Americanization on the Earnings of Foreign-Born Men," *Journal of Political Economy,* vol. 86, no. 5 (October 1978), pp. 897-922.

[3] A. Kahan, "Economic Opportunities and Some Pilgrims' Progress: Jewish Immigrants from Eastern Europe in the U.S., 1890-1914," *Journal of Economic History,* vol. 38, no. 1 (March 1978), p. 251.

[4] Chiswick, "Americanization."

[5] Barry R. Chiswick, "Sons of Immigrants: Are They at an Earnings Disadvantage?" *American Economic Review,* vol. 67, no. 1 (February 1977), pp. 376-380.

222

immigrants were largely unskilled and therefore, because of greater substitutability between unskilled labor and capital than between skilled labor and capital and/or less firm-specific skills, experienced greater unemployment during the depression years than their predecessors to the United States. (A. Kahan suggests that immigrant Jews were more skilled and more literate than other ethnic groups, which in part may explain their more rapid progress.) Second, Professor Chiswick's analysis of immigrants and the sons of immigrants has shown that in the U.S. labor market immigrants (and their sons) from English-speaking countries have an advantage over immigrants from non–English-speaking countries and their descendants.[6]

Turning to income differences, Professor Greeley finds that the family incomes of Jews, Catholics, Presbyterians, and Episcopalians exceed those of other Protestant groups, after standardizing for education, location, and background. The Presbyterian/Episcopalian result may largely reflect the sorting of high-income individuals within the spectrum of Protestant denominations. Excluding these two groups leaves a ranking of income by religion of Jews, Catholics, and Protestants. The intriguing question is, What are the underlying determinants of these differentials? Do they reflect differences in labor supply? in the quality of schooling? in ability? in entrepreneurship?

The data employed by Greeley are inadequate to answer these questions. Some insights can, however, be found in Paul Taubman's exhaustive analysis of the National Bureau of Economic Research–Thorndike-Hagan survey of World War II veterans.[7] In these data, holding constant education, ability, work experience, labor supply, health, marital status, location (city size and region), parental background, etc., Jews are found to earn 33–40 percent ($4,000) more—and Protestants 3–9 percent less—than Catholics. Some of these differentials appear to reflect differences in occupational choice: Jews are more likely to prefer to be self-employed and to be uninterested in job security. Even within occupations, however, Jews earn significantly more than Protestants: $6,400 more among self-employed businessmen and $7,300 more among managers. In contrast, the Protestant-Catholic differences are seldom significant *within* occupations. In addition, while the Jewish-Catholic differential is significant in all major census regions of the United States, the Protestant-Catholic differential was significant only

[6] Barry R. Chiswick, "The Economic Progress of Immigrants: Some Apparently Universal Patterns" in William Fellner, ed., *Contemporary Economic Problems 1979* (Washington, D.C.: American Enterprise Institute, 1979), reprinted in this volume; idem, "Sons of Immigrants."

[7] P. Taubman, *Sources of Inequality in Earnings* (Amsterdam: North-Holland Publishing Co., 1975).

in the north central region. These results suggest that a more detailed standardization by location may reduce or even eliminate the Protestant-Catholic differentials in Greeley's data.

On the basis of Taubman's analysis, it seems likely that the Jewish differential in the National Opinion Research Center–General Social Survey data reflects in part the returns on ability and quality of schooling.[8] One hypothesis that has been proposed to explain the Jewish/non-Jewish differential in earnings and occupational distribution is that, based on their cultural history, Jews invest a larger fraction of their total wealth in the form of embodied and mobile human capital. Certainly, the available evidence suggests greater investments in human capital. G. Catsiapis and C. Robinson find that, for the high-school class of 1972, Jewish parents made larger contributions to finance the college education of their children.[9] In addition, in the NBER-Thorndike data, the growth rate of the earnings of Jews throughout the life cycle exceeds that of Catholics by 21 percent—consistent with a greater acquisition of skills at an earlier stage in the life cycle. However, since the meager data available suggest that, other things being equal, Jews have greater financial wealth, even if the cultural history hypothesis is accepted as explaining the differential portfolio composition of total (human and nonhuman) wealth of Jews from that of non-Jews, there remains the further puzzle: Why does the total (human plus nonhuman) wealth of Jews exceed that of non-Jews?

Andrea Tyree

We have one paper of informed faith and another of informed pessimism. The one by Professor Greeley argues that, since such a wide variety of ethnic groups have found paths to socioeconomic success in the United States, without strong evidence to the contrary, we should assume other groups will do the same. The implicit admonition is to a sort of cultural benign neglect (curiously the invention of another Irish-Catholic social scientist). The second paper, by Professor Fogel, gives reasons to expect that Mexican immigrants to the United States will not fare well.

I should like to address my comments to the facts of the past discussed by Professor Greeley. Has socioeconomic achievement of immigrant ethnic groups been reached without the assimilation of the groups

[8] Ibid., pp. 173-175, 182-183.

[9] G. Catsiapis and C. Robinson, "Theory of the Family and Intergenerational Mobility: An Empirical Test," University of Western Ontario, Department of Economics Research Report, no. 7830 (London, October 1978).

into a homogenized purée or their acculturation to American ways and values? Professor Greeley says yes. He is surely right about the purée, though he does violence to how much we all share that was not shared by our grandparents.

The various European and Asian ethnic stocks are assimilated in the sense that their educational distributions are similar—except for Russians (largely Jews), who have more than everybody else, and people of Spanish origin, especially Mexican and Puerto Rican, who have less. All these ethnic stocks are also assimilated in the sense that they have similar occupational distributions, all with about 30 percent of their male labor force in professional or managerial occupations a decade ago—except again those Russians, with more than 56 percent and the Spanish, with 15 percent. They are assimilated in the sense that their income distributions are similar to one another's—with the same exceptions.

Ethnicity does not provide a basis for stratification in the United States. We do not have—for most white ethnic groups—ethnic stratification. There is reason to suspect that we did not have an ethnically based stratification system at the turn of the century when the Dillingham commission made such a consequential fuss.

Greeley disputes a myth created by W. I. Thomas and Florian Znaniecki in response to that commission and its supporters. The myth made social disorganization the fairly inevitable lot of a number of then-current immigrant groups and saw their salvation in Americanization. There is another myth sociologists interested in ethnicity have worked hard to perpetuate: that each immigrant group entered at the bottom of the social hierarchy of the United States and pushed everyone else, or at least almost everyone, up.

A student (Deborah Biele) spent last year with those Dillingham data. She had thirty-four national origin/generation groups, the first and second generations from seventeen European countries of origin. She examined the male occupational distribution of each of these groups in the 1900 census. She reduced the occupational diversity to some sensible dimensions, one of which is clearly a hierarchical one. It enabled her to rank the ethnic-generation groups in the American occupational hierarchy at the turn of the century.

As one might imagine, second-generation groups tend to be farther up the hierarchy than the first-, though the two sets overlap considerably, with some second-generation northern Europeans below a number of first-generation groups from western European origins—Scotland, England, Wales, English Canada, and France—as well as below one first-generation eastern European group, the Russians. Second-generation Swedes are nearly tied with first-generation Irish. The groups below these are largely immigrant, though they include second-generation Norwegians and Danes as well as Poles and French Canadians.

Since people from different countries tended to have different religions, a 1900 ethnic-religious socioeconomic hierarchy comparable to Greeley's should reflect Biele's hierarchy of national origins. Jews, solely by virtue of the Russians among them, should have been a bit above the middle. Earlier Sephardic and German Jews would have adjusted the overall position of the group upward a bit. Those Protestant denominations subscribed to by the more prosperous from the British Isles should have been high, as Greeley finds they are in the 1970s. Those Protestant groups made up of other western and northern Europeans should have been relatively low. Irish Catholics should have been somewhere in the middle, Italian Catholics well below them, with Polish Catholics yet lower.

Contemporary versus 1900 Characteristics

Some of the relative positions of national-religious groups that Greeley presents as characteristics of America in the 1970s seem to have been in place at the turn of the century, though there have surely been some changes in the total socioeconomic ranking in the course of time, with Jews and immigrant Catholic groups gaining on others, while holding something like their previous positions relative to one another. The continuities over the period may need little explanation; the changes surely do. In explaining how my view of the changes differs from Greeley's, let me begin with an aside.

My paternal grandfather was a Methodist minister with a church in Pikeville, Kentucky, and a circuit he rode thereabouts. Thus, I find myself in the second empirical section of Greeley's paper, being part of the benchmark middle, in an ethnic group neither advantaged nor disadvantaged, neither a success nor a flop. I seem to be a value about which squared deviations are minimized—a mean. One might imagine this is a good place from which to look up and down. It is not.

When the grandchildren of my grandfather's parishioners looked up and down, they saw Episcopalians and Presbyterians above, Baptists near below, with Pentecostals below them, overlapping with a considerable variety of blacks (also ranged by denomination). They did not see Irish Catholics or Italian Catholics, certainly not Polish Catholics. They did see a few German and French Catholics and some Jews, though not many. It is not that they were poor observers; where they were, all these "late" (1880–1920) immigrants were not to be found. These groups entered the United States at a time when the South was

226

in a severe decline, a hundred-year impecuniosity that understandably did not make the region attractive to immigrants.

There are two points from this personal perspective from the middle. First, ethnic occupational differentiation in the United States has not been a unidimensional phenomenon captured by a kind of social altimeter; it has been multidimensional. Second, socioeconomic achievement occurs in space; indeed, the industrial structure is transformed in space.

At the turn of the century, where an immigrant went and what he did was strongly influenced by where he came from. Northern Europeans kept going where previous northern Europeans had gone, to agricultural places. Agriculture was on the verge of decline. Their choice of destination did not bode well for the socioeconomic achievement of these groups during the twentieth century. Most of these northern Europeans were members of the Protestant denominations that Dr. Greeley finds near and below the middle of his national-religious hierarchy in the mid-1970s. Irish, Italians, and eastern European Jews went to urban industrial places just as urban-industrial America was expanding, booming. The Irish did enjoy pride of place; they got there first. The Italians and Jews turned up at about the same time. The skills they brought with them did influence how well they did and how quickly.

There the two groups were cheek by jowl in lower Manhattan in adjacent blocks. Italian men had worked mostly on farms in Italy. In Manhattan, they did manly things such as digging subways and sewers. Most Jewish men had been craftsmen, artisans, and small merchants. In Manhattan, they sewed and peddled. With probably more people with needle skills assembled in one place than ever before in the world, they created the ready-to-wear clothing industry. They were both in the right kind of place for the time and made the right occupational choices. Italians were also in the right place. While their occupational choices at first might not have been so promising, they were still there in urban centers when the subways were completed and the Jews were graduating from the machines in the garment industry. The northern European Protestants who had gone to rural America did not get to participate in this industrial expansion until they were forced off farms between 1930 and 1950. They often did not even get to be farmers but had to settle, along with the second-generation sons of their earlier arriving compatriots, for jobs as agricultural laborers.

The children of my grandfather's parishioners and their non-Methodist neighbors also did not get to participate in the industrial expansion. Pikeville, Kentucky, was the wrong place. So was most of the South, for its Methodists, Baptists, and Pentecostals (many of Dr. Greeley's other Protestants). The upward movement of Jews and the late-immigrant Catholic groups can be understood partly as a function of their location in the socioeconomically right places. The religious groups largely composed of either rural folk or Southerners were in the wrong places for those times.

Greeley shows that a number of late-arriving immigrant groups have done rather well. All other evidence supports the data he presents here. The social disorganization detailed by Thomas did not prove to be the impediment to socioeconomic assimilation of Polish Catholics that he anticipated. It might even be argued that it was necessary.

Concern with Social Disorganization

There is a kind of garrisoned conservatism to much sociological concern with social disorganization, as if the status quo is mutable only at intolerable risk. The tradition begun by Thomas has been elaborated recently by Morris Janowitz in *The Last Half-Century*. Here the emphasis is on the disarticulation of various social institutions and a consequent loss of social control. Janowitz is clearly worried. Once again, a half-century later, the worry is probably misplaced. The only condition under which the institutional articulation that he values could be expected or the absence of a certain amount of social disorganization is one of a social stability unseen since the beginning of the industrial revolution, at least. Changing circumstance promotes disorganization of social groups, just as life changes are temporarily disorganizing for individuals. This does not mean that the social fabric is about to fall apart, though it is likely that the next decade will not be quite like the last. Thomas's Polish-Americans did "Americanize" just fine, though not the way he advocated. Had they followed his advice, we should find them the socioeconomic peers of Baptists and Lutherans.

With new immigrant groups, we can expect evidence of social disorganization and should not leap to view it as a terminal disease. While I wish I could join Greeley in the happy prediction of success for all comers, I cannot. Whether Mexican, Haitian, Cuban, or Southeast Asian immigrants fare well or poorly will be influenced by where they settle, what skills they bring, the range of opportunities available to them, and possibly even the warmth of their welcome.

Greeley establishes facts of differential achievement of religious groups but curiously does not try to explain them. After control of a number of variables relevant to income, some groups still make a great deal more than others. The affluence of Presbyterians and Episcopalians can perhaps be understood as a consequence of both a sort of primitive accumulation and the denominational mobility of upwardly mobile Protestants. The residual income advantages of Jews and Irish Catholics cannot be explained so readily. It may be relevant for both groups that return to the country of origin was not a viable alternative to sticking out the frustrations of attempting to succeed in the United States. Jews clearly could not return to eastern Europe. While individual Irish could return, the numbers could not be large; Ireland was in the process of reducing her population by half, a decline dictated by an altered agricultural economy. The range of opportunities available to these two groups was reduced by one option, return; in northern cities, subsistence agriculture was also out. One had to earn a salary or turn a profit. We cannot predict the future success of current immigrant groups unless we understand, on a level abstract enough to make generalizations, the conditions promoting the differential achievement of previous immigrants.

José Alberro

Most of our people are reluctant to take dirty, low-paying and dead-end jobs. To fill these jobs, we need less choosy foreigners or the work won't get done.
                                          Forbes, August 15, 1977, p. 37

Professor Fogel's paper tries to establish three propositions: that contemporary migration from Mexico, especially that which is unsanctioned, is having important effects on U.S. population size and on low-skilled markets, that such migration is supply pushed, and that its effects are "unfortunate." As a policy prescription, he argues "for a large increase in authorized migration from Mexico along with an end to unsanctioned migration." [1]

The evidence presented to support these hypotheses is weak; there is evidence that contradicts the first two. Furthermore, since the policy prescriptions address neither the causes nor the consequences of undocumented migration, they are of little economic use. Professor Fogel has chosen to be a spokesperson for strong public sentiment that is not founded on scientific evidence and singles out Mexican migration for a series of evils. I disqualify myself from any discussion of such sentiments.

[1] See Walter Fogel, "Twentieth-Century Mexican Migration to the United States," this volume.

229

At the core of the explanation lies a description of labor markets that is worth examining carefully, since there is abundant theoretical and empirical work that calls it into question. Professor Fogel's explanation starts with the observation that the existence of unfilled jobs in the United States has brought Mexican migrants to this country and that those unfilled jobs have existed for almost a century. Finding workers willing to take those jobs has been a problem for most of that period: American employers have had to go to great lengths to fill those vacancies. The bracero program, emergency work programs, and recruitment drives into Mexico in the late nineteenth and early twentieth centuries are examples of such attempts.[2] That Mexican workers have been treated as a commodity "responsive to the labor needs of U.S. employers," that they have been thought of as having no "significant noneconomic need of their own," and that they have been prevented from exerting significant "demands on community housing and public services" [3]—we all agree. It is also known that twice before (during the 1930s and in 1954 with General Swing's Operation Wetback), we have repatriated "excess Mexicans" with extreme violence and little regard for their human, let alone legal rights, whether they were born in Mexico or in the United States.

The subject of our disagreement will be the "great strain [placed] on labor market absorptive capacity" by such migration.[4] Such a hypothesis should be simple to test: Those occupations, industries, and geographic regions where Mexican workers are more numerous should witness lower than average wage rates and/or higher than average unemployment. Professor Fogel produces no such evidence. The evidence shows that unemployment rates in "high impact areas" were 5 percent lower than the U.S. average for the period 1968–1977.[5] Contrary to Professor Fogel's long argument, there seems to be no evidence on wage rates. "Evidence on th[ese] point[s] is very difficult to produce," [6] he concedes. What are the foundations of the argument? "Theory, observation, and the protest of labor groups all suggest that, at times, Mexican migration has lowered unskilled wage rates and has exacerbated local unemployment." [7] Casual observation that suggests, at times, local

---

[2] Ibid.

[3] Ibid.

[4] Ibid.

[5] See Wayne Cornelius, "Mexican Migration to the U.S.: Causes, Consequences and U.S. Responses" (Cambridge, Mass.: Center for International Studies, MIT, 1978), p. 59.

[6] Fogel, "Mexican Migration."

[7] Ibid.

problems hardly seems to constitute scientific evidence useful for policy making.

Furthermore, Professor Fogel's description has been contradicted several times before. At the theoretical level, it remains to be shown that a partial-equilibrium, comparative-static argument is of any use in this context. Institutional descriptions and segmented labor markets arguments are much richer representations.[8] At the empirical level, it has been shown repeatedly that Mexican workers carry out the tasks that are "left over" by indigenous workers. They do not take jobs away from local workers, not even from unskilled ones. They labor where nobody else would under present social conditions.[9]

Migration Restrictions and Jobs

It is fallacious to argue that restrictions on migration would create more jobs. If all undocumented workers were expelled, native workers' employment would hardly increase. Obviously, there would be more job openings, but they would not be filled.[10] The reservation price of most native workers is substantially higher than the value of the marginal product of labor in those occupations. The vacancies would remain unfilled, the firms would go bankrupt, and low-skilled workers in the United States would be in no better position. Since most undocumented workers are employed by small, labor-intensive, marginal firms, the firms cannot upgrade the technology they use to productively employ higher skilled workers. Therefore, the unemployment rate would increase (because of the multiplier), and the price of several commodities in the basic basket of consumption of American workers would increase; social security contributions would decrease, and personal income tax receipts would also fall.[11] I fail to see how that would benefit native workers.

Professor Fogel argues that contemporary migration is different from earlier migration. It is not "a U.S. labor market phenomenon . . . as has heretofore been true" because it "apparently cannot be stopped and also appears to be larger in size." [12] To prove his hypothesis, he

---

[8] See Michael J. Piore, *Birds of Passage: Migrant Labor and Industrial Societies* (New York: Cambridge University Press, 1979).

[9] See Cornelius, "Mexican Migration," pp. 67-69.

[10] See Vic M. Villalpando et al., *A Study of the Socioeconomic Impact of Illegal Aliens on the County of San Diego* (San Diego: San Diego California Human Resources Agency, County of San Diego, 1977).

[11] At least two-thirds of the undocumented workers pay social security taxes and personal income taxes. See Cornelius, "Mexican Migration," p. 89.

[12] See Fogel, "Mexican Migration."

points out that the Mexican population has been growing as a fraction of the American population, that it is increasingly concentrated in the border, that there is a larger Mexican-American community in the United States that decreases set-up costs, and that the Mexican migrant is obtaining employment in nonagricultural jobs.

While it is difficult to believe that the Mexican-American community grew at an annual rate anywhere between 2.92 percent and 7.18 percent a year according to his estimates, the facts bear out his qualitative description of demographic trends. What the paper fails to prove is "that contemporary migration has built in its own momentum."[13] There is no evidence to support such a claim. If migration indeed were supply driven, there should be evidence of the excess supply it causes. As proof, Professor Fogel offers the displacement of other workers and the relatively falling wages about which labor leaders complain. Once more, anecdotal evidence and "common sense" have taken the place of scientific data.

As for the argument that more and more jobs are found in the nonagricultural sector, it has been well documented that "the proportion of Mexicans employed in the non-agricultural sector of the economy was probably as high or higher during the first 25 years of this century as it is today."[14] Mexican workers were brought to the United States to work not on specific industries but on specific tasks in different sectors: the mines, the foundries, the railroads, and also the fields. Migration was task specific, not industry specific.

Perhaps the most puzzling argument is that "increases in income (that result from migration) enlarge aggregate demand for goods and services, consequently increasing employment, including the employment of more migrants. Thus, the aggregate impact of Mexican migration adds to its self-sustaining nature."[15] In his haste to prove the evil of Mexican migration, Professor Fogel did not stop to include the increase in native employment that would result from an increase in aggregate demand.

Let us now examine the "detailed" analysis of the period 1965–1977 to determine whether it confirms the hypothesis that current migration is supply driven, while pre-1965 migration predominantly served the needs of American employers. If Mexican migration continues through recessions, how do undocumented workers provide for themselves when laid off, or why is it that they are less likely to be unemployed? Undocumented workers make little use of social services and they rarely

[13] Ibid.
[14] See Cornelius, "Mexican Migration," p. 53.
[15] See Fogel, "Mexican Migration."

get unemployment compensation when laid off.[16] When they are unemployed, they are likely to migrate back to Mexico. Clearly, that
evidence contradicts the labor market theories used in this paper, while
it is compatible with segmented market theories.

The dependent variable of the estimated regressions is the flow of
migrants to the United States. Careful researchers have tried to differentiate between total flows and net flows so as to avoid overestimat-
ing the number of migrants who stay permanently. Not willing to rely
on such data, Professor Fogel states that "informed estimates indicate
that the number of successful migrants is at least equal to the number
of apprehensions." [17] Those "informed estimates" are Professor Fogel's
own, based on "Border Patrol official *guesses*." [18] He then concludes
that "the apprehension data can be used to analyze the annual flow of
Mexican migration since 1965." [19] They cannot.

Researchers, however, have contested that apprehensions can be
used as a proxy for successful migration, let alone the net flow.[20] The
probability of apprehension has not remained constant over the twelve-
year period; the INS has gone through remarkable technological advances. The simplest proof is that the proportion of people arrested in
the first 72 hours after undocumented entry into the United States has
increased from 56 percent to 67 percent between 1972 and 1977.[21]
Therefore, the INS effectiveness is ill measured by constant dollar
spending; it has to be corrected by technological change. Since everybody agrees that undocumented workers are likely to attempt their
crossings several times until successful, we can see that, even as a
proxy, the number of apprehensions is of little use.

Significance of Independent Variables

The independent variables are not more encouraging. I cannot but be
puzzled at the statement that "a measurement of enforcement . . . was
not successful because of the high correlation between (it) . . . and the

[16] See David S. North and Marion T. Houstoun, *The Characteristics and Role of Illegal Aliens in the U.S. Labor Market* (Washington, D.C.: Linton and Co., 1976).
[17] See Fogel, "Mexican Migration."
[18] See Walter Fogel, *Mexican Illegal Alien Workers in the U.S.*, Institute for Industrial Relations, University of California—Los Angeles Monograph Series, no. 20 (Los Angeles, 1978), p. 61.
[19] See Fogel, "Mexican Migration."
[20] See Cornelius, "Mexican Migration."
[21] See Manuel García y Griego, "El volumen de la migración de Mexicanos no documentados a los Estados Unidos," Series ENEFNEU-CENIET, Secretaria de Trabajo y Previsión Social (1980), pp. 92-97.

explanatory variables." [22] In fact, how should we interpret a high correlation between the INS budget and the unemployment rate (or the wage rate for that matter) in the United States? Is there a close correlation with the Mexican population? Don't the other "independent" variables suffer from the same problem? It is unfortunate that such an important issue has been left to a passing comment.

Why was the Mexican labor force used, and not the unemployment rate that measures the excess supply of labor in Mexico? The latter exhibited procyclical behavior that would have affected the results substantially. Professor Fogel has biased the results in favor of his hypothesis since Mexican labor-force data are time interpolations between census data and not original data. It is also quite remarkable that the wages used are those for manufacturing, when 66.7 percent of the migrants were employed in Mexican agriculture[23] and 40 percent to 50 percent will end up working in the American fields.[24] Indeed, while the Mexican minimum wage for agricultural workers grew fivefold between 1965 and 1977, it only increased threefold in manufacturing. Once more, this biases the results in favor of not rejecting the hypothesis.

The results obtained are not impressive. At most, we can say that the evidence presented does not contradict the hypothesis that apprehensions have increased through time. That is the only meaning that can be attached to the reported R^2s. As for the hypothesis that migration responds to excess supply conditions, it remains a conjecture unrelated to the testing.

All the variables included but one (dependent and independent variables alike) have a strong trend component, biasing the specification against the unemployment rate in the United States ($U^{U.S.}$) that exhibits powerful cyclical behavior. The procedure tends to reject the hypothesis that the $U^{U.S.}$ is an important explanatory variable, which is what the author wants. The Durbin-Watson coefficients indicate autocorrelation in the residuals. If it were to be procyclical, it would indicate that the $U^{U.S.}$ is an important determinant of apprehensions. Unfortunately, no comment is made on the matter. Instead, reestimation was done by "smoothing out" the series, using two-year moving averages and thereby further biasing the test results in favor of the independent variables with a strong trend component.

[22] See Fogel, "Mexican Migration."
[23] See Carlos H. Zazueta and Rodolfo Corona, "Los Trabajadores Mexicanos en los Estados Unidos: primeros resultados de la Encuesta Nacional de Emigración (diciembre 1978–enero 1979)," Series ENEFNEU-CENIET, Secretaría de Trabajo y Previsión Social (1980), p. 114.
[24] See Cornelius, "Mexican Migration," p. 53.

234

INS real spending was not included because of a high degree of multicollinearity among the independent variables. There is still too much of it left in the specification for the test results to be useful. The multicollinearity results from the importance of the trend, but my suspicion is strengthened by the highly volatile estimates for the wage rates coefficients. Indeed, notice that, while the estimated coefficients for LF^{Mex} and $U^{U.S.}$ do not change systematically from one equation to the other, the coefficient of $W^{U.S.}/W^{Mex}$ varies between 159.53 and 0.09. As we know,

> the main consequences of multicollinearity are [that] the precision of estimation falls so that it becomes very difficult if not impossible to disentangle the *relative influence* of the various X variables. Investigators are sometimes led to *drop variables incorrectly* from the analysis because their coefficients are not significantly [different] from zero, but the true situation may be not that a variable has no effect but simply that the set of sample data has not enabled us to pick it up.[25]

To argue that demand-pull variables have taken second place to supply-push ones, multicollinearity has to be eliminated before policy recommendations are offered.

The traditional way to test whether parameters change over time is to carry out separate estimates for the different subperiods and to do paired F tests on them. Unfortunately, the procedure was not used. Instead, the 1965–1977 period was chosen on institutional grounds and not compared with any previous one.

Last, while the starting assumption was that apprehensions would be used as a proxy for successful migration, Professor Fogel then proceeds to use them as an actual count of total permanent migration on at least three occasions.[26] The numbers game has been played before with undocumented Mexican workers. Fortunately, most researchers have decided to stop guessing. Recent estimates put the stock of undocumented Mexican workers in the United States below 2.5 million. Hence, we should be very cautious of the "plausible estimates" in table 4.

Let me summarize my argument:

1. While data problems are enormous, we do have accumulated scientific evidence that contradicts several of Professor Fogel's arguments; he has chosen to disregard it. Indeed, there is a big difference between apprehensions and crossings, between the gross and net flow

---

[25] See J. Johnston, *Econometric Methods* (New York: McGraw Hill, 1972), p. 160. My emphasis.
[26] See Fogel, "Mexican Migration."

of immigrants, between temporary and permanent residents. Statistical analysis based on dubious methods and on shaky data is not illuminating. Increasing apprehensions are compatible with a growing net permanent flow of migrants, as the author would have it. They are also consistent with a constant flow of temporary workers who respond to an increasingly efficient INS by repeatedly attempting their crossings. There is evidence to refute the first hypothesis; there is little to refute the second.

2. It is unclear why undocumented Mexican workers are singled out for consideration. There has been over the period an important influx of immigrants to the United States, some with papers, some without. Most of them have had to work to survive and were likely to face the same environment as the Mexicans.

3. Why does the question of limiting migration arise in the first place? Professor Fogel argues that markets have become inadequate to regulate migration because of the externalities that it causes. He also argues that "the populace is no longer willing to trust the market mechanism to bring about a salutary balance." Given our ignorance as to whether these externalities are positive or negative, and our ignorance as to their magnitude, we should carefully specify our policy objectives for the short and the long run before we suggest changes in policy. Furthermore, we have to know that the policy prescription will indeed have an impact on the problem at hand. While it is suggested, for example, that unsanctioned migration be ended, there is no provision for a specific mechanism. There is little reason to believe that tripling the quotas we have will in any way solve "the problem." If our objective is to protect all workers in the United States, it would seem that the simplest policy is to extend the coverage of the National Labor Relations Board to all workers regardless of origin or legal status and to enjoin unions to defend the rights of all workers aggressively.

Markets may increasingly become incompatible with our political goals, but our actions may provoke political externalities on Mexico that could be internalized by its limiting the flows of commodities and investment to and from the United States. We should not forget that there is a flow of undocumented capital to Mexico and that we have traditionally resented restrictions on our investment mobility. The real reasons for the phenomenon seem to have been left out of this discussion. Mexico and the United States have had a symbiotic relationship for the last 150 years. Migration to the United States and our increasing interest in Mexican oil are only two facets of such a relationship. To think that we can limit undocumented workers by tripling quotas and put an end to unsanctioned migration amounts to breaking a thermometer to cure fever.

236

4. Research that purports to show a change in causality from demand-pulled to supply-pushed migration in 1975 should be extremely careful about the choice of the period and the nature (direction) of the causality. Fogel's paper assumes that changes in legal structures reflected changes in economic behavior but does not test that assumption.

Professor Fogel's main argument is that growing unsanctioned migration from Mexico, no longer demand pulled, is causing negative externalities on the U.S. labor market. Unfortunately, this paper is based on casual empiricism and common-sense theorizing, not the state of the art of our knowledge. Policy prescriptions based on such guesses do not come from a rational consideration of the issues.

Discussion

SIOBHAN OPPENHEIMER-NICOLAU, Ford Foundation: We may underestimate the influence of World War II on ethnic groups. We talk a great deal about the depression retarding the progress of Italians and Poles. After World War II, they began to go to college. Being in the service was an important resocialization tool for many people because it removed them from where they were, it placed them in a highly disciplined environment, and it provided learning and training experiences that would not otherwise have been available. A popular war gives one a certain kind of esteem and self-respect. How many of those who went to college after the war were beneficiaries of the GI Bill? The GI Bill may have been an important tool for social change for the Italians and Poles. How does this relate to the Hispanics, if we do not have another experience that actually pushes people up—although that was not the purpose of the war?

MR. GREELEY: I would not want to press the model of the Italians and the Poles, much less the Irish, for strict application to the Hispanics. I am not advocating a "just wait and see, they'll make it" policy of neglect. I am not advocating anything else either. Here is a historical development that showed that all the conventional wisdom was wrong. Maybe we ought to be a bit skeptical about the conventional wisdom for other groups.

One of the best things that ever happened to the Poles is that they got out of the neighborhoods before the New Deal came and tried to do "good things" for them. The Chicago School of Sociology led to a movement in the "helping professions" in which we were going to come in and do things for and to these poor, socially disorganized people that they could not do for themselves. One of the advantages of having good things done for a person is that it helps. One of the disadvantages is that it also hurts. It may well be that, if the Poles had been around to reap the full benefits of a lot of the social programs in the New Deal, however well intentioned, they might still be where they started.

I am skeptical about any intervention into an allegedly disorganized part of the population that is concerned about anything but calling forth the best resources in the values that are already in that population. When people come into a neighborhood and tell people how to act right, then they are probably going to do a lot more harm than good. I do not advocate benign neglect; I advocate the kinds of helping that call forth what is in a population, instead of trying to change the population's values and behaviors.

Everybody benefited from the GI Bill, but the slopes were going up anyhow. There does not seem to be evidence that anybody got special help, with the possible exception of the Italians and Poles. There was prosperity; there were scholarship funds available. The GI Bill seems to have been equally used across all society.

Education is surely essential to any kind of achievement, but the reasons people seek education are also important. It may be that the Jews sought education as an asset to the making of money but that the Poles turned to education as the result of having made money. If we are dealing with another group, I would like to see how motivation for education can fit into their preexisting values, rather than trying to obliterate these values and then make them think and act and value like others. How would that be done for Hispanics?

EDWIN P. REUBENS, City College, City University of New York: I would like to raise a few questions about Professor Fogel's suggestion about the flow of Mexicans into the United States. He was saying that, until about 1965, this was mainly a "pull" phenomenon and that, after 1965, it became mainly a "push" phenomenon related to conditions in Mexico. While he notes some pull effects in the latter period and some push in the earlier period, he has distinguished the strongest force in each period. Some points support that, and others raise real doubts as to whether there has actually been a shift in dynamics. What were these pull forces and how did they work in the period before 1965? Professor Fogel refers to employers seeking out the Mexicans. The one specific thing is a reference to labor contractors and the bracero system. For the rest, it was a period of "wetbacks"; wetbacks are presumably supply-pushed rather than demand-pulled. We will have to explain the existence of wetbacks as well as cite the labor contract system.

In the period after 1965, some of the factors seem relevant; others are doubtful—for example, the growth of the population in Mexico. The population increased from 17 million in 1930 to 25 million in 1950. On a simple average calculation, this is 2.5 percent a year, or about 2.0 percent compound rate, which is so little less than the recent 3 percent that there probably has not been a great transformation in population growth.

Perhaps the population problem can be viewed in a different way, not merely an increasing rate of growth but the level reaching a certain threshold. That is to say, the flow of Mexicans into the United States was something that was held back moderately effectively by the Immigration Service so long as it was a few thousand or even 100,000 a year. When it gets to the magnitude of apprehending 800,000 to 900,000 a year, the size and structure of the INS organization is no longer capable of controlling the border. The hillsides are covered with Mexicans crossing the border at dark; the immigration agents dart about picking up a handful here and a half dozen there but are quite incapable of containing that flow.

Little reference was made to the "coyote" system, the name for persons organizing the flow of migrants across the border. When they are helped by somebody who knows the way, migrants get through in large numbers.

The rising expectations of Mexican workers lead them to be discontented with their misery, as they are left behind by the progress of the Mexican economy, in which most have not participated. There are some factors that would amount to a stronger set of push elements. Yet it still seems that push has been a powerful factor driving Mexicans from that country into the United States for perhaps four decades, that is, since 1940; only an intensification has occurred, enough to raise the flood over the barriers or thresholds.

MR. FOGEL: The principal forces initiating migration were pull forces. It is difficult to distinguish between pull and push forces. In each of the three migration periods, migration was initiated essentially by demand of and recruiting by U.S. employers. Once that is initiated and has gone on for some period of time, information flows back. As there are people who want to improve their livelihood, some momentum occurs.

I was trying to determine whether the current migration that began in 1965 is qualitatively different. It is not different to any great extent, but there might be some small qualitative difference. The post-1965 migration also began, as the previous ones, by the pull factors. The growers in California and other locations wanted to replace the braceros. Have certain things occurred in the last fifteen years that make the current migration qualitatively a bit different, a bit more supply oriented? A dramatic shift backward in U.S. labor demand would have reduced the flow, but it would have to be quite a sizable reduction in labor demand. This is seen on the basis of logic, as empirical support is nonexistent. The regression analysis in my paper is not anything more than consistent with the hypothesis, but my arguments are that the effects of population change are tremendous.

JAMES BASS, Inter-American Development Bank: Walter Fogel's data on the rate of population increase are correct and consistent. The jump from 2.5 to 3.5 percent in the annual increase in population occurred in the 1950s, when the mortality rate was declining significantly in Mexico. The explosive birthrate that we saw in the 1950s and 1960s did produce fourteen years later the high labor-force increase that we have had.

MR. FOGEL: Population in Mexico grew from about 26 million in 1950 to 70 million in 1980, which is about a threefold increase over a thirty-year period. That is a substantially greater rate of increase than in the 1910 to 1930 period. At any rate, the population of Mexico is substantially greater now than in the migration periods in the 1950s and the 1920s. Migration from Mexico to the United States increased partly because of the large Mexican-American population in the United States. Migration from Mexico is becoming somewhat more like migrating from Indiana to California—not the same thing, by any means, but it has become a bit more like that. On the basis of that logic, there is a bit more of a supply orientation of the migration.

MR. ALBERRO: I am a little puzzled with the discussions about population. The geographical origin in Mexico of the undocumented workers does not seem to be closely associated with fertility rates, mortality rates, or population density. It is not the lower income people who come to the United States, it is not the people who come to the Mexican border who come to the United States, and it is not the people who are leaving the most densely populated states either. Who are they?

About 70 percent of them come from about six states that have historically (since the 1920s) been the main suppliers of migrants. If we are going to base our whole policy decision on the premise that the labor force has significantly increased in Mexico since 1965, we should be careful to provide a little better explanation than the one that has been offered as to why demographic forces are so powerful. It is not a clear-cut issue at all.

MR. BASS: I have no difficulty with the explosive, population surplus push arguments. When, however, I see an R^2 of .99, either I am awed or I want to question it. It is a mixture of the two. Where did Walter Fogel get his labor-force data?

He refers to the Mexican *Anuario Statistico*. If that is the source of the data, then those are census period estimates that are done every ten years. If, in fact, he was using annual observations, those annual observations usually come from the International Labor Organization's labor force projection report in which they decompose the data into annual average growth rates over two five-year periods. The census observations are broken down into annual observations by applying the estimated annual growth rate of the labor force. What he is doing is essentially picking up a strong time trend. The data could be cleaned up a great deal by changing estimating procedures.

MR. FOGEL: James Bass is probably right. The time factor is strong. We are not going to prove anything at all except that the increase in apprehensions of Mexican nationals is not inconsistent with my hypothesis about population growth and is the consequence of excess labor supplies being strongly correlated to the migration over the period of the 1970s.

WALTER G. REST, Travelers Aid Society, Chicago: Are the statistics that Professor Fogel got from the Immigration and Naturalization Service an unduplicated count? It has been our experience that people picked up by INS are deported or voluntarily return; then they return to the Chicago area in a few months. They are picked up again; it is a revolving process.

In August 1978, the INS raided the Arlington Park Race Track and deported fifty-four workers. We had a little bet among the staff as to when we would see the first one come back. I said a week and I lost; it took the first one ten days. Within two months, fifty of the fifty-four were back at the race track.

These people do not stay in the United States, most of them, when it begins to get cold up here (Chicago). They go home; we begin to see them come back in April. They are past masters at getting across the border. They know where to go and how to do it and have the resources to do it. They do not have to depend upon "coyotes." There is a large population that tends to migrate back and forth, much as the Appalachian workers come to Chicago and practically commute between here and Kentucky and Tennessee.

MR. FOGEL: As long as the INS makes apprehensions at Arlington Park Race Track only once a year, there is no duplication in my apprehension statistics. Of course, there are duplications because some of the observations represent people who have been arrested multiple times. The enforcement efforts vary according to resources available and according to political decisions that are made by the INS. That certainly affects apprehensions. The biggest problem of all is that trying to go from apprehension data, as weak as they are, to saying that they are some kind of an index of migrant flows is a big jump. The only excuse I have is that I do not know what else to do.

MR. ALBERRO: The flow count may be unbiased if arrests are made only once a year, but the illustration of the growth of the stock in Walter Fogel's paper may be substantially biased upward. In the recent Mexican household survey, one of the questions asked was how long they stayed in the United States. About 75 percent of the respondents who had been in the United States said less than one year. The survey also asked about relatives in the United States. The short length of stay in the United States suggests a high return rate and a slow growth of the stock of undocumented aliens in the United States.

DAVID NORTH, New TransCentury Foundation: I have done some work on apprehension statistics that I would like to share. One of the things that one wonders about is whether the increase in apprehensions relates to increasing flow, increasing effectiveness of the border patrol, or increasing resources. We divided the effective officer hours of the border patrol for a period of the 1970s into the apprehensions by the patrol. In 1970, it took 14.5 hours of border patrol agent time to apprehend someone on the Mexican border. By 1978, it was down to 4.5 hours. The border patrol has not suddenly gone from a second-rate police force to a bunch of supermen. There are few other variables with which to be concerned. What is happening is a lot more traffic; that should be borne in mind as we talk about these apprehension figures. They are going up steadily, year after year, but the resources used to make them are virtually flat.

JOAN NELSON, Johns Hopkins School of Advanced International Studies: I am glad to hear the topic of return migration brought into the picture. In some other parts of the world, there are extensive patterns of migration that are temporary in varying degrees. This is one of the interesting lines of analysis that is beginning to emerge in migration work concerned with Africa and Southeast Asia. It focuses on the relationships between degrees of commitment to the city and intended length of stay—whether for a short period of time to earn some money to serve a particular purpose, whether repeated back-and-forth migration of the kind that has been described here, or working-life migration

243

with an intent to retire at home. They do relate to the kind and degree of economic integration, as well as social and political integration, in the place of destination. That dimension is something to take into account in thinking about the prospects for Hispanics, and particularly Mexican groups, coming into the United States and comparing them with various other immigrant groups, current and past.

Another fact to keep in mind, drawn from comparative work in other regions, is that, although a number of groups may start with a high proportion of the migrants being temporary, intending to return home, there is a long-term trend toward permanence. Sometimes that trend is steep. Sometimes it takes a couple of centuries to convert a largely temporary flow to a largely permanent flow.

MR. CHISWICK: Regarding Andrew Greeley's paper and Andrea Tyree's comments, some groups in the United States are highly successful, such as the Jews and Japanese, both native-born and foreign-born. Mexicans, and possibly the Puerto Ricans, are at the other end of the scale in terms of educational attainment, occupational status, and earnings. Why are there different rates of success and what factors are responsible?

MR. GREELEY: My paper is intended to determine whether previous immigrant groups have been disadvantaged by their immigration. Apparently, they are not so disadvantaged. In his work Barry Chiswick speculates that this may be due to the selective recruitment of more ambitious people to be immigrants. That is one possibility that could explain the advantages of Catholics and Jews over Protestants in my data. It may also be, in the case of the Jews, that they came better equipped for the economic struggle. As Professor Tyree says, they were neither peasants nor rich. It is often argued by people like Irving Howe that they were the people with the book. They were people interested in learning—pragmatic, practical learning. This is what Rabbinic learning was. This may have given them some advantages. The Irish may have had advantages of language; maybe the Poles and Italians have had the advantages of a much more cohesive and clannish internal community organization. These are all possibilities, easy to speak on the tongue, difficult to test empirically.

One possibility, of course, is that the Jews and Catholics do better because they are more Protestant. They score higher on measures such as Max Weber's Protestant ethic. Weber said the Chinese were the Protestants of the Orient. David C. McClelland's national study did indeed show that on his achievement index, which he takes to be a functional surrogate for the Protestant ethic, the Jews and Catholics are the highest on the Protestant ethic and the Protestants are below them. That may push the need for an explanation back further: Why did that happen? This is a difficult question to answer.

MR. CHISWICK: Differential success is not accounted for solely by the human capital variables. My question can be rephrased into two. Why, for our simple-minded measures of human capital, are there such different levels of attainment? Even within our simple-minded human capital categories, why do we find different levels of success measured either by earnings or occupational attainment?

MR. FOGEL: This finding of less earning success for the third generation than the second generation is an interesting one that I did not expect. I have not seen any good explanation. Once we understand "motivation," maybe we will understand more about the differences across ethnic groups. Hours of work are less for the third generation, which may suggest something about motivation or it may say something about different occupational interests or different consumption functions for third-generation Americans. We have to have the sociologists answer some of these questions for us because they study matters such as discrimination, tastes for occupations, and motivation.

MS. TYREE: I have thought about the same question for a long time and I have included a few other groups. Why have Hawaiians done so poorly, and the American Indians? Also, why do even the full-time year-round women in the labor force with much the same education and human capital characteristics as men do badly?

Let me try out an idea I have been mulling over for some time. Certain groups, the ones I call "flops"—that would mean blacks, Mexican-Americans, American Indians, Hawaiians, and women—enter the labor force, enter the competition, trying to climb up a system with an option of going back to some safe, secure subsistence or socially acceptable role outside the labor force. Certain groups did not have an option to return. Eastern European Jews, for example, did not have this option. The Japanese are a little harder to explain, except that those who did stay through World War II had almost cut off the option of returning to Japan for cultural reasons, the way they are treated if they return.

The same two groups, eastern European Jews and Japanese—why did they do so well, why did others do so poorly? I am trying to attribute it all to this one principle: Do they have a chance to withdraw from the fray, withdraw from the conflict, when they find that making the next success is difficult? Some people do not have that option, withdrawing from the fray. It is a lot easier to sweep floors and be a housewife than to try to be an academic.

MR. FOGEL: There has been a fair amount of work that explains something like 60 to 70 percent of the Mexican-American Anglo earnings difference on the basis of schooling, age, location and language variables, leaving a residual of something under 30 percent to 40 percent.

I certainly did not mean to imply that all of the externalities of Mexican immigration or any immigration are bad. I did mention among my examples sociopolitical externalities; I had in mind California. The culture there is greatly enriched and livened by the existence of the Hispanic populations.

There is some evidence of wages for low-skilled workers compared with wages for high-skilled workers being a bit lower in areas that we think contain concentrations of illegal immigrants. The hard data in this field are difficult to obtain and perhaps we have not done all that we could with what does exist.

MR. GREELEY: My mandate was to examine whether immigration was a barrier to the achievement of religious ethnic groups. After establishing that it was not, there is another question that is quite different. Why have they not only done as well as they have, despite predictions to the contrary, but why have they done better than other people? That is much more difficult to analyze.

It is not a statistical artifact. One could examine the same thing, for example, just in the standard metropolitan statistical areas with over 2½ million people and get the same finding. That eliminates most farmers, size of place, and regional variations; one finds the same thing.

Why do Irish Protestants and Baptists do so poorly in big cities? Many of them are probably recent migrants to the city, from the South, from the rural regions; maybe many of them are cyclical migrants. One useful model for examining the cyclical migrations from Puerto Rico and the cyclical migration of unsanctioned workers back and forth across the border from Mexico, Canada, and the Caribbean would be based on proximity. It may parallel the cyclical migration of people from the hills of Kentucky to cities like Cincinnati, Chicago, and Detroit. They are people who come with considerable disadvantages, who do not propose to stay, and who have a different approach from those who cannot go back.

It may well be that what we have for the Irish Protestants and for the Baptists is a situation in which they are the victims of a cyclical migration or a recent migration that cannot be tested with our data.

As Professor Tyree said, there are even some reasons for the Irish to refuse to acknowledge their success. Why is this? We are a melancholy people, we like to think things are going badly. We have absorbed a fair amount of self-hate through the years, being occupied by a foreign power. Also, there is the New York and the Boston phenomenon. New York is the cultural-media capital of the country and Boston the intellectual capital. If a professor or a journalist looks at the Irish, and particularly if he is Irish himself, he sees Boston and New York. For a number of reasons, the middle western Irish do much better economically than the East Coast Irish. There may actually be a selected misperception.

Part
Three

The Economic Impact of Immigrants

Immigrant-Inequality Trade-Offs in the Promised Land: Income Distribution and Absorptive Capacity Prior to the Quotas

Jeffrey G. Williamson

Recent research on American inequality by Peter Lindert and myself has confirmed the Kuznets hypothesis, namely, rising inequality with the advent of early industrialization, relative stability at a high inequality plateau during the late nineteenth century, and a recent egalitarian leveling across the middle of the present century.[1] Thus, the antebellum period is characterized by a sharp increase in wealth concentration as well as what we have called "wage stretching"—a rise in the wage premium rewarding skilled and professional occupations relative to unskilled common labor. The "income revolution" following 1929 is characterized by a similar conformity among all inequality indicators—a reduction in the concentration of wealth, a leveling in the distribution of income and earnings, a diminution in the wage premium rewarding skills,

This paper draws heavily on collaborative research that Professor Lindert (University of California at Davis) and I have been pursuing since 1975. While some of the ideas here were first raised in my *Late Nineteenth-Century American Development: A General Equilibrium History* (Cambridge, England: Cambridge University Press, 1974), Professor Lindert has played an important role in sharpening the views contained in this paper. Indeed, one section draws wholesale from a recent joint paper (Peter H. Lindert and Jeffrey G. Williamson, "Trends in Pay Ratios: Modeling America's Past and Speculating on the Future," Institute for Research on Poverty, discussion paper no. 472-77 [Madison, Wis., 1979]). I gratefully acknowledge Professor Lindert's important contribution, although I am certain that he does not wish to be held responsible for any remaining errors. I also acknowledge the intelligent and cheerful research assistance of Kenneth Snowden, who has put up with outrageous demands to fulfill this paper's deadline.

[1] For a discussion of the Kuznets cycle see Moses Abramovitz, "The Nature and Significance of Kuznets Cycles," *Economic Development and Cultural Change*, vol. 9 (April 1961), pp. 225-248. For the Lindert-Williamson research see Peter H. Lindert and Jeffrey G. Williamson, "Three Centuries of American Inequality," in P. Uselding, ed., *Research in Economic History*, vol. 1 (Greenwich, Conn.: Johnson Associates, 1976); Jeffrey G. Williamson and Peter H. Lindert, "Long Term Trends in American Wealth Inequality (Paper presented to the National Bureau of Economic Research Conference on Income and Wealth, *Conference on Modelling the Distribution and Intergenerational Transmission of Wealth*, Williamsburg, Va., December 8-9, 1977; and Jeffrey G. Williamson and Peter H. Lindert, *American Inequality: A Macroeconomic History* (New York: Academic Press, 1980).

TABLE 1

WAGE STRETCHING, LABOR FORCE GROWTH, AND IMMIGRATION,
1820–1966

Period	Gross Annual Immigration per 1,000 U.S. Population (1)	Rate of Labor Force Growth (% per annum) (2)	Rate of Change in the Skilled-Wage Premium (% per annum) (3)
1820–1840	2.67	2.95	4.49
1840–1860	8.61	3.38	1.48
1860–1880	6.15	2.24	0.47
1879–1899	7.00	2.80	0.59
1899–1909	9.37	2.35	1.06
1909–1929	5.11	1.62	−0.09
1929–1948	0.62	0.32	−1.99
1948–1966	1.52	0.45	0.35

SOURCES: Column 1: Average annual gross immigration over period divided by midperiod resident population, *Historical Statistics* (1975, part one), Series C-89 and A-7, pp. 8, 105-106. Columns 2 and 3: Williamson and Lindert (1980), table 9.1.

and a relative rise in the real wage for low-skill work. Table 1 summarizes this inequality experience by reference to trends in the skilled-wage premium.

There is a long tradition in American historiography arguing that the mass migrations of the nineteenth century introduced inequality where little had previously prevailed. The same tradition reappears when labor historians attempt to account for the behavior of the wage structure after the turn of the century, when these mass migrations ceased. These and other strands of thought imply the operation of an "immigrant-inequality trade-off" in American history; the gross time-series correlation presented in figure 1 offers support for the position. Given how complex and numerous are the forces that influence inequality, the high correlation between labor force growth and inequality trends in figure 1 is quite remarkable. Furthermore, table 1 suggests that this historical correlation is closely related to immigration itself.

Is it possible that this correlation is spurious? How does the immigrant-inequality trade-off hold up under closer scrutiny?

Labor Absorption, Assimilation, and the Immigrant-Inequality Trade-Off. Even the most primitive comparative static model predicts that increased immigration should tend to breed cheap labor in the recipient

FIGURE 1
Wage Inequality and Labor Force Growth, 1820–1973

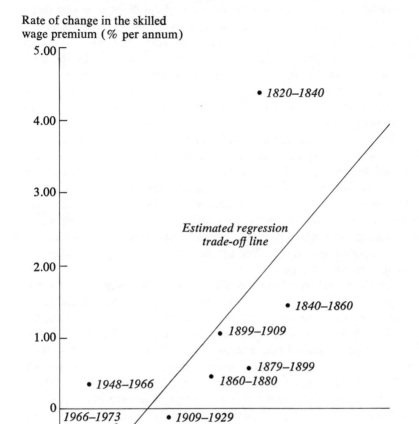

Rate of change in the skilled
wage premium (% per annum)

Rate of growth in the
labor force (% per annum)

SOURCE: Table 1. Estimated regression (*t*-statistics in parentheses):
$$y = -1.446 + 1.113\,x\,,\,R^2 = .483\,,\,DW = 1.556.$$
$$(1.351)\ (2.367)$$

253

country. In America between the 1830s and the 1920s, this should have been manifested in the short run by high unemployment among the new immigrants and the unskilled residents with whom the immigrants competed. It should also have been manifested by a high incidence of immigrants among low-skill service occupations, especially in the northeastern cities, the points of entry of the new immigrants. In the long run, immigration should have tended to lower real earnings of the unskilled, since immigrants tended to be concentrated among groups with relatively low human capital endowment, increasingly so as the century progressed.

The issue in American historiography, however, has never been whether immigration tended to suppress the rise in the real wage, thus augmenting earnings and income inequality. Surely, in the absence of mass migrations, the real wage would have risen faster and inequality trends would have been less pronounced. Rather, the debate has focused on absorptive capacity, assimilation, and the *extent* to which real wage growth was suppressed and inequality fostered. These are purely empirical issues, but they are no less interesting or relevant to forming contemporary policy.

Simple partial equilibrium analysis makes short work of the labor absorption problem: The only two parameter estimates required to evaluate America's absorptive capacity are the elasticity of demand for labor and, if we take immigrant labor supply as exogenous, the elasticity of supply of resident Americans. Figure 2 offers such a statement; it might prove a helpful cartoon around which to organize this paper's attack on the absorption issue. Suppose the domestic labor supply is augmented by an exogenous influx of European immigrants ("pushed" by the Malthusian devil), $\overline{M}$, and the domestic labor market is given sufficient time to surmount downward wage-rigidity. What real-wage decline is required to induce American firms to hire the immigrant-augmented labor force? The answer will define the immigrant-inequality trade-off; that trade-off is determined by the elasticities of S_N and D in figure 2. High native labor-force supply elasticities would imply "discouraged" native secondary workers being crowded out of the labor market by "unfair" foreign competition. Thus, the absorption would be accompanied by large changes in the composition of the labor force, as "old" residents are displaced by new immigrants; small real wage declines would be necessary to accommodate the immigrants. High-demand elasticities for labor would imply high absorption rates on the demand side, therefore inducing only modest crowding out of old resident workers and implying equally modest real-wage declines to accommodate the new immigrants.

FIGURE 2
LABOR ABSORPTION, WITH HOMOGENEOUS LABOR
AND EXOGENOUS IMMIGRATION

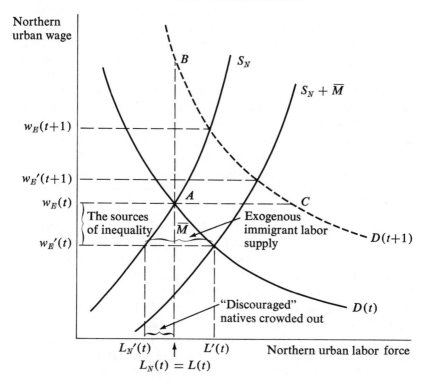

This simple partial-equilibrium analysis suggests one critical question that American historiography should be made to answer. Namely, how elastic was the aggregate derived demand for labor over the nineteenth and early twentieth centuries? After the 1840s, did the output mix shift in a fashion that tended to diminish over time America's ability to absorb immigrants? If so, what was the impact of these events on political attitudes toward "free" immigration and quotas?

Figure 2 employs simple comparative statics; $D(t)$ is drawn under the conventional assumptions of fixed endowments and constant technologies. This characterization is obviously inappropriate for a growing America that absorbed the immigrants while undergoing capital accumulation, land settlement, and technical progress. Suppose these buoyant growth conditions are characterized by $D(t+1)$ in figure 2. Assuming constant wage-elasticities on D and S_N, the impact of the immigrant influx on employment and the real wage is exactly the same

255

as before at $D(t)$. What is different about this case, however, is that the real wage rises despite the immigration. While voting attitudes toward free immigration may be influenced by American workers' perception of the size of $[w_E(t+1) - w_E'(t+1)] = [w_E(t) - w_E'(t)]$, what is likely to matter most is whether real wages rise in the presence of the immigration, that is, whether $w_E'(t+1)$ exceeds $w_E(t)$. This suggests another question that American historiography must be made to answer. Namely, did the rate of expansion in the derived demand for labor change significantly after the 1840s? Did it in fact decline over the century prior to the 1920s, thus encouraging the imposition of quotas? If so, what were the sources of the downward drift in the growth of derived labor demands? Exhaustion of the frontier? Retardation in the rate of accumulation? A change in the economic structure that served to diminish the elasticity of labor demand with respect to capital and land? Acceleration in the rate of labor-saving technological progress?

The issues of historical dynamics. Having focused attention on $D(t+1)$ in figure 2, we can hardly avoid issues of historical dynamics. To what extent was $D(t+1)$ influenced by the immigrations themselves? Accumulation rates may well have been raised, for if immigration tended to cheapen labor, profits were augmented; thus, both the profit share and the rate of return should have risen. Each of these forces was likely to have raised the domestic saving rate and thus the rate of accumulation. But by how much? How elastic *was* the rate of accumulation to changes in the immigration rate and did that elasticity change systematically over time? Furthermore, immigrants may have embodied capital to the extent that human capital investments had already been made in them prior to the move; this would have served to augment the stock of skills. There is also an active tradition in the historical literature that stresses the role of the frontier in "absorbing" the immigrants; that is, land stocks were elastic with respect to immigration. If these and other ameliorating dynamic forces were at work in nineteenth-century America, did their influence diminish with the passage of time, thus making the absorption task more difficult, reinforcing a pronativist movement?

Figure 2 also treats labor as homogeneous. Suppose instead we were to disaggregate labor into two types, unskilled and skilled. Suppose further we were to characterize new immigrants as being dominated by the unskilled and American residents as being dominated by the skilled. If unskilled labor (dominated by new immigrants) and skilled labor (dominated by natives and "old" foreign-born) are poor substitutes in production, then the immigrant absorption problem becomes more acute. There is, of course, a large historical literature that confronts this issue under the more colorful rubric of assimilation, mobility, and melting pots. Discrimination plays an important role in all of these accounts, though this paper later points out that a "revisionist" literature has recently cast some doubt on the conventional wisdom.

Figure 2 has served to motivate the outline of this paper. The immigrant absorption issue has typically been attacked by historians from two points of view, almost to the complete exclusion of a third. First, the microassimilation literature focuses on the labor market in isolation. The issues here are the extent to which the new immigrants suffered wage discrimination and barriers to occupational mobility. This paper later will briefly review this literature but will dwell instead on the macroassimilation issues. The literature here is surprisingly thin; there has been little or no attempt to analyze the problem of absorptive capacity within a general equilibrium system in which factor and product markets are allowed to interact. The time has come to take a more macro approach to the immigrant absorption issue in American history; thus, the third section expends considerable energy in that direction. While the model developed is quite simple, at least it offers a first step toward redressing the balance in the historical literature.

Second, there has been almost no systematic attention paid to the dynamic response of the American economy to an immigrant-swollen unskilled labor force. Given the long swing and business cycle tradition in the historical literature, it is surprising that there has been little effort to extend this tradition to the longer run growth and immigrant absorption issues. Indeed, most of the "new" cliometric literature on this and other historical problems conforms slavishly to comparative static paradigms. This paper expands on this theme by exploring domestic factor supply responses, while reviewing some foreign influences. Each of these warrants far more quantitative attention before American economic historians can offer any "lessons from history" to contemporary policy makers.

These important preliminaries dispatched, a simple three-sector general equilibrium model is later presented and used to explore empirically the immigrant-inequality trade-off. While this model is simple and tentative, it serves to direct attention to issues that partial equilibrium analysis obscures. This effort is extended by some quantitative experiments on the American nineteenth-century accumulation response, when the economy was shocked by mass migrations. These experiments are even more speculative than the analysis presented, but the effort is suggestive of the likely upper and lower bounds on America's accumulation response to nineteenth-century and early twentieth-century immigrations. The paper concludes with some contemporary morals.

The Growth Impact of the Immigrants and Dynamic Absorptive Capacity

What model is most appropriate to analyze the immigrant absorptive capacity of America? If our interest were only the short run—perhaps a year or two—then it would make obvious sense to choose a model in which industrial capacity by sector was limited. Capital stocks and technology would be taken as fixed, and elasticities of substitution between labor and capital would be set at levels approximating Leontief fixed coefficients. Furthermore, it would also make sense to embed labor immobility in the model, making it possible for excess labor demands to exist in some sectors or regions and unemployment in others. The longer the adjustment period admitted to the analysis, the less appropriate such "structuralist" models are. Our interest in this paper is in immigrant-absorptive capacity over episodes as long as two decades, episodes sufficiently long to make full economic adjustment—absorption—to a given mass migration possible. The model developed later will exploit all of the economic adjustments typically postulated in long-run neoclassical models. Thus, we shall assume complete labor mobility between sectors and across regions, full employment, market-clearing price adjustment in all commodity markets, capital mobility across industrial sectors, and high elasticities of substitution in both commodity and factor markets.

Comparative Statics, Dynamics, and Appropriate Counterfactuals. Long-run adjustments of a dynamic nature also have a hallowed place in traditional historiography. Some of these, however, have an impact only over epochs much longer than two decades. Some are influences about which we have only the vaguest notion and thus cannot be introduced with even any approximate precision into a macro model of immigrant-absorptive capacity. Four such influences will be discussed briefly in this section: farmland, western settlement, and the frontier; scale economies, the rate of productivity advance, and the factor-saving bias; demographic transition and "domestic" labor force growth; and capital accumulation. While the discussion of these dynamic influences is structured around the historical literature, it should be obvious that they deserve equal attention in analysis of contemporary immigration experience. The critical question in both cases is: How misleading are the answers that emerge from comparative static analysis of the immigrant absorption problem?

Frontier expansion and the "safety valve." The standard textbook in American economic history will tell us that natural resource abundance explains much of what was unique about the New World. Land abundance raised gross national product (GNP) per capita above levels in the Old World, where Malthusian forces had bred resource scarcity. Elastic land supplies implied rapid rates of farmland expansion and thus high rates of income growth. Elastic land supplies also served to place a "floor" under real wages in America since the disgruntled urban laborer could always migrate to the frontier, where a plot of abundant land awaited his arrival. The last of these influences is associated in particular with Frederick Jackson Turner's "safety-valve" thesis.[2] The thesis has become embedded in contemporary thought on American income distribution in the nineteenth century and on why labor was so "dear" on this side of the Atlantic.[3]

More recently, however, the thesis has taken its lumps. We are told that increases in the land stock in America never did contribute much to per capita income improvement, at least from the late nineteenth century onward.[4] Furthermore, it appears that even large changes in the historic rates of farmland growth would have mattered little to the trends in real wages across much of the nineteenth century.[5] If large changes in assumed exogenous rates of land stock growth cannot be made to influence the real wage or per capita incomes by much, it hardly seems worth the effort to struggle with an endogenous land supply specification in a model of immigrant absorption to be applied to an economy that, by the late antebellum period, was already extensively industrialized.

Technological change, scale economies, and factor-saving bias. It is hard to imagine how an immigrant-augmented population and labor force would influence the rate of total factor productivity growth unless

[2] Frederick J. Turner, *The Frontier in American History* (New York: Holt and Company, 1920); idem, *The Significance of Sections in American History* (New York: Holt and Company, 1932).

[3] H. J. Habakkuk, *American and British Technology in the Nineteenth Century* (Cambridge, England: Cambridge University Press, 1962).

[4] Edward F. Denison, *The Sources of Economic Growth in the United States and the Alternatives before Us* (New York: Committee on Economic Development, 1962); Lance Davis et al., *American Economic Growth: An Economist's History of the United States* (New York: Harper and Row, 1972), p. 39; and Williamson, *American Development*, chap. 5.

[5] Williamson, *American Development*, chap. 8; and Lindert and Williamson, "Trends in Pay Ratios."

the effect is translated through scale economies. Certainly, there are a number of scholars who support this position, among both development economists [6] and analysts of American history. The list is long, but these authors offer only assertions and beliefs.[7] Edward F. Denison, for example, tells us that 37 percent of the productivity change during the period 1929–1957 and 50 percent during the period 1909–1929 were attributable to scale economies, but both these numbers are pure speculation.[8] Simon Kuznets ventured the hypothesis that the rate of invention and innovation was stimulated by population size,[9] but, with one bold exception,[10] the hypothesis has never been tested. In short, while the belief persists that scale economies have significantly influenced America's productivity performance, a convincing quantitative test has yet to emerge. It would appear premature, therefore, to introduce scale economies into our immigrant-absorption model.

On the other hand, both John Hicks and H. J. Habakkuk have argued that the factor-saving bias in technological change is influenced by expectations about future relative factor scarcities, implying that increased labor abundance induced by mass migrations would tend to generate a diminution in the labor-saving bias of technological progress.[11] The only effective test of Hicks's thesis on American macro data is presented by M. Morishima and M. Saito.[12] Applying a multi-sectoral model embodying Hicks's theory of induced inventions, Mo-

[6] Ester Boserup, *The Conditions of Agricultural Growth* (London: Allen and Unwin, 1965); Colin Clark, *Population Growth and Land Use* (New York: St. Martin's Press, 1967); and Julian L. Simon, "Population Growth May Be Good for LDCs in the Long Run: A Richer Simulation Model," *Economic Development and Cultural Change,* vol. 24, no. 2 (January 1976), pp. 309-338.

[7] Moses Abramovitz, "Resource and Output Trends in the United States since 1870," *American Economic Review,* vol. 46, no. 2 (May 1956), pp. 5-23; Denison, *Sources*; Solomon Fabricant, "Study of the Size and Efficiency of the American Economy," in E. A. G. Robinson, ed., *Economic Consequences of the Size of Nations* (London: Macmillan and Company, 1963); and Zvi Griliches, "The Sources of Measured Productivity Growth: United States Agriculture, 1940-1960," *Journal of Political Economy,* vol. 71 (August 1963), pp. 331-346.

[8] Denison, *Sources,* p. 175.

[9] Simon Kuznets, "Population Change and Aggregate Output," in *Demographic and Economic Change in Developed Countries* (Princeton: Princeton University Press, 1960).

[10] Allen C. Kelley, "Scale Economies, Inventive Activity, and the Economics of American Population Growth," *Explorations in Economic History,* vol. 10, no. 1 (Fall 1972), pp. 35-52.

[11] John Hicks, *The Theory of Wages* (London: Macmillan, 1932); and Habakkuk, *American and British Technology.*

[12] M. Morishima and M. Saito, "An Economic Test of Hicks' Theory of Biased Induced Inventions," in J. Wolfe, ed., *Value, Capital and Growth* (Chicago: Aldine, 1968).

rishima and Saito find absolutely no support for the theory based on twentieth-century American data. In fact, *all* of the observed changes in rates of the labor-saving bias at the aggregate level from 1902 to 1955 were accounted for by changes in output mix between sectors of various factor intensity.[13] Morishima and Saito are telling us that, if there are endogenous forces influencing the aggregate factor bias, the source does not lie with Hicksian inducements at the firm level but rather with economywide changes in output mix.[14]

"Domestic" population and labor force growth. How might the "domestic" or "resident" American labor force and population respond to a mass migration from Europe? In the short run, if domestic labor supplies are upward sloping with respect to the wage, we might expect resident Americans to be "crowded" out of the labor market by new immigrants. Contemporary labor economists have struggled with this issue long and hard. It appears that income and substitution effects in contemporary America are such that labor-supply elasticities are low at best. In a nineteenth-century world of family farms, home enterprises, and low labor-market participation of married women, it seems unlikely that aggregate domestic labor-supply elasticities were higher than those estimated for the twentieth century.

Long-run influences on the domestic population are likely to have been even more tenuous. While the Walker thesis has a quaint corner reserved for it in literature, no one believes its operation to have been significant. The Walker thesis asserts that, in the absence of nineteenth-century immigrations, an offsetting rise in the American native population would have taken place.[15] General Francis A. Walker never offered an explicit statement of how the mechanism worked, but surely he had an economic model of "demographic transition" in mind, where economic variables play a critical role in influencing family formation rates and family size. Despite the ingenious efforts of Richard Easterlin and Peter Lindert, however, we have yet to be shown that fertility responds to income and "child costs" in the nineteenth century with

[13] Williamson and Lindert, *American Inequality,* chap. 7.

[14] This view is reinforced by recent econometric analysis at the industry level. One excellent example is offered by Hans Binswanger's analysis of American agriculture between 1912 and 1968. Binswanger concludes that "it is . . . clear from the series that it takes very substantial changes in factor prices in order to perceptibly influence the bias. The direction of technical change may respond only to massive changes in relative prices." (Hans P. Binswanger, "The Measurement of Technical Change Biases with Many Factors of Production," *American Economic Review,* vol. 64, no. 6 (December 1974), pp. 964-976; quoted, p. 975).

[15] Larry Neal and Paul Uselding, "Immigration: A Neglected Source of American Economic Growth," *Oxford Economic Papers,* vol. 24 (March 1972), pp. 68-88; and Williamson, *American Development,* chap. 11.

sufficient sensitivity to warrant inclusion in an immigrant-absorption model such as ours.[16] This statement does *not* deny the existence of a pronounced "demographic transition" across the nineteenth and well into the twentieth centuries; fertility rates do drift downward at a significant and persistent rate. Nor does it deny the existence of contemporary baby booms and busts. In any case, a domestic fertility response to immigrant-induced wage and earnings changes would take far longer than two decades to have any impact on domestic labor supply; that exceeds the time horizon adopted in the present paper.

Capital formation, population sensitive investment, and the accumulation response. As mentioned earlier, there has been almost no systematic attention paid to the dynamic response of the American economy to an immigrant-swollen labor force. This is certainly not true of the long swing and business cycle literature. Led by Moses Abramovitz, Easterlin, and Kuznets, that literature focused at length on the investment-demographic interactions over American business cycles and long swings.[17] Investment-demand-induced changes in capital stock growth, partially in response to immigration, are critical links in these models of macroinstability. There is absolutely no reason why we cannot appeal to these and other forces in modeling the long-run response of accumulation to immigrant-augmented labor force and population stocks and, thus, explicitly compare the long-run and short-run absorptive capacity problem. Indeed, one such effort has already been made that suggests that investment-demand forces—some of which are labor-force induced—were the key explanatory variables driving the savings rate upward across the nineteenth century.[18]

Our interest is in offering a simple but plausible accumulation response that can be reduced to a limited number of parameters with a

[16] Richard A. Easterlin, *Population, Labor Force and Long Swings in Economic Growth* (New York: National Bureau of Economic Research, 1968); idem, "Relative Economic Status and the American Fertility Swing," in E. B. Sheldon, ed., *Economics and Family Behavior* (Philadelphia: Lippincott, 1973); idem, "Population Change and Farm Settlement in the Northern U.S.," *Journal of Economic History*, vol. 36, no. 1 (March 1976), pp. 45-83; and Peter H. Lindert, *Fertility and Scarcity in America* (Princeton: Princeton University Press, 1978).

[17] Moses Abramovitz, "The Nature and Significance of Kuznets Cycles," *Economic Development and Cultural Change*, vol. 9, no. 3 (April 1961), pp. 225-248; idem, *Evidences of Long Swings in Aggregate Construction Since the Civil War* (New York: National Bureau of Economic Research, 1964); Easterlin, *Economic Growth*; and Simon Kuznets, "Long Swings in the Growth of Populations and in Related Economic Variables," *Proceedings of the American Philosophical Society* (February 1958), pp. 25-52.

[18] Jeffrey G. Williamson, "Inequality, Accumulation, and Technological Imbalance: A Growth-Equity Conflict in American History?" *Economic Development and Cultural Change*, vol. 27, no. 2 (January 1979), pp. 231-254.

sufficiently straightforward interpretation, so that we may debate their relative sizes. While we may disagree about these parameter values, we will at least be in a position of knowing exactly how our interpretation of the immigrant absorption problem is conditioned by our perception of these parameters. The model offered here is quite consistent with the long swing and business cycle literature cited, as well as with the conventional growth theoretic literature, which after all is based on the "stylized facts of history."

Let the (net) national saving function be specified by

$$S = Z r^{\varepsilon} Y_{P}^{\eta} \quad \text{for } \varepsilon \geq 0, \eta \geq 1 \tag{1}$$

where ε and η are the interest elasticity and the (property) income elasticity of saving, respectively. Dividing both sides of this expression by the initial (nonresidential) capital stock yields the per annum accumulation rates:

$$\overset{*}{K} = \frac{S}{K} = \frac{1}{K} \{ Z r^{\varepsilon} Y_{P}^{\eta} \} \tag{2}$$

$$\overset{*}{K}_{CF} = \frac{S_{CF}}{K} = \frac{1}{K} \{ Z r_{CF}^{\varepsilon} Y_{P,CF}^{\eta} \} \tag{3}$$

where CF refers to the counterfactual. Since our interest is in the impact of counterfactual changes in the level of immigration on accumulation response, we shall estimate that response by $d\overset{*}{K}_{CF} = [\overset{*}{K}_{CF} - \overset{*}{K}]$ as in equation 4:

$$\begin{aligned}
d\overset{*}{K}_{CF} &= \frac{Z}{K} \{ r_{CF}^{\varepsilon} Y_{P,CF}^{\eta} \} - \overset{*}{K} \\
&= \frac{Z r^{\varepsilon} Y_{P}^{\eta}}{K} \left\{ \left[\frac{r_{CF}}{r} \right]^{\varepsilon} \left[\frac{Y_{P,CF}}{Y_P} \right]^{\eta} \right\} - \overset{*}{K} \\
&= \overset{*}{K} \left\{ \left[\frac{r_{CF}}{r} \right]^{\varepsilon} \left[\frac{Y_{P,CF}}{Y_P} \right]^{\eta} \right\} - \overset{*}{K} \tag{4}
\end{aligned}$$

This can be further simplified to read

$$d\overset{*}{K}_{CF} = \overset{*}{K} \left\{ \left[\frac{r_{CF}}{r} \right]^{\varepsilon} \left[\frac{Y_{P,CF}}{Y_P} \right]^{\eta} - 1 \right\} \tag{5}$$

Finally, given that $Y = r \cdot K$, and as a first approximation letting $Y_{CF} = r_{CF} \cdot K$, we get

$$d\overset{*}{K}_{CF} = \overset{*}{K} \left\{ \left[\frac{r_{CF}}{r} \right]^{\varepsilon + \eta} - 1 \right\} \tag{6}$$

This paper will later put empirical teeth into equation (6) for various plausible values of ε and η.

A Free Lunch? Human Capital Imports and Foreign Investment. *Human capital imports, domestic saving, and skill supplies.* Recently, Larry Neal and Paul Uselding presented an interesting estimate of the human capital content of America's immigrants.[19] The question they posed was, If America had to develop in the absence of the immigrants and if the native born fully replaced the absent immigrants (the full Walker effect), by how much would the capital stock have been lowered?

The answer is based on two key steps. First, compute the "rearing costs" embodied in adult immigrants who would have required a resource commitment were they raised in America as native born. Second, by assuming that the saving rate from those rearing-cost committed incomes is that which actually prevailed in America, compute the saving and accumulation forgone. Their answer is startling: The 1912 capital stock would have been from 13.2 to 41.9 percent lower if the same labor force had been generated entirely by native born rather than in part by foreign born.[20] What this calculation implies is that the foreign born upon arrival were able to achieve higher savings rates since in effect dependency rates were lower (and "supernumerary" incomes higher).

One may wish to debate the mechanics of the Neal and Uselding calculation,[21] but it seems that these life-cycle and dependency rate effects might be well worth pursuing at greater length. Although this paper will not do so, the discussion suggests that the exclusion of these effects may serve to understate the accumulation response and thus overstate the long-run labor absorption problem.

While immigrants did indeed embody human capital,[22] did they enter at the average American skill levels or did they tend to dilute the "quality" of the labor force? The traditional position is, of course, that the immigrants entered the American labor force with distinctly inferior levels of health and education, especially when compared with the native labor force in northeastern cities.[23] It is also the consensus that the quality of the new immigrants drifted downward over time as the immigrant source shifted from the developed western European countries to the less developed eastern and southern countries. This is certainly

---

[19] Neal and Uselding, "Immigration."

[20] Ibid., p. 84.

[21] Robert E. Gallman, "Human Capital in the First 80 Years of the Republic: How Much Did America Owe the Rest of the World?" *American Economic Review,* vol. 67, no. 1 (February 1977), pp. 27-31.

[22] Paul Uselding, "Conjectural Estimates of Gross Human Capital Inflows to the American Economy: 1790-1860," *Explorations in Economic History,* vol. 9, no. 2 (Fall 1971), pp. 49-61.

[23] Gallman, "Human Capital."

what the inadequate occupation data suggest, but it is also suggested by the average per capita income of the sending countries. Peter Lindert has shown that the ratio of average GNP per capita in countries of immigrant origin to the United States per capita GNP declines from roughly 80 percent in the 1850s to about 40 percent shortly before World War I.[24]

Some evidence drawn from the American labor market confirms that the level of immigrant "quality" was significantly below the American average. If conventional wealth correlates with income, and income with skills, then the evidence from the 1860 and 1870 wealth censuses offer a confirmation. In 1860, for example, free males aged thirty–thirty-nine had average wealth equal to $2,444 and $1,051 for native born and foreign born, respectively.[25] Presumably, the difference would have been even greater had we information on new immigrants rather than simply the foreign born. Further evidence is available at the turn of the century, this time for annual earnings. The *Eighteenth Annual Report of the Commissioner of Labor* reports average annual earnings of male household heads (1903), for all workers with wage and salary income below $1,200 (which Stanley Lebergott suggests would represent something like 95 percent of nonfarm families in 1900).[26] While the foreign born were 94 percent of the U.S. average, foreign born from "new" countries—presumably more recent immigrants from poorer countries—had much lower incomes (Italy, 80 percent; Russia, 84 percent; and Austria-Hungary, 85 percent).[27] Finally, the foreign born in 1890 tended to be in "skilled" occupations much less frequently (40.5 percent) than were native-born whites (55.2 percent).

All of this evidence clearly supports the view that new immigrants had, on average, far lower skills than was typical of the resident labor force. This characterization holds, however, with far less strength for the first half of the nineteenth century. This should serve to motivate the approach used here to quantify the trade-off. First, we shall assume that the immigrants enter as "unskilled" common labor. Second, we shall assume that they enter at the American average skill level. The truth lies between these bounds, no doubt closer to the first assumption.

[24] Lindert, *Fertility and Scarcity*, p. 243.

[25] Lee Soltow, *Men and Wealth in the United States, 1850-1870* (New Haven, Conn.: Yale University Press, 1975), p. 77.

[26] Stanley Lebergott, *The American Economy: Income, Wealth and Want* (Princeton: Princeton University Press, 1976), p. 321.

[27] Peter J. Hill, "Relative Skill and Income Levels of Native and Foreign Born Workers in the United States," *Explorations in Economic History,* vol. 12, no. 1 (January 1975), p. 53.

This paper will later offer some guidance on the relative importance of the skill endowment assumption to the immigrant absorption issue.

Immigration and foreign investment. It is well known that immigrants and foreign investment tended to flow in the same direction in the nineteenth century; it seems apparent that foreign investment was responding to expected profitability differentials.[28] We would certainly expect an immigrant-swollen labor force to raise investment profitability, thus encouraging a foreign investment response and rapid domestic accumulation. Indeed, if one believes that world capital markets were perfect, then one would take American capital supplies as infinitely elastic. Except for some brief critical episodes in the first half of the nineteenth century, however, foreign investment was always a small share of total national investment, never exceeding 5 percent after the 1830s.[29] In any case, to use foreign capital to defend an elastic capital supply, or even a saving, specification would place far more weight on the efficient operation of international capital markets than the historical evidence can support.[30] We should keep the notion in mind, however, when establishing the relevance of experiments involving ε.

Absorbing the Immigrants

The traditional ethnic historian has tended to focus on the labor market in isolation; microassimilation issues have attracted his attention almost exclusively. In contrast, this paper focuses on the macroassimilation issues. Yet, there are elements of the traditional ethnic histories that warrant our brief attention since they will help motivate the macro model we have chosen to implement. The ethnic historian's thesis states that due to discrimination the melting pot worked imperfectly at best.[31] There are two critical premises underlying the thesis. First, discrimination played a significant role in determining the initial economic position of the immigrant since he received lower wages for the same work. Second, discrimination blocked the immigrant's efforts to scale the economic ladder since he was at least partially excluded from skilled occupations.

[28] Jeffrey G. Williamson, *American Growth and the Balance of Payments, 1820-1913* (Chapel Hill, N.C.: University of North Carolina Press, 1964), chap. 4.

[29] Williamson, "Inequality, Accumulation, and Technological Imbalance," p. 241.

[30] Michael Edelstein, "The Determinants of U.K. Investment Abroad, 1870-1913: The U.S. Case," *Journal of Economic History*, vol. 34 (December 1974), pp. 980-1007.

[31] Maurice R. Davie, *World Immigration* (New York: Macmillan, 1936); Oscar Handlin, *The Uprooted* (New York: Grosset and Dunlap, 1951); and Stephan Thernstrom, *The Other Bostonians: Poverty and Progress in the American Metropolis, 1880-1970* (Cambridge, Mass.: Harvard University Press, 1973).

Discrimination: How Did the Melting Pot Really Work? A revisionist literature has developed of late that appears to reject the first premise. Robert Higgs, Peter Hill, and Joan Hannon have found no turn-of-the-century evidence to confirm the view that immigrants were paid less for the same work.[32] Their econometric results suggest instead that there was *no* wage discrimination among employed workers, given age, sex, literacy, schooling, and on-the-job training. These revisionist results suggest that we treat new immigrants and resident Americans (of given skill) as perfect substitutes in production.

The revisionists have found it far more difficult to reject the thesis that immigrants found their path up the socioeconomic ladder blocked by discrimination. Indeed, Hannon has found abundant confirmation of discriminatory barriers to social mobility and thus limitations on the rate of human capital formation among the foreign born.[33] Such findings motivate the following simplification that first-generation immigrants cannot accumulate sufficient human capital to move from one skill status to another.

A Simple General Equilibrium Model of the Absorption Problem. This section [34] will offer a general equilibrium model that has been shown elsewhere to fit the long-run history of American prefiscal earnings inequality very well.[35] The model has several features that merit attention, although it has yet to be tested against competitors. One advantage of the model is that it is appropriate for explaining distributional events lasting longer than a decade. A second advantage is that the model not only fits past experience but also is especially convenient for the type of counterfactual analysis that this paper attempts. Finally, the model focuses on forces that are typically ignored in discussions of income distribution, in particular changes in labor force growth and technological performance over the course of economic development.

---

[32] Robert Higgs, "Race, Skills, and Earnings: American Immigrants in 1909," *Journal of Economic History,* vol. 31, no. 2 (June 1971), pp. 420-428; Hill, "Native and Foreign Born Workers"; and Joan Hannon, "The Immigrant Worker in the Promised Land: Human Capital and Ethnic Discrimination in the Michigan Labor Market, 1888-1890" (Ph.D. diss., University of Wisconsin, Department of Economics, 1977).

[33] Hannon, "Immigrant Worker."

[34] This section draws wholesale on Lindert and Williamson, "Trends in Pay Ratios," section 2.

[35] Jeffrey G. Williamson, "The Sources of American Inequality, 1896-1948," *Review of Economics and Statistics,* vol. 58, no. 4 (November 1976), pp. 387-397; Lindert and Williamson, "Trends in Pay Ratios"; and Williamson and Lindert, *American Inequality,* chap. 10.

The model is a variant of one initially suggested by Ronald Jones.[36] Four factors of production (i) are distinguished in our nineteenth-century variant of the Jones model: $i = J, K, L, S$, with farm land (J), excluding improvements other than initial clearing for cultivation or pasture; capital (K), consisting of all nonhuman asset services in the business and government sectors, other than farm land; unskilled labor (L), or total person-hours, compensated at the unskilled wage rate; and skills (S), or all attributes of labor input generating as much earnings as is received by an average skilled laborer in a base period.

The economy is disaggregated into three key sectors (j) whose technological attributes may affect relative factor rewards: $j = A, M, C$, with agriculture (A), or all gross national product originating in agriculture, forestry, and fisheries; industry, or the secondary or manufacturing sector (M), consisting of all gross national product originating in mining, manufacturing, transportation, communications, and utilities; and the tertiary sector (C), or all gross national product originating in construction, finance, trade, private services, and government. Land is confined to the agricultural sector. It is further assumed that skilled labor is mobile only between the industrial and tertiary sectors, since the available data make the measurement of agricultural skills extremely difficult. Unskilled labor and capital are assumed to be perfectly mobile among all sectors.

Besides the three sectoral output levels ($A, M,$ and C), the model determines various endogenous variables. For factor rents, $d =$ the real rental earned on an acre of cleared farm land, $r =$ the real rental earned on manmade nonhuman capital, $w =$ the real-wage rate for unskilled labor, and $q =$ the real-wage premium for skilled labor.[37] For output prices, $P_M =$ the price of industrial goods relative to agricultural goods ($P_A = 1$) and $P_C =$ the price of tertiary goods and services relative to agricultural goods.

Assuming perfect competition in product markets, the equality of price and average cost yields three cost equations:

$$1 = a_{JA}d + a_{KA}r + a_{LA}w, \tag{7}$$

$$P_M = a_{KM}r + a_{LM}w + a_{SM}q, \quad \text{and} \tag{8}$$

$$P_C = a_{KC}r + a_{LC}w + a_{SC}q \tag{9}$$

---

[36] Ronald Jones, "The Structure of Simple General Equilibrium Models," *Journal of Political Economy*, vol. 73 (December 1965), pp. 557-572.

[37] Skills are defined as attributes commanding pay above that of common labor. Thus, the return to skills is *not* the "skilled-labor" wage but rather its premium above the unskilled wage. If skilled workers earned $6 an hour and unskilled labor earned $4 an hour, the ratio q/w would be 0.50, not 1.50.

where the a_{ij}'s are physical input-output ratios. These expressions take on a convenient form when they are converted into rates of change involving sectoral factor cost shares, θ_{ij}, for the ith factor in the jth sector. These factors, or cost shares, add up to unity for each sector, since costs are assumed to exhaust the value of product. To explore linear approximations involving rates of change, we use the asterisk notation for rates of change per annum. Differentiating the cost equations and converting them into rates of change yields:

$$0 = \overset{*}{d}\theta_{JA} + \overset{*}{r}\theta_{KA} + \overset{*}{w}\theta_{LA} \qquad + \sum_i \overset{*}{a_{iA}}\theta_{iA} \qquad (10)$$

$$\overset{*}{P_M} = \overset{*}{r}\theta_{KM} + \overset{*}{w}\theta_{LM} + \overset{*}{q}\,\theta_{SM} + \sum_i \overset{*}{a_{iM}}\theta_{iM} \qquad (11)$$

$$\overset{*}{P_C} = \overset{*}{r}\theta_{KC} + \overset{*}{w}\theta_{LC} + \overset{*}{q}\,\theta_{SC} + \sum_i \overset{*}{a_{iC}}\theta_{iC} \qquad (12)$$

The $\sum_i \overset{*}{a_{ij}}\theta_{ij}$ terms are weighted sums of increases in physical input-output ratios. These become more familiar when each is expressed as *minus* the rate of increase in output-input ratios, weighting all ratios by input cost shares and holding prices constant. In other words, each of these expressions is simply the negative value of the rate of exogenous total factor productivity growth, $\overset{*}{T_j}$. Regrouping so as to put all terms involving endogenous variables on the left and all exogenous terms on the right, the cost equations simply become "price dual" expressions for sectoral total factor productivity growth:

$$\overset{*}{d}\theta_{JA} + \overset{*}{r}\theta_{KA} + \overset{*}{w}\theta_{LA} = \overset{*}{T_A} \qquad (13)$$

$$\overset{*}{r}\theta_{KM} + \overset{*}{w}\theta_{LM} + \overset{*}{q}\theta_{SM} - \overset{*}{P_M} = \overset{*}{T_M} \qquad (14)$$

$$\overset{*}{r}\theta_{KC} + \overset{*}{w}\theta_{LC} + \overset{*}{q}\theta_{SC} - \overset{*}{P_C} = \overset{*}{T_C} \qquad (15)$$

The next four equations are full-employment statements giving the division of the total supply of each factor into its employment in the various sectors:

$$J = a_{JA}\,A \qquad (16)$$

$$K = a_{KA}\,A + a_{KM}\,M + a_{KC}\,C \qquad (17)$$

$$L = a_{LA}\,A + a_{LM}\,M + a_{LC}\,C \qquad (18)$$

$$S = a_{SM}\,M + a_{SC}\,C \qquad (19)$$

Equations (16) through (19) can also be converted into more convenient expressions by introducing shares (λ_{ij}) and taking rates of change. In this case, the λ_{ij} are the shares of each jth factor used in the ith sector. Taking derivatives of equations (16) through (19) and dividing through by total factor supplies yields:

$$\overset{*}{J} = \overset{*}{A} + \overset{*}{a}_{JA} \tag{20}$$

$$\overset{*}{K} = \lambda_{KA} \overset{*}{A} + \lambda_{KA} \overset{*}{a}_{KA} + \lambda_{KM} \overset{*}{M} + \lambda_{KM} \overset{*}{a}_{KM} + \lambda_{KC} \overset{*}{C} + \lambda_{KC} \overset{*}{a}_{KC} \tag{21}$$

$$\overset{*}{L} = \lambda_{LA} \overset{*}{A} + \lambda_{LA} \overset{*}{a}_{LA} + \lambda_{LM} \overset{*}{M} + \lambda_{LM} \overset{*}{a}_{LM} + \lambda_{LC} \overset{*}{C} + \lambda_{LC} \overset{*}{a}_{LC} \tag{22}$$

$$\overset{*}{S} = \qquad\qquad\qquad \lambda_{SM} \overset{*}{M} + \lambda_{SM} \overset{*}{a}_{SM} + \lambda_{SC} \overset{*}{C} + \lambda_{SC} \overset{*}{a}_{SC} \tag{23}$$

Each of the rates of change in input-output ratios $(\overset{*}{a}_{ij})$ consists of two parts, one exogenous $(\overset{*}{b}_{ij})$ and the other an endogenous response to changes in relative factor prices $(\overset{*}{c}_{ij})$: $\overset{*}{a}_{ij} = \overset{*}{b}_{ij} + \overset{*}{c}_{ij}$. In what follows, we shall pull the $\overset{*}{b}_{ij}$ terms together into summary measures of the factor-saving resulting from exogenous productivity change. These factor-saving measures, Π_i, quantify the economywide savings on the use of each ith factor: [38] $\Pi_i = -\underset{j}{\Sigma} \lambda_{ij} \overset{*}{b}_{ij}$.

The induced part of each change in an input-output ratio is defined in terms of elasticities of factor substitution and factor price movements $(\overset{*}{v}_i)$: $\overset{*}{c}_{ij} = \underset{k}{\Sigma} \theta_{kj} \overset{j}{\sigma}_{ik} (\overset{*}{v}_k - \overset{*}{v}_i)$. A key parameter here is the elasticity of factor substitution, $\overset{j}{\sigma}_{ik}$. A large empirical literature tends to place these elasticities between zero and unity, closer to unity for long-run analysis. There is also some evidence that capital and skills tend to be less substitutable, and closer to being complements, than either of them is with unskilled labor.[39] We assume this to be the case

[38] Our measures of Π_i are derived from total factor productivity growth estimates in from three to twelve subsectors of the economy. We do not exploit factor-saving bias assumptions *within* sectors, though aggregate factor-saving appears in Π_i. In short, we assume that the rate of total factor productivity growth equals $-\overset{*}{b}_{ij}$ for all factors within any given sector.

[39] P. R. Fallon and P. R. G. Layard, "Capital-Skill Complementarity, Income Distribution, and Output Accounting," *Journal of Political Economy,* vol. 83, no. 2 (April 1975), pp. 279-301; and Jonathan R. Kesselman, Samuel H. Williamson, and Ernst R. Berndt, "Tax Credits for Employment Rather Than Investment," *American Economic Review,* vol. 67, no. 3 (June 1977), pp. 330-349.

for both the nineteenth and twentieth centuries.[40]

Product demands are endogenous. Each sectoral (per capita) demand equation takes the form

$$Q_j/POP = D_j(Y/POP)^{\eta_j} P_j^{\varepsilon_j} P_k^{\varepsilon_{jk}} \qquad (24)$$

where all prices are again relative to those of agriculture, and $D_j =$ an exogenous demand shift term, $Y =$ constant price gross national product,[41] $POP =$ total population, $\eta_j =$ income elasticity of demand for j, ε_j and ε_{jk} are the own-price and cross-price elasticities of demand for j.[42]

Converting the demand equations into rate-of-change form, and rearranging to put exogenous terms on the right-hand side, yields

$$(1 - \eta_M \phi_M)\overset{*}{M} - \eta_M \phi_A \overset{*}{A} - \varepsilon_M \overset{*}{P_M} - \varepsilon_{MC} \overset{*}{P_C}$$

$$- \eta_M \phi_C \overset{*}{C} = \overset{*}{D_M} + (1 - \eta_M) \overset{*}{POP} \quad \text{and} \quad (25)$$

$$(1 - \eta_C \phi_C)\overset{*}{C} - \eta_C \phi_A \overset{*}{A} - \varepsilon_{CM} \overset{*}{P_M} - \eta_C \phi_M \overset{*}{M}$$

$$- \varepsilon_C \overset{*}{P_C} = \overset{*}{D_C} + (1 - \eta_C) \overset{*}{POP} \qquad (26)$$

where the ϕ_j are initial final demand or sectoral output shares in GNP. These two demand equations and the national budget constraint make

---

[40] Specifically, we shall assume that the elasticities of substitution between capital and skills are one-half and that all other elasticities of factor substitution are unity. Sensitivity analysis with other parameter values is reported in Lindert and Williamson, "Trends in Pay Ratios."

[41] The expression for gross national product is $Y_A = A + P_M M + P_C C$. The national product concept more relevant for demand patterns is gross national product divided by prices of all goods and services consumed (Y). We simplify by assuming that foreign trade is initially in balance for each of the three sectors, so that shares in domestic absorption equal shares in domestic production, defined as the ϕ_j's. It follows that $Y = (A + P_M M + P_C C)/(\phi_A + \phi_M P_M + \phi_C P_C)$, and, if P_M and P_C are standardized to equal unity in the base period, then in growth rates we have:

$$\overset{*}{Y} = \phi_A \overset{*}{A} + \phi_M(\overset{*}{P_M} + \overset{*}{M}) + \phi_C(\overset{*}{P_C} + \overset{*}{C}) - \phi_M \overset{*}{P_M} - \phi_C \overset{*}{P_C}$$

$$= \phi_A \overset{*}{A} + \phi_M \overset{*}{M} + \phi_C \overset{*}{C}$$

This rate-of-change expression is used to derive equations (25) and (26).

[42] The own-price and cross-price elasticities are $\varepsilon_M = -1.3$, $\varepsilon_C = -1.0$, and $\varepsilon_{MC} = \varepsilon_{CM} = 0.5$. For the period 1839-1909, we shall set η_C at unity. We also assume that η_M equaled 1.60 around 1850 and 1.35 around 1900. These income elasticities have been chosen as to be consistent with an income elasticity of demand for agricultural goods of 0.50 for 1850 and 0.40 for 1900, values broadly consistent with a number of empirical studies.

the demand equation for agricultural products redundant. It should be noted, however, that the budget constraint implies that the economy's foreign trade is balanced and that net international capital flows are absent. The responsiveness of international trade to price and domestic income is implicit in the relatively high demand elasticities assumed in what follows.[43]

We have nine rate-of-change equations with nine endogenous variables: the three output growth rates, $\overset{*}{A}$, $\overset{*}{M}$, and $\overset{*}{C}$; the four factor price changes, $\overset{*}{d}$, $\overset{*}{r}$, $\overset{*}{w}$, and $\overset{*}{q}$; and the two product price changes, $\overset{*}{P}_M$ and $\overset{*}{P}_C$. Other variables of interest can, of course, be derived from this list, the annual rate of growth of GNP, $\overset{*}{Y} = \phi_A \overset{*}{A} + \phi_M (\overset{*}{M} + \overset{*}{P}_M) + \phi_C (\overset{*}{C} + \overset{*}{P}_C)$, for example, or the change in capital's share, $d\theta_K = \theta_K [\overset{*}{r} + \overset{*}{K} - \overset{*}{Y}]$ or the change in unskilled labor's share, $d\theta_L = \theta_L [\overset{*}{w} + \overset{*}{L} - \overset{*}{Y}]$. The exogenous variables are the sectoral rates of total factor productivity growth $(\overset{*}{T}_j)$, the rates of factor-saving produced by technological change (Π_i), the factor supply growth rates, the population growth rate, and the demand shift terms.

The entire nineteenth-century model is summarized in appendix table 1, while values of initial conditions and parameters are reported in appendix tables 2 through 4. When we turn to twentieth-century analysis, the model is slightly revised. First, farmland is purged from the model, aggregating its returns and its growth into the capital category. This simplification is justified on two grounds. Farmland growth was no longer an important constraint on American growth after the turn of the century; farmland growth, as we shall see shortly, had little impact on earnings inequality and employment growth even in the nineteenth century. Second, the demand parameters are revised. Agriculture's continued relative decline implies that lower income and price elasticities should be assumed for the industrial and tertiary sectors since they make up almost the entire economy by the mid-twentieth century. At the same time, the agricultural demand parameters are revised to reflect the apparent decline in the income elasticity of demand for agricultural goods over time. Third, while the three-

---

[43] Demand patterns are taken to be independent of the income distribution. It may appear that this assumption serves to dampen movements in inequality since it does not allow increasing inequality to shift demand away from unskilled labor-intensive agriculture, thus fostering additional inequality. Yet estimates reported elsewhere (Williamson and Lindert, *American Inequality*, chap. 8) suggest that the demand-independence-of-inequality assumption conforms to twentieth-century facts.

TABLE 2

IMMIGRANT ABSORPTIVE CAPACITY, GIVEN RESOURCE ENDOWMENTS,
AND TECHNOLOGY

Year	Impact Multipliers on the Real Unskilled Wage, $\overset{*}{w}$		Economywide Unskilled Labor-Demand Elasticities	
	$\overset{*}{L}$ alone (1)	$\overset{*}{L}$ and $\overset{*}{POP}$ jointly (2)	$\overset{*}{L}$ alone (3)	$\overset{*}{L}$ and $\overset{*}{POP}$ jointly (4)
1850	-0.257	-0.253	-3.90	-3.95
1900	-0.308	-0.333	-3.25	-3.01
1929	-0.626	-0.656	-1.60	-1.52
1963	-0.496	-0.515	-2.02	-1.94
1976	-0.413	-0.426	-2.42	-2.35

NOTE: Column 1 calculates the full general equilibrium impact of a change in $\overset{*}{L}$ by 1 percent per annum on the unskilled real wage, $\overset{*}{w}$, given resource endowments $(\overset{*}{S} = \overset{*}{K} = \overset{*}{J} = 0)$, technology $(\overset{*}{T_j} = \Pi_i = 0)$, and demand parameters $(\overset{*}{D_M} = \overset{*}{D_C} = 0)$, for example, $\partial w/\partial L$. Column 3 converts column 1 into more familiar elasticity form, for example, $\partial \overset{*}{L}/\partial \overset{*}{w}$; similarly for columns 2 and 4, although here both $\overset{*}{L}$ and $\overset{*}{POP}$ are jointly varied. The years refer to the source of parameter and initial condition estimates.

sector division is retained for the twentieth-century analysis, the transportation sector is now allocated to the tertiary (C) sector. This change seemed sensible since, in contrast with the nineteenth century, transportation now has a much lower capital intensity than other industrial sectors.

Quantifying the Immigrant-Inequality Trade-Off. Appendix table 3 reports the demand parameters and elasticities of substitution used in the empirical analysis. The reader will note that these vary hardly at all between the benchmark dates 1850, 1900, and 1929. Thus, changes over time in impact multipliers are to be explained by changes in the structure of the economy, that is, by changes in initial conditions describing the composition of final demand, the sectoral employment mix, the sectoral distribution of capital, and initial sectoral factor intensities and cost shares.

Immigrant absorptive capacity: comparative statics. How elastic was the aggregate derived demand for immigrant unskilled labor over the nineteenth and early twentieth centuries (the wage-elasticity of $D(t)$ in figure 2)? Table 2 reports the full general-equilibrium impact multipliers on the real unskilled wage from a 1 percent change in $\overset{*}{L}$ (for example, a rise in the per annum rate of growth for unskilled labor from the actual rate of 3.38 between 1839 and 1859, to 4.38). Clearly, the more pronounced the decline in the real wage in the face of a given change in immigration-induced $\overset{*}{L}$, the greater the immigrant-absorption problem. Table 2 (column 1) suggests that the absorptive capacity of the American economy drifted downwards across the nineteenth century. More importantly, table 2 also suggests that the immigrant-absorptive capacity dropped sharply between the turn of the century and the 1920s, the impact multiplier falling from -0.308 in 1900 to -0.626 in 1929. Column 3 of table 2 converts these impact multipliers into more familiar elasticity terms. The economywide wage elasticity of unskilled labor demand was high in 1850, -3.9,[44] but dropped sharply between 1900 and 1929. This exercise informs us that America's ability to absorb unskilled immigrants changed quite dramatically after the 1890s. Not only does this offer a likely explanation for the surge in inequality over the decade and a half prior to World War I, but it also offers a potential explanation for the timing of the immigrant restrictions. Perhaps the sharp decline in America's ability to absorb the immigrants after the 1890s explains the rise in the pronativist movement, the creation of an immigration commission whose charge appears to have been to collect data to support the pronativist

---

[44] Some readers may find the elasticities reported in table 2 too high to be believed. They range between -1.6 and -3.9, taking on values around -2 or -2.5 in the post–World War II period. Under Cobb-Douglass technologies, a two-factor model with unitary elasticities of substitution would imply labor demand elasticities of unity. How is it that we get economywide aggregate labor demand elasticities much higher? The answer might be best seen by looking at the determinants of the economywide elasticity of substitution, σ, in a two-factor and two-sector model (Jones, "Equilibrium Models," p. 564):

$$\sigma = (\theta_{LM}\lambda_{KM} + \theta_{KM}\lambda_{LM})\, \sigma_M + (\theta_{LF}\lambda_{KF} + \theta_{KF}\lambda_{LF})\, \sigma_F$$
$$+ (\lambda_{LM} - \lambda_{KM})(\theta_{LM} - \theta_{LF})\, \sigma_D$$

where σ_F and σ_M are the elasticities of substitution within the food and manufacturing sectors, respectively, and σ_D is the elasticity of substitution on the demand side,

$$\sigma_D = - \left[\frac{\overset{*}{M} - \overset{*}{F}}{\overset{*}{P_M} - \overset{*}{P_F}} \right]$$

Clearly, high-demand elasticities tend to raise the economywide elasticity of substitution above the levels prevailing in either of the two sectors. While our model has three sectors and four inputs, the implications are the same.

274

TABLE 3

IMPACT OF IMMIGRATION ON TRENDS IN VARIOUS INEQUALITY INDICATORS
(percent)

Impact of Joint 1 Percent per Annum Changes in $\overset{*}{L}$, $\overset{*}{S}$, and $\overset{*}{POP}$, Due to a Change in Immigration Rates, on:

Year	$\overset{*}{w}$	$\overset{*}{q} - \overset{*}{w}$	$d\theta_L$	$d\theta_K$	$d\theta_{L,N}$	$d\theta_{K,N}$

Assumption 1: all immigrants unskilled ($\overset{*}{L} = \overset{*}{POP} = 1\%$, $\overset{*}{S} = 0$)

Year	$\overset{*}{w}$	$\overset{*}{q} - \overset{*}{w}$	$d\theta_L$	$d\theta_K$	$d\theta_{L,N}$	$d\theta_{K,N}$
1850	−0.253	0.814	0.045	−0.046	−0.205	0.090
1900	−0.333	0.723	0.053	−0.048	−0.189	0.107
1929	−0.656	0.761	0.027	0.052	−0.190	0.110
1963	−0.515	0.869	0.016	0.020	−0.167	0.070
1976	−0.426	0.933	0.012	0.006	−0.217	0.072

Assumption 2: immigrants enter at the average American skill level
($\overset{*}{L} = \overset{*}{POP} = \overset{*}{S} = 1\%$)

Year	$\overset{*}{w}$	$\overset{*}{q} - \overset{*}{w}$	$d\theta_L$	$d\theta_K$	$d\theta_{L,N}$	$d\theta_{K,N}$
1850	−0.257	−0.223	0.115	0.034	−0.135	0.171
1900	−0.330	−0.448	0.101	0.096	−0.141	0.251
1929	−0.695	0.158	0.093	0.134	−0.124	0.192
1963	−0.705	−0.042	0.119	0.187	−0.064	0.237
1976	−0.579	−0.091	0.164	0.121	−0.064	0.187

NOTE: Columns 1 through 4 deal with changes in economywide inequality indicators: the real unskilled wage ($\overset{*}{w}$), the skill premium ($\overset{*}{q} - \overset{*}{w}$), unskilled labor's share ($d\theta_L$), and the profit share ($d\theta_K$). Columns 5 and 6 deal with trends in two inequality indicators *exclusive* of the new immigrants and their income. We assume here that the new immigrants laid no claim on returns to capital and land.

position, and the eventual passage and imposition of the quotas themselves following the war.

Table 3 expands the absorptive capacity measures to include the impact of immigration on other inequality indicators. These include per annum rates of change in the skill premium ($\overset{*}{q} - \overset{*}{w}$), as well as changes in factor shares, the latter reported for income recipients first including and then excluding the new immigrants. The calculations are reported under two assumptions motivated by previous discussion. Assumption 1 treats all immigrants as unskilled, and assumption 2 has the immigrants entering the labor force at average American skill levels. Not surprisingly, the two assumptions have quite different

275

implications for inequality trends. They can be summarized briefly by reference to the skill premium. Skilled immigrants tended to reduce the skill premium, causing a convergence of the pay structure by skill and thus, presumably, generating a leveling of earnings among wage and salary earners; unskilled immigrants had the opposite effect (table 3, column 2). It follows that the gradual decline in the skill endowment of immigrants across the nineteenth century tended to aggravate further immigrant-absorptive-capacity problems, adding fuel to the pronativist movement, just as the conventional literature suggests.

As a final comment, the reader should note the contrast between the impact of immigration on factor shares economywide and its impact on factor shares among the recipient population *excluding* the new immigrants. To the extent that the latter was far more relevant in influencing political attitudes toward open immigration, perhaps we should devote more attention to columns 5 and 6 in table 3. Unskilled immigrants tended to raise unambiguously the profit share among native Americans (including old foreign-born) and to erode the unskilled labor share sharply. The same is not always true of the *total* profit share or the *total* unskilled labor share (both including the new immigrants). The difference is important.

Immigrant-absorptive capacity: comparative dynamics. The previous paragraphs confronted comparative static measures of immigrant-absorptive capacity. There we measured the capacity of the American economy to absorb new immigrants, given technology and resource endowment. In effect, we estimated the elasticity of the derived demand for unskilled labor. In what follows, we raise a different question. What were the forces shifting that derived demand function over time? It turns out to be more convenient to measure those growth forces as vertical movements in the derived demand function. Thus, in figure 2, the shift in the demand for unskilled labor from $D(t)$ to $D(t+1)$ will be measured by the distance AB, rather than the more conventional measure, AC. To put it in somewhat different terms, column 1 in table 4 reports the per annum rise in the real wage for unskilled labor, given a fixed stock of unskilled labor but allowing the remaining exogenous variables to assume their actual historic per annum rates of change.

The total shift in the derived demand for unskilled (immigrant) labor reveals some striking patterns between the 1830s and the 1960s. The secular movements trace a rising rate of growth of absorptive capacity throughout the period but at a retarding rate since the turn of the century. Perhaps even more revealing, however, is the dramatic interruption in that trend immediately following the 1890s. Indeed, between 1899 and 1909, the per annum rate is *half* that of the antebellum period. This would appear to offer further support for the view that America's declining immigrant absorptive capacity following the 1890s had a significant impact on the timing of the quotas.

What were the sources of this dynamic absorptive capacity experience? Table 4 decomposes these sources into four component parts: accumulation rates $(\overset{*}{K})$, farmland growth $(\overset{*}{J})$, the rate and bias of technological change $(\overset{*}{T}_j$ and $\Pi_i)$, and other forces $(\overset{*}{S}$ and $\overset{*}{POP}$ combined). These potential influences were discussed earlier; some have popular places in the traditional literature. It appears that the steady rise in dynamic absorptive capacity across the nineteenth century is explained primarily by technological influences. In particular, the low dynamic absorption rate in the antebellum period appears to be explained by unbalanced sectoral rates of total factor productivity growth favoring the capital- and skill-intensive sectors at the expense of the unskilled-labor-intensive sectors. These conditions change across the late nineteenth century, such that more balanced total factor productivity growth generated a much more buoyant demand for unskilled labor. Capital formation rates had a mixed influence, the declining growth in farmland had a small negative influence, and the combined effects of skills and population growth had almost no influence at all.

The sources of the sharp decline in dynamic absorptive capacity growth after the 1890s are consistent with the longer-run nineteenth-century experience. While the decline in farmland growth (the "closing of the frontier") and the retardation in capital stock growth both tended to contribute to America's sharply reduced immigrant-absorptive capacity prior to World War I, technological conditions contributed the lion's share. The story is quite similar for the mid-twentieth century; the resumption of rapid rates of growth in unskilled labor absorption following 1929 does coincide with the "revolutionary leveling" of incomes in America between 1929 and 1948. *All* of this appears to be accounted for by sharply changing technological conditions, switching from the unskilled-labor-saving attributes of the nineteenth century. The character of technological progress—unbalanced total factor productivity growth across sectors—seems to be the key force driving dynamic immigrant-absorptive capacity following 1839 and up to the present. Paradoxically, the poor immigrant absorption conditions following the 1890s, that helped to produce the immigrant quotas in the 1920s, were followed in the mid-twentieth century by immigrant absorptive conditions buoyant even by the standards of the late nineteenth century.

277

TABLE 4

PER ANNUM GROWTH IN IMMIGRANT ABSORPTIVE CAPACITY OVER VARIOUS EPISODES
(percent per annum)

Period	Year Supplying Parameters and Initial Conditions	Total Shift in the Derived Demand for Unskilled Labor (1)	Sources of Shift in the Derived Demand for Unskilled Labor			
			$\overset{*}{K}$ (2)	$\overset{*}{J}$ (3)	Technological change (4)	Other ($\overset{*}{S}$ and $\overset{*}{POP}$) (5)
1839–1859	1850	1.209	0.752	0.474	−0.014	−0.003
1869–1899 (A)	1850	1.691	0.595	0.348	0.753	−0.005
1869–1899 (B)	1900	2.112	0.949	0.359	0.849	−0.045
1899–1909	1900	0.633	0.700	0.069	−0.098	−0.037
1909–1929	1929	2.411	2.197	0	0.361	−0.146
1929–1948	1929	2.735	0.647	0	2.189	−0.100
1948–1966	1963	3.003	2.100	0	1.182	−0.279

NOTE: The total shift in the derived demand for unskilled labor reported in column 1 should equal the sum of the four sources listed in columns 2 through 5, except in some cases due to rounding. "Technological change" refers to the combined effects of $\overset{*}{T_J}$ and $\overset{*}{\Pi_J}$, as discussed in the text.

Immigrant supplies: counterfactual analysis. Thus far we have discussed immigrant absorptive capacity. These demand conditions were such that America's absorptive capacity reached an all-time low from the 1890s to World War I, suggesting a likely source of the timing of the quotas. Paradoxically, long-run buoyant demand conditions returned to the American scene following the 1930s and have been typical for most of the post–World War II period. What has happened to the impact of immigrant *supplies?* The rate of immigration reached its peak in the years preceding World War I. Did these supply conditions account for a large share of the inequality trends and thus for the pronativist movement? Was the same true of the antebellum period?

Table 5 offers some experiments that should help to identify the impact of immigrant supplies on American inequality trends since 1839. Three important assumptions underlie those calculations and should be stressed. First, we assume that immigrants enter as unskilled labor (assumption 1 in table 3); this may tend to bias upward a bit their impact on inequality trends. Based on the previous discussion, the bias is unlikely to be large. Second, since the nineteenth-century immigration data are better documented for gross as opposed to net migration, we have used gross rates throughout. That the level of gross migration exceeded net is not a relevant issue in what follows; we only require that gross and net migration rates are highly correlated. Third, we assume that immigrants had the same labor participation rates as was true on average for America, an assumption, while convenient, clearly violated by fact. The procedure is, then, as follows. In 1839–1859, the ratio of gross immigration to population $(GM/POP =$ average annual immigration to midpoint average population) was 0.0086, thus contributing almost 0.9 of a percentage point to population growth rates over the period. If we take the labor participation rate to be constant, then a counterfactual antebellum world of no immigration $(GM/POP = 0)$ would imply $\overset{*}{POP}$ lower by 0.86 percent per annum and $\overset{*}{L}$ lower by the same amount. Table 5 computes the impact of such counterfactual experiments on various inequality indicators. The actual experiments reported there refer to the impact on inequality of the actual historic levels of $\overset{*}{J}, \overset{*}{K}, \overset{*}{L}, \overset{*}{POP}, \overset{*}{S}, T_j,$ and Π_i. The counterfactual experiments repeat the same values of $\overset{*}{J}, \overset{*}{K}, \overset{*}{S}, T_j,$ and Π_i but vary $\overset{*}{L}$ and $\overset{*}{POP}$ according to the GM/POP assumptions given in the table.

Consider the antebellum period first. It is true that, in the absence of immigration $(GM/POP = 0)$, real wages for unskilled labor would have expanded at a somewhat higher rate (0.56 percent rather than

279

TABLE 5

The Impact of Immigrant Labor Supplies: Actual and Counterfactual Experiments in Five Critical Epochs

	Impact of Immigration on:			
Period and Experiment	$\overset{*}{w}$	$\overset{*}{q} - \overset{*}{w}$	$d\theta_{K,N}$	$d\theta_{L,N}$
1839–1859				
Actual $(GM/POP = .86)$	0.342	1.109	0.316	−0.463
Counterfactual $(GM/POP = 0)$	0.560	0.409	0.238	−0.287
1899–1909				
Actual $(GM/POP = .94)$	−0.094	1.251	0.319	−0.497
Counterfactual $(GM/POP = 0)$	0.222	0.568	0.220	−0.316
1909–1929				
Actual $(GM/POP = .51)$	1.397	0.181	−0.279	−0.169
Counterfactual $(GM/POP = 0)$	1.732	−0.206	−0.335	−0.094
Counterfactual $(GM/POP = .94)$	1.115	0.508	−0.231	−0.233
1929–1948				
Actual $(GM/POP = .06)$	2.535	−1.232	−0.070	−0.029
Counterfactual $(GM/POP = 0)$	2.574	−1.277	−0.077	−0.020
Counterfactual $(GM/POP = .94)$	1.958	−0.564	0.026	−0.159
1948–1966				
Actual $(GM/POP = .15)$	2.780	−0.514	−0.075	−0.085
Counterfactual $(GM/POP = 0)$	2.875	−0.645	−0.085	−0.060
Counterfactual $(GM/POP = .94)$	2.373	0.172	−0.019	−0.217

NOTE: These experiments treat immigrants as unskilled (assumption 1 in table 3).

Only $\overset{*}{L}$ and $\overset{*}{POP}$ are changed in these experiments, while all other exogenous variables are allowed to grow at their historic rates. Initial conditions and parameters are described in table 4; $d\theta_{i,N}$ refers to the change in factor shares among income recipients *excluding* the new immigrants. See text.

0.34 percent per annum), but apparently demand conditions were such to have produced a relatively unimpressive rise in real wages. The same is true of inequality indicators. Wage "stretching" would have still taken place, although at a less dramatic rate (0.4 percent versus 1.1 percent per annum); the "domestic" (native-born and old foreign-born) labor share would still have fallen sharply; and the "domestic" profit share would have still undergone a dramatic rise. Antebellum immigration does not explain the rise in inequality associated with modern economic growth, but it helps. Similar findings appear for the 1899–1909 period. While the real wage actually fell during the period and while it would have risen a bit in the absence of immigration, pronounced inequality trends would have still characterized the period even in the absence of immigration. Immigrant-absorptive-capacity conditions appear to play an important role in the nineteenth century independent of the actual supply of immigrants which America was required to absorb.

While the quotas were imposed in the middle of the 1920s and while World War I interrupted the international flow of immigrants, the period 1909–1929 still registered a significant influx, although below that of the pre-war peak surge. In the absence of the war interruption and the quotas, suppose the pre-war peak immigration rates had continued up through the 1920s. What would American inequality experience have been like under those counterfactual conditions? Table 5 suggests $(GM/POP = 0.94)$ that inequality trends would have been somewhat more pronounced. Suppose instead we consider the implications of the imposition of quotas in 1909 rather than in the 1920s? In the *absence* of immigrants $(GM/POP = 0)$, it does appear that the secular revolutionary leveling of incomes would have appeared sooner, though it hardly would have been as pronounced as the actual leveling following 1929.

Perhaps most interesting are the experiments reporting America's counterfactual inequality experience had we chosen to accept immigrants between 1929 and 1966 at the same rate at which they entered during the peak pre–World War I episode. Great Depression aside, it seems quite clear that America could have absorbed even those mass migrations while still enjoying an egalitarian trend in the income distribution. True, the leveling would have been nowhere near as revolutionary. It is also true that real wage growth among the unskilled at the bottom of the distribution would have suffered—declining from 2.5 percent to 2 percent between 1929 and 1948, and from 2.8 percent to 2.4 percent between 1948 and 1966. This calculation offers an explicit measure of the trade-off between immigration, real wage growth, and egalitarian trends.

Speculating on the Accumulation Response. Perhaps we have overstated the impact of these counterfactual pre-quota immigration rates on real wages and inequality trends in mid-twentieth-century America. Suppose, for example, we believe that an immigrant-augmented population would induce higher saving and accumulation, thus creating a more buoyant absorptive capacity and a less pronounced impact on inequality. Similar questions could be asked of the nineteenth century. We concluded that inequality trends would have been less dramatic in the antebellum and post-1899 periods in the absence of the immigrants. These conclusions were, however, based on the assumption that the historic rates of accumulation achieved in the presence of the immigrants also would have been achieved in their absence. Yet, accumulation rates surely would have been lower, thus reducing dynamic absorptive capacity, implying that the more modest counterfactual inequality trends might never have been achieved. This section reports some speculations on the size of that accumulation response.

Equation 6 offered one device whereby the accumulation response might be estimated:

$$d\overset{*}{K}_{CF} = \overset{*}{K} \left\{ \left[\frac{r_{CF}}{r} \right]^{\varepsilon+\eta} - 1 \right\} \tag{6}$$

where $\overset{*}{K}$ is the actual rate of accumulation achieved in a given epoch in the presence of the immigrants, $d\overset{*}{K}_{CF}$ is the accumulation response as a deviation from that historic rate, and r_{CF}/r is the ratio of counterfactual to actual rates of return (both evaluated at the midpoint of the epoch). Clearly, the size of $d\overset{*}{K}_{CF}$ will be determined by our perception of the two parameters ε and η, the interest-elasticity and the income-elasticity of saving. The *lower bounds* are not at issue; $\varepsilon \geq 0$ and $\eta \geq 1$. But what happens with the *upper bounds*? Contemporary analysis rarely finds estimates of interest-elasticities exceeding unity; econometric analysis of the nineteenth-century United Kingdom offers similar results.[45] If we allow for the more elastic response of foreign capital to the rate-of-return differentials, perhaps a higher ε might be warranted, but surely the range $0 \leq \varepsilon \leq 5$ exhausts all reasonable cases. As far as income elasticities go, a range $1 \leq \eta \leq 2$ will satisfy even the most extreme view. Thus, table 6 experiments with $1 \leq \varepsilon + \eta \leq 7$.

While it is certainly true that accumulation rates would have been lower in the absence of the immigrants in either 1839–1859, 1899–1909, or 1909–1929, in only one of these periods—the antebellum years —is the accumulation response significant. There, a 1 percent decline in the accumulation rates (for $4 < \varepsilon + \eta < 5$) in the absence of the mass migrations would have lowered the growth in unskilled wages by 0.11 percent per annum (the impact multiplier of $\overset{*}{K}$ underlying the 1839–1859 calculations reported in tables 3 through 5). While that impact may appear to be small, a glance at column 1 in table 5 suggests that a good share of the difference between actual and counterfactual real wage growth (0.560 percent versus 0.342 percent) would have been lost as accumulation rates diminished. This result would appear to reinforce the view that demand conditions were far more fundamental

[45] Michael Edelstein, "U.K. Savings in the Age of High Imperialism and After," *American Economic Review*, vol. 67 (February 1977), pp. 288–294.

TABLE 6

ESTIMATING THE ACCUMULATION RESPONSE TO VARIOUS
IMMIGRANT COUNTERFACTUALS

A. Counterfactual Prequota Epochs without the Immigrants

$\varepsilon + \eta$	1839–1859, $\overset{*}{K} = 6.57\%$		1899–1909, $\overset{*}{K} = 3.84\%$		1909–1929, $\overset{*}{K} = 3.16\%$	
	$(r_{CF}/r)^{\varepsilon+\eta}$	$\dfrac{d\overset{*}{K}_{CF}}{\%}$	$(r_{CF}/r)^{\varepsilon+\eta}$	$\dfrac{d\overset{*}{K}_{CF}}{\%}$	$(r_{CF}/r)^{\varepsilon+\eta}$	$\dfrac{d\overset{*}{K}_{CF}}{\%}$
1	0.961	−0.26	0.977	−0.09	0.978	−0.07
2	0.924	−0.50	0.955	−0.17	0.957	−0.14
3	0.888	−0.73	0.933	−0.26	0.936	−0.20
4	0.853	−0.97	0.912	−0.34	0.916	−0.27
5	0.820	−1.18	0.892	−0.42	0.896	−0.33
6	0.788	−1.39	0.871	−0.49	0.876	−0.39
7	0.757	−1.60	0.852	−0.57	0.857	−0.45

B. Counterfactual Postquota Epochs with Immigration at Pre–World War I
Peak Levels

$\varepsilon + \eta$	1929–1948, $\overset{*}{K} = 0.93\%$		1948–1966, $\overset{*}{K} = 2.98\%$	
	$(r_{CF}/r)^{\varepsilon+\eta}$	$\dfrac{d\overset{*}{K}_{CF}}{\%}$	$(r_{CF}/r)^{\varepsilon+\eta}$	$\dfrac{d\overset{*}{K}_{CF}}{\%}$
1	1.038	+0.04	1.009	+0.03
2	1.078	+0.07	1.018	+0.05
3	1.120	+0.11	1.027	+0.08
4	1.163	+0.15	1.037	+0.11
5	1.208	+0.19	1.046	+0.14
6	1.254	+0.24	1.055	+0.16
7	1.302	+0.28	1.065	+0.19

NOTE: This applies equation (6) to the general equilibrium model's predictions on r and $\overset{*}{r}_{CF}$ as described in table 5. In panel A, all counterfactual "without immigrants" predictions on $\overset{*}{r}_{CF}$ use $GM/POP = 0$. In panel B, all counterfactual "with immigration at pre–World War I peak levels" use $GM/POP = 0.94$.

in driving American inequality in the antebellum period and that immigrant supply made a modest contribution to those inequality trends.

Table 6 also reports the accumulation response had the pre-quota peak levels of immigration been allowed to flood America in the mid-twentieth century. Once again, the accumulation response appears to be trivial and thus is unlikely to influence the main findings already reported.

Morals of the Story

One can find abundant time-series evidence confirming a high correlation between immigration rates and inequality trends in America since the early nineteenth century. Such correlations offer the inference that America was trading off equality to absorb Europe's mass emigrations. When America decided that the trade-off was no longer in her best interests, the quotas were imposed and egalitarian trends followed shortly thereafter. This paper has argued that such correlations do not warrant such inferences. *Demand* forces appear to have driven American inequality experience after the 1830s, not immigrant supplies. Furthermore, the timing of the quotas seems to correlate quite well with American experience with immigrant-absorptive capacity. Paradoxically, buoyant immigrant-absorptive-capacity returned to the American scene following the 1930s. The quotas, however, remained.

APPENDIX TABLE 1

The Nineteenth-Century General-Equilibrium Model in Rate-of-Change Form

	$\overset{*}{d}$	$\overset{*}{r}$	$\overset{*}{w}$	$\overset{*}{q}$	$\overset{*}{P}_M$	$\overset{*}{P}_C$	$\overset{*}{A}$	$\overset{*}{M}$	$\overset{*}{C}$		Endogenous Variables		Exogenous Shift Terms
$\overset{*}{d}$	θ_{JA}	θ_{KA}	θ_{LA}	0	0	0	0	0	0		$\overset{*}{d}$		$\overset{*}{T}_A$
0	0	θ_{KM}	θ_{LM}	θ_{SM}	-1	0	0	0	0		$\overset{*}{r}$		$\overset{*}{T}_M$
0	0	θ_{KC}	θ_{LC}	θ_{SC}	0	-1	0	0	0		$\overset{*}{w}$		$\overset{*}{T}_C$
g_{41}	g_{41}	g_{42}	g_{43}	0	0	0	1	0	0		$\overset{*}{q}$		$J + \Pi_J$
g_{51}	g_{51}	g_{52}	g_{53}	g_{54}	0	0	λ_{KA}	λ_{KM}	λ_{KC}	$=$	$\overset{*}{P}_M$		$\overset{*}{K} + \Pi_K$
g_{61}	g_{61}	g_{62}	g_{63}	g_{64}	0	0	λ_{LA}	λ_{LM}	λ_{LC}		$\overset{*}{P}_C$		$\overset{*}{L} + \Pi_L$
0	0	g_{72}	g_{73}	g_{74}	0	0	0	λ_{SM}	λ_{SC}		$\overset{*}{A}$		$\overset{*}{S} + \Pi_S$
0	0	0	0	0	$-\varepsilon_M$	$-\varepsilon_{MC}$	$-\eta_M \phi_A$	$(1-\eta_M \phi_M)$	$-\eta_M \phi_C$		$\overset{*}{M}$		$\overset{*}{D_M + (1-\eta_M)POP}$
0	0	0	0	0	$-\varepsilon_{CM}$	$-\varepsilon_C$	$-\eta_C \phi_A$	$-\eta_C \phi_M$	$(1-\eta_C \phi_C)$		$\overset{*}{C}$		$\overset{*}{D_C + (1-\eta_C)POP}$

(Table continues)

285

APPENDIX TABLE 1 (continued)

where

$$g_{41} = -(\theta_{KA}\sigma_{JK}^A + \theta_{LA}\sigma_{JL}^A), \quad g_{52} = -(\lambda_{KA}\theta_{JA}\sigma_{JK}^A + \lambda_{KA}\theta_{LA}\sigma_{KL}^A + \lambda_{KM}\theta_{LM}\sigma_{KL}^M + \lambda_{KO}\theta_{LO}\sigma_{KL}^C$$

$$= g_{42} = g_{43} \qquad\qquad = g_{51} \qquad\qquad\qquad\qquad\qquad\qquad\qquad = g_{53}$$

$$+ \lambda_{KM}\theta_{SM}\sigma_{KS}^M + \lambda_{KO}\theta_{SO}\sigma_{KS}^C),$$

$$= g_{54}$$

$$g_{63} = -(\lambda_{LA}\theta_{JA}\sigma_{JL}^A + \lambda_{LA}\theta_{KA}\sigma_{KL}^A + \lambda_{LM}\theta_{KM}\sigma_{KL}^M + \lambda_{LO}\theta_{KO}\sigma_{KL}^C) + \lambda_{LM}\theta_{SM}\sigma_{LS}^M + \lambda_{LO}\theta_{SO}\sigma_{LS}^C),$$

$$= g_{61} \qquad\qquad\qquad\qquad\qquad = g_{62} \qquad\qquad\qquad\qquad\qquad\qquad\qquad\qquad = g_{64}$$

$$g_{74} = -(\lambda_{SM}\theta_{KM}\sigma_{KS}^M + \lambda_{SO}\theta_{KO}\sigma_{KS}^C + \lambda_{SM}\theta_{LM}\sigma_{LS}^M + \lambda_{SO}\theta_{LO}\sigma_{LS}^C)$$

$$= g_{72} \qquad\qquad\qquad\qquad\qquad = g_{73}$$

APPENDIX TABLE 2
FACTOR PROPORTIONS IN THREE SECTORS OF THE U.S. ECONOMY, 1850 AND 1900

The Share of Factor i Employed in Sector j (λ_{ij})

1850

$j =$	$i = J$	K	L	S	All factors (ϕ_j)
A	1.0000	.1656	.5951	0	.4022
M	0	.5241	.1871	.2095	.2710
C	0	.3103	.2178	.7905	.3268
	1.0000	1.0000	1.0000	1.0000	1.0000

1900

$j =$	$i = J$	K	L	S	All factors (ϕ_j)
A	1.0000	.0755	.3762	0	.2172
M	0	.5002	.2807	.3811	.3721
C	0	.4243	.3431	.6189	.4107
	1.0000	1.0000	1.0000	1.0000	1.0000

The Share of Factor i's Compensation in the Income Originating in Sector j (θ_{ij})

1850

	$i = J$	K	L	S	
A	.1430	.1110	.7460	0	1.0
M	0	.5216	.3479	.1305	1.0
C	.0575	.2560	.3360	.4080	1.0
		.2697	.5041	.1687	1.0

1900

	$i = J$	K	L	S	
A	.1580	.1320	.7100	0	1.0
M	0	.5104	.3092	.1804	1.0
C	0	.3922	.3424	.2654	1.0
	.0343	.3797	.4099	.1761	1.0

SOURCE: Williamson and Lindert, *American Inequality* (1980, chap. 10, table 10.2).

287

APPENDIX TABLE 3

Factor Proportions in Three Sectors of the U.S. Economy, 1929 and 1963

		The Share of Factor i Employed in Sector j (λ_{ij})				The Share of Factor i's Compensation in the Income Originating in Sector j (θ_{ij})			

1929

| | | $i =$ | | | All Factors | | $i =$ | | |
		K	L	S	(ϕ_j)		K	L	S	
	A	.2684	.2260	0	.1202	A	.5977	.4023	0	1.0000
$j = M$	M	.3575	.3194	.3751	.3584	M	.2669	.1906	.5425	1.0000
	C	.3741	.4546	.6249	.5214	C	.1920	.1866	.6214	1.0000
		1.0000	1.0000	1.0000	1.0000		.2676	.2140	.5184	1.0000

1963

| | | $i =$ | | | All Factors | | $i =$ | | |
		K	L	S	(ϕ_j)		K	L	S	
	A	.0932	.0807	0	.0388	A	.4980	.5020	0	1.0000
$j = M$	M	.3978	.2806	.3718	.3551	M	.2324	.1909	.5767	1.0000
	C	.5090	.6387	.6282	.6061	C	.1742	.2546	.5712	1.0000
		1.0000	1.0000	1.0000	1.0000		.2075	.2416	.5509	1.0000

Source: Williamson and Lindert (1980, table 11.2).

APPENDIX TABLE 4

Parameter Assumptions: Demand and Production

Parameter	1850	1900	1929	1963
Demand				
ε_M	−1.3	−1.3	−1.3	−1.25
ε_C	−1.0	−1.0	−1.0	−0.3
$\varepsilon_{CM} = \varepsilon_{MC}$	0.5	0.5	0.5	0.5
η_C	1.0	1.0	1.0	1.03
η_M	1.6	1.35	1.3	1.03
Production				
$\sigma_{KS}^M = \sigma_{KS}^C$	0.5	0.5	0.5	0.5
σ_{ik}^j elsewhere	1.0	1.0	1.0	1.0

The Impact of Immigration
on the Level and Distribution
of Economic Well-Being

Barry R. Chiswick

This paper is concerned with the economic impact of immigration on the population of the receiving country. The analysis considers the effect of immigration on the level and distribution of income of the population of the receiving country under alternative assumptions as to the characteristics of the immigrants and public policy regarding both immigration and income transfers. It considers the implications of variations in the two major policy instruments regarding immigration— the number of visas issued and the criteria for rationing the visas.

There is a presumption that the immigrants themselves gain from the migration, where "gain" is defined broadly to include not only money income but also country-specific consumption (for example, climate), personal safety, and freedom.[1] Indeed, there would be no migration if the immigrants themselves did not expect the benefits from moving, net of the costs and risks inherent in the migration, to exceed the benefits from remaining in the place of origin. The Vietnamese and Cuban "boat-people" are the most recent examples of groups willing to incur high risks, both in terms of their lives and in terms of an uncertain future, to become international migrants.

The impact of international migration on the economic well-being of the native population of the receiving country and the remaining population of the sending country is less obvious. Public policy, often useful as a guide to actual impacts, may not be useful in this instance. At various times, countries have promoted or discouraged either immigration or emigration. In addition, political factors often unrelated to, or contrary to, apparent economic self-interest have determined immigration and emigration policies. The virtual prohibition for nearly a century of immigration into the United States of persons of Asian

---

[1] For many, international migration is reversible. If the actual experience in the destination falls short of expectations, many return to their countries of origin. For others, return migration occurs when target levels of skills, income, or other assets are acquired, or at retirement. Whereas the extent of return migration is low among immigrants to the United States from some countries (particularly eastern Europe and Cuba), it is high for others (particularly Canada and Mexico).

origin and Israel's policy of encouraging the immigration of Jews, no matter how poor, aged, or unskilled, are but two examples of immigration policies motivated by noneconomic considerations. In recent years, the expulsion of persons of South Asian origin from several East African countries and the restriction on emigration from the Soviet Union are two examples of emigration policies dictated by political considerations.

The Economic Model

The analysis of the impact of immigration will be based on theoretical models buttressed by empirical evidence. Understanding these impacts is important for reasons beyond intellectual curiosity. It is only when the costs and benefits of alternative policies can be ascertained that public policy can be based on a rational decision-making process.

For purposes of exposition, a model of the world in which there are only two homogeneous factors of production, labor and capital, is first developed to present a simple graphic treatment of the issue. This is followed by a more complex model in which workers are differentiated into those with high and low levels of skill. Although most of the essential elements in the conclusions do not change, this extension is necessary because much debate regarding immigration policy is based on the distinction between more-skilled and less-skilled workers.

These models will consider not only the effect of immigration on the aggregate income in the economy but also the effect on the distribution of this income. An immigration policy that would increase average income, but with gainers outnumbered by losers, may not be adopted in a democratic society unless it is linked to income redistribution policies that spread the benefits more widely. The analyses include summaries of empirical studies of the effects of changes in labor supply on relative wages, a key assumption of the theoretical model, and of the impact of immigration. A welfare and social service system that transfers income to the low-income population is also incorporated into the theoretical analysis. With the maximization of the income of the native population as the primary policy objective, the effect on the optimal number of immigrants of alternative mechanisms for rationing visas and alternative treatments of immigrants in the tax transfer system are considered.

An economic mechanism for rationing immigration visas that is not part of current policy is examined. The alternative is a large (rather than nominal) visa fee or a postimmigration surcharge on the income tax. Under this scheme, the native population would receive greater economic benefits from the immigrants and would favor a larger total immigration than at present.

FIGURE 1
Schematic Representation of the Effect of International Migration on the Level and Distribution of Income

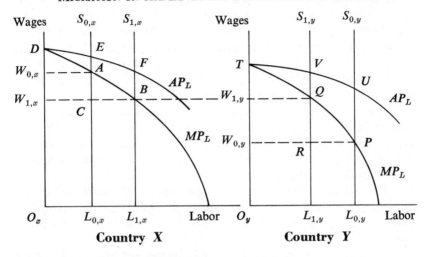

NOTE: AP_L = average product of labor
MP_L = marginal product of labor

Two Factors of Production. In a Ricardian model of the economy, there are two homogeneous factors of production, capital and labor, that are not perfect substitutes in production. For a given amount of capital, the marginal product of labor declines the greater the amount of labor in the economy, other things the same. The wage rate is determined by the intersection of the labor supply curve and the downward sloping curve for the marginal product of labor. This is shown schematically in figure 1 for two countries, X and Y. In the absence of international migration, the supply of labor in country X is $S_{0,x}$ and the supply of labor in country Y is $S_{0,y}$. Given their marginal product curves, the wage rates are $W_{0,x}$ and $W_{0,y}$, respectively. Since aggregate income in country X can be represented (figure 1) by the area under the marginal product of labor curve, total income is area $O_x DAL_{0,v}$, of which labor receives the rectangle area $O_x W_{0,x}AL_{0,v}$, and the return to the owners of the country's capital stock is the triangle area $W_{0,x}DA$. In country Y, total income is area $O_y TPL_{0,y}$, which is divided into labor's share, area $O_y W_{0,y}PL_{0,y}$, and capital's share, the triangle area $W_{0,y}TP$.

The situation portrayed by labor supply curves $S_{0,x}$ and $S_{0,y}$, is unstable if the present value of the stream of annual wage differentials $(D_0 = W_{0,x} - W_{0,y})$ exceeds the cost of migration. If there were no cost of migration (including no legal barriers), workers would move from country Y to country X until the wage differential were eliminated, as shown by the new labor supply curves $S_{1,x}$ and $S_{1,y}$ in figure 1. As a result of the migration, wages rise in the sending country and wages decline in the receiving country. At the margin, there is no longer any gain from migrating ($W_{1,x} = W_{1,y}$), and the net migration stream ceases. The earnings of the immigrants have increased, from a wage of $W_{0,y}$ to $W_{1,x}$. Costs of migration, including information about the labor market in the destination, can result in a persisting wage differential even if there are no legal barriers to migration.

The immigration has raised the aggregate income in the receiving country X, but it has also increased the number of workers. Because the capital stock was assumed unchanged, the marginal and average product of labor in X has declined. Average income has fallen from the length $L_{0,x}E$ to the length $L_{1,x}F$. Yet the native population is better off. The average income of the native population has increased because its aggregate income has risen from area $O_xDAL_{0,x}$ to $O_xDBCL_{0,x}$ (that is, the new aggregate income less the income received by immigrant workers).

In addition to the increase in the average income of the native population in the receiving country, there is a change in its distribution by economic function. The total income of capital increases (from area $W_{0,x}DA$ to $W_{1,x}DB$) and the total income of native labor decreases (from area $OW_{0,x}AL_{0,x}$ to area $OW_{1,x}CL_{0,x}$). The rise in the rate of return on capital provides incentives for more domestic investment and for the importation of foreign capital. This results in an outward movement of the marginal product of labor schedule and tends to increase wages for both native and foreign labor in the receiving country. The greater the extent of the increase in the capital stock, the smaller is the net decline in the wage received by native labor. In the limiting case, if the capital-labor ratio returns to its original level and if there are constant returns to scale in the economy, the wage rate returns to its original level. The favorable effect on wages of the growth of the capital stock would encourage additional migration. These second-order effects are not shown in the figure.

The effect of the change in the distribution of income by function on the personal (or household) distribution of income depends on the distribution of ownership of labor and capital. If each native household owned the same amount of labor and capital, the inequality in the personal distribution of income would not change. At the other extreme, if all the capital were owned by one household and labor was the only factor of production owned by the other households, the inequality in the personal distribution of income as measured by the share of income received by the top wealth holder would experience the

292

largest possible increase. Neither extreme characterizes the American economy, and, depending on how capital is measured, the economy is closer to one than the other.[2]

The level and distribution of income in the sending country also change in response to the emigration. As indicated in figure 1, the decline in the supply of labor raises the marginal product of labor from $W_{0,y}$ to $W_{1,y}$ and average income increases from $L_{0,y}U$ to $L_{0,y}V$. The rise in average income among those who remain is accompanied by a change in the distribution of income by function; labor gains and capital loses. The relative decline in the return on capital would discourage investments in country Y and encourage a flight of capital to country X. The effect on the personal distribution of income again depends on the distribution of ownership of capital and labor resources. The more highly concentrated is the ownership of capital, the larger is the decline in income inequality as a result of the emigration. Thus, in this model, emigration has the favorable effects of raising the level and narrowing the inequality of income.

For those accustomed to thinking in terms of "zero sum games," in which one party must lose if another party gains, the implication of the two-factor, two-country model in figure 1 would appear inconsistent. How can each of the three major groups in the international migration model gain? The gains arise from the movement of some workers from where they are less productive to where they are more productive. Because factors of production are not perfect substitutes for each other, marginal products change as factors move; this results in the gains to both the native population of the receiving country and the remaining population of the sending country.

Three Factors of Production. Although the two-factor model outlines the overall economic impact of immigrants on the native population, it is not useful for analyzing the differential impact on various groups in the labor market. A three-factor model, in which there is capital, less-skilled labor, and more-skilled labor, provides greater realism regarding the economy and highlights some important issues regarding the distribution of the economic impact between more- and less-skilled workers.

Recent research suggests that the U.S. economy can be well described by a three-factor constant-elasticity-of-substitution (CES) production function.[3] The three factors are high-level manpower (pro-

[2] The inequality in the ownership of capital is smaller if the equity of owner-occupied dwellings, automobiles, and wealth in asset-holding pension plans are included in the household's stock of capital.

[3] Using the Drymes-Kurz generalization of the constant-elasticity-of-substitution

293

fessionals, managers, and technical workers), all other manpower, and physical capital.[4] The production function and the algebraic manipulations needed to obtain the implications of immigration that are summarized here are presented in the appendix.

Within the context of a three-factor model, an increase in the supply of either type of worker due to immigration decreases the marginal product (wage) of that type of labor and increases the marginal product of both capital and the other type of labor. Since aggregate income in the economy increases by more than the total wages of the immigrants, the aggregate income of the native population is increased.

Thus, the immigration of unskilled workers widens the wage differentials between the two types of labor, increases the return to capital relative to the wages of the unskilled, raises the aggregate income of skilled workers and capital, and reduces the aggregate income of native unskilled workers. If the ownership of capital is concentrated, overall income inequality is increased. The immigration increases the return to investments in both physical and human capital. Unskilled native workers have a greater economic incentive to invest in schooling and on-the-job training, although this may be mitigated by the greater difficulty of self-financing human capital investments because of their lower level of wealth.

Suppose, however, the immigrants are skilled workers. This lowers wage differentials between skill levels and lowers the aggregate income of the native-born skilled workers but raises the income of unskilled workers and capital. The immigration raises the return on investment in physical capital relative to human capital. The aggregate income of the native population as a whole also increases. Income inequality in the lower part of the personal income distribution declines, but inequality in the upper part increases. The relative decline in the rate of return on human capital lowers the incentive for native-born unskilled

---

(CES) production function, C. U. Chiswick has shown that the data for U.S. manufacturing are consistent with a constant elasticity of substitution, where the pairwise elasticity is about 2.5. She used a two-equation supply-and-demand model in which the demand for professional manpower relative to other factors of production is derived from a three-factor production function in which nonprofessional manpower and capital are the other factors. See Carmel U. Chiswick, "The Rise of Professional Occupations in U.S. Manufacturing: 1900 to 1973," in I. Sirageldin, ed., *Research in Human Capital and Development,* vol. 1 (Greenwich, Conn.: JAI Press, 1979), pp. 191-217.

[4] For simplicity of exposition, the terms skilled and unskilled labor shall be used to designate high-level manpower and other workers, respectively. Thus, unskilled workers in this context are not workers without skill but rather with a lower level of skill.

workers to acquire additional schooling and on-the-job training, although their increased wealth facilitates the self-financing of the investments.

The analysis becomes somewhat more complex if it incorporates the finding that the skills of immigrants vary with the number of years they have been in the destination.[5] As a result, the initial impact of a cohort of immigrants differs from its ultimate impact. In an extreme example, if the immigrants are initially all unskilled when they arrive at their destination, they lower the earnings of unskilled native workers and widen wage differentials. As the immigrants adjust, their productivity rises, and in increasing proportion (in an extreme case, perhaps all) become skilled workers. As this occurs, wage differentials narrow, and the earnings of unskilled native workers increase. Ultimately, if the ratio of skilled to unskilled workers becomes larger among the immigrants than among the native population, relative wage differentials between skill levels are smaller, and the earnings of unskilled native workers are higher than prior to the immigration.

When there is a time path to the skill distribution of a cohort of immigrants, who gains and who loses among native workers, measured in terms of the present value of future income, depends on several factors. Of course, it depends in part on the initial and ultimate skill distribution of the immigrants compared with the native workers. It also depends on the time path of the change in relative skills of the immigrants. The greater the initial and ultimate skill level of the immigrants relative to native workers, and the faster they reach their ultimate skill level, the greater are the gains in income for native unskilled workers and the smaller the gains for skilled workers.

The discount rate of native workers, the rate at which they value today dollars received in the future, is also relevant. The higher the discount rate of unskilled native workers (that is, the smaller the present value of future income), the smaller is the gain to them from the type of immigration just described. Under a high discount rate, the declines in current income are less likely to be offset by the rise in future incomes as the immigrants become skilled workers. On the other hand, the higher the discount rate of skilled workers, the more they would gain from a policy that raised their earnings initially, even though it lowered them in the future.

---

[5] The pattern of low earnings on arrival in the United States and a subsequent rise in earnings with duration of residence is least intense for English-speaking economic migrants, more intense for economic migrants from non-English-speaking countries, and most intense for non-English-speaking refugees. See Barry R. Chiswick, "The Economic Progress of Immigrants: Some Apparently Universal Patterns," this volume.

Unskilled workers are likely to have a higher discount rate than skilled workers.[6] The difference in discount rates may account for the different level of investment in human capital. In addition, high discount rates may be a consequence of the lower level of wealth of those with less human capital.

If the divergence in discount rates by skill level is sufficiently large, that is, if the unskilled place little value on the higher incomes received in the future while the skilled place little extra value on receiving higher incomes in the present, it is possible for both skilled and unskilled native labor to lose because of the immigration. The income received, however, by the native population as a whole and by the owners of capital would be larger in each and every year; hence the present value of these incomes would also be larger with the immigration.

Immigrants and Investments. There is a presumption that immigrants have higher savings and investment rates than the native population. Immigrants appear to make greater investments in human capital, as evidenced by their investments in migration, including investments made to adjust for the imperfect transferability of the skills acquired in the country of origin. These greater investments may arise from a lower discount rate or from greater labor market ability, that is, a greater productivity of investments. The hypothesis that immigrants have a high savings rate and make greater investments in nonhuman assets is consistent with much folk wisdom regarding immigrants in the United States but has not yet been tested empirically.

The impact of immigrants depends in part on their propensity for saving relative to that of the native population.[7] Even if immigrants bring no nonhuman resources with them, if they have a higher savings rate than the native population, over time the capital stock increases faster than otherwise, increasing the ratio of immigrant-owned to native-owned capital. The increasing capital stock decreases the return on capital, and hence the income of native-born owners of capital and their incentive to invest in capital. As long as the per-capita capital stock is increased, however, the earnings of labor (native and foreign born) and the total income of the native population increase in response to the greater savings rate of immigrants.

---

[6] Gary S. Becker, *Human Capital* (New York: National Bureau of Economic Research, 1964), chap. 3; and David Caplowitz, *The Poor Pay More* (New York: The Free Press, 1967), chaps. 6-8.

[7] See, for example, Carlos Alfredo Rodríguez, "On the Welfare Aspects of International Migration," *Journal of Political Economy*, vol. 83, no. 5 (October 1975), pp. 1,065-1,072.

Applications of the Economic Models

The two- and three-factor models have been estimated empirically and have been used to analyze the effects of changes in population size on the level and distribution of income. This section reviews some of these applications.

Two-Factor Model. The two-factor model traditionally has been used to analyze empirically the effects of changes in population size on the level and distribution of income. Jack Hirshleifer, for example, used the model to analyze the impact of the Black Death in fourteenth-century Europe on the income of the remaining population.[8] The plague sharply reduced the population in parts of Europe but did not destroy the nonhuman factor of production—land. The effect would be the same as a mass emigration or the opposite of the impact of a mass immigration. Hirshleifer showed that the population changes due to the plague raised the real wages of labor (the bulk of the population), while land rents declined. Agricultural production shifted to less labor-intensive methods, for example, from tillage to pasture.

The two-factor model is useful for explaining an apparent paradox regarding immigration and the rate of growth of average income. Immigration raises the average income of the native population and, in comparison with their incomes in the country of origin, also the average income of the foreign-born population. Because the average income of the immigrants is less than that of the native population, the immigration lowers the average income of the total (native plus foreign) population. Thus, controlling for other effects, an analysis using a measure of the rate of growth of the income of the total population (for example, using data from national income accounts or household surveys) could show that it is negatively related to immigration and lead to the false conclusion that immigration retards the economic progress of the population.

Indeed, this may explain part (although probably only a small part) of the decline in the rate of growth of average real income as measured by conventional statistics in the decade after 1965. The 1965 amendments to the Immigration and Nationality Act resulted in a 25 percent increase in immigration (from about 300,000 per year to about 400,000 per year) and a shift in immigration in favor of those countries from

[8] Jack Hirshleifer, "Disaster and Recovery: The Black Death in Western Europe," Rand Corporation Memorandum RM4700-TAB (Santa Monica, Calif., February 1966). For similar findings regarding the effects of the 1918-1919 influenza epidemic in India, see T. W. Schultz, *Transforming Traditional Agriculture* (New Haven: Yale University Press, 1964), pp. 62-70.

which the skills of immigrants would be less readily transferable to the United States (that is, Asia). Both factors imply that the rate of growth of the average income of the total population would, for a time, lag behind the rate of growth of the average income of the native population.

Edward Denison used the two-factor model when he analyzed the impact of immigration in his path-breaking volume *The Sources of Economic Growth*.[9] He concluded that "larger immigration is among the most effective means available to stimulate the growth of the total product importantly. It is one of the few that, if continued, could boost the growth rates indefinitely, rather than only temporarily during a transitional period." He concludes that, although immigration might reduce per capita income, particularly if the immigrants are less skilled than the native population, "increased immigration would not reduce per capita income of the present population." [10]

Denison showed that, if immigrant labor is as productive as native labor, there are constant returns to scale, marginal products are nearly constant, and transitional adjustment costs are ignored, then a 1 percent increase in labor supply due to immigration would raise national income by 0.773 percent, that is, by labor's share of national income. If the supply of capital responds to its increased return so that the capital-labor ratio eventually returns to its original level, national income would increase by another 0.197 percent (capital's share). National income would then be higher by nearly 1 percent as a result of the 1 percent increase in the labor force.[11] When he assumes increasing returns to scale at a rate of 9 percent, a rate suggested by his analysis of scale economies, the 1 percent increase in labor inputs raises national income by 0.84 percent if the capital stock is not affected and by 1.06 percent if the capital-labor ratio is restored.

Denison estimated that a 1 percent increase in labor inputs due to immigration, currently about five years' immigration, would have the percentage effect on per-capita incomes shown in table 1.

Smith and Newman used an implicit two-factor model in their study of the effect of differential Mexican immigration on wages in four Texas standard metropolitan statistical areas (SMSAs), using data from the 1970 Census of Population.[12] Controlling for the person's own

[9] Edward Denison, *The Sources of Economic Growth in the United States and the Alternatives before Us* (Washington, D.C.: Committee for Economic Development, 1962), pp. 177-179, 275-277.

[10] Ibid., pp. 178-179.

[11] The increase would be 0.970 percent. The share of land sites is 0.03 percent of national income, and land sites would not increase in quantity in response to immigration.

[12] Barton Smith and Robert Newman, "Depressed Wages Along the U.S.-Mexican Border: An Empirical Analysis," *Economic Inquiry*, vol. 15, no. 1 (January 1977),

TABLE 1

Capital Accumulation	Returns to Scale	Increasing Returns to Scale (9 percent)
Rate unaffected	−0.20	−0.14
Capital-labor ratio restored	−0.03	+0.05

characteristics, they found that earnings are a statistically significant 8 percent lower in the three border SMSAs with a substantial proportion of Mexican-Americans than in Houston, which has a small proportion (9 percent) of Mexican-Americans. Even in the border areas, earnings are lower in Brownsville and Laredo (85 percent Mexican-American) than in Corpus Christi (33 percent). They attribute the outmigration of Anglos from the border area to the depressing effect on earnings of the Mexican immigration.

Three-Factor Model. The three-factor model of the economy, in which the factors are unskilled workers, skilled workers, and capital, has been shown to be a useful tool for describing the economy and recently has been used in analyses of immigration to the United States.[13] Over the past few decades, it has also been used in several studies of the labor market impact of immigrants in Israel.[14]

At the time of Israel's establishment in 1948, its Jewish population was composed primarily of immigrants from Europe. They came in large

---

pp. 51-66. For similar findings on earnings and unemployment, see Anna-stina Ericson, "The Impact of Commuters on the Mexican-American Border Area," *Monthly Labor Review,* vol. 93, no. 8 (August 1970), pp. 18-27. Larry Morgan and Bruce Gardner use a multisector two-factor model in their paper "Potential for a U.S. Guest-Worker Program in Agriculture: Lessons from the Braceros," this volume.

[13] See, for example, Jeffrey G. Williamson, "Immigrant-Inequality Trade-Offs in the Promised Land: Income Distribution and Absorptive Capacity Prior to the Quotas," and Robert S. Goldfarb, "Occupational Preferences in the U.S. Immigration Law: An Economic Analysis," both in this volume.

[14] For a summary of the literature on mass migration and income distribution in Israel, see Barry R. Chiswick, *Income Inequality* (New York: National Bureau of Economic Research, 1974), pp. 97-101. This includes summaries of Giora Hanoch, "Income Differentials in Israel," *Fifth Report, Falk Project for Economic Research in Israel* (Jerusalem: Falk Project, 1961), especially pp. 44-52; and Uri Bahral, *The Effect of Mass Migration on Wages in Israel* (Jerusalem: Falk Project for Economic Research in Israel, 1965).

299

numbers with relatively high levels of skill to an economy with a low capital-labor ratio. The result was a low skill differential.

The mass immigration after independence in 1948 consisted of persons with less schooling than those who came in the 1920s and 1930s. The average level of schooling of males aged fifteen and over was 6.6 years in 1957, but it was 7.8 years for those who immigrated prior to 1948. The new immigrants were also at a disadvantage in other forms of human capital. Many came from refugee camps in Europe and poor countries of the Middle East and North Africa. Their level of health was lower than that of the preindependence immigrants, and their postschool training had either depreciated in Europe during World War II or was of little relevance for Israel's rapidly developing economy.

The increased supply of unskilled workers after independence changed relative scarcities. Giora Hanoch wrote that "from a relative abundance of persons with secondary and higher education, and of experts, there developed a quite serious shortage." [15] Uri Bahral's analysis of wages shows that "the relative wage differentials of workers performing different jobs (when comparing high and low-wage groups), on the average widened during the first ten years of the state." [16] He adds that "this relative price of higher paid labor services in Israel should be stressed in view of the downward trend of occupational differentials found in most modern economies and in mandatory Palestine up to the end of the Second World War."

A study of the response of Swiss employers to the decline in the number of unskilled guest workers is also instructive.[17] As a result of the downturn in economic activity in 1973–1974, the Swiss government sharply limited the entry of guest workers, who are primarily unskilled. As a result, about one-quarter million guest workers who left Switzerland between 1973 and 1976 were not being replaced. The employers responded by raising the wages of unskilled relative to skilled workers and by "rationalizing production," that is, by increasing mechanization and automation.

Income Transfer System

Let us now introduce an income transfer system that taxes the population as a whole to subsidize low-income persons. The income transfer

15 Hanoch, "Income Differentials," p. 44.

16 Bahral, *Effect of Mass Migration*, pp. 5-6.

17 D. Maillat, C. Jeaurenand, and J. P. Widmer, "Reactions of Swiss Employers to Immigration Freeze," *International Labour Review,* November-December 1978, pp. 733-45.

system includes a welfare program or negative income tax,[18] social services targeted to the poor, or social overhead capital financed prior to the immigration. It will be assumed that the income transfer system is invariant with the immigration policy; that is, the criteria for eligibility and the schedule of benefits do not change as the number and characteristics of the immigrants change.

The immigration of unskilled workers can increase the aggregate income transfers in two ways. First, the immigrants themselves may qualify for benefits. Second, as the immigration depresses the wages of unskilled workers, a larger proportion of native unskilled workers qualify for some benefits, and some of those already receiving benefits may receive a larger transfer.

In the two-factor model of the receiving country in figure 1, through a tax on capital, each of the $L_{0,x}$ native workers can receive a subsidy of AC to raise their earnings to $W_{0,x}$, with capital still receiving a net increase in income, although the increase is reduced to area ABS instead of area W_1W_0AB. This can occur because aggregate income among the native population has increased. Thus, if the immigrants are excluded from participating in the transfer system, income could be transferred from skilled workers and capital to the unskilled, so as to make everyone at least as well off as before the immigration.[19]

Suppose, however, the transfer system is not permitted to differentiate between natives and immigrants.[20] If both native and immigrant unskilled workers are to be brought up to the income level of unskilled

[18] As a result of food stamps and other cash and in-kind income transfer programs, the United States has a negative income tax or a guaranteed annual income, even for two-parent working poor families. For the purpose of this discussion, any income- or earnings-contingent public transfer, including unemployment compensation, is treated as part of the transfer system. Reduced taxation of low-income workers has the same effect as increased welfare payments. For a description and analysis of the major welfare programs, see Barry R. Chiswick, "The Income Transfer System: Impact, Viability and Proposals for Reform," in William Fellner, ed., *Contemporary Economic Problems 1977* (Washington, D.C.: American Enterprise Institute, 1977), pp. 347-428.

[19] This assumes that there are no adverse labor supply or capital formation effects of the taxes and income transfers. The income of the native population is lowered to the extent that the tax and transfer systems reduce labor supply and capital formation. The larger these adverse effects, the smaller the optimal level of immigration.

[20] Under the current U.S. law, legal resident aliens generally have the same entitlement to welfare benefits as citizens. The number of illegal aliens receiving welfare benefits of one form or another is unknown. Temporary (guest) workers in the United States, as under the former bracero program, are not eligible for welfare benefits. For a discussion of the legal entitlement to welfare benefits, social services, and access to social overhead capital as of 1977, see David Carliner, *The Rights of Aliens: The Basic ACLU Guide to an Alien's Rights* (New York: Avon Books, 1977), chap. 12.

native workers prior to the immigration, the aggregate income (after taxes) of skilled workers and capital must be lowered. If all $L_{1,x}$ workers in figure 1 are to receive the subsidy of AC, the aggregate income of capital must be lower than before the migration.

When there is an income transfer system, the impact of immigrants can also be considered within the context of a three-factor production function. (See the appendix for the mathematical development.) Suppose the immigrants are unskilled workers and the transfers are to bring the earnings of unskilled native workers up to the level it would have been without the immigration, with the skilled workers and the owners of capital made no worse off than before. Because the aggregate income of the native population is increased, this can be accomplished if the immigrants are excluded from the income transfer system but not if they are included in it on the same basis as native workers. Thus, if the progressive-tax transfer system is invariant with immigration policy, the greater the extent to which unskilled immigrants are net recipients of income transfers (welfare benefits, social services, capital dilution), the smaller the optimal size of unskilled immigration.

If the immigrants are skilled workers, however, the wages of native-born skilled workers decline, while the wages of the unskilled increase. In an extreme case, the wage differential between skill levels becomes small (as in preindependence Israel) or even disappears. If the structure of the transfer system does not change, aggregate net transfers received by low-income native workers would decline as their earnings rise. The additional revenues from the taxation of the higher income of capital and lower transfer expenditures could be used to lower the tax rate paid by skilled labor. In principle, native-born skilled workers could be made at least as well off as before the immigration, without eliminating the net gain to the other factors of production.

The transfer system itself may serve as a means of attracting immigrants.[21] For some, the calculus of the costs and benefits of migration to the United States is the comparison of earnings in the country of

[21] As far as immigrants are concerned, it is largely immaterial whether the higher income in the destination is obtained from better job opportunities or a more generous transfer system. The recent increase in return migration from the mainland to Puerto Rico, for example, has been attributed to the 1974 extension to the island of the food stamp program with essentially the same income test and benefit structure as on the mainland. Using a simultaneous equations model, Richard Cebula found that nonwhite inter-SMSA migration between 1965 and 1970 was significantly positively related to the level of welfare benefits. See Richard J. Cebula, "Public Welfare and Non-White Migration: A Note," *Review of Business and Economic Research*, vol. 11, no. 1 (Fall 1975), pp. 97-101. For similar findings, using 1960 census data, see Robert Reischauer, "The Impact of the Welfare System on Black Migration and Marital Stability" (Ph.D. diss., Columbia University, 1971).

origin with income transfers in the United States. For others who intend to work in the United States, the potential availability of transfers acts as an insurance that cushions the loss of income due to unemployment.

The guest-worker programs in several European countries may have been designed with the foregoing model in mind. Under these programs, unskilled workers enter the country, but they do not bring their families with them and they are generally not eligible for income transfers.[22]

In the United States, the Bracero Program (1942–1964) and other temporary worker programs prohibit participants from receiving welfare benefits and most social services. The same situation exists de jure (although perhaps not de facto) for illegal aliens in the United States. If their status were "regularized" and they were allowed to bring their families with them, their greater use of welfare benefits and social services would reduce their net contribution to the economic well-being of the native population.[23] For illegal aliens with low levels of skill and nonworking dependents, the net impact on the native population is likely to change from positive to negative if they bring their dependent family members. This scenario may explain the reluctance of the political system to "regularize" the immigration status of illegal aliens currently in the country, while at the same time devoting so few

---

[22] As an alternative to excluding guest workers from the income transfer system, Melvyn Krauss and William Baumol consider an additional tax on their employment. In principle, this can provide guest workers with access to the social insurance programs without this access having adverse net effects on the native population. This alternative is likely to be easier to administer for short-term guest workers who do not bring dependent family members than for permanent immigrants. If dependent family members are included, unless the tax rises with family size, the program would encourage workers to bring a larger average number of relatives, thereby decreasing the likelihood that the migration is temporary. The employer-tax approach is not operative for guest workers who become unemployed but are discouraged from leaving the country by the availability of income transfers. See Melvyn B. Krauss and William J. Baumol, "Guest Workers and Income Transfer Programs Financed by Host Governments," *Kyklos,* vol. 32 (1979), pp. 36-46.

[23] Most studies of illegal aliens working in the United States suggest that they are disproportionately young males who leave their families in the home country and who make little use of income transfers and social services for fear of being apprehended. See, for example, David North and Marion T. Houstoun, "The Characteristics and Role of Illegal Aliens in the U.S. Labor Market: An Exploratory Study," mimeographed (Washington, D.C.: Linton and Co., 1976). For an econometric analysis of the earnings of illegal aliens, using the North-Houstoun data, see Barry R. Chiswick, "Illegal Aliens in the U.S. Labor Market," *Proceedings, 6th World Congress, International Economic Association, Mexico City,* August 1980 (in press).

resources to enforcing immigration law that the Mexican border is porous.

Immigrants consume a share, as a first approximation a proportionate share, of social overhead capital such as roads, schools, and flood control projects. In their analyses of the impact of immigrants, both Dan Usher and Julian Simon assume that this capital is paid for by the native population when it is constructed rather than by the total population when it is consumed.[24] The greater the magnitude of the "capital dilution," that is, the greater the extent to which immigrants receive benefits from social overhead capital without contributing to its cost, the smaller the net gain (or the larger the net loss) to the native population from immigration. Most social overhead capital is financed, however, by bonds that are retired by direct and indirect fees levied on the users (for example, gasoline taxes, water taxes), or through general taxes as the capital is consumed. Thus, immigrants pay for their consumption of social overhead capital. Social overhead capital that is paid for by the taxpayers as it is constructed can be subsumed within the income transfer system.

In summary, if immigrants are not included in the income transfer system, the increase in the aggregate income of the native population means that appropriate income redistribution policies can be devised to transfer some income from the native groups that gain, to the native groups that lose, so that no native group loses from the immigration. The welfare and tax systems can be the mechanism for this transfer. This cannot be accomplished, however, if the immigrants themselves are to be substantial recipients of income transfers, that is, if they receive an income substantially in excess of their productivity.

Even if immigrants are not recipients of any net income transfers, unskilled immigrants decrease the earnings and employment of unskilled native workers, thereby increasing the aggregate resources that flow through the income transfer system. The increased administrative costs and the adverse labor supply and capital formation effects of an enlarged tax transfer system reduce the aggregate net output of the native population. Thus, in terms of maximizing the income of the native population, the optimal level of immigration would be largest if the immigrants are skilled, smaller if they are unskilled but do not receive net income transfers, and smallest if they are unskilled and receive income transfers on the same basis as the native population.

---

[24] See Dan Usher, "Public Property and the Effects of Migration upon Other Residents of the Migrants' Countries of Origin and Destination," *Journal of Political Economy* (October 1977), pp. 1,001-1,020; and Julian Simon, "The Overall Effect of Immigrants on Natives' Incomes," in this volume.

The Economic Progress of Immigrants

The findings from recent research on the economic progress of immigrants have important implications for immigration policy.[25] Other things the same (including demographic characteristics and levels of schooling), the earnings of economic migrants generally catch up to the native born after eleven to fifteen years for men, and sooner for women, and then exceed the earnings of the native born. The native-born children of immigrants earn 5 to 10 percent more than the children of native-born parents. These patterns emerged for nearly all of the race/ethnic groups studied, with the exception of refugees, who tend to have lower earnings than economic migrants. The findings suggest that economic migrants are favorably self-selected in terms of ability relevant for the labor market and motivation for personal economic advancement. These characteristics would also tend to increase their favorable net effect on the overall economic well-being of the native population.

Refugees take longer to reach the earnings of the native born, if they ever catch up. Apparently this arises from the weaker transferability of their skills and the less intense favorable self-selection of refugees. This implies a less favorable net economic effect on the native population of refugees than of economic migrants with otherwise similar characteristics. Refugees are admitted, however, primarily for noneconomic reasons, such as humanitarian considerations and promotion of U.S. foreign policy objectives.

For reasons that are not yet understood, some immigrant groups are not as successful economically as others. In particular, persons of Filipino and Mexican origin, nearly exclusively economic migrants, apparently earn less in each immigrant generation than persons of Canadian, European, Japanese, and Chinese origin.[26]

Under current U.S. immigration law, less than 10 percent of the immigrant visas issued each year are allocated on the basis of the person's skills or economic opportunities in this country.[27] Nearly 90 percent of the visas are issued on the basis of kinship with a U.S. citizen, resident alien, or kinship with a new immigrant entering under the kinship, refugee, occupational, or nonpreference categories. Even the small number of immigrants who receive an occupational preference visa for

[25] The empirical findings reported in this section are drawn from Chiswick, "Economic Progress."

[26] For a history and analysis of the economic problems of Mexican immigrants, see Walter Fogel, "Twentieth-Century Mexican Migration to the United States," this volume.

[27] See Goldfarb, "Occupational Preferences," this volume.

their skills are not selected on the basis of their productivity in the United States. Indeed, it is difficult to rationalize the favorable treatment under current regulations of persons with advanced degrees in physical therapy and dietetics compared with others whose skills are more highly rewarded in U.S. labor markets. The economic success of a cohort of immigrants, and their favorable impact on the income of the native population, would be even greater if (nonrefugee) visas were issued primarily on the basis of the person's likely productivity in the United States rather than nearly exclusively on the basis of kinship criteria.

Property Rights and Political Rights

The rise in the average income of the native population as a consequence of immigration depends, of course, on the ability of the native population to retain its "property rights" to the nonlabor factors of production that it owned prior to the immigration. If the immigrants, either by themselves or in a coalition with native labor, can effect a nonreimbursed redistribution of the ownership of land and capital through force or the political process, the native owners of land and capital would incur a reduction in income. If this reduction is sufficiently large, the native population as a whole may lose. The greater this potential threat, the less inclined the owners of capital would be to favor immigration or to favor giving recent immigrants rights to participate in the political process.

These concerns are quite realistic. For several centuries, the American Indians were not able to enforce their property rights against the encroachment of Europeans/Americans and therefore lost much of their potential gain from the migration of whites. Mexico lost Texas, and subsequently what is now the southwestern part of the United States, as the result of the migration into Texas of foreigners (that is, U.S. citizens). The first federal legislation regarding immigration was the Alien and Sedition Act of 1798, which gave the president authority for two years to deport "undesirable aliens," that is, radicals who threatened the stability of the current economic order. It is not by coincidence that anarchists were included with criminals, professional beggars, prostitutes and procurers, and carriers of contagious diseases when the list of categories of persons barred from entry was lengthened in the early twentieth century. The adoption of guest-worker rather than permanent immigration programs in western Europe and the greater difficulty in acquiring citizenship in some of these countries (for example, France, Germany, and Switzerland) may be interpreted as an attempt to reduce the role of the foreign born in the political decision-making process.

306

The simple economic model also suggests why democratic governments are more likely to limit immigration than they are to limit emigration. Immigration results in a lowering of the income of labor, while capital gains. If capital is concentrated in the hands of a minority, more voters lose than gain, unless compensating income redistribution programs are linked to an easier immigration policy. Emigration, however, benefits the more numerous voting group that includes two sets of gainers, workers who expect to remain and those who expect to emigrate, while it is the less numerous group of owners of capital who lose.[28] On the other hand, regimes that have a larger aggregate income as a policy objective, either because they can support a larger military establishment or for other reasons, tend to discourage emigration.

Historically, the immigration policy of the United States has been consistent with this economic model. In the eighteenth and nineteenth centuries, there was little concentration of ownership of capital (land) among those eligible to vote. Those who had only labor services to offer were the native-born poor, recent immigrants, and blacks (first as slaves, then as free people), many of whom were largely disenfranchised through property, literacy, and citizenship requirements for voting, Jim Crow laws, and intimidation. Immigration restrictions were introduced only after an industrial labor force became sufficiently large and had sufficient voting strength to form an effective anti-immigration coalition with xenophobic nativist elements that had ineffectually opposed immigration for a century prior to the restrictions.

During the 1870s, in the absence of federal legislation, various states attempted to limit immigration directly, particularly the immigration of Asians to the Pacific Coast states. These state laws were ruled unconstitutional by the Supreme Court. Yet, from this period, and particularly from the 1890s, until the first major federal immigration restriction against eastern and southern Europeans (the quota law of 1921), those who opposed immigration were gaining political strength and attempting to use state legislation regarding property right as an indirect method of limiting immigration. Along the West Coast, for example, persons ineligible for citizenship were barred from owning land or from acting as trustees of land owned by their native-born children. Since only Asians were barred from citizenship, the clear intent of these laws was to discourage Asian immigration.

Elisabeth Landes reports that the number of states with legislation limiting the hours that women could work increased from eleven in

[28] This is an addition to (or an alternative to) Jagdish N. Bhagwati's social class hypothesis as to why the educated elites in the LDCs who do not expect to emigrate would oppose a tax that would discourage the emigration of those with high levels of skill. See the general discussion, part one, this volume.

1900 to forty (of forty-eight) and the District of Columbia by 1919.[29] Because of the lower income of their husbands, recent immigrant women wanted to work more hours than native-born women. Landes suggests that the hours legislation was introduced on a state-by-state basis to reduce the employment opportunities of foreign-born women and, hence, as a means of discouraging immigration.

An Alternative Rationing Mechanism

As an alternative, or an additional policy, to increase the gains to the native population from immigration, immigrants could be subject to either entry fees or differential tax rates.[30] The U.S. immigration visa is a scarce resource that substantially enhances the wealth of the lucky few who can qualify under the kinship criteria in current law and the even smaller number who enter under the refugee, occupational, and nonpreference categories. Indeed, substantial resources are sometimes expended to increase the probability of qualifying for a visa, and sometimes marriages occur that would otherwise not take place.[31]

The net impact of immigration on the overall income of the native population could be made more favorable if immigration visas were "sold" rather than rationed on the basis of nonpecuniary criteria. Then persons with the greatest expected increase in productivity from migrating to the United States would have the incentive to pay the largest entry fees and hence would be more likely to immigrate. This would not end the immigration of the relatives of U.S. citizens and resident aliens, as the U.S. relatives could pay for all or part of the visa fee if the immigrants themselves were unable to do so. It would, however, offer a market test to the value of family reunification by removing the kinship preference issue from the political arena and placing it in an economic context.[32] Indeed, in an earlier era when international migration was relatively more expensive and there were no public income transfers to assist immigrants during their adjustment, relatives who had arrived in earlier waves were an important source of financial assistance.

29 Elisabeth E. Landes, "The Effect of State Maximum Hours Laws on the Employment of Women in 1920," *Journal of Political Economy,* vol. 88, no. 3 (June 1980), pp. 476-494.

30 This section was not included in the version of the paper presented at the conference, but it was stimulated by the conference discussion.

31 The large economic rents are one of the issues of concern in J. Bhagwati, "Taxation and International Migration: Recent Policy Issues," this volume. Goldfarb, "Occupational Preferences," this volume, discusses efforts made to obtain an occupational preference visa.

32 As a variant, differential prices could be introduced where the entry fee is lower the closer the kinship to a U.S. citizen or resident alien.

308

Several objections may be raised against using visa fees as a means of rationing admissions. One is the capital market constraint. Because our institutional arrangements prohibit the enforcement of contracts creating slavery (including a fixed-period indentured service contract), human capital is poor collateral for a loan. Many productive immigrants would have difficulty financing a large entry fee. A second objection has to do with refugees who flee their home country, often because of personal danger, and lose their nonhuman assets. We would not want to bar persons whose lives or freedom are in danger because a hostile government in the country of origin has confiscated their assets.[33] A third has to do with the reversibility of migration. Many potential productive immigrants who are uncertain that their immigration is permanent would understandably be reluctant to pay a large visa fee, unless it were partially refundable upon return to the country of origin.

These concerns could be addressed by allowing immigrants to substitute an annual surcharge on their federal income tax as an alternative to the large entry fee.[34] To prevent the surcharge from encouraging unskilled migration and to reduce adverse labor supply incentives, the surcharge on earnings should be largely on a per-capita basis, although some component may be proportional to earnings as a partial insurance.

The visa fees could be set so as to maximize the net aggregate income of the native population. If this were done, the supply of immigrants would be smaller than under a laissez-faire immigration policy (under which anyone could enter), as the net gain from immigrating would be smaller. Under the visa-free system, however, the demand for immigrant labor by the native population would be greater and the number of visas would be larger than under the current nonprice rationing system. Under current policy, much of the gain from immigration

[33] One of the objections raised separately by Harry Gilman and Andrew Greeley at the conference to U.S. participation in Bhagwati's proposal for a brain drain tax is that refugees would object to making payments to a regime that oppressed them for political, religious, or racial reasons or to a foreign occupying regime. This objection would presumably not apply to the tax proposed here, as it would be levied by the country the refugee is willing to enter.

[34] The annual income tax surcharge would raise another objection, that it is unconstitutional. It is not obvious that the Supreme Court would rule it unconstitutional, as it would be a voluntary substitute for the visa fee. If it were ruled unconstitutional, however, it could be instituted after a constitutional amendment. Failure to pay the surcharge would presumably be treated in the same manner as failure to pay federal income taxes in general. Julian Simon's interpretation of the benefits to the native population from the social security taxes paid by immigrants is consistent with the proposed annual income tax surcharge. See Simon, "Effect of Immigrants," this volume.

is retained by persons who do not participate directly in the political decision-making process, the immigrants themselves and their relatives in the United States, many of whom are not citizens. The visa-fee rationing system would enable the native population to capture more of the gains and hence favor a larger immigration, that is, provide a larger number of visas. It is not obvious that a visa-free rationing system is less equitable than the current policy, as it substitutes a willingness to pay (by the immigrant or sponsors) for the kinship criteria that currently form the basis of immigration policy.

Overall Effects of Immigration

Immigrants do not have a uniform effect on the native population. Some native groups gain and others lose. The level and distribution of the effect depend on the relative skill characteristics and property rights of the immigrants and natives.

Although immigrant workers tend to raise the overall income of the native population, the incomes of native workers that are close substitutes in production for immigrant labor decline, while the incomes of other factors of production increase. If the immigrants are not substantial recipients of income transfers either owing to their high level of skill or to denial of access to these benefits, income redistribution programs can be designed to transfer resources from the native groups that gain to the native groups that lose, so that after the transfers no native group loses by the immigration. This cannot occur, however, if the immigrants themselves are to be substantial recipients of these transfers, whether they are welfare benefits, social services, or social overhead capital financed prior to the immigration.

Skilled immigrants tend to raise the level of income of the native population, reduce income inequality, and are not likely to be substantial recipients of income transfers. Unskilled immigrants tend to increase income inequality, are more likely to be substantial recipients of income transfers, and, as a consequence, have a smaller favorable effect (or a negative net effect) on the overall income of the native population. It is perhaps for this reason that several countries have developed guest-worker programs under which unskilled foreign labor can work for limited periods of time, but the participants are not eligible for most income transfers and are not permitted to bring their dependent family members.

The effect of immigrants on the native population changes with their duration of residence, as they acquire more skills specific to their country of destination. That is, as the average skill level of the immigrants relative to the native population rises the longer the duration of residence, the immigrants have a smaller adverse effect (or a larger favorable effect) on the wages of unskilled native workers, and they make smaller use of income transfers for the poor.

Among potential economic migrants, those selected on the basis of their likely productivity in the destination will tend to have a more favorable impact than immigrants selected under rationing mechanisms based on kinship (currently the primary criteria) or a first-come, first-served system. Economic migrants are likely to have a more favorable impact on the native population than refugees of the same demographic characteristics and level of schooling, as the former tend to have higher earnings. This situation presumably arises from the greater international transferability of skills and the more favorable self-selection in terms of labor market ability and motivation for personal economic advancement among economic migrants. Refugee preferences and the emphasis on kinship are included in the immigration policies of many countries because of humanitarian and foreign policy objectives and domestic social and political considerations. These objectives, however, are not without their economic costs.

As an alternative to the current policy of rationing immigration visas on the basis of nonpecuniary criteria, a large (rather than nominal) visa fee or, as a substitute at the immigrant's option, an annual immigrant income tax surcharge is considered. The overall productivity of immigrants would be likely to increase, as productivity criteria would increase in relative importance in allocating scarce visas. This change in rationing criteria is likely to increase the net gain to the native population from immigration both directly from the visa fee and indirectly from the increased productivity of immigrants. The increased benefits to natives from immigration would provide an economic incentive for an increase in the number of visas issued annually.

The change in rationing criteria would not end immigration motivated by a desire for family reunification but would place it in an economic context rather than its current political context, as the U.S. kinsmen who would presumably gain by the migration could assist the immigrant in paying the fee. The annual surcharge on the immigrant's income tax as a voluntary substitute for the visa fee has the advantage of avoiding problems of the capital market financing constraints. It also provides greater flexibility in terms of reemigration, although the visa fee should be partially refundable if reemigration occurs.

If the objective of immigration policy is to maximize the income of the native population, the optimal number of visas per year (that is, optimal annual immigration) would be greatest under a policy that favored skilled immigrants (particularly if it were coupled with the annual immigrant surcharge), smaller under a policy that was neutral with respect to skill but with immigrants denied access to the income transfer system, and smallest under a policy that was neutral with respect to skill but with immigrants given access to the income transfer system on the same basis as the native born. It is the last of these three alternatives that is the basis of current immigration policy.

Appendix: Aggregate Production Function Analysis of the Impact of Immigrants

Aggregate production functions are a useful means of describing the economy. The U.S. economy can be described by a three-factor constant-elasticity-of-substitution (CES) production function. The three factors are high-level manpower (professionals, managers, and technical workers), other manpower, and physical capital, and the pair-wise elasticities are consistent with a CES (σ) equal to about 2.5.[35]

Aggregate output (Q) may be written as

$$Q = \left[\beta_1 H_1^{-\rho} + \beta_2 H_2^{-\rho} + \beta_3 K^{-\rho} \right]^{-1/\rho} \qquad (1)$$

where $H_1 =$ low-level manpower, $H_2 =$ high-level manpower, $K =$ capital stock, and $\sigma = \dfrac{1}{1+\rho} =$ elasticity of substitution.

The marginal product of each factor of production is

$$MPH_1 = \beta_1 \left(\frac{Q}{H_1} \right)^{1/\sigma}$$

$$MPH_2 = \beta_2 \left(\frac{Q}{H_2} \right)^{1/\sigma}$$

$$MPK = \beta_3 \left(\frac{Q}{K} \right)^{1/\sigma} \qquad (2)$$

An increase in the quantity of unskilled labor, H_1, increases output Q, but at a smaller rate than H_1, so that Q/H_1 declines. Thus, an increase in H_1 due to the immigration of unskilled workers decreases the marginal product of unskilled labor, MPH_1, and increases the marginal product of skilled workers, MPH_2, and capital, MPK. If the number of unskilled workers increases from $H_{1,o}$ to $H_{1,n}$, aggregate income in the economy increases by the integral

---

[35] Carmel U. Chiswick, "The Growth of Professional Occupations in U.S. Manufacturing: 1900-1973," in I. Sirageldin, ed., *Research in Human Capital and Development* (Greenwich, Conn.: JAI Press, 1979), pp. 191-217; and Carmel U. Chiswick, "Some Time-Series Evidence on the Aggregate Production Function and Factor Substitution in the U.S. since 1900," mimeographed (Chicago: University of Illinois at Chicago Circle, 1981).

$$\int_{H_{1,o}}^{H_{1,n}} \beta_1 (Q/H_1)^{1/\sigma} dH_1$$

After the n immigrants arrive, the marginal product of unskilled workers is $MPH_{1,n} = \beta_1 (Q_n/H_{1,n})^{1/\sigma}$ and their aggregate wages are $(MPH_{1,n}) H_1$. Because of the decreasing marginal product of unskilled labor, the increase in aggregate income exceeds the total wages of the immigrants. The change in the aggregate income of the native population is

$$\int_{H_{1,o}}^{H_{1,n}} [\beta_1 (Q/H_1)^{1/\sigma} - \beta_1 (Q_n/H_{1,n})^{1/\sigma}] dH_1 \tag{3}$$

which is necessarily positive for any elasticity of substitution between zero and infinity.

Thus, immigration of unskilled workers widens wage differentials, increases the return to capital, and raises the aggregate income of native-born skilled workers, capital, and the native population. The aggregate income of native-born unskilled workers declines. Parallel changes occur if the immigrants are skilled workers.

If the unskilled immigrants are excluded from participating in the welfare system and if there are no adverse labor supply or capital formation effects of income transfers, enough income could be transferred from skilled workers and capital to unskilled native workers so as to make everyone at least as well off as before the immigration. This can occur because aggregate income among the native population has increased.

The rise in the aggregate income of skilled workers and capital exceeds the transfer that would return native unskilled workers to their preimmigration income but not the transfer required to bring all unskilled workers up to this level. That is, the gain in income exceeds the transfer of

$$\beta_1 [(Q_o/H_{1,o})^{1/\sigma} - (Q_n/H_{1,n})^{1/\sigma}] H_{1,o} \tag{4a}$$

but not the transfer of

$$\beta_1 [(Q_o/H_{1,o})^{1/\sigma} - (Q_n/H_{1,n})^{1/\sigma}] H_{1,n} \tag{4b}$$

that would be needed to bring the unskilled native workers and immigrants to the preimmigration level of earnings for unskilled native-born workers. Thus, if both native and immigrant unskilled workers are to be brought up to the income level of native-born unskilled workers prior to immigration, the aggregate income (after taxes) of skilled workers and capital must be lowered.

The Overall Effect of Immigrants on Natives' Incomes

Julian L. Simon

One of the two principal aims of inquiry into the economic effects of immigrants is to assess the overall effect of the newcomers upon the average income of natives. To do so, one must take into account all the important effects, rather than focusing only on those most easily embraced by theoretical and empirical devices. These important effects must be combined in order to arrive at an overall net calculation. To do this is the aim of this paper. The other main aim, understanding the distributive effects, is left to other papers in this volume.

The first section reviews the theory of the effect of the allocation of capital ownership and sketches a new way of calculating that effect for the United States. The second section discusses the intergenerational transfer effect. The following section discusses the effect of immigrants upon productivity, which has not been included in discussions of the topic but which is likely to be the most important effect in the long run. The next section combines all these elements into a simulation model that estimates the net on-balance effect of immigrants on the incomes of natives.

I appreciate a helpful, corrective reading by Paul Beckerman, capable computer programming by Joseph Ben-Ur, criticism at the conference by Warren Sanderson and other attendees, and useful suggestions by Barry R. Chiswick.

NOTE: The following notations will be used in this chapter:

A = level of technology and scale effects
d = discount factor
D_t = increase in total output in t due to immigration equal to $(Y_t^m - Y_t^n)$.
G_t = gross income in year t
K = capital
L = labor force
m = index indicating a situation with immigration
n = index indicating a situation without immigration
s = savings rate
T = taxation
v = index for native population
Y = national income

Z_m^v = lifetime income of natives if there is migration

Z_n^v = same but without migration

314

The Capital-Ownership Effect

The prevailing theoretical approach from Malthus until recently—and still the prevailing popular view—is that immigrants lower the income of natives through capital dilution and diminishing returns.[1] The given endowment of capital, combined with more workers, yields less output per average worker.

George Borts and Jerome Stein and then R. Albert Berry and Ronald Soligo pointed out that, if immigrants do not share in the returns to capital and yet are paid their marginal product, the total returns to capital are increased by more than the sum by which natives' wages are lowered; hence immigrants increase the average income of natives under these conditions.[2] This proposition is shown in figure 1, taken from Berry and Soligo, where the approximate triangle X represents the gain to natives as a whole.[3]

Berry and Soligo made it clear that whether immigrants obtain rights to the returns to the existing capital affects their impact upon natives' average income. Dan Usher suggested that the gain to natives from the triangle X is small compared to the loss to natives if immigrants capture part of the returns to capital, a demonstration I also made quantitatively in an analysis of the effect of Russian immigrants upon "veteran"

---

[1] By "native," I mean those residing in the country previous to the arrival of the immigrant in question. There is no good term in English to cover this concept. Israeli writers on immigration use "veteran," but this sounds unfamiliar in English. "Citizen" focuses attention on legal rather than residential status. "Native" seems to exclude prior immigrants, which I do not intend to do, but it seems to be the best term, nevertheless.

[2] George H. Borts and Jerome L. Stein, *Economic Growth in a Free Market* (New York: Columbia University Press, 1964); and R. Albert Berry and Ronald Soligo, "Some Welfare Aspects of International Migration," *Journal of Political Economy*, vol. 77 (September/October 1969), pp. 778-794.

[3] This line of reasoning implicitly assumes that there is only one wage-earning occupation in the economy. If this assumption is relaxed, the analysis is more complex. If there are a variety of occupations and the immigrants come with the same distribution of skills as the natives, then the result is the same as if there is only one occupation. But if the immigrants come with a different distribution of skills, then there are the same sorts of overall gains to trade that occur in international trade of goods. On the other hand, the occupations that are disproportionally represented by the immigrants suffer worse wage declines than do the average. The Vietnamese immigrants of the late 1970s and the Cuban immigrants of 1980 seem to have a broad spectrum of occupations, whereas the Mexican immigrants seem to be largely semiskilled laborers. Both sorts of cases seem to be important. The general question of an effect analogous to gains to trade was raised in conversation by Mark Rosenzweig, and to my knowledge has not been analyzed. Hence, I have no feeling for how important it may be. But, to the extent that it operates, it has a beneficial effect on the average native's income.

FIGURE 1
Total Returns to Capital from Immigrant Labor

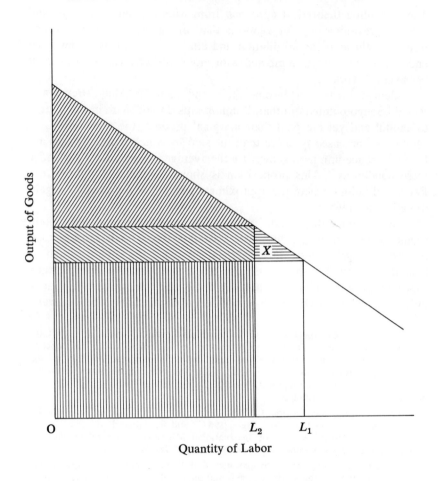

Output of Goods

O L_2 L_1

Quantity of Labor

Israelis' incomes.[4] The task, then, is to estimate the proportion of the return to capital that goes to immigrants. This is not a simple or straightforward task.

The Value of Capital Stock. Usher's approach was to estimate the value of the capital stock. This method necessarily is fraught with all

[4] Dan Usher, "Public Property and the Effects of Migration upon Other Residents of the Migrant's Countries of Origin and Destination," *Journal of Political Economy*, vol. 85 (1977), pp. 1001-1026; and Julian L. Simon, "The Economic Effect of Russian Immigrants upon the Veteran Israeli Population: A Cost-Benefit Analysis," *Economic Quarterly*, vol. 23 (August 1976), pp. 244-253, in Hebrew.

316

the well-known difficulties of valuing existing industrial capital, plus the special difficulties of valuing the physical and organizational capital of government and of farms and other land whose market price depends largely upon the value of the product rather than the cost of producing the capital. Usher's calculation of effective public ownership was therefore quite delicate and judgmental. Nevertheless, Usher made a back-of-the-envelope calculation that 58 percent of the capital in the United Kingdom is in effect publicly owned. If this were the appropriate figure, the loss to natives from immigrants would indeed be large relative to the "triangle" gain that would result if effective public-capital ownership by immigrants were zero.

Working with the streams of payments to capital owners and to labor would avoid some of the difficulties of valuing capital that arise in Usher's method; I tried to do this earlier. But both this and Usher's method now seem to me misdirected for illuminating the particular problem at hand.

Recall that the aim is to determine the effect of immigrants *upon natives' incomes*. A calculation of the sort that Usher made (based on the concept that I, too, used in my 1976 paper),[5] or the sort of calculation that I made working with streams of payments for the conference version of this paper, may reveal something about the benefits obtained from the capital *by the immigrants themselves*. But, the benefits to the immigrant are not the obverse of costs to natives.

Consider Usher's central statement:

> When a man migrates from one country to another, he abandons his share of public property—the use of roads and schools, the rights to a share of revenue from minerals in the public domain and so on—in the former country and acquires a share of public property in the latter, conferring a benefit upon the remaining results of the country from which he comes and imposing a cost upon the original residents of the country to which he goes.[6]

This assertion by Usher, to which I subscribed earlier,[7] no longer seems correct. The most obvious defect is that there are economies of scale in true public goods. The benefit that the immigrant receives when he sees the Statue of Liberty, for example, is not balanced by a corresponding cost to natives, even before or after the immigrant becomes a citizen and a part owner of the statue. To a greater or lesser extent,

5 Simon, "Russian Immigrants."
6 Usher, "Public Property and Migration," p. 1001.
7 Simon, "Russian Immigrants."

the same is true of roads, public television transmitters, museums, military real estate, and wilderness. Furthermore, there is no clear correspondence between the contemporary market value or the original cost of such public capital and the benefits derived from it. Therefore, we need a method that directly estimates the effect *upon natives* rather than an indirect estimate by way of the benefits obtained by immigrants. More specifically, we want to know the effects upon natives' money incomes, because estimating the costs or benefits to them of changes in physical and cultural environment caused by immigrants is not possible.

The matter turns out to be less inscrutable than it seems at first, however. The key to the analysis is observing that the total output of business need not be divided conceptually between the shares of capital and labor, that is, the return to labor and capital do not "exhaust the product" in this context. To put it differently, with respect to the difference D between total output Y^m with an immigrant and Y^n without him, the part that goes to capital and the part that goes to labor do not account for the whole. Rather, government gets a share; this share need not be seen as on a different footing than capital's and labor's shares. Rather, government can be seen as providing a third sort of service—security, organization, or whatever—for which it is paid the indirect and corporate taxes it receives. Government is providing a factor of production that a given business decides not to avoid using and paying for by moving offshore. The fact that the business decides to remain in the United States and pays for the privilege of doing so, as it pays for private capital as labor, makes clearer the status of the government services (or simply permission to do business) as a factor of production.[8]

This leaves us with difficulty only in the task of interpreting the business tax payments with respect to beneficiaries. The amounts paid by private business to immigrants can be interpreted as their marginal product; the returns to capital are capital's share. That is, in this interpretation, private capital's share is the amount that private capital receives, and the same for labor.

The government's take—14.6 percent of gross domestic product[9]— goes mostly for current expenditures; the extra taxes due to immigrants

[8] Access to the labor and services markets within the country are part of the decision to remain, of course, and one may not wish to consider these as a governmental service. This is a murky matter conceptually, but the argument does not depend upon this point. The important fact is that the firm must pay the government if it is to conduct its business, and the size of the payment depends on the size of the output, which in turn is influenced by the presence or absence of the immigrant.

[9] In 1979, $126.3 billion in indirect taxes plus $75.4 billion in corporate taxes divided by $1,380.3 GDP of nonfinancial corporate business. U.S., *Economic Report of the President*, 1980, p. 216.

are mostly offset by current expenditures on immigrants. Some of the tax payments finance government capital. Only the latter part of the government's share, from the entire additional output D, is a return to capital of which the immigrant gets a piece; this is likely to be small relative to D.

There is, however, a return to capital that immigrants employed by *government* obtain; for such immigrants there is *no* yield from capital that natives get and immigrants do not. The relevant estimate is the proportion of immigrants who work for the government, together with the return to government capital through taxes on private business—the latter a small part of the 14.6 percent government share, say 5 percent of D. Of the former, in 1979, 2,773 million persons and 12,840 million persons respectively worked in federal and state and local government, which is 17.4 percent of a total of 89,497 million employed persons.[10] A lower proportion of new immigrants than natives work for government. All told, this analysis suggests that immigrants capture less than 17.4 percent plus 5 percent of the return to capital, which is much less than the 35 percent that is the basic conservative or upper-limit figure used in the simulation.

This analysis is much compressed; a satisfactory treatment must be of article length elsewhere. Basically, the benefits to natives from the immigrants through the extra returns to private capital are not overstated by this analysis and by the 35 percent figure used.

The importance for natives' incomes of the extent of capital returns captured by immigrants can be derived from a Cobb-Douglas model, to be developed later. This partial effect corresponds to the proportion of the average immigrant's income that is transferred to or from the immigrant on one or another assumption of capital-returns capture. If the immigrant captures none of the returns to capital, the immediate effect is slightly positive (equal to 0.1 percent of the immigrant's income).[11] If the immigrant captures *all* the returns, there is a negative effect equal to 32 percent of the immigrant's income. For other capital-capture proportions, the effects on natives as proportions of the immigrant's first-year income are, respectively, 10 percent, −4 percent; 20 percent, −8 percent; 30 percent, −12 percent. At the 35 percent-capture rate that is an upper bound, the effect is a transfer to the immigrant equal to 14 percent of the immigrant's income.[12]

[10] *Economic Report of the President,* 1979, p. 242.

[11] The longer-run effects in years after entrance, and as the immigrant grows older, will be analyzed later.

[12] These calculations arise from runs of the model with a 4 percent savings rate. At a more realistic, higher savings rate, the capital-dilution effect on natives is less over the years.

These calculations agree with Usher's conclusion that the triangle of benefit to natives in the absence of returns to existing capital captured by immigrants is small relative to the capital dilution cost to natives at even small proportions of capital-returns capture. This effect is swamped by the sum of the other effects.

The Intergenerational Transfer Effect

Franco Modigliani and Paul R. Samuelson have shown in a different context that an additional person—and more generally, a positive population growth rate—will have a positive partial effect on incomes by way of existing patterns of life-cycle saving and consumption.[13] This argument has not previously been applied to immigrants, but in fact it applies even more strongly to immigrants than to native births because the childhood public-consumption portion of the life cycle is not present with immigrants, as we shall see later in the data on the age distribution of immigrants.

Though Modigliani and Samuelson talk about the saving of an additional person that makes him increase the incomes of others, *pure* saving is not meant here but rather a retirement system based on transfer payments. If one immigrates, builds a barn with his own hands (saving and investment), and then sells milk from it, no one benefits from the saving other than the individual. If one builds the barn and rents it, no one else's income is raised more than if one did the same construction work on salary for a construction company. It is one's immigrating and then *giving 10 percent of his salary* to the already fixed number of native retirees that increases the average income of the age cohort (by decreasing their contributions to the retirees) and therefore the incomes of the natives as a group.

The existence of this benefit from immigration depends on two assumptions. First, the public consumption patterns of children, adults, and retirees are such that an additional complete native family with a larger number of children than retirees—a family typical of population growth—transfers more to the rest of the economy in social security payments in a given year than it consumes in public expenditures on children plus transfers to retirees. This is the case in the United States,[14]

---

[13] Franco Modigliani, "The Life Cycle Hypothesis of Earning, the Demand for Wealth and the Supply of Capital," *Social Research,* vol. 33 (Summer 1966), pp. 160-217, and Paul A. Samuelson, "The Optimum Growth Rate for Population," *International Economic Review,* vol. 16 (December 1975), pp. 531-538.

[14] Robert L. Clarke and Joseph J. Spengler, "Dependency Ratios: Their Use in Economic Analysis," in Julian L. Simon and Julie DaVanzo, eds., *Research in Population Growth,* vol. 2 (Greenwich, Conn.: JAI Press, 1979).

TABLE 1
DISTRIBUTIONS BY AGE OF LEGAL IMMIGRANTS AT ENTRY AND OF U.S. POPULATION

Age	U.S. Population, 1970	Legal Immigrants to U.S., 1967–1973
0–19	38.0	35.5
20–39	25.6	46.4
40–59	22.2	13.8
60+	14.2	4.3

SOURCES: For U.S. population, U.S. Bureau of the Census, *Social Indicators, 1976* (1977), p. 32.

For immigrants, Charles B. Keely and Ellen P. Kraly, "Recent Net Alien Immigration to the United States: Its Impact on Population Growth, and Native Fertility," paper read to the Population Association of America, Atlanta, Ga., 1978.

though less so in European countries where child-support transfers are relatively larger than in the United States.

Second, the age distribution of immigrants when they arrive has more workers and fewer dependents than the age distribution of the native population. These are the most important reasons why this second assumption is overwhelmingly true. Even those retirees who do come with immigrant families are not entitled to old-age benefits; the age distribution of immigrants is much more heavily concentrated in the prime working ages than is the native population, as may be seen in table 1. On the average, it is the young, strong, and single who migrate. (This is especially true of illegals; more than 80 percent are male, half are single [most of the married men leave their wives and children in Mexico, for example], and most are youthful—less than 20 percent of the workers are over thirty-five, and they average perhaps twenty-seven.) Among the Vietnam refugees, only 12 percent are forty-five or over, compared with 32 percent for the forty-five-and-over age group in the U.S. population as a whole. (There is, however, a larger proportion of young children among the Vietnam refugees than in the citizen population.)

As to actual employment, one survey showed that 47 percent of the Vietnamese males fourteen years or older were working within three months of entry.[15] This rapid job-finding corresponds with the results

[15] *First, Second, Third, Fourth Wave Reports: Vietnam Resettlement Operational Feedback* (Washington, D.C.: Opportunity Systems, 1975-1977).

of studies of immigrant employment in Canada, Israel (Russian immigrants), and the United Kingdom (New Commonwealth immigrants).[16]

These data imply that immigrants constitute a class that, on net balance, contributes to natives by age-and-youth transfer payments. The sixth section will discuss whether there are offsetting negative transfer effects of immigrants through other social-welfare channels.

One may wonder whether the net flow of transfers caused by the immigrant cohort tends to balance out when the immigrants get older. This seems so if one looks only at the immigrants themselves, rather than at the whole sequence of events caused by the entry of the immigrants, which includes their children who then grow up into productive workers. When the immigrants get older, the immigrants' own offspring more than supply the necessary retirement transfers ("more" rather than "equal to" because of the effect of the first assumption, above). Were this system to be considered in an equilibrium context, this would not seem to be true. But it is in the nature of each immigrant's entry that it is a one-time disequilibrium event; the gains from the difference between it and an otherwise comparable equilibrium, that is, the system without the immigrant, constitute the transfers captured by the natives.

Perhaps a hypothetical example will clarify this important but elusive point. Imagine that a "native" family consists of husband and wife, both now aged thirty-five, three-year-old twins, and a retired grandfather. The immigrant family consists of a husband and wife, both aged twenty-five. Both families pay 20 percent of $20,000 yearly incomes in taxes. The native family now receives social security for the grandfather (and various minor support for the twins), whereas the immigrant family receives no such payments. On balance, the natives gain from the immigrants now. After a few years, the balance will become slightly more even as the immigrants also have two children. Forty years later, the yearly balance will become roughly equal after the two immigrants retire and collect social security. Since the native family was the net gainer in the early years—the years that weigh heaviest in a present-value calculation of the "investment" value to natives of admitting the immigrants, a calculation properly made at the time of the admission decision—the calculation is influenced positively by the social security effect (and to a much smaller extent, by the child welfare programs). The calculation for this one immigrant family is in no way altered by the fact that other immigrants may enter in future years.

---

[16] *Manpower and Immigration, Three Years in Canada* (Ottawa: Information Canada, 1974); Judith Shuval et al., *Adjustment Patterns of Immigrants from the USSR* (Jerusalem: The Institute for Applied Social Sciences, September 1973); and K. Jones and A. D. Smith, *The Economic Impact of Commonwealth Immigration* (Cambridge: Cambridge University Press, 1970).

The immigrant-saving effect is the opposite of the negative child-dependency effect that has been the mainspring of the Coale-Hoover argument against population growth in less-developed countries. The life-cycle facts may well be such that, even in developing countries, over his or her lifetime an additional child has a positive net transfer effect on the income of others.

The actual magnitude of the life-cycle saving effect is roughly equal to the proportion of an immigrant's salary that goes to fund social security and other federal old-age programs. At present, this is upward of 10 percent of the average salary;[17] the schedule is such that immigrants, who have relatively low incomes, pay a larger percentage than the average native. The social security percentage is almost sure to rise in the next few years. This positive effect is large and of the same order of magnitude as the negative capital-returns-capture effect seen earlier.[18]

---

[17] *Economic Report of the President,* 1977.

[18] No mention is made here of other taxes and transfers with respect to immigrants. For citizens as a whole, these flows balance out. Because of the "favorable" age distribution of immigrants and their high rate of employment, the net effect is almost surely that immigrants pay more in taxes than the cost of the other services they use. See Julian L. Simon, "Immigrants Don't Cost, They Pay" (Address to the Population Association of America, Atlanta, Ga., April 1978); "Economic Objections Fall Apart When Used against Immigrants," *Los Angeles Times,* July 1, 1980; and "Adding Up the Costs of Our New Immigrants," *Wall Street Journal,* February 26, 1981, p. 22.

A traditional, but fallacious, related argument in favor of immigration must be dealt with here. It has been alleged at least since Francis Walker, the first president of the American Economic Association, that immigrants are a better "buy" than additional children because immigrants arrive with the publicly financed portion of their educations already paid for by another country's public (or in more modern arguments, at a lower cost). This argument may be appropriate and relevant when historians (for example, Larry Neal and Paul Uselding, "Immigration: A Neglected Source of American Economic Growth, 1790-1917," *Oxford Economic Papers,* vol. 24 [1972], pp. 66-88) look backward, assume some substitution between additional children and additional immigrants, and reckon the advantage to immigrants. But, the argument is not relevant when the discussion is forward-looking (for example, Rudolph C. Blitz, "A Benefit-Cost Analysis of Foreign Workers in West Germany, 1957-1973," *Kyklos,* vol. 30 [1977], pp. 479-502), and the native fertility of the country of immigration is assumed invariant to immigration. It is then not reasonable to calculate apparent savings on the education of immigrants, because sunk costs are sunk for decision-making purposes. The only question for policy purposes is whether the *future* native incomes and outgoes will be on balance more positive or negative with the immigrant's presence, than without it. Of course, an immigrant's education and human capital have an effect through the gains to capital discussed earlier, as well as through possible gains to trade. But, these effects cannot be estimated by valuing the cost of the immigrant's education or the cost of the same education in the country of immigration.

The Most Important Effect: Long-Run Productivity

The likely most important long-run effect of immigrants has yet to be mentioned, here or in previous economic theorizing on immigration. This is the effect of immigrants (in their role of additional workers and consumers) upon the productivity of the country of immigration. To calculate the importance of this effect on native incomes over the years requires a dynamic analysis of the sort made elsewhere for general population growth in developed countries, though with a technical progress function less sensitive to population than used earlier.[19] As we shall see, this factor dwarfs all the others in a reasonably short span of time. This section lays the groundwork for the assumptions that are built into the model presented later.

Aside from their special characteristics as cultural newcomers and as nonowners of capital, immigrants represent additional people *as people*. Additional people are additional workers and consumers, who increase the size of the markets in which they produce and consume.

Productivity per worker is the key factor in the standard of living of a country. Economists at least as early as William Petty and Adam Smith have emphasized the importance of the size of the market in influencing productivity, due to the division of labor and other economies of scale. In more recent years, economists have also noted the influence of the size of the market—the total output and income in a market—on the decision to invest: "The inducement to invest is limited by the size of market."[20] Yet recent economists have not drawn the most obvious conclusion from this reasoning: Additional people lead to faster economic growth by increasing the size of the market and hence boosting productivity and investment.

Economies associated with larger plants are usually one's first thought when considering economies-of-market scale. Indeed, larger plants are more efficient, up to a point. The most important and interesting productivity advantages of larger markets arise at the *industry* level, or even the level of the market as a whole. Retail goods, and even most services, are distributed more cheaply in larger communities, once the wage effect is allowed.[21] In a general study of the costs of manufacturing production, Leo Sveikauskas found an eco-

[19] Julian L. Simon, *The Economics of Population Growth* (Princeton: Princeton University Press, 1977), chaps. 4-6.

[20] Ragnar Nurkse, "Growth in Underdeveloped Countries," *American Economic Review,* May 1952; reprinted in A. N. Agarwala and S. P. Singh, *The Economics of Underdevelopment* (New York: Oxford University Press, 1963), p. 20.

[21] Douglas Love, "City Sizes and Prices" (Ph.D. diss., University of Illinois, 1978).

nomically important advantage in efficiency in larger cities.[22] There is also evidence that less capital is needed to produce a given amount of output in larger cities.[23] The cost of capital is lower in larger communities, as measured by bank rates.[24]

Another important element is the greater density of communications and transportation networks that accompanies denser population. This may be seen casually in the larger number of radio and television stations in larger cities. David Segal found that standard metropolitan statistical areas (SMSAs) with populations of 2 million or more have 8 percent higher productivity than smaller SMSAs because "economies exist in transport and communications in the very largest cities."[25] A related phenomenon is the greater propensity to produce new ideas that accompanies living in larger cities of developing countries[26] and the greater propensity for new ideas and trends to diffuse and be adopted in larger cities.[27] In LDCs, Donald Glover and Julian Simon have shown in a cross-country study how road networks—a vital factor for agricultural development—are more dense where population is more dense.[28]

Larger markets also induce faster gains in productivity due to competition and to "learning by doing." An example of the competitive effect, the January white sale—a costless commercial innovation—was adopted decades earlier in big cities than in small cities, on the average;[29] the obvious explanation is the pressure of competition. As to learning, the more television sets or bridges or airplanes that a group of people produces, the more chance those people have to improve their skills

[22] Leo Sveikauskas, "The Productivity of Cities," *Quarterly Journal of Economics,* vol. 89 (1975), pp. 343-414.

[23] Summarized by William Alonso, "The Economics of Urban Size," in John Friedman and William Alonso, eds., *Regional Policy Readings in Theory and Applications* (Cambridge, Mass.: MIT Press, 1975).

[24] Jerry Stevens, "Demography, Market Structure and Bank Performance" (Paper prepared at the University of Illinois, 1978), and references therein.

[25] David Segal, "Are There Returns to Scale in City Size?" *Review of Economic Statistics,* vol. 58 (August 1976), pp. 339-350.

[26] Robert Higgs, "American Inventiveness, 1890-1920," *Journal of Political Economy,* vol. 79 (1971), pp. 661-667; and Allen Kelley, "Scale Economies, Inventive Activity, and the Economics of American Political Growth," *Explorations in Economic History,* vol. 10 (1972), pp. 35-52.

[27] Claude S. Fischer, "Urban-to-Rural Diffusion of Opinions in Contemporary America," *American Journal of Sociology,* vol. 84 (July 1978), pp. 151-159.

[28] Donald R. Glover and Julian L. Simon, "The Effect of Population Density upon Infrastructure: The Case of Roadbuilding," *Economic Development and Cultural Change,* vol. 23, no. 3 (April 1975).

[29] Julian L. Simon and Leslie Golembo, "The Spread of a Cost-Free Business Innovation: The Case of the January White Sale," *Journal of Business,* vol. 40 (October 1967), pp. 385-388.

with learning by doing, an important factor in the increase of productivity. The increased efficiency of production within firms and industries as experience accumulates has been well documented in many industries, starting with the air-frame industry in the 1930s.[30] The bigger the population, the more of everything that is produced, which promotes learning by doing.

The most relevant evidence on market size and economies of scale comes from studies of industries as wholes. It is an important and well-established phenomenon that industries that grow faster increase their efficiency faster—even compared with the same industries in other countries. The most complete analysis is that of Colin Clark, who compares the productivity of U.S. industries in 1950 and 1963 (and of U.K. industries in 1963), against U.K. industries in 1950.[31] The larger the industry relative to the 1950 U.K. base, the greater is the productivity difference, and the effect is large. This argues that faster population growth—which causes faster-growing industries—leads to faster growth of productivity.

Population Size and Growth. How do immigration, population size, and population growth come into the picture? [32] The source of improvements in productivity is the human mind. Because improvements—their invention and their adoption—come from people, it seems reasonable to assume that the amount of improvement depends on the number of people available to use their minds.

This is an old idea, going back at least as far as William Petty in 1682:

> As for the Arts of Delight and Ornament, they are best promoted by the greatest number of emulators. And it is more likely that one ingenious curious man may rather be found among 4 million than 400 persons. . . . And for the propagation and improvement of useful learning, the same may be said concerning it as above-said concerning . . . the Arts of Delight and Ornaments.[33]

[30] See, for example, references in Sherwin Rosen, "Learning by Experience as Joint Production," *Quarterly Journal of Economics,* vol. 86 (August 1972), p. 369.

[31] Colin Clark, *Population Growth and Land Use* (New York: St. Martin's 1967), p. 265. The U.S.-U.K. comparisons in the same year are relatively free of the potential bias arising from the fact that those industries where world technology grew faster exogenously were also those whose scale of production expanded faster, a bias that afflicts analogous time-series studies within a single country.

[32] The following paragraphs are taken from Julian L. Simon, "Population Resources, Environment," *Science,* vol. 208 (June 27, 1980), pp. 1431-1437.

[33] William Petty, "Another Essay in Political Arithmetic," in Charles H. Hull, ed., *The Economics Writings of Sir William Petty* (Cambridge: Cambridge University Press, 1899), p. 474.

More recently, this effect of population size has been urged upon us by Simon Kuznets.[34]

It cannot be emphasized too strongly that "technological advance" does not mean "science," and scientific geniuses are just one part of the knowledge process. Much of technological advance comes from people who are neither well educated nor well paid—the dispatcher who develops a slightly better way of deploying taxis in his ten-taxi fleet, the shipper who discovers that garbage cans make excellent cheap containers for many items, the supermarket manager who finds a way to display more merchandise in a given space, the supermarket clerk who finds a quicker way to stamp the prices on cans, the market researcher in the supermarket chain who experiments and finds more efficient and cheaper means of advertising the store's prices and sale items, and so on.

The potential contribution of additional producers of knowledge to resources and the economy is manifest. H. A. Bethe, who has excellent credentials to speak on the topic, says that the future cost and availability of nuclear power—and hence the cost and availability of energy generally—would be a better prospect if the population of scientific workers were larger. Talking specifically about nuclear fusion and a device called Tokamak by the Russians:

> Work on machines of the Tokamak type is also going forward in many other laboratories in the U.S., in the U.S.S.R. and in several countries of western Europe. If the problem can be solved, it probably will be. Money is not the limiting factor: the annual support in the U.S. is well over $100 million, and it is increasing steadily. Progress is limited rather by the availability of highly trained workers, by the time required to build large machines and then by the time required to do significant experiments.[35]

A casual inspection of the historical record confirms this speculation. There have been many more discoveries and a faster rate of growth of productivity in the past century, say, then in previous centuries, when there were fewer people alive. True, 10,000 years ago there was not much knowledge upon which to build new ideas. Seen differently, it should have been all the easier 10,000 years ago than now to find important improvements because so much still lay undiscovered. Progress surely was agonizingly slow in prehistory, however. Whereas we

[34] Simon Kuznets, "Population Change and Aggregate Output," in Universities–National Bureau of Economic Research, *Demographic and Economic Change in Developed Countries* (Princeton: Princeton University Press, 1960).

[35] H. A. Bethe, "The Necessity of Fission Power," *Scientific American,* vol. 234, no. 1 (January 1976).

develop new materials (metal and plastic) almost every day, it was centuries or thousands of years between the discovery and use of, say, copper and iron. It makes sense that, if there had been a larger population then, the pace of increase in technological practice would have been faster.

For the twentieth century, there is some statistical evidence. For the·period 1950–1962 for the United States, Edward F. Denison estimated yearly growth in output of 0.76 percent due to "advances in knowledge" (which excludes the effect of education on the labor force) and 0.30 percent due to "economies of scale," for a total just over 1 percent.[36] For northwest Europe, he estimated 0.76 percent due to "advances in knowledge," 0.56 percent due to "changes in the lag in application of knowledge, general efficiency, and errors and omissions," and 0.41 percent due to "economies of scale," for a total of something over 1.5 percent per year. Robert Solow's estimate of the increase in output in the United States due to increases in technical knowledge for the forty years from 1909 to 1949 is about 1.5 percent per year.

If a larger labor force causes a faster rate of productivity change, one would expect to see this reflected in observed changes in the rate of productivity advance over time in the United States as population has grown. Indeed, Solow concludes that the yearly rate of change of productivity went from 1 percent to 2 percent between the 1909–1929 and 1929–1949 periods. William Fellner found these rates of productivity increase: 1900–1929, 1.8 percent; 1929–1948, 2.3 percent; and 1948–1966, 2.8 percent.[37] These results are consistent with the assumption that the rate of increase of productivity is indeed higher when population is larger.[38]

The connections between numbers of scientists, inventors, ideas, and adoption and use of new discoveries are difficult to delineate clearly. The crucial links needed to confirm this effect seem obvious and strong, however. The data show clearly, for example, that the bigger the popu-

---

[36] Edward F. Denison, *Why Growth Rates Differ* (Washington, D.C.: The Brookings Institution, 1967), pp. 287, 298, 300.

[37] Robert Solow, "Technical Change and the Aggregate Production Function," *Review of Economics and Statistics*, vol. 39 (1957), p. 330; and William Fellner, "Trends in the Activities Generating Technological Progress," *American Economic Review*, vol. 60 (March 1970), pp. 11-12.

[38] The recent downturn in U.S. productivity change may be seen by some as a reversal in the long-term trend of an increasing rate of productivity change. To the extent that the data are meaningful rather than showing compositional effects, however, this downturn is more likely to be a pause than a basic change. The longest-term trends are the most reliable basis for characterizing basic economic forces; productivity seems to have been increasing at a continuous rate for hundreds of years.

lation of a country, the greater the number of scientists and the larger the amount of scientific knowledge produced; more specifically, scientific output is proportional to population size, in countries at the same level of income.[39] The United States is much larger than Sweden, and it produces proportionately more scientific knowledge.

In brief, the knowledge that leads to technological advance is created by people. Various readers may have reservations about one or another of the lines of evidence presented above, but they all fit together and confirm each other. Taken altogether, the evidence seems irresistible that the more people, the more technological advance and productivity increase, other things being equal. And immigrants are people.

The Integrated Model Including the Productivity Effect

If an economist is to be worth his keep, he must take into account the *size* and *importance* of the various effects and calculate the net effect. One can only obtain a satisfactory overall assessment of the effect of immigrants on the standard of living of citizens by constructing an integrated model of the economy and then comparing the incomes produced by the economy under various conditions of immigration and population growth.[40]

For simplicity and clarity, the model deals with a single cohort of immigrants; a continuous analysis yields similar results, however. Also for simplicity, I sometimes talk of a representative family instead of the cohort as a whole.

The question is whether the native population—that is, the people living in the United States *before* the immigrant family arrives—are

---

[39] Derek J. deSolla Price, "Measuring the Size of Science," *Israel Academy of Sciences and Humanities Proceedings,* vol. 4, no. 6 (1971), pp. 98-111; Douglas Love and Lincoln Pascute (pseudonym of J. Simon), "The Effect of Population Size and Concentration upon Scientific Productivity," in Julian L. Simon, ed., *Research in Population Economics,* vol. 1 (Greenwich, Conn.: JAI Press, 1978); Derek J. deSolla Price, *Science since Babylon,* enlarged ed. (New Haven: Yale University Press, 1975); idem, "Nations Can Publish or Perish," *Science and Technology* (1967), pp. 85-90; idem, "Measuring the Size of Science," *Israel Academy of Sciences and Humanities Proceedings,* vol. 4, no. 6 (1971), pp. 98-111; idem, "Some Statistical Results for the Numbers of Authors in the States of the United States and the Nations of the World," in *Who Is Publishing in Science?* (Philadelphia: Institute for Scientific Information, 1975), pp. 26-35.

[40] After finishing this article, I discovered an interesting model by Jan Ekberg ("Long-Term Effects of Immigration," *Economy and Society,* vol. 20, no. 1 [1977], pp. 3-22) that also makes technical progress endogenous in a migration context. Ekberg uses a Kaldor-like function, where the increment to technical progress depends upon the percentage change in the stock of capital, which I elsewhere argue is not appropriate for a study of this sort. My 1976 article on Russian immigration into Israel is the only other study of the sort that I know of (Simon, "Russian Immigrants").

better off or worse off economically if the immigrant comes or does not. In more precise terms, we wish to know if the lifetime income of the (average member of the) native population is higher or lower if the immigrant comes, that is, whether $Z_m^v > Z_n^v$ or $Z_n^v > Z_m^v$. Lifetime incomes with and without the immigration are, for our purposes here, functions of gross income less taxes

$$Z_m^v = (G_{m,t=1}^v - T_{m,t=1}^v) + d(G_{m,t=2}^v - T_{m,t=2}^v) + \ldots \text{ and}$$

$$Z_n^v = (G_{n,t=1}^v - T_{n,t=1}^v) + d(G_{n,t=2}^v - T_{n,t=2}^v) + \ldots.$$

Therefore, we must estimate the natives' yearly gross incomes and taxes if there are, and if there are not, immigrants.

The Effect of Immigration on Gross Incomes of Natives. We start with the effect of the immigrant on natives' incomes through the two major lines of influence: the capital-dilution effect and the economies-of-scale-and-productivity effect. I have estimated the combined effect of these two forces in a simple macro model. The main conventional element is a Cobb-Douglas function, whose labor and capital coefficients add to unity and where saving is a fixed steady-growth proportion of the prior year's output. A less conventional element is the effect of output and labor force on the technological-level coefficient, as discussed by Simon.[41] In other recent work, I have explored a wide variety of technological progress functions and have found that, in a policy context such as this one, the result is rather insensitive to the choice of function. I have chosen Edmund Phelps's well-known and elegant function, which is "conservative" in this sense: Phelps's function indicates that technical progress should have been progressively lower as population growth has declined in the twentieth century in the United States and in the Western world generally.[42] In fact, technical progress has apparently been higher

---

[41] Simon, *Economics of Population Growth*, chaps. 4-6.

[42] Phelps's original function is

$$\frac{A_t - A_{t-1}}{A_{t-1}} = \left(\frac{A_{t-w-1}}{A_{t-1}}\right) h\left(\frac{R_t}{A_{t-w-1}}\right)$$

The number of research workers, R, may be considered proportional to the labor force, and w is a retardation factor to represent the delay in adoption of newly produced knowledge. Edmund Phelps makes $h\left(\dfrac{R_t}{A_{t-w-1}}\right)$ a concave argument because, he says, this assumption is necessary if "an exponential growth of researchers will produce an exponential increase of the level of technology." Edmund S. Phelps, "Models of Technical Progress and the Golden Rule of Research," *Review of Economic Studies*, vol. 33 (April 1966), pp. 133-145.

This function has the realistic properties that more persons imply more

in the more recent decades than in the early decades of this century as discussed earlier. This implies that Phelps's function understates the contribution of population size and growth to the advance of economic welfare.[43]

In place of the size of the research force in Phelps's function, I have for simplicity used the size of the labor force. The function was written in Cobb-Douglas form to make its meaning obvious:

$$A_t - A_{t-1} = bA_{t-1}^{\gamma} L_{t-1}^{\Delta}, \text{with } \gamma, \Delta = 0.5$$

The exponents fit Phelps's requirement that the function be homogeneous of degree one and his assumption that "if the technology level should double we would require exactly twice the amount of research to double the absolute time rate of increase of the technology."[44] The assumption of the steady-state savings rate is also conservative in the sense that it is less advantageous to a larger population (and hence to immigrants) than would be a higher savings rate. This is reasonably clear upon inspection and is verified in other work by this writer. The coefficient b is that complement of the initial values chosen for A and L that start the simulation smoothly into motion and that correspond to the steady-state rate of change of A in the nonimmigrant case, which is equal to the rate of growth of the labor force in Phelps's model. It is kept the same in the plus-immigrants case, so as to hold all initial conditions exactly the same in the two cases, except the growth of the labor force. This, too, is a conservative assumption in the sense explained.

An iterative program is used to make investment approximately a function of current period income rather than prior period income, so that the computer model would approximate the steady-state analytic model. The results are much the same with and without this refinement, however.

The other equations and parameters of the model are as follows:

$$Y_t = A_t L_t^{\alpha} K_t^{\beta}, K_t = sY_{t-1} + K_{t-1}, \text{ and } L_t = L_{t-1} + 0.02 L_{t-1}$$

The initial values are $A_t = 1.0$, $K_t = 1000$, $Y_t = 500$, $\alpha = 0.67$, $\beta = 0.33$, $\gamma = 0.5$, and $\Delta = 0.5$; b is chosen so that the initial rate of

---

knowledge, there are diminishing returns at a given moment, and a larger stock of knowledge results in a larger increment of knowledge.

[43] Phelps's function can be made more realistic with the addition of arguments representing the effect of educational level and national income on the production of technology, with the function still retaining its convenient mathematical properties. See Gunter Steinmann and Julian L. Simon, "Phelps' Technical Progress Function Generalized," *Economic Letters*, vol. 5 (1980), pp. 177-182.

[44] Phelps, "Models of Technical Progress."

TABLE 2

The Effect of an Immigrant on the Incomes of Natives

at Various Assumptions about the Proportion of Capital Returns That Go to Immigrants
(Expressed as a Percentage of the Immigrant's Earnings)

Capture of Returns to Capital

Year	20% Capital Return			35% Capital Return			50% Capital Return		
	Income effect (%)	Social security	Total	Income effect (%)	Social security	Total	Income effect (%)	Social security	Total
1	− 7	+10	+ 3	−14	+10	− 4	−19	+10	− 9
2	− 7	+10	+ 3	−12	+10	− 2	−18	+10	− 8
3	− 5	+10	+ 5	−11	+10	− 1	−16	+10	− 6
4	− 4	+10	+ 6	−10	+10	0	−15	+10	− 5
5	− 2	+10	+ 8	− 8	+10	+ 2	−14	+10	− 4
6	− 1	+10	+ 9	− 7	+10	+ 3	−12	+10	− 2
7	1	+10	+11	− 5	+10	+ 5	−11	+10	− 1
8	2	+10	+12	− 4	+10	+ 6	−10	+10	0
9	4	+10	+14	− 3	+10	+ 7	− 8	+10	+ 2

10	+10	5	+15	−1	+10	+9	−7	+10	+3
11	+10	7	+17	0	+10	+10	−6	+10	+4
12	+10	8	+18	+2	+10	+12	−4	+10	+6
13	+10	10	+20	+3	+10	+13	−3	+10	+7
14	+10	11	+21	+4	+10	+14	−2	+10	+8
15	+10	13	+23	+6	+10	+16	−1	+10	+9
16	+10	14	+24	+7	+10	+17	1	+10	+11
17	+10	16	+26	+8	+10	+18	2	+10	+12
18	+10	17	+27	+10	+10	+20	3	+10	+13
19	+10	18	+28	+11	+10	+21	4	+10	+14
20	+10	20	+30	+12	+10	+22	6	+10	+16
21	+10	21	+31	+14	+10	+24	7	+10	+17
22	+10	23	+33	+15	+10	+25	8	+10	+18
23	+10	24	+34	+16	+10	+26	9	+10	+19
24	+10	25	+35	+18	+10	+28	11	+10	+21
25	+10	27	+37	+19	+10	+29	12	+10	+22
26	+10	28	+38	+20	+10	+30	13	+10	+23
27	+10	30	+40	+21	+10	+31	14	+10	+24
28	+10	31	+41	+23	+10	+33	15	+10	+25
29	+10	32	+42	+24	+10	+34	17	+10	+27
30	+10	34	+44	+25	+10	+35	18	+10	+28

change of A equals 0.02 yearly. The initial L equals 1,000 for the without-immigration case, and 1,020 for the with-immigration case.[45]

For the income-effect calculations, the increment of immigrant workers in period $t=1$ must be large enough so that the effects are not obscured by rounding error. It was therefore set equal to the 2 percent increase in native labor force in year $t=1$ (10 percent in some runs to show that the size of the increment matters little). Then the difference in citizens' incomes in future years between the situations if the immigrants do come in $t=1$ and if they do not come are calculated. The final calculation is in terms of the effect of one additional immigrant.

The third section discussed the extent to which immigrants gain the returns from the capital with which they work. Table 2 shows various calculations that should cover all possible values; 35 percent is the value with which I have continued to work because it is at the high end of probable values for the United States, in light of the earlier discussion. Any lower value shows immigrants to be even more favorable for natives' incomes.[46] On the latter assumption, the pretax effects on citizens' incomes amount to the percentages of the immigrants' net income, shown in column 4. Those figures may be interpreted as follows. In year one, citizens' incomes are (in the aggregate) lower by 14 percent of the income of the average immigrant, aside from taxes (though the effect on individual natives is small because of the small proportion of immigrants relative to natives). By year twelve, citizens' net incomes are higher than they would otherwise be, because of the immigrants. By year nineteen, citizens' incomes are higher by an amount equal to 10 percent of the income of each immigrant who arrives in year zero.

The Saving-and-Transfer Effect. We must take into account the immigrants' saving-and-transfer effect as discussed earlier. Social security is the main issue. Immigrants collect no social security, both because of age distribution and because they have no claims to benefits until they have worked for years. The immigrant family's contributions will be

[45] There would appear to be no danger here that the choice of production function forces the outcome, as in some studies of distributive shares. The cohort of immigrants whose effect is analyzed is small relative to the native population, hence its effect upon the overall distribution between capital and labor is small.

In addition, Ekberg experimented with a CES function and obtained the same results as with a Cobb-Douglas model (Ekberg, "Long-Term Effects of Immigration").

[46] The reader may wonder how the representative immigrant's share of capital, and the returns to it, changes with years of residence in the United States and whether this is reflected in the model. With time, the immigrant's share rises to 100 percent, of course. But this is counterbalanced by purchase payments by immigrants that are necessarily financed by higher-than-average saving. Hence, the result should be the same whether this is explicitly shown in the model or implicitly, as in the present model.

TABLE 3

RATES OF RETURN ON INVESTMENT IN IMMIGRANTS
FOR A VARIETY OF MODELS
(Increment of immigrants equal to 2 percent of labor force in $t = 1$)

| | | | | Rates of Return per Annum in Percent | |
| | | | Capital Capture | | |
b	s	γ, Δ	(%)	Without social security	With social security
0.02	0.04	0.5	0.2	18.4	28.4
0.02	0.04	0.5	0.35	9.3	19.3
0.02	0.04	0.5	0.5	5.1	15.1
0.02	0.07	0.5	0.35	12.2	22.2
0.02	0.07	0.5	0.5	7.3	17.3
0.02	0.10	0.5	0.35	14.8	24.8
0.01	0.04	0.5	0.5	1.5	11.5
0.01	0.04	0.4	0.5	0.0	10.0

roughly 10 percent of earnings. This makes the overall accounts positive in year five and thereafter and just *slightly* negative in years one through four, as seen in column 6.

The stream of negative and positive effects may be evaluated like any other investment, with negative outgoes at the beginning and positive incomes later on. On a capital-returns assumption of 35 percent, the rate of return on the investment decision to bring in an immigrant is 9.3 percent per annum without the social security effect and 19.3 percent with it, an excellent investment by any standard.[47]

The results of a variety of other specifications of the basic model with respect to savings rate, initial rate of technical progress, proportion of returns to capital captured by immigrants, and exponents of the technical progress function are shown in table 3. The lowest rate of return for any reasonable set of parameters is 0 percent (not a negative rate, however) for the results *without* the transfer-payment effect and 10 percent with it. Immigrants are an excellent 10 percent-return-per-annum investment even under these most conservative of parameters.

A Discussion of the Impacts

In discussions of the economic impact of immigrants on natives' standard of living, transfer payments and social welfare programs (other

[47] For the larger increment of immigrants, 11.1 percent and 21.1 percent.

than social security) are often suggested as a negative offset to the positive effects of the immigrants. In fact, however, immigrants seem to have an overall *positive* effect through these other transfers. One reason in the case of the United States is the simplest kind of economies of scale with respect to the defense budget—which is likely to be invariant to the number of immigrants, in which case immigrants reduce defense expenditures per citizen.

As to whether immigrants are disproportionate gainers from transfers because of low income, Barry Chiswick has shown that, only a few years after entry into the United States, immigrants typically approach or equal natives in income, at which time their taxes should be roughly equal.[48] Preliminary findings from my analysis of the 1976 survey of income and opportunity show that the difference between other welfare payments to immigrants and to natives is small compared to the difference in social security payments.[49]

Concerning illegals, David S. North and Marion F. Houstoun found that 73 percent of illegal aliens had federal income tax withheld and 77 percent paid social security tax—even though they can never collect on it.[50] On the other hand, the proportions who use welfare services are small: free medical, 5 percent; unemployment insurance, 4 percent; child schooling, 4 percent; federal job training, 1 percent; food stamps, 1 percent; and welfare payments, 1 percent. Practically no illegals, Cubans, or Indochinese are in a position to avail themselves of the most expensive welfare programs of all: social security and other aid to the elderly.

The reader may wonder whether a person need live in the United States in order that the United States get the benefit of the person's impact on productivity. The answer differs somewhat depending on the person's origin—that is, whether the person is from a more developed or a less developed country. The answer may also depend on the person's education and occupation, but the former is more clear-cut and probably much more important.

[48] Barry R. Chiswick, "The Effect of Americanization on the Earnings of Foreign-Born Men," *Journal of Political Economy,* vol. 86, no. 5 (1978), pp. 897-921.

[49] Julian L. Simon, "What Do Immigrants Take from, and Give to, the Public Coffers?" in Select Commission on Immigration and Refugee Policy, "United States Immigration Policy and the National Interest," Appendix D to the Staff Report of the Commission, *Papers on Legal Immigration to the United States* (Washington, D.C., 1981), pp. 223-262; idem, "Adding Up the Costs of Our New Immigrants."

[50] David S. North and Marion F. Houstoun, *The Characteristics and Role of Illegal Aliens in the U.S. Labor Market: An Exploratory Study* (Washington, D.C.: Linton and Company, March 1976).

Recall that a person may influence technical progress through both his demand for goods and his supply of knowledge. Let us consider each of these separately beginning with the more problematic case, that of the person who already lives in a more developed country, such as Sweden or Japan.

It is indeed true that there is international trade; a Swede's demand for goods may be satisfied in the United States. It is also true, and more relevant, that only a small proportion of U.S. goods are sold abroad. It is more likely that an increment of U.S.-made autos or newspapers or smoke detectors will be sold if a given person chooses to reside this year in the United States rather than in Sweden. This should be enough to make the point. An even more conclusive argument comes from a more general view of trade. If a person comes to the United States and still imports a Swedish auto, Sweden's imports (directly or indirectly) from the United States will rise by the amount of other goods equal in value to the auto. Total production in the United States, therefore, will rise by the amount of the immigrant's output and income, along with an effect through learning-by-doing and other demand-induced, productivity-increasing mechanisms.

We must also consider, however, whether the flow of technology among developed countries is so free that it does not matter in which country the technical progress is first made. By now there seems to be consensus among students of the subject that it does matter, for a variety of reasons. For one thing, there is a time lag of, say, a minimum of three years. Second, much technical progress is a matter of local adaptation, such as new agricultural varieties and techniques that depend on particular soil and climatic conditions; this is why even individual states within the United States can get a high return on research and development in agriculture.[51]

If a person goes from a poor country where little new technology is being created, to a rich country where much technology is being created, this argument is obviously even stronger. Here the United States benefits not merely by the person contributing to technology that will be differentially helpful to the United States but also by the absolute increment of technology that the person creates. The more technically advanced (relative to the state of the art) is the industry in which a person works, the greater the opportunity for that person to advance the state of the art, it would seem.

[51] Zvi Griliches, "Research Costs and Social Returns: Hybrid Corn and Related Innovation," *Journal of Political Economy,* vol. 66 (October 1958), pp. 419-431; and Robert E. Evenson, "The Contribution of Agricultural Research and Extension to Agricultural Production" (Ph.D. diss., University of Chicago, 1968), summarized in Yujiro Hayami and Vernon W. Ruttan, *Agricultural Development: An International Perspective* (Baltimore: Johns Hopkins University Press, 1971).

It is not a contradiction to this line of thought that the rate of economic growth per capita has been as high or higher in the poorer countries as in the United States in the post–World War II period. The poorer countries can take advantage of the technological progress in the richer countries much more than the reverse.

A more difficult question is, Should not the larger of two countries at the same level of per capita income grow faster, if this line of thought is correct? Yes, it should—and the evidence, sketchy as it is, seems to show that absolute size is an economic advantage, ceteris paribus.[52] In brief, on reasonable assumptions immigrants have a positive discounted effect on citizens' incomes, starting almost immediately and getting large quite rapidly.

Summary and Conclusions

In summary, the subject is the effect of an additional immigrant upon the incomes of natives of a country like the United States. This model confirms that the possible gain through increased returns to native capital, if the immigrants receive only their marginal product, is small relative to the loss if immigrants receive a realistic proportion of the returns to capital, as argued by Usher. But the life-cycle saving-and-transfer process works in a positive direction for natives and is of the same order of magnitude as the capital-dilution effect. Hence, adding the saving-and-transfer process almost, or more than, offsets the capital-dilution effect.

The effect of the immigrant upon productivity, however, must also be taken into account, though it has been omitted from previous theorizing. This is the sum of learning by doing, creation of new knowledge, and economies of scale of various sorts. Within a few years, the productivity effect comes to dominate the results and dwarfs the capital-dilution and saving-and-transfer effects, yielding a high rate of return to natives on investment in immigrants, on any reasonable parameters.

[52] Hollis B. Chenery, "Patterns of Industrial Growth," *American Economic Review,* vol. 50 (1960), pp. 391-416; and Denison, *Why Growth Rates Differ.*

Commentaries

Dan Usher

In commenting on Jeffrey Williamson's paper, I begin by pointing out several features of the model that may bias the estimate of the derived elasticity of demand for labor. Then I discuss the political premise of the model that the magnitude of the elasticity of demand for labor is the chief determinant of a country's willingness to accept immigration.

First, I am intrigued by the absence of land as a factor of production in agriculture in the twentieth century. The core of the model consists of a set of production functions, one for each industry, with land, labor, and capital as the possible factors of production. Land only appears as a factor in nineteenth century agriculture. In general, a factor may be excluded from a production function for one of two reasons; it is not necessary for the production of the good in question or it is superabundant. The former reason may justify Professor Williamson's exclusion of land from industries other than agriculture. The latter may on occasion justify its exclusion from the agricultural production function—just as air and sunlight are excluded.

Yet, it is strange that land is excluded from the agricultural production function in the twentieth century but not in the nineteenth. A better case could be made for the superabundance of land in the nineteenth century, when a farmer could always pack up his belongings and move to occupy a bit of free land out West. In the twentieth century, that is no longer true. Land is scarce and valuable, signifying that its marginal product is high and that it has come to play the role of a factor of production in its own right.

The presence or absence of land in the production function affects the estimate of the elasticity of the derived demand for labor; the elasticity would appear smaller when land is a factor, with a fixed supply and positive marginal product, than when land is superabundant. Professor Williamson's assumption about the role of land may have produced a downward bias in the estimate for the nineteenth century and an upward bias in the twentieth century.

Second, Professor Williamson may have underestimated the elasticity of demand for goods. His estimate was approximately −1.3, a not unreasonable estimate if one thinks of the United States as a closed economy. But the United States has never been a closed economy; it has always been actively engaged in world trade and, in the nineteenth century at least, may for some purposes be looked upon as a small country. Consequently, taking foreign and domestic demand together, it would seem that the elasticity of demand for U.S. agricultural products was closer to infinity than to one. An underestimate of the elasticity of demand for these products would impose a downward bias onto the estimate of the elasticity of the derived demand for labor.

Third, it is difficult to connect the equations depicting capital formation with the equations depicting the demand for goods. The capital formation equation tells us that the increase in something called capital depends on the rate of interest and the quantity of capital in existence. We are not told of what capital is made, or how outputs of manufactured goods, secondary industry, or agriculture are translated into capital formation. Capital formation floats free in the model, unconnected to what is actually produced during the year. It is not clear what effect, if any, this ambiguity has upon the estimate of the derived elasticity of demand for labor.

Finally, I am uneasy about the proxy for the rate of interest, R. This is defined as the ratio of income to capital, which, for the given definition of capital, may be high or low at any given time, regardless of the rate of interest as normally defined. Here too, there may be a bias in the estimate of the elasticity of the derived demand for labor, but neither the magnitude nor the direction is predictable.

Now I turn from the economic question of the accuracy of the estimate of the derived elasticity of demand for labor to the semipolitical question of why the magnitude of this elasticity might determine a country's willingness to accept immigration. Much depends on which social class within the United States plays the major role in opening or closing the tap. Suppose, first, it is unskilled labor. For the sake of the argument, ignore Barry Chiswick's evidence about how immigrants and their children advance within American society, so that immigrants are and remain the competitors of the unskilled in the labor market. If American unskilled workers decide whether to permit immigration and if they decide selfishly, the outcome is evident. No immigration will be permitted at all, regardless of the magnitude of the derived demand for labor, as long as the elasticity is less than infinite. On the other hand, if employers and owners of capital decide, the outcome is equally evident. Immigration is always permitted, again regardless of the elasticity of the demand for labor. Immigration makes labor worse off and capital better off in the context of Professor Williamson's model, so that the decision to permit immigration would seem to depend on which class has the upper hand.

It is not my intention to deny categorically the relevance of the magnitude of the derived elasticity of demand for labor to immigration policy. Lurking in the background of Professor Williamson's paper may be a well-developed theory of what motivated the U.S. government to turn on and off the tap at different periods; within this theory the derived elasticity of demand for labor may be the central determinant. Until the mechanism is set out, the evidence on derived elasticity of demand does not seem to bear one way or another on the issue.

There is, however, a general agreement among participants in this session about the significance of economies of scale for immigration policy. If there are significant increasing returns to scale in capital and labor together, then most of the original residents of the country will benefit from immigration. If, on the other hand, there are constant or decreasing returns to scale, most of the original residents are harmed by immigration. It is at least arguable that the closing of the frontier and the shortage of natural resources have together generated decreasing returns to scale in the twentieth century and that U.S. immigration policy has been determined accordingly. Everything does depend on one critical number, but it does not seem to be the number that Jeffrey Williamson has emphasized.

Allan G. King

I place my comments in the context of a simple model that emphasizes the economic consequences of immigration. From this perspective, a nation would find it in its interest to admit immigrants, so long as the marginal benefits to the resident population associated with the entry of an additional immigrant exceeds the marginal cost. As Barry Chiswick notes, the primary benefits of immigration accrue to the owners of productive factors that are complementary to the labor of the immigrant group. In contrast, the marginal product of substitute factors of production will decline as competitive labor is added to the economy. The value of the economic gains to the complementary inputs, however, will generally exceed the losses to the competitive inputs. So long as this is true, the native population will have gained income in the aggregate. This constitutes the primary economic benefit of immigration; optimal policy making must weigh these gains against the costs of immigration.

The costs of immigration are principally distributional. Although it is possible to envision a flow of immigrants that is neutral with respect to the distribution of income in the context of present-day immigration into the United States, the focus of this conference, this is manifestly not the case. When both legal and unsanctioned immigrants are considered, the flow of immigrants is far less skilled than the resident U.S. labor force. Consequently, there is a strong presumption that the lowest income groups will be adversely affected by the immigration of additional low-skilled labor. In contrast, owners of capital and, perhaps, highly skilled labor are likely to benefit. Persons who deem this capricious redistribution of income to be undesirable must consider this a cost of immigration policy, to be traded off against the aforementioned benefits.

The law of variable proportions suggests that the income gains to immigration should diminish as more immigrants are added to constant stocks of native capital, labor, and land. In contrast, the marginal costs of immigration may be expected to rise, since movements away from equality seem less tolerable the more unequal the existing distribution of income.

Under these assumptions, a nation is likely to find that a positive, although limited, rate of immigration is optimal when changes in both aggregate income and income distribution affect societal well-being. A critical task for policy makers is to identify the relevant costs and benefit schedules and to evaluate how they can be affected by qualitative and quantitative controls on immigration.

Barry Chiswick contends, correctly, that the maldistribution effects of immigration can be potentially eliminated through appropriately conceived tax and transfer policies. Yet, before one discounts the distributional costs of immigration, it is surely relevant to ask whether the existing system of taxes and transfers fits the bill. It does not. Although the tax system is mildly progressive and the transfer system is somewhat more so, the major transfer programs are still principally categorical in nature. Moreover, the gaps in the system are most severe in those categories into which adversely affected workers are most likely to fall— the working poor. Indeed, food stamps is the primary program for which such persons are eligible. Thus, the distributional costs of immigration will not be greatly mitigated by the present system of income redistribution.

If one accepts this analysis, then it follows immediately that, in the absence of controls on immigration by the receiving country, an optimal rate of immigration is unlikely. There is no mechanism that requires a potential immigrant to consider the distributional consequences of his decision, since they impinge on persons who are probably unknown to the immigrant. In this sense, undesirable income redistribution can be considered a negative externality that accompanies immigration. As is usual in such circumstances, the judicious intervention of government, which can maintain immigration below laissez-faire levels, will enhance economic well-being.

It is also worth considering how a government can minimize the distributional costs associated with a given number of immigrants by affecting the composition of the immigrant stream. Toward this end, a flow of immigrants that mirrors the skill distribution of the resident population would seem desirable. Let us consider a production function in which the labor inputs, say skilled and unskilled, are separable from capital. It follows that the ratio of labor's marginal products, and therefore wages, solely depends on the proportions in which these factors are employed. Since an immigrant stream that duplicated the domestic skill mix would leave these proportions unchanged, it would have no effect on the distribution of labor income. This desirable outcome would clearly require far greater control of immigration than the government exercises.

A minor issue raised by Barry Chiswick is that an inflow of unskilled labor will raise the rate of return to human capital and thereby enhance the incentive of domestic workers to invest in accquiring skill. Although this is true, it may *not* result in the expected increase in the number of domestic workers who invest in human capital. A great deal depends on the supply of training opportunities, a factor Barry Chiswick ignores.

Clearly, it follows that, if the supply of training opportunities is perfectly inelastic, then an increase in the rate of return will simply result in an increase in the cost of training and no additions to the ranks of the skilled. More generally, suppose the supply of training slots is not perfectly inelastic but increases as the demand for training shifts. The source of increased demand consists of two parts. One results from the increased rate of return, the second from an increase in unskilled labor that accompanies immigration. Unless the supply of training opportunities is sufficiently elastic, the net outcome could be a *reduction* in the amount of training received by native workers.

In summary, distributional issues must be accorded a primary place in discussions regarding immigration policy. I cannot share Barry Chiswick's optimism regarding the ability of the present system of taxes and transfers to redistribute income in a manner that offsets these effects. Finally, the passivity of present immigration policy and its inability to influence either the size or composition of the immigrant flow to the authority of the United States may bring significant harm to segments of the population that can least afford this burden.

Warren C. Sanderson

As usual, Julian Simon has presented us a particularly provocative paper. While others may respond differently, this paper, like much of Simon's recent work, provokes in me a reaction of severe and unmitigated schizophrenia. Although this response is preferable to the somnambulism or numbness that occasionally accompanies an attempt to digest other academic papers, it falls short of the feeling of pure excitement and exhilaration that authors attempt to induce in their readers.

My schizophrenia arises from two conflicting forces. First, Julian Simon's conclusions, on the extremely important point of the relationship between economic growth and population growth, may well be correct. If so, Simon's conclusions must be taken quite seriously. Second, the methodology used by Professor Simon to reach his conclusions is inadequate for the task. I am about to fill this discussion with criticisms of the methodology that leads Julian Simon to important and significant conclusions. The fact that the methodology does not imply the conclusions does not mean that the conclusions are incorrect; it only means that the conclusions remain unsupported.

The first section of Simon's paper contains a discussion of the capital ownership effect. This effect is, in principle, straightforward. If a group of migrants enters a country, their average product will, in general, exceed their marginal product. The difference between the average and marginal products provides a surplus that, at least potentially, can be redistributed among the preexisting populace. It is possible, however, for migrants to receive more than their average product if governmental programs supplement their earnings. In this case, the preexisting populace loses purchasing power because of the migrants.

The question, then, is whether the migrants receive more or less than the value of their average product. There is no government sector formally included in the analytics here, so this question gets translated into a question concerning what portion of the return to capital should be prorated as a supplement to the earnings of employees. Before we see how Julian Simon answers this question, it is useful to note that this is a rough translation indeed. Employers gets returns on the capital stock directly through the ownership of that stock or the ownership of this is a rough translation indeed. Employers get returns on the capital stock indirectly through institutions such as pension funds and insurance companies. Surely, it is not such assets that are immediately placed in the hands of the migrants when they enter this country. Instead, migrants receive a claim to a certain amount of government assistance.

Professor Simon computes the amount of money supplementing each employee's earnings—migrant and nonmigrant alike—from the following equation:

$$sup\ (t)\ =\ \frac{I_k(t)\cdot \sigma}{L(t)} \tag{1}$$

where $sup\ (t)$ is the per employee earnings supplement in period t, $I_k(t)$ is total income from capital in period t, σ is the share of capital income captured by employees, and $L(t)$ is the total number of employees in the economy in period t.

Equation (1) does not appear in the text but appears to be what the author is saying. What does appear in the text is a discussion of the derivation of an estimate σ from national accounts data for 1976. I do not understand the logic of this derivation. Let me try to reconstruct it, step by step.

First, the author computes ratio A as follows:

$$A = \frac{\text{total returns to capital (net of depreciation and indirect}}{\text{national incomes} - \text{social insurance payments}} \tag{2}$$

Next, Professor Simon computes ratio B as follows:

$$B = \frac{\substack{\text{total returns to capital in nonfinancial corporations} \\ \text{(including depreciation and indirect taxes)}}}{\substack{\text{gross domestic product originating in} \\ \text{nonfinancial corporations}}} \tag{3}$$

The third step is to subtract ratio A from ratio B. It is unclear what one obtains here, since the scopes of the two ratios are quite different. If the two ratios were comparable, one would obtain in the numerator the sum of the values of depreciation and taxes on capital. The author tells us that the difference between ratio B and ratio A is the share of total income that goes to supplement the earnings of laborers. The ratio σ is, then, defined as

$$\sigma = \frac{B - A}{B} \tag{4}$$

The relationship between corporate depreciation and taxes on capital and the concept Julian Simon wishes to express—governmental supplements of migrants' incomes—seems tenuous.

Intergenerational Transfer

The second section of the paper deals with the intergenerational transfer effect. The argument made here is that the social security system transfers income from immigrants to natives. Certainly this may be the case, but it does not follow logically from the argument made there. Consider a population in which people are either adults or "elderlies"; in which social security taxes are a fixed fraction, denoted t, of the incomes of adults; and in which social security payments are the same to natives and to immigrants.

First, for simplicity, let us treat the case where the age distributions of the natives and immigrants are identical and where immigrant adults earn less income than native adults. If social security income and expenditure are in balance, the tax rate on adult income may be written as

$$t = \frac{P \cdot (N_n^e + N_i^e)}{N_n^a I_n + N_i^a I_i} \tag{5}$$

where t is the social security rate, P is the social security payment, N_n^e is the number of elderly natives, N_i^e is the number of elderly immigrants, N_n^a is the number of adult natives, N_i^a is the number of adult immigrants, and I_n and I_i are the average incomes of adult natives and immigrants, respectively.

Immigrants receive $P \cdot N_i^e$ dollars from the social security system and pay into that system $t \cdot N_i^a \cdot I_i$ dollars. The amount transferred to the immigrants may be expressed as

$$TR_i = P \cdot N_i^e - t N_i^a \cdot I_i \tag{6}$$

$$= P \cdot N_i^e - \frac{P \cdot (N_n^e + N_i^e)}{N_n^a I_n + N_i^a I_i} \cdot N_i^a I_i \tag{7}$$

$$= \frac{P \cdot (N_i^e \cdot N_n^a \cdot I_n - N_n^e \cdot N_i^a \cdot I_i)}{N_n^a \cdot I_n + N_i^a \cdot I_i} \tag{8}$$

The assumption that the age distributions of the natives and migrants are identical allows us to take one further step. That is,

$$TR_i = \frac{P \cdot (I_n - I_i)}{N_n^a I_n + N_i^a I_i} \tag{9}$$

Clearly, since both the numerator and denominator are positive, the social security system transfers income to immigrants, not from them.

In the case of dissimilar age distributions, we can return to equation (8). It can be plainly seen there that income may be either transferred to or from immigrants, depending both on the relative age distributions of the two populations and their relative average incomes.

This conclusion does not emerge in Julian Simon's argument because the benefits to elderly migrants (who may have been in their country of residence for a considerable period of time) seem to be ignored. The transfer of resources from native-born child to foreign-born parents is indeed a real phenomenon that can be ignored only at the cost of realism.

Population and Productivity

The third section of the paper is essentially an argument that more rapid population growth causes more rapid productivity growth. While this may be true in some instances, it may be false in others; Julian Simon's evidence is not persuasive on this score. One important set of data—the relationship between indexes of scale and indexes of productivity, based on appropriate figures from the United Kingdom in 1950—is particularly weak in the context of the argument. The author argues that a high index of scale should imply a high index of productivity. The causation, however, can certainly run in the reverse direction, with relatively rapid rates of productivity growth leading to relatively great rates of output growth. This same sort of problem can even arise when considering the comparison of contemporaneous U.S. and U.K. data, especially if the lag of average-practice technology behind best-practice technology differs between the two countries. The data, then, do not unambiguously support the argument.

Further, the relation between economies of scale and a nation's demographic characteristics is unclear. Many countries achieve efficient market sizes through the specialization allowed by foreign trade. It is often said that the Japanese and Korean steel industries are more efficient than the steel industry in the United States. Economies-of-scale problems and learning-by-doing difficulties do not seem to hamper them, even though their populations are considerably smaller than the U.S. population. The relatively slow growth of the West German population does not seem to have hampered it in maintaining a quite dynamic automobile industry. Indeed, more rapidly growing Indonesia does not seem to have achieved a faster rate of technological progress than less rapidly growing Taiwan. The relationship between population growth and productivity growth is undoubtedly a complex one. The task remains for further research to discern where the truth lies.

The next section of the paper builds into a simplistic one-sector model, the assumption that the rate of technological progress over time asymptotically approaches the rate of population growth. Thus, when the simulation without immigration assumes a 2 percent rate of popula-

347

tion growth and the simulation with immigration assumes a 4 percent rate of population growth, it is not surprising to find that immigration can be a force that raises the incomes of both the natives and the newcomers. Indeed, in the Simon specification, we would be better off yet, if migration were sufficient to double our population every year.

Given that Professor Simon's arguments are not sufficient to convince us of his conclusions, in what light should we view those conclusions? They may be true or they may be false. Unfortunately, the evidence presented in the paper does not greatly aid us in choosing between these alternatives. The paper, though, is bold in its conception. Perhaps population growth did influence productivity growth in the past. Perhaps it will do so again. Julian Simon has not proven his case to be true, but neither has anyone proven it to be false. Perhaps it is a good thing to be reminded from time to time of those matters that we have yet to understand. As the author's work makes clear, these can indeed be quite important.

Discussion

NIGEL TOMES, University of Western Ontario: I want to make one comment on Barry Chiswick's paper with which he should agree. We realize that workers' skills are not immutable characteristics but are acquired over the life cycle as young unskilled workers progress to become older skilled workers. This suggests that the immigration of a young cohort of workers will influence the wages of the corresponding birth cohort of native workers throughout its life cycle. Those who initially suffer by the immigration of young unskilled workers are the unskilled young native workers. As both immigrants and natives acquire skills during their lifetime through on-the-job training and additional schooling, the same birth cohort of natives that has acquired skills suffers as a consequence of competing with a greater number of skilled foreign-born workers. Although we talk about skilled and unskilled workers, the workers who actually suffer and gain in terms of birth cohorts need to be identified. Viewed from this perspective the immigration of a particular birth cohort inflicts losses on the corresponding birth cohort of natives, while gains may accrue to preceding and succeeding birth cohorts of the native population. There is a symmetry between immigration as one source of changes in the age (and therefore skill) structure of the labor force and variations in the birth rate of the native population—for example, the postwar "baby boom" and subsequent "bust."

MR. CHISWICK: A cohort of young workers that is confronted with a large influx of young immigrants will throughout the life cycle have lower wages than otherwise.

WALTER G. REST, Travelers Aid Society: A large portion of immigration into this country in the near future will be refugees. Professor Simon's formulations about the favorable impact on immigrants through the social security system does not take into consideration what we will be paying under Title XX of the Social Security Act for refugee resettlement. Those costs are going to be high. Until two years ago, the use of sponsors seemed to reduce the reliance on public assistance. This is no longer a safety net; practically every refugee goes on public assistance. They are tribesmen from Southeast Asia, who in some instances do not even read and write their own language. In some instances, they do not have a written language. This is a new kind of immigrant; the costs of this have to be figured in the calculations. It remains to be seen whether the American public as a matter of policy and on a humanitarian level is going to be willing to pay these costs.

JOAN NELSON, Johns Hopkins School of Advanced International Studies: As part of his presentation, Professor Williamson said that microdata evidence strongly suggests rather limited mobility from unskilled to skilled status among first-generation immigrants. In his paper, Professor Chiswick was arguing rather the contrary. Were the two drawing on different kinds of evidence? Is there a reconciliation?

MR. WILLIAMSON: I was referring to detailed microdata drawn from a whole host of state labor surveys starting in the mid-1870s. In her doctoral dissertation, for example, Joan Hannon looked at Michigan data drawn from the late 1880s and early 1890s for a group of five industries that suggest quite strikingly that the immigrants had low skill levels and limited mobility.[1]

MR. CHISWICK: It is not that each immigrant goes from unskilled to skilled in five, ten, or thirteen years, but that, as a group, immigrants have reached earnings parity with the native born after eleven to fifteen years, whether one looks at turn-of-the-century or contemporary data.

Francine Blau's study of immigrants using data from the 1911 Dillingham commission report indicates that male immigrants reach earnings parity with the native-born after eleven to thirteen years.[2] Her findings are strikingly similar to what I found in the 1970 Census of Population. Although different methodologies are used, the state labor force studies I have seen for turn-of-the-century data are consistent with her findings.

MR. WILLIAMSON: My model takes an extreme position; I do not know what other position it should take, given the evidence we have. There

---

[1] Joan Hannon, "The Immigrant Worker in the Promised Land: Human Capital and Ethnic Discrimination in the Michigan Labor Market, 1880-1890" (Ph.D. diss., Department of Economics, University of Wisconsin, 1977).

[2] Francine Blau, "Immigration and Labor Earnings in Early Twentieth Century America," in Julian L. Simon and Julie DaVanzo, eds., Research in Population Economics, vol. 2 (Greenwich, Conn.: JAI Press Inc., 1980), pp. 21-41.

are lots of allegations but little evidence on the nineteenth-century immigrant experience. We cannot identify the skill mix of immigrants into America; we allege that they were relatively unskilled, based on highly deficient data on the occupational status of the immigrants. Though we are aware that their skill level varied over time because they came from different places and some did not speak English, we do not know much about human capital acquisition in the nineteenth century. We need to look at human capital accumulation and the skill mix of immigrants. That would be obviously one of the first research avenues to pursue.

MR. CHISWICK: Paul Douglas, whose production function has been used in at least four or five of the papers presented in this conference, published an article in 1921 entitled "Is the New Immigration More Unskilled than the Old?"[3] He found that, with occupational classifications as the measure of skill, immigrants coming at the turn of the century from eastern and southern Europe were more unskilled than the immigrants coming at that time from northwestern Europe but not more unskilled than the immigrants who came twenty years earlier from northwestern Europe.

MS. NELSON: These different assumptions play some role in each of the two analyses. Also, the economic adjustment of immigrants is linked through a political mechanism to immigration policy. If one were to trace a cohort of immigrants over time, the balance of costs and benefits for the native population would shift. If one wants to analyze what is happening in a particular decade, he has to cumulate the effects of the series of cohorts that have come in previous decades.

Suppose the costs come early and the benefits come much later, as is believed to be the case. It is those costs transparently associated with the immigration that have a political effect. The economic analysis of the long-run mobility and long-run contributions is important for an objective analysis of the gains and losses from immigration, but, from a political perspective, it is the early and transparent costs on which one would want to focus.

MR. WILLIAMSON: It is one of our great responsibilities as economists to point out constantly some of the longer run consequences and use the discount rate to show how the long-run and the short-run are linked. That is a contribution we can make.

[3] Paul H. Douglas, "Is the New Immigration More Unskilled Than the Old?" *Journal of the American Statistical Association,* vol. 16 (June 1919), pp. 393-403.

LORENE YAP, Urban Institute: I am uncomfortable about Julian Simon's assumption of economies of scale with population growth. Even for manufacturing, there are some limits. Also, GNP is composed of services and not just manufacturing; that is a large and increasing part of GNP. Few people think that the service sector becomes more productive with increasing size. All the empirical evidence for services shows that there is a point where you should stop or costs escalate; that point is low.

MR. SIMON: That comment goes to the heart of the issue. The economies from additional people, in my paper, do not refer simply to physical economies of scale at the manufacturing plant level due to larger and more efficient machinery. Rather, I am concerned with the changes in productivity that come from additional people that show up in a longer-run context. These effects are not dealt with well in our standard way of thinking about economies of scale.

As to services, they are difficult to analyze because it is not clear what services are. We once thought, for example, that a person adding up a string of figures was performing a service. Now we have computers that perform those same activities, with a vast multiplication of our human capacities to obtain this service. In many other service sectors, for example, communications, we see enormous gains in productivity. We should not think only of haircuts and similar personal services. Services are not inherently different from other kinds of goods.

BRUCE L. GARDNER, Texas A & M University: In his discussion, Professor King mentioned an "optimal" level of immigration, and I have not heard that from anyone else. He said there is no reason to think that any level of immigration would have any particular optimality characteristics because the consequences are all external. All of the consequences we have been talking about are pecuniary externalities. Does everyone agree that Professor King is correct and that we can say nothing about the optimality characteristics of, say, laissez-faire immigration?

MR. KING: We are talking about optimality from the perspective of the people who are not involved in the migration decision. We are talking about optimality from the point of view of the natives. There is no way for the natives to communicate their preferences to others who participate in that same market, as do buyers and sellers in a market of a given commodity. I am concerned about the effects on the wages of the nonimmigrants and the returns to the capitalists who reside in the receiving country. Those are the two major impacts that are external to the immigrant. They are, however, not external to the economy.

The Bhagwati emigration tax approach is an attempt to get the immigrants to internalize the externalities that they are imposing on nonmigrating peoples. That is how a tax system is often used—to internalize externalities.

MR. CHISWICK: Jacob Mincer asked me the same question yesterday. My initial reaction was that, in the absence of an income transfer system providing benefits for low-income immigrants, a laissez faire immigration policy would be close to optimal. He raised some objection.

JACOB MINCER, Columbia University: I am comparing the national with the international system. Under the international system, clearly there would be no objection at all. The same applies in interregional migration. Do we have the same problem with internal migration? Should we regulate that?

MR. KING: I am not interested in regulating interregional migration; the same thing is true of international trade. There is a certain sovereignty that attaches to a nation that for one reason or another we have not attributed to a state. We are interested in considering the well-being of people as a collectivity within the nation, rather than just a state. If I were satisfied with the redistributional mechanisms, I do not think that would be a problem. There is, as Barry Chiswick has pointed out, the potential to redistribute the gains to the loser. In the absence of the redistributional mechanism, these externalities do exist; in principle, they need to be taken into account. I would not open up immigration until the law were in effect.

MR. USHER: In regard to the optimum, the effects of migration are frequently analyzed with the aid of a one-good–two-factor model in which the optimal amount of immigration is either zero or unlimited. That is not illogical, though it may be inexpedient in a context where migration is limited but never prevented altogether. It is conceivable, for example, that the marginal cost and marginal benefit curves not cross at all—for one to be uniformly above or uniformly below the other. If there are sufficiently large increasing returns to scale, the optimal size of immigration is infinite. If returns to scale are zero or negative and if certain other conditions hold, the optimal amount of immigration is zero. By modifying the simple model, one can generate cases in which the optimal immigration is a finite number between these limits. There are even a few queer cases where immigration is beneficial if it is large but harmful below a certain level. In principle, the analysis of migration may be improved through the introduction of a better model. Possibly not much is gained by crossing marginal cost and marginal benefit curves, unless these curves are grounded in and derived from a general equilibrium model in which it is clear who is maximizing what.

MR. SIMON: I agree with the last point but from a different point of view. As soon as you treat knowledge as endogenous in a system, there are no limits whatsoever to the amount of immigration that will benefit a country. This is implicit in Phelps's model, where the rate of productivity increase equals the rate of population growth without any limit whatsoever.[4] That may be one of the reasons why such models have been uncongenial to economists who instinctively believe that there must be some sort of a limit, some sort of optimal level.

JOHN F. McDONALD, University of Illinois at Chicago Circle: Bruce Gardner's point is right. The kind of externalities that we worry about are externalities that are not captured in the market mechanism, for example, if the immigrants cause more traffic congestion. That is the kind of migration that one would want to regulate, whether one is talking about international flows or regional flows. There is a whole literature about optimal city size. We do not ordinarily worry as much about pecuniary externalities. What externalities are of concern?

MR. KING: An externality is a consequence of an agent's action that is not entirely experienced by that agent. Why is it bad if I make someone late for work by adding to traffic congestion and he loses a dollar, but not if I do it by competing his wage down?

MR. McDONALD: In the traffic congestion case, one can make everybody better off by regulating traffic flow. One cannot in the other case.

MR. CHISWICK: The traffic congestion case is a waste of resources; the person is sitting idly in his car for an hour. That is the externality about which we worry.

MR. WILLIAMSON: Allan King paints me as an optimist in the sense that I want to take nineteenth-century experience and use it to suggest

---

[4] Edmund S. Phelps, "Models of Technical Progress and the Golden Rule of Research," *Review of Economic Studies,* vol. 23 (April 1966), pp. 133-145; and Gunter Steinmann and Julian L. Simon, "Phelps' Technical Progress Model Generalized," *Economic Letters* (forthcoming).

that we ought to free up immigration policy. He should take a closer look at the paper.

If one wants a relevant historical example for the 1980s, the better one is *not* the nineteenth century as a whole, but rather the episode from the 1890s to World War I. That was a period of technological retardation, especially in unskilled labor-intensive sectors. Also, it was a period of decline in labor-intensive sectors. It was a period of retardation in the growth of the capital stock. It seems to have precisely the attributes of the contemporary decade—capital shortage and technological retrogression. I do not offer any explanation of why that is going on now nor why it went on then, but it has the same implications for immigration.

Dan Usher has raised four interesting points, three of which I can deal with easily and one I cannot. First, on his point on price elasticities of commodity demand, if one does not like the ones in the paper and wants to raise them—fine; it will reinforce the findings. The paper stresses the importance of technological forces in driving the rates of change in the derived demand for labor, unskilled labor in particular. The main force in yielding those technological effects is the unbalanced character of technological progress across sectors. The size of the commodity price elasticities will influence the importance of technological imbalance in determining the aggregate derived demand for labor. In a model like this, higher elasticities reinforce the importance of these technological forces.

The second issue was the capital formation response. It is an appendage to the model. I was trying to get some notion of what the likely capital accumulation response might have been to an increase in immigration. I convinced myself that it is trivial, and so I could ignore it. It is true I never ask how those capital goods would have been produced, but its influence on my results is not so clear.

Suppose the capital formation response on which one is focusing is human capital. Human capital formation is skilled labor-intensive. Any effort to augment, in the short run, the stock of human capital, and thus presumably to lower the premium on skills, will be met with failure. In the short run, the derived demand for skilled labor is driven up, as the capital goods sector gears up to augment the supply of skilled labor. That is exactly what happened in the 1960s (and my salary benefited enormously). The same thing is true of conventional capital.

The third point was the issue of land. The issue is whether one can aggregate land with capital and talk about returns to both factors as a bundle. There is a literature that worries a lot about landowners as a separate recipient of income in the nineteenth century, with important regional implications. It does not seem to play a big role in the twentieth century, so land and capital were aggregated. Contrary to what Dan Usher thinks, there were not free lunches at the frontier in the nineteenth century, as there never were anywhere. Land was not free.

The fourth point is the one I cannot handle: political theory. Should we restrict the comment to only the irrelevance of the derived demand for labor? Should we extend it and ask why the quotas were imposed anyway? My paper offers an argument that the derived demand conditions may have been pushing that legislation. Others have argued that supply conditions produced that legislation. Dan Usher seems to be arguing that it was neither.

In the short run, it may be obvious. Immigrants are coming into the cities. They dilute the capital stock. They tend to stretch public goods, increase congestion, and the like. There was an accumulation of adverse impacts in the cities, a big one during this time, and the immigrants therefore had a cost. The question is, Who paid the cost? My paper is mute on that issue. Incidentally, the development literature is confronting exactly these issues on third world urbanization: the capital requirements of rapid urbanization in the third world and whether actual urbanization is "overurbanization" and suboptimal.

MR. CHISWICK: The three-factor model and the analysis of the gainers and losers provide implications for the political decision making. My "political model" relates to the expanding voting rights (the removal of property requirements and greater literacy) and the growing industrial workforce. The trade union workers on the one hand and the xenophobic racist elements that had been around for 100 or 200 years on the other hand formed a coalition to reduce immigration. The first step was to reduce the least-skilled immigration and this involved not just restrictions on Asians. The first binding immigration law on Europeans was in 1917, when health standards were strengthened and a literacy requirement was introduced. With certain exceptions, immigrants had to demonstrate literacy in any language. The quota law of 1921, of course, went much further.

Julian Simon reports data on productivity for three subperiods from 1900 to 1966. His interpretation is that productivity is higher, the larger the population. In the period since 1966, however, although population has increased, productivity has fallen. The decline started nearly a decade before the 1973 oil embargo. The productivity data for the four periods suggest that the growth in productivity was smallest in the period when immigration was greatest relative to the population

(1900–1929) and was highest in the period (1948–1966) when immigration was smallest relative to the population.

I agree with Allan King that current immigration policy is not explicitly tied to the tax transfer policy. That does not mean that there is no implicit relation. Somehow, decisions are made about a whole range of issues and, in some way, these issues are interrelated.

We talked about the laissez-faire approach to migration. I do not know of anybody who advocates a laissez-faire policy in the presence of the current income-transfer system.

There are many policy instruments that can be used to change the tax benefit burden on low-income workers. I certainly agree with Professor King's point that we will not be able to devise a precisely optimal tax transfer structure. I have never known any government agency to devise a precisely optimal anything. The question is, Can we move closer to optimality? I suspect that we can.

It sounded as if Professor King were saying that there is a fixed number of jobs in the economic system. We know, however, that there is an elasticity to the demand curve for skilled labor, so that a new person coming in with a skill may lower the wages of all skilled workers, but it does not result in a one-for-one removal of a native skilled worker from the skilled labor force.

Allan King mentioned an immigrant's coming in and lowering the wages of unskilled workers; then he gets skills and so lowers the wages of skilled workers. That was a double whammy. He is trying to have it both ways. If the immigrant hurts the unskilled native worker when the former is unskilled, he is presumably benefiting the skilled native worker. If the immigrant then becomes skilled, he will ease the burden that he had previously imposed on the unskilled worker.

MR. SIMON: I am looking at the social security matter in the decision-making context of what will happen, taking into account what is now fixed. One of the things that is fixed is the number of immigrants already here. Those immigrants are working now; in the future, they will get pensions whether or not more immigrants come. If we take this decision-making viewpoint, the social security reckoning that I built in makes sense.

I wish to comment also on the matter of reverse causality for the data relating productivity in the United States and the United Kingdom to their different market sizes. The first studies of market size and production that were done a long time ago were comparisons within a given country; they are indeed subject to the charge of reverse causality, that is, that the more productive sectors were the ones that grew in size. It is for exactly that reason that people began to compare industries across countries, in Clark's case, comparing the United States in 1950 with the United Kingdom in 1950, the United States in 1963 with the United Kingdom in 1963. For the most part, that eliminates the reverse causality because it is not a matter of a rate of change but a comparison of two different levels.

It is clear that in using a model like Phelps's, a higher population growth (or more people) will eventually lead to higher productivity. What is not so clear, however, is how fast the positive effects will overcome the negative effects. We have to evaluate the near and far future together by computing present values.

Part Four

Alternative Immigration Policies

Potential for a U.S. Guest-Worker Program in Agriculture: Lessons from the Braceros

Larry C. Morgan and Bruce L. Gardner

The large and apparently increasing flow of illegal immigration from Mexico to the United States suggests a need for fairly substantial policy adjustments. The options range from legalizing the status of current illegals and liberalizing immigration restrictions to making strong attempts to repatriate current illegals and to tighten the restrictions on further legal and illegal immigration. An option that falls between these extremes is provided by the examples of guest-worker programs in the United States and Europe, particularly that of the Bracero Program employed in the United States between 1942 and 1964. (Mexican farm workers contracted for temporary farm work in the United States are called braceros.) Although the Bracero Program was restricted to the temporary employment of Mexican workers in U.S. agriculture, it could be used in the future to supplement the domestic nonfarm labor supply.

The implementation of a guest-worker program involves many positive issues of economic analysis as well as normative issues requiring explicit value judgments. The primary goal of this paper is to explore the positive issues, which may be stated as follows: If a guest-worker program were initiated, what effects could be expected on wage rates in U.S. farm labor markets; on employment in these markets; and on the returns to employers, the prices paid by consumers, and the real incomes of U.S. natives? Estimates of these effects can then be used to identify the expected gainers and losers in such a program, and the extent of the gains and losses.

This paper first presents a brief history of the Bracero Program. The second section describes, first in general terms and then more specifically, the authors' model of the economic environment of labor use in agriculture. In the third section the Bracero Program is incorporated into an empirical analysis of the farm labor market in the principal states using braceros. The fourth section estimates the effects of the Bracero Program on farm labor markets, and the final section discusses the implications for evaluating possible guest-worker programs for future use.

History of the Bracero Program

The Bracero Program must be analyzed in the context of the historical pattern of Mexican immigration to the United States.[1] During the nineteenth century most alien farm workers were recruited from China, Japan, and the Philippines. The Alien Contract Labor Law of 1885 represented the first attempt to restrict the recruitment of alien labor and protect domestic labor markets. Meager immigration records were kept during this period, but there appears to be little doubt that Mexican immigration to the United States was minimal compared with European, Canadian, and Chinese immigration.

Immigration records before World War II, although of questionable accuracy, indicate that about 24,000 Mexicans immigrated to the United States during the period 1900–1909. From 1910 through 1919, the Mexican revolution, the influenza pandemic, and the greater demand for labor caused this immigration to increase to about 174,000. During the 1920s, with the rapid growth of prosperity in the United States and the dramatic increase in the demand for farm labor in the Southwest, particularly in California, legal Mexican immigration rose sharply to about 488,000.

With the advent of the Great Depression of the 1930s, there was intense political pressure to reduce immigration to the United States. With stricter enforcement of quotas, Mexican immigration dropped to about 28,000 during the decade. Annual reports of the U.S. Immigration and Naturalization Service (INS) indicate that about 123,000 Mexican immigrants were either deported or required to leave the United States during the period 1930–1939 (table 1). The official INS data on Mexican deportation or repatriation probably underestimate the true number of aliens expelled. Deportation methods used by INS during this period caused such bitter resentment in Mexico that much of Mexico's present distrust of the United States stems from this period.[2]

Immediately following U.S. mobilization for World War II, as U.S. farm workers began entering military service and stronger national security laws restricted the supply of illegal alien labor, growers in the Southwest began to request temporary admission of unskilled Mexican workers under provisions of the Immigration Act of 1917. Initially,

[1] Walter Fogel, "Twentieth-Century Mexican Migration to the United States," in this volume; and David M. Reimers, "Recent Immigration Policy: An Analysis," in this volume.

[2] G. C. Kiser and M. W. Kiser, eds., *Mexican Workers in the United States: Historical and Political Perspectives* (Albuquerque: University of New Mexico Press, 1979).

TABLE 1

MEXICAN IMMIGRATION TO THE UNITED STATES

Years	Immigration			Aliens Expelled[a]		
	Mexican	Total	Percent Mexican	Mexican	Total	Percent Mexican
1820–1900[b]	28,003	19,123,606	0.1			
1900–1909	23,991	8,202,388	0.3			
1910–1919	173,663	6,347,380	2.7	4,715	27,845	16.9
1920–1929	487,527	4,295,510	11.3	20,530	78,288	26.2
1930–1939	27,937	699,375	4.0	122,750	222,885	55.1
1940–1949	54,290	856,608	6.3	913,100	1,018,217	89.7
1950–1959	293,469	2,499,268	11.7	4,167,283	4,462,493	93.4
1960–1969	436,959	3,204,749	13.6	767,939	1,170,586	65.6
1970–1977	483,275	3,274,211	14.8	4,678,734	5,066,352	92.3

[a] "Aliens Expelled" includes aliens "deported," "required to depart" and "directed secure return." The third category denotes illegal aliens apprehended or identified along U.S. borders and is chiefly Mexican. Therefore the number of Mexicans expelled includes a small number of non-Mexican aliens not identified in INS reports.

[b] No Mexican immigration records are available for 1886-1893.

SOURCE: Leo Grebler, *Mexican Immigration to the United States: The Record and Its Implications*, Advance Report 2, Mexican-American Study Project (Los Angeles: University of California at Los Angeles, Graduate School of Business Administration, 1966), pp. 8, 22; and U.S. Department of Justice, Immigration and Naturalization Service, *INS Annual Report*, various issues.

Mexico resisted U.S. attempts to import Mexican labor because of resentment over the massive reverse migration of Mexican workers during the 1930s.[3] In addition, Mexican workers were less willing to enter the United States because they would be vulnerable to induction into U.S. military service.

United States diplomats quickly placated Mexican complaints of discrimination against Mexican workers and laid the foundations for the so-called Bracero Program, which was formed by international agreements signed in August 1942 and April 1943 and by Public Law 45 (the Farm Labor Bill of 1943) which was enacted in April 1943. The program called for minimum housing, sanitary, and medical services; in addition, braceros were guaranteed the same benefits as U.S. workers, as well as exemption from U.S. military service. In deference to Mexico's insistence that the program contribute to its economic devel-

[3] R. B. Craig, *The Bracero Program: Interest Groups and Foreign Policy* (Austin: University of Texas Press, 1971), p. 41.

opment, braceros were guaranteed the prevailing wage in the local U.S. labor market or a minimum hourly wage of thirty cents, whichever was higher. (The daily cash wage for farm workers without board was about $3.27 in 1943.) A savings fund, consisting of 10 percent of each bracero's wage, was withheld and transferred to individual, apparently noninterest-bearing, accounts in Mexico's Agricultural Credit Bank. Braceros were guaranteed employment for at least 75 percent of the contract period and a subsistence payment of three dollars per unemployed day.

Craig details the emptiness of many Bracero Program guarantees.[4] The subsistence payment guarantee specified that braceros would receive the same pay as domestic workers, who enjoyed no such subsistence guarantee. Mexico insisted that braceros be guaranteed the same protection against occupational accidents and diseases as U.S. farm workers, who again did not receive such protection.

The Bracero Program was initially administered by the Farm Security Administration (FSA) of the U.S. Department of Agriculture (USDA). The U.S. Employment Service was charged with certifying growers' requests for braceros. The FSA was designated as the employer and was responsible for enforcing all program guarantees within the United States. Transportation and living expenses from Mexican recruitment centers to work destinations in the United States were paid by FSA. Because growers were critical of the widely held image of FSA as a social reform agency, USDA transferred the Bracero Program to the newly created Agricultural Labor Administration in March 1943.[5]

Braceros were recruited and were directed to strategically located centers in Mexico under the direction of Mexico's Ministry of Foreign Affairs and Departments of Labor and Interior, according to a quota assigned to each Mexican state. Mexican officials monitored the program to prevent drafting of braceros into U.S. military service, discrimination against braceros, and failure or refusal on the part of the United States to pay minimum wages and transportation expenses.

About 4,200 braceros were admitted to the United States in 1942, the program's first year of operation (table 2). A peak was reached in 1944, when some 62,000 braceros were contracted. The number of workers declined to about 20,000 in 1947 when the international agreements of 1942 and 1943 ended.

From 1948 through 1950, braceros continued to enter the United States under a series of informal agreements with Mexico that were

[4] Ibid., pp. 44-45.

[5] W. W. Wilcox, "The Wartime Use of Manpower on Farms," *Journal of Farm Economics*, vol. 28 (August 1946), pp. 729-30.

administered by the U.S. Department of Labor (DOL). A peak number of 113,000 braceros were contracted in 1949, followed by only 76,000 in 1950.

During 1948–1950, growers gained increased flexibility by directly recruiting braceros. The minimum wage guarantee was dropped, but growers now had to pay all transportation costs between the point of contact in Mexico and the place of employment. As the program operated during this period without formal supervision by a U.S. agency to ensure that braceros returned home at the end of the contract, growers were required to post a $25 bond for each bracero. The bond

TABLE 2
MEXICAN ALIEN WORKERS IN U.S. AGRICULTURE, 1942–1977

	Foreign Workers Admitted for Temporary Employment[a]			Deportable Mexican Aliens Apprehended by U.S. Border Patrol		
Year	Mexican	Total	% Mexican	Farm worker	Total	% Farm worker
1942	4,203	4,203	100.0			
1943	52,098	65,624	79.4			
1944	62,170	83,206	74.7			
1945	49,454	72,900	67.8			
1946	32,043	51,347	62.4			
1947	19,632	30,775	63.8			
1948	35,345	44,916	78.7			
1949	107,000	112,765	94.9			
1950	67,500	76,525	88.2			
1951	192,000	203,640	94.3			
1952	197,100	210,210	93.8			
1953	201,380	215,321	93.5			
1954	309,033	320,737	96.4	349,543	1,022,267	34.2
1955	398,650	411,966	96.8	88,833	221,674	40.1
1956	445,197	459,850	96.8	11,953	62,625	19.1
1957	436,049	452,205	96.4	7,595	38,822	19.6
1958	432,857	447,513	96.7	6,310	32,556	19.4
1959	437,643	455,420	96.1	4,935	25,270	19.5
1960	315,846	334,729	94.4	4,402	22,687	19.4
1961	291,420	310,375	93.4	5,162	23,109	22.3
1962	194,978	217,010	89.8	5,574	23,358	23.9
1963	186,865	209,218	89.3	9,143	31,910	28.7
1964	177,736	200,022	88.9	10,689	35,146	30.4

(*Table continues*)

365

TABLE 2 (continued)

Year	Foreign Workers Admitted for Temporary Employment [a]			Deportable Mexican Aliens Apprehended by U.S. Border Patrol		
	Mexican	Total	% Mexican	Farm worker	Total	% Farm worker
1965	20,284	35,871	56.5	14,248	44,161	32.3
1966	8,647	23,524	36.8	24,385	71,233	34.2
1967	6,125	23,603	26.0	27,830	86,845	32.0
1968	0	13,323	0.0	39,301	113,304	34.7
1969	0	15,830	0.0	50,881	159,376	31.9
1970	0	17,474	0.0	53,674	219,254	24.5
1971	0	13,684	0.0	74,423	290,152	25.6
1972	0	12,526	0.0	84,084	355,099	23.7
1973	0	13,551	0.0	101,220	480,588	21.1
1974	0	13,197	0.0	111,289	616,630	18.0
1975	0	12,423	0.0	116,250	574,448	20.2
1976	0	16,145	0.0	140,260	848,130	16.5
1977	0	12,266	0.0	103,300	792,613	13.0

[a] Data prior to 1973 are from Rasmussen and U.S. Department of Labor; data from 1973 onward are from *INS Annual Report* (see Sources).

SOURCES: W. D. Rasmussen, *A History of the Emergency Farm Labor Supply Program, 1943-1947,* U.S. Department of Agriculture, Bureau of Agricultural Economics, Agricultural Monograph, No. 13 (Washington, D.C.: USDA, 1951), p. 199; U.S. Department of Labor, *Farm Labor Developments,* various issues; and U.S. Department of Justice, *INS Annual Report,* various issues.

was forfeited if the worker departed before the contract expired. If such a worker was apprehended in the United States, the grower was required to pay the costs of apprehension and return to Mexico. The increased costs of using braceros and the absence of any prohibition (as under P.L. 45) against the use of alien labor to depress wages and working conditions for domestic labor combined to make illegal immigrants, or "wetbacks," a more attractive source of labor during this period.[6]

In 1951 the Korean War was cited by growers as a justification for restoring some of the original programs conducted under P.L. 45. The enactment of Public Law 78 (P.L. 78) in July 1951 established the basis for reinstituting a formal bracero program. In August, Mexico and the United States signed the Migrant Labor Agreement of 1951 and renewed the contracting of Mexican workers for U.S.

[6] Craig, *Bracero Program,* pp. 57-60.

farm jobs under a bilaterally administered program. Mexico supported the program operations through its Departments of Interior, Labor, Public Health and State.

United States involvement in the Bracero Program increased in detail and coordination. The U.S. Department of Labor was assigned chief responsibility for recruiting, certifying need, maintaining a revolving fund, and monitoring U.S. compliance with P.L. 78. The U.S. Department of Agriculture was charged with assisting growers in presenting requests for workers to DOL. The Justice Department determined the admissibility of braceros, and the U.S. Department of Health, Education, and Welfare (HEW), through the Public Health Service, conducted admissions examinations and provided required health services. The State Department monitored the relevant treaties with Mexico.

P.L. 78 had originated as an amendment to the Agricultural Adjustment Act of 1949. The political consensus that had made P.L. 78 possible had come about as an attempt to resolve three conflicting goals: (1) reduction of the U.S. farm labor shortage; (2) protection of domestic farm workers from adverse effects of bracero labor; and (3) reduction of illegal Mexican immigration to the United States. After 1951, organized labor, various religious and social reform groups, and one agricultural organization—the National Farmers Union—opposed seven extensions of P.L. 78 before it expired at the end of 1964.[7]

The opponents of P.L. 78 attempted to weaken or nullify the Bracero Program through regulatory changes when, early in the program, it became apparent that agricultural interests exercised sufficient political influence to prevent its outright repeal. Mexico aided the anti-bracero cause in 1953 when it unsuccessfully demanded higher, uniform wages for braceros. After the program operated for one year on a unilateral basis, Mexico in 1954 signed a bilateral agreement that excluded the demands for higher wages.[8]

During the period 1951–1953, about 200,000 braceros were contracted annually. Despite grim predictions on the part of growers of high food prices without bracero labor, the program was used far less than was expected: the main reason seems to have been the availability of wetbacks along the border. The number of illegal Mexican immigrants apprehended and deported increased from about 500,000 in 1951 to about 840,000 in 1953, according to INS annual reports.

In 1954 the newly appointed INS commissioner, General Joseph

[7] Ibid., pp. 142-43, 175-76, 197.
[8] Ibid., pp. 105-23.

Swing, led the U.S. Border Patrol in Operation Wetback and apprehended more than 1 million wetbacks, much to the consternation of growers along the border who had been accustomed to hiring wetbacks rather than contending with the higher costs and the administrative burdens imposed by the Bracero Program.[9] As a result of Operation Wetback, bracero contracts increased to about 400,000 in 1955 while apprehensions of illegal Mexican immigrants fell to about 165,000. Between 1956 and 1964 the annual number of Mexican illegals remained at less than 60,000.

As the demand for bracero labor increased, DOL instituted regulations that substantially raised the cost of hiring braceros,[10] and in 1956 DOL issued housing regulations that caused more than 200 bracero camps in California and Arizona to close.

In 1958 the U.S. secretary of labor began to issue a series of prevailing wage regulations that effectively reduced the gap between domestic and bracero wage rates. These regulations were directed initially at the largest bracero markets with the intent of forcing growers to attract domestic workers by offering higher wages. In 1962 DOL began issuing statewide adverse wage rates under the revised provisions of P.L. 78. The new minimum wages ranged from sixty cents per hour in Arkansas to one dollar per hour in most of the other twenty-three states that employed braceros in 1961, compared with the U.S. wage rate of about $1.01. The issuance of statewide adverse wage rates marked one of the major turning points in the Bracero Program. The legal basis for such rates was supported by P.L. 78, as well as by court decisions affirming DOL's establishment of an adverse wage rate for growers in Dona Ana County, New Mexico, in 1961.

From 1956 (the peak year of P.L. 78) through 1961 the number of bracero contracts declined at an annual rate of almost 7 percent. Between 1961 and 1962 total contracts declined by 33 percent. Growers using bracero labor sensed the increasing political opposition to P.L. 78 and began adopting more mechanized production methods or shifting to less labor-intensive enterprises. Bracero contracts increased from 192,000 in 1951 to a peak of about 445,000 in 1956, but fell to about 178,000 when P.L. 78 expired at the end of 1964.

Merits and Demerits. The Bracero Program, a unique chapter in U.S. immigration history, created intense political confrontations between southwestern growers and a coalition of labor unions, religious organizations, and social reform groups.

[9] J. McBride, *Vanishing Bracero* (San Antonio: Naylor Company, 1963), pp. 11-17.
[10] Craig, *Bracero Program,* pp. 151-55.

Most arguments about the merits and demerits of the Bracero Program were devoid of positive economic analysis, but it seems clear who the principal gainers and losers were. Growers obviously benefited from the program to the extent that uncertainty regarding production planning decisions was reduced,[11] as were wage rates. Throughout the duration of the Bracero Program, growers argued that the declining agricultural labor supply was raising their costs; this argument was supported by a general trend of rising real wages and a declining supply of hired farm workers in the U.S. farm labor market. Growers also benefited from the transportation cost savings under P.L. 45. Under P.L. 78 a revolving fund was created by DOL to cover the U.S. government costs of recruiting, screening, and transporting braceros.[12] An initial fee of $7 was collected from growers for each bracero contract. In 1959 this fee was raised to $12 per bracero. While growers considered the fee to be a tariff, it was undoubtedly less than the government's cost of administering the program. The program excluded most nonworking members of a bracero's family, thus reducing growers' housing costs in comparison with their costs of using domestic migratory farm workers.

The principal arguments against the Bracero Program centered on its adverse effects on domestic workers (that is, depressed wage rates and displacement of domestic farm workers with few employment alternatives). While the qualitative effects seem clear, Mamer was unable to find reliable studies of the program's impacts.[13]

Most P.L. 78 braceros were employed in picking vegetables, fruits, cotton, and sugar beets.[14] Vegetables and fruits are still relatively labor intensive, but cotton and sugar beets underwent major mechanization as the Bracero Program began to decline. Mechanical strippers were available to cotton growers in 1958, but were not widely used at the time. Only thirty-five cotton mechanical strippers were used, and they were in the northern-most cotton regions where frost defoliated

[11] D. Zilberman and R. E. Just, "Agricultural Products Markets and the Demand for Seasonal Labor" (Paper presented at the U.S. Department of Labor/University of Florida Conference on Seasonal Agricultural Labor Markets, Arlington, Va., January 1980).

[12] J. M. Vigro, "Economic Impacts of International Manpower Flows: A Consideration of the Bracero Program" (Ph.D. diss., Claremont Graduate School, Claremont, California, 1972), pp. 25-27.

[13] G. W. Mamer, "The Use of Foreign Labor for Seasonal Farm Work in the United States: Issues Involved and Interest Groups in Conflict," *Journal of Farm Economics,* vol. 43 (December 1961), pp. 1204-10.

[14] R. C. McElroy and E. E. Gavett, *Termination of the Bracero Program: Some Effects on Farm Labor and Migrant Housing Needs,* Agricultural Economic Report no. 77 (Washington, D.C.: U.S. Department of Agriculture, Economic Research Service, 1965), pp. 18-22.

the plants prior to harvest. McBride argues that growers continued to use braceros to harvest cotton, even under growing regulatory pressure from DOL, as long as hand-picked cotton received a premium price over dirtier machine-picked cotton.[15] By 1962 the increased cost of bracero labor encouraged a dramatic shift toward mechanical cotton harvesters and new ginning equipment that would handle the extra trash. Had P.L. 78 not been enacted, this technological change probably would have occurred earlier.

Immigration Trends. Legal Mexican immigration to the United States increased from about 54,000 during 1940–1949 to about 293,000 during the 1950s (table 1). Since 1954, legal immigration has remained stable at about 49,000 per year.

Illegal Mexican immigration has been much more variable. About 913,000 illegals were expelled during 1940–1949, but almost 4.2 million were expelled during 1950–1959. After Operation Wetback in 1954, illegal immigration fell to 165,000 in 1955 and 59,000 in 1956. During the remaining years of P.L. 78 illegal immigration from Mexico remained at less than 51,000 per year. After 1964 the number of illegal immigrants detected increased rapidly, reaching almost 957,000 in 1978.

North and Houstoun interviewed 481 illegal Mexican immigrants in 1975 and found about 24 percent employed as farm laborers.[16] Statistics on the employment status of deportable Mexican aliens apprehended by the U.S. Border Patrol indicate that the proportion of illegals classified as farm workers dropped to about 19 percent at the height of P.L. 78 enforcement, then rose to a peak of about 34 percent following the termination of P.L. 78, and then declined to about 13 percent in 1977 (table 2). These trends, while most applicable to border counties, suggest that agriculture has significantly reduced its dependence on alien labor.

A Model of International Labor Flows

Our approach to the market context of labor movement is in the general spirit of Krauss and Johnson or Krauss and Baumol, and our view of the appropriate modeling of the migration process follows Sjaastad

---

[15] McBride, *Vanishing Bracero*, pp. 21-31.

[16] D. S. North and M. F. Houstoun, *Illegal Aliens: Their Characteristics and Role in the U.S. Labor Market: An Exploratory Study* (Washington, D.C.: Linton and Company, 1976), p. 110.

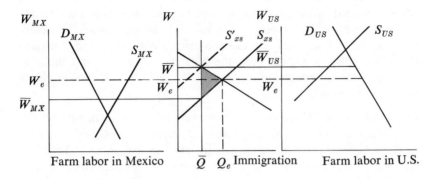

FIGURE 1
UNITED STATES/MEXICO LABOR MARKET INTERACTION

Farm labor in Mexico $\bar{Q}$ Q_e Immigration   Farm labor in U.S.

and subsequent work in a similar vein.[17] The basic idea is that there exists an excess supply of Mexican farm labor at U.S. farm wage rates. The relevant wage rate refers to Mexican labor-market adjustments. The adjustment involves currency translation from the peso to the dollar and the transportation and other costs necessary to put Mexican labor in a position to enter the U.S. market.

The relationship between the labor markets can be represented diagrammatically by the same kind of excess supply and demand approach used in the partial equilibrium analysis of trade in goods. Figure 1 shows the supply of immigrants to the U.S. farm sector as an excess supply curve of Mexican farm labor, S_{xs}. The demand for immigrant farm labor is the excess demand function for U.S. labor in agriculture. The flow of immigrants in the absence of constraints on international migration would equate the U.S. excess demand and the Mexican excess supply of agricultural labor. The resulting equilibrium wage rate would be higher in Mexico and lower in the United States than each country's farm wage rate would be with no migration. The wage rates would not be the same in the two countries, however; they would result in a differential in which the gains from discounted expectations of future increased earnings offset the costs of migration for marginal immigrants. Wage differentials reflecting the skill mix of the U.S. and Mexican farm labor forces would also persist.

[17] M. B. Krauss and H. G. Johnson, *General Equilibrium Analysis* (London: George Allen and Unwin, 1974), pp. 199-205; M. B. Krauss and W. G. Baumol, "Guest Workers and Income Transfer Programs Financed by Host Governments," *Kyklos*, vol. 32, no. 1-2 (1979), pp. 36-46; and L. G. Sjaastad, "The Costs and Returns of Human Migration," *Journal of Political Economy*, vol. 70 (October 1962, Supplement), pp. 80-93.

Because immigration is restricted, the equilibrating process is incomplete. A quantitative restriction to $\bar{Q}$ in figure 1 (or an implicit tax on immigration, in the form of penalties imposed on and wasted effort expended by captured illegal migrants, that would shift the supply of immigrants to S'_{xs}) would put constraints on equilibration of skill-adjusted wage rates between the countries. With restricted immigration there exists a gap between the Mexican wage rate and the U.S. wage rate (net of migration costs) which can be a powerful incentive to illegal migration.

Empirical Issues. There are two main sets of issues to be considered. First, what determines the wage and employment effects of a change in $\bar{Q}$ in figure 1, that is, a change in immigration policy? This is a question of the comparative statics of the model. Second, since changes will be observed in circumstances that involve shifts in the supply and demand functions in figure 1, how can we hold exogenous dynamic influences constant so that comparative-statics results will be meaningful? This is a question of identifying and validating an econometric model that embodies the supply and demand functions for immigrants. To analyze the comparative statics of the model, we begin with the excess demand function for farm labor in the United States, which is

$$L_M = L^D_{US} - L^S_{US}$$

To examine small changes in response to price, we have

$$\frac{dL_M}{dW_{US}} = \frac{dL^D_{US}}{dW_{US}} - \frac{dL^S_{US}}{dW_{US}}$$

converting to elasticities

$$\frac{dL_M}{dW_{US}} \cdot \frac{W_{US}}{L_M} = \left(\frac{dL^D_{US}}{dW_{US}} \cdot \frac{W_{US}}{L^D_{US}} \cdot \frac{L^D_{US}}{L_M} \right) - \left(\frac{dL^S_{US}}{dW_{US}} \cdot \frac{W_{US}}{L^S_{US}} \cdot \frac{L^S_{US}}{L_M} \right)$$

The left-hand sides are $\% \Delta L_M / \% \Delta W_{US}$, which can be expressed as

$$\eta_M = \eta_{US} K^D_{US} - \varepsilon_{US} K^S_{US} \qquad (1)$$

where η_M is the elasticity of the U.S. demand for imported farm labor, η_{US} is the total elasticity of demand for farm labor in the United States, ε_{US} is the elasticity of the supply of U.S. farm labor, K^D_{US} is the reciprocal of the share of U.S. farm labor accounted for by immigrants, and K^S_{US} is the ratio of U.S. to immigrant farm labor. Thus, if the United States has 1.6 million domestic farm workers and 0.4 million immigrant workers, for a total of 2.0 million, then K^D_{US} is 5 and K^S_{US} is 4.

The supply function of U.S. immigrants is the Mexican excess supply of farm labor, which is

$$L_M = L_{MX}^S - L_{MX}^D$$

Going through a derivation analogous to that which generated equation (1) yields

$$\varepsilon_M = \varepsilon_{MX} K_{MX}^S - \eta_{MX} K_{MX}^D \qquad (2)$$

where ε_M is the elasticity of Mexican supply of farm labor to the United States, ε_{MX} is the total elasticity of supply of farm labor in Mexico, η_{MX} is the elasticity of demand for farm labor in Mexico, K_{MX}^S is the reciprocal of the share of Mexican farm labor that migrates, and K_{MX}^D is the ratio of labor used in Mexico to labor emigrating.

The interaction between the U.S. demand for immigrant labor and the Mexican supply of such labor is influenced by U.S. immigration policy. If we suppose that the policy is a quantitative restriction, so that L_M becomes an exogenous policy-determined variable, then the effect of a change in the controlled immigration L_M on wage rates in the United States is determined by η_M, the elasticity of excess demand for U.S. farm labor. From equation (1), this elasticity will be larger, and hence the U.S. wage effect of a change in immigration will be smaller the greater the elasticities of demand and supply for U.S. farm labor and the smaller the share of the U.S. farm labor force accounted for by immigrants. With plausible values for the parameters, η_M is large; for example, Tyrchniewicz and Schuh estimate the short-run elasticity of demand for U.S. hired farm labor to be -0.26 and the short-run elasticity of supply to be 0.65.[18] If we use a share of bracero labor of 0.20, η_{US} is $(-0.26)(5) - (0.65)(4) = -3.9$. Thus, a 10 percent increase in U.S. farm labor via increased immigration would be expected to reduce U.S. farm wages by about 2½ percent.

The effect of an implicit tax on immigration, consisting of penalties and lost time, costs, and effort when illegal immigrants are apprehended, is slightly more complicated. The excess demand function for immigrant labor can be expressed as

$$L_M = D(W)$$

the function of whose elasticity is η_M. The supply of immigrant labor can be written as

$$L_M = S(W')$$

[18] E. W. Tyrchniewicz and G. E. Schuh, "Econometric Analysis of the Agricultural Labor Market," *American Journal of Agricultural Economics,* vol. 51 (November 1969), pp. 770-87.

whose elasticity with respect to W is ε_M. The wage rate in the demand function is the U.S. market wage including the implicit tax, W, while the immigrant workers can expect to receive only the wage rate minus the tax rate, that is,

$$W' = W(1-t)$$

To analyze the effect of a change in t (for example, stricter enforcement of immigration laws), equate the supply and demand of immigrants under the constraint imposed by t, and differentiate with respect to t. The result, expressed in terms of elasticities, is

$$E(W,t) = \frac{-1}{\dfrac{\eta_M}{\varepsilon_M}-1} \cdot \frac{1}{1-t} \tag{3}$$

when t is the tax rate as a percentage of W. The notation $E(W,t)$ means a percentage change in W resulting from a 1 percent change in t. Thus, let us suppose that W is \$4.00 per hour and t is 0.30. The 30 percent tax resulting from penalties that illegal immigrants face means that the expected value of the wage rate to immigrants is \$4.00 $(1-t) = \$2.80$.

Equation (3) provides the estimated effect of a change in the penalties on the wage rate. Let us suppose that $\eta_M = -1$ and $\varepsilon_M = 2$. Then, using $t = 0.30$, we have $E(W,t) = (-2)/[(-3)(0.7)] = 0.952$. This says that if we reduce the implicit tax on immigration by 5 percentage points to 0.25 (by relaxing border patrol activity, for example) we expect to see the U.S. farm wage rate fall by about 4¾ percent. If the U.S. wage was \$4.00, it falls to \$3.81.

By substituting from equations (1) and (2) into equation (3), we obtain a relationship between the underlying supply/demand parameters for the two countries and the wage effects of immigration policy. Generally, an easing of entry into the United States will tend to reduce U.S. farm wage rates by a greater amount; this can be stated as follows:

1. the less elastic the supply of domestic farm labor in the United States
2. the less elastic the demand for farm labor in the United States (for example, the less substitution there is between labor and nonlabor inputs)
3. the greater the share of the U.S. farm labor force accounted for by immigrants
4. the more elastic the supply of Mexican farm labor
5. the more elastic the demand for Mexican farm labor
6. the smaller the share of Mexican labor that emigrates.

Much discussion of the pros and cons of immigrant labor policy options can be expressed in terms of disagreement about the magnitudes of these parameters. For example, those who emphasize the trade-off between mechanization and the availability of immigrant labor are suggesting a relatively high value for the elasticity of U.S. farm labor demand: if less immigrant labor is available then mechanization will occur and there will not be much more work or higher wages for U.S. workers. Those who stress, usually in a short-run context, the necessity of maintaining foreign labor sources are suggesting a low elasticity of demand for labor (with very limited substitution possibilities) together with a low elasticity of supply of U.S. farm labor, so that η_M tends to be small and the U.S. wage is sensitive to immigration policy. Another special case is the model of Krauss and Baumol, which assumes that $\varepsilon_M \to \infty$ (that is, in our example that U.S. immigration policy would have no effect on Mexican wage rates).[19]

The validity of these or other assumptions about the determinants of wage rate effects is of course an empirical matter. A broader empirical issue is the general applicability of the supply/demand model to the farm labor market and to the place of immigrant labor within the market. The main purpose of the remainder of this paper is to explore these empirical questions.

Before we turn to this empirical discussion, more should be said about the general issue of the relationship between international labor flows and international trade in products. The factor–price equalization literature has examined this issue extensively. In the case of U.S./ Mexican labor mobility, it appears in a particular microeconomic, albeit international, context. The demand functions for U.S. farm labor in figure 1 are derived demands, the relevant product markets being those for agricultural commodities. In the case of the U.S. products in which immigrant workers are most heavily engaged, there is movement of both workers and products, particularly winter season vegetables, from Mexico to the United States. While these flows can substitute for one another to some extent, they raise quite different policy issues. U.S. workers can agree on being opposed to liberalization of international flows at both levels, and U.S. consumers can agree on favoring both. But U.S. vegetable growers tend to favor liberalized immigration while opposing liberalized commodity trade (although some Texas growers are engaged in farming on both sides of the border, which provides a policy hedge and also blunts their interest in achieving any particular policy regime).

---

[19] Krauss and Baumol, "Guest Workers."

FIGURE 2
SIMULTANEOUS EQUILIBRIUM OF PRODUCT AND DERIVED
INPUT MARKET, WITH TRADE IN PRODUCTS AND
CONSTRAINED MOBILITY OF LABOR

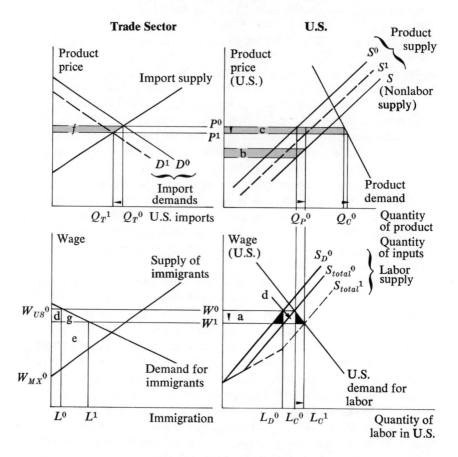

The issues involved can be illustrated by means of a simple derived-demand model of U.S. farm labor demand[20] coupled with the excess demand for farm labor and agricultural products. In figure 2 an initial equilibrium position is shown with restricted immigration but free trade in commodities. The superscript 0 identifies the resulting commodity price (P). Other variables are the U.S. wage rate (W); product quantities imported, produced, and consumed (Q_T, Q_P, Q_C); and labor immigrating from Mexico, domestic labor, and total labor

[20] M. Friedman, *Price Theory* (Chicago: Aldine, 1962), chapter 8.

376

used in U.S. production (L, L_D, L_C). Let us suppose that immigration is liberalized by permitting L^1 instead of L^0 workers to enter the United States. Then the U.S. farm wage rate declines and U.S. labor use increases, which results in increased production and a reduced excess demand for imported farm products. Consequently, U.S. commodity imports decline and commodity price falls. The net result is that U.S. consumers gain area c and Mexican producers (including losses to Mexican workers) lose area f in the product markets. In the input markets, U.S. farm workers lose area a and U.S. producers (including owners of all nonlabor inputs) gain area b. Newly immigrating Mexican workers gain area e. The net welfare gain to the United States and Mexico jointly (the sum of all gains and losses) is e plus the two small darkened triangles. The net welfare gain to U.S. citizens is $c + b - a$.

There is always a net gain to the U.S. citizens taken together, and to Mexican workers newly migrating to the United States. Mexican workers will tend to gain as the move from L^0 to L^1 drives up the Mexican wage rate as the supply of labor declines, but the reduction in product trade reduces the derived demand for Mexican workers. The net effect on Mexican wages is uncertain in the absence of further assumptions. The result is a shift to the right in the excess supply of Mexican workers, S_{MX}, but this has no effect on the constrained market equilibrium with immigration held at L^1. The net effect in Mexico depends on whether the shift in S_{MX} outweighs the movement along the unshifted S_{MX} (that is, whether the dotted curve intersects L^1 at a wage higher or lower than W_{MX}^0.

The same kind of comparative-statics results can be used to analyze a tariff or quantitative restraint on U.S./Mexican trade in agricultural commodities. Restricting trade increases the derived demand for U.S. labor and hence increases immigration (in the absence of restrictions). Liberalizing commodity trade reduces the demand for immigrants; it also increases the demand for labor in Mexico. Thus, liberal trade in commodities serves as a substitute for liberalizing immigration and lessens the distortion created by a given set of immigration restrictions.

The quantitative significance of such policy moves in actual U.S./Mexican relations depends on empirical matters—the size and stability of elasticities and behavioral functions of U.S. and Mexican workers, farmers, and consumers. There is hope for placing empirical substance in these considerations, because some experience has been accumulated on international flows of labor between Mexico and the United States in the course of the Bracero Program. We now turn to an analysis of this experience.

Estimation of Effects of the Bracero Program

In analyzing the effects of the Bracero Program it is necessary to specify the market situation into which immigrant workers are introduced. This necessity creates problems which cannot be resolved in a completely satisfactory manner. Braceros were employed in many geographically specific areas and in commodity specific activities. This suggests that we might need to consider independently such issues as the effects of bracero labor in the Rio Grande Valley citrus industry, in the California lettuce industry, in the High Plains cotton industry, etc. On the other hand, there are important interrelationships, especially with respect to wage rates and employment, among these sectors. Thus, if an influx of immigrant workers is contracted for in California tomatoes, the domestic workers who would otherwise have been employed in tomatoes become available elsewhere and change labor market conditions in other commodities and areas.

There is evidence that an effective informal information system existed under the P.L. 78 Bracero Program that resulted in quite rapid cross-market adjustment. McBride provides a colorful description of the South Texas cotton industry's adjustment to a declining labor supply.[21] When INS halted the entire supply of wetback labor in July 1954, cotton association managers responded over the weekend by placing orders for 60,000 braceros. By 1958 the Bracero Program was effectively reducing the supply of Mexican labor. The industry reacted by mechanizing, as most other cotton regions had already done. McBride estimates that less than 10 percent of South Texas cotton was mechanically harvested in 1958. By 1962 more than 90 percent of the crop was mechanically harvested.

There is no reason why the cross-market adjustments to braceros need be confined to agricultural labor markets or even to those sections of the United States that employed braceros. If we were to take the entire country as the relevant labor market, however, the effects of bracero labor would be diluted to such an extent as to be lost in other disturbances in employment and wage rates during the bracero period, which were quantitatively much more important. Eliminating 200,000 braceros from the U.S. civilian labor force changed it by less than one-half of 1 percent. Consequently, we will take the general level of nonfarm wages in the United States as an exogenous variable influencing but not influenced by the supply of braceros.

The aggregation of regions and farm commodities of the United States to specify a single U.S. agricultural labor market yields a total

[21] McBride, *Vanishing Bracero.*

of about 2.5 million hired farm workers in the bracero period. We may expect a few hundred thousand braceros to have a more noticeable impact in this smaller market, unless wages in the farm labor market adjust so fully to nonfarm labor market conditions that the farm wage rate cannot depart significantly from nonfarm wage rates for comparable workers in comparable working conditions. Empirical studies of the farm labor market suggest a less than perfectly elastic supply of agricultural workers with respect to the farm wage rate, if nonfarm wage rates are held constant,[22] so that we may justifiably expect to find exogenous events changing agricultural wage rates specifically.

Morgan considered the effects of foreign temporary agricultural workers in a national model of the agricultural labor market.[23] The hired farm labor demand elasticity is estimated, from 1949–1978 data, to be −2.77 at the means. The elasticity of the hired farm labor supply with respect to foreign agricultural workers is 0.08, indicating that a 1 percent increase in the supply of foreign agricultural workers (which amounts to 2,000 foreign workers at the mean) will decrease the hourly wage rate by 0.03 percent. While these results have the expected signs and are significantly different from zero at the 1 percent confidence level, the impact of foreign labor is difficult to assess in a national model because this labor was not evenly distributed throughout the United States.

State data on the use of bracero labor are available only from 1953. Seven states—Arizona, Arkansas, California, Colorado, Michigan, New Mexico, and Texas—used 92 percent of all bracero labor in 1953. In all successive years these states used at least 96 percent of all bracero labor entering the United States.

Table 3 shows the numbers of braceros by state. In addition to being concentrated by region, braceros were employed in particular types of agriculture. Since there are presumably economic reasons for this fact, an economic model which accounts for them should be able to give a fuller and more satisfactory account of the consequences of P.L. 78. Our analysis makes use of state-aggregate data.

Serious problems are created by the use of states as units of labor market observation. For some purposes they are disaggregated to too great an extent. If 20,000 braceros are employed in West Texas, this

[22] G. E. Schuh, "An Econometric Investigation of the Market for Hired Labor in Agriculture," *Journal of Farm Economics,* vol. 48 (May 1962), pp. 307-21; and Tyrchniewicz and Schuh, "Econometric Analysis of the Agricultural Labor Market."

[23] L. C. Morgan, "Income Maintenance Programs and Farm Labor Markets" (Paper presented at the U.S. Department of Labor/University of Florida Conference on Seasonal Agricultural Labor Markets, Arlington, Va., January 1980).

TABLE 3

NUMBER OF BRACEROS CONTRACTED UNDER P.L. 78, BY STATE, 1953–1964

Year	Arkansas	Arizona	California	Colorado	Michigan	New Mexico	Texas
1953	27,706	12,141	52,452	3,248	2,568	23,599	62,854
1954	22,668	16,181	77,423	2,818	5,093	18,946	158,704
1955	30,218	18,584	109,677	3,908	6,818	19,230	200,470
1956	30,289	22,279	150,877	7,368	7,025	19,907	193,344
1957	23,658	23,108	149,067	8,189	10,686	19,444	188,824
1958	15,480	27,176	138,328	7,689	8,167	20,218	206,331
1959	27,387	24,630	136,012	8,168	8,212	18,290	205,959
1960	27,413	19,324	112,995	8,492	4,815	10,404	122,755
1961	26,849	16,747	98,733	9,083	6,744	7,503	117,368
1962	8,850	11,985	116,455	9,119	9,968	1,634	30,152
1963	5,806	15,857	110,823	9,337	9,932	1,823	26,084
1964	4,572	16,768	112,096	8,615	9,939	1,437	18,171

SOURCE: U.S. Department of Labor, Bureau of Labor Statistics, *Farm Labor Developments*, various issues.

will create an excess supply of labor at the previously existing wage rate and hence will tend to drive down the West Texas farm wage rate. Adjustments will tend to create an excess supply of labor in New Mexico at the previously existing wage rate there, and hence will drive down New Mexico's farm wage rates. Michigan, which traditionally obtains a significant amount of seasonal labor from Texas migratory workers, would tend to receive more workers from Texas's excess supply. Therefore, it may be misleading to estimate the effects of the Bracero Program in a state by considering the number of braceros in that state alone. This is especially true in such a case as New Mexico, where the total hired farm labor force is only 8,000 workers. The general problem is that neighboring states may be more appropriately treated with New Mexico as part of a single labor market, or at least as submarkets too closely related to be treated as independent areas with their own supply/demand equilibria.

On the other hand, for some purposes states may be aggregated to too great an extent. There are within-state regional variations in labor market conditions; in particular, there is evidence of notable wage-depressing effects resulting from proximity to the Mexican border.[24] In

[24] B. Smith and R. Newman, "Depressed Wages along the U.S.-Mexico Border," *Economic Inquiry,* vol. 15 (January 1977), pp. 51-66.

estimating bracero effects, the issue is whether the whole state's wage rate structure responds proportionally to braceros or whether the border areas absorb the wage and employment effects, with a significantly lesser impact in areas far from the border. In addition, a state as a unit of observation aggregates many agricultural commodities that employ labor with differing skills, with differing seasonal patterns, and under differing working conditions.

Although twenty-four states used braceros at some time during the lifetime of P.L. 78, it serves no useful purpose to discuss the Bracero Program on a national basis if (as mentioned earlier) more than 90 percent of all braceros were employed in four border states—Arizona, California, New Mexico, and Texas—and three interior states—Arkansas, Colorado, and Michigan. These seven states, denoted hereafter as "bracero states," are selected as the relevant geographic market for braceros. The border states employed most of their bracero labor in vegetable, cotton, and citrus harvesting. Colorado and California relied on braceros for sugar beet harvesting. The Arkansas bracero demand came primarily from cotton and vegetable harvesting requirements, and Michigan used most of its bracero workers in harvesting vegetables and fruit.

Although the Bracero Program originated in 1942, braceros were not significant components of state hired farm labor markets until P.L. 78 was enacted in 1951. Before 1953, records do not show use of braceros by state; therefore, any attempt to measure program effects at the state level must be restricted to post-1952 data. The twelve-year period 1953–1964 is too short for adequate modeling of many of the structural and institutional changes—such as the delayed adoption of new labor-saving harvesting and processing techniques—caused by P.L. 78 in bracero state farm labor markets. Moreover, the post–P.L. 78 period was certainly influenced by the program. Several studies conducted shortly after P.L. 78 was terminated had to rely on analyses using market information taken from the last years of the program and the first post-program years for an estimate of program effects.[25] Our study covers the time period 1953 through 1978, the last year for which data are available for many attributes of the market.

[25] L. B. Jones, "Mexican-American Labor Problems in Texas" (Ph.D. diss., University of Texas, Austin, Texas, 1965, reprinted by R and E Research Associates, San Francisco, 1971); W. E. Martin, "Alien Workers in United States Agriculture: Impacts on Production," *Journal of Farm Economics,* vol. 48 (December 1966), pp. 1137-45; C. V. Manes, "The Short-Run Effects of the Termination of Public Law 78 on the Texas Migrant Farm Labor Market" (Master's thesis, University of Texas, Austin, 1967); and R. Geenan, "Economic Adjustments to the Termination of the Bracero Program" (Ph.D. diss., University of Arkansas, 1967).

Specification of the Model. To estimate the effect of P.L. 78 on the wage rate and the quantity of workers in the hired farm labor market, it is necessary to hold constant other relevant factors affecting labor supply and demand. On the demand side the relevant variables include three main types: shifters of final-product (food and fiber) demand, which change the derived demand for farm labor; exogenous changes in the markets for nonlabor inputs which substitute for farm labor; and technological change in agricultural production.

Final-product demand effects. These effects are most straightforwardly represented as prices received by farmers. Product and factor prices are mutually determined, however, so that it is questionable whether to represent the wage rate as determined by product price as an independent variable. The identification problem is lessened by the sequential nature of farm production. The most important labor use decisions of farmers are made before output and the resulting market-clearing prices are observed. Labor use decisions are therefore more properly specified as a function of anticipated prices. The latter may be represented by lagged prices. While reasonable objections may be raised to the use of lagged prices as an indicator of price expectations, lagged prices are exogenous variables, predetermined when labor use decisions are made.

Product demand considerations are complicated by the heterogeneity of agricultural production. Farm labor is used to produce many different products, some of which are actually inputs into others (feed crops in livestock production); also, the crop mix differs in the different states that we consider. It is inappropriate, therefore, to use a single, overall agricultural product price index for all states.

Our approach is to introduce two state-specific product price variables. First, an index of prices received for farm commodities was created for each state by weighting the U.S. indexes for eight major farm commodities by their relative market shares in each state. Second, an attempt was made to measure the labor intensity of the crop mix in each state by the share of each state's total farm production expenditures accounted for by hired labor. This second variable once again raises the problem of mutual determination. In our context, a labor-intensive crop mix increases the demand for labor; but an increased quantity of labor available tends to encourage production of labor-intensive crops.

Substitute input effects. During recent decades, purchased inputs such as fertilizer, pesticides, and mechanical equipment have tended to become cheaper in relation to farm labor. At the same time energy became relatively expensive in the 1970s. To hold input market effects constant, we introduce two variables. First, for inputs that are relatively elastic in supply in the long run—the manufactured inputs—we use a price index as a labor demand shifter. Second, for inputs that are relatively inelastic in supply—notably land—we use a quantity index as a labor demand shifter. Ideally, the prices and quantities of all farm inputs should be treated as mutually determined. We believe, however, that the index of prices paid by farmers for purchased inputs and the quantity of land in production are both too little influenced by farm labor market conditions during our period of analysis to create significant simultaneous equations bias.

Technological change. Much of the change in agricultural production processes in the post–World War II period may be explainable in terms of reduced prices of purchased nonlabor inputs. The results for labor demand would be incorporated in the input price effects discussed in the preceding paragraph. Over and above the effects of input price changes, there are changes in the quality of inputs and in production processes which are likely to have influenced labor demand in agriculture. Unfortunately, it is difficult to obtain an exogenous indicator of technological change; indeed, it is impossible if technological change is induced by changes in labor markets. Even apart from this problem, output per unit of labor, a commonly used indicator of productivity in nonfarm U.S. industry, is surely an inappropriate indicator of exogenous technological change for our purposes. For the farm sector there exists an index of total factor productivity which seems more likely not to be a function of farm labor market events, and so is more nearly suitable as an exogenous variable. This index (the USDA's *Changes in Farm Productivity*), which is available annually by U.S. region, is our indicator of technological change.

Shifters of farm labor supply. The most important exogenous variables on the labor supply side—apart from the availability of Mexican labor, which it is our primary purpose to explore—pertain to the opportunity costs of committing labor to agriculture. These involve the returns from nonagricultural employment. The opportunity wage rate should reflect the options actually open to farm workers. A very broad index of nonagricultural wage rates would be an inappropriate measure of the opportunity wage because the schooling, work experience, and other characteristics of farm workers limit their options considerably. On the other hand, no narrow occupational wage would be appropriate, since various options are open and the available alternatives change over time. As a compromise, the wage of production workers in manufacturing is used as an indicator of what farm workers may expect to earn in nonfarm employment. The relevance of this wage rate is conditioned by the availability of nonfarm work. In order to take into account the probability of a farm worker's not obtaining nonfarm work, we include as an exogenous variable the unemployment rate in the nonfarm sector of each state.

The availability of braceros shifts the supply of U.S. farm labor, but the quantity of braceros is not necessarily an exogenous variable. In terms of figure 1, above, where $\bar{Q}$ is shown as a wholly regulated level of immigration, the number of immigrant workers is a policy determined exogenous variable. In the Bracero Program as it actually operated, however, there was no quantitative constraint on the number of immigrant workers. The quantity supplied was free to respond to shifts in demand for bracero labor. Our model for bracero demand makes it simply a component of total labor demand. There is no distinction in theory or in data between a bracero employed on a farm and a domestic farm worker of equivalent skills. The data reflect— indeed, assume—an essential homogeneity of farm labor in that the U.S. Department of Agriculture statistics on farm employment are obtained by asking farmers about the number of workers employed on the farm surveyed. Domestic workers, braceros, and illegals are all, in principle, counted as equivalent and are aggregated uniformly to obtain the estimated U.S. farm labor force.

On the supply side there are several exogenous variables relevant to the use of braceros. Bracero supply depends on opportunities not only in the United States but also in Mexico; also, the costs of migration from Mexico to the relevant U.S. labor market may be important. A full specification of bracero supply should include, in addition to the wage rate prevailing in the United States, distance between the U.S./ Mexican border and the state, P.L. 78 regulations, and the Mexican wage rate. Unfortunately, we have no time series data on market wage rates in Mexico that might be directly relevant to braceros. The best data available are the official minimum daily wage rates applicable to hired farm labor in Mexico. While it is obviously a crude variable, this regulated wage rate may serve as a useful proxy for labor market conditions in Mexico. During the last three decades the real hired farm hourly wage rate for the United States has generally been about four times greater than the real minimum farm daily wage rate for Mexico. This difference is consistent with the immense difference in real wage rates between the two countries suggested by data not available in time series.

The Bracero Program experienced numerous administrative changes, as was discussed earlier. The most important of these changes was the U.S. Department of Labor ruling on adverse wage rates in the 1961

Dona Ana County, New Mexico case.[26] This ruling is generally agreed to have been a major step toward elimination of the program, thus, all states would be expected to receive fewer braceros after 1961 because of the *Dona Ana* ruling.

Our model of bracero labor supply is specified as

$$LB_{jt} = f(WMM_t, WH_{jt}, PL78_t, DA_t, SD_j) \qquad (4)$$

where *LB* is thousands of bracero workers contracted;[27] *WMM* is the minimum hired farm daily wage in Mexico in 1977 pesos converted to dollars;[28] *PL78* is 1 if P.L. 78 was in effect, otherwise zero; *DA* (*Dona Ana*) is 1 if the year is later than 1961, otherwise, zero; *SD* is a state dummy variable for each state except California; *j* is 1, 2, ..., seventh state; and *t* is 1, 2, ..., twenty-sixth year ($1 = 1953$, $26 = 1978$).

The structural equation for U.S. farm labor demand is

$$LH_{jt} = g(WH_{jt}, LS_{jt}, PR^*_{jt}, PP_t, HA_{jt}, AP_{jt}, SD_j) \qquad (5)$$

where *LH* is thousands of hired farm workers;[29] *WH* is the hourly hired farm wage rate in 1977 dollars;[30] *LS* is hired labor's share of farm production expenses;[31] *PR** is product price expectations, measured by the index of prices farmers received, where $1977 = 100$,[32] lagged one year; *PP* is the index of prices paid by farmers for production items (excluding labor, land, interest, and taxes) where $1977 = 100$;[33] *HA* is millions of acres of cropland harvested,[34] with linear interpolation be-

[26] U.S. District Court for the District of Columbia, *Dona Ana County Farm and Livestock Bureau, et al. vs. Goldberg, Secretary of Labor,* Civil Action No. 2538-61, 200 Fed. Supp. 210 (District Court, District of Columbia, December 21, 1961).

[27] U.S., Department of Labor, Bureau of Labor Statistics, *Farm Labor Developments,* various issues.

[28] International Monetary Fund, *International Financial Statistics* (Washington, D.C.: International Monetary Fund, various issues); International Labor Organization, *Yearbook of Labor Statistics* (New York: International Labor Organization, various issues); and U.S. Department of Agriculture, Economics, Statistics, and Cooperatives Service, *Hired Farm Labor,* various issues.

[29] U.S. Department of Agriculture, Economics, Statistics, and Cooperatives Service, *Farm Labor,* various issues.

[30] Ibid.

[31] U.S. Department of Agriculture, Economics, Statistics, and Cooperatives Service, *State Farm Income Statistics,* various issues.

[32] U.S. Department of Agriculture, Economics, Statistics, and Cooperatives Service, *Agricultural Prices,* various issues.

[33] Ibid.

[34] U.S. Department of Commerce, *Census of Agriculture,* 1949-1974.

tween census years; and AP is the index of agricultural productivity, where $1977 = 100$.[35]

The equation for the U.S. farm labor supply is

$$LH_{jt} = h(WH_{ht}, WI_{jt}, U_{jt}, LB_{jt}, SD_j) \tag{6}$$

where WI is the hourly manufacturing wage rate in 1977 dollars;[36] U is the percent of unemployment among the work force covered by unemployment insurance;[37] and LB is the number of braceros, the dependent variable in the first structural equation above.

The USDA farm labor survey does not classify workers by country of origin or immigrant status. Thus, the data on LH include both domestic U.S. workers and braceros (as well as illegals). The coefficient of LB would be 1 if a bracero simply added the equivalent of one U.S. worker to the U.S. farm labor supply. The braceros, however, tended to be short-term workers: the minimum bracero contract was usually six weeks and the maximum was usually six months, although a few one-year contracts were issued and still fewer contracts were written for up to eighteen months. In most cases the bracero returned to Mexico immediately after completing a contract and received only one contract per year. Elac estimates that the average bracero contract lasted about three and one-half months.[38]

Since the number of braceros is a variable, as are LH and WH, ordinary least squares (OLS) estimation of the structural equations is suspect. We experimented with OLS, two-stage least squares (2SLS), and instrumental variable estimation techniques. An instrumental variables rationale leads to the replacement of LB in the equation for U.S. farm labor supply (3), by the exogenous Bracero Program variables $PL78$ and DA, and the Mexican minimum wage rate WMM.

Hired farm labor's share (LS) of the agricultural product is determined exogenously, although in the limiting case in which an aggregate Cobb-Douglas production function is applicable, LS of total product would be constant. It is possible that a Cobb-Douglas production function could be applicable to each commodity separately, yet LS would not be constant because different commodities have different

[35] U.S. Department of Agriculture, Economics, Statistics, and Cooperatives Service, *Changes in Farm Production and Efficiency, 1978,* Statistical Bulletin, no. 628, January 1980.

[36] U.S. Department of Labor, Bureau of Labor Statistics, *Employment and Earnings: States and Areas, 1939-78,* 1979.

[37] U.S. Department of Labor, *Employment and Training Report of the President,* various issues.

[38] J. C. Elac, "The Employment of Mexican Workers in U.S. Agriculture, 1900-1960: A Binational Analysis" (Ph.D. diss., University of California, Los Angeles, 1961; reprinted by R and E Research Associates, San Francisco, 1972).

labor intensities. Then a state's labor share would change with the product mix of the state's agriculture. *LS* of the agricultural product should also depend on the price and availability of substitute inputs.

Our model for labor's share of the agricultural product is specified as

$$LS_{jt} = f(WH_{ht}, PP_t, HA_{jt}, AP_{jt}, SD_j) \qquad (7)$$

where *LS, WH, LB, PP, HA, SD, j,* and *t* are as defined above.

Estimation of the Model. The foregoing discussion specifies the economics of braceros in U.S. labor markets in terms of variables that seem the best available proxies for the relevant economic concepts. We tried a few alternatives, such as use of a quantity index for nonlabor purchased inputs instead of the input price index, *PP*. The only substantive change in the models as outlined above is that the rates of lagged prices received to prices paid (*PRL/PP*) were used instead of the two variables (*PR** and *PP*, separately), which seemed highly co-linear in our data so that using them separately might not yield reliable estimates of independent regression coefficients.

Table 4 shows regression results for reduced-form equations of the four endogenous variables—*LB, LH, WH,* and *LS*—as functions of

TABLE 4

ESTIMATED REGRESSION COEFFICIENTS FOR REDUCED-FORM
EQUATIONS, SEVEN-STATE[a] MODEL, 1953–1978

Independent Variables	Equation 8 Bracero Supply (LB)	Equation 9 Labor Quantity (LH)	Equation 10 Wage Rate (WH)	Equation 11 Labor Share (LS)
Constant	−183.15 (−2.39)**	163.96 (4.43)***	1.01 (2.66)***	0.042 (0.64)
WMM	−1.71 (−0.42)	−0.031 (−0.02)	0.017 (0.83)	−0.004 (−1.02)
PL78	29.86 (3.19)***	17.03 (3.76)***	−0.182 (−3.91)***	0.013 (1.68)*
DA	−18.46 (−2.16)**	−4.66 (−1.13)	−0.076 (−1.78)*	−0.042 (−5.74)***
WI	17.63 (2.31)**	−6.80 (−1.85)*	0.110 (2.89)***	0.029 (4.55)***

(*Table continues*)

387

TABLE 4 (continued)

Independent Variables	Equation 8 Bracero Supply (LB)	Equation 9 Labor Quantity (LH)	Equation 10 Wage Rate (WH)	Equation 11 Labor Share (LS)
U	−0.609	0.618	−0.020	−0.002
	(−0.34)	(0.72)	(−2.26)**	(−1.24)
PRL/PP	−7.46	1.20	0.039	0.094
	(−0.21)	(0.07)	(0.22)	(3.14)***
HA	20.82	6.74	0.008	0.002
	(7.86)	(5.27)***	(0.59)	(1.05)
AP	−0.192	0.303	0.015	−0.001
	(−0.44)	(1.43)	(6.95)***	(−2.17)**
State Dummies				
AR	31.65	−151.95	−0.679	−0.050
	(1.70)*	(−16.94)***	(−7.37)***	(−3.16)***
AZ	110.19	−141.08	−0.602	−0.036
	(4.96)***	(−13.16)***	(−5.47)***	(−1.92)*
CO	10.47	−180.98	−0.467	−0.134
	(0.77)	(−27.56)***	(−6.92)***	(−11.63)***
MI	−30.62	−165.65	−0.291	−0.158
	(−3.20)***	(−35.89)***	(−6.13)***	(−19.51)***
NM	124.17	−164.10	−0.783	−0.052
	(4.96)***	(−13.57)***	(−6.30)***	(−2.47)***
TX	−247.74	−180.32	−0.818	−0.128
	(−7.14)***	(−10.77)***	(−4.31)***	(−4.37)***
R^2	0.66	0.97	0.92	0.87

[a] States are Arkansas, Arizona, California, Colorado, Michigan, New Mexico, and Texas.

 * t is significant at the 10 percent level (t-values are in parentheses).

 ** t is significant at the 5 percent level (t-values are in parentheses).

 *** t is significant at the 1 percent level (t-values are in parentheses).

the exogenous variables WMM (Mexican minimum wage), PL78 (Bracero Program dummy), DA (Dona Ana ruling dummy), WI (nonfarm wage rate in the United States), U (unemployment rate), PRL/PP (output/input farm price ratio), HA (crop acreage), AP (agricultural productivity), and state dummies. Each observation is one of the seven states using braceros in one of the years 1953–1978, yielding pooled cross-section/time series regressions with $7 \times 28 = 196$ observations.

The main variable of interest is *PL78*. Its coefficient of 17 in the labor quantity regression (table 4, equation 9) suggests a point estimate that the Bracero Program increased the farm labor force on average during the years 1953–1964 by 17,000 workers in the seven-state market. Its coefficient in table 4, equation 10, suggests that the Bracero Program reduced the average farm wage rate in the seven states by 18.0 cents per hour. While the effects are significantly different from zero at the 1 percent significance level, the standard errors are too large for confidence about the point estimates. For example, the standard error of the *PL78* coefficient in the wage equation (table 4, equation 10) is 4.6 cents, so that the range of the wage effect covering two standard errors or a 95 percent confidence interval is that P.L. 78 reduced farm wage rates between 9.0 and 27.4 cents per hour.

Normal expectations for the other exogenous variables are that labor demand-increasing variables (*PRL/PP, HA*) should have positive coefficients in equations (9) and (10), and the farm labor supply-reducing variables (*WI*) should have a positive coefficient in equation (10) but a negative coefficient in equation (11), while the farm labor supply-increasing variable (*U*) should have a negative coefficient in equation (10) but a positive coefficient in equation (11). These expectations are all borne out although some of the coefficients are not statistically significant, notably those of *PRL/PP*. The productivity variable (*AP*) is acting as a farm labor demand-increasing variable. This does not mean that technical change has increased the demand for farm labor, but it does suggest that technical change *would have* increased the demand for farm labor if farm product prices and input prices had been held constant.

Table 5 presents two-stage least squares (2SLS) estimates of the structural equations as specified earlier. The bracero supply equation (12) has the signs expected. The *PL78* dummy is naturally associated with more braceros, and the *Dona Ana* dummy (*DA*) indicates the expected reduction in braceros associated with this ruling. The estimated effects of the U.S. and Mexican wage rates indicate that braceros were indeed responsive to economic opportunities and were not wholly policy-determined. The positive coefficient of *WH* indicates positive response to higher U.S. wages, and the negative coefficient of *WMM*, although not statistically significant, is consistent with the idea that the bracero supply responded to Mexican labor market conditions.

In the farm labor supply equation (table 5, equation 13), the coefficient of 0.35 indicates that each 100 braceros resulted in a net increase of 35 in the farm labor supply. The meaning of this effect (Why isn't

TABLE 5

ESTIMATED REGRESSION COEFFICIENTS FOR STRUCTURAL EQUATIONS,
SEVEN-STATE[a] MODEL, 1953–1978

Right-Hand Side Variables	Equation 12 Bracero Supply (LB)	Equation 13 Labor Quantity (LH)	Equation 14 Labor Demand (LH)	Equation 15 Labor Share (LS)
Constant	−82.70 (−1.14)	239.25 (13.68)***	204.65 (7.44)***	0.382 (10.77)***
LB		0.346 (6.96)***		
WH	53.12 (2.14)**	6.66 (0.85)	−75.77 (−7.45)***	−0.019 (−0.70)
LS			165.12 (3.01)	
WMM	−4.47 (−1.05)			
PL78	44.35 (3.19)***			
DA	−27.35 (3.19)***			
WI		−12.38 (−3.20)***		
U		1.50 (1.77)*		
PRL/PP			0.835 (0.08)	
HA			7.34 (7.59)***	0.006 (2.56)***
AP			1.52 (5.53)***	−0.002 (−2.89)***
State Dummies				
AR	6.05 (0.25)	−155.06 (−20.18)***	−187.37 (−15.71)***	−0.122 (−4.68)***
AZ	−14.72 (−0.89)	−168.07 (−26.29)***	−174.77 (−16.23)***	−0.023 (−0.84)
CO	−31.29 (−2.50)***	−175.84 (−29.04)***	−190.56 (−19.63)***	−0.121 (−6.87)***

(*Table continues*)

TABLE 5 continued)

Right-Hand Side Variables	Equation 12 Bracero Supply (LB)	Equation 13 Labor Quantity (LH)	Equation 14 Labor Demand (LH)	Equation 15 Labor Share (LS)
MI	−33.48 (−2.83)***	−154.04 (−22.99)***	−163.54 (−18.80)***	−0.143 (−14.52)***
NM	−2.19 (−0.10)	−193.63 (−26.70)***	−206.19 (−15.15)***	−0.069 (−2.04)**
TX	49.38 (2.23)**	−93.92 (−14.54)***	−222.75 (−12.50)***	−0.214 (−6.00)***

[a] States are Arkansas, Arizona, California, Colorado, Michigan, New Mexico, and Texas.

  * t is significant at the 10 percent level (t-values are in parentheses).

 ** t is significant at the 5 percent level (t-values are in parentheses).

*** t is significant at the 1 percent level (t-values are in parentheses).

the coefficient unity?) is discussed later. The nonfarm wage rate (WI) and the unemployment rate have the expected effects in equation (13). The strength of these variables is consistent with the findings of Tyrchniewicz and Schuh, Morgan, and other econometric work on the U.S. farm labor market.[39] The estimated own-price supply elasticity of farm labor supply, however, is not consistent with previous estimation models. The coefficient of WH in equation (13) is not significantly different from zero. The point estimate of elasticity of supply is 0.2 at the data means.

The farm labor demand equation (14) has the expected signs, although the PRL/PP variable is insignificant. The point estimate of the elasticity of farm labor demand is −2.3 at the sample means, somewhat more elastic than has typically been found by previous investigators, although some recent work has obtained elasticities of this order of magnitude in aggregate U.S. data.[40]

Two-state model. The seven states pooled in the regressions of tables 7 and 8 vary greatly in the size of their farm labor force. The raw data and statistical theory suggest a likelihood of considerably greater measurement error in the farm labor force and farm wage rates

[39] Tyrchniewicz and Schuh, "Econometric Analysis of the Agricultural Labor Market"; and Morgan, "Income Maintenance Programs."

[40] T. M. Hammonds, R. Yadav, and C. Vathana, "The Elasticity of Demand for Hired Farm Labor," *American Journal of Agricultural Economics,* vol. 55 (May 1973), pp. 242-45; and Morgan, "Income Maintenance Programs."

TABLE 6

ESTIMATED REGRESSION COEFFICIENTS FOR REDUCED-FORM
EQUATIONS, TWO-STATE[a] MODEL, 1953–1978

Independent Variables	Equation 16 Bracero Supply (LB)	Equation 17 Labor Quantity (LH)	Equation 18 Wage Rate (WH)	Equation 19 Labor Share (LS)
Constant	−138.73	284.91	0.648	0.161
	(−0.76)	(3.37)	(0.88)	(1.97)*
WMM	−0.843	3.67	0.035	0.0001
	(−0.11)	(1.03)	(1.14)	(0.03)
PL78	81.46	28.31	−0.136	0.007
	(3.97)***	(2.99)***	(−1.65)	(0.74)
DA	−78.00	−1.46	−0.058	−0.0004
	(−4.19)***	(−0.17)	(−0.77)	(−0.06)
WI	61.34	−37.65	0.290	−0.026
	(2.64)***	(−3.50)***	(3.10)***	(−2.45)**
U	−0.391	5.84	−0.074	0.001
	(−0.07)	(2.29)**	(−3.35)***	(0.59)
PRL/PP	−114.57	−47.46	−0.028	0.027
	(−1.49)	(−1.34)	(−0.09)	(0.80)
HA	0.012	7.99	0.006	0.015
	(2.98)***	(4.36)***	(0.37)	(8.65)***
AP	−1.24	0.955	0.010	0.001
	(−1.69)*	(2.82)*	(3.45)***	(1.58)
State Dummy				
TX	−96.58	−206.29	−0.814	−0.329
	(−1.72)*	(−7.96)***	(−3.61)***	(−13.08)***
R^2	0.87	0.95	0.96	0.97

[a] States are California and Texas.
* t is significant at the 10 percent level (t-values are in parentheses).
** t is significant at the 5 percent level (t-values are in parentheses).
*** t is significant at the 1 percent level (t-values are in parentheses).

in the smaller states, particularly New Mexico and Arizona. Yet these observations count equally with those for the larger states in the pooled regressions.

To obtain results not sensitive to the small states, we fit a two-state pooled regression on California and Texas only, by far the most important bracero states (table 6). This reduces the number of observations from 196 to 56, but should provide data more free of errors in variables.

TABLE 7

ESTIMATED REGRESSION COEFFICIENTS FOR STRUCTURAL EQUATIONS,
TWO-STATE[a] MODEL, 1953–1978

Right-Hand Side Variables	Equation 20 Bracero Supply (LB)	Equation 21 Labor Supply (LH)	Equation 22 Labor Demand (LH)	Equation 23 Labor Share (LS)
Constant	−36.81 (−0.27)	291.65 (4.38)***	209.26 (3.09)***	0.186 (6.82)***
LB		0.255 (2.65)***		
WH	48.38 (1.02)	89.39 (2.44)**	−72.31 (−3.01)***	−0.054 (−4.44)
LS			929.68 (2.29)**	
WMM	−11.27 (−1.43)			
PL78	79.08 (2.92)***			
DA	−67.05 (−3.82)***			
WI		−73.78 (−3.75)***		
U		15.73 (3.63)***		
PRL/PP			−54.07 (−1.71)*	
HA			−6.45 (−0.96)	0.017 (11.61)***
AP			1.35 (2.88)***	0.001 (2.17)***
State Dummy				
TX	45.55 (1.15)	−39.40 (−1.57)	44.72 (0.30)	−0.371 (−22.12)***

[a] States are California and Texas.

* t is significant at the 10 percent level (t-values are in parentheses).
** t is significant at the 5 percent level (t-values are in parentheses).
*** t is significant at the 1 percent level (t-values are in parentheses).

In the reduced-form equations reported in table 6 we find that R^2 is in fact increased in three of the four equations. The number of significant coefficients (apart from state dummies), however, is not increased. The estimated coefficients are basically similar, although the nonfarm wage is much stronger in the two-state model.

The two-state structural equations, reported in table 7, are basically similar to the seven-state results. The most important difference is that the farm labor supply equation (21) yields better results and the farm labor demand equation (22) worse results in the two-state model. The farm labor supply equation now has a significantly positive own-price elasticity of 1.2. The estimated elasticity of farm labor demand in the two-state model (-0.8) is less than in the seven-state model and the *PRL/PP* and *HA* coefficients now have the wrong signs, with the former statistically significant.

Three-region model. As has been discussed earlier, the farm labor markets of the states analyzed are not wholly independent, as they ought to be for the pooled seven-state model to be fully appropriate. We chose the seven-state approach as the most promising of the set of imperfect options available. To obtain some indication of possible problems created by treating mutually dependent state wage rates as independent, we estimated a regional model which aggregates bracero-using states known to be linked by migrant labor flows. One such region is Texas–Arkansas–Michigan. While these states are geographically distant, there is evidence that events in farm labor markets in Texas influence the seasonal movement of labor north to Arkansas and Michigan. We constructed a second region composed of Arizona, Colorado, and New Mexico, and left California as a third region.

The reduced-form and structural equations for the three-region model are shown in tables 8 and 9. The reduced-form results are basically the same as the state-level regressions. The *PL78* effect of 17,000 workers per state in equation (9) is roughly equivalent to the 43.6 thousand workers for each of the three regions in equation (25). The former coefficient implies a total U.S. effect of $17 \times 7 = 119$ thousand workers, while the latter implies a total U.S. effect of $43.6 \times 3 = 132$ thousand additional farm workers resulting from P.L. 78 while it was in effect. The estimated wage effect of *PL78* in equation (26), however, is somewhat smaller than in equation (10) or equation (18).

The structural equations for the three-region model yield perhaps the most reasonable results of any of the models. All of the variables for which there are a priori expected signs do, in fact, have the expected signs. The own-price elasticities of farm labor supply and farm labor

TABLE 8

ESTIMATED REGRESSION COEFFICIENTS FOR REDUCED-FORM EQUATIONS, THREE-REGION[a] MODEL, 1953–1978

Independent Variables	Equation 24 Bracero Supply (LB)	Equation 25 Labor Quantity (LH)	Equation 26 Wage Rate (WH)	Equation 27 Labor Share (LS)
Constant	111.94 (0.61)	692.93 (2.95)***	0.673 (1.40)	0.334 (2.32)**
WMM	−2.11 (−0.28)	0.340 (0.04)	−0.003 (−0.15)	−0.002 (−0.33)
PL78	47.00 (2.64)***	43.62 (1.91)*	−0.107 (−2.29)**	0.010 (0.74)
DA	−28.51 (−1.69)*	58.10 (2.69)***	−0.019 (−0.43)	−0.024 (−1.84)*
WI	−1.29 (−0.06)	−116.03 (−4.21)***	0.168 (2.99)***	−0.031 (−1.84)*
U	8.47 (2.09)**	9.99 (1.93)*	−0.012 (−1.16)	−0.001 (−0.17)
PRL/PP	−127.14 (−1.76)*	153.81 (−1.67)*	0.201 (1.06)	0.039 (0.70)
HA	19.08 (5.09)***	27.59 (5.76)***	0.030 (3.11)***	0.004 (1.30)
AP	−1.21 (−1.50)	0.197 (0.19)	0.010 (4.85)***	0.0001 (0.20)
Region Dummies				
AZ-CO-NM	5.00 (0.28)	−119.88 (−5.19)***	−1.67 (−35.39)***	−0.132 (−9.32)
TX-AR-MI	−460.96 (4.78)***	−506.95 (4.11)***	−2.49 (−9.88)***	−0.224 (−2.96)
R^2	0.32	0.94	0.99	0.89

[a] Regions are California, Arizona–Colorado–New Mexico, and Texas-Arkansas-Michigan.

　* t is significant at the 10 percent level (t-values are in parentheses).

　** t is significant at the 5 percent level (t-values are in parentheses).

　*** t is significant at the 1 percent level (t-values are in parentheses).

TABLE 9

ESTIMATED REGRESSION COEFFICIENTS FOR STRUCTURAL EQUATIONS,
THREE-REGION[a] MODEL, 1953–1978

Right-Hand Side Variables	Equation 28 Bracero Supply (LB)	Equation 29 Labor Quantity (LH)	Equation 30 Labor Demand (LH)	Equation 31 Labor Share (LS)
Constant	−207.81 (−1.17)	240.91 (1.78)*	1281.87 (1.81)	0.59 (5.26)***
LB		0.767 (4.02)***		
WH	105.44 (1.69)	167.70 (2.83)***	−690.34 (−2.21)**	−0.209 (−2.73)***
LS			−1061.25 (−0.86)	
WMM	−9.09 (−1.14)			
PL78	81.00 (3.31)***			
DA	−60.59 (−3.44)***			
WI		−99.20 (−3.65)***		
U		4.63 (0.79)		
PRL/PP			72.32 (0.31)	
HA			53.58 (3.02)***	0.013 (3.41)***
AP			7.42 (1.90)*	0.001 (0.96)
Region Dummies				
AZ-CO-NM	140.85 (1.35)	167.85 (1.82)*	−1396.82 (−2.10)**	−0.465 (−3.36)***
TX-AR-MI	206.39 (1.86)**	479.92 (4.82)***	−2478.14 (−2.31)	−0.818 (−4.53)***

[a] Regions are California, Arizona–Colorado–New Mexico, and Texas-Arkansas-Michigan.

* *t* is significant at the 10 percent level (*t*-values are in parentheses).

** *t* is significant at the 5 percent level (*t*-values are in parentheses).

*** *t* is significant at the 1 percent level (*t*-values are in parentheses).

demand, 2.3 and —9.5 respectively, are larger than in the state-level models, contrary to expectations. The estimated effect of braceros on U.S. farm labor quantity implies that 100 additional braceros adds 77 to the U.S. farm labor force, a larger effect than that found in the state-level models.

The labor-share equations—(15), (23), and (31)—have not been discussed because we did not have a priori expectations on the signs and because the bearing of labor's share in total production costs on braceros is only indirect. It may be worth pointing out that the estimated effect of productivity change is ambiguous—significantly positive in equation (23) and significantly negative in equation (15). This suggests a specification problem in the *LS* equations. It should be noted also that the coefficient of *WH* is an estimate of $(1-\sigma)$, where σ is the elasticity of substitution between labor and nonlabor inputs in farm production under the maintained hypothesis of a constant elasticity of substitution production function.[41] Under this hypothesis, the negative coefficient of *WH* in equations (15), (23), and (31) implies that $\sigma > 1$.

Consequences of the Bracero Program

Interpretation of the econometric evidence may be aided by referring back to figure 2. The lower right-hand panel of the diagram shows the effects to be expected in the U.S. farm labor market. The principal empirical questions are:

1. How far did the program shift the supply of U.S. farm labor to the right?
2. What is the elasticity of the U.S. farm labor supply (which determines the extent to which domestic workers are displaced by braceros)?
3. What is the elasticity of the demand for U.S. farm labor (which determines the extent to which an expanding labor market will accommodate immigrant workers)?

The effect of the bracero program on the U.S. farm wage rate depends on the answers to all three questions, as indicated by equation (1) in the theory section. The reduced-form equations provide a direct estimate of this effect, while the structural equations provide the data needed for an indirect estimate via questions 1–3.

The results of fitting the regression in tables 4–9, and other specifications not reported there, do not yield estimates of program effects

[41] K. Arrow et al., "Capital-Labor Substitution and Economic Efficiency," *Review of Economics and Statistics,* vol. 30 (August 1962), pp. 291-99.

that are as precise as might be hoped, but the principal estimated effects are quite robust in that the same direction and order of magnitude of effects result from a range of model specifications.

The *LB* coefficients in the structural labor quantity equations— (13), (21), and (29)—suggest that each bracero leads to an increase of 0.25 to 0.80 of a worker in the farm labor force *given the farm wage rate*. Thus, the horizontal shift in the farm labor supply curve from a program of 300,000 braceros (about the mean number in 1953– 1964) is 75,000 to 240,000 workers. The coefficient is less than unity because, as was mentioned earlier, braceros worked in the United States an average of only about three and one-half months. This coefficient should not, however, measure the displacement of domestic farm workers (because the wage rate is held constant).

The net displacement of workers and the jointly determined decline in the farm wage rate depend on the elasticities of supply of and demand for farm labor in the United States. During the period 1953–1964, the estimated own-price elasticity of farm labor supply in the bracero states ranges from 0.2 to 1.0, depending on the model, and the elasticity of demand ranges from -0.8 to -3.2. The three-region model yields estimates of supply and demand elasticities of 0.8 and -3.2, respectively, which is roughly consistent with recent empirical works at the national level. These values simplify the following wage rate effects. A shift of 300,000 (the mean number of braceros in 1953–1964) in the U.S. supply of braceros (wages constant) amounts to about 50 percent of the mean hired farm labor force, but a coefficient of 0.7 on *LB* in the *LH* equation—equation (28)—implies an effective increase of $50 \times 0.7 = 35$ percent in labor available. The structural estimate of the wage rate effect is 35 divided by $\eta - e$, which is $35/(-3.2 - 0.8) \cong -8.8$ percent. Thus, the farm wage rate, whose mean value was about $1.440 per hour (three-region mean in 1977 dollars) during 1953–1964, would have been about $0.14 per hour higher in the absence of P.L. 78, according to this estimate. A more direct effect of the estimated wage effect is available from the reduced-form wage rate equation. For the three-region model the *PL78* coefficient implies that the program reduced wages by $0.11 per hour.

The reduction of domestic farm workers from a 10.0 percent wage decline is 8.0 percent with an elasticity of supply of 0.8. This amounts to about 51,000 workers for the entire seven-state area directly affected by the program. A labor demand elasticity of -3.2 implies that an 8.8 percent decline in wages associated with braceros expanded the total demand for farm workers by 26.0 percent (that is, that about 120,000 jobs in the seven-state area were created and were eliminated when P.L. 78 ended). This relatively high demand elasticity and job creation effect is consistent with the informal observation that braceros were a substitute for mechanization, notably in High Plains cotton, and that the end of the program substantially accelerated the mechanization of Texas cotton.[42] This is also the period in which the tomato harvester came into widespread use in California.[43]

The preceding inferences about labor use effects can be checked against the more direct estimate available from the reduced-form equation (22) explaining U.S. farm labor quantity (table 10). The coefficients of *PL78* indicate that the Bracero Program added an average of about 122,000 farm workers to the United States compared with about 120,000 inferred in the preceding paragraph. The coefficients of *PL78* in the two-state *LH* equation (17) yields a smaller but still significantly positive effect. This is confirming evidence that the demand for farm labor is sufficiently elastic for the labor market to create new jobs to accommodate immigrant labor supplies without facing the necessity of drastically lower farm wages.

Our best estimates of the effects of the Bracero Program on farm wage rates and employment are presented in table 10. The reduced-form equation estimates of the effects of P.L. 78 are made by evaluating the differences between the mean wages and quantities of each model and the implied wage and employment levels in the absence of P.L. 78. The structural equation estimates of program effects are made by evaluating the differences between the mean wages and quantities of each model and the implied wage and employment levels, via elasticity estimates, of a 100 percent decrease in the bracero supply.

One of the problems in assessing the influence of braceros on the labor market stems from the role of illegal alien farm workers. During P.L. 78's existence the illegal worker problem was not a major political issue after Operation Wetback in 1954. The low levels of illegals apprehended by INS during 1955–1964 (see table 2) may reflect the success of P.L. 78 in slowing down this supply. After 1964, however, the apprehension of illegals began to rise rapidly. During the first years following the termination of the Bracero Program, border states responded by making greater use of "green card" workers and illegals.[44]

Although the numbers of illegal Mexican immigrants began to increase after the termination of P.L. 78, there are no conclusive data available for measuring how much of this impact was due to events in agriculture. During 1953–1964 the number of apprehended illegals

[42] See, for example, McBride, *Vanishing Bracero.*

[43] A. Schmitz and D. Seckler, "Mechanized Agriculture and Social Welfare: The Case of the Tomato Harvester," *American Journal of Agricultural Economics,* vol. 52 (November 1970), p. 520.

[44] Martin, "Alien Workers," p. 1143.

TABLE 10

ESTIMATED IMPACTS OF P.L. 78 ON HIRED FARM LABOR WAGE
AND QUANTITY[a] AT THE MEANS OF EACH MODEL, 1953–1964

Item	Seven-State Model[b]	Two-State Model[c]	Three-Region Model[d]
Reduced-Form Equation Estimates of Program Effects			
Wage change (WH)	−$0.18	−$0.14	−$0.11
% wage change	−8.5%	−6.2%	−6.9%
Quantity change (LH) (thousands)	+17.0	+28.3	+41.8
% quantity change	+25.8%	+17.3%	+68.2%
Structural Equation Estimates of Program Effects			
Wage change (WH)	−$0.23	−$0.54	−$0.13
% wage change	−10.3%	−20.6%	−8.0%
Quantity change (LH) (thousands)	+12.9	+26.5	+63.0
% quantity change	+18.4%	+16.0%	+25.3%
Mean LB (thousands)	44.2	120.7	103.1
Mean WH	$1.96	$2.07	$1.44
Mean LH (thousands)	83.0	192.3	312.5

[a] Quantity effects are estimated on the basis of each model's observational unit.
[b] States are Arkansas, Arizona, California, Colorado, Michigan, New Mexico, and Texas.
[c] States are California and Texas.
[d] Regions are California, Arizona–Colorado–New Mexico, and Texas-Arkansas-Michigan.

had a downward trend. During that period, also, the seven-state bracero total was slightly negatively correlated with the number of apprehended illegals ($r = -0.23$). Northwestern and midwestern states lost part of their domestic interstate migrant farm labor supply at the termination of P.L. 78 as the migrant supply states, mainly California and Texas, began to use more migrant labor to replace braceros.[45]

By the time P.L. 78 had ended, cotton harvesting was almost completely mechanized, thus irreversibly eliminating a large component of

[45] E. W. Hawley, "The Politics of the Mexican Labor Issue, 1950-1965," *Agricultural History*, vol. 40 (April 1966), pp. 157-76.

the earlier demand for bracero or illegal labor. Although vegetable, fruit, and citrus harvesting methods have been relatively slow to mechanize, the development of tomato, carrot, and lettuce harvesting machinery has countered some earlier expectations that vegetable crops would always be hand harvested.

The effects of the Bracero Program on the well-being of U.S. farm workers are not adequately measured by either the wage-rate effect or worker-displacement effect alone. It will generally be the case that when workers are unresponsive to economic incentives (elasticity of supply is low) there will be little displacement but substantial wage declines when immigrant workers arrive. If domestic workers are responsive (elasticity of supply is high) the wage effect will be smaller but the displacement will be larger. The best overall indicator of domestic farm worker losses that are due to immigrant workers is area a in figure 2. The preceding estimates that seem most reasonable—a wage effect of about 8 to 9 percent, an elasticity of labor demand of -3.2, and an elasticity of labor supply of 0.8—imply that area a plus losses to nonbracero immigrants—area d—is about 6 to 7 percent of total wages paid to farm workers in the bracero states, which amounts to about $139 million per year (1977 dollars) in the bracero period.

The estimated losses did not all accrue to native U.S. workers: the Bracero Program evidently had a substantial effect in reducing employment for illegals, who are included in the labor quantity estimates. Table 2 shows this effect in lower numbers of illegals in farm work apprehended during the bracero period.

What were the gains from the Bracero Program? Employers obtained more workers at lower wages. The preceding estimates are that they hired some 120,000 additional workers (for the United States as a whole) at $.15 to $.20 less per hour. With a mean bracero state labor force of about 580,000 during the P.L. 78 period, the wage bill is reduced by $185 million per year.

The gains to labor users exceed the losses to domestic farm workers because (1) some of the losing workers are illegals, and (2) there are net gains in efficiency from reallocating labor from lower-value (Mexican) to higher-value (U.S.) activities at the margin. In terms of figure 2, the losses of a to domestic workers and d to nonbracero immigrants sum up to the $139 million per year calculated above. The darkened triangles measure item 2, above. With the elasticities and wage effects as estimated, the area of the left triangle is about $12.5 million and that of the right triangle is about $33.5 million, so that the total area $a + d +$ triangles equals $185 million.

This $185 million per year in reduced wage costs will not accrue entirely to employers. Prospective profits will tend to be dissipated by product price declines as output expands. Hence, the transfer resulting from immigrant farm workers is in part from domestic farm workers to domestic food consumers. The upper right-hand diagram in figure 2 shows the division of the gains from lower wages between food consumers and owners of nonlabor inputs into farming. These gains are *not* in addition to the gains of $185 million measured in the lower right-hand panel but are rather a depiction of their division between the two gaining groups.

Our labor market model does not provide econometric evidence of the effects of the Bracero Program on consumer prices or farmers' returns; thus, we cannot provide estimates of the distribution of Bracero Program gains. We did estimate an OLS regression of the prices received by farmers in the bracero-using states, as follows (*t* ratios are in parentheses):

$$PR = 23.2 - 3.5 \, PL78 + 0.6 \, DA + 1.06 \, PP + 0.21 \, HA \quad (32)$$
$$(-1.5) \qquad (0.2) \qquad (19.2) \qquad (0.4)$$

$$-0.15 \, AP \qquad R^2 = .953$$
$$(1.3)$$

where PR is the U.S. Department of Agriculture index of farm prices received, 1977 = 100 (mean value 66.9), and the other variables are as defined earlier. The prices-paid index (PP) dominates the regression (this relationship is the reason for using PRL/PP in the labor models), but $PL78$ and AP (productivity index) are marginally significant with the correct signs. The $PL78$ coefficient implies a point estimate that farm prices in the bracero states were about 5 percent lower because of the Bracero Program. While this is a very uncertain estimate, it does suggest that consumers did in fact share in the gains from the Bracero Program.

It is not completely consistent with economic theory to treat these consumer gains as diagrammatically as has been done in figure 2. Figure 2 was derived on the basis of a proportional correspondence between quantity of farm labor and quantity of farm output; that is, it assumes that labor and nonlabor inputs are used in fixed proportions in production. We have strong reasons to believe, however, that labor and nonlabor inputs are in fact substitutable in production. Indeed, as was discussed earlier, the labor-share equation suggests an elasticity of substitution between labor and nonlabor inputs of more than 1, the point estimate being 1.2.

The simplest way of analyzing factor price/product price relationships in this context is by means of a mathematical model along the lines of Floyd.[46] Without going into the derivation, we can describe the effect of a bracero-induced change in the wage rate, *WH*, on product price, *PR*, in such a model as

$$\frac{\% \Delta PR}{\% \Delta WH} = \frac{LS\,(\sigma + e')}{e' + LS \cdot \sigma - (1 - LS)\,\eta}$$

where σ is the elasticity of substitution in production; η is the elasticity of demand for farm products; e' is the elasticity of supply of nonfarm labor input; and LS is hired labor's relative share in production costs. The LS equations above suggest that σ is about 1.2 and LS in the P.L. 78 period was 0.15. There exist estimates of η at the U.S. aggregate level of about -0.25, but the elasticity of demand for the output of the bracero states should be greater. Unfortunately, we do not have quad estimates of it, nor of e'. As an illustrative calculation, if $\eta = -0.5$ and $e' = 1.0$, inserting the values in equation (32) yields

$$\frac{\% \Delta PR}{\% \Delta WH} = \frac{.15(1.2 + 1)}{1 + .15(1.2) - .85(-.5)} = 0.21$$

that is, a 9 percent decline in the farm wage rate reduces prices for bracero-state products by about 2 percent. Generally, we know that reduced farm wage rates will result in some addition to output and that additional output will clear the commodity markets at lower prices. Therefore, consumers must capture some of the $185 million gain. But any quantification of the consumer gain is very much a matter of conjecture in view of our lack of information on key parameters.

The net welfare gain to U.S. residents of $46 million per year seems quite small, although the differing gains and losses to employers and domestic workers appear large enough for each group to be concerned about. An overall calculation of the welfare effects of the Bracero Program, however, should also take into account the gains of Mexican workers. These are depicted diagrammatically in the lower left-hand panel of figure 2 as area $e - d$. Our empirical model does not permit a quantitative assessment of the net gain. The main missing data are the opportunity wage rates of Mexican farm workers. If for the sake of an illustrative calculation we suppose that braceros had a mean opportunity wage in Mexico of half the U.S. farm wage rates, the 300,000 average number of braceros at three and one-half months each of forty-hour weeks gained $300,000 \times 3\frac{1}{2} \times 4.33 \times 40 \times \$1 = \$182$ million per year, or about $600 per bracero. The amount of this $182 million per year that represents a net gain to Mexico would depend on the extent to

[46] J. E. Floyd, "The Effects of Farm Price Supports," *Journal of Political Economy*, vol. 73 (April 1965), pp. 148-58.

which braceros replaced other Mexican immigrant workers in the U.S. farm labor market. It seems unlikely that more than a third of the $139 million loss to U.S. farm workers would have been borne by non-bracero Mexicans. This would amount to about $46 million, which suggests a minimum net gain to Mexico of $182 - 46 = \$136$ million.

The total welfare gain from the program in both countries implied by the preceding calculations is $136 + 46 = \$182$ million per year. It is a conservative but plausible estimate of the sum of the two darkened triangles plus area e in figure 2 (it can be represented also as $e + g$ in figure 2 or as the hatched triangle in figure 1). The $182 million is net gain in the sense that it measures economic gains of permitting the immigration of workers that are not affected by losses to domestic U.S. farm workers.

Lessons from the Bracero Program

A guest-worker program is worth considering today as a means of regularizing the status of Mexican citizens who wish to work in the United States—some of whom will do so illegally in any case. Since the Bracero Program was in fact a guest-worker program, the following question arises: What lessons must be learned about the likely consequences of a new program of this type? We will consider three broad issues: (1) the political forces that will be brought to bear on the program; (2) the probable economic consequences of the program; and (3) the social welfare issues involved. These areas are obviously interrelated: the most important political forces are those of economic interest groups. It is useful, nevertheless, to consider these topics separately.

Political Forces. The Bracero Program had its beginnings during the darkest days of U.S. involvement in World War II. Organized labor offered little opposition to the program because it was nonindustrial; a relatively small number of foreign workers was involved; and additional labor would strengthen national security by ensuring an adequate supply of agricultural products. A diminished sense of crisis that had fostered the program through the Korean War and a growing concern for civil rights and adverse wage effects on U.S. farm workers finally combined to end P.L. 78. Producers supported the Bracero Program because it enabled them to obtain workers at lower cost. Braceros, although largely unskilled and untrained for operating tractors and other farm machinery, were consistently acknowledged by their employers to be hard-working and industrious. Although the Bracero Program guaranteed nonwage benefits exceeding those that domestic farm workers received, it does not appear that those guarantees were even partially fulfilled. Mexico consistently pressed for improved housing conditions for braceros, but because most braceros entered the United States without family members, farmers were able to provide dormitory style housing that was modest by most standards.

Adequate health services for braceros were continually demanded by Mexico. The United States generally dealt with this issue by screening all braceros before they entered the country. All unhealthy workers were refused entry to the United States, which greatly reduced health costs for braceros who received contracts.

Increased regulatory action by the U.S. Department of Labor obviously reduced producer benefits after 1956. There is evidence that producers viewed the program only as a short-run benefit and that they began to make resource adjustments after 1956. Additional mechanized harvesting technologies were adopted, and, although INS statistics show low apprehensions of Mexican illegal aliens during 1960–1964, the border states probably employed more illegals. Producer costs for participating in the program consisted of a fee of $7 per bracero collected by the DOL bracero revolving fund. In 1956 producers paid about $4.2 million into the fund. During the final year of P.L. 78 the value of the program to producers fell, but producer costs of program participation rose because of a higher revolving fund fee of $12 per bracero. Although the bracero revolving fund was designed to pay all U.S. administrative costs of the program, the scope of DOL program operations suggests that program costs exceeded revolving fund contributions.

Craig and Hawley argue that the Bracero Program was terminated because agricultural interest groups benefiting from the program suffered a loss of political power.[47] In retrospect this argument would appear to be simplistic as an explanation of producer response to the program. While the major bracero-intensive commodities (vegetables, fruit, citrus, and cotton) are produced in narrow geographic areas that are relatively less interdependent with nonbracero commodities, there is ample evidence of successful lobbying efforts on the part of producers of such isolated, nonbracero commodities as tobacco and sugar cane. A more plausible explanation for the decision of farm interest groups to abandon P.L. 78, we believe, can be found in the relatively small size of producer benefits from the program, as was discussed in the preceding section.

A new guest-worker program would revive the political arguments surrounding the Bracero Program and would provide some new ones. First, nonfarm labor representatives may take a greater interest in such a program—even one limited to agricultural workers. As was men-

[47] Craig, *Bracero Program*; and Hawley, "Mexican Labor Issue."

tioned earlier, there appears to be an increasing tendency for illegal aliens with rural backgrounds to go to cities and search for nonfarm employment. This development parallels the increasing farm-to-nonfarm mobility of U.S. farm workers. This points to the fact that a new Bracero Program would be more likely to have an impact on urban labor markets than did P.L. 78.

A second new issue is likely to take the form of intensified scrutiny of social services provided to guest-workers, particularly from the point of view of the United States as being overcrowded, threatened environmentally, and pressed by scarcity. This point of view may not be dominant today, but it can be expected to play an important political role that scarcely existed during the P.L. 78 period. The social service issues are discussed after the next section.

Economic Consequences. The data evidence for the P.L. 78 period and its aftermath tells a story which, in its broad outlines, is coherent and consistent with economic theory, but we do not have precise point estimates of the relevant behavioral parameters. Beyond the statistical source of error in our best estimates, it is questionable to what extent a Bracero Program today would have the effects that P.L. 78 had. The central issue is the extent to which the structure of the U.S. farm labor market has changed.

The principal relevant structural elements are the elasticity of demand for U.S. farm labor and the elasticity of supply of domestic labor to farm employment. Both of these elasticities appear to have been relatively high—in the neighborhood of 1 for supply and greater than 1 (in absolute value) for demand—for the bracero states under P.L. 78. The importance of a high demand elasticity is that it permits guest workers to be absorbed with a relatively small decline in wage rates, as compared with a less elastic demand function. The importance of a high labor supply elasticity is that it indicates an ability on the part of U.S. farm workers displaced by guest workers to move readily to nonfarm employment.

It may be questioned whether the demand for farm labor will be as elastic in the 1980s as it was during the 1953–1978 period. The types of substitutions of capital for labor that have occurred since that period do not seem readily reversible. The question is whether there are further prospective shifts from use of labor to capital that could be postponed or made uneconomic by the availability of guest workers. Some surveys of actual and potential harvest mechanization suggest that there are.[48]

[48] M. Zahara and S. S. Johnson, "Status of Harvest Mechanizations of Fruits, Nuts, and Vegetables," *Horticultural Science,* vol. 14 (October 1979), pp. 578-82.

Another element of labor demand elasticity is derived from the elasticity of demand for the farm products that guest workers would produce. The major structural change in this area is probably that, instead of being used in cotton production, guest farm workers in the 1980s would be used almost exclusively in the production of border state fruits and vegetables. These are the very products for which there is the greatest likelihood that imports will replace domestic production; therefore, the elasticity of product demand in relation to guest workers is likely to be higher in the 1980s than it was during P.L. 78. Indeed, it is possible that a failure to institute a guest-worker program, if coupled with increased measures against illegals, could lead to a substantial move of production to Mexico.

On the labor supply side there is reason to believe that the elasticity of supply of workers to agriculture has increased since the P.L. 78 period. The farm labor force has experienced a marked trend toward more part-time workers and more highly schooled and skilled workers. The fraction of farm workers who are full-time farm residents or migrants has steadily declined.[49] These changes have been accompanied by the increasing wage rates of farm workers in relation to non-farm workers—even before and outside the region of unionization of farm workers. Indeed, the most dramatic wage gains have been in the southeast and the south central states.[50] These changes suggest an environment in which farm workers are better integrated with the non-farm labor market. As farm workers are now more sensitive to off-farm employment opportunities, there is a more elastic supply function of farm labor than was the case in the P.L. 78 years.

In summary, while today's farm labor market is smaller than that of the 1950s and 1960s, so that a given number of guest workers would have larger wage effects, the elasticities of demand and of supply are likely to be larger, which would ease the burden of adjustment to be borne by domestic workers. Indeed, the increase in elasticity of demand resulting from the greater potential for importing bracero-produced products could imply that, with free trade in products but restrictions on the use of foreign workers, the market for domestic workers in these products could be sharply reduced in any case.

The effect of more elastic labor demand and supply curves on the gains, losses, and welfare costs as calculated above are as follows. First, the importation of a given percentage of the farm labor force will have

[49] G. Rowe, "The Hired Farm Labor Force of 1977," U.S., Department of Agriculture/Economics, Statistics, and Cooperatives Service Report, no. 437, 1979.

[50] See B. L. Gardner, "Seasonal Farm Labor and U.S. Farm Policy" (Paper presented at the U.S. Department of Labor/University of Florida Conference on Seasonal Agricultural Labor Markets, Arlington, Va., January 1980).

smaller wage effects the more elastic the supply and demand for labor are. Therefore, the losses to U.S. farm workers measured by area *a* in figure 2, the gains to employers and consumers, and the net gain to U.S. welfare will *all* be smaller than they were under P.L. 78. Second, however, if the United States simply opens the border, higher elasticities imply that the influx of guest workers will be larger as a percentage of the U.S. farm labor force than they were under P.L. 78. This will tend to make the losses and gains greater than under P.L. 78 and will tend to increase the potential gains to Mexican workers from the opportunity to work in the United States.

Both advocates and opponents of more liberal immigration of workers sometimes put the issue in terms of "labor shortages." Employers argue for (and DOL will acquiesce in) the temporary importation of workers if a case can be made that domestic workers are not available for the job. In economic terms, the ideas of availability of workers and shortages of workers have no meaning apart from particular wage rate levels.

Social Welfare Issues. Broader social welfare issues are less easily analyzed than is the Bracero Program. Society has pluralistic views on social welfare. At the most fundamental level, Mexico's position throughout the operation of P.L. 45 and P.L. 78 included strong demands for social and economic fringe benefits comparable to those received by U.S. farm workers. There is no evidence that Mexico would be less insistent on such benefits in any future program.

The much broader range of income maintenance benefits available to U.S. citizens and permanent resident aliens will also be an important factor in any new guest-worker program. These programs are generally funded by the U.S. Treasury, and thus they raise a question about the equity of the nonagricultural public paying the majority of benefits received by guest workers. It is not beyond possibility that agricultural interests might be able to persuade nonproducers to pay for these benefits if a crisis such as World War II were to occur.

Under P.L. 45 and P.L. 78 some social services, mainly medical services and housing, were guaranteed to braceros, but there is little evidence that they were delivered. If future guest-worker programs are structured to admit mostly single, male, young adults, many social service issues will be simplified; however, any attempt to allow workers' families to accompany them will greatly increase the need for medical and educational services.[51] Producers will argue that providing medical

[51] Barry R. Chiswick, "The Impact of Immigration on the Level and Distribution of Economic Well-Being," in this volume.

services for guest workers involves public goods issues that justify public (that is, U.S.) funding. School districts will balk at providing educational services for alien children, and case law offers little hope that state or federal governments can force them to provide such services.

If the total costs of these social services programs were charged to the employers of braceros, the wage differentials that we have estimated suggest quite low producer willingness to pay. Thus, it is apparent that any new agricultural guest-worker program that provides substantially broader social services and fringe benefits than were delivered under the Bracero Program would require public funding similar to U.S. domestic worker programs. Payments by employers would amount to a tax on imported workers (that is, a guest-worker tariff that could be levied to compensate the United States for social benefits). For guest workers to enter the country under a tariff system, the U.S. wage rate would have to equal or exceed the guest-worker opportunity wage outside the United States plus the tariff. The large gap between U.S. and Mexican real wages suggests that a tariff system would still permit substantial numbers of Mexican workers to enter the United States.

A new guest-worker program would have important implications for the social welfare of illegal immigrants. Such a program would aid in reducing illegal immigration to the extent that illegals are employed in agriculture. Indeed, a major labor displacement effect of the Bracero Program was probably a reduction in demand for illegal alien farm workers. It could well be that many of the individuals now employed as illegals would become braceros (although a tariff on workers would encourage a continuation of illegals, and the higher the tariff the greater would be the incentive). It would seem that a regularization of the status of Mexican workers would be a significant improvement psychologically and socially for the immigrant workers and for the communities in which they live.

The most important social welfare issue that would arise with a new guest-worker program would be the psychic costs that inevitably would be imposed upon those domestic farm workers who were displaced occupationally or geographically by the guest workers. While these costs would, in our judgment, be more than offset by gains to food consumers and employers—not to mention the Mexican immigrants—the losses to this relatively disadvantaged class of U.S. workers must be taken seriously.

It should be noted that the losses measured by area a in figure 2 are not losses to displaced farm workers but to those who retain agricultural employment. Compensation for displaced workers is ostensibly provided through DOL training programs and various income maintenance programs. The dual market argument that immigrant workers perpetuate a market for "bad" jobs[52] does not rule out the possibility of displaced domestic workers moving "up" to "better" or "good" jobs. The rural-to-urban migration experience in the United States has generally consisted of poor rural people leaving "bad" jobs in isolated, monopsonistic rural labor markets to take "better" or "good" jobs in more competitive urban labor markets; however, the U.S. workers who remain in agriculture would receive lower incomes as a result of competition from guest workers, and would typically not be fully compensated under U.S. income maintenance programs. In this respect, the worst situation for U.S. farm workers under a guest-worker program would occur with a very inelastic domestic labor supply function. There would be little displacement, but there would be substantial uncompensated decline in U.S. farm wage rates. However, as has been discussed above, the elasticity of U.S. farm worker supply was fairly high during the P.L. 78 period and is probably even higher today.

The issue of social service use by immigrant workers is further complicated by the present hodgepodge of conflicting policies at various governmental levels. School districts in counties near the Mexican border often encourage the enrollment of illegal alien children or conveniently decline to screen against them because their bureaucratic objectives stress increased organizational size, which increases their ability to secure additional nonlocal funding. States, however, have consistently argued against public expenditures for illegal aliens.

Under present administrative procedures in the Food Stamp Program, when Spanish-speaking persons apply for food stamps, their inability to speak English is not used as the sole basis for inquiring into their legal rights to be in the United States. There are no reliable estimates on how many illegal Mexican immigrants receive food stamps, but food stamp administrative procedures are regularly explained to Spanish-speaking communities by numerous civil rights and social welfare advocacy groups.

The conflicting views over the administration of the 1980 Census of Population is a prime example of how governments and special interest groups maneuver in their efforts to tailor the immigrant worker issue to their own objectives. Because of increasing public distrust of government and private survey research, the U.S. Bureau of the Census has not attempted to ascertain the immigration status of respondents. Since the census is used to reapportion legislative seats, a larger proportion of

---

[52] P. L. Martin and M. Miller, "Regulating Alien Labor in Industrial Societies" (Paper presented at the annual Industrial Relations Research Association meeting of the Industrial Relations Research Association, Atlanta, Ga., December 1979), p. 7.

legislative seats will go to regions that have relatively higher proportions of aliens, if the aliens respond to the census. States with relatively high proportions of illegal immigrants have attempted to minimize reapportionment by urging the Census Bureau to estimate the population by citizenship, although these same states welcome the count of illegals as a basis for appealing for federal funds to provide social services to illegals.

If a new guest-worker program were to be initiated, a major inequity in the tax procedures followed by many employers of illegal workers would be reduced. Employers typically withhold income and social security taxes from the pay of illegal immigrant workers but do not report these withholdings.[53] Although numerous studies have reported that tax payments for illegal immigrants are approximately the same as those for domestic workers with similar incomes, the proportion of withholdings kept by employers is probably high for the former. While illegal immigrant workers may be relatively low social service claimants, the widely reported net gains in tax revenues from illegals based on withholdings probably have an upward bias. A formal guest-worker program would provide a means of ensuring that public treasuries, rather than employers, received these tax withholdings.

Implications for Immigration Policy. The Bracero Program's history offers a unique opportunity to evaluate many questions of paramount importance to immigration policy. Unfortunately, much of the debate over the Bracero Program's merits and liabilities has centered on normative issues without the benefit of a positive economic analysis of its labor market effects. The program offers valuable background for the design of a future guest-worker program. A final note of caution is that any attempt to create a new guest-worker program would have to give prime consideration to the industrial sectors that would employ such workers.

The nature of the Bracero Program limits the application of that experience to a national guest-worker program. Nevertheless, our reading of the data evidence indicates that the United States and Mexico benefited from the freer mobility of labor between the two countries under P.L. 78. This lesson should not be lost in any future guest-worker program, or, for that matter, in the handling of illegal immigration.

[53] P. L. Martin and D. S. North, "Nonimmigrant Aliens in American Agriculture" (Paper presented at the U.S. Department of Labor/University of Florida Conference on Seasonal Agricultural Labor Markets, Arlington, Va., January 1980).

Occupational Preferences in the U.S. Immigration Law: An Economic Analysis

Robert S. Goldfarb

The large majority of legal migrants to the United States enter under provisions whose primary stated motivation is not economic. For example, many legal migrants are covered by provisions promoting the reunification of families. There are, however, a number of "occupational preference" categories allowing entry by individuals trained in occupations allegedly useful to the domestic economy. In view of the supposedly economic motivation for these provisions, it is odd that economists have devoted very little attention to analyzing them. This "shortage" of attention from economists has had the following unfortunate consequence: analysts perceptive about legal, social, and other aspects of immigration law are sometimes unaware of or misinformed about the economic implications of occupational preference types of provisions.

The aim of this paper is to provide an economic evaluation of these occupational preference provisions. The discussion begins with a description of these provisions. Following this, the economic evaluation is carried out in three steps. First, a number of conceivable economic rationales for an occupational preference system are presented; as part of this discussion, the relevance of each rationale as a basis for a general U.S. immigration policy is explored. Second, certain broad policy implications of relevant rationales are explored. Third, the effectiveness of the actual features of the U.S. occupational preference system as a method for carrying out relevant rationales is evaluated—that is, do the actual provisions make sense as a basis for an economically motivated immigration policy?

This method of procedure has a useful by-product in that it raises the following question: How much immigration of trained individuals is economically beneficial to the receiving country? This paper will

I received helpful comments on an earlier draft of this paper from Barry Chiswick, Marsha Goldfarb, Daniel Hamermesh, Oli Havrylyshyn, Jim Hosek, David Lindauer, Salih Neftci, David North, Richard Scheffler, Katherine Swartz, and Harry Watson. Linda Liner's comments at the conference led to several changes in the paper. I alone am responsible for remaining errors. I am especially grateful to Barry Chiswick for suggesting this topic.

412

argue that economic analysis *does* indicate, at least in principle, how economically beneficial immigration levels can be determined. While this assertion will not surprise economists, perceptive immigration analysts from other fields are not necessarily aware that the question can be usefully addressed. For example, in a thoughtful article about the immigration laws two legal specialists assert that "the simple fact is that there is no scientific or objective way to determine how many immigrants should be admitted or can be 'absorbed' by the United States."[1]

Occupational Preference in the U.S. Immigration Laws

There are two groups of legal aliens admitted to the United States. Those in the first group, referred to here as permanent immigrants or PIs, have obtained the right of permanent residency. Those in the second group, referred to here somewhat imprecisely as visitors, are admitted for only a specified limited time.[2] Occupational preference migrants are a subset of PIs (visitors *are not* occupational preference migrants). Other subsets of PIs are those with specified family ties to current U.S. residents, as well as certain classes of refugees.

In principle, the occupational preference categories exist to allow or to promote the migration of individuals whose labor services are likely to be valuable to the U.S. economy.[3] To evaluate the labor market effects of occupational preference, we must consider the size of the flows involved. The law specifies an upper limit of 290,000 immigrants in specified occupational preference, family preference, and refugee preference categories combined. Actual flows of PIs in recent years have been in the neighborhood of 400,000, because certain close relatives of U.S. citizens (in particular, unmarried children under twenty-one years of age, spouses, and parents of citizens over twenty-one) are not

---

[1] Elliot Abrams and Franklin S. Abrams, "Immigration Policy: Who Gets In and Why?" *The Public Interest,* no. 38 (Winter 1975), p. 6. The quote is at the end of a section which deals with population pressure in general and not with labor market considerations specifically. Our claim that economic analysis can show how economically beneficial immigration levels can be determined is qualified by the phrase "at least in principle." This qualification is needed because (as is pointed out in this paper) various complex *empirical* (as opposed to theoretical) issues need to be resolved before dependable *quantitative* estimates can be derived.

[2] Visitors are sometimes referred to as nonmigrants or nonmigrant aliens in the migration literature and the relevant legislation. Some visitors later succeed in changing their status to that of permanent immigrant.

[3] Some of the visitor categories can also be viewed as promoting migration of individuals providing valuable labor services, but such provision is supposedly only temporary.

limited by any numerical quota. Row 1 of table 1 gives the total number of PIs for fiscal years 1971–1977, while row 2 indicates the number of close relatives admitted outside of numerical limits.[4] Row 3, derived by subtracting row 2 from row 1, indicates that the 290,000 limit came close to being met in each of the listed years. The small shortfalls *do not* indicate that no one was waiting for visas: in fact this was far from being the case.[5]

How many occupational preference migrants might there be out of the total PI flow of approximately 400,000? The law specifies that the two explicit occupational preference categories, the third and sixth preferences (described in detail below), can provide no more than 20 percent of the 290,000 numerical limit on admissions. This suggests a maximum number of 58,000. There is a factor, however, that can raise this total by an amount which varies by year. The 80 percent of the possible PI slots not set aside for occupational preference are reserved for specific family and refugee preference categories. (A complete list of these categories is provided in table 2.) If these specific categories are not fully subscribed—that is, if fewer than 290,000 slots have applicants —the leftover slots become available to "nonpreference immigrants," some of whom must meet criteria similar to those required to qualify for the formal occupational preference categories. Row 4 of table 1 shows estimates of the overall flows in recent years. *It should be noted that these flows count the worker and the worker's family,* so that the number of workers involved is considerably smaller than the figure given. Netting out an estimate of other family members indicates that the occupational preference provisions result in the admission of fewer than 50,000 (and in recent years, considerably fewer) workers per year.[6] In other words, the occupational preference program is relatively

---

[4] Our discussion describes the law as of Fall 1979, whereas the table reflects some provisions no longer in effect by 1979. See note 5 and the notes to table 1 for one important example.

[5] For example, before 1977 Western Hemisphere immigration operated under a somewhat different system. A 1976 Congressional Report indicates that there was a two-year waiting list for visas under that system and that nearly 300,000 people were on the list. See U.S., Congress, House, *Immigration and Nationality Act Amendments of 1976,* Report no. 94-1553, 94th Cong., 2d sess., pp. 2-4. See also the text discussion below of the current system's country limit, which can result in waiting lists for visas.

[6] The estimate of other family members is from North and LeBel and is based on an assumption that for every ten workers admitted approximately another nine family members are admitted. These estimates actually yield numbers whose minimum value is slightly higher than the North estimates of numbers of labor certificates actually used. See David North and Allen LeBel, *Manpower and Immigration Policies in the United States,* Special Report, no. 20 (Washington, D.C.: National Commission for Manpower Policy, February 1978).

TABLE 1
PERMANENT IMMIGRANTS TO THE UNITED STATES, FISCAL YEARS 1971–1977

Category	1971	1972	1973	1974	1975	1976	Transition Quarter 1976	1977
1. Total PIs	370,478	384,685	400,063	394,861	386,194	398,613	103,676	462,315[a]
2. Relatives admitted outside numerical limits	86,425	96,726	112,989	116,206	100,197	110,438	30,159	115,105[b]
3. PIs admitted under numerical limits (row 2 − row 1)	284,053	287,959	287,074	278,655	285,997	288,175	73,517	279,252[b]
4. Occupational preference plus labor-certified nonpreference immigrants[c]	91,296	87,175	73,028	65,141	67,846			
5. Number of labor certificates used by PIs	48,430	44,964	34,991	30,668	29,680			
6. Occupational preference and nonpreference immigrants, Eastern Hemisphere only[d]	69,282	71,101	64,130	54,957	55,295	52,136	11,777	42,974

[a] The figure includes the Cuban refugees described in note b.

[b] The figure omits 67,958 Cuban refugees exempt from numerical limitations, retroactive to 1968, court mandate September 21, 1976.

[c] This is an overestimate, as it counts all nonpreference immigrants as being labor certified.

[d] This row is included because before 1977 the Western Hemisphere did not have a preference system or a country quota. Instead, there was a ceiling of 120,000 on total Western Hemisphere immigration, and labor certification for nonrelatives was required. Thus, the Eastern Hemisphere data better illustrate the workings of the preference system.

SOURCES: Data for 1971-1975 are from David North and Allen LeBel, *Manpower and Immigration Policies in the United States,* Special Report, no. 20 (Washington, D.C.: National Commission on Manpower Policy, February 1980). Data for 1976-1977 are from U.S. Department of Justice, Immigration and Naturalization Service, *1977 Annual Report* (1979).

TABLE 2

PREFERENCE CATEGORIES

Order	Category	Percentage
First preference	Unmarried sons and daughters[a] of U.S. citizens and their children	20
Second preference	Spouses, unmarried sons and daughters of resident aliens, and their children	20
Third preference	Immigrants in professions	10
Fourth preference	Married sons and daughters[a] of U.S. citizens, their spouses, and their children	10
Fifth preference	Brothers and sisters of adult U.S. citizens, their spouses, and their children	24
Sixth preference	Other workers	10
Seventh preference	Refugees	6
Nonpreference		0[b]

[a] Citizens' unmarried children below the age of twenty-one face no numerical limits.

[b] Visas allocated to but unused by the first seven categories are available for the nonpreference category.

SOURCE: Category descriptions are reprinted from North and LeBel, *Manpower and Immigration Policies*, p. 50. These descriptions are used because of their conciseness.

small in comparison with labor force growth. For example, the average yearly growth in the civilian labor force from 1969 through 1977 was 2,085,500; workers added by occupational preference amount to less than 2.5 percent of this number.[7]

There is another important numerical constraint on immigration. Not only is there a 290,000 overall limit, but each country is limited to 20,000 immigrants. This would seem to translate into a limitation of 4,000 per country in the two occupational preference categories (plus any slots left over for nonpreference immigrants). This maximum of 4,000 plus, however, *only applies if the country hits its 20,000 overall*

[7] Labor force data were calculated from U.S. Department of Labor, *Employment and Training Report of the President, 1979,* table A-1, p. 233. If this calculation were instead done for relatively skilled white and blue collar workers, the 2.5 percent would rise to around 7.0 percent, since such workers were approximately 36.0 percent of employment in 1969 and 1977 (see table A-16, p. 260, in the same source).

416

limit the year before.[8] In any case, the fact that a country using its 20,000 limit repeatedly will have a numerical limit on occupational preference quotas means that it is possible for there to be a long waiting list for occupational preference visas in country A while some of country B's slots go unused. Indeed, if some countries have excess applicants while others do not use their slots, row 2 in table 1 could consistently show numbers less than 290,000 while long waits for visas existed in selected countries.

Finally, there is an obvious sense in which particular countries may face constraints much more severe than the 20,000 limit. The fact that only 290,000 PI visas are to be issued to other than close relatives would allow a maximum of only fourteen countries to have full quotas of 20,000—yet far more than fourteen countries have citizens who want to emigrate to the United States. Visas are apparently made available to individuals in a particular preference category on a first come, first served basis until some relevant numerical quota (a country quota, a world quota, etc.) is reached.

The Labor Certification Requirement. Labor certification is required if an immigrant is to qualify for occupational preference status. The Immigration and Nationality Act contains the following provision:

> Certain aliens may not obtain a visa for entry into the United States in order to engage in permanent employment unless the Secretary of Labor has first certified, by granting a labor certification, that: (1) there are not sufficient United States workers who are able, willing, qualified, and available to perform the work; and (2) the employment of the aliens will not adversely affect the wages and working conditions of United States workers similarly employed.[9]

Workers who obtain labor certification can then seek entry under the occupational preference categories or as nonpreference immigrants. There are no upper limits on the number of labor certifications which can be issued. Row 5 of table 1 shows the number of labor certificates used by permanent immigrants for fiscal years 1971–1975.[10]

The workings of labor certification are extremely complex. There are two routes by which labor certification can be obtained. A special and extremely restricted set of occupations listed in Schedule A (table 3)

[8] This rule allows for the possibility that the number of occupational preference visas available to a country could actually fall if the country bumped its 20,000 constraint.

[9] *Federal Register,* vol. 42, no. 12 (January 18, 1977), p. 3440.

[10] North and LeBel, *Manpower and Immigration Policies,* p. 57, based on their estimation technique.

TABLE 3

Schedule A Jobs

The schedule now contains four categories:

Group I

1. Aliens who have received an advanced degree (equivalent to a Ph.D. or Master's degree conferred by a United States college or university) in dietetics;
2. Aliens who have received a degree (equivalent to a Bachelor's degree conferred by a United States college or university) in physical therapy;

Group II

1. Aliens (except for aliens in the performing arts) of exceptional ability in the arts or sciences including college and university teachers of exceptional ability who have been practicing their art or science during the year prior to the application and who intend to practice the same art or science in the United States;

Group III

1. Aliens who seek admission to the United States in order to perform a religious occupation, such as the preaching or teaching of religion and aliens with a religious commitment who seek admission into the United States in order to work for a nonprofit religious organization;

Group IV

1. Aliens who have been admitted to the United States in order to work and who are currently working in managerial or executive positions for organizations with which they were continuously employed for one year before they were admitted;
2. Aliens who will be employed in the United States in managerial or executive positions with the same international corporation or organization with which they have been continuously employed for the immediate prior year.

NOTES: Physicians were included on Schedule A until passage of the Health Professionals Education Assistance Act (1976), which declared the end of the physician shortage. In a *Federal Register* notice of proposed rulemaking (vol. 42, no. 15, January 22, 1980, pp. 4918-4929), the Labor Department has proposed removing dieticians from Schedule A, and allowing physician specialists "in geographic areas certified by the Secretary of Health, Education, and Welfare (HEW) as shortage areas for the alien's medical specialty" to be on Schedule A. The applicant would have to obtain a signed statement from the Regional Health Administrator of the Public Health Service that the position was eligible for Schedule A treatment. Similar treatment of registered nurses is also proposed. It is important to stress that these are only *proposed* changes, open for public comment and discussion.

SOURCE: Reprinted from U.S. Department of Labor, "Processing Department of Labor Applications for Alien Employment Certifications," mimeographed (Washington, D.C.: U.S. Department of Labor, n.d.).

is predetermined by the U.S. Department of Labor (DOL) to be acceptable for labor certification. An individual fitting one of these categories can receive labor certification by filing directly with a consular office abroad or with a U.S. Immigration and Naturalization Service office in the United States. The individual need not file with the Labor Department. Moreover, if the applicant is seeking a nonpreference visa, he or she need not show evidence of a specific job offer. If, instead, the individual is seeking an occupational preference visa, then an employer must submit a form indicating a job offer, but the individual need not submit other documentation required for a non–Schedule A job.

The second more widely applicable route, for jobs not listed in Schedule A, requires that employers file detailed applications for labor certification. The documentation required must include evidence of the following points:

> 1. The employer has been recruiting at the prevailing wage, and at prevailing working conditions, and has reason to think it will continue to be unsuccessful in its recruiting of U.S. workers through the public employment system and/or . . . through recruitment sources normal to the occupation. . . .
> 3. The wage offered . . . will equal or exceed the prevailing wage which is applicable at the time the alien begins work. . . .
> 7. The job opportunity has been and is clearly open to any qualified U.S. worker;
> 8. The job opportunity has been and is being described without unduly restrictive job requirements; . . .
> 9i. The employer has advertised and is still advertising the job opportunity without success in such media as newspapers of general circulation, and ethnic and professional publications.[11]

There are sixteen items in this list of required evidence, and item 9 includes several specific requirements as to the nature of the advertising required. The evidence is submitted to the local employment service office "serving the area where the alien proposes to be employed."[12] That office then calculates, "to the extent of its expertise using wage information available to it, the prevailing wage."[13] If the application meets the various requirements, the local public employment office tries to recruit U.S. workers for thirty days (minus any days during which an order for the job was already on file). If recruitment is not successful the application goes to a regional office, where a certification decision is

---

[11] *Federal Register,* vol. 42, no. 12 (January 18, 1977), p. 3445.
[12] Ibid.
[13] Ibid.

made. There is then a review process which the employer can initiate for denied applications.[14] In short, the labor certification process is quite complex and usually requires that a specific employer certify that there is a job opening for the occupational preference applicant.

Current Criticisms of the Occupational Preference System. It may be useful to review briefly some current criticisms of the existing system made by lawyers and other noneconomists and to contrast these with several features striking to an economist. The following criticisms made by noneconomists can be found in various commentaries on the occupational preference and labor certification system:

1. Because it requires case-by-case review, labor certification is both expensive to administer and time-consuming.

2. The entire system is questionable because there is no guarantee that an individual will remain in the occupation for which he or she is certified once he or she has obtained a permanent visa.

3. The Labor Department certification procedures are arbitrary and lead to innumerable legal challenges which are frequently lost by DOL in the courts. In particular, determinations of availability of U.S. workers are based on inadequate data, the legal requirement that U.S. workers be not only available but "willing" is largely ignored, and specific requirements stated by employers are often ignored.[15]

4. The decentralization of certification decisions into regional offices leads to contradictory policies.[16]

5. Occupational preference covers only a small percentage of permanent immigrants and an even smaller percentage of immigrants plus visitors. Since many PIs admitted under family or refugee quotas end up in the labor market, occupational preference has little power to control labor market effects.

---

[14] In addition to Schedule A there exists a Schedule B, which lists forty-nine occupations (for example, guards, ushers, yard workers, clerk-typists, porters, chauffeurs, and taxicab drivers) for which the Department of Labor will not usually issue certificates because sufficient U.S. workers are believed to be available. Employers can still apply for labor certification in these occupations but must do so directly to the regional area certifying officer. It is an interesting fact that although cab drivers are on Schedule B there seem to be a large number of recent immigrants driving taxicabs in Washington, D.C. While this probably reflects the labor market activities of visitors or of immigrants in other categories, it may also reflect the fact that occupational preference immigrants are not wedded to a specific occupation.

[15] A variety of examples are given in Peter Rodino, "The Impact of Immigration on the American Labor Market," *Rutgers Law Review,* vol. 27 (Winter 1974), pp. 245-74, and in "Note: Alien Labor Certification," *Minnesota Law Review,* vol. 60 (May 1976), pp. 1034-60.

[16] Rodino, "Impact of Immigration on the American Labor Market," p. 256.

6. Since employers must, in most cases, file requests for certification, the program expects employers "to know about a worker who is outside the nation." This leads to a situation in which a substantial percentage of labor certification applications are filed *after* the worker has been hired, so that, to some extent, "the labor certification program is now operating as a specialized amnesty program for illegal aliens of more-than-average skills."[17] Even if the program were not used by illegal aliens, it promotes transfers by visitors (especially students) to PI status.

7. The program "makes no labor market impact in that it has no impact on the total number of immigrants coming to the country or the total number of new alien admissions to the labor market, in that unused worker visas are used by other would-be immigrants."[18]

What is an economist to make of this list? A number of these criticisms involve administrative matters which might be made far less troublesome under a system which made more *economic* sense. For example, item 3 stresses the arbitrariness of DOL rulings, but this is in good part due to the fact that the act requires DOL to do case-by-case certifications on criteria which are often *in practice* economically meaningless. If the act were changed to recognize this, items 1 and 4 might also become moot. In contrast, I should like to present the following listing of features striking to an economist.

First, an economist's immediate reaction to a system for limiting immigration on *economic* grounds is that one must consider limiting *categories* of workers. Such categories can be either aggregate (for example, skilled versus semiskilled versus unskilled labor) or occupation-specific (for example, physicians versus lawyers versus French chefs). The choice of an occupation-specific versus an aggregate skill class system would depend on one's theory or rationale for limiting immigration and on one's view of the production structure of the economy. The U.S. system has no explicit numerical limitations by occupation or by broad skill category. It is legally possible that, in one year, a large number of occupational preference immigrants could be physicians, while in another year some other occupation could predominate. If numerical limitations by occupations (or more aggregate skill class) were set at the beginning of a year, the whole case-by-case labor certification exercise would be virtually unnecessary.

Second, the *overall* numerical limits set by the system are not based on any sensible *economic* criteria. While 20 percent of 290,000 has the advantage of being an even number, it has virtually nothing else to

[17] North and LeBel, *Manpower and Immigration Policies,* p. 58. The authors provide some data in their footnote 50, on the basis of U.S. Government Accounting Office investigations.
[18] Ibid.

recommend it economically over 21 percent, or 13 percent, or 93 percent of 290,000, or 450,000, or another figure. Even if 20 percent of 290,000 were a "correct" number, it would rarely be achieved because non-worker family members enter under the occupational quota—and there is the additional complication of nonpreference immigrants.

Third, if one is worried about labor market impacts one should have a means of taking account of the impact of family or refugee preference immigrants on the labor market. The current system does not do this, whereas an occupational or skill class quota system could, at least in principle, set occupational quotas *net of the expected occupations of family and refugee PIs.*

Fourth, whenever a system limits available slots to a number smaller than the number of demanders, there is a problem of allocating these slots. "Better" allocation systems result in a "better" quality of labor being admitted. The current system "solves" this allocation problem by ignoring it. Moreover, whenever there are scarce slots, there is a likelihood "rents" will arise owing to the value of the scarce slots. Some systems allow these payments or rents to be collected by the government (for example, through the use of large immigration fees), while other systems allow them to be expropriated by private agents. It is striking that virtually none of the legalistic writing, so apparently concerned with equity, even asks the question, "Who gets the rents?" Having reviewed the details of the current system, together with some criticisms of its workings, this discussion turns to the following issue: What kinds of plausible rationales, if any, are there for an occupational preference system?

Alternative Rationales for an Occupational Preference Policy

For the purpose of evaluating alternative rationales for the occupational preference system, it is useful to have a simple description of an immigration-limiting system which can be used as a reference point. The following is our version of such a description of the U.S. system. The United States limits relatively skilled immigration, but *does not* de facto limit relatively unskilled immigration—that is, while there are legal limits on both skilled and unskilled immigration, large flows of illegal immigrants, believed to be largely relatively unskilled, destroy any effective limits on unskilled immigration. While some relatively skilled immigrants (for example, a carpenter willing to work in the informal sector) may also enter illegally, many skilled individuals are precluded from so doing because of a need to enter the formal sector and obtain formal credentials (doctors, with their need for licensing to enter private practice, provide an obvious example). This discussion will therefore concentrate on the question: What are the rationales for a system that limits relatively skilled immigration?

Rationales for occupational preference type provisions fall into two broad categories: rationales based on aggregate economic effects and rationales based on specific occupations. The first category focuses on the aggregate volume of skilled immigration and stresses the possible aggregate economic benefits of such immigration—that is, it focuses on the aggregate number of immigrants and the aggregate mix of trained versus untrained immigrants. The second category focuses on specific occupations or sectors and stresses the possible effects of influencing the number and mix of particular types of trained immigrants.

Rationales Based on Aggregate Economic Effects. This section discusses two rationales: one having to do with aggregate production and income and the other concerned with training costs.

The aggregate production and income rationale. An economy can be viewed as producing output (perhaps measured as GNP) by using the services of inputs such as various kinds of labor and machines. As more inputs are used, more output can be produced—at least within certain ranges of inputs and output. In particular, more labor inputs can produce more output. Since immigration can increase labor inputs, it can raise output. The promise of output effects provides a possible rationale for allowing immigration. The implication of this rationale needs to be carefully spelled out, however, since such a rationale does not provide a blanket endorsement of immigration under all circumstances, nor does it necessarily suggest unlimited immigration. Indeed, this rationale is, at least in principle, capable of suggesting a meaningfully derived numerical limit on the immigration of trained individuals.

In exploring this approach it is useful to consider a simple situation. Let us suppose that we are dealing with an economy that continuously maintains full employment; in this economy the relationship between inputs and output could be described by a production function:

$$Q = f(K, L_1, L_2)$$

where Q is output, L_1 is unskilled labor, L_2 is skilled labor, and K is all other (nonlabor) inputs. For ease of analysis, let us assume that this general production function in fact has the specific form

$$Q = AK^a L_1^b L_2^c \qquad a, b, c < 1$$

where A, a, b, and c are particular numerical parameters. This is the

423

so-called Cobb-Douglas production function.[19] The broad conclusions we will draw from our analysis are not dependent on the use of the Cobb-Douglas function.

For the above production function, additional K, L_1, or L_2 all raise Q, but with diminishing effectiveness as input quantities rise:

$$\frac{\partial Q}{\partial K}, \frac{\partial Q}{\partial L_1}, \frac{\partial Q}{\partial L_2} > 0$$

$$\frac{\partial^2 Q}{\partial K^2}, \frac{\partial^2 Q}{\partial L_1^2}, \frac{\partial^2 Q}{\partial L_2^2} < 0$$

We assume, moreover, that each factor is paid according to its contribution to the raising of output (in technical terms, each factor is paid its marginal product).

How much (if any) immigration of skilled (L_2) labor should be allowed? *It can be shown that the preferred immigration policy depends on what economic variable the society is trying to maximize.* Three of many possible maximands are: (1) aggregate output; (2) output per capita; and (3) output per capita going to the native population. These three maximands are useful for illustrative purposes; there is no claim that they are necessarily the most appropriate maximands.[20]

---

[19] The Cobb-Douglas production function represents a major simplification and is adopted here only for ease of illustration. A particular weakness of the Cobb-Douglas is its failure to allow for the possibility that K and L_2 are complements, while L_1 and L_2 are substitutes. The Cobb-Douglas form "assumes away" this possibility. L. Epstein in "Some Economic Effects of Immigration: A General Equilibrium Analysis," *Canadian Journal of Economics,* vol. 7 (May 1974), pp. 174-90, has examined the effects of immigration in a world in which these complement-substitute relations hold.

[20] For example, one argument for using a per capita output maximand (rather than per capita output for natives alone) is that one may want to "count" the welfare of immigrants (who, after all, become residents and even citizens) as well as the welfare of natives. Per capita output, however, provides a flawed measure of changes in welfare for natives and migrants. Per capita output can *fall* while income of both groups is *rising* (see Barry R. Chiswick, "Impact of Immigration on the Level and Distribution of Economic Well-Being," in this volume, for an explanation). A better measure would involve aggregating income gains for each group. In any case, we use a per capita income maximand only to indicate that different maximands (whatever their precise merits) produce different optimal immigration levels.

In addition, while an economist's instinctive reaction may be to discount the aggregate output maximand (because output per person is more closely related to individual welfare), J. H. Dales has argued that the Canadian government over the period 1926-1955 behaved as though aggregate output rather than per capita income was its maximand:

> The question now arises as to why any excess demand for labour in Canada that arises from the interaction of the Canadian tariff and differentially favourable technological trends should be satisfied by immigration rather than by a differentially large increase in wages in

To analyze the first maximand, aggregate output, we must consider several scenarios. The first scenario involves output maximization *regardless of political consequences.* Specifically, if enough skilled immigrants are admitted, the marginal product of a skilled immigrant (and therefore this immigrant's wage and the wage of all skilled workers) will fall until it becomes equal to the unskilled wage. At this point a further increase in skilled immigration would force some skilled individuals to switch to unskilled work. If this did not happen, the wage of skilled workers would fall below that of unskilled workers. Forcing some native skilled workers to switch to unskilled status is politically unpalatable and is likely to result in a *political* constraint on immigration. Scenario one ignores the possibility of such a constraint. In this case, it can easily be shown that the optimal policy is to allow open immigration of trained individuals—that is, to let in all trained individuals who want to immigrate. (An appendix available from the author demonstrates this result and those following.)

In scenario two it is again assumed that skilled workers will switch to unskilled jobs if the remuneration on unskilled jobs is above that on skilled jobs. It is further assumed, however, that a situation in which domestic skilled labor is displaced (that is, forced into unskilled jobs) by immigrants is unacceptable, so that immigration policy is set to maximize output subject to the *political* constraint that no domestic skilled workers are displaced. That is, a policy is chosen that maximizes output subject to the constraint that the remuneration on skilled jobs

---

Canada. The answer seems to be: "an unwitting conspiracy" by business, labour, and government. If differentially favourable technological trends reduce Canadian costs of production relative to American costs of production in most industries, management in these industries will be able to "afford" to reduce the Canadian-American wage differential. However, they would probably prefer, if possible, to enhance their status by increasing output on the basis of immigrant labour at the going wage rate (and selling the additional output to the additional population) rather than to increase their wage-bill at the existing output. . . .

On the whole, therefore, business probably prefers an increase in immigration to an increase in wages. . . .

Government's role in the mechanism seems to reflect an interest in a Big Canada—a willingness, up to a certain point, to increase Canada's population even if that involves a lower standard of living for Canadians than would otherwise be possible. In any event, Government's willingness to solve the recurring problem of an excess demand for labour in Canada by promoting immigration whenever the economy can "absorb" more people at the going wage rate, rather than by allowing nature to take its course (which would involve an increase in wages and a reduction of the Canadian-American income gap), clearly fits in with the main preconception of business, rather than labour, as to the proper cure for "wage inflation." J. H. Dales, *The Protective Tariff in Canada's Development* (Toronto: University of Toronto Press, 1966), pp. 120-22.

remains above the initial (pre-immigration) wage on unskilled jobs. In this case, skilled immigrants should be admitted so long as

$$\frac{cL_1}{b} \geq L_2 + N$$

that is, the maximum number of skilled immigrants that should be let in is

$$N = \frac{cL_1}{b} - L_2$$

It should be noted that, under this scenario, if L_2 is large enough in relation to L_1, N could be zero.

A third scenario (less plausible to this writer) is also analyzed for completeness. Let us assume that skilled workers continue to work as skilled workers even if their remuneration falls below that of unskilled workers. In this case the optimal policy is to allow open immigration of trained individuals (that is, to let in all trained individuals who want to immigrate).

A second possibility is to maximize output per capita (the second possible maximand mentioned above).[21] Under scenario one, this can be shown to generate the solution

$$N = [c/(1-c)]L_1 - L_2$$

so long as $1 - c > b$, which is extremely likely.[22]

Under scenario two, maximization of per capita output suggests letting in N immigrants, where N is the lesser of the following two amounts:

$$N = \text{minimum of } \left(\frac{c}{1-c} L_1 - L_2, \frac{cL_1}{b} - L_2 \right)$$

Since $1 - c$, however, is quite likely to turn out to be greater than b (by the argument in note 22), this condition reduces to

$$N = \frac{c}{1-c} L_1 - L_2$$

This is also the required condition under scenario three. Once again, if L_2 is large enough in relation to L_1, then N could be zero. It should be noted that this condition is different from the condition that would be

---

[21] In our calculations we assumed that the relevant population equaled the number of workers so that maximizing output per capita is identical with maximizing output per worker. Letting population exceed the labor force is solved through the use of precisely analogous techniques.

[22] The statement $1 - c > b$ encompasses decreasing, constant, and moderate increasing returns to scale for a variety of values of a, b, and c. (It should be remembered that a, b, and c were individually assumed to be less than 1.)

required if total output rather than per capita output were to be maximized.

A third possibility—in some ways the most politically plausible one—is to maximize output per capita *going to the native population* (nonmigrants). This result is identical with the three scenario solutions we obtained under our first maximand, where output per se was maximized.

The cases studied immediately above yield several useful implications regarding the analysis of immigration. First, before discussion of an economically optimal immigration policy can even begin, a decision must be made as to what economic magnitude is to be maximized. The three alternatives discussed above do not exhaust the possibilities. Second, if we assume that a maximand is chosen, for an economy with a determinate and known production function *there is likely to be a specific immigration policy which is optimal in an economic sense.* It is simply not true that, as was quoted early in this paper, "there is no objective . . . way to determine" an optimal level of immigration. Our example used a particularly simple hypothetical production function (the Cobb-Douglas function) to illustrate what optimal levels might be, and different production functions would produce different levels, but the crucial point is that such specific levels do in general exist.[23]

A third implication that can be drawn from the cases just studied is that purely economic considerations may yield implications for immigration that are politically unpalatable. Specifically, some of our cases showed native skilled labor being displaced because of open immigration. In such cases it is likely that political considerations would override economic considerations in setting immigration limits, unless there were some mechanism to enable immigrants to buy off potential displacees.

A fourth implication concerns the notion of absorptive capacity, a term which always seems to crop up when numerical limits on immigra-

---

[23] Our analysis embodies a large number of simplifying assumptions, but the "moral" that optimal immigration levels exist would hold up for a much more general analysis. We discuss a number of complicating factors appropriate to a more general analysis below. Two other complications deserve mention: (1) we assumed a simple division of classes of labor, but here again more complex divisions do not change the existence of an optimal solution (for example, there might be several classes of skilled and unskilled labor and *separate* classes of skilled and unskilled immigrants); and (2) economists might worry that the analysis assumes that L_1 and K are exogenous to the decision about N (for example, if skilled immigrants bring capital with them, or if large N raises the return on capital [since it raises its marginal product], capital might flow into the country). If such effects are expected they could be built into the solution technique. Finally, we would stress again that the Cobb-Douglas function is much too simple and is used only for illustration (see note 19).

tion are discussed and which was used in connection with rationalizing the numerical limits in the 1965 Amendments to the Immigration and Nationality Act.[24] Our example indicates that the term is not meaningful with respect to *economic* determinants of numerical limits. The issue is not how many immigrants the economy can put up with, but how many immigrants should be let in to promote economic goals—and this number varies according to what is to be maximized. With most of the rules that we analyzed, the optimal number *does not* represent the reaching of some imaginary "capacity."[25]

A number of qualifications and comments should be added to the simple economic approach to the question of immigration limits illustrated above. The first comment concerns actual quantitative estimates. Unfortunately, although economic analysis suggests a way of approaching the problem of setting immigration quotas if the goals are economic, it is not possible currently to present a specific simple, but dependable, numerical estimate of these optimal immigration quotas. Existing production function estimates are not designed for this purpose, nor are they readily adaptable.[26]

A second comment concerns issues of income distribution. Let us suppose that we pick an immigration rule that maximizes output per

[24] Abrams and Abrams, in "Immigration Policy," p. 4, point out that the term absorptive capacity appears in a congressional report on the 1965 Immigration and Nationality Act.

[25] Jeffrey G. Williamson, in "Immigrant-Inequality Trade-Offs in the Promised Land: Income Distribution and Absorptive Capacity Prior to the Quotas," in this volume, uses the term absorptive capacity in a quite different way, one that does not represent an absolute limit or capacity being reached. His usage seems to differ very much in character from the legislative discussion. A very different interpretation of absorptive capacity conceivably consistent with the concern in the legislative discussion would involve short-run adjustment costs which would arise because large numbers of immigrants would enter in short periods of time, causing short-run crowding of facilities, temporary unemployment, etc. (See note 29 below for another author's description of these effects.) This type of absorptive capacity problem can be avoided by limiting the flow of immigrants in any short time period rather than limiting cumulative flows. A second interpretation consistent with the legislative discussion would arise in models where the marginal product of labor could fall to zero, generating long-term unemployment.

[26] While a large number of such estimates exist in the literature, they generally apply only to manufacturing, and the labor categories used are not necessarily appropriate for migration policy. For example, it may be that a production function disaggregating labor into five (or eight or . . .) occupation groups provides a more useful description of the economy for setting immigration policy than does one with fewer labor groups. Unfortunately, existing empirical production function studies are not designed to deal with this issue. See Daniel Hamermesh and James Grant, "Econometric Studies of Labor—Labor Substitution and Their Implications for Policy," *Journal of Human Resources*, vol. 14 (Fall 1979), pp. 518-42, for a useful summary of the literature; and see Epstein, "Some Economic Effects of Immigration," for an attempt to build an analysis for Canada based on "plausible numbers."

native, subject to the political constraint that skilled wages do not fall below initial unskilled wages. This does not mean that all natives fare equally well under the quota. In fact, with our simple Cobb-Douglas framework, unskilled native workers and owners of capital will have their incomes increased while skilled natives will suffer wage decreases when compared with the no-immigration case. It is, of course, perfectly possible to put distributional desiderata into the determination of what is to be maximized in the first place.

A third comment on our economic approach to the question of immigration limits concerns its effects on other nations. The focus in this paper is on U.S. interests, not on the interests of the migrant's country of origin. The effects of U.S. immigration policy on the welfare of other (especially less developed) nations is a legitimate concern, however. Readers who believe that there are harmful effects on LDCs from "brain drains" and related phenomena,[27] and who believe that the United States should take these effects into account when designing policies, will want to modify this paper's analysis to include consideration of such effects. Such modification might involve choosing maxi-

---

[27] There are conflicting views on the welfare losses (to the country of emigration) associated with brain drains. At least three identifiable positions seem to exist in the literature:

1. A straightforward position based on simple economic theory. In cases where migration is very small in relation to the size of the labor force, and the migrant was earning his marginal product, there is no effect on the welfare of those left behind. For larger movements, however, "the different models seem to lead to a prima facie presumption of a loss to those left behind even under conditions of perfect competition" (Jagdish N. Bhagwati and Carlos Rodriguez, "Welfare Theoretical Analyses of the Brain Drain," *Journal of Development Economics,* vol. 2 [1975], pp. 195-221. The quotation is from p. 207.)

2. A position that holds that damaging effects of the brain drain may be more imaginary than real because skilled professionals are in excess supply in many less developed countries. Thus, we find doctors driving cabs in Manila.

3. A response to this second position which holds that the outflow of unemployed or "taxicab-driving" doctors from Manila will still involve an economic loss to the Philippines. There are several different strands to this argument. First, Jagdish N. Bhagwati and Koichi Hamada, in "The Brain Drain, International Integration of Markets for Professionals, and Unemployment," *Journal of Development Economics,* vol. 1 (1974), pp. 19-42, and Bhagwati and Rodriguez, in "Welfare Theoretical Analyses of the Brain Drain," suggest that if doctors can migrate this raises the expected returns of becoming a doctor, other things being equal. This in turn may lead to further expansion of training facilities for doctors —a costly use of scarce domestic capital. Second, Bhagwati and Hamada discuss a possible "emulation effect" on LDC wages, which would cause these wages to be higher than they would be in the absence of migration. Perhaps even more compelling is the argument in Bhagwati and Rodriguez that the doctor would not, in the absence of migration possibilities, continue driving a cab in Manila forever. "He is almost certainly 'waiting' . . . to migrate to the U.S. If the possibility of migration to the U.S. were not available, he would at some stage stop wasting his skills and . . . migrate internally: to the smaller cities where he could practice medicine" (Bhagwati and Rodriguez, p. 208).

mands which incorporate the interests of both the United States and other nations.

A fourth comment is concerned with additional complications which the judicious analyst might want to include in a fuller analysis. We shall limit ourselves to mentioning four possibilities. The first is that if there is high and continuing unemployment, careful consideration of the employability of skilled immigrants and of their effect on nonimmigrant unemployment is necessary. It is important, however, to avoid the "kneejerk reaction" that the existence of unemployment indicates that skilled immigration is counterproductive. (High aggregate unemployment can coexist with virtually zero real unemployment of skilled individuals; in addition, even if unemployment is positive "today" for skilled workers, skilled workers may not remain unemployed for a significant period of time.) [28]

Adjustment costs are the focus of the second complication. Let us suppose that we believe that importing skilled labor always raises aggregate income in the medium run, but that large importations create temporary adjustment costs because the labor market (or even the housing market) cannot adjust rapidly to very large inflows: for example, a very large influx of a particular skill might push up unemployment rates temporarily, until market adjustments allowed all immigrants to be placed in jobs. In addition, the productivity of immigrants and their ability to adjust rises with duration of residence as skills become transferable or individuals acquire new skills. If we have a sense of the magnitude of these adjustment costs as a function of the size of the immigrant group, these costs can be incorporated into our formal production function analysis framework.[29]

---

[28] Any unemployment rate consists of a combination of a number of individual unemployment spells and an average duration per spell. Skilled workers can have positive unemployment *rates* because of frequent job changes but can have very low duration per unemployment spell: another way of putting this is to say that skilled workers may be only "frictionally unemployed."

[29] Mishan and Needleman stress the possibility of these effects. "First, there are consequences, readily classified as external diseconomies, which are associated with immigrant settlement in the host country and which are noticeable wherever large numbers attempt to settle within limited areas of a few large towns. . . . In the 'short period' immigrants concentrated in certain districts may aggravate further an existing housing shortage and impose additional burdens on an already crowded public transport system. In addition, they may reduce for some time the standard of environment and the amenity of the neighborhoods in which they settle. . . . Such disutilities as are suffered by . . . the indigenous population . . . are quite unambiguously a part of the costs of absorbing immigrants." E. J. Mishan and L. Needleman, "Immigration: Some Long Term Economic Consequences, Part B," *Economica Internationale* (August 1968), pp. 515-24; quoted p. 515.

A third possible complication involves regional differences. The aggregate production function analysis assumes that the nation can be usefully treated as one economy for present purposes; but if immigrants go to particular locations in disproportionate numbers, a regionally disaggregated approach might be needed, at least to model short-run impacts. In the longer run there should be internal migration in response to regional imbalances.

A fourth possible complication concerns the usefulness of aggregate production functions versus that of more disaggregated descriptions of economic activity (for example, descriptions using separate production functions by sector or industry). While we have employed an aggregate production function for illustrative purposes, an approach that disaggregates economic activity is in principle likely to give more dependable results. The important point, however, is that a disaggregated model could provide estimates of optimal immigration levels, just as our rather aggregate approach did. In addition, even if an aggregate production function framework is chosen, it is important when trying to derive actual immigration rules to use more general and flexible production function forms than the Cobb-Douglas, which, as has been mentioned, was used above only for ease of exposition.

The economizing on training costs rationale. The discussion above has ignored the existence of training costs, yet the saving of such costs is often mentioned as a benefit of skilled migration. As Abrams and Abrams have stated it, "The advantage of the present system is clear: it provides the United States with highly trained new workers. . . . Further, it does so at relatively little cost to us, since most of the individuals will have been trained elsewhere."[30] Training costs can be added to the analytical framework set forth above. While this involves a considerable increase in complexity, the gain is a unified treatment of training cost savings with production and income gains.

In an appendix available from the author, a simplified model incorporating training costs is specified and solved for two different maximands: total output and per capita output.[31] The case with training costs suggests, just as the no-training case did, that optimal immigration depends on choice of maximand, that optimal levels of immigration are derivable once a maximand is chosen, and that political considerations

[30] Abrams and Abrams, "Immigration Policy," p. 10.

[31] The simplifications are: (1) a multi-period problem is reduced to a single-period problem, and (2) a particularly simple relationship among training costs, wage differentials, and volume of training is assumed. It should be noted that the model *determines* the volume of training undertaken by the native population, and this volume is affected by the volume of immigration because the volume of immigration affects wage differentials.

431

may well override economic ones in the setting of immigration levels. In addition, the training cost model makes two points clear. The first is that immigration does indeed cut training costs by reducing the number of trainees below its zero-immigration level.[32] Moreover, the reduction in trainees in our model is less than one-for-one: one immigrant displaces a fraction of a trainee. The second point is that, because it suggests decreased domestic training, our model supports the claim that immigration reduces training for natives. In the context of opening training opportunities to (native) minority groups, this is sometimes seen as a serious drawback of increased immigration. One consistent analytical way of viewing this decreased opportunity is to see it as another example of an income distribution effect of immigration (discussed in the previous section as a qualifying comment on the question of immigration limits). This view has the advantage of forcing the analyst to decide how he or she values income distribution gains and losses versus output considerations.

Rationales Based on Specific Occupations. Unlike the aggregate rationales in the previous section, those considered here stress special situations in particular skilled occupations. Several different rationales for particular skilled immigration policies in specific occupations will be discussed.

The shortage rationale. The U.S. economy has periodically generated perceived shortages of skilled personnel. Scientific and engineering manpower, teachers, doctors, and skilled computer personnel are examples of groups which have been perceived to be in shortage at some point in the last several decades. A typical scenario seems to be that there is a large-scale increase in demand for the services of this group. In the case of teachers this increase was generated by the post-war baby boom. In the case of doctors it was generated partially by a large upward shift in demand for medical services accompanying the use of so-called third party payments, including Medicare and Medicaid. In the case of engineering and scientific manpower, the post-Sputnik stress on R & D seems to have been responsible. With computer personnel, a revolution in computer technology was the cause. Typically, employers' additional requirements for personnel at current salary levels

[32] In note 18 to "The Overall Effect of Immigrants on Natives' Incomes," in this volume, Julian Simon contends that the argument that education costs are saved by immigration is frequently fallacious because it assumes that fewer children will be produced domestically because of immigration (and, therefore, that less education will be required). Our model is not subject to Simon's criticism and does identify a true training cost saving, because it treats population size as exogenous to immigration but postulates an endogenous volume of domestic training which varies with real returns to training (and therefore with immigration)

outrun the additional supply being generated by current training sources. These perceived shortages generally provoke considerable expansion in training facilities, so that over periods ranging from a few years to several decades the alleged shortage seems to disappear.[33] While the existence of skilled manpower shortages associated with cobweb patterns has also been claimed, these shortages, because of their temporary or "cycling" nature, are less relevant to immigration policy.

Immigration policies might be used to mitigate such perceived shortages. For this to be at all possible, there must be a trained labor supply in other countries ready and willing to migrate. (In the case of computer personnel such a supply was probably not available.) In addition, it may take time for immigrants to adjust their skills to U.S. requirements; such adjustment lags lessen the ability of immigration to quickly mitigate shortages.

Let us suppose, however, that immigration can be used to mitigate perceived shortages. What are the advantages and disadvantages of such a policy? If there is a ready supply of migrants, then one advantage of opening immigration to meet shortages is the gain in output in the short run because strategic labor supplies are increased: in the absence of immigration, domestic supply would have been considerably lower for several years until domestic training sources caught up. A second, longer-run effect (which may not be an advantage, depending on what is to be maximized) is the substitution of immigrants for natives in the particular occupation. As our training cost model in the previous section suggested, the inflow of migrants should result in a lessening of incentive for natives to enter the occupation. This has the advantage of saving training costs, but the diminution of opportunity to native individuals is sometimes seen as a disadvantage.

The advantages and disadvantages mentioned above would accrue in a world in which all individuals and government decision makers made accurate calculations of degree of shortage, gains from undertaking training, and related matters. In fact, when we consider the uncertainties involved and the way in which perceived historical shortages seem to

---

[33] For a discussion of the disappearance of shortage in the computer case, see Sheldon Haber and Robert Goldfarb, "Labor Market Responses for Computer Occupations," *Industrial Relations,* vol. 17, no. 1 (February 1978), pp. 53-63; for a discussion of the college teacher case, see Allan Cartter, "The Supply of and Demand for College Teachers," *Journal of Human Resources,* vol. 1 (Summer 1966), pp. 22-38; and for a discussion of engineers and technical workers, see Glen Cain, Richard Freeman, and W. Lee Hansen, *Labor Market Analysis of Engineers and Technical Workers* (Baltimore: Johns Hopkins University Press, 1973). Richard Scheffler has pointed out to me that another reaction to perceived shortage may be the growth of paraprofessional categories. Once the perceived shortage becomes a perceived surplus, this growth is discouraged. Physicians' assistants are a case in point.

turn fairly quickly into perceived surpluses, a number of additional effects and complications need to be considered. First, all sorts of calculation errors are possible: this suggests that benefits are likely to be considerably smaller than in a world of perfect certainty. For example, the widespread perception of shortage by the relevant decision makers may come only when the shortage is well on its way to being eliminated, so that by the time the immigrant "spigot" is turned on, there may be little remaining potential gain to capture. Since the United States does not have a dependable system for precisely forecasting or measuring shortages, the potential for such errors is clearly present.[34] If such errors are made, not only will there be far less benefit from increased output, but the presumed longer-run savings in training costs may not materialize. Along the same lines, even if the forecasters correctly identify a shortage, determining the appropriate number of migrants to admit is extremely complex.

A second complicating factor concerns the ability of the immigration authorities to manage the flow of immigration. The current U.S. system, for example, is not set up to establish and enforce numerical limits on *particular* occupations, yet a system to combat shortages may imply such numerical quotas or limits. Even if such limits were allowable de jure, the ability of the immigration system to enforce them might be limited. As has been pointed out above, the U.S. system admits individuals under categories other than occupational preference and also allows some individuals to come in temporarily outside the occupational preference quotas. One's faith in the government's ability to design and administer control systems would have to be very strong indeed for one to believe that a precise quota system efficacious for meeting shortages could be made operational.

Yet another complication arises when the quality of labor trained overseas is uncertain. In such cases, providing an individual trained abroad to fill an expected vacancy may result in a different level of output or quality of output than if that vacancy is filled by someone trained in the United States. Changes in output level or quality affect the attractiveness of the use of immigrants to counteract shortages.

A fourth complicating factor is that political considerations rather than economic conditions may be prime determinants of occupations

---

[34] U.S. Department of Labor, Bureau of Labor Statistics, *Occupational Outlook Handbook,* various years, stresses projections of level of employment but has difficulty dealing with any supply response induced by employment growth. Moreover, changes in hours worked and productivity per hour may be important but are extremely difficult to predict. These changes themselves may be functions of endogenous wage changes. For an attempt to describe induced supply response in the computer case, see Haber and Goldfarb, "Labor Market Responses for Computer Occupations."

chosen as being in shortage. In addition, it should be borne in mind that individuals immigrating under a particular occupational quota are perfectly free to enter an entirely different occupation.

An example of recent U.S. immigration experience that bears on the fruitfulness of using immigration to alleviate shortages is the policy regarding foreign doctors. The United States has allowed a large number of foreign (foreign born) medical graduates (FMGs) to migrate during a period of perceived doctor shortage. Moreover, the perception of shortage apparently helped provoke an easing of immigration restrictions, while a perceived ending of the shortage has resulted in attempts to tighten immigration of FMGs.

It is useful to examine some numbers to assess the relative importance of physician immigration in building up the stock of U.S. doctors. In 1977 there were approximately 390,000 active physicians in the United States—up from 323,000 in 1970 and 259,000 in 1960. Approximately one in five of these physicians was an FMG (foreign born).[35] Licensure statistics of 1974 indicate that more than 40 percent of all new medical licenses were being granted to FMGs.[36]

Many users of the U.S. Immigration and Naturalization Service data on physician immigrants failed to realize that these data have reflected some double counting, since they did not net out foreign physicians who enter on exchange visas and, once they are here, switch their status to permanent immigrant, thereby showing up twice in the data. Table 4, based on the work of Stevens, Goodman, and Mick,[37] corrects for this double count. It shows numbers of new entrants (immigrants plus those on temporary visas) and compares these numbers to total U.S. medical school graduates for the years 1965–1973.

Several comments on table 4 are in order. First, the table reveals that, for a number of years in the 1960s, total new entrants of FMGs were about the same as U.S. medical school output as a source of new physicians; moreover, the total of 66,757 new entrants for the period 1965–1973 is clearly an important source of increase in the stock.[38]

[35] Richard Scheffler et al., "Physicians and New Health Practitioners: Issues for the 1980s," *Inquiry,* vol. 16 (Fall 1979), pp. 196, 199. We stress, in this paper, the fact that the term FMG is used to mean *foreign-born* foreign medical graduate, as contrasted with U.S. citizens who obtain training abroad.

[36] I. Butter, C. Wright, and D. Tasca, "FMGs in Michigan: A Case of Dependence," *Inquiry,* vol. 13 (March 1975), pp. 439-42.

[37] Rosemary Stevens, Louis Goodman, and Stephen Mick, "Physician Migration Reexamined," *Science* (October 1975), pp. 439-42.

[38] According to Ruby and Dolan, in 1974-1975 new permanent migrant physicians averaged 3,404 annually. Gloria Ruby and Katherine Dolan, "An Analysis of the Distribution of Foreign Medical Graduates in the U.S.," mimeographed (Washington, D.C.: National Academy of Sciences Institute of Medicine, December 1977).

TABLE 4

ENTRY OF FOREIGN MEDICAL GRADUATES INTO THE UNITED STATES
COMPARED WITH SIZE OF MEDICAL SCHOOL GRADUATING CLASSES,
1965–1973

Fiscal Year	Number Recorded (1)	Net New Entries (2)	Other Visas (3)	Total New Entries (col. 2 + col. 3) (4)	Total U.S. Medical Graduates (5)
1965	2,012	1,900	4,114	6,014	7,409
1966	2,549	2,075	4,553	6,628	7,574
1967	3,325	2,484	5,361	8,115	7,743
1968	3,060	2,408	5,997	8,405	7,973
1969	2,756	2,180	4,759	6,939	8,059
1970	3,155	2,265	5,365	7,630	8,367
1971	5,748	2,846	5,033	7,879	8,974
1972	7,143	2,754	4,270	7,024	9,551
1973	7,119	2,979	5,144	8,123	10,391
Total	36,867	21,891	44,866	66,757	76,041

NOTE: Column (2) represents number recorded (column 1) less adjustments of status. Column (4) is the sum of columns (2) and (3).

SOURCE: Rosemary Stevens, Louis Goodman, and Stephen Mick, "Physician Migration Reexamined," *Science* (October 1975), table 1, p. 440.

Second, the large jump in column 1 between 1970 and 1971 apparently represents an easing of the regulations for switching from temporary to permanent immigrant status.[39]

A third point is that the large number of new entrants in column 3 leads one to ask how likely these people are to remain in the United States for relatively long periods, since they are on "temporary" visas. While no definitive answer is possible, several pieces of available evidence suggest that very high percentages will end up staying, barring new and effective legal restrictions. Haug and Stevens find that, of a cohort of FMGs in the United States in 1963, over 80 percent were still there in 1971.[40] Stevens, Goodman, and Mick's study of a sample of FMGs

[39] "Before 1971 an exchange visitor who wanted to become an immigrant was required to leave the United States for a period of 2 years before applying for admission as an immigrant. . . . The 1970 law (Public Law 91-225) virtually abolished the two year requirement." Stevens, Goodman, and Mick, "Physician Migration Reexamined," p. 440.

[40] James Haug and M. Stevens, "Foreign Medical Graduates in the U.S. in 1963 and in 1971: A Cohort Study," *Inquiry*, vol. 10 (March 1973), pp. 26-32.

working on hospital staffs in 1973–1974 found that, although less than 30 percent of their sample planned to stay in the United States when they first decided to migrate, this figure had risen to 75 percent by the date of interview.[41] The large number of switches to permanent immigrant status (column 1 minus column 2 in table 4) is again consistent with the existence of considerable desire to switch to permanent status, though the percentages of the relevant population switching cannot be determined solely from the table.

A fourth comment on table 4 is that the growth in U.S. medical school output revealed in the table has continued. As a result of strong federal support to expand training in medical schools in response to the perceived shortage, the number of first year medical students in the United States has risen from 8,772 in academic year 1963–1964 to over 16,000 in 1977–1978.[42]

Clearly, there has been a large influx of FMGs—but was this inflow coincidental with the perceived shortage, or was it at least in part provoked by it? That is, did federal officials try to respond to the shortage by opening immigration? One factor was that in 1965 a fundamental revamping of the law took place which abolished the old national origin quota system and substituted a system that included occupational preference. This allowed a much larger number of Asians (a major source of FMGs) to enter and also allowed preference to be given to FMGs. While the fact that this major immigration law revision took place in the midst of a perceived physician shortage was no doubt coincidental, several important specific changes in law and administration increased the FMG flow; these changes were apparently provoked by the perception of shortage.

In 1965 the U.S. Department of Labor declared a physician shortage in hospitals; this, of course, meant that physicians could readily obtain labor certification for permanent immigrant visas under occupational preference. In 1970 an amendment to the Immigration and Nationality Act allowed the exchange visa visitor "coming to the U.S. with private funds from countries where his special skills were not in short supply to convert to the immigrant visa without leaving for two years"; previously, such a two year hiatus would have been required.[43] The impression that the federal government was trying to use immigration to cope with the shortage is further supported by the fact that,

---

[41] Rosemary Stevens, Louis Goodman, and Stephen Mick, *The Alien Doctors* (New York: John Wiley & Sons, 1978), p. 252.

[42] Scheffler et al., "Physicians and New Health Practitioners," p. 195.

[43] Ruby and Dolan, "Analysis of the Distribution of Foreign Medical Graduates," quoted, p. 4. There is, however, some doubt about how strictly the two-year requirement was enforced.

when the perceived shortage began to turn into a perceived surplus, the law was again amended (in 1976). At this time, medical examination requirements were stiffened considerably and exchange visitors were subjected to numerous additional requirements involving such matters as limits on maximum length of stay and "commitment to return." The quantitative effects of these legislative changes are of course far from clear. Writing in December 1977, Ruby and Dolan suggest that "the full effect of the provisions on the aggregate supply of FMGs will not be known for the next five years."[44] The very appearance, however, of such legislative changes is consistent with the existence of attempts to "manage" a shortage by changing immigration flows.

If we accept the assumption that a doctor shortage was with intent offset by immigration policy, what implications does the experience suggest? First, it seems fairly clear that, because of the importation of FMGs, the benefit of greater physician services was achieved while the alleged shortage lasted. Second, if the notion of a developing "surplus" is taken seriously, then some of the supposed savings in training costs have not materialized: to the extent that "too many" doctors are being trained domestically, training costs are incurred beyond levels necessary to produce an "adequate" supply. Before making too much of this point, however, one needs to consider whether the notion of "surplus" makes sense in this context. When laymen and health practitioners refer to surplus, they apparently mean more doctors than are "needed," where "needed" is apparently someone's idea of a desirable physician–population ratio.[45] To an economist this reaction does not make much sense. If more of a particular kind of skilled labor providing services is supplied, the result ought to be higher output and lower prices for that service; from the consumer's point of view, this is a good thing.

There are several additional meaningful interpretations of surplus, however. First of all, it would be possible from the economist's point of view to produce too many of these skilled laborers if the social cost of producing one more skilled laborer was greater than the social value of the stream of output that laborer would provide, but such a sophisticated view of overproduction does not seem to be the basis for cries of physician surplus.[46] Moreover, if it *were* the basis for such cries, it

[44] Ibid., p. 7.

[45] In fact, "needs" are often above-market estimates based on judgments of physicians.

[46] A related argument about the nature of surplus is based on the idea that, when an occupation is growing rapidly, individuals undertaking training may systematically underestimate the effect on post-training income and employment opportunity of induced increases in occupational supply. See Haber and Gold-farb, "Labor Market Responses for Computer Operations," for a discussion in the computer case.

would be consistent with substituting immigrant doctors for those trained domestically (because imported labor is "cheaper" to "produce" for the society). Second, our aggregate rationale suggested an (implicit) notion of surplus involving a number of immigrants too large for maximizing the chosen maximand (indeed, this is a useful version of the social value of output mentioned in the interpretation of surplus given in this section).

Finally, there is a specialized interpretation of surplus for health occupations only based on a view of health care services as a commodity that consumers have great difficulty evaluating. Paul Feldstein and Irene Butter have commented as follows:

> A different (and contrary) concern with the consequence of a surplus of physicians is that many people believe that physicians can create their own demand. Given the general lack of knowledge by patients, physicians are both their advisors and suppliers of medical services. Further, the traditional method of payment for physician services, fee-for-service, creates an incentive for the physician to supply such services. In a shortage situation, it is believed, physicians will have no need to create additional demand for their services, since they will be able to work at capacity or at the level they desire. Under surplus conditions, however, the fee-for-service system and the lack of patient information increases the potential for abuse, as it offers monetary incentives toward misuse of the physician's relationship with the patient. This increased care when paid for by the government can result in greater budgetary requirements under government payment programs than are believed necessary. Thus, the federal government, as a payor for Medicare and Medicaid (and also for a possible national health insurance system), might also be expected to be concerned with a possible surplus of physicians.
>
> Still another concern with the consequences of a physician surplus is that quality of care may decline. For example, if excess capacity exists among surgeons then they will perform fewer surgeries and be less experienced. Further, physicians will be less likely to refer patients if they are concerned about losing them.[47]

In any case, cries of physician surplus in the health literature rarely concern themselves with true economic surpluses (with the exception of the Feldstein–Butter arguments, which are controversial). Instead, some of these complaints of surplus come from physicians and

---

[47] Paul Feldstein and Irene Butter, "The Foreign Medical Graduate and Public Policy: A Discussion of the Issue and Options," University of Michigan School of Public Health Discussion Paper, no. D-4 (Ann Arbor, January 1975).

439

from physician organizations that do not want their members to lose business and income. In trying to limit physician supply, physicians are motivated at least in part by private concerns. What is good for doctor incomes, however, is not necessarily good for consumers.

The doctor shortage experience does point up some additional difficulties involved in pursuing an immigration policy aimed at ameliorating shortages. One problem is the lack of numerical quotas by occupation in the United States. If policy makers determine a target number of immigrants, and if exceeding this number by large amounts is seen as harmful, then a problem with the present U.S. immigration system is that it does not provide for the setting of specific numerical limits by occupation. A second problem is that permanent immigrants qualified to pursue a particular occupation need not enter through occupational preference.

A more complex problem involves the coordination of immigration policy and policy concerning the expansion of domestic training. When a shortage exists, supply can be increased by various combinations of immigration and increased domestic training. Yet the system's ability to coordinate these two supply sources may be limited. Let us assume that the immigration authorities are given the authority to set occupational quotas on the basis of perception of shortages. Interest groups pressing for expansion of domestic training would be unlikely to anticipate any increase in immigration, and it is unlikely that the immigration authorities would take account of and accurately forecast growth in domestic supply sources.[48]

What conclusions can be drawn from this experience on the possibility of a general continuing policy of using immigration policy to combat shortages? This writer would conclude that chances for a successful continuing anti-shortage policy are very small. For "success," the shortage must be large, quickly diagnosed, and long-lasting (so that the spigot is turned on soon enough before the shortage disappears to produce some benefits) and must be in an area in which a large elastic supply of acceptably trained immigrants exists overseas. Of the four shortages listed earlier—doctors, teachers, scientists, and computer personnel—only doctors and possibly scientists fit the supply requirement. Indeed, this writer would expect that, if an anti-shortage policy were institutionalized and assigned to an executive agency such as the

---

[48] In the physician case, there has in fact been some coordination of training and immigration decisions, but only because of special congressional actions affecting *both* immigration and doctor training (in particular, the Health Professions Educational Assistance Act of 1976). Such "special attention" and coordination on the part of Congress could not be expected if immigration authorities routinely acted on predicted shortages.

Department of Labor or the Department of Health and Human Services, one of two possible scenarios would emerge. The first assumes that an activist department would be chosen to administer the policy. This scenario would involve a series of false alarms regarding emerging shortages and resulting inflows of individuals in occupations not in fact in shortage. A second scenario assumes a cautious department. Here, shortages would rarely be diagnosed and declared, so that the anti-shortage policy would have little effect. Perhaps the best to be hoped for is that, if unusual occupational situations such as the doctor shortage arise, the legislature will recognize them and will take reasonably sensible action with respect to immigration policy.

The anti-monopoly rationale. Let us consider a country in which the supply of a particular skill is limited because of control of entry to the occupation. For example, we might suppose that current practitioners through the political power of their professional organizations had managed to prevent the "sufficiently rapid" growth of training institutions, so that the supply of this type of skilled labor was well below the competitive level. Immigration policy could conceivably be used to increase the supply of this category of skilled labor. To continue our use of the physician example, if physician organizations used their political power to block medical school expansion, FMGs might be admitted to help overcome this supply restriction.

There are several sizable impediments to the use of immigration policy to combat monopoly in the United States. First, if supply is in fact held down because of the political power of skilled labor lobbies to stop entry, the same political power is likely to be able to prevent the opening up of immigration to increase supply. Second, professional organizations often control state licensing, so that even if migration flows are increased the professional organization may be able to prevent large effects on supply by creating requirements which result in denying licenses to migrants. The FMG case provides one example of the possible relevance of anti-monopoly strategy. It seems quite clear that the increase in FMG migration took place only so long as the physician lobby perceived a shortage.[49] Once the danger of a so-called surplus

[49] One can, of course, ask why the physician lobby did not fight tooth and nail to cut off *any* immigration, as a more severe shortage would appear even more likely to raise incomes. This question is beyond the scope of this paper (and is outside the author's field of expertise). Plausible answers, however, can be imagined, for example: (1) physician fear that rapidly rising prices might provoke government demands for expanded training facilities which, once established, would be harder to shut down than an immigration spigot is to turn off; (2) fears that rapid rises in demand without at least limited supply expansion might bring about government pressure for unattractive changes in practice techniques in order to increase patients per doctor. Marsha Goldfarb suggests another

was perceived, the considerable political power of the physician lobbies was exerted to help restrict immigration. In short, if politically powerful professional organizations exist, it is unlikely that immigration policy could be readily and explicitly used to help ease monopoly positions.

Other rationales. There are any number of other conceivable rationales for skilled immigration of specific occupations: three examples will suffice. The first of these is the interest group rationale. Particular groups of workers or consumers may favor or oppose the importation of particular kinds of skilled labor. Buyers of violins may well favor allowing skilled violin makers to immigrate. Lovers of French cuisine would no doubt wish to see a great number of French chefs, while the unions representing chefs would oppose this. (In fact, migration of French chefs has apparently been an issue in immigration policy.)[50] Physicians may or may not favor large-scale immigration of nurses, depending on the particular physician's views of complementarity versus emerging competition.[51] More generally, identifiable interest groups have strong opinions about migration of occupational groups because the supply of these particular occupational groups noticeably affects the real income of the interest group.

A second example of a possible rationale concerns infant industries and return to scale arguments. Let us assume that country A is the leading producer of a technologically sophisticated product such as computers. Let us assume further that (1) the computer science industry exhibits huge economies of scale, so that, if other countries are to compete, their domestic industry must be quite large; and (2) that highly skilled manpower trained specifically for that industry (computer programmers) is essential to provide that industry's services. Then coun-

---

explanation. She argues that, within medicine, there are some jobs which are more desirable than others. Because FMGs tend to staff many of the less desirable jobs (hospital staff work, asylum work, etc.), U.S. physicians can pursue private practice and not be pressured into filling these less desirable positions. See Feldstein and Butter, "Foreign Medical Graduate and Public Policy," for a discussion of the claim that FMGs do jobs that U.S. doctors "don't want to do."

[50] See Pamela Bujarski, "The Haute Cuisine Restaurants Here Are Up against the Kitchen Wall," *New York Times Magazine,* February 20, 1972. Bujarski refers to a "severe shortage of chefs." She then argues that "a prospective chef cannot be admitted without certification from the New York State Department of Labor that no unemployed American chef would thereby be deprived of a job. The difference in viewpoint over what constitutes a qualified chef is roughly the difference between bureaucracy and artistry."

[51] That is, use of nurses may raise a doctor's net income from solo practice. If more nurses are let in, nurses' wages will grow less rapidly, which would increase doctors' income. On the other hand, if larger nurse supplies are seen as encouraging forms of practice that compete with solo physicians, then physicians might oppose nurse immigration.

tries trying to develop their industry should encourage migration of computer specialists from country A. Moreover, if country A is trying to prevent the emergence of competition abroad, it should encourage migration to country A of foreign-trained computer specialists. This "beggar thy neighbor's industry" policy might be called the "strategic specialist economies-of-scale" rationale.

A third example concerns specialized training available abroad but not available (or not as cost-effectively provided) in the United States. It may be, for example, that French chefs are best trained in special schools, but the demand for French chefs in Mexico (or the United States) is not large enough to support a chef's school. A dynamic version of this argument would hold if an infant industry which needed skilled labor was starting to develop.

None of these rationales seems very relevant for fashioning U.S. skilled labor immigration policy "in the large."

Implications of the Rationales Discussion. Our review of aggregate output versus occupation-specific economic rationales suggests that none of the occupation-specific rationales provides a suitable basis for overall U.S. immigration policy. The shortage and anti-monopoly rationales are both subject to serious doubts about the ability to successfully apply them. The other rationales listed are far too specific in focus to provide a general basis for immigration policy. Indeed, if the shortage and anti-monopoly rationales were enforceable they would be irrelevant to the large majority of occupations. The limiting of immigration only to those occupations covered by these two rationales would sacrifice potential economic benefits (identified in the aggregate rationale discussion) from immigration of other occupations. It seems clear that if an economic rationale is to be used to help set immigration quotas, it apparently will have to be based on an aggregate output rationale.

Two clarifying comments on the use of the aggregate output rationale are appropriate. First, in principle the nature of the economy's production structure (its production function) determines whether an aggregate output rationale merely sets numerical limits on broad categories of labor (skilled versus semiskilled versus unskilled, for example) or whether it sets limits on much narrower occupational categories or groups. Even if such limits are set by very narrow occupational groupings, however, *it is still an aggregate output rationale so long as the motivation and focus is on an aggregate maximand.*

How is it to be decided whether the economy's production structure implies limits on narrow versus broader occupation groups? In principle, this should depend on the degree of "substitutability" (elasticity of substitution) among particular occupation groups. If a narrowly defined skilled occupation A turns out to be a close substitute for a narrowly defined skilled occupation B (that is, there is a high elasticity of substitution between them), separate immigration limits for each occupation are unnecessary. Unfortunately, the econometric literature on production functions has not come anywhere near performing the background studies (appropriately disaggregated by detailed occupation group) needed for these choices about appropriate occupation groups.

The second point that should be made on the use of the aggregate output rationale is that our analysis frequently has suggested letting in everyone who wants to immigrate. This implication of a laissez-faire immigration policy, however, will depend on the nature of aggregate production relations. We have implicitly assumed situations in which aggregate production allowed considerable factor substitution and always positive factor marginal productivity. We believe these assumptions are likely to be correct for describing the U.S. economy in the long run. Not all observers of the labor market agree, however, with this assessment: for example, radical economists and dual labor market theorists might not accept them. If these implicit assumptions in fact turn out to be incorrect, economic immigration limits are likely to be generated even in the case in which total output is the maximand.

The Present Occupational Preference System as a Mechanism for Achieving Aggregate Output Rationale Goals

Our analysis suggests that an aggregate output rationale is the most plausible *economic* basis for a system limiting immigration. How well designed is the U.S. immigration system for implementing such a rationale? The current system reveals several major weaknesses with respect to the aggregate output rationale. A first weakness is that current numerical limits seem unrelated to any meaningful choice of *economic* maximand. There appears to be no relation between the occupational preference limits the system sets and any notion of optimizing some aggregate output maximand. Thus, before such a system could function to carry out the details of an aggregate output rationale, a maximand would have to be chosen, its numerical quota implications would need to be deduced, and immigration limits would have to be set according to these quota implications.

Inability of the Current System to Set Effective Numerical Limits. Let us assume that an appropriate maximand has been chosen and its numerical implications deduced. A number of additional difficulties with the existing system would remain. First, as the system is currently designed, there is no provision for setting explicit numerical limits by broad or narrow occupational category—although there is a list (Schedule B) of prohibited occupations. Instead, (1) labor certifications are given on a case-by-case basis apparently with no consideration of whether other certification recipients have obtained visas, and (2) the numerical limits on visas are themselves not subject to controls on numbers per occupation. Until the system is redesigned to remedy this, it cannot serve effectively to limit immigration by broad or narrow occupational category. Second, even if such numerical limits were in fact set, there would remain the fact that occupational preference covers only a minority of immigrants. To begin to cope with this problem, the system would have to find a way of netting out the expected occupational distribution of family and refugee preference immigrants in setting occupational preference numerical limits. In the same way, some correction must be made for the expected distribution of nonpreference immigrants, or that category itself must be changed or eliminated.

Selection of High Quality Immigrants and the Incidence of Rents. The issues raised above relate to the system's ability to pick an "economically rational" numerical limit and then enforce it. There are two other classes of issues which arise regardless of whether an economically rational numerical limit is set. The first concerns the system's ability to select "higher" rather than "lower" quality immigrants within any (economically rational or irrational) numerical limits that are set. The second issue involves the generation of "rents" from an immigration-limiting system. Specifically, as rents are inevitably generated, who does and who should collect these rents?

As currently designed, the U.S. immigration system fails in several ways to choose high quality over low quality immigrants, where quality refers to skill rankings within appropriately defined occupational groups. If we were to assume that mean quality and the associated distribution of potential immigrants per occupation were constant across countries, then maximizing the quality of labor for a limited number of slots would imply admitting individuals by country *in proportion to the country's population of potential immigrants*. If, instead, some countries had a higher mean quality of particular occupations, a strategy designed to maximize quality would admit larger than proportional numbers of potential immigrants in the relevant occupations for the countries with the higher distribution. The U.S. system is virtually guaranteed to fail to do either of these things, since it sets a constant *numerical* limit of 20 percent of 20,000 for each country instead of setting limits related to the potential population of skilled migrants. In particular, countries with small populations and low percentages of skilled labor have the same limits as large countries with large percentages of skilled individ-

445

uals. Thus, for example, India, Germany, Denmark, Haiti, and Portugal all have the same maximum limits. Only a particularly odd distribution of talent across countries and of propensities to migrate would allow this quota system to pick relatively high quality immigrants for the United States.

If it is argued instead that the 20,000 limit is, typically, not reached because the 290,000 "world" limit is bumped first, there is still no reason to expect the U.S. system to successfully choose relatively high quality immigrants within each occupation. Within occupational preference, immigrants are apparently chosen on a first come, first served basis—a system which, while politically attractive, makes no pretensions to selecting high quality immigrants from among all applicants.

Limits per country based on a "quality-adjusted" potential migrant population would seem to make much more economic sense than a blanket 20,000 limit. It can also be asked, however, whether there are ways of ranking potential migrants *from one country* which would ensure that higher quality potential migrants *from that country* would be chosen over lower quality potential migrants. While this topic is beyond the scope of this paper, a thorough treatment would consider the following possibilities: (1) Could a testing system be used? (2) More generally, could a "screening" system, based on a series of qualifications, be used to indicate quality? (3) Are there incentive systems which could be used to further encourage higher quality individuals to "self-select" themselves?[52]

There is one feature of the current U.S. system which may, in fact, serve as a partial, imperfect screen. This is the requirement for the majority of labor certifications that an employer petition be included indicating the existence of a job opening. This indicates at least that the individual meets some employer's hiring standard, but it does not guarantee that excluded individuals might not look even more attractive to the same employer. Whether or not this requirement serves as a partial screen, there is a more general issue of the desirability of this kind of regulation. Although it does serve to indicate the existence of a job opening for the potential PI, its administration consumes large amounts of private and public sector real resources and sets up the Catch-22 situation that immigrants must be known to employers *before* obtaining legitimate PI status.[53] Indeed, fiscal year 1977 data on occu-

[52] For a discussion of incentive structures promoting self-selection in labor markets, see Joanne Salop and Steven Salop, "Self-Selection and Turnover in the Labor Market," *Quarterly Journal of Economics,* vol. 90 (November 1976), pp. 619-28.

[53] It is also possible that immigration lawyers serve as partial screens by picking and choosing the cases they accept. I owe this point to discussions with Salih Neftci. Obviously, this kind of screen would also be quite imperfect.

pational preference (third and sixth preference) migrants indicates that out of 11,227 labor certificates used, 5,762—more than half—represented adjustment of status.[54] Table 4 provides data for a specific occupation—physicians: subtracting column 2 from column 1 indicates that roughly one in four immigrants were adjustees during 1968–1970, but that more than half were adjustees during 1971–1973. Thus, the current system does encourage granting PI status to those already in the United States.

Finally, we should consider the issue of rents. Whenever there are fewer opportunities than there are applicants, payments are likely to arise from the value of these scarce slots. These payments or rents often arise out of competition for the scarce slots. Under the current U.S. system, individuals competing for status as permanent migrants are willing to pay sizable sums for legal services to aid in getting visas. The amounts they are willing to pay are related to the value of obtaining a scarce visa. Thus, the legal profession is a major recipient of the rents from the U.S. immigration system. A reasonable question is whether the system could and/or should be redesigned so that rents would flow to recipients other than lawyers; for example, a system that required immigrants to pay to the U.S. government a sum reflecting the value to the immigrant of the scarce slot would reduce the rent available for lawyers. A more economically desirable payment scheme would impose a surcharge on the income tax, thereby making the payment a function of income achievement in the United States and also avoiding capital market imperfections associated with an initial lump sum payment requirement. Unfortunately, this economically desirable surcharge is almost certainly unconstitutional. Schemes of this type would redistribute rents from lawyers to the public or government.[55] The reader can decide whether such reassignment of rents would be attractive.

[54] Because the Western Hemisphere was included under the preference system only for part of fiscal year 1977, the reported data (from U.S., Immigration and Naturalization Service, *1977 Annual Report,* table 8A) is dominated by Eastern Hemisphere immigrants. However, 1978 data to be included in the 1978 Immigration and Naturalization Service *Annual Report* indicate that this figure rose to 65 percent in fiscal year 1978. It should be noted that the data for *both* years excludes nonpreference immigrants, and also that an individual who comes to the United States temporarily and then returns home for a period before receiving a job offer is *not* counted as an adjustee, even though that person is likely to be previously known to an employer.

[55] Another way of decreasing lawyers' opportunities for capturing rents would be to reduce their usefulness in helping to obtain visas. Any change in the system which would make obtaining a visa more of a *truly random system* would tend to do this (assuming this randomness were widely recognized by potential immigrants). Thus, for example, distributing visas by a true lottery would probably decrease the usefulness of legal expertise.

Summary

Our analysis of the occupational preference system began with a search for plausible economic rationales for limiting the volume of skilled immigration. Evaluation of alternative rationales produced the result that only the so-called aggregate output rationale provides a conceivably suitable economic basis for U.S. immigration policy. An important implication of the aggregate output rationale is that determinate optimal immigration levels do in principle exist, although the exact level depends on the choice of maximand.

The paper then investigated the ability of the current system to effectively apply an aggregate output rationale. Sources of difficulty include the current system's inability to effectively set numerical limits and the lack of incentives for selecting high quality over low quality potential migrants. Finally, there is a discussion concerning who receives the rents generated by the system. As currently designed, the system funnels what is probably a substantial amount in rents to lawyers rather than to the government or the native population as a whole.

Commentaries

Linda S. Liner

The major premises of Dr. Goldfarb's discussion can be summarized in the following way. It is possible to derive some optimal level and mix of immigration with the objective of making our immigration policy more economically rational. The optimal level and mix will be dependent on the particular economic maximand chosen. With a Cobb-Douglas production function as an analytical framework and aggregate output as the key maximand, in most cases it is economically desirable to admit unlimited numbers of skilled immigrants into the United States. Finally, the economic rationale based on maximizing aggregate output is superior to one based on alleviating shortages in specific skilled occupation categories.

The Social Welfare Function Relevant to Immigration Policy

Our current immigration policy reflects a number of values held by the public and the government of the United States. The level and composition of people admitted for permanent resident status reflects a desire to promote family reunification, to provide asylum for political refugees, and, to a lesser extent, to supplement the U.S. labor force. The United States also admits thousands of foreign nationals (nonimmigrants) each year on a temporary basis. Our nonimmigrant policy seems to reflect our desire to promote tourism, international commerce, and cultural and educational exchange, and to reduce excess demand for labor in certain occupations and industries. Our de facto immigration policy also allows for the admission of a relatively large inflow of primarily unskilled workers as undocumented aliens.

There is considerable evidence that the current immigration statutes and procedures do not adequately reflect current values of the public. In the past five years we have witnessed several major attempts on the part of policy makers to try to assess what the optimal immigration policy ought to be. (These groups have included the Domestic Council

Committee on Illegal Aliens, the Interagency Task Force on Immigration Policy, the Select Committee on Population, and the Select Commission on Immigration and Refugee Policy.) While there still does not appear to be a consensus regarding what our ideal immigration policy ought to accomplish, several major themes reappear during each policy assessment.

- Foreign nationals should be able to join their immediate relatives in the United States.
- The United States should be a haven for the politically oppressed.
- The level of immigration should be geared toward reducing population and labor force growth and ameliorating environmental problems.
- Immigration should not contribute to unemployment and underemployment, particularly among economically disadvantaged groups such as blacks, Hispanics, teenagers, and women.
- Immigration should not have an "adverse" impact on wages and working conditions, particularly among economically disadvantaged groups.
- Immigration should not contribute to the public burden (welfare payments, food stamps, costs of operating educational and medical facilities, etc.).
- Immigration should not have an "adverse" impact on distribution of income.
- Immigrants should be admitted to benefit certain sectors of the economy.

While the above list may not be all-inclusive, it illustrates several important considerations. First, the public desires a policy that will serve both humanitarian and economic goals. Obviously, several of these goals conflict. With respect to economic goals, the primary concern appears to be with perceived short-term effects of immigration—unemployment, wages and working conditions, and public assistance. To a lesser extent the desire to satisfy temporary needs of certain economic sectors is stressed. Notably absent from the above list is the economic goal of maximizing aggregate output.

It is difficult to dispute the point that an optimal immigration policy is derivable provided we define the maximand and make some assumptions about the behavior of our economy. It must be stressed, however, that the most difficult problem we are likely to confront in this exercise is in defining the social welfare function. Humanitarian and noneconomic considerations aside, the task is still rather formidable. Attempts to derive an economically rational immigration policy which ignore economic variables of importance to the U.S. public, such as

450

unemployment, wages and working conditions, impact on public burden, and income distribution, are not likely to receive much serious attention from policy makers.

On a more positive note, it should be stressed that the social welfare function reflects values of the public and that these values are, at least in part, a function of current knowledge and information pertaining to any particular policy variable. Certainly in the past fifty years we have seen our immigration policy evolve in response to changing values and perceptions regarding immigration and its effects on public welfare. To the extent that immigration affects aggregate output and economic growth, and to the extent that these variables remain important goals of the public as regards the U.S. economy, it is extremely useful for economists to demonstrate the relationship between immigration and economic growth and to communicate their findings to the public and to policy makers.

The Cobb-Douglas Specification

The conclusions drawn from an analysis of the optimal level and mix of immigration will be dependent on the choice of the model describing production relations in the economy as well as on the choice of the maximand. The particular model employed in Dr. Goldfarb's analysis is the Cobb-Douglas production function. This specification is commonly used by economists not so much because of its accuracy in describing production relations but because of its simplicity as an analytical tool. This particular attribute may also lead to conclusions which are overly simplified.

One of the major characteristics of the Cobb-Douglas function concerns the responsiveness of factors of production to relative changes in factor prices. Specifically, the mathematical properties of the function yield an elasticity of factor substitution equal to -1. This value implies a great deal of responsiveness and may be unrealistically high, particularly for the short and medium runs. If we drop the assumption that the elasticity of factor substitution is high, our conclusions regarding the optimal level and mix of immigration may change accordingly.

Let us assume that the U.S. economy is divided into two sectors.[1] The secondary sector tends to generate jobs characterized by insecurity, lack of advancement opportunity, poor working conditions, and menial or degrading social status. Generally, we would find competitive, labor-intensive industries in this sector. In some cases such as in agriculture or

[1] Testimony by Michael J. Piore, "Undocumented Workers and U.S. Immigration Policy" in *Immigration to the United States: Hearings Before the Select Committee on Population,* 95th Congress, 2nd session, April 4–7, 1978 (1978), p. 473.

construction, the industry's production will be cyclical, contributing to a fluctuating demand for labor. Because these industries tend to be low-profit, labor-intensive, and cyclical, they require a labor force which is highly mobile and relatively cheap. The primary sector, which comprises the majority of economic activity in advanced industrial economies, is characterized by a higher level of stability and organization. Jobs in this sector tend to be higher paying, to offer opportunities for career advancement, and to be more stable.

Let us further assume that the elasticity of labor supply from the primary sector to the secondary sector is very low. Native-born workers —even the hard-core unemployed and underemployed—are reluctant to accept jobs in the secondary sector. This reluctance may be a function of social factors (the disutility in accepting a low status job may be greater than the disutility of being unemployed). In addition, there are economic incentives which reduce mobility between the two sectors: if workers' reservation wages should exceed going wages in the secondary sector and if transfer payments such as unemployment insurance and welfare are available, many members of the labor force would be willing and able to remain unemployed rather than accept jobs in the secondary sector. Thus, it is possible for an advanced capitalistic economy to have a sustained excess demand for unskilled labor.

Traditionally, foreign-born labor has been employed by advanced industrial societies to meet this excess demand. Often, these migrant populations view their stay in the host country as temporary. They are not necessarily seeking job security; they are less affected by the job's menial status because they "view themselves in the social setting of their home country from which they derive their identity and self image."[2] Moreover, the option of transfer payments may not be viable to this group of workers, either because of different attitudes or because of legal constraints (undocumented aliens and nonimmigrant aliens do not qualify for most types of transfer payments).

If this source of mobile, low-cost labor were not available, it is questionable whether the domestic labor supply would adjust, even in the long run. For example, the level to which wage payments would have to rise in order to attract native-born workers may exceed the level which would yield normal profits for many firms. To the extent that these industries face foreign competition from countries with large, mobile supplies of low-cost labor, the problem is exacerbated.

In the long run, the firms in the secondary sector may react to a reduction in the supply of low-skilled, foreign-born labor in several

[2] Ibid., p. 474.

ways. They may alter production techniques; they may relocate abroad to nations with a more accommodating supply of labor; they may relocate to the primary sector; or they may go out of business. Depending upon the extent to which production techniques can be altered and the ease with which firms can relocate, the United States may experience a decrease in output in this sector. To some extent the decline in the secondary sector will "free up" resources which could be used in the primary sector and, consequently, will increase output in the primary sector in the long run. Complementarities may exist, however, between the two sectors: a decline in output in the secondary sector may result in a decline in output in the primary sector. For example, the availability of foreign-born private household workers allows many women who might otherwise be tied to household work to enter the labor force. Consequently, a decline in the availability of foreign-born private household workers may result in a decline in the female labor participation rate and a resulting decline in output. The sheepherding industry relies heavily on foreign-born labor. A decline of such labor in this activity may affect employment and output in the garment industry. Such arguments can be applied to many other fields as well.

At this point the net effect on output of a supply of unskilled (or low-skilled) foreign labor is unclear. An empirical production model which more fully addresses the structural attributes of the economy described above may give some indication regarding the net output effect of changes in the supply of unskilled foreign labor. It is entirely possible that such a model would lead to conclusions significantly different from those reached by Dr. Goldfarb's model. For example, keeping aggregate output as the maximand, we may want to admit skilled immigrants up to a certain point and then switch to unskilled workers for the secondary sector. The point at which switching to unskilled labor becomes desirable will depend on the following factors:

- the magnitude of the elasticity of factor substitution between the primary and secondary sectors
- the extent to which resources freed from a declining secondary sector move to the primary sector, increasing output in the primary sector in the long run
- the extent to which complementarities exist between the primary and secondary sector which could result in declines in output in the primary sector as output declines in the secondary sector.

These are empirical issues which must be addressed before we can make a more realistic determination regarding the optimal mix of immigrants to the United States.

ALTERNATIVE IMMIGRATION POLICIES

The Desirability of Admitting Immigrants in Special Occupational Categories

Dr. Goldfarb stresses that the following conditions are necessary for it to be worthwhile to admit immigrants in specific occupational categories: quick diagnoses of shortages, long-lasting shortages, and a large elastic supply of acceptably trained immigrants from abroad. Dr. Goldfarb's own analysis, which focused on skilled occupations, led him to the conclusion that the required conditions do not exist to make such admissions worthwhile.

If we accept the view that a long-term excess demand for some groups of unskilled labor prevails in our economy, as was suggested in the previous section, then the idea of admitting immigrants (or non-immigrants) into specific occupational categories in the secondary sector may become feasible. There is evidence that the requisite conditions exist, and can be stated as follows:

- the shortage in the secondary sector has tended to be long-lasting because it is the result of long-term structural problems in the economy. There are cyclical variations in the size of the shortage in some industries such as construction and agriculture, but, at least in the latter case, the fluctuations are fairly predictable.
- there appears to be a large elastic supply of foreign-born labor at the appropriate skill levels to meet the excess demands. This supply is evidenced by the apparently large inflow of undocumented aliens.

In view of these conditions it seems feasible to implement a program to admit foreign-born labor to work in specified industries in the secondary sector. One possibility would be the expansion of our current H-2 program (temporary workers) into which aliens could be admitted for specific periods of time to work in specific industries. There are many considerations other than that of increasing output in the secondary sector that must be addressed if we are to fully assess the desirability of this sort of program, and the political obstacles are serious. It is beyond the scope of this paper to address these points.

Conclusions

Dr. Goldfarb's paper yields some useful insights with respect to making immigration policy more economically rational. Most important, he shows that it is analytically possible to devise a policy that can increase the economic benefits resulting from immigration. This framework

454

could make further contributions to our knowledge if it were to be expanded to consider additional economic variables to be maximized (or minimized) and if it were to be altered to reflect some of the structural conditions present in our economy.

Philip L. Martin

Immigration is one of the major unresolved issues remaining from the 1970s. Inadequate theory, data, and analysis have thus far precluded any professional or popular consensus on the numbers and characteristics of illegal aliens, their labor market and other economic impacts, and the effects of alien labor on the nation's sociopolitical fabric. Legal immigrants, whose numbers are swelled by unprecedented waves of refugees, are focusing renewed attention on the debate between U.S. "humanitarians" and "utilitarians." The two papers reviewed here explore the economic dimensions of illegal and legal migration to the United States.

Guest-Worker Program

Morgan and Gardner recognize the reality of illegal immigration and suggest that U.S. policies should be changed to cope with it. In particular, Morgan and Gardner ask how a 1980s guest-worker program will affect wages, employment, prices, and incomes in agricultural labor markets.

U.S. farm wage rates are currently four or five times as much as Mexican wages for similar work. If free labor mobility were permitted, Mexicans would be expected to come to the United States, thereby increasing wages and reducing unemployment in Mexico and decreasing wages and jobs (for U.S. workers) in the United States. If the wage and employment impacts of Mexican labor were concentrated by area, industry, or occupation, we would expect an outflow of domestic workers from these areas, industries, and occupations. The empirical question is estimating the schedule linking *numbers* of Mexican workers and their *impacts* on U.S. wages, jobs for natives, and internal U.S. migration patterns.

Estimating such a schedule· on the impacts of numbers poses several statistical conundrums. Information is desired on future impacts; the United States, however, used easily measurable numbers of alien workers only between 1942 and 1964. Estimates made for that period are not likely to be a reliable predictor of 1980s impacts because: (1) there have been important changes in agricultural labor markets since the early 1960s (massive out-migration, new technologies, new labor laws and unions, less migrancy); (2) the braceros working in the United States between 1942 and 1964 were concentrated in certain crops in southwestern states, which makes it difficult to predict their current impacts; (3) legally admitted braceros were joined by illegal aliens (1 million were apprehended in 1953), which makes the underlying data suspect.

The empirical work presented by Morgan and Gardner is not sufficiently cognizant of these underlying statistical difficulties. The first exercise, a calculation of a "flexibility coefficient," indicates that farm wages would decrease 2.5 percent if the U.S. labor force were increased by 10 percent more (alien) workers. This assumes an equilibrium for calculating the underlying elasticities in spite of the obvious disequilibrium manifested in migration. If we assume that one simply estimates a flexibility coefficient (a change in price when quantity changes) by inverting an elasticity estimate, more realistic *shares* of U.S. and Mexican labor increase the wage depression estimate 2.5 times—if 400,000 aliens worked in a southwestern agricultural *harvest* work force of 1 million, the estimated wage depression from a 10 percent work force increase is 6.3 percent instead of 2.5 percent. It is doubtful that the *total* U.S. elasticities used are relevant for harvesting agriculture in the Southwest, and they are probably wrong for 1980s predictions.

I agree with Morgan and Gardner that more alien workers will tend to depress wages, but even very minor changes in estimates dramatically change the estimated effect on wages. I believe that these simple elasticity estimates are as likely to mislead as to inform.

Morgan and Gardner's primary empirical effort is an attempt to estimate the state-by-state impacts of braceros on wage rates from 1953 through 1964. While they recognize that states are too aggregated for some purposes and not aggregated enough for others, they proceed to estimate state-by-state effects. While they make honest attempts to find the "best" data series to estimate the supply of alien labor available, the U.S. demand for farm labor, and the U.S. supply of farm labor, none of the series is without (acknowledged) defects. For example, the U.S. labor supply equation makes the U.S. Department of Agriculture count of hired farm workers dependent on both agricultural and manufacturing wages (to account for nonfarm opportunities), on unemployment covered by unemployment insurance, and on an estimate of the legal bracero work force. The model is estimated over the period 1958–1978, with 1961 serving as a "break." Unfortunately, this model only indirectly accounts for any unmeasured effects of illegals in the late 1960s and 1970s.

Most of the estimates go in expected directions. Many of the continuous economic variables (wages, unemployment, etc.) were not significant. Using fairly low estimates of farm labor supply (0.8) and high estimates of demand (-3.2), Morgan and Gardner estimate that every three braceros created about 1.2 new farm jobs, that farm wages were lowered fifteen to twenty cents per hour because 300,000 braceros worked in southwestern agriculture, and that this wage decline reduced the domestic farm work force by 12 percent. Farmers saved an estimated $185 million annually because braceros lowered their wage bill. Some of these wage savings were passed on to consumers in the form of lower prices; others may have increased taxes because some crops are subsidized (for example, cotton).

Morgan and Gardner's labor demand estimate is probably too high for most agricultural uses of aliens in future years. In some instances (Florida sugar cane, wine grapes, lettuce, and tobacco) mechanical harvesting devices are available but are waiting for rising farm wages to make them profitable. These crops have high labor demand elasticities (as did processed tomatoes and cotton in the past); for other crops, labor replacement may be more difficult, making labor demand far more inelastic.

Assuming a high demand elasticity means that the depressing effects of bracero labor on U.S. agricultural wages will be partially offset by increased farm employment. Assuming a high supply elasticity means that a little wage depression will lead to relatively large reductions in the number of U.S. workers who want to do farm work (conversely, a small wage increase will bring a flood of new workers into agriculture). If both demand and supply elasticities are so high, *why not simply increase farm wage rates, simultaneously decreasing demand and increasing the supply of U.S. agricultural workers?* The reader could not be faulted for considering this paper an "empirical justification" for a new bracero program when all the arguments are couched in terms of "easing the burden of adjustment to be borne by domestic workers," when a wage increase imposed on farmers would, under the same assumptions, "ease the adjustment burdens imposed on *farmers*"!

Guest workers are individuals entering a country to work for a particular employer (or in a particular area) for one or two years. *If* the aliens displace few natives, and *if* they in fact leave after one or two years, the labor-host nation derives net economic benefits (profits to employers, wages to complementary workers, taxes to governments). These benefits, so immediate and tangible, are predicated on the system's rotating workers as planned. The bracero program *did* rotate temporary alien workers through temporary U.S. jobs, providing economic benefits but raising complaints of "exploitation" and wage depression.

The 1980s present a very different picture. Most studies suggest that the vast majority of illegal aliens work in nonseasonal, nonagricultural jobs. A new guest-worker program will have to rotate temporary workers through relatively *permanent* jobs. Even a guest-worker program confined to agriculture will have to be "done up right" this time, meaning that minimum wage and working condition standards may be enforced.[1]

Guest workers provide short-term benefits but may produce long-term infrastructure and integration costs. Immigrants, on the other hand, often impose short-run costs but promise long-term economic benefits. Guest workers can be converted into immigrants, but such an adjustment-of-status provision allows a select group of employers to pick (some of) the nation's immigrants.

Occupational Preferences

Legal immigration is at its postwar zenith just when the United States is experiencing a series of seemingly intractable economic problems. What economic role do immigrants play? More specifically, what is the rationale for favoring the entry of "needed" immigrants?

Robert Goldfarb provides a sensible analysis of the issues surrounding the admission of skilled workers through the occupational preference system. He notes that the current certification system applies to only a small fraction of all immigrants who eventually work, that the administration of the system is widely criticized, that the underlying premise of certification—the assumption that labor markets can be "tested" to see if domestic workers are available—may be misleading, and that economic criteria play only an indirect role in the immigration system's goals. Goldfarb dismisses the economic effects of unskilled migrants and concentrates instead on the reasons for regulating skilled immigration.

An immigration policy with an economic basis can have several objectives. Goldfarb rejects any occupation-specific rationales for regulating skilled migration, arguing that the only *economic* basis for immigration policy is one based on aggregate output. (I suggest that regional policy can also be a rationale, since it can minimize the internal migration required of the domestic population by letting presumably mobile migrants go to areas needing labor.) Goldfarb suggests that to maximize aggregate output, the United States should have some selection process that picks the "best and brightest" among potential

---

[1] For an overview of these administrative issues, see Philip Martin, *Guestworker Programs: Lessons from Western Europe,* U.S. Department of Labor, Bureau of International Labor Affairs, 1980).

immigrants. While it is true that such a selection process will maximize immigration's contribution to U.S. economic growth, any such system is likely to be opposed by generally poorer sending countries (in other words, the economic criterion is politically infeasible). In a similar way, the suggestion that immigrants come to the United States for a trial period before they can obtain permanent immigrant status runs into the very practical but real enforcement problem of assuring exit for those deemed unfit.

The current certification system does not maximize the economic contributions of immigrants. But Goldfarb's suggestions for working in a maximizing direction are likely to be politically unpopular or administratively impossible, or both. Goldfarb's second concern, the generation of rents because entry to the United States is restricted, seems at first glance to be more amenable to some sort of regulation. But the suggestions for reform are not practical: Can a system be designed so that immigrants really pay the U.S. government the personal value of a scarce visa? Requiring a period of public service from all immigrants does more to alter the immigrant queue than to change the distribution of rents to U.S.-based assistors. Finally, a lottery may reduce rents but may make it impossible to restrict the applicant pool to the "best and brightest."

Goldfarb has looked at our system for admitting skilled immigrants and found it wanting: it does not achieve its stated goals, nor does it achieve any broader economic goals. Goldfarb suggests ways of putting the skilled admissions process on more economically rational grounds. I believe that most of his suggestions will prove politically and/or administratively impossible. As Barry Chiswick notes, the United States pays a price for a noneconomic immigration policy (at least for skilled workers).[2] The country has apparently elected, however, to pay the price to be humanitarian rather than utilitarian. Since the 1920s, immigration policy has reflected domestic goals and aspirations: first in the 1920s attempt to protect and preserve a perceived national heritage and then in the 1960s repudiation of national origins quotas in an era of concern for equal rights. It could be argued that illegal immigration makes the United States humanitarian in spirit but utilitarian in practice. Although immigration criteria will continue to reserve some slots for investors and those likely to make extraordinary economic contributions, the United States does not yet appear willing to endorse a *radical* change to an economically based immigration policy.

[2] See Barry R. Chiswick, "The Impact of Immigration on the Level and Distribution of Economic Well-Being," in this volume.

David S. North

It is always a pleasure to watch a fresh mind struggle with an old problem; Robert Goldfarb, who is new to the field of immigration, has made an important contribution in what I gather is his first paper on this subject.

He is an economist. He deals with inputs, outputs, and formulas. Labor is an input; immigrant workers are a particular kind of input, the supply of which, incidentally, is more easily regulated than that of native-born workers, a point the author does not make.

It is a delight to watch Goldfarb's mental processes as he seeks to make sense (from an economist's point of view) of the manner in which we choose our immigrants. The only economic sense he can make out of it is that it is a financial boon to the legal profession!

Goldfarb notes that whereas it would be possible to work out a rational distribution of at least some of the immigrant slots by occupation (so many physicians, so many bricklayers, and so many economists), no such rationality is in fact at work in the selection process. His description of the process is largely a negative one in that he notes in detail what the system does not do (in terms of economics) rather than noting what it does (in terms of augmenting the families of recent immigrants), and why it works (in terms of politics).

Goldfarb's two principal contributions are his recognition that immigration could be regulated to meet a number of *different* economic goals, and his reminder to us that the current immigration system focuses its economic benefits on private parties rather than on the public at large.

As to the first point, Goldfarb points out that immigration could be regulated to meet a number of different economic goals, or maximands. He discusses three of them—aggregate output, output per capita, and output per capita for residents.[1]

For each maximand there is likely to be a specific optimal immigration policy, he says. The numbers and types of workers to be admitted could be arranged in such a way as to best meet the specific economic goal. For example, dealing only with the question of the size of the flow of skilled workers, he shows us, with a blizzard of equations (which I am not qualified to evaluate), that the most appropriate scenario for securing the maximum aggregate output would be to admit all skilled workers who desire to immigrate. He notes, however, that

---

[1] He uses the terms "nonimmigrants" and "nonmigrants" to identify the resident population; I prefer the term "residents." "Nonimmigrants," in the immigration business, means temporary, legal alien visitors.

political considerations would enter the decision-making process as the reward for skilled labor dropped below that for unskilled labor. (In real life we have watched the American Medical Association move effectively to limit the influx of foreign medical graduates, which might decrease the wages paid to the skilled workers in the association.)

Regarding the second point mentioned above, Goldfarb states:

> Whenever there are scarce slots [that is, a limited number of visas], there is a likelihood that "rents" will arise owing to the value of the scarce slots. Some systems allow these payments or rents to be collected by the government . . . while other systems allow them to be expropriated by private agents. It is striking that virtually none of the legalistic writing, so apparently concerned with equity, even asks the question, Who gets the rents?

This is important, and is rarely discussed, although Philip Martin, of the University of California at Davis, has also pointed out that the economic benefits of immigration are narrowly focused (on the immigrants themselves and their employers).[2]

Stimulating though Goldfarb's paper is, I wish that instead of concentrating on manipulating the flows of skilled workers he had directed more effort to discussing the various impacts on the economy of widening or narrowing the flow of *unskilled* immigrants. In the real world it is the millions of unskilled immigrants (mostly illegal) who are making a more significant impact on the U.S. economy, and who are the major source of controversy in the migration field today. My own worry is that the illegal entrants are numerous enough and concentrated enough so that they often drive down the price of labor, both for themselves and for the disadvantaged U.S. workers who are in the same market. This, of course, increases the profits of their employers and tends to widen the income gap between the working poor and the balance of the population. I would like to see an economist like Goldfarb tackle those issues.

Whatever such an economist finds, however, may be stated in terms of the general good, and I despair of the political utility of such work. This is the case because in immigration policy, as in gun control and energy conservation and many other public policy issues, the mobilized private interests (of gunowners and gunmakers, for example) will always outshout and outmaneuver the disorganized public interest forces (of those who want to avoid being killed by guns, for example).

---

[2] Philip Martin, *Guestworker Programs: Lessons from Western Europe*, U.S. Department of Labor, Bureau of International Labor Affairs (mimeograph, 1980).

This is the case despite the fact that the private interests often represent a tiny percentage of the population.

Nevertheless, it is encouraging to see a new face and to hear a different point of view in this field of ours.

Edwin P. Reubens

The two papers presented at this session—one by Robert Goldfarb and the other by Larry Morgan and Bruce Gardner—taken together with several related papers given earlier at this conference, reflect the strengths and limitations of welfare economics and of econometric models in the area of human capital.

Economists who start out with an a priori formal theory or model resemble the political and moral philsophers who reason from what they believe to be first principles: that is, they try to draw rational conclusions for real world policy in just those areas where real world data are inadequate and actual experience is limited. Indeed, if we allowed history to teach us anything we would know that nothing is more dangerous and potentially misleading than an absolute trust in one's own opinions—however much they are bolstered by claims of being "obvious" or "self-evident" or "plausible." The graveyard of such opinions ranges from the belief that "the earth is flat" to the assertion that foreigners and other minorities are "inferior and wicked," and that "their gain is our loss"; likewise, in more technical economics today, consider the faith that "what goes up must come down"—despite the evidence of cumulative inflation; or, again, consider the neoclassical supposition that an increase in the supply of labor must lead to a fall in wages—despite the well-known stickiness of wages and the associated unemployment. Yet these skeptical remarks are not intended to rule out rational methods but rather to invest them with a healthy respect for reality and experience.

Mr. Goldfarb's paper is concerned with certain aspects of occupational preferences in U.S. immigration law and practice. He begins with a brief review of the existing law and its alleged defects. But, oddly, he entirely omits here the category of temporary admission—the H-1 visas for highly skilled workers, the H-2 visas for less skilled workers, and the status of exchange visitor for certain specialties (notably for foreign doctors). It is an omission which, despite some statistical references to temporaries in his later pages, tends to plague much of his subsequent discussion whenever he claims that immigration practices are inflexible and ill-adapted to occupational requirements, because he is thinking mainly, if not entirely, of immigration for settlement.

Next Mr. Goldfarb, seeking what he calls rationales for immigration rules, turns to the possible maximands. In an extremely simplified taxonomic discussion, he points to three macro-criteria: aggregate output, aggregate output per capita, and aggregate output per capita going to the native population. He then mentions some micro-criteria, which seem to be mostly maximizing output by industry, alleviating industrial "shortages" of labor, and fighting "monopoly." Among all these, he settles on maximizing aggregate output as "the most plausible economic basis for a system limiting immigration," but gives no observable reason for selecting this maximand or for calling it plausible except as he asserts that all other criteria are "uncertain," "full of errors," and "administratively difficult." Yet he asserts much the same points about aggregate output when he comes to his ultimate question, which is: "How well designed is the U.S. immigration system for implementing such a rationale?" Of course his answer is in the negative—as anyone would expect who realized that the present system or any alternative system represents many social objectives besides maximizing aggregate output!

Indeed, this whole paper would appear to be little more than a verbally elaborate way of restating the well-known fact that our immigration rules give only minor attention to settlement admissions for occupational reasons. And we might leave it at that were it not for the pretentious way in which Mr. Goldfarb sets himself to disprove the proposition that "there is no scientific or objective way to determine how many immigrants should be admitted or can be absorbed by the United States." He attempts this disproof by selecting his own maximand, and, assuming that the economy has "a determinate and known production function," assigning to this function all the familiar, convenient neoclassical characteristics with only the slightest hesitation or doubt. Within this invented world, Goldfarb resolves some of the most difficult questions: "capacity to absorb immigrants," "benefits and costs of the brain drain," and, finally, "rational immigration quotas." His treatment is simply macro even for particular structural vacancies—whether for physicians or for laborers. Indeed, Mr. Goldfarb and some other welfare economists seem to have little awareness of the arrogance of their model-building method and little patience for dealing with the complex and troubled world, which they quickly reject whenever it fails to conform to their a priori Platonic ideas.

The paper by Morgan and Gardner is more empirical, being concerned with the historical Bracero Program and with an effort to find in that program lessons that are applicable to present-day proposals for a new guest-worker program. Observing the evolution of this paper was illuminating, as it moved from an earlier version, which arrived at strong conclusions regarding costs and benefits of the Bracero Program, to the later version, which avoids strong conclusions and ties up all implications in alternative possibilities concerning the elasticities of supply and demand. Indeed, there is some internal evidence in these versions that the authors began with the familiar working hypothesis that the braceros must have had large adverse effects on the wages and employment of American farm workers; but the authors were actually driven by their data and their calculations toward a finding of weak effects on Americans (and strong beneficial effects on Mexicans), as is indicated in the closing section of their early version. In the later version the authors appear to have backed away into the wilderness of elasticity suppositions and neoclassical assumptions.

Their econometric method is complex and laborious. It frequently inserts assumptions where crucial data are unavailable and ignores weather and seasonality in farming and unemployment of displaced workers; yet the outcome is an estimate of net welfare benefits but in a remarkably small figure. This figure is so small that it is dubious for arguing the pros and cons of the bracero or guest-worker programs. Yet it is significant at least in showing a positive net benefit as against the usual suppositions of great harm. More specifically, Morgan and Gardner find that (1) the Bracero Program had, at most, a slight depressing effect on farm wages and a small displacement effect on American farm workers, while American producers and consumers and the Mexican labor force benefited substantially; and that (2) the biggest effect appears to have been the displacement of illegal entrants (wetbacks) while the Bracero Program functioned.

These findings are of great importance for present proposals to set up a large new program of guest workers, or "limited-visa foreign workers" (LVFWs), in order to meet U.S. vacancies in low-level jobs by a legitimate procedure that would in some degree dry up the inflow of illegals. Their findings are the more encouraging for such programs if we free ourselves from the supposition that any gross inflow into a labor category must depress wages there. The fact today seems to be that Americans are withdrawing from low-level jobs—whether in farm work or in cleaning work or in garment sewing—and aliens are taking their places; this is taking place without much displacement and without actual depression of real wages—and without much resistance from local labor unions, which are proceeding to sign up the new aliens! An LVFW program would regularize this process while providing safeguards, along H-2 lines, to prevent or to minimize exploitation of the foreigners, adverse effects on the U.S. workers, and social costs to the United States.

Discussion

CARMEL U. CHISWICK, University of Illinois at Chicago Circle: Listening to Edwin Reubens's proposal for guest workers, thinking about the nature of the Bracero Program and some of the other points that have been made about skilled versus unskilled immigrants, it occurs to me that the guest-worker proposal is based on some empirical propositions about the supply of immigrants to this country and the demand for immigrant labor by American employers.

In particular, it assumes no firm-specific or country-specific on-the-job training. A guest-worker program is only relevant if there is a large pool of illegals and potential illegals who do not mind going home after a year or two, or whatever the presumably very short period is that they are allowed to stay, with whatever skills they may have acquired while here. It also assumes that employers do not mind losing these workers. If workers acquire substantial country-specific skills while they are here they will try to stay on, legally or otherwise, and employers will have no incentive to send them back. If they acquire firm-specific skills the employers will do their best to keep them. In either event, the de facto result would be something other than the guest-worker program that has been proposed.

Another difficulty introduced by the possibility of investment in human capital is that the current wage differential may be an imperfect indicator of future wage differentials, and the present value of these differentials, faced by potential immigrants. Whether because of lower discount rates or better potential returns, some immigrant groups have been quite articulate on this point: they come here not expecting very high wages for themselves but, rather, opportunities for their children. I like to call this the "land-of-opportunity" model of immigration as contrasted with the "streets-are-paved-with-gold" model where high current wage differentials are expected. Other things being equal, the land-of-opportunity model implies a higher savings rate and higher future income, suggesting that a current subsidy of immigrants (through the tax-and-transfer system) is more likely to disappear in the long run. Immigrants focusing primarily on current incomes (that is, the streets-are-paved-with-gold model) would be a less good investment on the part of the American taxpayer.

It seems to me that the supporters of liberal immigration policies view the land-of-opportunity model as the more relevant while the supporters of restriction favor the streets-are-paved-with-gold model. Unfortunately, I see no way to screen for this distinction in designing an immigration policy. Opening the doors to immigration certainly does not screen out people who are coming here to get rich, nor should it. Limiting the duration of a worker's stay in the United States will not effectively screen out people who are coming here to settle. Many of the 7 or 8 million people here on temporary visas, or even as guest workers, can be expected to be lining up a job so that they can then immigrate, or to be learning the ropes so that when they do immigrate they will have a competitive advantage. If they want to migrate for the opportunity motive they will do so, legally or illegally, once they see how to do it, even if they have come in under a guest-worker type of program.

With that background, I will ask my question. My impression is that historically a fairly large component of the immigration from Mexico came here for a high current wage as modeled in the Morgan-Gardner paper. They left their families in Mexico, sent remittances home, and had no compunction about returning home after a while, which resulted in movement back and forth across the border. My impression from the media coverage is that today there are many more families who want to be treated as permanent residents and who are probably here because they want their children to have a future in this country. Is my impression from the media accurate? Does anyone know which type of immigration is involved for all these illegals from Mexico that everyone is talking about?

MR. REUBENS: The illegals coming into this country are not mostly bringing their children in order to take advantage of American schools. All you have to do is go out on the patrol on the border. There are hillsides swarming with Mexican persons crossing the border in the dark by the thousands, visible through the infrared telescopes, visible from the helicopter that flies over, and visible from the hilltops. There are almost no children. When I was touring the San Diego border in 1978 I did not find a single INS agent who told me that he had arrested a school-age child. Justice Department data on aliens arrested this year imply that at most 6 percent are juveniles.[1] The notion that the

---

[1] *New York Times*, August 4, 1980.

big bulk of illegals are coming in bringing their children to use American schools, American hospitals, American pediatricians, American restaurants (to get hamburgers at Hamburger Heaven), or whatever, is false.

The only approach through which numerous illegals can come with children, who might then become social dependents, is to come in as visitors and overstay their visa. You are never going to have a border so tightly sealed that you do not have some people who come in with a valid visa for what is supposed to be a three-month or six-month stay, and then overstay. That is a tiny fraction of the illegals who are entering.

I presume that social dependence is what you had in mind when you talked about the costs of bringing these people in and your willingness or unwillingness to subsidize them. I suggest that an illegal adult comes in to work, and that this is exactly the same as coming to a "land of opportunity" and the same as "benefiting our economy." They come because of the opportunities here—whether or not they are H-2 or braceros. And they stay for the sake of jobs and income here— whether or not they acquire specific skills here. Probably 85 to 90 percent of them take jobs, and the unemployment rates are very low. What costs are they imposing? The evidence from sample studies is that the illegals more than pay the taxes to cover whatever very meager social services they use. It is really a "When did you stop beating your wife?" kind of question to ask whether we should subsidize their costs, since in fact most of them do not impose any real costs.

MR. NORTH: I would disagree with a lot of that. First of all, the metaphor of the border is a very strong one. The families that come illegally to the United States come largely, but not totally, through the ports of entry bearing documents of some kind, legitimate or illegitimate, which they either honor or subsequently dishonor and, therefore, become illegals. I think that there is a fairly substantial number of such people.

There is a maturing of migration streams in which more family members are involved; we are starting to see more in the way of demands for social services. The suits in the Texas schools are part of it. Largely unknown is the fact that in California they are starting to find a substantial number of people who are applying for Aid to Families with Dependent Children. Los Angeles County alone was detecting 1,300 applicants for AFDC a month last year, which works out to the country's quietly turning down $50 million worth of AFDC claims annually. We are starting to see this occasionally because some people are looking at systems such as the welfare system in Los Angeles County, and some of them are looking at undocumented populations within this country. The Van Arsdol study found that 8.9 percent of the males that they talked to were receiving or had received welfare of some kind; 18.5 percent of the women in their survey similarly had received or were receiving welfare.[2]

The image of the migration as being that of single males is certainly passing, and I think the newspapers are picking it up.

WALTER FOGEL, University of California, Los Angeles: The ability of Mexican illegal aliens to adjust to cultural life in the United States may be related to the size of the ethnic group that is already here. If so, the acculturation process may be easier in the future, and the extent of return migration may be smaller as a greater proportion feel at home in American society.

DAN USHER, Queen's University: This afternoon's session and this morning's session were allegedly on the same subject, but the treatments in the papers were so different that it was barely possible to recognize the subjects as the same or to know how arguments in one session relate, by reinforcement or contradiction, to arguments in the other. There is, however, a direct comparability between Barry Chiswick's paper and the Morgan-Gardner study. Morgan and Gardner were estimating the triangles in Barry Chiswick's paper in a context in which many of the factors discussed in Chiswick's paper (sources of externality, the redistributive system, the role of taxes), and everything that Julian Simon talked about (in particular, problems of economies of scale), were assumed away, leaving only the derived demand for labor in a model with constant returns to scale. On these assumptions, one triangle showed a benefit to the United States and the other triangle showed a benefit to Mexico, as they should.

But there was much said this afternoon and nothing in any of the models this morning about the lowering of prices. It was not even in Jeffrey Williamson's paper, though he could perfectly well have calculated the drop in prices had he chosen to do so. I think Williamson did not do so for the very good reason that it would have been double counting in the context of his model. Those two little triangles constitute the whole of the benefits from migration; any changes in prices, up or down, are irrelevant because they are just changes in relative prices. Any lowering of the price of food is necessarily an increase in the relative price of manufactures; the two cancel out in the valuation of the net benefit from migration.

There is, however, one important exception that was discussed this afternoon and largely ignored this morning. Much of this after-

[2] Maurice D. Van Arsdol, Jr., et al., *Non-Apprehended and Apprehended Undocumented Residents in the Los Angeles Labor Market: An Exploratory Study* (Los Angeles: University of Southern California, 1979), table 26, page 89.

noon's discussion was about how ostensibly identical workers are not really identical or could be differentiated. The Bracero Program is a way of keeping the wages of unskilled migrants below the wages of unskilled Americans. The pickle example is a good one. If migrants and their children are denied access to any jobs but picking pickles, and if, as a result, the wage of migrants falls well below the wage of unskilled Americans, none of whom picks pickles, then there may be a genuine benefit to veteran Americans. I think it was taken as axiomatic by this morning's speakers that such a differentiation would not be maintained in the long run—that within a generation migrants and veterans are indistinguishable.

DAVID REIMERS, New York University: The whole discussion here about undocumented aliens really focused on Mexicans. I think there might be real differences between New York and California. I don't believe any of these wild stories of the estimates of the illegals in New York City. Guest-worker models might not fit New York. I think that a different kind of situation may be important. Fragmentary studies that we have had indicate that the kind of people coming are somewhat different from Mexican illegals in the Southwest. They are more traditional immigrants and are not coming for a temporary stay.

BARRY CHISWICK, University of Illinois at Chicago Circle: Robert Goldfarb, did I hear you correctly when you said that an objective of a good occupational preference system would be to indicate in which occupations we need people and set quotas within occupations—so many economists, so many doctors?

MR. GOLDFARB: If in fact it is legitimate to assume that there are alternative maximands, and you are willing to pick one, and you have a world in which you are not doing anything about the supply of unskilled workers, it is conceivable that you might have preferences about the supply of skilled workers. That is one point. The second point is that it is all very nice for us to sit here and talk about skilled and unskilled workers as though that is the obvious description of the American economy we want to work with, but I certainly don't know the appropriate description, the right aggregate production function. I don't know if it is in skilled versus unskilled or if it is in five categories or ten categories or fifteen.

In order to do what I was claiming you could do (that is, pick an optimal number of relatively skilled workers), I would need the right production function with the right degree of disaggregation. That degree of disaggregation conceivably might have physicians separately from all other skilled manpower; I just don't know. If it did, then my aggregate rationale would suggest that the model might tell me how many doctors we might want to admit.

MR. CHISWICK: I like your proposal in one regard: I think that it would be a fantastic subsidy to the economics profession. We probably should push it. But the problem I have with it is that attempts to estimate "shortages" within broad occupational categories are a tortuous exercise at best. Within more narrowly defined occupations I find it even more difficult.

MR. GOLDFARB: I wish we wouldn't use the word shortages. Shortages to me are things which take place because there has been a shift in demand, and domestic supply hasn't kept up with it; it usually involves issues of shorter-run adjustment to shifts in demand. Another issue concerns what the socially optimal equilibrium level of immigration is in the absence of short-run adjustment problems. Suppose that all domestic doctors make exactly the right calculation, from their private point of view, about the cost of training versus the returns; and exactly the "right" number of doctors get trained. It still seems to me that if we get foreign doctors without paying for their training it might raise national output to admit another foreign doctor. I may be missing something but it seems to me that this is at least possible.

Since Jeffrey Williamson used the term "absorptive capacity," and since I really don't understand it, I would like to hear what he means by it. Are your way of using it and my way of using it in conflict? How is that for a nonquestion?

JEFFREY WILLIAMSON, University of Wisconsin, Madison: My use of the term "absorptive capacity" refers to the effects of immigrants on the wages of the domestic (native) workers. If absorptive capacity is high, a large in-migration will have little if any depressing effect on wages; if absorptive capacity is low, wages fall sharply in response to the same immigration. Absorptive capacity is high, by this definition, if the native labor force has a high supply elasticity, that is, if the native secondary workers are crowded out of the labor force. High demand elasticities for labor would also imply high absorption rates. A high demand elasticity implies there is little "crowding out" of native workers and modest real wage declines in response to the immigration.

Absorptive capacity in a dynamic model is also greater if there is a high elasticity of response of land and capital with respect to immigration. High response rates imply a smaller decline in the land/labor and capital/labor ratios as a consequence of immigration and hence a smaller decline in the wages of native workers.

MR. REIMERS: In the legislative process absorptive capacity is, of course, a political definition. By putting the determination of the occupation categories in the Labor Department they knew it would be quite limited.

MR. REUBENS: There is another way of handling that in terms of costs and benefits. It is possible to define capacity in terms of how much it would cost to introduce another 1 or another 10 or another 1,000 as against how much benefit it would yield. Either at the point where the MR/MC ratio for a given occupation equals that of all other occupations, or at the point where the additional costs get to exceed the additional benefits, I suppose you would say that the country has reached its absorptive capacity for that category. It doesn't mean that physically you have reached it, because you could force in more doctors, for example, if for some health reason you wanted them, and you might conclude that your costs are now running higher than the additional benefits but you could continue to do it with subsidies. The difficulty is a confusion between absorptive capacity in some physical or very nearly physical sense as against this economist's measure of shifts in the ratio of benefits to cost at the margin for any given occupation. Once the point is reached where that ratio becomes equal to all other occupational ratios, or actually equal to unity, I suppose you could settle on that as being absorptive capacity. You have to know what you are maximizing.

MR. CHISWICK: How can one design an occupational preference system that would not be captured by the groups that have the incentive to close off immigration? Dieticians and physical therapists with advanced degrees are politically weak groups in the United States. The more narrowly defined the occupational category, the easier it is for that occupation to capture a sufficient number of legislators to pass a special bill to close it off, or to corner the secretary of labor at lunch and effectively do the same thing.

MR. GOLDFARB: I think one has to differentiate between the questions being asked. To say: If I were a benevolent dictator and had the power to set this number, there is a conceptual way in which I would do it— that is one question. A second question is: As a political economist, can you ever conceive of such a scheme working? That seems to be your question, and I agree with what you said. On the other hand, I think there is some sense to calculating how many of those people you (as a benevolent dictator) might want to let in, because it gives you an idea of the cost to the economy of not letting those people in.

MR. MORGAN: Econometric models of the U.S. farm labor market typically include a variable to represent the cyclical relationship between the farm and nonfarm sectors. The urban unemployment rate has often been used to specify this feature of the market. I interpret the results of these models to suggest that an increase in the urban or overall unemployment rate does not increase the supply of labor in rural areas, but rather slows the dissipation of labor out of those markets.

Philip Martin talked about the wage impacts of the Bracero Program by crop. If I had wage and quantity data by crop for our cross-section of states, I would specify a model accordingly to investigate crop effects of the program. Unfortunately, only California has labor wage and quantity data for specific crops. In addition, the procedures used to generate the California data are too biased to be considered in our study. Donald Wise's study, which is reported by us,[3] used crop-specific labor market data that should be viewed with great caution. I would point out to you that in our proxies for price ratios, prices received were weighted by the eight major agricultural commodity groups in each of the states. I know of no way to develop a reliable estimate of the amount of labor used per crop by state. USDA has some measures of farm labor utilization for various crops, but these estimates are not uniform over time or crop, and cannot be reasonably allocated by state. I would simply say that if wage-quantity data were available by crop and state, over time, they should be incorporated into models such as ours. Given the data limitations, we have made a reasonable attempt to reflect the mix of crops within each labor market.

MR. GARDNER: To add to that point, we shouldn't carry this issue of not aggregating crops too far. If we did have the individual crop data we would still have to aggregate as we did. The reason is, if you want to look at the overall effect of the Bracero Program, you can't do that crop by crop. If we said: First we'll look at the cucumber pickers and see what happened to their wages as a function of the number of braceros there, and then we will look at the carrot pickers and we'll look at their wages as a function of the number of braceros in that crop, and similarly for other crops; and for crops for which there are no braceros used we say there is no bracero effect: If we did this we'd be wrong. Braceros have ripple effects on all the crops in an area, even

---

[3] D. E. Wise, "The Effect of the Bracero on Agricultural Production in California," *Economic Inquiry,* vol. 12 (December 1974), pp. 547-58.

ones they aren't working themselves. The question is, What is the relevant labor market? There is likely to be a relatively high cross-elasticity in the supply of labor between an area's crops, so if the pre-bracero cucumber workers aren't picking cucumbers they are probably picking something else. Workers in all crops are doing closely related activities, so you have to somehow put them all together.

MR. REUBENS: It seems to me that if you take that line you are again implicitly assuming that the entry of other workers, foreign workers, means the displacement, either one-for-one or in some large proportion, of American workers. I suggest to you that in most of the cases in the Bracero Program, and in the present illegal inflow, it is not the displacement of American workers but rather the withdrawal of the American workers that left "vacancies" which were filled by the foreign workers. This is to amend Robert Goldfarb's earlier comment that shortages result from a shift in demand not met by a shift in supply: our vacancies for aliens mostly result from falling labor supply and virtually steady demand in particular occupations.

The Bracero Program started in the Second World War when the withdrawal of the young adult males was the cause of shortage of farm labor. The braceros were brought in simply to replace them, not to displace the workers that were already there. In fact, the farmers were not contracting for more workers than they could use, given the labor supply they had from American sources to which they then had to add braceros. Consequently, there is no a priori assumption that the entry of a farm worker displaces Americans, or even that it reduces the wage rate. You are not shifting the supply to the right, you are simply replacing the supply which had shifted to the left and you are bringing it back to its previous position.

That is equally true, I think in large part, of the present flow of illegals. They are coming into low-level occupations from which Americans are dropping out because of the preferences of American workers and the alternatives open to them. The illegals are simply replacing them, and they replace them at the same wage or at the generally rising wage which is currently rising for various reasons. They are not pushing many American workers out of occupations so far as I can see. I think the garment industry is probably the most fully developed example of that.

MR. CHISWICK: Do you mean that even if there were no braceros the wages in these jobs would not rise and that one or both of two things would not happen: these sectors would to some extent shrink and to some extent the higher wages would attract workers either from other sectors or outside the labor force?

MR. REUBENS: I would respond to that in terms of the smoothness and continuity of the supply curves you are supposing. I would suggest that in 1942 you could not have obtained farm workers to replace those young men who had gone off into the service without some enormous increase in the farm wage. I have no doubt that if you were prepared to pay in those days $8 or $10 per hour instead of what was then the going $1.50 or $2.00 per hour that you could have lured away some auto workers—which, of course, would have reduced the military effort in producing tanks—or you could have lured away some communications workers, who would then make the country incapable of communicating through the telephone system. Small marginal increments, which is what the neoclassical economist always uses, would have produced almost no effect.

Likewise, today in the garment industry there is very little prospect for increasing the supply of women to do sewing unless you are prepared perhaps to double the wage. The International Ladies' Garment Workers Union would be delighted to hear you propose that, but they are not proposing it. The union doesn't suggest that what we ought to be doing is doubling the wage of garment workers so as to preclude the necessity of falling back on the illegals, and it is a dream world to suppose that a small change, say a 10 percent increase in wage, would enlarge the supply of labor by 10 percent or even by 5 percent. The market for low-level labor does not work that way.

This is a structured labor market with a great deal of rigidity and a great deal of immobility. If you want to push up wages high enough to accomplish that shift of workers you must recognize what effects you would be having on inflation and the repercussions throughout the rest of the economy where you would be dislocating workers. I suggest that you just can't fall back on a simple marginalist textbook model.

HARRY GILMAN, U.S. Department of Labor: An argument given by manufacturers is the substitutability of the importation of goods for the importation of labor. Indeed, on the value-added-to-import tax, where you do have a factory on the American side of the border where you are cutting suits, you take it across to the Mexican side of the border where the sewing is done, you bring it back, and you pay the tariff on the value-added, which is on the lower wages. So you do have to extend the model to include the substitutability of the importation of goods and services for the importation of labor.

PHILIP MARTIN, University of California, Davis: Just a couple of very quick notes. One is that I agree with Morgan and Gardner's leaving out specific crops from the equations. What I was trying to point out was that their analysis is simultaneously too broad and too narrow. It is too narrow in the sense that braceros were used only in particular crops, confining their impacts; it is not broad enough in the sense that bracero impacts could spill over into the nonfarm sector. I am saying that the analysis may be a good approximation—however, it is hard to say it is an accurate approximation. A whole series of things could have happened and are not captured in the analysis. That was the only point I was trying to make.

A second point concerns aliens and wages. There was an official report of the U.S. Department of Agriculture in 1940 that said the agricultural labor shortage for the Bracero Program could be due to the farmers' wanting to continue peacetime methods of employment, with what USDA called underemployment and low wages. This was official USDA recognition that there was a potential for labor rationalization but that the farmers preferred braceros.

The third point that Harry Gilman raised is relevant, too: the potential of trade in place of migration. One of the things to keep in mind when making predictions about the future of international labor flows is that a service-oriented economy offers fewer opportunities for trade in place of migration because services have the quality that labor has to be at the site of consumption. You can't separate production and delivery, so when you get an economy in which 60 percent of the work force is in services it gets harder and harder to think of significant trade in place of the migration. The sectors around the world that employ the largest number of illegals, or temporary-type workers (with the exception of Western Europe), are largely construction, services, and agriculture. Agricultural products could be imported but land prices may change. Only in Western Europe are guest workers employed in manufacturing to a significant extent.

MR. GOLDFARB: I guess I just wanted to say that, with respect to Linda Liner's comments, I certainly think that the Cobb-Douglas production function does give oversimplistic results. It was really just used illustratively, to show once again that different maximands are likely to give different results. To actually derive precisely appropriate rules to maximize welfare from immigration, you have to know the right production structure of the economy—which is quite a difficult problem. One further comment: At this session Linda Liner seemed to agree with me that determining the appropriate maximand is a very difficult problem. One thing puzzles me about the discussion this morning. In response to

475

Allan King's comments, some seemed to be asserting there was a very obvious maximand and there really wasn't much of an issue here. I strongly disagree with that.

I have two reactions to Phil Martin's helpful comments. First, he describes the kind of analysis I propose as trying to put economic values on decisions based in good part on noneconomic criteria. This is certainly a useful point, but I believe the analysis is still very helpful. If you don't try to figure out what an optimal policy from some economic point of view would be, you are going to have a tough time figuring out the real costs of applying those noneconomic criteria. Second, he said that one of the things he would like to add to the maximand is something about regional distribution of immigrants. If you impose on incoming immigrants a requirement that they have to go to locations that they didn't want to go to, that is a way of capturing some of the economic rents.

A NOTE ON THE BOOK

*The typeface used for the text of this book is
Times Roman, designed by Stanley Morison.
The type was set by
Hendricks Miller Typographic Company, of Washington, D.C.
R.R. Donnelley & Sons Company of Harrisonburg, Virginia,
printed and bound the book,
using paper manufactured by the S.D. Warren Company.
The cover and format were designed by
the AEI Publications staff
with Pat Taylor.
The manuscript was edited by
the AEI Publications staff.*

SELECTED AEI PUBLICATIONS

AEI ASSOCIATES PROGRAM